Global Issues, Local Arguments

Readings for Writing

Third Edition

June Johnson
Seattle University

PEARSON

Boston   Columbus   Indianapolis   New York   San Francisco   Upper Saddle River
Amsterdam   Cape Town   Dubai   London   Madrid   Milan   Munich
Paris   Montréal   Toronto   Delhi   Mexico City   São Paulo   Sydney
Hong Kong   Seoul   Singapore   Taipei   Tokyo

Senior Acquisitions Editor: Brad Potthoff
Senior Development Editor: Marion B.
  Castellucci
Development Editor: Kassi Radomski
Senior Marketing Manager: Sandra McGuire
Senior Supplements Editor: Donna Campion
Production Manager: Denise Phillip
Project Coordination and Electronic Page
  Makeup: Element LLC
Cover Design Manager: John Callahan

Cover Images (from left to right): bonsai/
  Shutterstock, © SCPhotos/Alamy,
  Andrea Danti/Shutterstock,
  FotograFFF/Shutterstock
Photo Researcher: Integra
Senior Manufacturing Buyer: Roy Pickering
Printer and Binder: R. R. Donnelley and Sons
  Company—Harrisonburg
Cover Printer: R. R. Donnelley and Sons
  Company—Harrisonburg

This book was typeset in 10.5/12 Minion Pro Regular.

For permission to use copyrighted material, grateful acknowledgment is made to the copyright
holders appearing on the appropriate page within text and on pp. 506–508, which are hereby
made part of this copyright page.

Library of Congress Cataloging-in-Publication Data
Johnson, June
    Global issues, local arguments : readings for writing / June Johnson, Seattle University. —
Third edition.
      pages cm
    Includes index.
    ISBN 978-0-205-88615-9 (alk. paper)
  1. History, Modern—21st century—Sources. I. Title.
      D861.4.J65 2013
      909.831—dc23
                                                                                        2012030391

10 9 8 7 6 —DOH—16 15

ISBN-13: 978-0-205-88615-9
ISBN-10:   0-205-88615-9

Contents

iii

4 Crossing Borders

Immigration   135

Readings   147

5 Protecting the Environment
Water Issues and Competing Energy Technologies 202

Readings 215

6 Merging and Clashing Cultures
Graffiti, Comics, and Music 264

International Voices

Readings   276

Chapter Questions for Reflection and Discussion   317
Writing Assignments   318

7 Global Netizens
Social Media's Role in Social and Political Change   322

Readings   333

8 Defending Human Rights
Human Trafficking, Forced Child Labor, and Rape as a Weapon of War   384

Preface

As global issues intersect with our local spaces and increasingly demand our informed responses, we, as writing teachers, wrestle with *how* to teach these issues productively in our writing classes. I and others have discovered that global issues have potential to spark students' interest and motivate learning. Our students have both a need and a desire to understand the multiple ways that our states, regions, and country are part of the larger world. Daily, the media bombard us with stories and images that relate to controversies over global economic problems, free trade, outsourcing, immigration, energy, human rights problems, and health. These issues, I have found in my writing classes, intellectually challenge students and elicit lively writing from them. Some of these controversies are new and intriguing to students: How does shopping at the local mall affect workers in clothing factories in China? How does the lack of safe water in Africa threaten global security? Is the Internet fueling political protest in the United States and Islamic countries? Some controversies are immediately relevant: How will sending businesses and jobs to Mexico and India affect the number of jobs available to young adults in the United States and Canada? Should we rebuild our manufacturing sector? Some have urgency: What energy technologies should we be investing in to meet energy needs and to protect the environment for future generations? These issues, connecting "over there" with "home here," appeal to today's students, whose generation has been shaped by images from around the world and who are faced with an increasingly complex, interdependent world.

Global Issues, Local Arguments is based on three main premises. First, to prepare our students for taking their place in the world, we need to equip them with the critical thinking and writing skills to sort out for themselves how global issues touch them and how our local decisions as consumers and voters have far-reaching consequences. Second, studying the public *arguments* on these issues—both civic and academic—in our writing classrooms enables students to engage with global controversies and their local connections. Third, because these controversies come to us rhetorically packaged, we can most productively approach global issues rhetorically: examining how invested stakeholders write out of powerful motivating occasions, in various genres, for the purpose of changing readers' perspectives and winning adherents to their views.

WHAT'S NEW IN THE THIRD EDITION?

This third edition of *Global Issues, Local Arguments* preserves the approach and structure of the second edition, while it incorporates several new features, new chapters, and new readings:

- **A new Chapter 7: "Global Netizens: Social Media's Role in Social and Political Change."** This chapter explores the important timely issues of global digital rights, connectivity, the relationship between Facebook, YouTube, and Twitter and social/political activism, and the Internet's vulnerability to cooptation by commercial forces and authoritarian governments. This chapter asks: Can the Internet foster democratic movements? Why is equal access to the Internet important? What role does the Internet play with regard to mainstream news? High-interest readings in this chapter also examine the commonalities in the recent movements that have used Facebook and Twitter, such as the Occupy Wall Street movement and the Arab Spring.

- **A new Chapter 9: "Fighting Global Disease: Pandemics, Antibiotic Resistance, AIDS, and Maternal Health."** This chapter examines the threat of pandemics, the danger of increasing resistance to antibiotics, and the ongoing need to combat AIDS and attend to global maternal health.

- **A substantially revised Chapter 6: "Merging and Clashing Cultures: Graffiti, Comics, and Music."** This chapter focuses on three issues: international graffiti cultures, cartoons and comics, and rap music. It asks students to consider the main paradigms for cultural interaction—conflict and lasting difference, assimilation and dominance, and hybridization and ongoing mixing—as they explore the controversies over graffiti as an artistic, political, or criminal activity; comic strips as cultural propaganda or a means of nurturing cultural understanding; and rap as a commercial, artistic, or political instrument.

- **New issues in Chapter 5: "Protecting the Environment: Water Issues and Competing Energy Technologies."** In addition to the focus on the availability of fresh water, this chapter now includes readings on the Keystone XL Pipeline controversy, on shale and fracking as a source of energy, and on post-Fukushima disaster perspectives on nuclear power.

- **A new Thinking Visually feature in the introductions to the readings (Chapters 3–9), which invites students to think about how photos and images contribute to global–local public controversies.** These Thinking Visually exercises include short headnotes that put the image in context, a provocative photo or poster, and questions for discussion that engage students in thinking about how images can be used rhetorically to support different arguments.

- **New reflective writing prompts throughout the book and especially in the Writing Assignments section at the end of readings chapters.** These reflective exercises and writing assignments foster students' personal investment in the global issues; help them forge their own local to global links; push them to wrestle with readings; prod them to articulate their own values in preparation for writing meaningful arguments; and by acknowledging the affective dimension of writing, enable students to lay a motivational and personal foundation for their own civic and academic arguments.

- **New samples of student writing that show how students have engaged with and explored global issues.** In this edition, there are twelve Student Voice essays, a number of them new to this edition: two new personal narratives in chapter introductions; a new rhetorical analysis essay of a reading in the text, and a new researched argument in MLA style. A number of the Student Voices from the last edition are available in the *Instructor's Manual.*

- **New questions on readings and new writing projects throughout.** Updated headnotes provide current contextual information on the authors and the readings; new questions encourage students to analyze, reflect on, and personally apply the new readings to their lives; and new writing projects invite students to add their voices to the argumentative conversations of the readings.

- **Thoroughly updated readings.** This edition includes over 70 new professional visual and verbal arguments, representing multiple argument genres, diverse stakeholders, and current global and local developments on the issues. Readings chosen for high student appeal include controversies over free trade and American jobs, the potential of Twitter and Facebook to fuel social and political activism, local/national campaigns to confront the Internet sex ads trafficking minors, the problem of resistance to antibiotics, and the need to prepare for pandemics like the one portrayed in the film *Contagion.*

WHAT *GLOBAL ISSUES, LOCAL ARGUMENTS* OFFERS WRITING INSTRUCTORS AND STUDENTS

Global Issues, Local Arguments has grown directly out of my experiences as a writing instructor grappling with the ongoing challenge of teaching my students to be successful writers. I have designed *Global Issues, Local Arguments* with the following goals in mind: reaching a wide range of students with current, high-interest material; introducing students to global studies, which intersects with many disciplines and careers important to students; encouraging students to be involved citizens; fostering critical thinking; and, most of all, building students' rhetorical knowledge and helping students develop as writers and arguers.

Reaching Students with a Wide Range of Interests and Majors Many instructors are seeking accessible, stimulating, current issues to explore in their courses and looking for ways to teach college reading and writing to students heading for diverse fields. This text has grown out of my work in writing classrooms with students whose interests range widely, from nursing to education, social work, engineering, environmental science, business, marketing, law, and communication. The public controversies in this book provide significant, complex, and lively readings that span fields, many of which will require students to have a background in global studies.

Encouraging Students to Be Involved Citizens The local and global issues in this book exemplify argument as an active, productive instrument to build communities of supporters and bring about change. Understanding stakeholders' investments in issues—why they care—and how they try to change their readers' thinking and move them to action can help students find their own investment in arguments they write. In its chapter introductions, readings, discussion questions, and writing assignments, this text pushes students to ponder their local connection to global issues. In its reflective and narrative writing prompts, it urges students to find their personal investment in these issues, which can then generate motivated academic and civic writing.

Helping Students Develop as Critical Thinkers The layered, multifaceted, and often controversial issues that bridge local and global communities are ideal for teaching critical thinking. To prepare students to write about these issues, this text encourages students to examine different perspectives and consider the emotional impact of arguments. Recent studies such as those by political psychologist Drew Westen underscore how our "passionate minds" govern our response to public arguments much more than our dispassionate processing of reasons and evidence.* These studies suggest that critical thinking needs to address the emotional component of arguments. Similarly, studies measuring undergraduate learning and satisfaction (for instance, the National Survey of Student Engagement) point to the need to address moral reasoning and intercultural effectiveness as well as problem-solving and evaluative/analytical skills. This enlarged sense of critical thinking is infused throughout the pedagogy of this text, in its chapter introductions, the discussion questions, and writing prompts. For example, recognizing the emotional component of arguments and the controversial nature of these global issues, I have invited students to write reflectively about their values, experiences, and responses to readings as preparation for constructing effective arguments.

Helping Students Develop as Writers and Arguers Most important, this book functions as a tool to teach writing in three main ways:

- *It helps students analyze the rhetorical power of arguments and think about how to infuse that power into their own arguments.* Focusing on how arguments are constructed rhetorically encourages students

---

*Drew Westen, *The Political Brain: The Role of Emotion in Deciding the Fate of the Nation* (New York: Public Affairs, 2007).

to become more sophisticated readers and to find their own ways to contribute to these dynamic discussions in their writing. Chapter introductions, headnotes to readings, discussion questions, and writing assignments direct students' attention to the ways that the structure, content, and depth of arguments are shaped by the target audience, the genre, and the publication. The multisided arguments in each chapter demonstrate the importance of rhetorical context and are particularly good at showing how language frames issues and how writers tailor their claims, reasons, evidence, and emotional and imaginative appeals to move their readers to think from new perspectives. In addition, each chapter's readings represent diverse argument genres for students to analyze and respond to, such as op-ed pieces, editorials, researched arguments, policy analyses from news commentary magazines, advocacy Web site policy statements, posters, and political cartoons.

- *This text works on the principle that students write best when they acquire a solid base of knowledge on issues.* Because global issues involve geopolitical knowledge, each chapter gives students a running start on understanding the issues and prepares them to wrestle with the complexity of the arguments: Chapter introductions, headnotes, and questions provide context for the readings, help students understand the controversies—some of the big underlying questions—and the stakeholders, and prepare students to find their own connections and delve deeply in their analyses. Suggestions for writing assignments provide prime opportunities for students to use writing to learn and rhetorical analyses of print and visual texts as preparation for writing their own arguments.

- *Global Issues, Local Arguments* *helps students develop as arguers.* It moves them beyond the tendency to think of argument as pro–con debate or to reach closure quickly on issue questions. It pushes students to listen carefully to views and reflect on them in order to clarify their own values and deepen their own perspectives. Featuring global–local issues that do not have simple solutions, this book emphasizes the intellectual work involved in reading and writing arguments and shows how argument is connected to problem solving as well as persuasion. In studying multisided issues, students work their way toward more complex, informed views and toward writing richer arguments.

PEDAGOGICAL FEATURES OF *GLOBAL ISSUES, LOCAL ARGUMENTS*

Chapter Introductions Give Background Information and Context The introduction that opens each chapter has four main objectives: (1) to provide historical information, explanations, and definitions of terms to equip students with the knowledge base they will need to understand the readings and write about the issues; (2) to spark students' intellectual curiosity about each chapter's subject; (3) to make these global issues appealing and accessible to instructors and students; and (4) to help students find their own personal engagement with these issues. Each chapter introduction includes the following features:

- **Context for a Network of Issues** sketches the current status of the issues, provides brief historical information, and explains key terms such as *free trade*, *nongovernmental organizations*, and *offshore outsourcing*.

- **Stakes and Stakeholders** illuminates some of the main controversies and issue questions that people are arguing about to spark students' thinking about the global and local ties and to prepare students to analyze how people's investments in these issues shape their arguments.

- **Thinking Visually** engages students in applying their understanding of the chapter's issues to images as they consider how visual texts can be used rhetorically to support different arguments.

- **Student Voice** presents a student's personal narrative response to, or reflection on, the issue to convey its experiential reality and to inspire students to look for their own connections with global issues.

- **International Voices** presents brief views from another part of the world in interviews and newspaper articles, bringing a concrete, human dimension to these issues.

- **Global Hot Spot** uses an excerpt from a news service or Web site to zoom in on a main region or country grappling with this global issue to show its complexity and to engage students emotionally and intellectually.

Context and Discussion Questions for Each Reading Brief introductory headnotes with preview questions and follow-up questions for discussion accompany each visual and verbal text to help students analyze the rhetorical context and the rhetorical features of these arguments. These For Class Discussion items focus students' attention on how each piece works as an argument, how each contributes to the global conversation on the issue, and often how readings talk to each other. Rhetorical terms are intentionally generic (for example, "author's reliability and credibility" instead of "appeals to *ethos*") to enable instructors to use this text in a range of writing courses.

Three Student Essays Using MLA Style Chapters 2, 4, and 5 offer student-researched writing in the form of researched proposal arguments driven by significant, complex issue questions. These papers offer examples of MLA documentation style.

Questions Concluding Each Chapter Each chapter's Chapter Questions for Reflection and Discussion pose questions that encourage students to see relationships among readings, to explore points of agreement and disagreement among these arguments, and to frame their own questions for further research.

Chapter Suggestions for Multiple Writing Assignments To give instructors maximum flexibility in using this text, the writing assignments at the end of each chapter offer options for instructors and students who are using the chapter's material early in the course as well as those using it later. Brief Writing Assignments include suggestions for short, informal writing; for reflective and narrative pieces; for writing-to-learn pieces; and for writing that can help students generate ideas for their longer, more formal writing assignments. These writing assignments also lead students to find their own local stakes in these global matters and to think out their own views.

The suggestions for Writing Projects also offer a range of writing assignments:

- **Reflective writing prompts** ask students to explore their experiences, think out their responses to issues and readings, and probe these responses.

- **Rhetorical analysis assignments** ask students to examine one or more arguments in terms of their rhetorical strategies and effect on particular audiences.

- **Analysis and synthesis prompts** ask students to rethink one reading in light of another and to draw their own conclusions based on both arguments.

- **Argument assignments** ask students to construct their own arguments for different audiences by delving deeper into one of the chapter's subissues.

- **Civic argument assignments** foster civic engagement through letters to political representatives or op-ed pieces directed to university or regional newspapers.

- **Community-based assignments** lend themselves to service learning and call for fieldwork, interviews, surveys, and research into local conditions.

- **Research projects** broaden and deepen the chapter's issues, often through Web research on international and local organizations or advocacy groups.

Glossary The Glossary of this text provides brief definitions of rhetorical analysis and argument terms and of key economic, political, and cultural terms related to globalization.

A list of films (now in the *Instructor's Manual*) related to each chapter's issues provides ideas for further exploration.

INSTRUCTOR'S MANUAL

The *Instructor's Manual* suggests ideas for course designs with sample syllabi, examines the many local-to-global connections in the readings, provides rhetorical approaches to the articles, and discusses how issues have potential for local community involvement. Additional suggestions for class discussion, in-class activities, research activities out of class, and resources, including additional student models, aid instructors in tailoring the text to different course designs.

PEARSON MYLABS

The Pearson English MyLabs empower students to improve their skills in writing, grammar, research, and documentation with market-leading instruction, multimedia tutorials, exercises, and assessment tools. Students can use the MyLab on their own, benefiting from self-paced diagnostics and extra practice in content knowledge and writing skills. Instructors can use MyLabs in ways that best complement their courses and teaching styles. They can work more efficiently and more closely with students by creating their own assignments and using time-saving administrative and assessment tools. To learn more, visit www.pearsonhighered.com/englishmylabs or ask your Pearson representative.

ACKNOWLEDGMENTS

I have been fortunate to have Michael Caster, a recent graduate of the master's program in conflict studies and human rights at the University of Utrecht in the Netherlands, and now a human rights worker and a cultural critic blogger, work closely with me on this edition. Michael's sociological, political, and cultural knowledge and his experience living in different countries are reflected in the new "Global Netizens" chapter, which he researched and developed; in the treatment of graffiti in the chapter titled "Merging and Clashing Cultures" to which he contributed a blog analysis and photos of street art from around the world; and in the subissues explored in the human rights chapter. I am grateful to my colleague at Seattle University, Hilary Hawley, for her research and development of the environmental and global health chapters. Hilary's experience teaching composition and argument, her strong rapport with her students, her commitment to environmentalism, and her experience working with me on the second edition of this book greatly benefited this third edition. In addition, I want to thank Kris Johnson for his creation of the Global Pursuit Quiz from his perspective as a professional writer and cosmopolitan citizen, and my colleague, Tara Roth, who offered her keen civic awareness and shared her experiences teaching this book in her first-year writing seminars.

I am appreciative of my academic institution, Seattle University, particularly for its commitment to social justice, its support of first-year writing seminars, and its ever-deeper investment in global education. The ideas of numerous scholars, writers, and activists have contributed to my understanding of global issues and of the importance of seeing the world through the eyes of other cultures.

Recent and former students played a significant role in this revision through their writing and research. I owe special thanks to Lydia Wheeler for her research and her rhetorical analysis in Chapter 2; to Carlos Sibaja Garcia for his researched argument refuting Arizona's ban an ethnic studies; to Tine Sommer in Denmark for her research on graffiti and European immigration; and to Danielle Bowlden for her research on global health. I am grateful to those students with origins outside the United States for constantly challenging my classes to see other and bigger pictures of the world than our local and national ones. I also appreciate the insights of the students who have contributed their reflective narratives to this book, exemplifying how students interact with global issues and personalize them.

I have great respect for the pedagogical experience of the people who reviewed this book. Whenever I could, I followed their insightful and very useful suggestions, and I am grateful to these scholars and teachers: Jane Kretschmann, Edison Community College; Melissa Miller-Waters, Houston Community College; Connie St. Clair-Andrews, Flagler College; Lynn West, South Puget Sound Community College; and Chris Williams, University of Wisconsin–Stevens Point.

I am also grateful to my skillful Pearson team, especially to my development editor, Kassi Radomski, for her insights, timely aid, and cordial encouragement.

Finally, I want to thank my parents, brother, husband, and daughter for their continued interest in and support of my work. My deepest gratitude goes to my husband, Kenneth Bube, who has been a wonderful intellectual and domestic partner, standing by me at every step of this project. My daughter, Janie, an environmental studies major in college, shared her ideas and experiences from her classes and her field studies work abroad.

JUNE JOHNSON
Seattle University

Exploring and Defining Globalization

*Almost overnight, globalization has become the most pressing
issue of our time, something debated from boardrooms to op-ed
pages and in schools all over the world.**

—Joseph E. Stiglitz, Nobel Prize–winning economist

In this statement, Joseph E. Stiglitz succinctly articulates the immediacy, scope, and importance of globalization. **Globalization**—the increasing interconnectedness of all parts of the world in terms of communication, trade, business, politics, travel, and culture—affects us every day although its presence is sometimes masked. Globalization influences the food we eat, the clothing we wear, the jobs we have, the people we live near, and so on.

This text invites you to join worldwide conversations about globalization by examining many of the major global issues people are arguing about, and by adding your own voice to the public dialogue through your writing about these issues. As you read and enter into these conversations, this text will continuously draw your attention to its overall thesis: that global issues affect us locally and that local matters have global consequences. For example, think about these hypothetical but realistic problems:

- When the payroll department of a software company moved overseas, your mother lost her job, yet this offshore outsourcing has brought new career opportunities and vital income to some workers in India.

- Some of the fruits and vegetables you regularly eat were grown by chemical-using agribusinesses in Nicaragua that have displaced and impoverished small subsistence farmers. You wonder if you should investigate produce grown organically by local farmers.

**Globalization and Its Discontents* (New York: Norton, 2002), 4.

- Your city has experienced an influx of immigrants from different parts of the world. You wonder what forces are driving these people to leave their countries and how your city can more effectively integrate immigrant children into the schools.

What do these experiences have in common? They are instances of the global connections that increasingly link the everyday lives of Americans with the lives of people around the world: In short, they are examples of globalization. They also suggest some of the problems of globalization that call on us to be informed, to seek solutions, and to make decisions.

Before you embark on your examination of the global issues in this book, this chapter offers three exploration activities to spark your thinking about the relationship between your local space and global concerns, the process of globalization, the idea of multiple perspectives, and the way values shape perception.

This introduction also asks you to consider what people mean by the term *globalization*. It briefly sketches the major controversies surrounding the concept of globalization itself and the big-picture questions that underlie global issues. Thinking about what scholars, analysts, and activists are saying about globalization will prepare you to explore the issues and arguments presented in the chapters' readings.

EXPLORATION ONE: HOW WIDE IS YOUR GLOBAL VIEW?

As Americans, we sometimes forget that people living in other countries view the world differently than we do. Globalization draws all parts of the world closer together, and yet reduced transportation time and rapid communication should not fool us into believing that there is only one perspective on events, people, and problems. This first exploration activity resembles a newspaper quiz or Trivial Pursuit game with global subject matter. As you answer the questions that follow, explore how wide your global view is. Try to think beyond an American or Western-dominated perspective of the world. Working individually, with a partner, or with a group, you may want to search for answers to some of these questions by using the Web and by checking general reference books in a library.

 Global Pursuit

1. Nestlé is the world's largest food company. Where is its corporate headquarters?

   a. Paris, France
   b. Atlanta, Georgia
   c. Tokyo, Japan
   d. Vevey, Switzerland
   e. New Delhi, India

2. Match these world cities with their country of location.
   a. Lahore   China
   b. Guayaquil   Romania
   c. Ho Chi Minh City   Pakistan
   d. Tianjin   Ecuador
   e. Bucharest   Vietnam

3. A raga is
   a. a kind of tropical storm that can cause immense damage.
   b. an Italian dish made with beef in red wine.
   c. an annual Scandinavian cultural festival.
   d. a particular kind of melody in Indian music.

4. Rank these international sports in terms of estimated global popularity.
   a. Volleyball   c. Cricket
   b. Basketball   d. Surfing

5. Which country is *not* one of the world's top oil-producing countries?
   a. Norway   e. Kazakhstan
   b. Brazil   f. Russia
   c. United Arab Emirates g. Canada
   d. India   h. China

6. How many American states border Canada?

7. Nasi Goreng is considered the national dish of which country?

8. Which of these nations is *not* a member of NATO?
   a. Albania   c. Luxembourg
   b. Australia   d. Slovakia

9. The United States owes billions of dollars around the world. China is by far its largest creditor. What country is number two?

10. Pop star Lady Gaga was born in which country?
    a. Britain   c. Germany
    b. United States   d. Canada

11. Which country has the largest Muslim population in the world?
    a. Iran   d. Indonesia
    b. Bangladesh   e. Pakistan
    c. Egypt   f. Iraq

12. Which country on the continent of Africa is newly formed since 2008?
    a. Eritrea   d. Republic of South
    b. Algeria   Sudan
    c. Swaziland   e. Sierra Leone

13. The International Dateline generally runs which way?
    a. East–west along the equator
    b. North–south along the 180 degrees of longitude while skirting around Russia
    c. Diagonally across the Pacific

14. What do Guam, Puerto Rico, and the Virgin Islands have in common?

15. In 2011, which nation experienced a significant popular political and cultural revolution?
    a. Mexico   c. Egypt
    b. Chile   d. Cambodia

16. African mango refers to a
    a. popular dance craze that originated in London via West Africa.
    b. controversial diet aid or weight-loss program.
    c. style of African cinema that has been likened to India's Bollywood.
    d. radical political group based in Nigeria opposed to commercial exploitation on the continent.

17. Anders Behring Breivik achieved international notoriety for what?
    a. Marrying Sandra Bullock
    b. Mass murder
    c. Winning the Tour de France
    d. Receiving a Nobel Prize for stem cell research

18. What does Pai Gow refer to?
    a. Style of Thai cooking
    b. Famously polluted river in Cambodia
    c. Chinese gambling game
    d. Human trafficking in Malaysia

19. What is Hamas?
    a. The Algerian independence movement in France
    b. An Arab-originated food dip made from cooked and ground chickpeas
    c. The Palestinian Sunni Islamic party that governs the Gaza Strip
    d. A world animal rights organization

20. Muammar Gaddafi, the assassinated dictator, was the head of state of which country?

Reflective Writing. After you have located answers for the quiz, write informally for ten to fifteen minutes in response to these questions:

1. Which quiz questions and answers surprised you the most?

2. Why was (or was not) this information part of your regular cultural knowledge?

3. Have these questions made you think of other parts of the world as familiar or unknown, as close to home or far away?

4. How did searching for answers to these questions affect your thinking about the importance of being knowledgeable about the world?

After you have responded to these self-reflection questions, your class might discuss your quiz answers, where you found them, and what insights this activity has given you about other parts of the world.

EXPLORATION TWO: GLOBALIZATION AT WORK

One term that often comes up in discussions of globalization is **glocalization**. The Pulitzer Prize–winning journalist Thomas L. Friedman gives his explanation of glocalization in his book *The Lexus and the Olive Tree*:

> I define healthy glocalization as the ability of a culture, when it encounters other strong cultures, to absorb influences that naturally fit into and can enrich that culture, to resist those things that are truly alien and to compartmentalize those things that, while different, can nevertheless be enjoyed and celebrated as different. The whole purpose of glocalizing is to be able to assimilate aspects of globalization into your country and culture in a way that adds to your growth and diversity, without overwhelming it.*

Working individually or in groups, examine these two images of globalization: photos of a global franchise in Beijing, China, and an advertising banner for a global franchise that sells coffee, pizza, and books in Dhaka, Bangladesh. Then answer the following questions in preparation for a class discussion. (For the second photo, note that Ramadan is a month-long religious observance for Muslims that involves prayer and fasting from dawn until sunset. Iftar is the meal after sunset that breaks the fast.)

Starbuck's in Beijing, China

---

*Thomas L. Friedman, *The Lexus and the Olive Tree* (New York: Random House, 1999), 295.

Sign in Dhaka, Bangladesh

1. Describe the visual details of each photo.
2. What influences of globalization do you see in these photos?
3. Now consider whether these images do (or do not) represent success-ful examples of "healthy glocalization" according to Friedman's expla-nation. Create mini-arguments for the following different audiences by formulating at least two reasons for each position you are taking: (a) a U.S. audience thinking about each business; (b) a group of Chi-nese citizens considering this Starbucks; and (c) a group of Bangladeshi citizens considering the business advertising the "Ramadan Special."
4. What additional information about these photos would you find helpful in discussing them in terms of glocalization?

The following sections offer several different definitions of globalization, introduce you to the disagreements over these definitions, and prepare you to think about arguments over global issues.

WHAT DOES *GLOBALIZATION* MEAN?

When people argue about globalization "from boardrooms to op-ed pages and in schools all over the world," what exactly are they arguing about? On the most general level, people are debating the meaning of globalization itself. Disagreements may focus on any or all of these major underlying questions about globalization:

Underlying Controversies About Globalization

- Is globalization a new phenomenon? Or is it simply an accelerated stage in a centuries-long process?
- What forces are driving globalization?
- Is globalization inevitable and uncontrollable? Or is it the product of human decisions and therefore controllable?
- Is globalization harmful or beneficial, a problem or the solution to problems?
- Are there clear winners and losers in globalization?
- How can global and national interests be balanced?
- How is globalization changing our perceptions and behavior, and most other aspects of our lives?
- Is globalization in its current form sustainable?
- Should we welcome, applaud, encourage, resist, protest, or seek to change globalization?

These questions are the foundation of all the global issues explored in this book. As you discuss the global-to-local connections in the chapters' readings, think about how specific issues and individual arguments tap into these foundational questions.

Controversies over Definitions and Interpretations of Globalization

Most books about globalization begin with the author's definition of globalization as both a process and a phenomenon. Indeed, the term *globalization* has sparked intense discussion and argument. Let's consider three different definitions and a visual interpretation of globalization.

One common definition of globalization explains it as the new, defining phenomenon of our historical moment. Thomas L. Friedman, author and foreign affairs journalist and columnist for the *New York Times*, articulates this vision of globalization:

Thomas L. Friedman's Definition of Globalization

It is the inexorable integration of markets, nation-states and technologies to a degree never witnessed before—in a way that is enabling individuals, corporations and nation-states to reach around the world farther, faster, deeper and cheaper than ever before and in a way that is enabling the world to reach into individuals, corporations and nation-states farther, faster, deeper, and cheaper than ever before.*

The Lexus and the Olive Tree (New York: Random House, 1999), 9.

Note that Friedman emphasizes "integration" and pervasive, expansive, and accelerated connections. In his view, all parts of the world are being drawn ever closer together by unstoppable historical processes.

Another common definition of globalization zeros in on the *economic* features and forces of globalization. Jagdish Bhagwati, a professor of international economics and a former special adviser to the United Nations on globalization, distinguishes between the revolution in communication of the recent past and present, cultural globalization, and the profound, powerful economic changes referred to as **economic globalization**:

Jagdish Bhagwati's Definition of Economic Globalization

Economic globalization constitutes integration of national economies into the international economy through trade, direct foreign investment (by corporations and multinationals), short-term capital flows, international flows of workers and humanity generally, and flows of technology.*

Still other prominent voices in the globalization debate emphasize the *problems of defining globalization.* Cynthia Moe-Lobeda, a professor of theology and ethics, argues that it is crucial that we distinguish between two main definitions of globalization: (1) the "intercontinental connections," the way that transportation, communication, and technology have facilitated the movement of materials, goods, and ideas around the world and among continents and countries (basically Friedman's definition); and (2) the dominant model and system of economic globalization (Bhagwati's definition). Moe-Lobeda asserts that the first kind of globalization describes a process of modernization and technological change that is inevitable and beneficial in many ways, whereas economic globalization is not inevitable and not universally beneficial. She contends that it matters *how* we define globalization, because Friedman's and Bhagwati's definitions of globalization mask who is controlling global economic forces and reaping the most rewards from increased global integration. Moe-Lobeda and other opponents of economic globalization believe that it needs to be described in terms that reveal how it distributes economic and political power.† David Korten, a scholar, an activist, and a well-known critic of economic globalization, provides such a description:

David Korten's Definition of Economic Globalization

[Economic globalization refers to] the forces of corporate globalization advanced by an alliance between the world's largest corporations and the most powerful governments. This alliance is backed by the

---

In Defense of Globalization (New York: Oxford University Press, 2004), 3.

†"Defining Globalization: A Faculty Roundtable," in "Debating Globalization: An Interdisciplinary Dialogue" (conference, Seattle University, April 16–17, 2004).

power of money, and its defining project is to integrate the world's national economies into a single, borderless global economy in which the world's mega-corporations are free to move goods and money anywhere in the world that affords an opportunity for profit, without governmental interference.*

Economic globalization as an economic model and system is sometimes called "corporate globalization" or "neoliberalism." Among its main principles, **neoliberalism** as a political-economic philosophy maintains that governments should stay out of trade and give markets free rein; that resources and services such as railroads, electricity, and water should be controlled by private companies; and that capitalism and unregulated trade will lead to beneficial economic and social development.

In addition to verbal definitions, visual images define and interpret globalization. Scholar Wolfgang Sachs asserts that the "the image of the blue planet"† has become a rich symbol adopted by diverse stakeholders who assert different views of the globe and globalization. For example, for environmentalists, the image of the blue and green globe symbolizes the earth as a planet with limited water, air, livable land, and natural resources. Environmentalists want to convey that because the earth is all we have, we must work together to preserve it. However, for another group of stakeholders—the corporations that do business in countries all over the world—the image of the globe symbolizes the expansive potential of business territory and trade. Sachs explains that depicting the world in its entirety as a blue and green ball of continents and oceans with no country borders enables the business community to communicate the message that the entire world is open and available for economic growth.

In this text, the term *globalization* refers both to Friedman's definition of a technologically advanced, increasingly interconnected world and to economic globalization. Several chapters specifically examine the interplay between globalization and the environment and globalization and culture. Although economic globalization influences globalization in all its forms, also keep in mind the other definitions as you read and discuss the arguments in this book.

Controversies over Responses to Globalization

One reason that globalization is so controversial is that the lived experience of it differs depending on people's country, economic class and status, race, gender, age, and even religion. In the last three years, and especially since

---

When Corporations Rule the World (San Francisco: Berrett-Koehler, 2001), 4.

†"Globalization and Sustainability," in *The Globalization Reader*, ed. Frank J. Lechner and John Boli, 2nd ed. (Malden, MA: Blackwell, 2004), 398. What Does *Globalization* Mean?

the global economic crisis of 2008 exploded, arguments about globalization have intensified as people worldwide ponder the positive and negative effects of globalization on their countries, cultures, and individual lives. The responses to globalization and the suggestions for how to manage it range along a continuum.

Strong Supporters of Globalization. On one end of the continuum, supporters praise globalization's sharing of knowledge and technologies. They point to the growth of industries and new markets and the rate at which developing countries are being integrated into the international economy. Arguing that globalization has improved the standard of living and increased the life span of many, they promote expanded globalization. Taking a strong stand in favor of economic globalization and open markets, they warn developing countries, as well as developed countries such as the United States, not to erect barriers to international trade that would interrupt the process of globalization. Instead, more open exchanges of goods, people, and culture should be welcomed.

Supporters of Globalization as a Process. Another group of globalization advocates emphasizes the *process* of globalization. Its members contend that most of the problems countries are experiencing with globalization are temporary setbacks related to the current stage of globalization. Advocates of globalization, such as Jagdish Bhagwati, argue that the problems people attribute to globalization, such as world poverty and hunger, will diminish and that more people will benefit from globalization as these developing countries participate more in the international economy.

Envisioning integration into the global economy as a "development ladder" that countries need to climb to reach full economic and industrialized maturity through the collaboration of governments and private business and the spreading of scientific and technological advances, economist Jeffrey Sachs offers a hopeful win–win vision of globalization that involves "shared prosperity" rather than simply a redistribution of wealth from rich countries to developing ones.*

Moderate Critics of Globalization. These people acknowledge the gains and benefits of globalization but voice objections, mainly about the unequal distribution of benefits and about problems with the global market. For example, George Soros, an entrepreneur, billionaire, activist, philanthropist, and author, sees globalization as an opportunity for greater freedom for everyone; however, he argues that the public good and social well-being of people in developing countries especially have been overrun by market

---

*Peter Sachs, *The End of Poverty: Economic Possibilities for Our Time* (New York: Penguin Press, 2005), 18; *Common Wealth: Economics for a Crowded Planet* (New York: Penguin Press, 2008), 205.

forces. Similarly, Joseph E. Stiglitz, in his book *Making Globalization Work* (2006), argues that globalization as it has been conducted has favored industrialized nations over developing nations, which lack the economic advantages to compete; economic globalization so far has resulted in "unbalanced outcomes, both between and within countries."*

Soros, Stiglitz, and many other analysts of globalization call for a revision of the system. First, they say we must reform the institutions of global governance, such as the International Monetary Fund, the World Bank, and the World Trade Organization, which put decision-making power into the hands of an elite financial community unaccountable to the people whose lives are most directly affected. Pushing these organizations toward more democratic participation would provide checks and balances on market forces and protection for the public good of people in developing countries and poor people everywhere.

Strong Critics of Globalization. Toward the other end of the globalization continuum, some people vehemently challenge economic globalization. Environmentalists, advocates for social justice, spokespeople for preserving cultural identities and heritages, representatives of indigenous peoples and developing countries, political activists, and some economists see economic globalization as a warping of the market itself. Furthermore, Cynthia Moe-Lobeda, David Korten, Indian activist Vandana Shiva, and others believe that economic globalization, with its emphasis on immediate profits, is, in Korten's words, "enriching the few at the expense of the many, replacing democracy with rule by corporations and financial elites, destroying the real wealth of the planet and society to make money for the already wealthy."† In short, they see economic globalization in its current form as inherently flawed, strongly antidemocratic, and harmful to people and the environment. They believe that people everywhere must reject the principle of economic growth, reduce consumption, and commit to preserving the environment and working for social justice in order to end world hunger and poverty.

Proponents of a Local Vision. On the far end of the globalization continuum, some critics are calling for a rethinking of globalization and new investment in local communities. Critics such as Gustavo Esteva and Madhu Suri Prakash focus on the ways that global forces have threatened "local spaces." They claim that it is arrogant and impossible to think "globally" because "we can only think wisely about what we can know well." They say that global policies represent small groups foisting their

---

***Making Globalization Work* (New York: Norton, 2006), 8.

†*When Corporations Rule the World*, 5. What Does Globalization Mean?

local views and interests on other places and peoples. Esteva and Prakash envision an antiglobalization movement composed of "people thinking and acting locally, while forging solidarity with other local forces."* They urge all of us to resist global policies and forces at the local level as we make our decisions about what we eat, what we buy, and how we live.

Navigating the Controversies. As you read the arguments in this text about global issues and their local repercussions, you will see that these divergent definitions of and responses to globalization are embedded in these readings. Try to place the issues in the context of these big-picture questions about globalization: What assumptions have the writers made about the meaning of globalization? Are they assuming that globalization is inevitable? Do they believe that globalization is basically a good thing? Also examine the way their arguments pursue solutions to global problems, strive to win adherents to their views, and expand and clarify your thoughts.

The exploration activity that follows can be used to prepare you to investigate the multisided arguments in this book and the way these issues influence your life.

EXPLORATION THREE: YOUR GLOBAL POSITIONING PROFILE

Our backgrounds, beliefs, and values influence the lenses through which we read arguments about global issues. Playing off the idea of a GPS system for identifying your location, this exercise asks you to sketch a Global Positioning Profile that will help you be conscious of your own values and assumptions. This self-awareness profile will in turn enhance your critical thinking as you encounter and consider new perspectives throughout this book.† To create your own Global Positioning Profile, write brief answers to the following questions:

1. Where do you come from and where have you lived? (Think about your home country, your current country, your state/region, and city, rural versus urban origin.)

2. How would you describe your family background and social connections? (Think about your heritage, ethnicity, class, family composition [for example, number of siblings], gender, age group, education, religious affiliation, and political and ideological leaning.)

---

*"From Global to Local: Beyond Neoliberalism to the International of Hope," in *The Globalization Reader*, 2nd ed. (Malden, MA: Blackwell, 2004), 412–16.

†Chapter 2 identifies a writer's lens or filter on an issue as his or her **angle of vision**. Karen Gookin of Central Washington University originated a version of this exercise in her Research and Reasoning classes.

3. What are your interests and values (for example, pop culture, sports, the arts, the outdoors, independence, volunteerism, free time, the right to vote, social justice, business success)?

Reflective Writing. Choose one of the following global issues and write informally for ten to fifteen minutes, exploring what you currently think about it. Speculate about how your Global Positioning Profile influences your assumptions about, and views on, this global issue.

1. The company making the household appliances your family uses has closed its last factory in the United States and moved to Mexico, leaving hundreds of American workers without jobs. Will you continue to buy this company's products?

2. Following the example of some European cities that have reduced oil consumption and carbon emissions, your city is proposing establishing a daily car-free district downtown between 10 a.m. and 6 p.m. Will you support this proposition?

3. Some policymakers argue that the best way to curb the power of the drug cartels in Mexico and Central America is to decriminalize marijuana in the United States. Do you agree with this approach to the war on drugs?

2

Analyzing and Writing Arguments

*Argument is an ethically powerful way of using conflict to conduct learning and inquiry, and to create change and newness.**

—James Crosswhite

Should U.S. cities follow Paris's example in becoming a bicycle zone with thousands of bikes to rent inexpensively? Should the United States grant more visas to highly educated immigrants? Can the Internet drive political and social change for social justice around the world? How can the global community prepare for pandemics? Global issues like these, as you will discover as you read this book, are producing many public arguments.

Because arguments seek to shape readers' views of controversial issues, they can best be understood in rhetorical terms. The terms **rhetoric** and **rhetorical** refer to the persuasive use of language to accomplish certain ends in specific situations. Aristotle explained rhetoric as "the faculty of discovering in any particular case all the available means of persuasion." Scholar and rhetorician Lloyd Bitzer has expanded on Aristotle's definition and elaborated on the power and importance of rhetoric: "Rhetoric is a mode of altering reality, not by the direct application of energy to objects, but by the creation of discourse which changes reality through the mediation of thought and action."†

What these and many other definitions of rhetoric have in common is a focus on the use of language to persuade, to mold the way people see the world. Because rhetoric is enlisted all around us in arguments attempting to "change our reality," as a citizen and a student you will benefit from acquiring rhetorical skills to interpret and produce arguments.

To study arguments rhetorically means to realize that arguments are always produced in contexts. Reading rhetorically involves attending

---

*James Crosswhite, *The Rhetoric of Reason: Writing and the Attractions of Argument* (Madison: University of Wisconsin Press, 1996), 9.

†Quoted in Wayne Booth, *The Rhetoric of Rhetoric: The Quest for Effective Communication* (Carlton, Victoria, Australia: Blackwell, 2004), 8.

closely to the writer, the writer's purpose, the audience, and the genre or type of writing. When we think of an argument rhetorically, we think of it as written by someone who has a stake in the issue, to an audience, for a purpose, in a genre (for example, op-ed pieces, policy analyses, advocacy fliers and open letters). Writers of arguments tailor their arguments to change readers' views and move them to action. However, these arguments can be skillfully, shoddily, responsibly, or deceptively constructed. Thinking rhetorically will enable you to examine arguments to determine how and why they are persuasive.

This chapter will introduce you to the main tools of civic and academic argument. First, it will explain the elements of an argument and the features to examine in analyzing an argument rhetorically. The second part of the chapter will provide some steps and strategies you can use to summarize arguments, write rhetorical analyses, and generate and structure your own arguments in response to the arguments you are reading. Knowing how to analyze arguments rhetorically will help you become a stronger, more sophisticated reader. Knowing how to speak back to texts and to construct your own reasoned and audience-based arguments will help you become a more confident, versatile writer.

A BRIEF INTRODUCTION TO ARGUMENT

The first step in understanding arguments rhetorically is to move beyond a casual understanding of argument. In everyday conversation, argument often refers to an opinion, a disagreement, or a fight. However, the discipline of writing and rhetoric has a more specialized and complete meaning for **argument**: a persuasive text that makes a claim and develops it with reasons and supporting evidence. In addition, argument is multisided, not merely two-sided. Usually, there are many positions that can be argued on any issue, not simply a pro and a con. Global issues tend to generate multiple views because these issues are complex and touch the lives of many people, groups, and institutions, all of whom have stakes in these issues.

Issue Questions, Claims, and Stakeholders

Arguments originate in issue questions. Unlike an information question, which merely calls for an explanation, an **issue question** is a controversial question that could have many contestable answers. These controversial questions are behind every argument: no controversy, no argument. Writers form claims in answer to issue questions. You can think of a **claim** as a statement that asserts an arguable answer to an issue question.

Global issues are highly controversial and generate many issue questions. For example, urban farming is a controversial issue globally. Even though cities around the world—Vancouver, Canada; Beijing, China; Rosario, Argentina; Kyoto, Japan; and many others—are practicing urban farming, support for urban farming and systematic planning are lacking in many cities. Some cities have outlawed agriculture and others consider it unimportant. Here are two issue questions related to urban farming: Can urban farming meet the world's growing need for food? What are the most effective ways to encourage urban farming? Notice how each question can be answered with different claims that would lead to different arguments.

Issue Questions	Claims
Can urban farming meet the world's growing need for food?	Urban farming cannot contribute substantially to feeding the world's growing population.
	Urban farming can be a partial solution in feeding the world's growing population.
	Urban farming can be a main solution in feeding the world's growing population.
What are the most effective ways to encourage urban farming?	In order for urban farming to succeed, the rate of growth for cities must be slowed by helping people continue living in more rural areas.
	In order to promote urban gardening as a source of food, city planners and politicians must set aside land in cities for urban gardening.
	To encourage urban farming, all new city buildings should be designed for roof-top gardens.

To think about arguments rhetorically means to think in terms of who is arguing and who cares—in other words, who are the **stakeholders**, or people who have investments in the answers to these questions. Issue questions become claims when people who care about them—stakeholders—decide to take a stand on them. The stakeholders in any argument include the people who are motivated to write about the issues and the people affected by the issues. The following stakeholders are people who have stakes in the arguments about urban farming:

- city dwellers who stand to benefit from growing their own food or buying locally produced food
- environmentalists who want to preserve the environment by using it wisely

- urban planners who could help make this farming possible
- businesses and city residents buying land and buildings in cities
- politicians who make city laws

For each argument you read, try to state the issue question behind the claim and identify the writer's stake and others' stake in the issue: To whom does this argument matter?

Discussing and Writing

Determining Issue Questions, Possible Claims, and Stakeholders

We frequently buy new electronic gadgets to replace broken or outdated ones. Where should we dispose of these old computers, televisions, cell phones, digital cameras, and game systems? Can these be recycled in environmentally friendly ways? Currently, some of this electronic trash (e-waste), much of it containing toxic chemicals, is dumped in poor developing countries. The reading that follows argues that disposal of e-waste plunges us into environmental, legal, economic, and human rights problems.

Read the following advocacy statement posted on the Web site for Basel Action Network (BAN), an environmental watchdog group dedicated to alerting American consumers about the problems of e-waste. After reading this campaign piece, follow these steps:

1. State at least five issue questions related to e-waste.

2. List at least five stakeholders—people involved in these issue questions in one way or another.

3. Formulate at least five possible claims, answers to these issue questions that stakeholders might want to argue.

Remember that an issue question should have at least two different answers, and a claim should be a controversial, arguable statement. (Later in this chapter, we will return to this article and these issues.)

The e-Waste Crisis
Basel Action Network

Every year, an estimated 400 million units of obsolete electronics are scrapped. Four billion pounds of electronic waste, or e-waste, was discarded in the United States in 2005, accounting for between 2% and 4% of the municipal solid waste stream. As much as 87.5% of this was incinerated or dumped in landfills. Of the remaining 12.5% collected for "recycling," industry sources claim that about 80% is exported to developing countries where it is processed in primitive conditions, severely endangering the environment, workers and communities. Pollution created by irresponsible e-waste processing can also come back to haunt those in the exporting countries as well in the form of air pollution fallout via long-range transport.

The world faces an e-waste crisis because of the following factors:

- **Huge volumes:** The dual forces of rapid obsolescence of electronic gadgetry combined with astronomically burgeoning use have created mountains of e-waste—the largest growing waste stream our economy produces.

- **Toxic design:** Electronic equipment contains some of the most toxic substances known: mercury, lead, cadmium, arsenic, beryllium, and brominated flame retardants, among others. Thus, when this equipment becomes waste, it is toxic waste. When burned, even worse toxins can be formed such as dioxins and polycyclic aromatic hydrocarbons that can cause cancer and birth defects. Until recently, far too little emphasis has been placed by manufacturers on eliminating toxic materials.

- **Poor design and complexity:** E-waste is full of many different materials (such as multiple kinds of metals, plastics, and chemicals) that are mixed, bolted, screwed, snapped, glued, or soldered together. This makes separation for recycling difficult. Further, little attention has been paid to designing equipment for recycling. Therefore, recycling either requires intensive labor or sophisticated and costly technologies.

- **No financial incentive to recycle:** There's usually not enough value in most electronic waste to cover the costs of responsibly managing it in developed countries unless laws require such management as a service industry. For this reason it is exported to countries where workers are paid low wages and the infrastructure and legal framework are too weak to protect the environment, workers and communities.

- **Reuse abuse:** Sending equipment and parts for reuse—an important solution—can easily be abused by falsely labeling scrap as reusable or repairable equipment. Often this "reusable" equipment ends up getting dumped in countries lacking any infrastructure to properly manage it.

- **Policy of "free trade in toxic waste":** In the U.S. and Canada, the laws governing export of trade in hazardous electronic waste are tragically inadequate, and thus these two countries are the primary sources of the global crisis. The U.S. is the only developed country in the world that has failed to ratify the 1989 Basel Convention, an international treaty controlling trade in hazardous waste from richer to poorer countries. In 1995, that treaty adopted a full ban on exports from rich to poorer countries. Both the U.S. and Canada actively oppose this pro-hibition. In Canada, the Basel Convention is not properly im-plemented, allowing almost all e-waste to flow abroad freely. In both countries, then, it is perfectly legal for businesses to maxi-mize profit by exporting toxic electronics to developing coun-tries, even when this export is a violation of the laws of import-ing countries. The export of toxic electronic waste to developing countries disproportionately burdens them with a toxic legacy and allows for externalization of real costs.

- **Prison laborers employed to process e-waste:** Unlike other countries in the world, the U.S. sends much of its hazardous e-waste to U.S. prisons to process in less-regulated environments without the worker protections and rights afforded in the pri-vate sector. Moreover, such operations amount to government subsidies, undermining the development of responsible private-sector recycling infrastructure and distorting the economics of recycling.

- **Private data is imbedded in electronic devices:** Comput-ers, PDAs, mobile phones, and even printers and fax machines hold private data such as social security, bank account, and credit card numbers and private emails. These can be used by criminals involved in identity theft to hijack bank accounts and conduct blackmail and extortion if this data is not completely eradicated. Loss of confidential data is another form of liability and irresponsibility stemming from improper e-waste disposal.

- **Lack of regulation requiring proper management:** U.S. regulations mostly exempt the electronic waste stream from en-vironmental laws and active OSHA* oversight. Further, accord-ing to the laws of Canada and the U.S., most toxic electronic waste is still perfectly legal to dispose of in nonhazardous waste landfills and incinerators.

DOCUMENTED HARM

In 2002, the Basel Action Network (BAN) and the Silicon Valley Toxics Coalition released the ground-breaking report and film *Exporting Harm: The High Tech Trashing of Asia,* which exposed the toxic "recycling" of discarded electronics in China. A second film and report released in 2005 by BAN, *The Digital Dump: Exporting Reuse and Abuse to Africa,* showed similar tragic results happening in Africa, this time in the name

---

*OSHA is the Occupational Safety and Health Administration, part of the United States Department of Labor. It was created in 1971 to protect workers on the job.

of 'reuse' and 'bridging the digital divide.' Images of men, women, and children burning tons of toxic circuit boards, wires, and plastic parts exposed the fast-cheap-and-dirty side of our consumption of computers, televisions, faxes, printers, etc. Furthermore, BAN analyzed hard drives from exported computers collected in Africa and found massive amounts of private data freely available for criminal exploitation. We have also discovered that when U.S. prisoners are used as cheap labor, they are exposed to these poisons as well. The Federal Prison Industries' UNICOR, which processes much of the e-waste in the U.S., is now the focus of a Department of Justice investigation for the toxic exposures prisoners suffer. Finally as much as 87 percent of discarded toxic e-waste is simply dumped in municipal landfills or incinerators, ill equipped to contain or destroy such toxic waste.

Unfortunately this grossly irresponsible waste mismanagement and toxic trade is the norm in the North American recycling industry. It is still all too commonplace for recyclers and even electronics manufacturers, aided by the inadequate or non-existent policies of the Canadian and U.S. governments, to leave the dirty and dangerous work of managing our toxic waste to the poorest of the poor in developing countries. The resulting environmental hazards and social injustice ravage the land and people in these developing nations. Furthermore, these poisons come back to our shores and into our bodies via long-range air and ocean pollution, toxic imports, and contaminated food.

GOVERNMENT FAILURE: EXTERNALIZING OUR TOXIC IMPACTS

To date, unlike the 27 member countries of the European Union, the United States and Canada have failed to create legislation providing a national system to finance and responsibly deal with toxic e-waste. Instead, an e-waste anarchy is sanctioned, where we can exploit the cheap and dirty 'solutions' that 'externalize' (or pass on) the real toxic impacts and their costs to others—poor communities in developing countries, disempowered prisoners in this country, or local municipalities and taxpayers who suffer from this material getting dumped in local landfills or incinerated, polluting soil, air and water. Further, the U.S. and Canada have failed to ratify or properly implement the Basel Convention that prescribes international rules to prevent such toxic waste trade.

U.S. Congress' watchdog agency, the Government Accountability Office (GAO), recently published a report entitled, "Electronic Waste: EPA Needs to Better Control Harmful U.S. Exports through Stronger Enforcement and More Comprehensive Regulation." The GAO report describes, in no uncertain terms, the complete inadequacy of legislation to control e-waste exports and the lack of EPA enforcement of the minimal regulations that do exist, resulting in a flood of toxins to the developing world.

Instead of properly regulating electronic waste management and trade, the EPA has tried to bring interest groups together to create voluntary solutions. These efforts have ended in failure or have produced little more than minimalist, 'lowest-common denominator' standards, which seemingly please everyone, including waste exporters, but result in continued abuse to the environment and human health. One of these efforts is the recently released "R2" Standard for Responsible Recycling.

Meanwhile, in lieu of an appropriate federal response, states and municipalities must cope with the national failure by passing a variety of local laws and state laws. However, the U.S. Constitution forbids these local governments from legislating international trade, so states and municipalities are helpless to prohibit the flood of e-waste leaving our shores. It is in this unregulated landscape that responsible electronics recycling companies are challenged to compete against unscrupulous brokers and exporters and those who deceptively call themselves "recyclers." These bad actors simply load up seagoing containers and ship U.S. hazardous electronics to the highest bidders globally. Almost always, this results in the wastes shipped to a developing country to be processed by cheap, unprotected labor to maximize profits. These "low road" operators are thriving while the responsible companies, with their safer, more expensive methods, struggle. ■

The Core of an Argument: A Claim with Reasons

To move from a claim to an argument, you need reasons to support the claim. We say that the core of an argument consists of a claim with **reasons**. A claim answers an issue question and becomes an argument when it is supported implicitly or explicitly by reasons. In reconstructing the core of arguments you read and in creating your own arguments, it is helpful to state reasons as *because* clauses. *Because* clauses help show the logical and arguable reasons justifying the claim. In order for arguments to be persuasive, the claims and reasons that writers craft should be tailored to the values, assumptions, and interests of their chosen audience; in other words, they should be audience-based reasons. What reasons would make this audience consider this claim?

Let's take the example of the controversies over bottled water. People are arguing about how the corporate bottling of water—taking it from the ground and selling it in bottles—is exploiting sources of water in rural regions, including in developing countries like Kenya. They are also arguing about the production, recycling, and disposal of tons of plastic bottles. The following chart presents some examples of claims and audience-based reasons in response to this issue question: Should universities and college students continue to buy bottled water? Notice how the reasons change depending on the audience.

Issue question: Should universities and college students continue to buy bottled water?	
Audience and Stakeholders	**Argument Cores: Claim and Reasons**
Audience: University administration considering getting rid of vending machines with bottled water **Stakeholders:** The university administration, college students, and bottled water companies	**Claim:** Universities and college students should continue to purchase bottled water. **Reasons:** Because bottled water conveniently fits students' on-the-go schedules. Because students think bottled water tastes better than tap water.
Audience: University administration considering reducing the use of bottled water on campus **Stakeholders:** College athletic departments, college athletes, the university administration, and bottled water companies	**Claim:** College athletic departments should continue to purchase bottled water for athletic teams. **Reasons:** Because bottled water provides an ever-ready beverage that athletes especially need while engaged in strenuous physical activity. Because bottled water comes with good financial deals between the companies and universities purchasing bottled water in bulk.
Audience: Residence halls exploring ways to promote the university's commitment to global sustainability and healthy living **Stakeholders:** Student environmentalists, other college students, university administrations	**Claim:** College students should not continue to purchase bottled water. **Reasons:** Because the bottled water industry is producing tons of plastics that are damaging the environment worldwide. Because bottled water is often less healthful and safe than publicly regulated tap water.

These examples show a few of the argument cores that could be constructed in response to this issue question. Each argument core would lead to a different argument with different reasons that would appeal to a different audience. Note that an argument core could have one or many reasons.

Assumptions in Argument

Besides claims and reasons, there are other parts of arguments to consider when thinking of arguments rhetorically. In addition to choosing audience-based reasons related to the beliefs, values, and interests of their intended audience, writers should think out the assumptions behind their reasons and determine if the audience shares these assumptions. You can think of **assumptions** as the principles behind the reasons. These principles are usually connected to values (for example, priority on convenience, low costs, environmental protection, human rights, humane treatment of animals, free speech, and so forth). Does the audience share the writer's values? If yes and if these principles are acceptable to the audience, then the reasons will seem good and logical and will function as strong justification for the claim.

> **Example of a claim and reason:** We should have mandatory labeling stating the country of origin for all imported foods because such labeling would improve the monitoring of food safety in the global food system.
>
> **Assumption/principle:** Monitoring food safety in the global food system is important and beneficial.

Assumptions may be buried inside the argument or overtly discussed. Thinking out these assumptions and figuring out if they, too, need to be argued and supported often makes the difference between a successful argument and an unpersuasive one. In the following examples, the rationale explains possible problems with the argument that might emerge related to the assumptions behind the reasons.

Audience: University administration considering getting rid of vending machines with bottled water.	
Claim: Universities and college students should continue to purchase bottled water.	

Audience-Based Reasons	**Thinking Out Assumptions**
Because bottled water conveniently fits students' on-the-go schedules	**Assumption 1:** Convenience for busy students is a high priority for the university.
Because students think that bottled water tastes better than tap water	**Assumption 2:** Providing products that appeal to students' tastes is important to the university.
	Rationale: If the university administration does not value student convenience and satisfaction above other things, then the reasons will not be workable, or the writer will need to justify the assumptions as well as support the reasons.

Audience: University administration considering reducing the use of bottled water on campus.

Claim: College athletic departments should continue to purchase bottled water for athletic teams.

Audience-Based Reasons	Thinking Out Assumptions
Because bottled water provides an ever-ready beverage that athletes especially need while engaged in strenuous physical activity	**Assumption 1:** Conveniently meeting the physical needs of university athletes is important to the university.
Because bottled water comes with good financial deals between the companies and universities purchasing bottled water in bulk	**Assumption 2:** Saving money is important to the university. **Rationale:** If the needs of university athletes and the finances of the university are not top priorities, then other reasons would be more persuasive, or these reasons will require justification and supporting evidence.

Audience: Residence halls exploring ways to promote the university's commitment to global sustainability

Claim: College students should not continue to purchase bottled water.

Audience-Based Reasons	Thinking Out Assumptions
Because the bottled water industry is producing tons of plastics that are damaging the environment worldwide	**Assumption 1:** Producing tons of plastic and damaging the environment are undesirable consequences.
Because bottled water is often less healthful and safe than publicly regulated tap water	**Assumption 2:** Choosing the most healthful and safe water is important. **Rationale:** Most likely the audience would agree that these consequences are negative. This argument, then, would concentrate on establishing exactly *how* bottled water's tons of plastic hurt the environment, and on *how* bottled water is unsafe and unhealthful, not on whether these effects and qualities are bad.

When you analyze an argument, determining the assumptions behind the reasons, which will often be implied and not stated, can help you understand how well an argument is constructed. Writers can build stronger arguments by adjusting their reasons and assumptions to their audience and in some cases, by defending and developing the assumptions as well as the reasons—in effect, carrying on a two-tier argument.

Discussing and Writing

Thinking Out Argument Cores and Assumptions

Working individually or in groups, take three of the claims that you formulated in the exercise on page 17 in response to the e-waste article. For each of these claims, do the following tasks:

1. Develop at least two reasons that would support the claim.

2. For each reason, state what you think is the assumption—the principle behind the reason that an audience would have to accept to find the reason persuasive.

The Development of an Argument: Evidence

Another important part of an argument is the kind, amount, and quality of supporting evidence that writers use to make their arguments persuasive. **Evidence** can take the form of examples, facts, numerical data, testimonies and quotations, or further reasoning. Writers choose their evidence to meet the needs of their audience. What constitutes good evidence? Rhetorician Richard Fulkerson offers helpful criteria for evaluating the evidence in an argument, which he calls the **STAR criteria**.*

STAR CRITERIA FOR EVALUATING EVIDENCE IN AN ARGUMENT
• **Sufficiency**: Is there enough evidence for this audience?
• **Typicality**: Is the evidence typical or is it extreme and deceptively chosen?
• **Accuracy**: Is the evidence accurate and current?
• **Relevance**: Is the evidence related to the claim, reasons, and assumptions?

*Richard Fulkerson explains these criteria in more detail in his book *Teaching the Argument in Writing* (Urbana, IL: National Council of Teachers of English, 1996), 44–50.

Applying the STAR criteria to evidence in the arguments you read and later to your own arguments will help you assess the effectiveness of the arguments. The key rhetorical question, though, is "For whom is the evidence persuasive?" As with the other parts of an argument, evidence is also rhetorical in that what an audience considers persuasive evidence depends on its values, interests, and beliefs. Arguments that succeed with their audiences include appropriate audience-based evidence. As we saw in the charts on pages 23–24, writers may need to create additional subarguments to support their assumptions with evidence; in other words, other parts of the argument, besides the reasons, may call for evidence to make the whole argument persuasive.

Responses to Alternative Views

The final structural part of an argument is the writer's recognition of alternative or opposing views. Although not all arguments acknowledge opposing views, the presence or absence of these acknowledgments and responses to these views often makes the difference between a persuasive argument and a weak one. Because arguments are controversial and arguers most likely will be writing to an audience who is uninformed, undecided, or opposed, it is important for writers to show their awareness of alternative views and respond logically and authoritatively to them. Writers may either concede to those views by accepting their validity and then shift the focus back to their own case, or they may rebut them with counterreasoning and counterexamples (see the chart on page 27). For example, if a writer is arguing the claim that her university should stop supplying bottled water in vending machines, she would need to anticipate objections that students and the university might make. She could either concede and admit that these objections do make sense and then shift back to her own views, or she could argue directly against these objections in a rebuttal, using her own reasons and examples. How much space a writer devotes in an argument to opposing views also depends directly on the audience.

Arguments Tailored to Audiences

The whole construction of an argument—its degree of edginess and development—is a function of the writer's relationship to his or her purpose, audience, and choice of the type of argument (flier, formal researched argument, editorial, and so forth). We can think of arguments as ranging on an argument continuum, with positions on the continuum representing the writer's specific purpose and relationship to the audience. On one end of the continuum, the arguer would have an exploratory purpose and would imagine a cooperative or collaborative relationship with the audience. In effect this writer says, "Think this issue out with me." On the other end of the continuum, the arguer is basically writing propaganda with a hard-sell purpose that blasts the audience, denying any space or value to audience members. This writer says, "You have to see this issue my way, the only way." The more the writer engages in dialogue with the audience and seeks to see the issue from this alternative perspective, the more the argument will convey a problem-solving, inquiry approach. When writers are assured of their audience's agreement, they may choose not to include alternative views.

The argument continuum shown on pages 28–29 demonstrates the range of possible purposes and relationships with the audience. All arguments fall somewhere on this continuum. When you are reading an argument, determine the purpose of the argument and the stance the writer is taking toward the audience. Is the writer trying to solve a problem of interest to the audience? Is the writer mostly in an inquiring mode, entertaining differing perspectives on the issue question, or is the writer shoving a view at the audience? How firmly and aggressively is the arguer asserting a claim? How does the engagement with alternative or opposing views enrich the argument?

Now that we have examined the structure of arguments in some detail, you may be wondering, Does everyone who writes and publishes an argument plan the argument as systematically as this explanation suggests? The answer is no. However, writers who construct successful arguments for their audiences have most likely thought carefully about their issues in ways that reflect the deep structure of their arguments. You will have the greatest success with your own arguments if you think of planning them in terms of claims, reasons, assumptions, evidence, and acknowledgment of alternative views. (The last section of this chapter offers suggestions to help you with this planning.)

RESPONSES TO ALTERNATIVE OR OPPOSING VIEWS	
Claim: The university should stop selling bottled water in vending machines.	
Example of Concession	**Example of Rebuttal**
It is true that busy students are often racing around campus to classes and activities. I know that sometimes fountains are difficult to find, might not work, or might be dirty. I also recognize that being thirsty can impair a student's ability to concentrate. One day when bad traffic made me late to campus and I had to run to class, all I could think about during my class was Gatorade, Pepsi, and water. Nevertheless, it is easy to carry aluminum reusable water bottles, which are inexpensive.	Although students get thirsty amidst their busy schedules, the university could try harder to maintain drinking fountains in clean, working order, and students could carry water in reusable aluminum containers, reducing their need to buy bottled water.

Truth Seeking

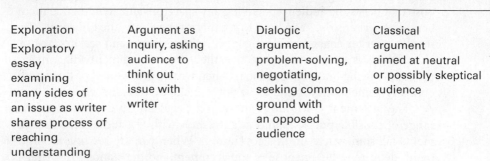

Exploration	Argument as	Dialogic	Classical
Exploratory essay examining many sides of an issue as writer shares process of reaching understanding	inquiry, asking audience to think out issue with writer	argument, problem-solving, negotiating, seeking common ground with an opposed audience	argument aimed at neutral or possibly skeptical audience

The Argument Continuum: From Exploration to Problem-Solving and Persuasion

Discussing and Writing

Analyzing an Argument's Structural Parts

The following argument presents a citizen's and consumer's perspective on the problem of sweatshop-made goods. The writer is addressing the issue questions, *Should we care whether our goods are made in sweatshops, and how can we reduce companies' use of sweatshops?* Sweatshops are highly exploitive factories with extremely long working hours and days, unsafe conditions, low and/or unreliable wages, and management control of workers. As you study this argument, you will see that the writer, Ed Finn, proposes that we change our buying habits for three main reasons.

Working individually or in groups, read the following example of a well-crafted argument and analyze it by identifying these parts of the argument:

1. the claim

2. the reasons

3. the assumptions behind the reasons

4. several pieces of evidence used to support each reason

5. the alternative/opposing views; and the writer's response to these views

This argument first appeared in June 2003 in the *Canadian Centre for Policy Alternatives Monitor,* a progressive monthly journal focusing on social and economic justice. According to its Web site, this organization's motto is "Think again," and it seeks to inform people of alternatives "to the message that we have no choice about the policies that affect our lives." Ed Finn is the senior editor of this publication.

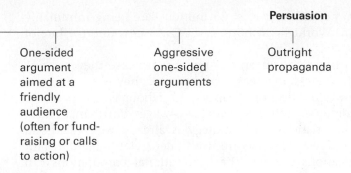

Persuasion

One-sided argument aimed at a friendly audience (often for fund-raising or calls to action)

Aggressive one-sided arguments

Outright propaganda

Harnessing Our Power as Consumers: Cost of Boycotting Sweatshop Goods Offset by the Benefits
Ed Finn

Being follicly challenged, I can't venture out in the noonday sun without a cap. So I went looking for one. My shopping foray took nearly two weeks. Not because headgear was hard to find in Ottawa, but because I wanted a cap made by workers who were fairly paid and well-treated—and that kind of headgear is hard to find.

Had I been content to buy a cap made in a sweatshop in China, Haiti, Malaysia, or some other Third World nation, it would have been easy. The stores were full of them. But I wanted a cap made preferably by a unionized worker in Canada, or, failing that, in another country with decent labour standards.

After visiting a score of clothing shops, I finally located such a cap. It was made in England. I had to pay nearly $40 for it, four or five times more than a comparable cap from an Asian sweatshop would have cost. But the Brit beanie was far more comfortable and durable. It comes out of the washing machine looking as good as new. I bought it four years ago and it still shows no sign of wearing out. So, even from an economic standpoint, I didn't suffer for sticking to my "buy non-sweatshop" principles.

Most Canadians, sad to say, don't make any effort to find domestic apparel. Or they give up after visiting their third or fourth clothing store, where the racks are crammed with shirts, pants, sweaters and jackets sewn by underpaid and abused workers in Asia or Latin America.

Imported outfits do cost less. They appeal to anyone looking for the cheapest item and indifferent to how and where it was made. Even when reminded that millions of children under the age of 14—the

UN estimates they number at least 25 million—are being inhumanly exploited in Third World sweatshops, most Canadians find the lure of a "bargain" irresistible.

They should be more concerned—not just because they want to help mistreated workers overseas, but because they want to help themselves. The exploitation of cheap foreign labour is part of a vast global strategy designed ultimately to force wages down in Canada and other Western nations. This strategy is already well advanced. Freed from national restrictions by free trade, deregulation, and instant global communications systems, the transnational corporations can now relocate production to countries and regions where wages, taxes, and environmental laws are the lowest.

This corporate mobility has eroded the power of Canadian workers and their unions to protect their jobs, benefits, and working conditions.

As consumers, however, we are far from powerless. We can refuse to buy the products of child labour, prison labour, and sweatshop labour in the Third World. In the short term, this will unavoidably increase our living expenses, but in the long term it could save our jobs and prevent our wages from plummeting further.

The corporations are counting on us to keep our needs as consumers entirely separate from our needs as workers. And, unfortunately, up to now, most of us have done just that—in the process unthinkingly worsening our own financial security. The more sweatshop goods we buy, the more we reward the corporations for their downsizing here and their cheap labour strategy abroad. And—contrary to some right-wing pundits—we aren't doing any favours to oppressed foreign workers, either. We are in effect perpetuating their serfdom.

Some politicians, business leaders and academics argue that, if we boycotted goods made by underpaid foreign workers, we would be depriving them of their livelihood, as meagre as it may be.

But this claim is as spurious today as it was in Victorian times, when it was advanced to rationalize the use of child labour. ("Take away these kids' jobs and they'll starve to death or turn to lives of crime.")

The same flawed reasoning was trotted out by conservatives to oppose the economic boycott of the apartheid regime in South Africa. Had their arguments been heeded, that country would still be ruled by a brutal and racist government, and Nelson Mandela would still be in prison.

The leaders of opposition movements in developing nations ruled by dictators know that boycotts of sweatshop goods would temporarily add to their people's woes. But they also know that, in the long run, such boycotts offer the best hope of toppling the dictators and thereby vastly improving their people's lives.

One such leader is Nobel Peace Prize winner Aung San Suu Kyi, who heads the National League for Democracy in Burma. Like Mandela, she too was jailed by that country's ruthless military rulers and still endures their harassment. She favours the same kind of economic sanctions that finally got rid of apartheid in South Africa, even if they temporarily cause more hardship for Burma's sweatshop workers.

"All profits from business enterprises in my country," she said recently, "go to a small privileged elite. Companies that continue to invest here only serve to prolong the agony of my country and its people by encouraging the military regime to persevere in its atrocities."

She could have said the same thing about consumers in Canada and other developed nations, who also prop up Burma's dictatorship when they buy made-in-Burma merchandise.

It's time for us to look at the labels of the goods we buy. If we stopped buying sweatshop products, we would accomplish three things: 1) we would be helping to slow down and eventually stop the export of jobs from Canada; 2) we would be helping the oppressed people in the Third World to throw off the yoke of military and corporate tyranny; and 3) we would be effectively challenging the corporations' global low-wage strategy.

Granted, such a change in our shopping habits would involve some additional costs to us as consumers. But these costs would eventually be offset by the gains we would derive as workers—and the gains that would be made by brutally mistreated workers in the Third World. ◼

A BRIEF INTRODUCTION TO RHETORICAL ANALYSIS

As you read in the introduction to this chapter, to analyze a piece of writing—a verbal or a visual text—rhetorically means to examine closely how the text is put together to create a specific effect. Although any text—a billboard, a course syllabus, a personal ad, a sermon, a travel brochure, a phone book—can be analyzed rhetorically, this section of the chapter will prepare you to analyze the arguments on global issues you will encounter in this book.

The Importance of Thinking and Reading Rhetorically

Before we look at how to read rhetorically, let's consider two important principles about rhetoric.

1. **Language plays an important part in constructing reality.** Language presents visions of what is real and shapes how we see the world. Taking a rhetorical approach to reading and writing emphasizes the knowledge-making, constructive potential of language and argument. As rhetorician James Berlin explains, "truth is dynamic and dialectical" and "truth is always truth for someone standing in relation to others" in a context that is shaped by language.*

---

*James Berlin, "Contemporary Composition: The Major Pedagogical Theories," *College English* 44, no. 8 (December 1982): 774.

2. **Every argument you read is actually a voice in a larger, ongoing public conversation.** No argument represents a complete answer or total view, and knowledge grows through these many contributions.

These two principles show that rhetoric is not decorative, static, or extraneous but part of our ongoing effort to make sense of the world. As contributions to larger conversations, arguments are moments of meaning-making in that effort. To take a rhetorical approach to arguments is to think about each argument as a part of an ongoing, situated conversation.

The rhetorical tools you will learn in this section will help you understand how arguments grow out of and contribute to these specific global conversations. These tools will help you evaluate the usefulness and value of these arguments for you and others. When rhetoricians talk about argument, they think, as rhetorician John T. Gage explains, in terms of "the sequence of moves which the writer has controlled for the purpose of leading the reader to assent."* Rhetorical reading, then, becomes a useful process for you as a citizen, student, and later a professional, of determining when an argument is well constructed and when it deserves your "assent" because it has legitimately persuaded you. In addition, when reading and analyzing an argument, you will be able to determine when the writer is trying to solve a problem and when he or she is mostly selling his or her views, or even more, foisting them on you as if they were the only views possible.

In the next sections, you will learn how to apply your understanding of the structural parts of arguments and of some additional rhetorical principles to the analysis of arguments. For every argument you read, consider these key questions:

- How is this argument constructed to have certain effects on readers?
- For whom would this argument be persuasive? What values, beliefs, and assumptions would an audience have to hold to find it persuasive?
- Why is (or is not) this argument persuasive for you?

Becoming adept at answering these questions for the arguments you read will spur your growth as a reader and writer. The following sections explain the foundational rhetorical concepts to help you examine the arguments you read. The examples of these concepts draw on the variety of stakeholders, views, and arguments on the problem of illegal immigration in the United States.

Identifying the Writer and the Writer's Angle of Vision

When you read an argument, you need to consider who is arguing. Begin with the writer of the argument. Figure out the writer's identity and

---

*John T. Gage, "Freshman English: In Whose Service?" *College English* 44, no. 5 (September 1982): 472.

background. In every argument, the writer expresses an **angle of vision**, which is the lens of values through which he or she is interpreting the issue.

CONSIDERING THE WRITER'S IDENTITY AND ANGLE OF VISION	
Rhetorical Concept and Working Definition	**Example Using the Illegal Immigration Issue**
Writer: Who is the writer or creator of the text? What is his or her background, profession? What knowledge or authority does he or she have?	Policymaker, immigration lawyer, Pulitzer Prize–winning journalist, Jesuit priest, film celebrity, advocacy organization in favor of immigrant rights
Angle of vision: All arguments have an angle of vision. Angle of vision refers to the selective seeing of the writer; the writer's angle of vision determines how the argument is framed and what is emphasized and what is omitted. The writer's stance on the subject is influenced by his or her values, beliefs, background (family history, education, gender, religion, age, class), ethnicity, political leanings.* For every argument, we can ask, What is the writer's angle of vision, lens, filter, or perspective? How much does the angle of vision control or dominate the argument?	A Border Patrol agent "sees" illegal immigration differently from the way an economic analyst or the owner of a construction company sees it. A nativist organization wanting to restrict all immigration, especially illegal immigration, focuses on social problems such as crime rates and public costs and connects these to immigration. An environmental organization sees immigration through the lens of population growth and use of natural resources. For example, an environmental angle of vision might stress the damage to the desert plants and animals (including fires and garbage) caused by the many people illegally crossing the deserts on the border.

Often, as in this book, introductory material for each argument provides information about the writer of the argument and helps you determine the writer's angle of vision. The writer's angle of vision can be perceived in every choice the writer has made in the argument: from the claim to the reasons and evidence; the way this evidence is presented to look positive or negative; the points emphasized; the consideration of alternative views; and the fairness or extremism of the language. Some arguments will not let you forget for a minute what the writer thinks of the issue and will make a conscious effort to shape your views at every point. Others will sequence and frame the evidence but also maintain a less insistent and aggressive presence. If the angle of vision of a writer does not coincide with your own values and views, you may find it more difficult to listen to the argument and find yourself talking back to the writer.

---

*The Global Positioning Profile activity at the end of Chapter 1 asks you to explore your angle of vision.

Identifying the Rhetorical Context

Another key part of thinking rhetorically is realizing that texts grow out of and operate in social contexts; therefore, we need to approach arguments as voices in controversial conversations. Arguers are moved to write by **motivating occasions**; they may be responding to a specific public event, private circumstance, or experience. Identifying the motivating occasion—the event, occasion, problem, or condition that prompts the arguer to speak out—can help you understand the argument. Related to the motivating occasion is the timeliness of the argument, what rhetoricians call the *kairos* or "why now" of the argument. You should also try to determine the specific **purpose** of the argument. Is the writer trying to change people's view of the issue, move them to action, or search for and work out an answer to a problem? Another part of the rhetorical context is the **audience** the writer has in mind, the people to whom he or she is directing the argument, sometimes called the target audience. Often, arguments have a primary and secondary audience, as in the genre of the open letter, which is written to a specific person although it will be read by a larger reading public. The audience—whether neutral, friendly, or antagonistic, uninformed or knowledgeable—influences the argument. Finally, the **genre** or type, kind, or category of argument also is related to the audience and purpose. Is this argument an editorial in a big city newspaper, a policy statement, a blog, an advocacy advertisement, a scholarly argument in a journal in a discipline, or is it a visual argument?

EXAMINING RHETORICAL CONTEXT	
Rhetorical Concept and Working Definition	**Example Using the Illegal Immigration Issue**
Audience. Who are the intended readers? What does the writer know about these readers' background knowledge, their interest in the subject, and their values, beliefs, and assumptions? Beyond the target audience, who might read this text?	Is the text directed toward a large, general audience of newspaper readers or toward scholars with years of background in the field? For example, does the audience already share the writer's belief that a strong physical barrier at the border will not solve the illegal immigration problem?
Writer's motivating occasion and purpose. What is the occasion or event (also called exigency), the external or internal cause, that compelled the author to write? What is the change the writer wants to bring about in the readers?	Is Congress voting on an immigration reform bill? Does the writer want to influence voters? What has the news reported on how many illegal immigrants have died recently crossing the border through the desert?

Kairos. *Kairos,* a term from classical rhetoric, refers to the "rightness" of the argument for the moment and the situation—its timeliness and appropriateness. What is the kairotic moment for the argument? Why is this argument being written now for this audience?	Luis Alberto Urrea wrote his book *The Devil's Highway* after the incident of the Wellton 26, when fourteen "walkers" died hideous deaths trying to cross the border in the desert. He wanted to give readers a deeper understanding of the immigrants who risk their lives to enter the U.S. and of the Border Patrol whose job it is to intercept them.
Genre. Genre refers to the category/kind/form of the text (for example, news report, editorial, political cartoon, formal speech, and so forth). Genres have conventions (rules) that bring readers' expectations and that are intended to have social effects. Genre determines length, formality, treatment of sources, style and document design. What is the genre of an argument?	Is this text an op-ed piece (short, provocative, urgent) in the local newspaper about deported immigrants? Or is it a policy proposal for a think tank (researched, thorough, supported by statistics and studies)? Is the genre personal or public, entertaining or motivational?

Examining the Use of Classical Appeals to *Logos, Ethos,* and *Pathos*

Some final basic concepts to consider when reading an argument are the arguer's use of the classical appeals to *logos, ethos,* and *pathos.* The Greek philosopher Aristotle outlined the importance of these appeals to the rhetorical effectiveness of arguments.

- **Appeals to *logos*** refer to the logical structure, consistency, and development of an argument.

- **Appeals to *ethos*** refer to the ethical character of the writer that comes across in the argument. For the writer to convey an ethical, positive *ethos,* he or she must be fair to opposing views, be credible and knowledgeable, and use evidence in a reliable manner.

- **Appeals to *pathos*** refer to how the writer engages the emotions and imaginations of the audience by evoking sympathy and how the writer taps into the audience's values. Writers can use case studies, extended examples, narratives, quotations, descriptions, figurative language, and images to make issues real and meaningful to the audience.

The role that these appeals play in particular arguments can vary enormously. For example, it is possible for an argument to be dominated by *logos* with few appeals to *pathos,* making the argument very intellectual, complex, or even dry or dull. Conversely, an argument can emphasize appeals to *pathos* and have little logical substance, trying only to work the audience's emotions. An argument can rest on the authority and reputation of the writer, relying on appeals to *ethos*. It can gain persuasiveness through a writer's use of reliable evidence, or it can lose persuasiveness through a writer's unfair attack on opponents or use of scanty or unverifiable evidence.

The following chart summarizes the classical appeals and how they can be used to explore the effectiveness of an argument.

EXAMINING THE USE OF CLASSICAL APPEALS	
Rhetorical Concept and Working Definition	**Example Using the Illegal Immigration Issue**
Logos *of the Argument* (the logical appeal): What is the logical structure of the argument? What is the main claim? What reasons support this claim and how are they tailored to the audience? Is the evidence sufficient and accurate to make the claim and reasons persuasive? Are opposing views recognized and answered persuasively with counterreasoning?	A policy analyst at a research institute might argue that only a thorough overhauling of U.S. hiring and labor practices will address the illegal immigration problem. She might cite studies and statistics.
***Appeal to* Ethos** (the ethical appeal): The writer's *ethos* is shown in how he or she presents himself or herself as knowledgeable about the subject, treats alternative views responsibly, and reaches out to the audience by grounding the argument in shared values and assumptions. Has the writer given signs of having listened to other views? How well does the writer gain the readers' trust? How authoritative, credible, and fair is the writer?	If the writer is arguing about changes in policies at the border, has he or she lived or worked in Arizona or Texas on the border? Has the writer researched problems with illegal immigrants and quoted and cited verifiable sources?
***Appeal to* Pathos** (emotional, imaginative appeal): How does the writer appeal to readers' emotions, imaginations, beliefs, and values? Has the writer used audience-based reasons? How prominent and effective is the writer's use of specific, vivid language; narratives and illustrations; humor? How much has the writer humanized the argument?	In the book *The Devil's Highway,* Urrea devotes fifteen pages to describing in detail what it is like to die of hyperthermia. He uses the pronoun "you" throughout to put the reader in place of the illegal immigrant whose blood is boiling and skin melting in the desert. The reader cannot remain detached. This scientifically accurate, graphic description evokes intense compassion for the immigrants risking their lives in the desert.

A Consideration of Style

Style is an elusive quality that is often noticed by readers but is difficult to describe in words. It is related to the writer's *ethos* and closely related to genre, which often dictates features of the style. The style of an argument can be very formal or very casual and conversational; it can be very intellectual and discipline-specific (suited to one field such as psychology or economics), using terminology from the field; or it can be very readable and suited to a popular audience. The following chart shows additional points that help create and distinguish the style of a piece of writing.

Rhetorical Concept and Working Definition	Example Using the Illegal Immigration Issue
Style: Style refers to the level of formality of the writing, the complexity, the tone of the text (humorous, serious, mocking, ironic), and the use of language. It includes the length and complexity of sentence structure and the sophistication of the vocabulary. Style is closely related to genre because many genres dictate style: for example, the appealing readability of editorials in general circulation newspapers or the authoritative declarations of a policymaker in a white paper sketching out an organization's view of an issue.	Does the editorial writer attack opponents using colloquial language or use many Spanish words to convey the immigrants' culture? Is the policy statement packed with complicated statements in legal jargon, calling for a reform of the laws governing visas, or complex economic terms about remittances (the money immigrants send back to their communities and families in their countries of origin)?

Style can make an argument readable or tough going for readers. It can enhance the effectiveness of an argument, highlighting points in humorous, memorable, or powerful ways, or it can call attention to itself and distract readers.

Although you may not have time methodically to answer each of the questions about rhetorical features for each argument you read, the more attention you pay to these features, the more you will find yourself understanding the arguments and how they work. Furthermore, a sound rhetorical understanding of an argument will enable you to assess how much influence this argument should have over your own views—how much "assent" it merits. The following activity will give you an opportunity to practice what you have learned about the main features of arguments and rhetorical analysis.

Discussing and Writing

Conducting a Rhetorical Analysis

Working individually or in groups, return to the argument written by Ed Finn, "Harnessing Our Power as Consumers" on pages 29–31. Using the questions for rhetorical analysis in the charts on pages 33–37 take notes on how you think the writer's identity and angle of vision, the rhetorical context, argumentative strategies, and style are working in this text. Also, determine how well the appeals to *logos, ethos,* and *pathos* are working in this argument: How logical, well structured, and well supported is the argument? How ethical, responsible, and reliable is the writer? How does the writer appeal to readers' emotions and values? Sum up your rhetorical analysis by writing a paragraph explaining the appeal of this argument to its target audience. What specifically makes it persuasive? Then comment briefly on how persuasive this argument would be for other audiences.

WRITING A SUMMARY

You will find that writing summaries is a key part of writing both rhetorical analysis essays and arguments. In fact, summary writing is one of the most useful writing skills you can learn for academic and professional success. Many other academic and professional genres, such as papers to be presented at conferences and proposals for grants or projects, also draw on summary writing skills.

Using Summaries in Rhetorical Analyses

Before you can critique an argument to determine how well it is written and why it is persuasive for certain audiences, you need to have a sound understanding of the argument. This kind of understanding can be fostered through writing a summary of the argument. In writing a summary, you listen carefully to the argument, withholding your own views and judgments, simply trying to grasp what the argument is saying. In a rhetorical analysis essay, you can use your summary to ground readers in the argument, to build a base from which to launch your rhetorical critique. You usually include your summary, which can range from one or two sentences to a full paragraph, early in your essay to give readers a basic understanding of the argument so they will be able to follow and appreciate your analysis.

Using Summaries in Arguments

The process of summarizing and the summaries you produce also play a major role in writing arguments. Listening carefully and sympathetically to the arguments of others represents a critical step in entering argumentative conversations. Your understanding of multiple perspectives should inform the claims and reasons that you develop in your own arguments. Often, you will summarize views you are applying or enlisting in support of your position. You will also summarize opposing views that you are conceding to or refuting. In addition, incorporating a fair and accurate summary of a text into your own argument helps establish your positive *ethos*.

How to Write a Summary

As you are learning to write summaries, you should follow a deliberate and methodical process. Later you may develop your own effective shortcuts. The following chart proposes steps and strategies to write a summary of an argument.

STRATEGIES FOR WRITING A SUMMARY

- Read the article you are summarizing at least two times.
- Either in your head or on paper, map out the shape or structure of the article by determining how each paragraph and section of the article functions.
  - How many paragraphs are introductory?
  - What is the thesis-claim—if it is stated?
  - Which paragraphs develop the writer's reasons?
  - Is there an alternative views section? Or are opposing points and objections woven throughout the article?
  - How many paragraphs make up the conclusion?
- Go back through the article, paragraph by paragraph or section by section, and translate the writer's ideas into your own words. Try to state in one sentence the main point of each section or paragraph.
- Take stock of the length of the summary you will be writing. Choose the drafting approach that works best for your needs.
  - To produce a summary of 200–350 words, draft your summary by combining your point statements from each paragraph. Once you have strung together these sentences, experiment with ways to combine and condense them into clear, concise, coherent statements.
  - For a one- to two-sentence summary, you can condense your paragraph summary down to the overall thesis-claim of the argument. Alternatively, you can try to identify, extract, and reformulate that main idea after achieving a good understanding of the article.

(continued)

(continued)

- Begin your summary by identifying the writer, the title of the article, and your own statement of the writer's overall thesis-claim.

- In revising your summary, be sure you have used **attributive tags** (Finn argues … , Finn asserts … , According to Finn, …) every few sentences to indicate that the ideas you are expressing belong to the writer, not to you.

- In revising your summary, check it for these features:

  - neutrality (you should keep your own views and judgments out of a summary)

  - fair and balanced coverage (your summary should be true to the importance of the ideas in the original article)

  - conciseness (you should use language economically—use the most direct, clear language with no wasted words)

  - coherence with smooth, logical movement from sentence to sentence

  - minimal or no quotations (quote only if you want to give the flavor of the article or if you can't do justice to the writer's ideas otherwise) and citation of page numbers using the documentation system your instructor specifies (Modern Language Association, American Psychological Association, or *Chicago Manual of Style*)

Test of a good summary: Would the writer of the article accept your summary as an accurate and fair abstract of his or her argument?

The following example is a summary of the article "The e-Waste Crisis." The annotations help identify the features of an effective summary.

Example of a Summary

First sentence identifies the article and author and states the main idea.

Attributive tag focuses on the author.

Attributive tag focuses on the author.

In the article "The e-Waste Crisis," Basel Action Network claims that the United States and Canada lead the world in the environmental destruction and social injustice caused by the dangerous dumping and exporting of toxic electronic waste. According to BAN, four billion pounds of e-waste, the largest single type of waste, were produced in 2005. Over 85% of it was burnt or deposited in landfill and 12% of what was recycled ended up in developing countries. The toxins in this waste endanger the environment and communities where it is dumped, the workers handling it, and even the rest of the world through polluted air, water, and food. BAN asserts that many complex factors are compounding the e-waste crisis. First, electronic gadgetry is made up of highly toxic substances such as lead, mercury, and arsenic. This gadgetry, which rapidly goes out of date, is labor intensive to take apart to recycle parts, and the market for this equipment is growing, creating more e-waste. Second, lack of regulation also removes any incentive to recycle this waste and falsely labeled recycling hides the disposal methods. The biggest problem, according to BAN, is that the United States is the only developed country that did not ratify the 1989 Basel Convention, controlling trade of e-waste and prohibiting the exporting of hazardous waste from rich to developing countries. The Basel Action Network and the Silicon Valley Toxics Coalition have documented on film the exporting of this waste to poorer countries in Southeast Asia and Africa where children and adults are exposed to dangerous toxins as they cheaply and primitively disassemble and burn this waste. BAN calls for legislation and a national system to confront this crisis. Finally, BAN argues that states, cities, U.S. prisons where the waste is often handled, poor countries around the world, and a few responsible companies, responding to the EPA's weak voluntary solutions, should not have to bear the brunt of the e-waste problem. (321 words)

> Transitions help organize the summary.

> Additional transitions and attributive tags keep the focus on the main points.

> Concluding sentence wraps up the summary.

Example of a One-Sentence Summary

In its Web article "The e-Waste Crisis," Basel Action Network claims that the United States, which has refused to adopt global regulations, leads the world in the discarding of toxic electronic waste in municipal dumps and the exporting of this toxic waste to poorer countries, and consequently contributes substantially to environmental destruction and social injustice.

Discussing and Writing

Summarizing an Argument

Working individually or in groups, return to Ed Finn's argument "Harnessing Our Power as Consumers" on pages 29–31. Follow the steps and strategies for writing a summary explained in this section.

1. Write a 250–300 word summary.

2. Then write a one-sentence summary that captures the main claim of the article.

3. **Reflective Writing.** Write a short reflective paragraph discussing the challenges you faced writing these summaries. What was difficult? How did you solve any problems?

WRITING A RHETORICAL ANALYSIS

This section discusses the main thinking and writing moves of a rhetorical analysis essay. Particularly, it explains how to find a focus and formulate a thesis statement for your essay. It concludes with an example of a student's rhetorical analysis, an essay by Lydia Wheeler analyzing the rhetorical effectiveness of an argument by Ha-Joon Chang (in Chapter 3, pages 100–104).

The Purpose and Audience of a Rhetorical Analysis

A rhetorical analysis is basically an interpretive argument, written for an audience who is assumed to be neutral or uninformed yet receptive, rather than hostile and antagonistic. Because a rhetorical analysis essay is an interpretation—your interpretation of someone else's argument—it has a persuasive purpose. Your main strategy is to make your interpretation persuasive by providing textual evidence and good discussions of all your points. Your goal is to make your audience see the argument you are analyzing your way. However, your essay may be as heavily analytical as it is persuasive.

Purpose. Your motivation and specific purpose for writing a rhetorical analysis may be described in one of several ways:

1. You may be writing as a student producing an academic essay critiquing an argument to show your understanding of the argument and how it works rhetorically.

2. You may be writing as a citizen or student trying to make sense of an argument as you develop your own views on the issue in preparation for joining the public conversation on the issue with your own argument.

Audience. The usual audience for a rhetorical analysis is other people who are seeking a deeper understanding of the argument and who want to know what it contributes to the public conversation on this controversy. Your audience might be other citizens and students who like yourself want to sort out the various public arguments to choose the most reasonable, informed view. Or occasionally, you may have a more specific audience in mind, such as a defined group of stakeholders (potential volunteers with refugees in the community, potential vegetarians, commuters who drive cars to campus, and so forth).

The Structure of a Rhetorical Analysis

In envisioning a structure for your rhetorical analysis, think of your essay as having these main parts:

- An **introduction** providing a brief context for the argument and perhaps for your analysis (a statement explaining your interest in the article and its timeliness and relevance for you and your audience)

- A **brief summary of the argument** to provide your readers with a foundation and basic understanding of the argument you are analyzing
- A **thesis statement** that indicates the focus of your analysis and perhaps maps out the points you will discuss
- A **well-developed main section** devoted to your analysis of the article and evaluation of the rhetorical strategies, perhaps considering the article's rhetorical context, purpose, and target audience
- A **brief conclusion** that wraps up your analysis and possibly comments on the significance of the article's argument

Analyzing the Argument

A rhetorical analysis essay should reflect your close examination of and deep thought about a piece of writing. Here are some strategies that will help you engage thoughtfully with an argument. Note how these strategies incorporate the summary writing strategies from the preceding section of this chapter.

STAGE 1: STRATEGIES FOR ANALYZING AN ARGUMENT

1. *Reach a thorough understanding of the article you are analyzing.* Familiarize yourself with the article and its argument by reading it several times.

2. *Follow the strategies for writing a summary on pages 39–40.* Map out the shape of the argument, identify its main points, and try to get inside the argument to grasp the writer's perspective. Write a summary of the argument, perhaps both a longer summary of 150–250 words and a short one-sentence summary.

3. *Examine the article's presentation of its argument.* Using your understanding of the main elements of an argument, ask yourself questions and jot down notes:

   - What is the question-at-issue? What is the writer's core argument? What reasons and evidence does the writer present?

   - Because all stakeholders are driven to present their views to change readers' perspectives, the question is not, Is this writer biased or passionate? (Of course, arguers are passionate!) Ask instead, Is this writer arguing rationally with evidence to support reasons or only ranting and name calling, skewing evidence? Is the writer aware of alternative views and fairly representing and refuting them?

   - How responsibly does the writer develop the *logos* of the argument and use appeals to *pathos*?

(continued)

(continued)

4. ***Examine your response to the construction or ideas of the argument by freewriting answers to these questions:***

   - What features stand out as most important to the way this argument makes its appeals to readers?

   - Where does your interest shift to a higher gear, or where do you disengage in frustration or disagreement?

   - What will you remember about this argument? What leaves you thinking?

Now that you understand what argument the writer is making and have explored your response, you can dig deeper into its rhetorical construction.

Choosing a Focus for Your Rhetorical Analysis and Writing a Thesis Statement

Your goal at this point is to reach a thorough understanding of this article and to discover some independent perceptions that you can share with your readers. As you apply the rhetorical concepts and the questions presented in the charts in the section "A Brief Introduction to Rhetorical Analysis" (pages 31–38), try to refine your thinking about the argument you are analyzing and zero in on a focus. A typical focus for a rhetorical analysis essay is either (a) why and how an argument works for its target audience or (b) why and how the argument works for you or others who are not part of its target audience. Basically, *how* does this argument contribute to the public conversation on this issue?

STAGE 2: STRATEGIES FOR FOCUSING YOUR RHETORICAL ANALYSIS AND WRITING A THESIS STATEMENT

1. ***Think about the rhetorical context of the argument:*** the writer, the writer's angle of vision, the motivating occasion and writer's purpose, the *kairos* of the argument, and the target audience.

   - Analyze how rhetorically effective the argument is. Most writing on global issues in the public sphere has a civic component, appealing to readers as citizens, voters, or consumers. How is the argument working to persuade them?

   - Who are the stakeholders in this argument?

   - What values and assumptions would readers have to hold to be moved by this argument?

(continued)

- Think about how this argument fits in the larger public conversation on the issue. How is the writer framing the issue or articulating the problem? How does this argument intersect with other arguments you have read on the same issue?

2. ***Think about your relationship to the target audience and the argument's effectiveness for you.*** If you are not part of the target audience (for instance, not a supporter of the advocacy group or not a regular reader of the news commentary journal where the argument appears), ask yourself questions like these:
   - What features of this argument make it a reliable, responsible view on this issue?
   - Where do the reasons, evidence, or argumentative strategies (for example, handling of alternative views) seem effective and persuasive to you?
   - What points need more development or verification?

3. ***Choose several important features of the article that you want to discuss in depth in your essay.*** Identify points that grow out of your rhetorical thinking about the argument. These points should go beyond the obvious and should bring something fresh and insightful to your readers that will help them see this argument with new understanding. You may want to list your ideas and then look for ways to group them together around main points.

4. ***Write a thesis statement for your analysis.*** Given that you cannot discuss every rhetorical feature of the argument, select main points from your notes and freewriting to be the focus for your analysis.

   - Which points do you think shed important light on the rhetorical effectiveness of the argument you are analyzing?
   - For your audience, which features of this article's argument merit interpretation and discussion?

   In your thesis statement, you may choose to map out two or more points that you will explore in your essay. You may need two sentences to present these points.

Here are some examples of thesis statements for a rhetorical analysis essay.

Three Sample Thesis Statements

1. Ed Finn's editorial "Harnessing Our Power as Consumers" works beautifully to persuade an audience sympathetic to social justice issues by using Finn's personal experience to build a positive *ethos* and by making points about historical labor struggles, boycotts, and the causal link between cheap products and overseas labor.

2. Ed Finn's editorial "Harnessing Our Power as Consumers" will not reach dissenting readers because he fails to acknowledge opposing views of sweatshops, relies heavily on his own experiences as a consumer, and does not address readers' real financial need for cheap products.

3. Although PETA's (People for the Ethical Treatment of Animals) You-Tube video *Meet Your Meat* makes powerful verbal and visual appeals to *pathos,* the film fails to persuade meat eaters to change their ways because it distorts its evidence and disregards all other perspectives.

Drafting a Rhetorical Analysis

Once you have drafted a strong working thesis statement, you are ready to write a complete draft of your rhetorical analysis essay following the suggested structure on pages 42–43. The main writing moves that will make your rhetorical analysis essay persuasive as well as engaging are (1) setting up your points clearly and delivering on your readers' expectations by following through with lively explanations of them; and (2) using specific textual evidence, both examples and quotations, to give validity and credibility to your points.

An Example of a Rhetorical Analysis Essay

The following rhetorical analysis essay by student writer Lydia Wheeler examines an argument that is an excerpt from a book by Ha-Joon Chang, *Bad Samaritans: The Myth of Free Trade and the Secret History of Capitalism* (2008). The chapter excerpt that Lydia analyzes, "My Six-Year-Old Son Should Get a Job: Is Free Trade Always the Answer?" appears in Chapter 3 of this book, pages 100–104. Lydia's rhetorical analysis represents one of the most frequently assigned types of academic writing assignment. Notice how the title sets up her focus. Other features of Lydia's analysis are identified by annotations.

 STUDENT VOICE: Ha-Joon Chang's Vital Discussion of Free Trade and Developing Nations: A Rhetorical Analysis by Lydia Wheeler

Since the highly controversial North American Free Trade Agreement (NAFTA) went into effect in January 1994, the United States has signed into law eleven other free trade agreements (FTAs) and the massive South Korea–United States FTA (KORUS), which may go into effect in early 2012, could be the twelfth. In addition, the United States is currently in talks to create or join more than fifteen free

> Writer addresses the *kairos* or timeliness of the issue.

trade agreements around the globe. Clearly, FTAs have become an integral part of the global economy. As responsible citizens of the U.S. and the world we need to learn not just what free trade agreements can do for us, but what they may do *to* the other countries that sign them. Many of the principles we must consider while tackling the question of FTAs are presented by South Korean economist Ha-Joon Chang in his book *Bad Samaritans: The Myth of Free Trade and the Secret History of Capitalism* (2008). In one chapter of this book, "My Six-Year-Old Son Should Get a Job: Is Free Trade Always the Answer?,"* Chang illustrates the dangers of free trade agreements with an analogy that casts developing nations as young children and the developed world as their negligent parents. Chang asserts that both children and newly established national industries need protected opportunities before fending for themselves—in careers or less regulated markets. In the second half of the chapter, Chang provides evidence that liberalization (the practice of reducing or removing government restrictions on the production and free flow of goods) has not sparked the growth its proponents claimed it would in developing nations, and discusses additional problems liberalization causes in developing nations.

> Writer introduces Chang's argument, which she is analyzing rhetorically, and briefly summarizes it.

Although Chang's decision to open with an emotionally charged analogy is rhetorically risky, and some readers may be confused about his focus and tone or feel manipulated, most readers will likely find that, "My Six-Year-Old Son Should Get a Job" offers an illuminating argument on free trade economics that employs well-balanced appeals to *pathos, logos,* and *ethos.* Chang successfully engages our emotions, supports his knowledgeable case against liberalization, and all the while maintains a fair, balanced approach.

> Writer presents her two-sentence thesis statement setting up the points she will discuss in her rhetorical analysis.

The first key to Chang's success is the emotional appeal he makes to readers in his opening analogy. At its most basic, the analogy simply introduces one relationship and superimposes onto it the dynamic of a different, but similar, relationship: Chang introduces his father/son relationship with his hypothetical story about his little son Jin-Gyu, then draws parallels to what free trade economists propose should be the relationship between developed nations and currently developing nations. Through the father/son analogy to industrialized/developing nations, Chang makes some economic

> Writer discusses her first main point about Chang's use of an analogy argument as an appeal to *pathos.*

---

*This chapter appears as a reading in Chapter 3 of this book on pages 100–104.

problems glaringly—even absurdly—obvious. After all, who would say that a six-year-old boy should be forced to compete in an adult economic world? Chang establishes himself as an exploitive, callous father threatening to harm Jin-Gyu. This situation generates sympathy—and possibly even affection or worry—for his son, effectively making the readers allies with Jin-Gyu against his uncaring father. As an economic issue, free trade is often discussed in very cold-blooded terms, with statistics and dry projections of economic growth. Opening with such a strong appeal to readers' sympathy for Jin-Gyu—and by extension, for developing nations—is a powerful reminder that international trade policies can have direct, and sometimes devastating, effects on people around the world.

> She explains how the analogy argument works rhetorically.

When Chang later acknowledges the absurdity of his assertion that Jin-Gyu should be forced to work, he shifts the relationship he created with his readers and comes to side with them against the idea of pushing Jin-Gyu into the workforce. Working through his analogy, Chang replaces Jin-Gyu with developing nations and replaces dangerously lax parents with the free trade economists of developed nations. From the start, Chang's analogy serves to foster sympathy for countries ill-treated through FTAs. By the fourth paragraph of this chapter, he has also managed to generate sympathy for his own points, and may have engendered negative feelings for the policies he will argue against.

> Writer elaborates on and extends her point about the emotional effectiveness of Chang's analogy.

An argument relying entirely on emotional appeals, however, wouldn't convince many readers, so Chang also appeals to *logos* with developed and substantiated reasoning. In the second half of the chapter, Chang explains his objections to liberalization as an unjust and unsuccessful policy foisted upon developing nations. He analyzes numerous indicators of economic health in economies which have been extensively liberalized to belie the myth that free trade is inherently good. While some readers may find the extensive use of economic terms and heavy use of data slow-going, the use of hard evidence provides ballast against the emotional weight of the opening analogy and builds on the theoretical points Chang has laid out through the analogy. In this part of his argument, Chang develops and supports his view with extensive, verifiable data, showing how his theories are applicable to the real world. He focuses on the case of Mexico, which he calls "the poster boy of the free trade camp" (102) because Mexico seems to have all the ingredients for prosperity according to free trade theory: the

> Writer discusses her second main point about the logical effectiveness of Chang's argument. She analyzes Chang's use of evidence to substantiate his views about free trade's damage to developing countries.

workers, the proximity to the large market of the United States, and the North American Free Trade Agreement. However, Chang cites the slow rate of growth, the loss of jobs, and the damage to Mexican agriculture to support his view that free trade policy is not working. Chang further builds his case by mentioning similar problems in Ivory Coast and Zimbabwe that occurred when these countries experienced the implementation of free trade policy. Far from being the cure for economic ills it is made out to be, free trade may be inflicting damage of its own on the developing nations it supposedly helps, Chang argues.

The real rhetorical power of Chang's argument lies in his refocusing of the free trade conversation. At the beginning of this piece through his analogy, Chang directs readers' ire at the mistreatment of Jin-Gyu onto free trade policies; at the end of this piece, he refocuses the entire discussion of free trade agreements between developed and developing nations. He looks beyond income and job generation in developing nations to spotlight rarely examined effects of liberalization on developing countries. Chang points to a pattern common in many developing nations: tariff reductions mandated by FTAs eventually lead to less spending on infrastructure, health care, and education in the nations "helped" by liberalization. Chang's final point—that liberalization can lead to reduced funding for education in developing nations—also builds on and brings readers back to his opening analogy. If Jin-Gyu drops out of school to join the workforce, "he may become a savvy shoeshine boy or even a prosperous street hawker, but he will never become a brain surgeon or a nuclear physicist" (101). And if a nation must reduce funding to education and infrastructure in order to qualify for the "benefits" of free trade agreements, will any jobs gained be worth the loss in potential they may cost?

> Writer explains how Chang connects the parts and levels of his argument—his analogy and his economic data and examples about problems with free trade in developing countries.

In addition to weaving together the *pathos* and *logos* of his argument, Chang also conveys a positive *ethos*; he is clearly knowledgeable and he is also fair in his treatment of opposing views. A Cambridge University educated economist who grew up during South Korea's own period of economic development, Chang demonstrates his trustworthiness as an analyst of free trade agreements. For example, he cites sources opposed to his views such as a study by the IMF, an organization which avidly promotes rapid liberalization in developing nations. Additionally, Chang concedes that "the protection I provide to Jin-Gyu (as the infant industry argument itself says) should not be used to

> Writer discusses her third main point about the rhetorical effectiveness of Chang's *ethos*, achieved through his concessions and acknowledgment of opposing views and evidence.

shelter him from competition forever" (101). He admits that both over-protective parents and over-protective governments can become "dysfunctional" (101). Chang also demonstrates his consideration of opposing views as he concludes the piece, when he concedes "it is perfectly possible that *some* degree of *gradual* trade liberalization may have been beneficial, and even necessary, for certain developing countries in the 1980s—India and China come to mind" (104). This willingness to acknowledge when liberalization may be appropriate serves to illustrate Chang's trustworthiness as a source on free trade.

"My Six-Year-Old Son Should Get a Job" starts with an original, commanding appeal to *pathos*, one Ha-Joon Chang carefully balances with appeals to *logos* and *ethos*, to create a rhetorically effective argument against unchecked free trade. The brilliance of his analogy argument, his inclusion of extensive support, and his measured avoidance of extremes demonstrate the value of Chang's perspective in the discussion we must continue to have about the dangers of free trade and liberalization for as long as the United States proposes and promotes the establishment of new free trade agreements around the world.

> Writer briefly sums up her points and reiterates the significance of Chang's argument.

Work Cited

Chang, Ha-Joon. "My Six-Year-Old Son Should Get a Job: Is Free Trade Always the Answer?" *Bad Samaritans: The Myth of Free Trade and the Secret History of Capitalism.* New York: Bloomsbury Press, 2008: 65–69. Rpt. In *Global Issues, Local Arguments.* June Johnson. 3rd ed. New York: Pearson Education, 2013. Print.

> Writer includes a citation using the documentation style of the Modern Language Association.

Discussing and Writing

Generating Ideas for a Rhetorical Analysis Essay

Choose one of the arguments in this chapter—"The e-Waste Crisis" or "Harnessing Our Power as Consumers: Cost of Boycotting Sweatshop Goods Offset by the Benefits"—or an argument specified by your instructor. Then using the Stage 1 and 2 Strategies charts on pages 43–45, do the following writing tasks in preparation for writing a rhetorical analysis essay:

1. Write your own 150-word summary of the article's argument.

2. Analyze the argument's parts based on the questions under 3 in the Stage 1 chart on pages 43–44.

3. Freewrite—that is, write in rapid, nonstop, free associational, uncensored mode for a certain period of time, say fifteen or twenty minutes—thinking about important features of the argument, using the suggestions in question 4 on page 44.

4. Take notes about the rhetorical features of the argument using the Stage 2 questions on pages 44–45.

5. Then choose several analytical points about the rhetorical features of the argument or its ideas that have emerged from your note taking and free-writing, and draft a thesis statement you could develop in a rhetorical analysis essay.

WRITING AN ARGUMENT

In your academic career and very likely in your professional life, you will be called upon to construct arguments, some informal and some formal. In some situations, you may be writing an argument to support a cause you believe in or inventing a solution to a problem of interest to you. Sometimes you will be engaging in soul-searching and examination of your own values and experiences to figure out your stand on an issue. Other times, you will be researching an issue to develop your view and take an informed position on it. In all these cases, the thinking and writing moves explained in this section can help you write a rhetorically effective argument. This section will walk you through these strategies:

1. Posing a significant, perplexing issue question
2. Using reflective or narrative writing to discover your interests
3. Examining multiple perspectives on your issue by immersing yourself in the issue, by adopting different views, and by using brief informal and formal writing to think out your own views
4. Analyzing your audience, purpose, and genre
5. Constructing an argument core attuned to your audience's interests, values, and assumptions

After you have used these various approaches to discovering what argument you want to make, you will be better prepared to structure and draft your argument and then revise it. This section will briefly explain these approaches and will show you an example of student writer Lindsey Egan's policy proposal* argument on water usage in the American Southwest.

---

*A policy proposal—unlike a practical proposal that outlines an action to solve an immediate, local problem—presents a broad plan of action that tackles a big, public social, economic, or political problem.

Posing a Significant, Perplexing Issue Question

Your argument will achieve more depth and complexity if it grows out of a significant, perplexing issue question. The most successful, responsible arguments have developed through genuine inquiry—true engagement with the issue question and searching for an understanding of the issue. The question should be significant to you and other stakeholders so that the "Who cares?" "What are the stakes?" dimension is built into your argument from the beginning.

Using Reflective or Narrative Writing to Discover Your Interests and Values

One way to discover significant issue questions and probe the connections between global and local issues is to start from what you care about and from your own experiences. In this text, discussion questions after readings and at the ends of chapters and many of the writing assignments will spur you to find your own personal and local angles on global issues and will ask you to reflect on how your thinking about these issues is evolving. Simply discovering how many of the products we use, from food to technology, are not made locally or domestically can lead you to vital issue questions. This text, your other courses, and casual reading, radio, television, the Web, and local events can also lead you to think about issues that matter to you. Writing informal reflections exploring your thoughts and feelings about an event or issue can lead you to a deeper understanding of your values and to questions that fascinate or disturb you. Similarly, recreating an experience in narrative form can help you discover your own investment in an issue. For example, you might reflect on a question like this one: Why is your city's decision to halt its acceptance and resettlement of refugees perplexing to you? Or you might reflect on your experience attending a professional soccer game and your identification with South American soccer fans.

   In the following narrative, student writer Lindsey Egan uses her own experience to help her discover an issue question that interests her and that relates to her class's focus on environmental sustainability and water.

 STUDENT VOICE: Informal Writing to Discover Personal Investment in an Issue Question by Lindsey Egan

Growing up, I spent early-summer weekends with my dad fly-fishing the Priest River at Binarch Creek. The small stretch of water is piercingly cold, clear as crystal, and loaded with deep, emerald pockets of water shaded by granite boulders—the seemingly perfect environment for sizeable cutthroat trout. I would tie on an elk hair caddis and cast my line, placing the fly right at the seam of the rapid, hoping to tempt hungry trout as my fly floated into the eddy downstream. Cast after cast, my line would drift, and I would wait … and wait. As a kid I wondered why I never caught a fish in that river.

My family discovered a few years later that the river is dammed upstream in order to regulate the flow of water into Priest Lake—where thousands of people spend their summers recreating at local resorts and privately owned cabins. Closing the dam in the summer lowers the water in the Priest River, diminishing it so far that bedrock is exposed by July, and in August a person can walk across the riverbed without ever touching water. The water temperature rises. Insects and fish eggs can't survive. The river can't sustain much life. Kayakers, rafters, and people fly-fishing must share their source of recreation with those using the lake (and, all the while, the native plant, fish, and wildlife populations are displaced from *both* environments).

This early experience exposed me to the debate over water usage. Who should have the right to use our freshwater, and why? Why does our culture value water for private lawns and jet-skiing over sustaining natural habitats? Sure, relatively few people depend on the Priest River for water. On the other hand, my reading has shown me that the Colorado River is highly disputed and increasingly overused. I wonder if other parts of the world have similar problems with overused water sources. What can we learn from their problems? What should the American West do about its water policies?

In this informal narrative, Lindsey draws on her personal experience and her reading to ponder local, global, and national connections to the problem of water usage. Often, writing from personal experience and writing reflectively in response to reading you have done can lead you to find your own personal stakes in issues with local and global dimensions.

Examining Multiple Perspectives

Whether you are trying to deepen your view of an issue, determine where you stand on it, or come up with a solution to a problem, your argument will be stronger if you truly explore the issue by looking at it from multiple perspectives. There are a number of reasons for dwelling with your issue question—for leaving it open for a while, for not taking a position on your issue early, and for letting your stand on your issue evolve before you try to formulate a claim: (1) seeing your issue from the vantage point of different stakeholders will help you question your values and assumptions, perhaps change or enlarge your view, and ultimately construct a more reasonable case; (2) seeing your issue through the eyes of different stakeholders will also enable you to construct an argument tailored to your audience's values and assumptions; (3) exploring an issue will enable you to recognize and answer alternative views effectively; (4) finally, thinking dialectically about an issue as you purposefully take on different perspectives restores to argument its ethical social function as a sincere search for the most valid solution to problems.

Because arguments gain depth when you approach your issue question with an open mind and a willingness to change views or let your views develop in unexpected ways, you should have a repertoire of strategies such as the following to help you encounter multiple perspectives.

STRATEGIES FOR EXPLORING AN ISSUE FROM MULTIPLE PERSPECTIVES

1. ***Deliberately seek out different points of view on your issue.*** Consult varied stakeholders and read sources by people who see your issue from different angles. Explore different forums (letters to the editor; editorials and op-ed pieces; articles in public affairs magazines, in scholarly journals, and in popular magazines; white papers produced by organizations; blogs; policy arguments and campaigns posted on advocacy Web sites; public affairs advocacy ads; speeches; even documentary films). Seek out sources from different political perspectives. Try to understand alternative and opposing views and see the issue from their frame of reference.

2. ***Play rhetorician Peter Elbow's Believing and Doubting Game.**** In this exercise, you deliberately adopt opposing perspectives on an issue and force yourself to dwell with a claim. As you believe the claim, you agree with it and seek to understand it by exploring it, supporting it, and applying it, adding your own examples. What would the world look like if you truly agreed with this claim? After freewriting for a certain length of time (usually fifteen or more minutes) from this assenting view, you then deliberately set out to doubt the claim and disagree with it. In your doubting freewrite, you challenge and question the claim, find holes in its view, and think of counterreasoning

---

*Rhetorician and compositionist Peter Elbow introduced his Believing and Doubting Game in his classic book *Writing Without Teachers* (Oxford University Press, 1973) in his appendix essay: "The Doubting Game and the Believing Game—An Analysis of the Intellectual Enterprise." In this essay and throughout his writing, he advocates resisting the urge to want immediate answers. He argues that only by trying to understand or "believe" views that clash with our own can we achieve an understanding of our own views and move toward the best solutions to problems.

and counterexamples. Try to freewrite for an equal amount of time believing and doubting. See what ideas and new insights about your issue emerge from this exercise.

3. *Use informal writing to respond to and interact with your sources.* Purposeful note taking (using your summary writing and rhetorical reading skills) can encourage you to track your evolving understanding of your issue. Novice writers and researchers tend to gather numerous sources and then try to wade through them hurriedly, often becoming overwhelmed and confused by the volume of material and the complexity of the different views on the issue. More experienced writers and researchers know the importance of processing their sources and responding in writing to them as they read. Freewriting, journaling, and summarizing of your sources as you read each one can help you enlarge and deepen your understanding of your issue. Some writers find double-entry journals helpful. In a double-entry journal, you divide your pages into two columns. In one column you write a quotation, idea, or fact (with the citation) that seems important to you. In the second column, you respond to that piece of information with your own thinking, as if you are talking back to your source or carrying on a conversation about it.

4. *Evaluate the material you encounter in sources as you read and research.* For each source you read, examine it for these qualities:

   - **Reliability:** Are the factual data accurate? Can you verify them by checking other sources?

   - **Credibility:** Does the writer inspire confidence through his or her tone, reasonableness, and fair treatment of alternative views?

   - **Angle of vision and political stance:** How do the writer's underlying values, assumptions, and political stance shape the writing?

   - **Degree of advocacy:** Is the writing inquiry-based and exploratory? Committed to a position but reasonably persuasive? Insisting on one view only and dragging the reader along?

   Assessing a source on these points will help you decide how much influence this source should have on your own thinking about an issue.

5. *Use incremental formal writing such as annotated bibliographies or brief rhetorical analyses of sources to complicate and clarify your thinking on your issue.* Brief formal writing can help you build your argument and also figure out what parts of your issue you still need to investigate. In an annotated bibliography, you formally cite each source, briefly summarize it, and then evaluate it, explaining how it has shaped your thinking, why it is valuable, and how you might use it in your own argument.

Analyzing Your Rhetorical Context

As you feel that you are moving closer to the claim and reasons you want to assert, you will probably want to firm up the rhetorical context for your argument—your target audience, specific purpose, and genre—and have this context consciously influence the development of the argument. Usually, audience, purpose, and genre are closely intertwined, with the genre itself holding certain reader expectations for depth and complexity of the argument, level of formality, and kinds of documentation. For example, an op-ed piece would target a general readership and would take a bold, appealing "broadstrokes" or a "small piece of the issue" approach and would not include extensive examples or formal documentation. The following questions can help you think out the rhetorical context that will shape your argument.

QUESTIONS TO HELP YOU TAILOR YOUR ARGUMENT TO YOUR AUDIENCE, PURPOSE, AND GENRE

1. Who is your target audience and what background knowledge of your issue does this audience have?

2. What are your audience's values and beliefs that pertain to this issue?

3. What is your specific purpose; that is, what would you like your audience to think about your issue after reading your argument? What are you asking your audience to do?

4. What genre of argument is called for to reach this audience and carry out this purpose? Are you writing a formal scholarly argument, a policy proposal that might appear in a news commentary magazine or on an advocacy Web site, an op-ed piece for the local newspaper, or a brochure advertising a campaign for an issue?

5. How agreeable or antagonistic is your audience? With what parts of your argument is your audience most likely to agree? To disagree?

6. To persuade this audience, what rhetorical use will you make of the ideas and material from your sources? Which will provide background information, which will supply evidence, and which will help you formulate your own argument or represent opposing arguments?

7. How can you elicit your audience's agreement or support for your argument?

Constructing an Argument Core

Another strategy that can help you create a strong argument is constructing an argument core. Usually after you have consulted multiple perspectives, done some preliminary writing in response to your sources, and thought about your rhetorical context, you are ready to commit to a claim and to formulate reasons in support of it. Construct an argument core with a main claim and at least several audience-based reasons. To develop your argument core further, you could identify the assumptions or principles behind your reasons, sketch out the kinds of evidence and support you will need for those reasons, and even imagine the alternative views you will need to address. An argument core enables you to focus your argument and envision its scope. Adding assumptions and evidence will help you determine if you will need to provide support for your assumptions as well as for your reasons. The explanation of the parts of an argument on pages 15–17 at the beginning of this chapter can guide you in thinking of your argument as a persuasive structure.

Structuring and Drafting Your Argument

An argument core provides the deep structure, the essence of your argument; however, it does not outline your argument for you. It informs you what needs to be present in your argument for it to be persuasive for your audience, but it does not tell you how to arrange these parts. As you draft your argument, you will have to make a number of important decisions.

DECISIONS TO MAKE WHILE DRAFTING YOUR ARGUMENT

1. How will you establish the *kairos* of your argument, connect with your audience, and set up your claim early in your argument?

2. In what order will you develop your reasons? Which is the strongest reason from your audience's perspective?

3. If you have to provide support for your assumptions, where will you include it?

4. How will you select evidence to meet the STAR criteria (that is, evidence that is sufficient, typical, accurate, and relevant for your audience)?

5. How will you incorporate material from sources so that it serves your argument? How will you frame your evidence and keep the focus on *your* points while strengthening your case with this material?

6. How will you introduce and give credit to your sources to meet the audience's expectations for documentation?

7. How will you make your argument come alive and make it memorable? How will you appeal to the imaginations, emotions, and values of your audience?

(continued)

(continued)

8. What alternative views do you need to consider, given your intended audience? Where in the argument will you address them? How will you respond to them to return the focus to your own argument?

9. How specifically will you build a positive *ethos*?

10. How will you title this argument to introduce your issue and claim and attract your audience?

Reviewing and Revising Your Draft

As with any piece of formal writing, your argument will benefit from having several different readers, preferably members of your audience, at the complete draft stage. To elicit the most helpful responses, address some specific questions to your reviewers such as, Where could the evidence for my reasons be more persuasive? Where might I give more attention to alternative views? Once you have given your argument a test drive, so to speak, you can revise with your reviewers' suggestions in mind.

An Example of a Student's Researched Argument

Here is Lindsey Egan's researched argument about water use written for the general public, including her student peers. Her purpose is to persuade her audience to accept her view of the problem. Note how the title suggests the focus and main claim of the argument. Annotations point out the way she has developed and structured this argument.

STUDENT VOICE: American Privilege Dangerously Perpetuates Water Inefficiency by Lindsey Egan

Frequently, newspaper articles from around the world confront us with stories about food shortages. Pasta, bread, and meat become too expensive for many people, who are forced to change what and how much they eat. Often, these food shortages are the consequence of a lack of water to grow crops for human and animal consumption. For example, the recent food shortage in Egypt, driving people to stand in line for daily rations of bread, has been caused by this region's water scarcity. For decades, the ten countries sharing the Nile River Basin have diverted its waters to make farming possible in desert regions like the Sahara

> Introduction makes the problem come alive in a global context.

and Sinai. As a result of water overuse, the dry countries of Northern Africa have to import much of their food. As the population here and around the world continues to grow, the combined problem of water and food increasingly becomes a global crisis.

What if a crisis like this happened right here in the United States? In a land where our freshwater seemingly flows freely, a food crisis may seem like a far-off implausibility, but the West's largest source of freshwater, the Colorado River, is also being overused and mismanaged to the point where it is nothing more than a trickle by the time it finds its way to the parched delta south of the U.S. border. Along with the Nile River in Egypt, the Colorado River has, as Marc Reisner, author of *Cadillac Desert*, notes, "more people, more industry, and a more significant economy dependent on it than any comparable river in the world" (120). Consequently, the American Southwest must make environmental sustainability its first priority in water usage for three main reasons: first, population growth is going to make increased demands on the river; second, changing climate patterns related to global warming are decreasing the water resources in this area; and third, the current emphasis on economic growth is leading the region on a course toward disaster.

The Colorado River, the single-most disputed and legislated river on Earth, is inevitably a battle-site for cities, farmers, electric companies, environmentalists, and Native Americans—all of whom claim rights to the river and contest the amount to which they are entitled. As a result of the Colorado River Compact of 1922, the river was apportioned among seven states: Colorado, Utah, Wyoming, New Mexico, California, Nevada, and Arizona. It now generates electricity throughout many major cities in the West and irrigates the land used for much of America's agricultural production—just like the Nile. In fact, farmers claim around eighty percent of the river's entire water supply ("Water Use in the West" 1). While food is certainly a necessity, the water used for irrigation does not return to the river (Burness 115). Once the water is depleted, then, farming in such an arid region will become virtually impossible.

The current use of water resources in this area poses a major problem, particularly in light of the past and future population growth in this region. Government officials overestimated the river's capacity at the time the Colorado

> Thesis: policy proposal claim presents three causal reasons: (1) population growth will increase (2) climate change will affect the available water (3) current view of economic progress is dangerously dominating water use.

> Writer provides background on the demands on available water.

River Compact was signed. During that time, the region had experienced record precipitation for several years in a row, causing officials to overestimate the typical flow of the river. The region's urban populations, moreover, have since skyrocketed to levels no one living in 1922 could have predicted. The current population of California, for example, is around 36 million but is expected to rise to 60 million by 2050 (Gertner 3). When Californians in Los Angeles are using around 125 gallons of water per person per day (Gertner 4), the steady increase in population causes an immense increase in the amount of water needed for daily living. These miscalculations mean that today the river is unable to support all those who depend on it, and that population will inevitably increase, making the problem worse.

> Writer develops her first reason about the problem posed by increasing population growth.

Furthermore, related to the continuing population boom are the ever-worsening effects of global warming. Global warming currently causes more rain and snow to fall in regions near the poles, but areas closer to the equator are drying out—as is happening around the Colorado and Nile Rivers. In fact, recent scientific evidence suggests that "periodic long, severe droughts have become the norm in the Colorado River basin" (Archibold 2), thus worsening the water shortage and intensifying the need to solve disputes over rights.

> Writer develops her second reason about the problem posed by the changes in climate patterns due to global warming.

The most important reason that Americans need to change water policy in the American Southwest to value conservation and sustainability first is that the current emphasis on economic progress in terms of profit, luxury, and convenience is following a foolishly disastrous course. Water use in Las Vegas best exemplifies the dangers of prioritizing capital over sustainability. Located in the Mojave Desert—one of the hottest regions on Earth—Las Vegas is one of America's fastest growing cities. It requires tremendous amounts of energy generated from the Hoover Dam to keep its casinos and hotels brightly lit and air-conditioned and its fifty golf courses well-watered (each course soaking up millions of gallons of water each day). In an effort to bring life to the desert, the Venetian Hotel uses water to recreate the canals of Venice; Mandalay Bay fills live aquatic tanks; Treasure Island flaunts its pirate lagoon; Luxor runs an imitation Nile River; the Bellagio showcases an enormous choreographed fountain display every fifteen minutes; and the Mirage has an erupting volcano made entirely out of water. Residential housing developments are

> Writer moves to her third and most important reason: the consequences of bad policies of economic growth.

built around artificial lakes,* and residents also use about 100 gallons of water per day per person just to maintain their lawns and gardens (Revkin 2). In a region that receives a mere average of four inches of rain each year (Robbins 1), plants and animals struggle to survive in nature as it is—yet people continue to pump this scarcity *out* of nature and into homes and hotels so that people can enjoy life in the desert.

Water policy in this region is entirely wrong. With the Colorado River's water supply tapped out, however, Las Vegas looks to bring more water into the city—instead of looking to reduce the city's water usage. Patricia Mulroy, general manager of the Las Vegas Valley Water District since 1989, plans to tap 65 billion gallons of water a year through a 280-mile-long pipe drawing from a natural underground reservoir on the Nevada-Utah border—taking water away from both farmers and the natural environment. According to Howard Berkes of National Public Radio, Mulroy claimed in 1991 that "there is an *economic imperative* to taking water from rural counties largely dependent on ranching, and bringing it to the big city" (1, emphasis mine). Evidently, Mulroy disregards the need for water in nature and for agriculture in favor of economics—that is, making profit from tourists. Once again, progress is measured in terms of luxury and capital instead of sustainability.

> Writer continues to develop her third reason.

Conservationists warn that adding to the water capacity of Las Vegas will promote more growth in a region that cannot sustain it. The Pacific Institute and Western Resource Advocates contend that "if Las Vegas adopted more aggressive indoor and outdoor water conservation measures, it could, in essence, harvest some 28 billion gallons a year without laying a single costly pipeline" (Revkin 1). In fact, as Andrew Revkin of the *New York Times* reports, "the installation of water-efficient fixtures and appliances could cut indoor water use by 40 percent in single-family homes and 30 percent in hotels and casinos" (2).

> Writer continues to develop her third reason.

Granted, there have been some movements toward conservational water use. The MGM Mirage Company has installed drip irrigation and low-flow bathroom fixtures in its eleven hotels (Robbins 2). The regional water

---

*One neighborhood known as "The Lakes" was constructed around three miles of synthetic shoreline (Robbins 2).

agency in Las Vegas is also "removing the equivalent of a football field of grass every day from front lawns, playgrounds, and golf courses to save on outdoor watering" (Johnson "Drought" 3). Mulroy has even waged several water-conservation campaigns to combat the wasteful use of water on private lawns, and she implemented a "return-flow credits"* system to recycle the city's wastewater. Still, research shows that not enough is being done individually or collectively to avert the growing crisis. Even these practices are done in the name of economic growth—not sustainability. When enticing tourists (and their money) to Las Vegas is the primary objective in implementing "sustainable" practices, the actual conservation of water becomes secondary. Yes, the installation of water-efficient showerheads is a start. But lavish fountains still spew twenty-four hours a day, and fifty golf courses remain in operation (because tourists could not possibly choose from a mere twenty). If real solutions are to be found, revenue—although a practical concern—cannot motivate our reasons for conserving the environment. When the matter threatens the next generation's ability to enjoy clean drinking water, shouldn't cutting back on our pirate lagoons and artificial volcanoes at least be an option?

> Writer addresses alternative views and refutes them with counterreasoning and counterexamples.

Although Las Vegas is the most flagrant example of wastefulness and disregard for sustainability, this city is not the only culprit in the region. In 2001, for instance, a dispute emerged between the city of Los Angeles and Calpine Company (a giant energy corporation based in California) that exemplifies how America's prioritization of profit limits sustainable solutions. Despite opposition from environmentalists and a thirsty Los Angeles desperate for more drinking water, Calpine planned to pump fresh water from a Colorado River canal for the purpose of cooling a planned 530-megawatt power plant† in the Palm Desert. According to Gerald Meral, the executive director of the Planning and Conservation League, an environmental group in Sacramento, there are other environmentally safe

> Writer elaborates on the third reason, enlarging the scope of the problem.

---

*A system that allows the city's wastewater to be treated, returned to Lake Mead, and used again.

†California has laws that minimize the use of scarce water resources for power generation, but Calpine arranged to build this plant and two other facilities on Indian reservations where state regulations do not apply. Since water rights are a precious commodity, tribes—desperate for income—are selling their rights to companies like Calpine.

methods to cool power plants: Utilizing wastewater or dry-cooling technology, for example, uses ninety-five percent less water but is, admittedly, more expensive (Khan B.1). A substantial amount of Colorado River water could have been saved, but Calpine chose to save money instead. Once again, concern for the bottom line has taken precedence over environmental conservation, thus inhibiting real, sustainable solutions.

If the United States intends to avoid food and water crises, Americans ought to demand that governmental policies reflect these interests. The former Bush administration, though, certainly did not foster environmental sustainability when it passed policies to loosen the federal government's claim on rivers by ceding water rights to Western states in 2002. As Douglas Jehl of the *New York Times* writes, these policies "give the states more latitude to transfer water to their *cities* and away from national parks, forests, wildlife refuges, and other federal lands" (1, emphasis mine). When states have more control over where and how the water is apportioned, state officials typically draw water away from national parks and forests in order to support their cities—centers of profit and economic growth. Such losses of water threaten the natural beauty and environmental health of the parks. Certainly, more water is necessary in urban areas to sustain mass populations, but, when cities like Las Vegas and Los Angeles squander their resources in the name of luxury and convenience, Americans ought to ask themselves whether their casinos and private swimming pools are worth destroying our nation's last remaining natural sanctuaries.

> Writer continues to elaborate on the third reason.

Americans ultimately have a choice: We can use our privilege to solve the earth's freshwater crisis, or we can use it to perpetuate the problem. In choosing the latter, Americans have foolishly disregarded warnings around the globe and are headed toward disaster. When only 0.01 percent of the earth's total water supply is available for human consumption (Johnson *Global* 203), *no one* can afford to waste the one vital resource on which all life depends. The quest for profit—although inevitable and necessary in a capitalist society—is clearly useless if people will not have the resources to sustain future generations. According to Micah Morrison, the Environmental Protection Agency reports that Americans tend to use on average 90 gallons of water daily, Europeans, 53, and sub-Saharan Africans, 5 (Johnson *Global* 213). It is obviously possible,

> Writer concludes the argument with a call for changes in attitude, practice, and policy.

then, for humans to survive with a more modest use of water—without round-the-clock choreographed fountain displays. If Americans do not reconfigure social and economic development in terms of environmental sustainability, "progress" may send us, too, into breadlines.

Works Cited

Archibold, Randal C., and Kirk Johnson. "An Arid West No Longer Waits for Rain." *New York Times*. New York Times, 4 Apr. 2007. Web. 19 Jan. 2009.

Berkes, Howard. "Las Vegas Water Battle: 'Crops vs. Craps.'" *Morning Edition*. Natl. Public Radio, 12 June 2007. Web. 23 Jan. 2009.

Burness, H. Stuart, and James P. Quirk. "Water Law, Water Transfers, and Economic Efficiency: The Colorado River." *Journal of Law and Economics* 23.1 (1980): 111-34. Web. 21 Jan. 2009.

Gertner, Jon. "The Future Is Drying Up." *New York Times*. New York Times, 21 Oct. 2007. Web. 19 Jan. 2009.

Jehl, Douglas. "U.S. Eases Way for West to Control Big Volumes of Water." *New York Times*. New York Times, 13 Oct. 2002. Web.19 Jan. 2009.

Johnson, June. *Global Issues, Local Arguments: Readings for Writing*. New York: Pearson Education, 2013. Print.

Johnson, Kirk, and Dean E. Murphy. "Drought Settles In, Lake Shrinks and West's Worries Grow." *New York Times*. New York Times, 2 May 2004. Web.19 Jan. 2009.

Khan, Mahvish. "California's Needs for Water and Electricity Pit One Against the Other." *Wall Street Journal* 1 Aug. 2001: B1. Print.

Reisner, Marc. *Cadillac Desert*. New York: Penguin, 1993. Print.

Revkin, Andrew. "A 'Hidden Oasis' in Las Vegas' Water Waste." Dot Earth blog posting. *New York Times*, New York Times, 5 Nov. 2007. Web. 19 Jan. 2009.

Robbins, Ted. "Stakes High for Las Vegas Water Czar." *Morning Edition*. Natl. Public Radio, 11 June 2007. Web. 23 Jan. 2009.

"Water Use in the West." *Issues & Controversies on File*. Facts on File, 23 Aug. 2004. Web. 23 Jan. 2009.

Writer provides a Works Cited and complete documentation for this researched argument, using Modern Language Association citation style.

Discussing and Writing ▰▰▰▰▰▰▰▰

Creating an Argument Core and Shaping an Argument

This role-playing exercise asks you to try your hand at shaping an argument in the genre of a flier for a specific target audience. This genre calls for a concise, tightly structured argument that presents its case very clearly with several strong reasons and minimal but well-chosen evidence. Visually appealing through the layout and use of images, a flier is also expected to change views and influence action. Working individually or in groups, choose one of the stakeholders and audience pairs below. Then follow the strategies on pages 54–58 for deepening your understanding of the issue and for shaping your argument for your audience. The underlying issue question is, What should be done to improve the United States' handling of e-waste? Consumers, high-tech manufacturers, lawmakers, environmentalists—indeed, all people—are stakeholders in this controversy.

STAKEHOLDERS AND TARGET AUDIENCE	
Arguers/Stakeholders	**Target Audience**
You are a high-tech company that needs to charge more for your products to cover the costs of recycling.	Your audience is American consumers interested in buying high-tech products such as LCD monitors and televisions, keyboards and mice, game systems, printers, and scanners.
You are part of a group of environmentalists concerned about the pollution from high-tech products in third world countries.	Your audience is American consumers who regularly buy high-tech products such as LCD monitors and televisions, keyboards and mice, game systems, printers, and scanners.

1. To help you become familiar with the issue and think dialectically about it, you may want to reread the argument "The e-Waste Crisis," examine the following photos from the Basel Action Network carefully, and consult the Web sites listed here or others related to e-waste:
   - Basel Action Network (www.ban.org)
   - ReLectronics in Bellingham, Washington (www.relectronics.org/)
   - GreenBiz.com (www.greenbiz.com)
   - EuBusiness.com (www.eubusiness.com)
   - "The Story of Electronics" (www.storyofstuff.org/movies-all/story-of-electronics) (animated video)

2. In response to these photos and the information and arguments you find on several of the Web sites, do a fifteen- or twenty-minute freewrite about two or three of these sources. What view of the e-waste problem does each photo and Web site present? How does each substantiate its view?

3. Briefly analyze your audience and decide on your purpose. What assumptions and values do you believe your audience holds on this issue?

Copyright Basel Action Network

Copyright Basel Action Network

Copyright Basel Action Network

4. Now construct an argument core for the argument you would present in your flier. Include a claim, at least two audience-based reasons, and a description of the kinds of evidence you would need to support your claim and reasons. If you need to support your unstated assumptions, how would you do it?

5. Decide how you would build a positive *ethos*, and explain how you would use appeals to *pathos*. Which, if any, of these photos would you consider using and why?

6. Your instructor may ask you to share your sketched out argument with the class or to flesh out and complete it as an actual short argument flier.

3

Trading Goods and Jobs

Sweatshops, Corporate Responsibility, and Consumerism

CONTEXT FOR A NETWORK OF ISSUES

Free trade and economic globalization (corporate globalization) affect us every day—what we eat, wear, buy, and what jobs are available and how much they pay. **Free trade** refers to the economic philosophy and practice of reducing barriers such as tariffs, taxes, subsidies, and quotas so that raw materials, goods, and services can move unhampered across national borders. Supporters of free trade point out that facilitating the movement of goods around the world stimulates economies by opening markets and enlarges the variety of available products—for example, bringing American consumers a choice of cars from South Korea, Japan, and Germany; a choice of wine from Australia, Italy, and France; and a choice of kiwis and apples from New Zealand when it is winter in the United States. Free trade also helps lower the cost of goods so that consumers can buy more things and have a higher standard of living.

However, hidden costs of these benefits have increasingly surfaced. In the last ten years, the media and advocacy groups have exposed the production processes that create the goods that make our lives comfortable. Frequent news stories and even legal cases have given glimpses of the exploitation, injustices, and abuses—**sweatshop** conditions—experienced by workers in factories throughout Central America, China, East Asia, and Southeast Asia: twelve- to eighteen-hour shifts; minimal or no overtime pay; housing in stark, barricaded dormitories; working amid poisonous chemical waste and hazardous conditions; dangerous, poorly maintained equipment; minimal or no compensation for occupational injuries; and firing in response to unionization efforts. While these factory and assembly plant jobs provide employment that has represented a chance for developing countries to enter the global economy, the exploitation and sacrifices of these workers, as documented in films like *China Blue*, remain conditions for consumers in developed countries to interrogate and monitor.

A second sobering reality of free trade has been the corporate **outsourcing** of jobs from countries with high wages and production costs to countries with fewer environmental and legal restrictions and abundant low-wage workers. As part of free trade's global movement of money and goods, since the 1980s, many of the garments, toys, footwear, computer components, electronic equipment, and appliance parts that Americans buy have been made in factories located in countries such as Mexico, Nicaragua, the Philippines, Indonesia, Pakistan, and China. In the late 1980s and 1990s, call centers (customer service departments of companies such as help desks for computer software that are accessed by phone) and business processing also moved to other countries with lower wages.

More recently, corporations, especially high-tech companies, have transferred some of their departments to countries such as India, the Philippines, Hong Kong, Taiwan, South Korea, and Singapore, where a qualified, and often highly educated, labor force can do the same work for salaries often only one-tenth to one-fifth as much as American or western European salaries. Both the manufacturing sector and white-collar jobs have lost jobs to overseas, called **offshore outsourcing**, a term applied especially to white-collar jobs. Advances in the Internet, technology, and communication have made conducting work in real time possible from sites on the other side of the world. According to A. T. Kearney, a global management consulting firm in choosing an offshoring site, American firms look for low costs; availability of people with the necessary skills in mathematics, science, and reading; English-speaking workers with an understanding of American culture; economic and political stability; and good tax rates. Based on these criteria, in 2011 A. T. Kearney's Offshore Location Attractiveness Index gave these countries the top-ten ranking for offshoring sites: India, China, Malaysia, Egypt, Indonesia, Mexico, Thailand, Vietnam, Philippines, and Chile.

Furthermore, a complex network of economic issues related to global free trade, corporate responsibility, and the United States' trade deficit, which endangers the United States' long-term economic security, has been exposed by the fallout of the global financial crisis of 2008. Economists say that Americans' habit of borrowing against their homes and living on credit masked the growing income gap between the rich and the rest of America, which is now the greatest since before the Great Depression. However, corporations have profited handsomely from the global free trade system, with low corporate taxes and high CEO wages in part fueling the concentration of wealth in the hands of the top 1 percent of Americans, with the greatest gains to the top 0.1 percent (corporate executives, investment bankers, real estate investors, etc.) while the wealth and income of the 99 percent has stagnated or declined. This income disparity has been fed by the high unemployment rate, estimated to be somewhere between 8.5 and 9.5 percent in winter 2012, to which the continuous outsourcing of jobs has contributed.

A third trade-related piece of this economic puzzle is the United States' **trade imbalance**, which continues to grow. In the 1970s, the United States ran a trade surplus, manufacturing and selling abroad more goods than it bought; however, now with fewer goods made here and more money being paid out to trading partners for their goods, we have become a nation in debt to other countries. Our current **trade deficit** is running over $45 billion.* Trade policy analysts and economists are debating what we should do: Create more exports?† Emphasize new free trade agreements that give the United States more access to other countries' markets? Most people agree that continuing to increase trade deficits is not sustainable and will lead to economic insecurity, giving other countries control of our economy.

Free Trade Theory in Brief.   Before we examine problems with the workings of economic globalization's free trade, it is helpful to have a basic understanding of free trade as a philosophy and a global economic system. Free trade theory emphasizes continuous economic growth and believes that this growth is the solution to world poverty. In metaphoric terms, the "pie" of global wealth-earning potential needs to grow bigger so that more countries can have a piece, and the world needs to grow "flatter" so that all countries can share economic and technological benefits.‡

Proponents of free trade regularly cite the theories of eighteenth-century Scottish economist Adam Smith (author of the 1776 book *The Wealth of Nations*) and David Ricardo, a nineteenth-century British economist. Smith argued that if government stays out of trade, then wealth created by private businesses and trade will benefit the public. Ricardo asserted that countries need to specialize in the goods that they can produce most efficiently and cheaply and that when countries trade their specialties, all will benefit (a principle called **comparative advantage**). Another free trade economic principle called **creative destruction** posits that the

---

*U.S. Census Bureau: Foreign Trade, www.census.gov/foreign-trade/balance. On this site, users can investigate the trade balance for the United States and all its trading partners by the month.

†A very helpful article on this problem is multi-billionaire Warren E. Buffett's well-known proposal "America's Growing Trade Deficit Is Selling the Nation Out from Under Us. Here's a Way to Fix the Problem—and We Need to Do It Now," in *Fortune* (November 10, 2003).

‡Thomas L. Friedman proclaims this equalized vision of global development in his book *The World Is Flat: A Brief History of the Twenty-First Century* (New York: Farrar, Straus, and Giroux, 2005).

offshore outsourcing of jobs will spur innovation in business and prompt the creation of new jobs that demand a higher skill level and more education to create higher-value goods. Free trade theory claims that economic competition with minimal government intervention will lead to greater efficiency, productivity, and innovation; will reduce costs for consumers; and will free up more capital for further investment. Free trade's removal of **trade barriers,** such as tariffs, should promote economic growth, foster a cooperative spirit among nations, help developing nations become independent economies, and end poverty around the world.

Some Key Free Trade Agreements and Institutions.   As citizens and consumers, we also need a basic understanding of how free trade has become the global trading system. In 1944, the global economic institutions and agreements that have implemented this theory of free trade—the **International Monetary Fund (IMF)**, the **World Bank**, and the **General Agreement on Tariffs and Trade (GATT)**—were launched. The International Monetary Fund and World Bank were intended to further economic progress in poorer countries by lending them money to help them through economic crises and help them build the systems (called **infrastructure**) such as roads, power plants, ports, and education that provide the foundation for economic development. In 1947, GATT, accepted by **developed countries** (also called "industrialized" or "first world" countries) and **developing countries** (also called "unindustrialized" or "third world" countries or "emerging economies"), sought to shape international trade by minimizing trade barriers, especially tariffs. In 1994, this agreement became an institution, the **World Trade Organization (WTO)**. By removing barriers to trade, the WTO seeks to create "a level playing field"—that is, equal opportunity for businesses in all countries. Additionally, free trade agreements provide many benefits for large corporations, including the establishment of **Export Processing Zones (EPZs)** that are tax-free locations for factories producing goods for big retailers.

Besides the WTO, many other free trade agreements create free trade zones and regional partnerships among groups of countries. The **European Union (EU)** is a trading bloc among twenty-seven countries throughout Europe that was formed to coordinate these countries' political and economic affairs. Another trading bloc, the **North American Free Trade Agreement (NAFTA)** among the United States, Canada, and Mexico, took effect in 1994. The **Central America–Dominican Republic–United States Free Trade Agreement (CAFTA-DR)** took effect in 2006. The United States currently has eleven free trade agreements with seventeen countries and other free trade agreements in various stages of negotiation, approval, and implementation: the KORUS with the Republic of Korea; the U.S.–Colombia Trade Agreement; the Panama Trade Promotion Agreement; and the Trans-Pacific Partnership with Australia, Brunei Darussalam, Chile, Malaysia, New Zealand, Peru, Singapore, and Vietnam. Among other benefits, these trade partnerships offer the United States expanded markets for U.S. goods and services and protection for investors and intellectual property rights.*

STAKES AND STAKEHOLDERS

People throughout the world, businesses and multinational corporations, national and local governments, whole countries, and individual citizens and consumers are directly affected by free trade's principles, policies, and practices. Here are some of the significant issue questions revealing current conflicting interests.

Is Free Trade a Universally Good Global Economic System?   This major controversy over who benefits from free trade is complex partly because the information used to measure growth and success varies. What is problematic about the accumulation of wealth in the hands of a small group of privileged worldwide elites? Some political analysts and social activists representing workers and indigenous peoples around the world argue that free trade is creating winners (in particular, big corporations) and losers (indigenous peoples and poor workers in developing countries). Environmentalists and social activists challenge free trade's goal of continuous economic growth with its drain on the earth's resources. Political analysts such as David Korten believe that free trade theory misinterprets and misapplies the theories of Adam Smith and David Ricardo. For instance, Korten asserts that Smith disliked corporations and believed in local investment and production so that business owners and managers would be responsible to the people most affected by industrial activity. Many critics contend that free trade enables powerful corporations called **transnationals** or **multinationals** to exploit poor developing countries' resources and workers and to dominate their own nations' politics.

How Can the Global Free Trade System Be Improved?   Stakeholders differ in the problems they identify and the solutions they propose.

- **Trade reforms to distribute opportunity more evenly among countries.** Some leaders and citizen groups in developing countries accept the model and goals of free trade but argue that the rules and agreements currently favor rich countries and large corporations. Farmers in developing countries protest that they cannot compete with U.S. and European farmers, whose governments give them tax cuts and **subsidies** (financial support). Furthermore, rich countries put high

---

*"U.S. Free Trade Agreements," Export.gov, accessed January 24, 2012, http://export .gov/FTA/index.asp.

tariffs on competing foreign goods (called **protectionism**) while at the same time demanding that developing countries lower their tariffs on American and European products. For small farmers and factories in developing countries such as Mexico, free trade can mean losing out to low-priced agricultural goods from the United States and Europe, going bankrupt, and falling into poverty. Since 2001, in what is called the Doha Round (from Doha, the capital of Qatar where the trade talks began), the developing countries met to compel developed countries represented by the United States, the European Union, and Japan to lower tariffs and remove agricultural subsidies.

- **Alternatives to free trade.** Other groups favor alternatives to free trade such as fair trade and direct trade. **Fair trade** seeks to connect farmers, artisans, and workers in developing regions more closely with markets in developed nations in long-term, transparent relationships to establish dependable markets and a living wage. However, as fair trade products expand to include bananas, cocoa, cotton, tea, sugar, and cut flowers, and big chains such as Walmart, McDonald's, and Dunkin' Donuts buy in bulk, some critics believe that fair trade principles have been compromised, favoring large plantations. Other activists and businesses embrace **direct trade**, which restores control to individual sellers and growers through respectful, private price-setting agreements. However, skeptics argue that fair trade networks and direct trade cannot realistically compete with the scope, capital, and efficiency of free trade.

How Has Corporate Globalization Created Economic Problems for the United States? While corporate domination of global free trade has increased income inequality in most industrialized countries, the increase is the most extreme in the United States, and the nation faces an identity crisis as well. Studies from reputable think tanks and government surveys have amassed data on the growing income disparity and loss of economic mobility in the United States that threatens the American Dream at the heart of our national identity. Many citizens and analysts are asking, "What kind of country do we want to be?" The Pew Charitable Trusts' Economic Mobility Project has identified that, "In the United States, there is a stronger link between parental education and children's economic, educational, and socio-emotional outcomes than in any other country investigated"*; and the 2010 U.S. Census found that more than one in five children in the

---

*"Does America Promote Mobility as Well as Other Nations?" The Pew Charitable Trusts, *The Economic Mobility Project* (November 2011), www.economicmobility.org/reports_and_research/other?id=0017. Other nations compared were the United Kingdom, France, Germany, Sweden, Italy, Finland, Denmark, Australia, and Canada.

United States lives in poverty. Downward mobility, growing poverty, and high unemployment are seen by some policymakers, analysts, economists, and worker organizations to be connected to the corporate practice of out-sourcing jobs and lowering of wages. The global distribution of wealth, dividing the workers everywhere from corporations, managers, owners, and stockholders, and the unemployment of even those with college educations became key protest points of the **Occupy Wall Street Movement** in fall 2011. Forces for democracy are drawing attention to numerical facts about the contrast between corporate and average-American prosperity and are calling for more corporate responsibility:

- Corporations continue to prioritize CEO salaries and bonuses, share-holders, and profits above workers and the nation; the following pros-perous companies recently moved assembly plants to Mexico, where the average factory worker makes $3 per hour compared to $18 in the United States: Whirlpool, Coca-Cola, Ford, RCA, General Motors, General Electric, and Nokia.*

- The United States collects fewer corporate taxes as a share of gross domestic product (GDP) than all but one (Iceland) of the twenty-six developed countries measured by the Organization of Economic Co-operation and Development (OECD).†

- In 2010, the annual CEO compensation was 243 times that of the com-pensation for the average American worker.‡

Increasingly, progressive news commentators and economists see the emergence of an economic and political profile for the United States that resembles a **banana republic**, a term used to describe Latin American countries that exported one crop and raw materials and had a vast eco-nomic divide between a small ruling elite of economic-political leaders and the masses. People who identify corporate responsibility as a major economic problem point out that the current economic order is self-perpetuating as big money distorts the political system by buying political support, lobbyists, and favorable laws and policies and tax codes, as seen in the Supreme Court's decision in *Citizens United* v. *Federal Election Commission*.

---

*Dustin Ensinger, "Whirlpool Moving Jobs to Mexico," *Economy in Crisis* (February 22, 2010), accessed October 28, 2011, http://economyincrisis.org/pring/content/whirlpool-moving-jobs-mexico.

†"U.S. Is One of the Least Taxed Developed Countries," *Citizens for Tax Justice* (June 30, 2011), accessed January 27, 2012, www.ctj.org.

‡ Josh Bivens, "CEOs Distance Themselves from the Average Worker," Economic Policy Institute (November 9, 2011), accessed January 27, 2012, www.epi.org.

However, some economists and analysts argue that economic factors are too complex to pin income inequality and loss of economic mobility on free trade policies. Advances in global technology have influenced the loss of jobs and the lower pay that lesser-skilled workers receive, not just outsourcing, which can be used as a scapegoat. Some commentators claim poverty levels are exaggerated and suggest that American workers are complacent and too entitled. They justify tax breaks to corporations and the wealthy as "job creators." Corporate leaders and some political leaders and economists claim that offshore outsourcing spurs innovation in business, prompts the creation of new jobs, and enables corporations to lower costs for consumers. Proponents of free trade and supporters of offshore outsourcing argue that outsourcing jobs to other countries helps the United States by creating new markets for goods from developed countries, substantially enhancing the economic development and political stability of those countries, and promoting peaceful global relations. Yet critics, while acknowledging these benefits, point to the erosion of local, state, and federal tax bases when businesses are relocated abroad and average income declines; and loss of tax bases leads to further elimination of jobs and services.

Should Nations Protect Their National Prosperity and Citizens' Economic Opportunities? Citizens of all countries are invested in this key question.

- **Government intervention in corporate responsibility.** Free trade advocates and corporate leaders believe that markets will regulate and fix themselves; government intervention would harm global competitiveness and the flow of inexpensive goods, which Americans value. Part of the issue is how corporations can be run for profit *and* for the economic prosperity of their countries. Some political leaders are recommending that federal regulation of corporations and the tax code fill the corporate tax loopholes, encourage companies to stay or return to the United States, build at home, and expand research and development through tax breaks. Political will is building to curb corporate irresponsibility as several recent national polls confirmed.

- **National versus global interests.** The balance between national and global interest is being hotly debated, with some policymakers and workers asserting the country's need to rebuild American industries and "Buy American." As analysts and economists argue, the powerful new economies of China and India are highly state-regulated for their own benefits, and charges of protectionism should begin with those countries that invest heavily in their own industries. China manipulates its currency, imposes tariffs and restrictions on foreign goods and services, protects and nurtures its solar energy and wind power, and now is the world's leading producer of wind turbines. In addition it has heavily invested in its infrastructure, building roads and high-speed trains. Shouldn't the United States prioritize its own future economic security, too? Many Americans recognize the need to rebuild the nation's infrastructure, especially roads and transportation, and invest in clean-energy jobs and high-tech manufacturing. But controversies focus on whether federal policies, programs, and assistance would be affordable and successful, and whether public or private investment is called for. Counterviews like those expressed by Sir Nigel Sheinwald, the British ambassador to the United States, warn that protecting domestic industries leads to nurturing unsuccessful companies, endangering open markets and risking retaliatory protectionist measures from other countries ("trade wars"), and thus hurting jobs and raising prices at home. The European Union has also experienced serious tensions as individual countries have put their national interests above the EU market as a whole.

- **National responses to global job competition.** Although the United States still manufactures machines, chemicals, and transportation equipment (airplanes), the number of workers in manufacturing dropped from 19.6 million in 1979 to 11.8 million at the beginning of 2012.* With the offshore outsourcing of increasingly diverse and sophisticated jobs—technical support for computer companies, software and data management, medical transcription, reading of X-rays and CAT scans, and now product design—and with the growing number of low-cost educated global workers, some people are wondering if any jobs in the United States and developed countries are secure. They are questioning the reality and quality of replacement jobs. Faced with such enormous foreign job competition, will education and training be any insurance that Americans can find and maintain jobs?

  Many stakeholders are proposing means to retain and create jobs. Some economists and strategists point out that jobs will return as the wages and cost of doing business abroad rises (called **reshoring**). Other analysts and policymakers recommend attracting more foreign investment in manufacturing, increasing the trade provisions for the export of services (U.S. engineers working abroad, for instance), infusing substantial national investment into our educational system and retraining of workers, and supporting small businesses. Some people, such as Jim Clifton in his book *The Coming Jobs War* (2011), are emphasizing the importance of local communities and businesses in job creation as a countermeasure to the loss of jobs through global competition and the outsourcing that big corporations do. As represented by the slogan "eat local, buy local, and bank local," the organizations promoting local business in a variety of states offer a means to reinvigorate the economy at the local level through keeping jobs and money in the community.

---

*Floyd Norris, "U.S. Manufacturing Shows Growth," *Seattle Times*, January 6, 2012, A11.

What Responsibility Do Consumers and Citizens Have in How Global Trade Is Conducted?

- **Ethical shopping and support for global workers.** Many analysts, businesses, and activists argue about the benefits and problems of the way that free trade incorporates workers in developing countries into the global supply chain. Are grueling, low-paid, dangerous jobs a necessary stage in development or, as other analysts, social activists, and workers contend, are market competition, corporate greed, and consumers in developed countries creating these sweatshop conditions in foreign factories? Moving factories to the countries with the cheapest labor and fewest regulations on worker health and safety has created a "race to the bottom" with workers competing against each other to work longer hours for less pay, and developing countries exploiting their own workers. How much is this global competition driven by the consumer habits of developed nations? Advocates of the free market and corporations believe that consumers are *helping* workers in developing countries when they buy the products these workers make. Anti-corporate activists and labor supporters say we need to use our consumer power to influence the improvement of factory conditions around the world. However, these human rights advocates, union supporters, worker organizations, and consumer groups disagree about *how* to use consumer power and *how* to change consumer habits: Should we boycott abusive companies, demand corporate accountability, buy only union-made goods, and/or be willing to pay higher prices for goods to ensure fair wages for workers?

- **Ethical shopping's influence on economic policies.** Commentators disagree about the importance of shopping with our values. For instance, what contribution have Americans made to China's dominance of our markets? What if we were willing to try harder and pay more to buy American? Author and political critic John Atcheson faults Americans for elevating consumption over production and for adopting the attitude that we believe we can buy our happiness: "The *entire* U.S. economy is now organized around the notion that getting U.S.' cheap stuff—the more the better—is the sine qua non of economic policy."* Studies of values in the EU countries and other parts of the world show that many countries have cultures that put a high priority on savings. Maybe Americans should take more responsibility for how we handle our money. If we buy fewer new gadgets and "stuff," reduce our support for corporate products and bank locally, for instance, maybe large groups of Americans could influence economic policies that involve social justice at home and abroad.

---

*"The Walmartization of America Redux: How the Relentless Drive for Cheap Stuff Undermines Our Economy, Bankrupts Our Soul, and Pillages the Planet," Common Dreams.org (December 16, 2011), accessed December 17, 2011.

Thinking Visually ▮▮▮▮▮▮▮▮▮▮▮▮▮▮▮▮▮

Working Conditions in Global Factories

This photo taken in 2004 shows workers in a garment factory in Saipan, part of the U.S. Commonwealth of the Northern Mariana Islands in the Pacific Ocean and an Export Processing Zone. Workers come from China, Thailand, the Philippines, Vietnam, and other Asian countries to make garments in some thirty factories for big-name retailers such as Abercrombie & Fitch, Calvin Klein, Gap, J. Crew, The Limited, Liz Claiborne, and Tommy Hilfiger. Recent lawsuits have yielded improvements in the sweatshop conditions in these factories: better dormitories, improved water and food, overtime pay for work over forty hours a week, protection from sexual abuse, and payment of back wages.

© June Johnson

Garment Factory in Saipan

Questions to Ponder

1. How would a journalist who wanted to use this photo for the rhetorical purpose of criticizing the treatment of workers in factories in Export Processing Zones (EPZs) interpret this photo? In contrast, what would a journalist who wanted to use this photo for a different rhetorical purpose—in praise of improved conditions in foreign factories—choose to describe and emphasize?

2. What questions about the production of goods today does this photo inspire you to ask and investigate?

The three sections that follow—Student Voice, International Voices, and Global Hot Spot—help you explore ways our lives are touched by global production, free trade policies, corporate choices, and consumerism.

 ## STUDENT VOICE: Thinking Beyond My American Consumerism by Tiffany Anderson

Some Americans, as Tiffany Anderson shows, are beginning to question our participation in the unequally distributed benefits of free trade.

I spent the summer of my sophomore year of college working stock at the Gap Outlet in the nearby mall. Although I complained of the early morning hours, the stifling heat of the back room, and the physical labor it required, I was secretly proud to be a part of our all-girl stock team. We worked hard, but our shifts resembled the ambiance of sleepovers; we gossiped, joked around, and blasted the top-40 station as we unpacked boxes of clothing and accessories. On days when shipments of new products came in, we each took turns passing snap judgments on the cuteness of the new items. On this particular day, I knew it was going to be rough because we were getting one of the biggest shipments for the Back to School season. I pulled on my black apron and searched for my exacto-knife, eyeing the seemingly endless stacks of boxes. There was nothing to do but start.

I hummed along to the new Christina Aguilera song as I pulled corduroy pants from their protective plastic wrapping, wrinkling my nose at the sour smell of newness that clung to them. I finished unpacking the box, broke it down, threw it onto the garbage heap, and ripped open the next box on my stack. I tore off the lid and froze as a numbing chill enveloped my perspiring body, and I yelled, "Oh, you guys. Look."

My coworkers gathered around, anticipating my horror at an atrocious sweater or some ill-advised pants. Instead, I pointed to a few lines scrawled across the inside lid of my box in navy blue pen and in a foreign language that I couldn't translate or decipher. The language looked Thai, or maybe Vietnamese ... something Asian, I was sure. The tags on the clothing were of little help. In the one box alone, there were tags from Indonesia, China, Vietnam, and Thailand.

"What do you think it says?" asked Amy.

Each of us knew The Gap had been cited repeatedly as a major employer of sweatshop labor, although we rarely acknowledged this fact to each other.

"Do you think it's a cry for help?" I sensed the author's presence, as if the sight of the blue right-slanting writing had freed the author from her prison, like the rubbing of a lamp releases a genie. I pictured a woman, my age but skinny, with sunken eyes and black hair, locked into a blindingly hot factory until she met her daily quota. I thought about her family of five she had to feed on a skimpy wage, children raised by a mother who was practically absent as she tried to provide for them. We went through the possible scenarios, embarrassed by our frequent references to our own jobs as "sweatshop labor." An unsettling silence descended on the room, and all you could hear was the tearing of plastic and cardboard. Before I recycled the box, however, I tore off the piece with the message and put it in my locker, hoping to find a translation, although I never did.

As the day progressed, I couldn't shake the feeling that I had been chosen to open that box, that I now had a responsibility to my friend overseas, trapped in a situation she couldn't free herself from. Maybe I was being melodramatic, but the problem was I had very little information on the actual working conditions of the people who made my clothes. Now I could no longer ignore the fact that I didn't know.

As an American, I realized that I had the privilege to listen to the radio at work and chatter with my coworkers. My biggest complaints consisted of feeling tired after a six- or seven-hour day, or of having to drive home sweaty and dust-covered. I worked to make money so I could go out dancing during the school year and get a discount on Gap jeans. I now felt guilty that my $30 pair of jeans paid a marginal fraction of the profit to the person who had made them. It slowly began to occur to me that I had a choice of which companies to support and that I had a responsibility as a consumer to know what sort of practices my money supported. While research only complicated these issues further for me, I at least think now that consumer consciousness is encouraging. Nothing will change if I continue to ignore the problem, unwrapping khakis and singing along with the radio, as if I'm the only person in the world.

INTERNATIONAL VOICES

China, with the world's second largest economy after the United States, steams ahead at a growth rate averaging between 9.7 and 9.1 percent of GDP in 2011 contrasted with the U.S. growth of between 1.3 and 2.0 percent, according to CNNMoney. China also continues to be a major site of global manufacturing, attracting consumer electronics corporations such as Dell, Hewlett-Packard, Nintendo, Nokia, Samsung, and Apple, among others. Although the wages of Chinese workers have risen in the last few years, conditions in assembly plants and factories are often dangerous, showing the problems with oversight of the supply chain, and raising questions about the complicity of governments, corporations, and consumers in global trade. The following excerpt comes from the *New York Times* article "In China, the Human Costs That Are Built Into an iPad" by Charles Duhigg and David Barboza, which appeared January 26, 2012, and was reprinted in papers around the country.

Apple's Manufacturers in China Reveal Disregard for Workers

More than half of the suppliers audited by Apple have violated at least one aspect of the code of conduct every year since 2007, according to Apple's reports, and in some instances have violated the law. While many violations involve working conditions, rather than safety hazards, troubling patterns persist.

"Apple never cared about anything other than increasing product quality and decreasing production cost," said Li Mingqi, who until April worked in management at Foxconn Technology, one of Apple's most important manufacturing partners. Mr. Li, who is suing Foxconn over his dismissal, helped manage the Chengdu factory where the explosion occurred.

"Workers' welfare has nothing to do with their interests," he said. . . .

When Mr. Lai [who died in May 2011 in an explosion caused by aluminum dust in the air] landed a job repairing machines at the plant, one of the first things he noticed were the almost blinding lights. Shifts ran 24 hours a day, and the factory was always bright. At any moment, there were thousands of workers standing on assembly lines or sitting in backless chairs, crouching next to large machinery or jogging between loading bays. Some workers' legs swelled so much they waddled. "It's hard to stand all day," said Zhao Sheng, a plant worker.

Banners on the wall warned the 120,000 employees: "Work hard on the job today or work hard to find a job tomorrow."

GLOBAL HOT SPOT: The United States

While workers in developing countries contend with exploitive working conditions, Americans have struggled through the Great Recession, which began in 2007 and has left many without jobs, with unemployment benefits expired, and with homes in foreclosure. In the following excerpt from an op-ed piece, "Making the Case for the 99ers," published in the *Seattle Times*, on November 4, 2011, Susan Wilkinson exemplifies the downward mobility and income inequality experienced by many in the United States.

At the end of October, I became a 99er. The unemployment check I received on Oct. 28 was the 99th and final installment of my extended unemployment benefits. I still haven't found work.

I was laid off from my last job as an administrative assistant in November 2009. Before this, I had a solid 25-year-plus work history, with progressively more responsible positions. I owned my own home, had excellent credit, and worked full-time while taking 10 credit hours per quarter in the evening at community college.

Ninety-nine weeks of unemployment later, I've had my home foreclosed, spent my meager retirement savings and filed for bankruptcy. And after 99 weeks of contacts, searches, and sending out my resume, I still haven't found a good job.

The stress of living for two years in economic uncertainty has taken its toll on my health and well-being. It has taught me a few things, too. In the beginning, I was ashamed of my lack of funds and inability to honor my financial obligations. Now I see them for what they were: the result of a system weighted heavily in favor of the top 1 percent, designed to make getting ahead nearly impossible for the rest of us. . . .

You hear lots of talk about what the protesters [Occupy Wall Street] want. I'm just one protester, but I can tell you what I want: I want a system where the vast chasm between CEO salaries and workers' salaries is narrowed. Where people can get jobs doing the work that needs doing in our communities. Where jobs pay a living wage, and where banks and Wall Street are under our control instead of the other way around. Mot of all, I want a system where our voices and lives matter. . . .

The readings in this chapter explore the constellation of issues connected to free trade, corporate responsibility, and consumerism, inspiring you to expand your knowledge base and evaluate how arguments frame the problems and argue for solutions.

READINGS

Sweat, Fire and Ethics
Bob Jeffcott

Bob Jeffcott works with Maquila Solidarity Network, a labor and women's rights organization, based in Toronto, Canada, that "supports the efforts of workers in global supply chains to win improved wages and working conditions and a better quality of life" (en.maquilasolidarity.org). This editorial appeared in the April 2007 issue of *New Internationalist*, a progressive British publication with a focus on issues of world poverty and inequality.

How does this editorial add context to the photo of garment workers in Saipan (on page 78)?

At the Maquila Solidarity Network, we get phone calls and emails almost every day of the week from people wanting to know where they can buy clothes that are Fairtrade-certified or sweatshop-free. Alter-native retail outlets even contact us to ask whether we have a list of 'sweatfree' manufacturers. So, what are we to tell them? Unfortunately, there are no easy answers.

First, there's the cotton used to make the clothes. If you live in Canada, you may soon be able to buy a T-shirt at your local Cotton Ginny store that is both organic and Fairtrade Cotton certified. If you live in Britain, you can already purchase T-shirts and other apparel products bearing the Fairtrade Cotton label, not only through alternative fairtrade companies, but also at your local Marks & Spencer shop.

This is all to the good, isn't it? Growing organic cotton is better for the environment, and farmers are no longer exposed to dangerous chemicals. Fairtrade certified cotton goes a step further—a better price and a social dividend to small farmers in the global South.

But what happens when cotton goes downstream? What does the Fairtrade Cotton label tell us about the working lives of the young women and men who spin the cotton into yarn in China, or those who cut the cloth and sew the T-shirt in a Bangladeshi factory before it's shipped to my local Cotton Ginny store in Toronto?

Unfortunately, very little. The Fairtrade Cotton certification is about the conditions under which the cotton was grown, not how the T-shirt was sewn.

To use the Fairtrade Cotton label, a company does have to provide evidence that factory conditions downstream from the cotton farms are being monitored by a third party; but the kind of factory audits currently being carried out by commercial social-auditing firms are notoriously unreliable. In other words, my organic, Fairtrade Cotton certified T-shirt could have been sewn in a sweatshop by a 15-year-old girl who's forced to work up to 18 hours a day for poverty wages under dangerous working conditions. So what's a consumer to do?

Well, maybe we could start by admitting the limitations of ethical shopping. Isn't it a little presumptuous of us to think that we can end sweatshop abuses by just changing our individual buying habits? After all, such abuses are endemic to the garment industry and almost as old as the rag trade itself.

The term 'sweatshop' was coined in the United States in the late 1800s to describe the harsh discipline and inhuman treatment employed by factory managers, often in subcontract facilities, to sweat as much profit from their workers' labour as was humanly possible.

Sweatshop became a household word at the beginning of the 20th century when the tragic death of over a hundred garment workers became headline news in the tabloid press across the US. On 25 March 1911, a fire broke out on the ninth floor of the Asch Building in New York City, owned by the Triangle Shirtwaist Company. Unable to escape through the narrow aisles between crowded sewing machines and down the building's only stairway, 146 young workers burned to death, suffocated, or leapt to their doom on to the pavement below. Firefighters and bystanders who tried to catch the young women and girls in safety nets were crushed against the pavement by the falling bodies.

GLOBALIZATION AND FREE TRADE

In the decades that followed, government regulation and union organizing drives—particularly in the post-World War Two period—resulted in significant improvements in factory conditions. This period, in which many—but not all—garment workers in North America enjoyed stable, secure employment with relatively decent working conditions, was short-lived.

Globalization and free trade changed all that. To lower production costs, garment companies began to outsource the manufacture of their products to subcontract factories owned by Asian manufacturers in Hong Kong, Korea and Taiwan. Companies like Nike became 'hollow manufacturers' whose only business was designing fashionable sportswear and marketing their brands. Other retailers and discount chains followed Nike's lead, outsourcing to offshore factories. Competition heightened. Asian suppliers began to shift their production to even lower-wage countries in Asia, Latin America and Africa. A race to the bottom for the lowest wages and worst working conditions went into high gear.

Today, countries like Mexico and Thailand are facing massive worker layoffs because production costs are considered too high. While most production is shifting to China and India, other poor countries like Bangladesh attract orders due to bargain-basement labour costs.

On 11 April 2005, at one o'clock in the morning, a nine storey building that housed the Spectrum Sweater and Shahriar Fabrics factories in Savar, Dhaka, Bangladesh, collapsed, killing 64 workers, injuring dozens and leaving hundreds unemployed. Just 16 hours before the building crumbled, workers complained that there were cracks in the structure's supporting columns. Despite the lack of an adequate foundation and the apparent lack of building permits, five additional storeys had been added. To make matters worse, heavy machinery had been placed on the fourth and seventh floors.

The Spectrum factory produced clothes for a number of major European retailers, all of whose monitoring programmes failed to identify the structural and health-and-safety problems.

'Negligence was the cause of the 11 April tragedy,' said Shirin Akhter, president of the Bangladeshi women workers' organization, Karmojibi Nari. 'This was a killing, not an accident.'

In February and March 2006 there were four more factory disasters in Bangladesh, in which an estimated 88 young women and girls were killed and more than 250 were injured. Most of the victims died in factory fires, reminiscent of the Triangle Shirtwaist fire, in which factory exits were either locked and blocked.

Twelve years ago, when we started the Maquila Solidarity Network, the word 'sweatshop' had fallen out of common usage. When we spoke to high school and university assemblies, students were shocked to learn that their favourite brand-name clothes were made by teenagers like themselves, forced to work up to 18 hours a day for poverty wages in unsafe workplaces.

BADLY TARNISHED BRANDS

Students who had proudly worn the Nike swoosh wrote angry letters to Nike CEO Phil Knight declaring they would never again wear clothes made in Nike sweatshops. But the big brands weren't the only villains: the clothes of lesser-known companies were often made in the same factories or under even worse conditions.

Twelve years later, the Nike swoosh and other well-known brands are badly tarnished, and the word 'sweatshop' no longer needs explaining to young consumers. Companies like Nike and Gap Inc are publishing corporate social responsibility reports, acknowledging that serious abuses of worker rights are a persistent problem throughout their global supply chain.

Today some major brands have 'company code of conduct compliance staff' who answer abuse complaints almost immediately, promising to investigate the situation and report back on what they are willing to do to 'remediate' the problems.

Yet, despite such advances, not much really changes at the workplace. On the one hand, a little less child labour, fewer forced pregnancy tests or health-and-safety violations in the larger factories used by the major brands. But, on the other hand, poverty wages, long hours of forced overtime and mass firings of workers who try to organize for better wages and conditions remain the norm throughout the industry.

Recent changes in global trade rules (the end of the import quota system) are once again speeding up the race to the bottom. The same companies pressuring suppliers to meet code-of-conduct standards are also demanding their products be made faster and cheaper, threatening to shift orders to factories in other countries. Conflicting pressures make suppliers hide abuses or subcontract to sewing workshops and homeworkers. The name of the game remains the same: more work for less pay.

Targeting the big-name brands is no longer a sufficient answer. Given how endemic sweatshop abuses are throughout the industry, selective shopping isn't the answer either.

We need to start by remembering that we are not just consumers: we are also citizens of countries and of the world. We can lobby our school boards, municipal governments and universities to adopt ethical purchasing policies that require apparel suppliers to disclose factory locations and evidence that there are serious efforts to improve conditions. We can write letters to companies when workers' rights are violated and in support of worker's efforts to organize. And we can put pressure on our governments to adopt policies and regulations that make companies accountable when they fail to address flagrant and persistent violations of workers' rights.

We should worry a little less about our shopping decisions, and a bit more about what we can do to support the young women and girls who labour behind the labels that adorn our clothes and sports shoes.

For Class Discussion

1. How does Jeffcott's review of the history of clothing manufacturing and recent developments in sweatshops and trade lead persuasively into his main claim? What is that claim?

2. How does Jeffcott establish a connection with his audience? How does he then employ this connection to make readers question their own values and motivations?

3. What conflicts of interest does Jeffcott identify for brands that have established "codes of conduct" for their manufacturing facilities?

4. How does Jeffcott both seek to enlighten readers and complicate their understanding of free trade, sweatshops, and consumer responsibility? How does his use of examples enhance his credibility and authority?

5. This article concludes with a different kind of call to activism than is usually made in arguments about sweatshops. What does Jeffcott propose that consumers do to address the issue?   ▪

Bangladesh: On the Ladder of Development
Jeffrey D. Sachs

Jeffrey D. Sachs is the director of The Earth Institute, Quetelet Professor of Sustainable Development, and Professor of Health Policy and Management at Columbia University. He is also Special Advisor to United Nations Secretary-General Ban Ki-moon. From 2002 to 2006, he was Director of the UN

Millennium Project and Special Advisor to United Nations Secretary-General
Kofi Annan on the Millennium Development Goals. A leading voice for combining economic development with environmental sustainability, Professor Sachs
was named one of the one hundred most influential leaders in the world by
TIME magazine in both 2004 and 2005. His books include *Common Wealth*
(2008) and *The End of Poverty* (2005), from which this excerpt is taken. The
book, intended for a general audience, presents Sachs's plan to eliminate extreme poverty around the world by 2025 and outlines the roles of globalization,
the United Nations, the International Monetary Fund (IMF), the World Bank,
and both wealthy and developing nations in achieving that goal. In the chapter
from which this excerpt is taken, Sachs presents Bangladesh as a case study
of the second rung on his well-known ladder of economic development. The
African country, Malawi, represents extreme poverty at the bottom of the ladder; both India and China represent stages of greater economic progress.

How does Sachs hook your interest in Bangladesh?

A few thousand miles away from this perfect storm is another scene of
poverty. This is poverty in retreat, where the fight for survival is gradually
being won, although still with horrendous risks and huge unmet needs.
This struggle is being waged in Bangladesh, one of the most populous
countries in the world, with 140 million people living in the flood plains
of the deltas of the two great rivers, the Brahmaputra and the Ganges,
that flow through Bangladesh on their way to the Indian Ocean.

Bangladesh was born in a war for independence against Pakistan in
1971. That year, it experienced massive famine and disarray, leading an
official in Henry Kissinger's State Department to famously label it an
"international basket case." Bangladesh today is far from a basket case.
Per capita income has approximately doubled since independence.
Life expectancy has risen from forty-four years to sixty-two years. The
infant mortality rate (the number of children who die before their first
birthday for every 1,000 born) has declined from 145 in 1970 to 48 in
2002. Bangladesh shows us that even in circumstances that seem the
most hopeless there are ways forward if the right strategies are applied,
and if the right combination of investments is made.

Still, Bangladesh is not out of the grip of extreme poverty. Although
it has escaped the worst of the ravages of famine and disease in the past
generation, it faces some profound challenges today. A few months after
my visit to Malawi, I was up at dawn one morning in Dhaka, Bangladesh,
to see a remarkable sight; thousands of people walking to work in long
lines stretching from the outskirts of Dhaka and from some of its poorest
neighborhoods. Looking more closely, I noticed that these workers were
almost all young women, perhaps between the ages of eighteen and
twenty-five. These are the workers of a burgeoning garment industry in
Dhaka who cut, stitch, and package millions of pieces of apparel each
month for shipment to the United States and Europe.

Over the years, I have visited garment factories all over the developing world. I have grown familiar with the cavernous halls where hundreds of young women sit at sewing machines, and men at cutting tables, where the fabrics move along production lines and the familiar labels of Gap, Polo, Yves Saint Laurent, Wal-Mart, J.C. Penney, and others are attached as the clothing reaches the final stages of production. There is nothing glamorous about this work. The women often walk two hours each morning in long quiet files to get to work. Arriving at seven or seven-thirty, they may be in their seats for most of the following twelve hours. They often work with almost no break at all or perhaps a very short lunch break, with little chance to go to the lavatory. Leering bosses lean over them, posing a threat of sexual harassment. After a long, difficult, tedious day, the young women trudge back home, when they are again sometimes threatened with physical assault.

These sweatshop jobs are the targets of public protest in developed countries; those protests have helped to improve the safety and quality of the working conditions. The rich-world protesters, however, should support increased numbers of such jobs, albeit under safer working conditions, by protesting the trade protectionism in their own countries that keeps out garment exports from countries such as Bangladesh. These young women already have a foothold in the modern economy that is a critical, measurable step up from the villages of Malawi (and more relevant for the women, a step up from the villages of Bangladesh where most of them were born). The sweatshops are the first rung on the ladder out of extreme poverty. They give lie to the Kissinger state department's forecast that Bangladesh is condemned to extreme poverty.

On one visit to Bangladesh, I picked up an English-language morning newspaper, where I found an extensive insert of interviews with young women working in the garment sector. These stories were poignant, fascinating, and eye-opening. One by one, they recounted the arduous hours, the lack of labor rights, and the harassment. What was most striking and unexpected about the stories was the repeated affirmation that this work was the greatest opportunity that these women could ever have imagined, and that their employment had changed their lives for the better.

Nearly all of the women interviewed had grown up in the country side, extraordinarily poor, illiterate and unschooled, and vulnerable to chronic hunger and hardship in a domineering, patriarchal society. Had they (and their forebearers of the 1970s and 1980s) stayed in the villages, they would have been forced into a marriage arranged by their fathers, and by seventeen or eighteen, forced to conceive a child. Their trek to the cities to take jobs has given these young women a chance for personal liberation of unprecedented dimension and opportunity.

The Bangladeshi women told how they were able to save some small surplus from their meager pay, manage their own income, have their own rooms, choose when and whom to date and marry, choose to have children when they felt ready, and use their savings to improve their living conditions and especially to go back to school to enhance their literacy and job-market skills. As hard as it is, this life is a step on the way to economic opportunity that was unimaginable in the countryside in generations past.

Some rich-country protesters have argued that Dhaka's apparel firms should either pay far higher wage rates or be closed, but closing such factories as a result of wages forced above worker productivity would be little more than a ticket for these women back to rural misery. For these young women, these factories offer not only opportunities for personal freedom, but also the first rung on the ladder of rising skills and income for themselves and, within a few years, for their children. Virtually every poor country that has developed successfully has gone through these first stages of industrialization. These Bangladeshi women share the experience of many generations of immigrants to New York City's garment district and a hundred other places where their migration to toil in garment factories was a step on the path to a future of urban affluence in succeeding generations.

Not only is the garment sector fueling Bangladesh's economic growth of more than 5 percent per year in recent years, but it is also raising the consciousness and power of women in a society that was long brazenly biased against women's chances in life. As part of a more general and dramatic process of change throughout Bangladeshi society, this change and others give Bangladesh the opportunity in the next few years to put itself on a secure path of long-term economic growth. The countryside that these women have left is also changing quickly, in part because of the income remittances and ideas that the young women send back to their rural communities, and in part because of the increased travel and temporary migration between rural agriculture and urban manufactures and services.

In 2003, my colleagues at Columbia and I visited a village near Dhaka with one of the leaders of an inspiring nongovernmental organization, the Bangladeshi Rural Advancement Committee, now known universally as BRAC, There we met representatives from a village association, which BRAC had helped to organize, in which women living about an hour outside the city were engaged in small-scale commercial activities—food processing and trade—within the village and on the roads between the village and Dhaka itself. These women presented a picture of change every bit as dramatic as that of the burgeoning apparel sector.

Wearing beautiful saris, the women sat on the ground in six rows, each with six women, to greet us and answer questions. Each row represented a subgroup of the local "microfinance" unit. The woman in the front of the row was in charge of the borrowing of the whole group behind her. The group in each line was mutually responsible for repayments of the loans taken by any member within the line. BRAC and its famed counterpart, Grameen Bank, pioneered this kind of group lending, in which impoverished recipients (usually women) are given small loans of a few hundred dollars as working capital for microbusiness activities. Such women were long considered unbankable, simply not credit-worthy enough to bear the transaction costs to receive loans. Group lending changed the repayment dynamics: default rates are extremely low, and BRAC and Grameen have figured out how to keep other transaction costs to a minimum as well.

Perhaps more amazing than the stories of how microfinance was fueling small-scale businesses were the women's attitudes to child rearing. When Dr. Allan Rosenfield, dean of Columbia University's Mailman School of Public Health and one of the world's leading experts on reproductive health, asked the women how many had five children, no hands went up. Four? Still no hands. Three? One nervous woman, looking around, reluctantly put her hand in the air. Two? About 40 percent of the women. One? Perhaps another 25 percent. None? The remainder of the women. Here was a group where the average number of children for these mothers was between one and two children.

Rosenfield then asked them how many they wanted in total. He again started at five—no hands, Four? No hands. Three? No hands. Two? Almost all the hands went up. This social norm was new, a demonstration of a change of outlook and possibility so dramatic that Rosenfield dwelt on it throughout the rest of our visit. He had been visiting Bangladesh and other parts of Asia since the 1960s, and he remembered vividly the days when Bangladeshi rural women would typically have had six or seven children.

The jobs for women in the cities and in rural off-farm micro-enterprises; a new spirit of women's rights and independence and empowerment; dramatically reduced rates of child mortality; rising literacy of girls and young women; and, crucially, the availability of family planning and contraception have made all the difference for these women. There is no single explanation for the dramatic, indeed historic, reduction in desired rates of fertility: it is the combination of new ideas, better public health for mothers and children, and improved economic opportunities for women. The reduced fertility rates, in turn, will fuel Bangladesh's rising incomes. With fewer children, a poor household can invest more in the health and education of each child, thereby equipping the next generation with the health, nutrition, and education that can lift Bangladesh's living standards in future years.

Bangladesh has managed to place its foot on the first rung of the ladder of development, and has achieved economic growth and improvements of health and education partly through its own heroic efforts, partly through the ingenuity of NGOs like BRAC and Grameen Bank, and partly through investments that have been made, often at significant scale, by various donor governments that rightly viewed Bangladesh not as a hopeless basket case but as a country worthy of attention, care and development assistance.

For Class Discussion

1. What is Jeffrey Sachs's main claim in this excerpt from his book? How does he defend the existence of "sweatshops" even as he critiques them?

2. In this excerpt, Sachs blends vivid narrative with detailed presentation of evidence. What examples of this strategy can you cite? How does this argumentative strategy affect readers? How persuasive is it?

3. What assumptions does Sachs make about his audience's position on the existence of sweatshops, and how does he address these concerns?

4. How does he link developing countries' labor issues to other issues such as women's rights and economic futures? What might readers find problematic about his discussion of women?

5. This excerpt participates in the controversy over the responsibility of the developed world to the developing world. Sachs concludes his case study with an assertion of the real responsibility of "rich-world protesters" to the poor of Bangladesh. How might these protesters respond to his ideas?

6. How has this reading influenced your view of free trade, sweatshops, and American consumerism? ■

We Are What We Trade
David Sirota

David Sirota, host of a morning news commentary talk show in Denver, continues to be ranked as a top influential journalist. He is a nationally syndicated progressive newspaper columnist, whose writing regularly appears in *The Huffington Post*, *The Nation*, *The American Prospect*, *The Washington Post*, and *Salon.com*, among other publications. He is senior editor of *In These Times* magazine, "a nonprofit and independent newsmagazine committed to political and economic democracy and opposed to the dominance of transnational corporations and the tyranny of the marketplace over human values" ("About Us"). He has authored three books: *Hostile Takeover* (2006); *The Uprising* (2008); and *Back to Our Future: How the 1980s Explain the World We Live in Now—Our Culture, Our Politics, Our Everything* (2011). Before becoming a full-time journalist, he worked as a Democratic political strategist, campaigner, and press secretary for various politicians running for Congress. This op-ed piece appeared in the *Denver Post* on November 7, 2009.

> What does Sirota mean by saying "we are what we trade" and what other popular phrase is he alluding to?

Trade and globalization: When not referencing blockbuster sports transactions or raucous street protests, debates over these abstract terms can give Ambien and Jack Daniels a run for their money as a cure for insomnia. Of course, that's the problem—the rules governing what we buy and sell are now playing such a decisive role in almost every major policy that we're falling asleep at our peril.

Most are familiar with trade and globalization, if at all, through the prism of heavy manufacturing in the "old economy." We know, for instance, how NAFTA-style pacts helped destroy our factory job base. The economics were unabashed and straightforward: By eliminating the tariffs we charged for goods made in countries with negligible wage and human rights laws, Washington removed disincentives for mass offshoring. With "free trade," our government effectively encouraged corporations to transfer production facilities abroad so as to cut costs via the cheap labor, slave working conditions and rampant union busting that flourishes in the developing world.

No surprise—two decades into this allegedly glorious "free trade" era, an ever-bigger swath of Flyover America looks just as flicks like "Roger and Me" predicted: rusted, abandoned, boarded up, and/or otherwise resembling a nuclear test site. Even less shocking, that apocalyptic reality has been largely ignored by a political and media establishment that believes economic emergencies are only those that threaten Wall Street bankers. Indeed, if the Beltway chattering class has paid attention to trade reform at all, it has portrayed the cause as a boring "special interest" crusade of supposedly selfish unionists and crazed anarchists.

Circumstances, however, have undermined the narrative power of that deliberately dishonest cliché.

In 2009, trade and globalization have transcended their "old economy" ghetto and become central to the "new economy," health care and even the Earth's very survival.

Remember the stimulus bill that promised a job-supporting down payment on the infrastructure and technology needed to rebuild our country? Yeah, well, the success of lobbyists in neutering the legislation's "Buy American" provisions in the name of "free trade" has steered much of that money into subsidizing job growth offshore.

Worried about skyrocketing health care costs? If you are, then you ought to be wondering about laws that bar Americans from using "free trade" to purchase lower-priced medicines from abroad.

And what about reducing greenhouse gas emissions? You interested in avoiding a climate catastrophe? Then realize the planet's future has far more to do with good old-fashioned tariffs than any neoliberal techno-babble about "cap and trade."

That's right, because global climate change is just that—global—we must both reduce our own pollution and compel other nations to reduce theirs. We can certainly try that through saccharine promises in a treaty, but it's far more effective to use the market.

That's the beauty of Ohio Sen. Sherrod Brown's proposal. A new levy on goods made in ways or in nations that ignore greenhouse gas caps doesn't merely discourage American companies from moving jobs to countries whose domestic laws tolerate pollution. It also economically advantages green products/companies/nations, raises revenues for clean energy innovation and—most important—appreciates the borderless nature of the crisis.

"Carbon dioxide emissions expand if a company closes down in Toledo, Ohio, and moves to Shanghai, where the emissions standards are weaker," Brown, a Democrat, says.

Put another way, as coma-inducing as the words *trade* and *globalization* may seem, we are what we buy and how we buy it. That means the cause of trade reform isn't everything—increasingly, it is the only thing.

By permission of David Sirota and Creators Syndicate, Inc.

For Class Discussion

1. What assumptions does Sirota make about his audience's knowledge and interests?

2. According to Sirota, what false story about the importance of trade reform has been spread and by whom?

3. As part of Sirota's effort to deliver a forceful message in the brevity of an op-ed piece, what emotionally charged language does he use? What's the rhetorical risk and rhetorical gain for using this language?

4. What network of issues does Sirota construct around trade and globalization?

5. For you, why does this piece succeed (or not succeed) in conveying the urgency of decisions about trade?

Top Twelve Reasons to Oppose the World Trade Organization
Global Exchange

This policy statement is taken from the Web site for Global Exchange, an international human rights organization that works toward a "people centered globalization that values the rights of workers and the health of the planet; that prioritizes international collaboration as central to ensuring peace; and that aims to create a local, green economy designed to embrace the diversity of our communities" (www.globalexchange.org/about). Global Exchange seeks to stir up public awareness about injustices and elicit support for fair trade. This campaign policy flier was downloaded April 30, 2009.

This flier lays out a case against the World Trade Organization in broad, sweeping points. For what purpose and for what audience would it be particularly effective?

TOP TWELVE REASONS TO OPPOSE
THE WORLD TRADE ORGANIZATION

The World Trade Organization is writing a constitution for the entire globe. The trade ministers and corporate CEOs who control the WTO would like you to believe that its purpose is to inspire growth and prosperity for all. In reality, the WTO has been the greatest tool for taking democratic control of resources out of our communities and putting it into the hands of corporations. But an international movement is growing to oppose the corporate rule of the WTO and replace it with a democratic global economy that benefits people and sustains the communities in which we live. And importantly, we are winning!

1. The WTO Is Fundamentally Undemocratic

The policies of the WTO impact all aspects of society and the planet but it is not a democratic transparent institution. The WTO's rules are written by and for corporations with inside access to the negotiations. For example, the US Trade Representative gets heavy input for negotiations from 17 "Industry Sector Advisory Committees." Citizen input by consumer, environmental, human rights and labor organizations is consistently ignored. Even simple requests for information are denied, and the proceedings are held in secret. Who elected this secret global government?

2. The WTO Will Not Make Us Safer

The WTO would like you to believe that creating a world of "free trade" will promote global understanding and peace. On the contrary, the domination of international trade by rich countries for the benefit of their individual interests fuels anger and resentment that make us less safe. To build real global security, we need international agreements that respect people's rights to democracy and trade systems that promote global justice.

3. The WTO Tramples Labor and Human Rights

WTO rules put the "rights" of corporations to profit over human and labor rights. The WTO encourages a 'race to the bottom' in wages by pitting workers against each other rather than promoting internationally recognized labor standards. The WTO has ruled that it is illegal for a government to ban a product based on the way it it produced, such as goods produced with child labor. It has also ruled that governments cannot take into account "non commercial values" such as human rights, or the behavior of companies that do business with vicious dictatorships such as Burma when making purchasing decisions. The WTO has more power to punish countries that violate its rules than the United Nations has to sanction violators of international human rights standards.

4. The WTO Would Privatize Essential Services

The WTO is seeking to force national governments to privatize essential public services such as education, health care, energy and water, so that these sectors are open to multinational corporations. The WTO's General Agreement on Trade in Services, or GATS, includes a list of about 160 threatened services including elder and child care, sewage, garbage, park maintenance, telecommunications, construction, banking, insurance, transportation, shipping, postal services, and tourism. When free trade and corporate globalization turn public services over to private for-profit corporations, those least able to pay for vital services—working class communities and communities of color—are the ones who suffer the most.

5. The WTO Is Destroying the Environment

The WTO is being used by corporations to dismantle hard-won local and national environmental protections, by attacking them as "barriers to trade." The very first WTO panel ruled that a provision of the U.S. Clean Air Act, requiring both domestic and foreign producers alike to produce cleaner gasoline, was WTO-illegal. The WTO also declared illegal a provision of the Endangered Species Act requiring shrimp sold in the United States to be caught with an inexpensive device allowing endangered sea turtles to escape. The WTO is now attempting to deregulate service industries such as logging, fishing, water utilities, and energy distribution, leading to further exploitation of natural resources.

6. The WTO Is Killing People

The WTO's fierce defense of Trade Related Intellectual Property rights (TRIPs)—patents, copyrights and trademarks—comes at the expense of health and human lives. The WTO has protected pharmaceutical companies' 'right to profit' against governments seeking to protect their people's health by providing life-saving medicines in countries in areas like sub-saharan Africa, where thousands die every day from HIV/AIDS. Developing countries won an important victory in 2001 when they affirmed the right to produce generic drugs (or import them if they lacked production capacity), so that they could provide essential lifesaving medicines to their populations less expensively. Unfortunately, in 2003, many new conditions were agreed to that will make it more difficult for countries to produce those drugs. Once again, the WTO demonstrates that it favors corporate profit over saving human lives.

7. The WTO Is Increasing Inequality

Free trade is not working for the majority of the world. During the most recent period of rapid growth in global trade and investment (1960 to 1998) inequality worsened both internationally and within countries. The United Nations Development-ment Program reports that the richest 20 percent of the world's population consume 86 percent of the world's resources while the poorest 80 percent consume just 14 percent. WTO rules have hastened these trends by opening up countries to foreign investment and thereby making it easier for production to go where the labor is cheapest and most easily exploited and evironmental costs are low.

8. The WTO Is Increasing Hunger

Farmers produce enough food in the world to feed everyone—yet because of corporate control of food distribution, as many as 800 million people worldwide suffer from chronic malnutrition. According to the Universal Declaration of Human Rights, food is a human right. In developing countries, as many as four out of every five people make their living from the land. But the leading principle in the WTO's Agreement on Agriculture is that market forces should control agricultural policies—rather than a national commitment to guarantee food security and maintain decent family farmer incomes. WTO policies have allowed dumping of heavily subsidized industrially produced food into poor countries, undermining local production and increasing hunger.

9. The WTO Hurts Poor, Small Countries in Favor of Rich Powerful Nations

The WTO supposedly operates on a consensus basis, with equal decision-making power for all. In reality, many important decisions get made in a process whereby poor countries' negotiators are not even invited to closed-door meetings—and then 'agreements' are announced that poor countries didn't know were being discussed. Many countries do not have enough trade personnel to participate in all the negotiations or to even have a permanent representative at the WTO. This severely disad-vantages poor countries from representing their interests. Likewise, many countries are too poor to defend themselves from WTO challenges from the rich countries, and are forced to change their laws rather than pay for their own defense.

10. The WTO Undermines Local Level Decision-Making and National Sovereignty

The WTO's "most favored nation" provision requires all WTO member countries to treat each other equally and to treat all corporations from these countries equally regardless of their track record. Local policies aimed at rewarding companies who hire local residents, use domestic materials, or adopt environmentally sound practices are essentially illegal under the WTO. Developing countries are prohibited from creating local laws that developed countries once pursued, such as protecting new, domestic industries until they can be internationally competitive. California's Former Governor Gray Davis vetoed a "Buy California" bill that would have granted a small preference to local businesses because it was WTO-illegal. When the WTO was created in 1995, entire sec-tions of U.S. laws were rewritten. Many countries are even changing their laws and constitutions in anticipation of potential future WTO rulings and negotiations.

11. There Are Alternatives to the WTO

Citizen organizations have developed alterna-tives to the corporate-dominated system of global economic governance. Together we can build the political space that nurtures a democratic global economy that promotes jobs, ensures that every person is guaranteed their human rights to food, water, education, and health care, promotes freedom and security, and preserves our shared environment for future generations. Check out the International Forum on Globalization's Alternatives to Economic Globalization: A Better World is Possible (available on the Global Exchange online store).

12. The Tide Is Turning Against Free Trade and the WTO!

International opposition to the WTO is grow-ing. Massive protests in Seattle of the 1999 WTO Ministerial brought over 50,000 people together to oppose the WTO—and succeeded in shutting the meeting down. In 2001, the WTO had to go to Qatar—a country that effectively lacks freedom of speech rights—to launch a new round of ne-gotiations. The WTO met in Cancún, Mexico in September of 2003, and met thousands of activists in protest. Developing contries refused to give in to the rich countries' agenda of WTO expansion and the talks collapsed! Find out how you can help Stop the WTO!

GET INVOLVED!!

EDUCATE your community and connect with local corporate issues through bringing speakers, videos, and books like GX's *Globalize This! The Battle Against the World Trade Organization and Corporate Rule,* available on our website.

*SPEAK OUT to your Member of Congress about the WTO and other trade issues. Urge him or her to reject the expansion of the WTO and other Free trade agreements. Find helpful resources for these and more ideas at www.globalexchange.org.

*LEARN MORE at www.globalexchange.org.

For Class Discussion

1. What goals and principles of free trade policy does Global Exchange challenge in this flier? Or to put it another way, what alternative views does it articulate and rebut?

2. What policies and course of action does this piece advocate?

3. What effect do the enumerated reasons in bold type have on readers? What are the strengths and limitations of this genre of argument?

4. How effective is this piece in influencing your view of free trade? What issues does it inspire you to investigate further?

Made in China
Matt Wuerker

Matt Wuerker is a political cartoonist and illustrator based in Washington, DC, where he is the staff cartoonist and in-house illustrator for the newspaper/ Web site, *Politico* (www.politico.com). Two collections of his cartoons have been published: *Standing Tall in Deep Doo Doo: A Cartoon Chronicle of the Bush Quayle Years* (1991), and *Meanwhile in Other News: A Graphic Look at Politics in the Empire of Money, Sex and Scandal* (1998). His political cartoons are published on the Web by The Cartoonist Group. This cartoon first appeared in 2002 (see page 97).

To what extent has this cartoon maintained, or even increased, its relevance in the last ten years?

For Class Discussion

1. Who are the characters and what is the "storyline" of this cartoon? What is this cartoon arguing about the role of the American consumer in global production and trade?

2. How would you describe the tone of this cartoon? What details of the drawing influenced your interpretation?

3. Cartoons often employ exaggeration or humor to make their point. What or whom does this cartoon appear to be satirizing?

4. What audience would find this cartoon meaningful? What audience might be offended?

5. What readings in this chapter would this cartoon agree with or support?

STUDENT VOICE: Uncove[RED]
by Nicole Cesmat

Student writer Nicole Cesmat is interested in the medical field. She developed her concern for social justice and public health in Africa on a summer service trip to Uganda. She wrote this argument for a writing assignment that called for a personal response to the role of American college students in global trade, basically answering the question, "Where should we shop?" This op-ed piece, imagined as a newspaper article written for the university community, draws on personal experience, fieldwork, reading, and research.

> How does Nicole establish the motivating occasion for writing, and how does she build a bridge to her audience with the opening of her op-ed piece?

Like so many other Americans who occasionally turn on the Oprah show, I was incredibly excited when my mom wanted to show me the episode about the (RED) campaign, pioneered by Bono and supported by Oprah and a number of corporations. The participating businesses are Dell and Microsoft, Hallmark, Motorola, Armani, American Express, Apple, Converse, and Gap. Each company involved gives a percentage of its sales of certain designated (RED) products to AIDS medication for Africa. The percentage varies product to product, but Gap usually gives about 50 percent whereas Armani gives 40 percent and Converse gives 15 percent, etc. Because not all people need a new credit card or can afford to buy a new Razr cell phone or iPod or shop at Armani, Gap has received the most publicity with its consumer participation.

In addition to being the most affordable of the (RED) product stores, Gap also sells products that make it easiest for consumers to wear the cause on their sleeves. Their t-shirts bearing phrases such as "Inspi(red)" and "Empowe(red)" can easily be recognized anywhere. Wearing products that support charitable causes has become trendy and popular in recent years, such as the army of people in yellow rubber Livestrong bracelets that could be found in numerous U.S. cities a few years ago. The recent popularity of products like these makes Gap's (RED) t-shirts especially appealing. To enhance the popularity even more, all the models used to display the products in Gap's advertising are huge celebrities such as Dakota Fanning, Penelope Cruz, and Chris Rock, to name a few.

I can't help wondering, though, if Gap is in it for the publicity or is really changing its ways and becoming more involved in social justice issues. I believe we as consumers must question corporate practices and think about what we are buying into.

Undoubtedly, the (RED) campaign has benevolent and inspirational goals. In a world of consumerism, what better way to raise money for countries in need of aid than to sell people popular items that donate part of the profits to charity? I am not questioning the intentions of product (RED) itself. However, past accusations regarding Gap's manufacturing practices (and those of its related companies, Old Navy and Banana Republic) have made me increasingly suspicious of the company's motives for their involvement in the (RED) campaign.

Gap's involvement has benefited its business a great deal and there has been little if any sacrifice involved. I know that when I first went to check out the products that Gap had supporting product (RED), I became frustrated that in a store of $20 T-shirts and $60 to $70 jeans, the (RED) brand t-shirts were $30 and the jeans were $98. Why should we have to pay more for these products? I'm sure that the company can afford to keep the price down and still make the donation to the Global Fund that product (RED) supports. It seemed to me that all Gap was really doing was tacking on a built-in donation for each customer. I worry that these more expensive prices may deter numerous customers from purchasing the (RED) products and send them over to the sales racks where their money will support nothing but the business of the Gap Corporation. How do we as consumers know that Gap is a company we should be supporting? Even if a portion of the sales does go to a good cause for these limited products, do the rest of the profits from each purchase go back to supporting Gap's sweatshops, its exploitation of laborers, and its abuse of the environment? What is it that we are accomplishing by spending an extra $10 on our T-shirts? I wondered if it would be better to purchase my clothes somewhere else and donate some money directly to the Global Fund.

Now it is true that while Gap engages in sketchy manufacturing practices and is far from ideal, in the corporate world it is not the worst of evils. It is turning in the right direction. *Coopamerica.org* says that Gap has shown interest in addressing labor issues (key word here is *interest*) and has become an EPA climate leader, taking steps to make environmentally sound practices a top priority. Both of these accomplishments are very promising, considering the corporation's history.

As consumers we have a lot of power in the corporate world. It is our job to keep Gap heading in this right direction. If these issues are important to consumers, they become important to the company. If Gap, a huge corporation, changes its practices, it may lead other companies to do so as well. One way you can help is to write to Gap and say that this progress is important to you as a customer. An easy way to do this is to visit *organicconsumers.com* on its Clothes for Change page to find information on how to contact current Gap executives.

I'm not going to tell you that purchasing (RED) designated products at the Gap, or anywhere else for that matter, is wrong. I hope, though, that you might begin to question corporate actions such as Gap's involvement in charity fundraisers. What are you willing to support with the second 50 percent of the money you hand over for a T-shirt just to say that the first 50 percent went to Africa to fight AIDS? Think about that.

For Class Discussion

1. What is Nicole's main claim in this argument?

2. How does she convey her personal investment in and knowledge of the subject? How does she win readers' consideration of her view?

3. Nicole uses questions as a rhetorical strategy to get her readers to engage with the issue. If you consider yourself a member of her target audience, how effective is this strategy in drawing you in? What does she gain by taking a reflective, rather than a hard sell, tone in this piece?

4. What concessions does she make in analyzing the Gap Corporation's motives?

5. What contribution does Nicole make (along with Sachs, Jeffcott, Wuerker, and Finn, in Chapter 2) to the larger conversations about the influence consumers in developed countries may wield in shaping the ethics of shopping in this global economy?

My Six-Year-Old Son Should Get a Job: Is Free Trade Always the Answer?
Ha-Joon Chang

Ha-Joon Chang was born in the Republic of Korea, and he holds a doctorate in economics from Cambridge University, where he also works as a Reader in the Political Economy of Development. He has served on the editorial board of the *Cambridge Journal of Economics* and as a consultant to the World Bank, the Asian Development Bank, and the European Investment Bank as well as to Oxfam and various United Nations agencies. He is also a fellow at the Center for Economic and Policy Research in Washington, DC. This excerpt is from Chang's book *Bad Samaritans: The Myth of Free Trade and the Secret History of Capitalism* (2008), which refutes the neoliberal claim that the United States and Britain became powerful in the nineteenth century through unrestricted free trade. He argues that wealthy countries that preach free trade and free markets to developing countries are acting as "Bad Samaritans." Their real goal, he asserts, is to capture larger market shares in these developing countries and preempt competition rather than to nurture these countries' economic development.

> What is surprising, shocking, or appealing about Chang's opening to his argument? How effective is it in launching his argument?

I have a six-year-old son. His name is Jin-Gyu. He lives off me, yet he is quite capable of making a living. I pay for his lodging, food, education and health care. But millions of children of his age already have jobs. Daniel Defoe, in the 18th century, thought that children could earn a living from the age of four.

Moreover, working might do Jin-Gyu's character a world of good. Right now he lives in an economic bubble with no sense of the value of money. He has zero appreciation of the efforts his mother and I make on his behalf, subsidizing his idle existence and cocooning him from harsh reality. He is over-protected and needs to be exposed to competition, so that he can become a more productive person. Thinking about it, the more competition he is exposed to and the sooner this is done; the better it will be for his future development. It will whip him into a mentality that is ready for hard work. I should make him quit school and get a job. Perhaps I could move to a country where child labour is still tolerated, if not legal, to give him more choice in employment.

I can hear you say I must be mad. Myopic. Cruel. You tell me that I need to protect and nurture the child. If I drive Jin-Gyu into the labour market at the age of six, he may become a savvy shoeshine boy or even a prosperous street hawker, but he will never become a brain surgeon or a nuclear physicist—that would require at least another dozen years of my protection and investment. You argue that, even from a purely materialistic viewpoint, I would be wiser to invest in my son's education than gloat over the money I save by not sending him to school. After all, if I were right, Oliver Twist would have been better off pick-pocketing for Fagin, rather than being rescued by the misguided Good Samaritan Mr. Brownlow, who deprived the boy of his chance to remain competitive in the labour market.

Yet this absurd line of argument is in essence how free-trade economists justify rapid, large-scale trade liberalization in developing countries. They claim that developing country producers need to be exposed to as much competition as possible right now, so that they have the incentive to raise their productivity in order to survive. Protection, by constrast, only creates complacency and sloth. The earlier the exposure, the argument goes, the better it is for economic development.

Incentives, however, are only half the story. The other is capability. Even if Jin-Gyu were to be offered a £20m reward or, alternatively, threatened with a bullet in his head, he would not be able to rise to the challenge of brain surgery had he quit school at the age of six. Likewise, industries in developing countries will not survive if they are exposed to international competition too early. They need time to improve their capabilities by mastering advanced technologies and building effective organizations. This is the essence of the infant industry argument, first theorized by Alexander Hamilton, first treasury secretary of the US, and used by generations of policy-makers before and after him, as I have just shown in the previous chapter.

Naturally, the protection I provide to Jin-Gyu (as the infant industry argument itself says) should not be used to shelter him from competition forever. Making him work at the age of six is wrong, but so is subsidizing him at the age of 40. Eventually he should go out into the big wide world, get a job and live an independent life. He only needs protection while he is accumulating the capabilities to take on a satisfying and well-paid job.

Of course, as happens with parents bringing up their children, infant industry protection can go wrong. Just as some parents are over-protective, governments can cosset infant industries too much. Some children are unwilling to prepare themselves for adult life, just as infant industry support is wasted on some firms. In the way that some children manipulate their parents into supporting them beyond childhood, there are industries that prolong government protection through clever lobbying. But the existence of dysfunctional families is hardly an argument against parenting itself. Likewise, cases of failures in infant industry protection cannot discredit the strategy *per se*. The examples of bad protectionism merely tell us that the policy needs to be used wisely.

FREE TRADE ISN'T WORKING

Free trade is good—this is the doctrine at the heart of the neo-liberal orthodoxy. To the neo-liberals, there cannot be a more self-evident proposition than this. Professor Willem Buiter, my distinguished former colleague at Cambridge and a former chief economist of the EBRD (European Bank for Reconstruction and Development), once expressed this succinctly: 'Remember: unilateral trade liberalization is not a "concession" or a "sacrifice" that one should be compensated for. It is an act of enlightened self-interest. Reciprocal trade liberalization enhances the gains but is not necessary for gains to be present. The economics is all there.' Belief in the virtue of free trade is so central to the neo-liberal orthodoxy that it is effectively what defines a neo-liberal economist. You may question (if not totally reject) any other element of the neo-liberal agenda—open capital markets, strong patents or even privatisation and still stay in the neo-liberal church. However, once you object to free trade, you are effectively inviting ex-communication.

Based on such convictions, the Bad Samaritans have done their utmost to push developing countries into free trade—or, at least, much freer trade. During the past quarter of a century, most developing countries have liberalized trade to a huge degree. They were first pushed by the IMF and the World Bank in the aftermath of the Third World debt crisis of 1982. There was a further decisive impetus towards trade liberalization following the launch of the WTO in 1995. During the last decade or so, bilateral and regional free trade agreements (FTAs) have also proliferated. Unfortunately, during this period, developing countries have not done well at all, despite (or because of, in my view) massive trade liberalization, as I showed in Chapter 1.

The story of Mexico—poster boy of the free-trade camp—is particularly telling. If any developing country can succeed with free trade, it should be Mexico. It borders on the largest market in the world (the US) and has had a free Trade Agreement with it since 1995 (the North American Free Trade Agreement or NAFTA). It also has a large diaspora living in the US, which can provide important informal business links. Unlike many other poorer developing countries, it has a decent pool of skilled workers, competent managers and relatively developed physical infrastructure (roads, ports and so on).

Free trade economists argue that free trade benefited Mexico by accelerating growth. Indeed, following NAFTA, between 1994 and 2002, Mexico's *per capita* GDP grew at 1.8% per year, a big improvement over the 0.1% rate recorded between 1985 and 1995. But the decade before NAFTA was also a decade of extensive trade liberalisation for Mexico, following its conversion to neo-liberalism in the mid-1980s. So trade liberalization was also responsible for the 0.1% growth rate.

Wide-ranging trade liberalization in the 1980s and the 1990s wiped out whole swathes of Mexican industry that had been painstakingly built up during the period of import substitution industrialization (ISI). The result was, predictably, a slowdown in economic growth, lost jobs and falls in wages (as better-paying manufacturing jobs disappeared). Its agricultural sector was also hard hit by subsidized US products, especially corn, the staple diet of most Mexicans. On top of that, NAFTA's positive impact (in terms of increasing exports to the US market) has run out of steam in the last few years. During 2001–2005, Mexico's growth performance has been miserable, with an annual growth rate of *per capita* income at 0.3% (or a paltry 1.7% increase in total over five years). By contrast, during the 'bad old days' of ISI (1955–82), Mexico's *per capita* income had grown much faster than during the NAFTA period—at an average of 3.1% per year.

Mexico is a particularly striking example of the failure of premature wholesale trade liberalization, but there are other examples. In Ivory Coast, following tariff cuts of 40% in 1986, the chemical, textile, shoe and automobile industries virtually collapsed. Unemployment soared. In Zimbabwe, following trade liberalization in 1990, the unemployment rate jumped from 10% to 20%. It had been hoped that the capital and labour resources released from the enterprises that went bankrupt due to trade liberalization would be absorbed by new businesses. This simply did not happen on a sufficient scale. It is not surprising that growth evaporated and unemployment soared.

Trade liberalization has created other problems, too. It has increased the pressures on government budgets, as it reduced tariff revenues. This has been a particularly serious problem for the poorer countries. Because they lack tax collection capabilities and because tariffs are the easiest tax to collect, they rely heavily on tariffs (which sometimes account for over 50% of total government revenue). As a result, the fiscal adjustment that has had to be made following large-scale trade liberalization has been huge in many developing countries—even a recent IMF study shows that, in low-income countries that have limited abilities to collect other taxes, *less than* 30% of the revenue lost due to trade liberalization over the last 25 years has been made up by other taxes. Moreover, lower levels of business activity and higher unemployment resulting from trade liberalization have also reduced income tax revenue. When countries were already under considerable pressure from the IMF to reduce their budget deficits, falling revenue meant severe cuts in spending, often eating into vital areas like education, health and physical infrastructure, damaging long-term growth.

It is perfectly possible that *some* degree of *gradual* trade liberalization may have been beneficial, and even necessary, for certain developing countries in the 1980s—India and China come to mind. But what has happened during the past quarter of a century has been a rapid, unplanned and blanket trade liberalization. Just to remind the reader, during the 'bad old days' of protectionist import substitution industrialization (ISI), developing countries used to grow, on average, at double the rate that they are doing today under free trade. Free trade simply isn't working for developing countries.

For Class Discussion

1. Ha-Joon Chang creates an extended analogy between his six-year-old son and developing countries, claiming that for both, rapid growth is harmful. What are the advantages of this analogy? What are the analogy's limitations or difficulties?

2. How does Chang refute the claims of free trade proponents that trade liberalization accelerates growth in developing nations? What examples does he employ to measure or quantify growth and support his own argument?

3. What economic terms does Chang use in his argument and what do they suggest about his readers?

4. Chang, an economist, is well known for his approach of placing sociopolitical and moral issues at the center of discussions regarding economics and policy. How does this approach influence his authority, credibility, and impact on readers?

5. How has this argument influenced your views on free trade?

Let's Admit It: Globalization Has Losers
Steven Rattner

Steven Rattner has been as an investment banker, financial adviser, and co-founder and director of a number of corporations. For example, he started his career in investment banking at Lehman Brothers, and then went on to be General Director of Morgan Stanley. Rattner has also worked as a reporter for the *New York Times*, and he contributed a monthly column to the *Financial Times* and served as the economic analyst for MSNBC's *Morning Joe*. Most recently, Rattner played a key role, as Counselor to the Secretary of the

Treasury, in the recent rebuilding of the auto industry, which he chronicles in his book *An Insider's Account of the Obama Administration's Emergency Rescue of the Auto Industry* (2010). He is described as a veteran of Wall Street and a political campaigner and contributor to the campaigns of Democrats John Kerry and Hillary Clinton. This op-ed piece appeared in the *New York Times* on October 15, 2011.

What does Rattner's use of the "winner" and "loser" language in reference to globalization contribute to the persuasiveness of his argument?

For the typical American, the past decade has been economically brutal: the first time since the 1930s, according to some calculations, that inflation-adjusted incomes declined. By 2010, real median household income had fallen to $49,445, compared with $53,164 in 2000. While there are many culprits, from declining unionization to the changing mix of needed skills, globalization has had the greatest impact.

Yes, globalization. The phenomenon that free traders like me adore has created a nation of winners (think of those low-priced imported goods) but also many losers. Nowhere have these pressures been more intense than in the manufacturing sector, which I saw firsthand as head of President Obama's Auto Task Force.

A typical General Motors worker costs the company about $56 per hour, which includes benefits. In Mexico, a worker costs the company $7 per hour; in China, $4.50 an hour, and in India, $1 per hour. While G.M. doesn't (yet) achieve United States-level productivity in China and India, its Mexican plants are today at least as efficient as those in the United States.

G.M. has responded with inarguable logic. While reducing its United States hourly work force to 50,000 from 89,000 over the past five years, its Mexican hourly head count has risen, to 9,235 from 9,073.

Pressed by high unemployment and eager to keep jobs in this country, the United Auto Workers agreed that companies could cut their costs by hiring some workers at $14 an hour, with lower benefits. Most recently, Volkswagen arrived in Chattanooga, Tenn., with 2,000 much-welcomed jobs—but all with starting pay of $14.50 per hour. At this pay rate, although some workers will quickly exceed it at that plant, yearly income would be $30,000 per year, hardly the American dream of great middle-class jobs.

In these troubled times, any jobs are surely welcome. But we need to reverse the decline in incomes, and this requires a more thoughtful approach than the pervasive, politically attractive happy talk nostalgically centered on restoring lost manufacturing jobs.

So let's start by acknowledging that just as occurred decades ago with agriculture, the declining role in our economy of manufacturing, which over the last half-century is down from 32 percent of the work force to 9 percent, will continue. Let's also recognize that retreating into protectionism would turn a win-lose into a lose-lose.

And even if organized labor could force wage rates back up, that would hardly help domestic manufacturing compete against lower-cost imports.

Instead, we should follow the example of successful high-wage exporters in concentrating on products where we have an advantage, as Germany has done with products like sophisticated machine tools.

While America still leads in sectors like defense and aviation, our greatest strength, and a source of high-paying jobs, lies in service industries with high intellectual content, like education, entertainment, digital media, and yes, even financial services. Facebook, Google and Microsoft are all American creations, as are the global credit card companies American Express, Visa and MasterCard.

Achieving higher wages also requires a greater commitment to education; wages for those with college degrees rose 1.4 percent between 2000 and 2010, after inflation. Following the German model of greater emphasis on engineering and technical training would also be advantageous.

Finally comes the tricky question of what role government should play. The prospect of Washington lurching into the private sector is terrifying, as illustrated by the debacle of Solyndra, the solar energy company that failed with $535 million of taxpayer loans. While countries like China have put large resources behind industries they want to nurture, we should resist the temptation to plunge deeply into industrial policy. Particularly in its current dysfunctional condition, Washington is ill-equipped to pick winners and should concentrate its capital on infrastructure and other public investments that the private sector won't make.

To assist the private sector, particularly young companies, which are the biggest source of new hiring, tax incentives could be used to foster the creation of well-paying jobs.

In addition, the Kauffman Foundation, which focuses on entrepreneurship, has identified other possible solutions, including providing visas to entrepreneurs, easing access to public financing markets and reform of the patent and regulatory apparatus. Sadly, Congress shows little sign of addressing all of this.

With global competition and its pressure on American wages intensifying, American workers deserve a more focused approach from Washington.

For Class Discussion

1. What does Rattner gain in terms of readers' interest and willingness to listen to his argument by his self-identification as a "free trader" and a supporter of the very globalization that has contributed to the loss of manufacturing jobs and decline in American middle-class incomes?

2. How does his direct, blunt presentation of numerical data on wages and jobs serve his argument rhetorically?

3. What claim undergirds the second half of his argument and functions as a solution of sorts to the problem addressed in the first part of this op-ed piece?

4. What use of language in this piece conveys Rattner's (a) knowledge of the global economy and (b) desire to forge a moderate economic policy that takes both workers and corporations into account?

5. How successfully does he make his views appealing to you?

Watching Greed Murder the Economy
Paul Craig Roberts

Paul Craig Roberts, who holds a PhD from the University of Virginia, has been prominent in academic scholarship, public journalism, politics, and research for major think tanks. A leader in formulating economic policy, he served as assistant secretary of the treasury for economic policy under President Reagan. He has held prestigious research positions at the Center for Strategic and International Studies (1982–1993); the Cato Institute (1993–1996); and, currently, the Institute for Political Economy, Stanford University's Hoover Institute, and the Independent Institute. He has written numerous academic articles for economic, finance, and law scholarly journals. Author of the *The Tyranny of Good Intentions* (2000) with Lawrence Stratton, among other books, he is a syndicated columnist, winner of the Warren Brookes Award for Excellence in Journalism in 1993, among other awards, and a regular contributor to the *Wall Street Journal, Bloomberg Businessweek, Investor's Business Daily*, and *National Review*. Roberts is a conservative who is known as a critic of both Republicans and Democrats and an initiator of bipartisan economic policies. This editorial was posted on the Web site for *Counterpunch* (www.counterpunch.org), on July 10, 2008. *Counterpunch* claims to be "America's Best Political News letter." In its bi-weekly news commentaries, it takes a muckraking approach, criticizing both major parties as well as U.S. economic and foreign policy.

Although Roberts's affiliations include conservative and libertarian think tanks, what are his criticisms of free trade ideology's policies on offshore outsourcing in this piece?

The collapse of world socialism, the rise of the high speed Internet, a bought-and-paid-for US government, and a million dollar cap on executive pay that is not performance related are permitting greedy and disloyal corporate executives, Wall Street, and large retailers to dismantle the ladders of upward mobility that made America an "opportunity society." In the 21st century the US economy has been able to create net new jobs only in nontradable domestic services, such as waitresses, bartenders, government workers, hospital orderlies, and retail clerks. (Nontradable services are "hands on" services that cannot be sold as exports, such as haircuts, waiting a table, fixing a drink.)

Corporations can boost their bottom lines, shareholder returns, and executive performance bonuses by arbitraging labor across national boundaries. High value-added jobs in manufacturing and in tradable services can be relocated from developed countries to developing countries where wages and salaries are much lower. In the United States, the high value-added jobs that remain are increasingly filled by lower paid foreigners brought in on work visas.

When manufacturing jobs began leaving the US, no-think economists gave their assurances that this was a good thing. Grimy jobs that required little education would be replaced with new high tech service jobs requiring university degrees. The American work force would be elevated. The US would do the innovating, design, engineering, financing and marketing, and poor countries such as China would manufacture the goods that Americans invented. High-tech services were touted as the new source of value-added that would keep the American economy preeminent in the world.

The assurances that economists gave made no sense. If it pays corporations to ship out high value-added manufacturing jobs, it pays them to ship out high value-added service jobs. And that is exactly what US corporations have done.

Automobile magazine (August 2008) reports that last March Chrysler closed its Pacifica Advance Product Design Center in Southern California. Pacifica's demise followed closings and downsizings of Southern California design studios by Italdesign, ASC, Porsche, Nissan, and Volvo. Only three of GM's eleven design studios remain in the US.

According to Eric Noble, president of The Car Lab, an automotive consultancy, "Advanced studios want to be where the new frontier is. So in China, studios are popping up like rabbits."

The idea is nonsensical that the US can remain the font of research, innovation, design, and engineering while the country ceases to make things. Research and product development invariably follow manufacturing. Now even business schools that were cheerleaders for offshoring of US jobs are beginning to wise up. In a recent report, "Next Generation Offshoring: The Globalization of Innovation," Duke University's Fuqua School of Business finds that product development is moving to China to support the manufacturing operations that have located there.

The study, reported in *Manufacturing & Technology News,* acknowledges that "labor arbitrage strategies continue to be key drivers of offshoring," a conclusion that I reached a number of years ago. Moreover, the study concludes, jobs offshoring is no longer mainly associated with locating IT services and call centers in low wage countries. Jobs offshoring has reached maturity, "and now the growth is centered around product and process innovation."

According to the Fuqua School of Business report, in just one year, from 2005 to 2006, offshoring of product development jobs increased from an already significant base by 40 to 50 percent. Over the next one and one-half to three years, "growth in offshoring of product development projects is forecast to increase by 65 percent for R&D and by more than 80 percent for engineering services and product design-projects."

More than half of US companies are now engaged in jobs offshoring, and the practice is no longer confined to large corporations. Small companies have discovered that "offshoring of innovation projects can significantly leverage limited investment dollars."

It turns out that product development, which was to be America's replacement for manufacturing jobs, is the second largest business function that is offshored.

According to the report, the offshoring of finance, accounting, and human resource jobs is increasing at a 35 percent annual rate. The study observes that "the high growth rates for the offshoring of core functions of value creation is a remarkable development."

In brief, the United States is losing its economy. However, a business school cannot go so far as to admit that, because its financing is dependent on outside sources that engage in offshoring. Instead, the study claims, absurdly, that the massive movement of jobs abroad that the study reports are causing no job loss in the US: "Contrary to various claims, fears about loss of high-skill jobs in engineering and science are unfounded." The study then contradicts this claim by reporting that as more scientists and engineers are hired abroad, "fewer jobs are being eliminated onshore." Since 2005, the study reports, there has been a 48 percent drop in the onshore job losses caused by offshore projects.

One wonders at the competence of the Fuqua School of Business. If a 40–50 percent increase in offshored product development jobs, a 65 percent increase in offshored R&D jobs, and a more than 80 percent increase in offshored engineering services and product design-projects jobs do not constitute US job loss, what does?

Academia's lack of independent financing means that its researchers can only tell the facts by denying them.

The study adds more cover for corporate America's rear end by repeating the false assertion that US firms are moving jobs offshore because of a shortage of scientists and engineers in America. A correct statement would be that the offshoring of science, engineering and professional service jobs is causing fewer American students to pursue these occupations, which formerly comprised broad ladders of upward mobility. The Bureau of Labor Statistics' nonfarm payroll jobs statistics show no sign of job growth in these careers. The best that can be surmised is that there are replacement jobs as people retire.

The offshoring of the US economy is destroying the dollar's role as reserve currency, a role that is the source of American power and influence. The US trade deficit resulting from offshored US goods and services is too massive to be sustainable. Already the once all-mighty dollar has lost enormous purchasing power against oil, gold, and other currencies. In the 21st century, the American people have been placed on a path that can only end in a substantial reduction in US living standards for every American except the corporate elite, who earn tens of millions of dollars in bonuses by excluding Americans from the production of the goods and services that they consume.

What can be done? The US economy has been seriously undermined by offshoring. The damage might not be reparable. Possibly, the American market and living standards could be rescued by tariffs that offset the lower labor and compliance costs abroad.

Another alternative, suggested by Ralph Gomory, would be to tax US corporations on the basis of the percentage of their value added that occurs in the US. The greater the value added to a company's product in America, the lower the tax rate on the profits.

These sensible suggestions will be demonized by ideological "free market" economists and opposed by the offshoring corporations, whose swollen profits allow them to hire "free market" economists as shills and to elect representatives to serve their interests.

The current recession with its layoffs will mask the continuing deterioration in employment and career outlooks for American university graduates. The highly skilled US work force is being gradually transformed into the domestic service work force characteristic of third world economies.

For Class Discussion

1. In the third paragraph, Roberts rehearses the classic rationale for offshore outsourcing jobs. What points does he include?

2. What counterclaim to the value of outsourcing does Roberts assert in this editorial? How would you articulate what Roberts values in the U.S. economy?

3. What evidence does Roberts muster to rebut the policy of offshore outsourcing endorsed by the American business community and academic economists?

4. Roberts uses a vehement and bleak tone in this piece. How does it suit the publication? How rhetorically effective do you think it is for both its target audience and a wider general audience?

5. How has this argument influenced your understanding of U.S. corporations' policies on jobs?

A Time for Action: Jobs, Prosperity, and National Goals
Ralph E. Gomory

Ralph E. Gomory holds a PhD in mathematics from Princeton University. From 1959 to 1989, Gomory held various leadership positions at IBM: director of the mathematical sciences department; director of research; and vice president and senior vice president for science and technology. With eminent economist William J. Baumol, he authored the book *Global Trade and Conflicting National Interest* (2001), which is gaining traction in political circles. In addition to being president of the Albert P. Sloan Foundation—a grant-giving research organization devoted to science, technology, and the economy, he is a part of the eleven-member Horizon Project, whose mission is "to provide the new Congress with a legislative agenda to ensure that America continues to be the preeminent economic power in an era of globalization" and to prompt action in order "to stave off the erosion of our competitive advantages and the loss of the nation's middle class base" (www.horizonproject.us). This proposal argument was posted on *The Huffington Post*, a liberal news commentary site, on October 24, 2011.

> How does Gomory try to reframe the debate over free trade in a way that will lead to positive action?

Here in the United States, we talk endlessly about the importance of free trade and of government not interfering with the market. But while we are talking, other nations are busy subsidizing and building up key sectors of their economies, and in this process destroying key sectors in our own economy. These nations have grasped the obvious: that a country which leads the world in the most productive sectors of the economy will be rich, while countries that are confined to what is left will be poor. And while this is going on we continue to pursue more "sophisticated" but misleading ideas like comparative advantage.

We have too many people today who see in the destruction of our key industries by well-organized and highly subsidized actions from abroad nothing more than the effect of free trade and the operations of a perfectly free market. This is a delusion and a dangerous one. We also have an elite industrial leadership that too often sees itself with no other duty than maximizing the price of their company's stock, even if that means offshoring the capabilities and know-how for advanced production to other nations that have no free markets themselves.

OUR NATION'S FAILURE

Although I have just named foreign subsidies and American corporate leadership as part of the problem, the heart of the problem is the lack of leadership from our own government. Despite the importance of economic progress, our government, unlike many others, has no clear economic goals for our nation. But economic progress is essential, and to make that progress in today's world we need economic goals that we steadily pursue and support.

I believe that our government should visibly and clearly adopt two national economic goals:

1   To be a productive nation steadily growing a large per capita Gross Domestic Product (GDP).
2   To share widely the prosperity made possible by that productivity.

Both are essential and measurable goals. By adopting and pursuing these goals our government can visibly align itself with the interests of the American people.

THE ROLE OF THE CORPORATION

The principal actors in attaining these economic goals must be our corporations. But today our government does not ask U.S. corporations, or their leaders, to build productivity here in America; much less does it provide incentives for them to move in that direction. Rather, our government, captured by the delusion that they are watching free trade and free markets at work, has too often simply stood by and allowed one-sided destruction to go on.

They do not realize that the corporate goal of profit maximization at all costs does not serve the interests of the nation. *They do not realize that the fundamental goals of the country and of our companies have diverged.* The sole focus on profit maximization, which leads to offshoring and holds down wages, does not serve the nation. This must change. And it must change before the damage to our economic ability is irreversible. And, in light of the recent Supreme Court decision on campaign financing, we must also act before the increasing influence of global corporations on our government becomes irresistible.

We must act to realign the goals of *company and country*.

REWARD PRODUCTIVITY AND HIGH-WAGE JOBS

I am not suggesting that our government step in and run our industries. What I am suggesting is that we need economic goals. Then, given those goals, we should reward those corporations that, acting freely and competitively, contribute strongly to those goals, productivity in America being high among them.

Our government should not pick companies to favor; I do not think we have the history or inclination to do what some countries can do successfully, which is to pick and sustain national champions. Rather we should use traditional means to directly serve national goals.

For a long time we have used the corporate income tax rate to spur R&D in any company. Building on that familiar approach we could, for example, use the corporate income tax rate to reward any corporation, large or small, that maintains high-value-add-per-U.S.-employee. These companies are the strong contributors to GDP per capita. Many variations on this approach are possible, including many that are revenue neutral, but the essential point is to use corporate tax rates to reward the corporations whose actions support national goals. We do not select national champions; rather, we reward any entity that contributes strongly to the national goals. If we can agree on goals, enunciate them, keep them in mind and measure them, we will find many ways to provide rewards to corporations that contribute to those goals.

Some nations target the growth of specific industries that are productive. But let us go one better and make our country a place where any productive entity is rewarded. Much of manufacturing has the high productivity that will earn it incentives under this approach. We should clearly reward productive manufacturing and end this endless discussion about whether we do or do not need manufacturing. But we should also reward intelligent users who use tools and ingenuity to become more productive in whatever they do.

We should make sure that in our country productivity and high-wage jobs in the United States become the path to profitability.

BALANCE TRADE

One unpleasant aspect of reality is that we cannot have success with any real economic policy, if we do not balance trade. Foreign governments can be extreme in their quest for dominance in specific industries. And we see every day the destructive effect of their actions.

By balancing trade we guarantee that any inflow of goods is matched by an equivalent export of goods made here in the United States. Balancing trade, coupled with rewarding productivity, will move us a long way toward ending both the one-sided destruction of industry by subsidized competition with its consequent loss of jobs, and the growth of our indebtedness to other nations. And this indebtedness leads to a diminution of our actual independence and of our ability to control our own future.

There are many ways to approach the balance of trade. Many measures have been discussed. Prominent in these discussions is the need to obtain a realistic exchange rate. Clearly, major movement in that direction would serve our national goals. However, other nations—China is the best example—see it in their interest to have their currencies undervalued and hence their products underpriced. Years of talks with China with no results should make clear to us that the exchange rate is something we do not control. We should realize that the approach of trying to "level the playing field" may simply not apply when we are dealing with countries that work hard to keep the playing field slanted in their direction, and when they have many ways beyond the exchange rate to do just that.

We may very well need to tackle the trade issue in the direct and head on way that Warren Buffet suggested in his insightful *Fortune* article in 2003. In this article he described his Import Certificates plan. The Buffet plan is something that we can carry out without the agreement of other nations, and it is something that would actually balance trade. The time has come to take this plan seriously in place of the endless talk that only postpones the day of reckoning.

THE MORAL DIMENSION

And let us not neglect the moral dimension. Let us make it right and admirable for corporations to consider high wages for Americans as part of their job, and for outstanding products to be something in which they take pride. Those who cannot remember may think I am dreaming, but I am not. Until the 1980's the dominant view of the role of corporations was the stakeholder view, which included, along with profits, all the considerations I have just named and more.

CONCLUSION

The time has come for us to shake ourselves free from the delusions that shackle us; let us act before it is too late. Let us urge government to visibly announce and then support and measure goals of productivity and widespread prosperity. Let us reward those who provide high-wage employment in the United States. Let us urge on our government the necessity of balanced trade, and let us do that in spite of the cries from those who currently find it more profitable to participate in and develop unbalanced trade. Let us all in our various ways start to clarify the role of the American corporation and find ways for our companies to serve not only shareholders, but also their employees, and the nation. Let us act before it is too late.

For Class Discussion

1. How does Gomory propose to tackle the problem of corporate responsibility to the nation in order to change both the current corporate approach and the U.S. government's approach to trade? What claim does he make?

2. What reasons and evidence does Gomory offer that his proposal will be beneficial to the nation and to ordinary Americans?

3. How does knowing that Gomory has a background as a corporate leader himself contribute to his reliability, credibility, and authority in this argument?

4. He concludes this argument with a call to action. What would you say is the tone of Gomory's conclusion? How rhetorically effective is it?

5. Gomory emphasizes that in the last decades some major changes happened in the way corporations conducted business. What values is he appealing to in his readers? Why is this perspective important in the current debates over corporate responsibility and national choices?

Buy American Hurts America
Daniella Markheim

Daniella Markheim holds the position of Jay Van Andel Senior Trade Policy Analyst in the Center for International Trade and Economics at The Heritage Foundation, a conservative think tank with the mission "to formulate and promote conservative public policies based on the principles of free enterprise, limited government, individual freedom, traditional American values, and a strong national defense" ("About"). Analysts like Markheim are part of the foundation's research and educational program, providing reports and analyses to "members of Congress, key congressional staff members, policymakers in the executive branch, the nation's news media, and the academic and policy communities" ("About"). This researched policy statement appeared on January 30, 2009, on The Heritage Foundation Web site. The immediate motivating occasion of this piece was the stimulus package of 2009, early in Obama's presidency as the country struggled to recover from the global economic crisis of 2008, yet the problems of trade imbalance, unemployment, and increasing income equality have reinvigorated and heated up the Buy American issue.

> What is Markheim's major concern about the United States' participation in global trade?

Looming large in the stimulus package passed by the U.S. House of Representatives Wednesday—and currently under consideration in the U.S. Senate—is the expansion of "Buy American" provisions that discriminate against foreign goods and services in U.S. government procurement. House legislation would require that only iron and steel products made in America be used in the myriad public works projects funded in the stimulus package—unless domestic steel adds more than 25 percent to the cost of the project. The Senate version is even more restrictive, banning the use of *any* import in stimulus-funded projects.

Advocates of Buy American rules claim that limiting competition for U.S. government contracts to domestic firms will protect U.S. jobs and help prop up firms in troubled industries. Regrettably, the cost of such protectionism will be inflicted on the American public, who will fail to get the best value for their hard-earned taxpayer dollars; the U.S. workers who lose their jobs when the companies they work for go out of business as countries retaliate in kind; and the economy as a whole, which will become less productive.

Rather than expand on the Buy American provisions the U.S. has long maintained, a better approach would be to open competition in government-funded projects even wider. This expansion will help ensure that America gets the most benefit it can from vast new government spending. It will also send a critical message to the world that the U.S. is committed not only to its own welfare but to that of the international economic system as well.

PROTECTIONISM IS NOT THE RIGHT ANSWER

The devastating economic effects of such protectionist measures are well-documented. The Smoot–Hawley Tariff Act of 1930, for instance, raised U.S. tariffs on more than 20,000 imported goods to record levels. Introduced as a means to reduce imports and protect American businesses and jobs,* Smoot–Hawley did cut the amount of imports between 1929 and 1933 in half. At the same time, exports dramatically

---

*The justification for Smoot–Hawley is laid out in the 1928 Republican Party Platform: "[W]e realize that there are certain industries which cannot now successfully compete with foreign producers because of lower foreign wages and a lower cost of living abroad, and we pledge the next Republican Congress to an examination and where necessary a revision of these schedules to the end that American labor in the industries may again command the home market, may maintain its standard of living, and may count upon steady employment in its accustomed field." "Republican Platform [of 1928]" in Arthur M. Schlesinger, Jr., Fred L. Israel, and William P. Hansen, eds., *History of American Presidential Elections, 1789–1968*, Vol. 3 (New York: Chelsea House, 1971).

declined,* and unemployment grew from 3.2 percent in 1929 to 8.7 percent in 1930 and peaked at 24.9 percent in 1933—the heart of the Great Depression.† Large majorities of economists and historians now say that Smoot–Hawley played a significant role in worsening the Great Depression.‡ While not the same, the expansion of the Buy American program represents a step toward the same type of destructive protectionism instituted by Smoot–Hawley.

With countries' economic vitality linked through trade and investment, the need for all nations to protect open markets is crucial to helping the global economy recover and return to a path of growth. Therefore, given the effects of previous protectionist schemes, expanding the Buy American program as part of a *stimulus package* is perverse.

LEADING BY EXAMPLE

In November 2008, the U.S. and other leaders in the G-8 publicly acknowledged the role trade plays in mitigating the cost of economic contraction and committed to avoid any new protectionist measures in their plans to spark their domestic economies. According to recent reporting from the WTO, although the economic downturn has prompted a few instances of protectionism, nations are largely sticking to that promise.§

That said, the longer it takes for the world's economies to recover, the higher the risk that trade and investment barriers will find their way into domestic stimulus schemes. While some countries may cave to the temptation to protect the special interest groups and industries clamoring for assistance, the U.S. cannot afford such a response. Implementing new, more restrictive Buy American provisions not only breaks the promise America made to the world in November, but it also opens the door for other nations to introduce similar domestic bias in their own recovery plans.

Such retaliatory measures would result in U.S. firms being denied the chance to compete for billions of dollars in foreign government

---

*Tim Kane, Brett D. Schaefer, and Alison Acosta Fraser, "Myths and Realities: The False Crisis of Outsourcing," Heritage Foundation *Backgrounder* No. 1757, May 13, 2004, at *http://www.heritage.org/Research/Economy/bg1757.cfm*.

†*Ibid.*, footnote 28.

‡Robert Whaples, "Where Is There Consensus Among American Economic Historians? The Results of a Survey on Forty Propositions," *The Journal of Economic History*, Vol. 55, No. 1 (March 1995), pp. 139–154, at *http://www.jstor.org/stable/2123771* (January 26, 2009).

§International Centre for Trade and Sustainable Development, "WTO Report Finds 'Limited Evidence' of Protectionism amidst Economic Crisis," January 28, 2009, at *http://ictsd.net/i/news/bridgesweekly/38844* (January 29, 2009).

contracts in support of stimulus projects in Australia, China, France, Germany, the U.K., and elsewhere around the world. While the Buy American provisions might protect 3 million U.S. manufacturing jobs (as claimed by White House spokeswoman Jen Psaki*) by shutting out foreign competition, it would threaten many of the more than 57 million Americans employed by firms that depend on international trade if nations retaliate against U.S. protectionism.[†]

Moreover, while much of the U.S. economy has retrenched since the current crisis started, U.S. export performance has improved—a source of economic strength that has so far helped mitigate the cost of the downturn. However, as countries fall prey to global economic weakness, it will be increasingly difficult for U.S. firms to find customers abroad. Opportunity to participate in other nations' stimulus projects would provide a new source of foreign demand as traditional international markets weaken.

NO NEW TRADE RESTRICTIONS

Tougher Buy American provisions protect the few at the expense of the many. Under these provisions, regardless of whether America protects only steel or a broad swathe of industry, American families already struggling to make ends meet will have to pay more for goods and services. U.S. businesses and their employees that depend on global markets will find it harder to stay afloat, and economic recovery will take much longer to come to fruition. Economic recovery depends not only on preserving a competitive, transparent business climate in the U.S. but on preserving the open markets on which so much of our prosperity is based and which even now are helping keep the U.S. from slipping deeper into recession.

For Class Discussion

1. Summarize the case (claim and main reasons) that Markheim has constructed against the move to install "Buy American" clauses in our trade policies. Why should the United States not adopt Buy American policies?

2. What values and assumptions about global trade and the measuring of economic prosperity, shared by The Heritage Foundation, underlie this argument? What stakeholders might be left out of these assumptions?

3. Where does Markheim address alternative views in this argument?

---

*Anthony Faiola, "'Buy American' Rider Sparks Trade Debate," *The Washington Post*, January 29, 2009, at *http://www.washingtonpost.com/wp-dyn/content/article/2009/01/28/AR2009012804002.html?hpid=topnews* (January 29, 2009).
†Council of Economic Advisors, "Economic Report of the President," February 2007, p. 169, at *http://www.gpoaccess.gov/eop/2007/2007_erp.pdf* (October 24, 2008).

4. What is the rhetorical effect of Markheim's scholarly citations?

5. Markheim's argument against Buy American rests in part on three facts she claims: (1) that the Smoot-Hawley Tariff Act of 1930, intended to protect "American businesses and jobs," hurt the economy and increased unemployment; (2) that the main stakeholders pushing Buy American laws are "special interest groups and industries clamoring for assistance"; and (3) that "tougher Buy American provisions protect the few at the expense of the many." Based on other readings in this chapter and your own research, who would contest these "facts" and what alternative interpretations of them would they give?

Buy American, Buy Union
Rebecca Cook, Reuters

Rebecca Cook is a Detroit-based photographer who has been photographing Detroit area news events and major league sporting events for Reuters global-news service since 1990. Her freelance work has appeared in *USA Today*, the *New York Times* and *TIME* magazine. This photo was taken in early June 2009 and accompanied an article titled "Canadians Angered over 'Buy American' Rule" in the *NewsDaily* on June 6, 2009. The person whose arm is pictured in this photo is Don Skidmore, president of United Auto Workers union local 598. Variations on this image appeared in June 2009 alongside stories about a provision in a U.S. economic stimulus package passed in February of 2009 that requires public works projects to use iron, steel, and other goods made in the United States. The provision has engendered controversy with U.S. trade partners, particularly Canada.

What are your first impressions of this image?

Rebecca Cook/Reuters/Corbis

For Class Discussion

1. How do the image of the tattoo and the appearance of the arm in this photo influence your idea of Skidmore's beliefs and values?

2. This image makes a proposal claim, but it relies largely on an implicit argument. Using ideas from the other readings in this chapter, reconstruct this argument and the opposing case. What are the stakes in this issue?

3. List two to four ways that this photo asks individual American consumers to participate in the debate over production, consumerism, values, national economic prosperity, and corporate responsibility to workers and the nation.

4. Organizations such as the Level Field Institute (www.levelfieldinstitute.org) supply background data on the value and effect of buying American-made automobiles. Investigate the Web site for this organization or one for another organization like it, and make connections between the organization's angle of vision and supporting information and this photo's argument.

Gallup's Jim Clifton on *The Coming Jobs War*
Dan Schawbel

This piece, an interview, has two authors in effect—Dan Schawbel, the conductor of the interview, and Jim Clifton, the person who is setting forth the arguments about jobs. Dan Schawbel has a growing reputation in the business community as a leading authority on personal branding. He publishes *Personal Branding Magazine* and an award-winning blog with the same title, is a syndicated columnist for *Metro US*, and a frequent contributor to *Bloomberg Businessweek*, the *New York Times*, the *Wall Street Journal*, and *Details Magazine*. He is often a keynote speaker and has appeared on MSNBC, Fox, ABC News, and NPR. His book *Me 2.0: Build a Powerful Brand to Achieve Career Success* (2009) is a best seller. Jim Clifton, as CEO of the well-known polling company the Gallup Organization, has created the Gallup Path, an economic model to measure worldwide business outcomes, and the Gallup World Poll, which asks questions about "individual and social needs, including food and shelter, safety and security, mental and physical health, education, jobs, economics and finance, transportation, water and air quality, hope and futurism, leadership approval, religion, and war and peace" (Speaker Biography http://worldcongress.com/). This interview, focusing on Clifton's recent book, *The Coming Jobs War* (2011), appeared in *Forbes* magazine, the nation's foremost business magazine, on October 26, 2011.

Why is Dan Schawbel an appropriate interviewer and *Forbes* a likely forum for this interview?

I recently caught up with Jim Clifton, who has served as the CEO of Gallup since 1988. His most recent innovation, the Gallup World Poll, is designed to give the world's 6 billion citizens a voice in virtually all key global issues. Under Mr. Clifton's leadership, Gallup has achieved a fifteenfold increase in its billing volume and expanded Gallup from a predominantly U.S.-based company to a worldwide organization with 40 offices in 30 countries and regions. Mr. Clifton serves on several boards and is Chairman of the Thurgood Marshall College Fund. His latest book is called *The Coming Jobs War*. In this interview, Jim talks about why jobs are so important for leaders, how leaders can create more jobs than competitors, and much more.

WHY ARE JOBS THE NEW GLOBAL CURRENCY FOR LEADERS?

Gallup has discovered that having a good job is now the great global dream; it's the number one social value for everyone. This is one of our most powerful findings ever. "A good job" is more important than having a family, more compelling than democracy and freedom, religion, peace and so on. Those are all very important but they are now subordinate to the almighty good job. So it follows that everything turns on delivering this ultimate need. Stimulating job growth is the new currency of all leaders because if you don't deliver on it you will experience instability, brain drain, sometimes revolution—all of the worst outcomes of failed leadership. At the very least you will have no followers and no chance of re-election.

HOW DOES A LEADER CREATE MORE JOBS THAN THE COMPETITION?

By creating more customers. Almost no one knows this. Keep in mind that no business is trying to create jobs. They are all working all day and every weekend to create new customers. New customers are the real goal of a nation. Because jobs always follow customers. Too few leaders have this figured out and it is at the very core of our failure to fix this seemingly colossal American problem. To create authentic, organic, real job growth—not pretend jobs made by government—city and country leaders need to focus on customers.

WHAT OBSTACLES DO LEADERS HAVE WHEN TRYING TO CREATE MORE JOBS?

There are no real obstacles. Just wrong thinking, bad assumptions. When you build strategies and policies on wrong assumptions, the more you execute, the worse you make everything, which is what we are doing now. There are three wrong assumptions that cause all the current job creation attempts to not work.

1. Innovation is not scarce. Entrepreneurship is scarce. We are spending billions and wasting years of conversations on innovation and it isn't paying off. Great business people are more valuable and rarer than great ideas.

2. America has about six million active businesses. Ninety-nine percent of them are small businesses. An incalculably huge mistake leaders are making now is spending time, money, strategies, and especially policies for those who need "help" getting a job. A useful way to look at any citizen is this, "Can she herself create jobs or does she need a job created for her?" We are spending all our time on the cart and doing little or nothing on the horse. We have our assumptions and futurism that backward. "The horse (small and medium business) stopped, so we fix the cart (jobs)." If we change all our strategies and policies to favor the job creators (small and medium businesses) the horse and cart will get moving again. We have our compassion right, but the logic is staggeringly stupid.

3. It is wrong thinking to imagine that Washington has solutions. Job creation is a city problem. There is great variation in job creation by city in the United States. San Francisco and the greater Valley keep pumping away while Detroit isn't. Austin's cart works while Albany's doesn't. Cities need to look inwardly and say, "What can I do to create great economic energy, to bring new customers for all existing companies and start-ups?"

CAN YOU EXPLAIN THE GLOBAL COMPETITION FOR JOBS? SINCE MANY JOBS HAVE MOVED TO ASIA, HOW DO WE GET THEM BACK?

According to Gallup's World Poll, there are three billion people out of seven billion who want a good job. There are only 1.2 billion jobs to go around. So there's a short-fall of 1.8 billion jobs. The question is who gets those new jobs as they emerge. The second part of this macroeconomic phenomenon is that the world currently has a GDP of $60 trillion and it will grow to $200 trillion GDP over the next 30 years. So there is an incoming $140 trillion of new equity, sales, and profit, but most importantly new products and customers and subsequently the appearance of new good jobs. God is going to rain $140 trillion of new economic energy on earth over the next 30 years and the question is, who gets these jobs? The competition or "war" for good jobs lies exactly there. To be more specific, it is a war for the best customers first. He who wins that war, wins the jobs war. Almost no leader has this figured out.

But how do we get back the jobs that moved? We won't—they're not coming back. We will do well just to hold on to what we have. Building strategies around "bringing back manufacturing" is a losing proposition. That's more strategy and policy around wrong assumptions that make everything worse. America has to create the next generation of customers who cause new human development, such as the Internet, the auto and aeronautical industries, transistors, satellites, Facebook, everything Apple makes, world-class code, etc. And then go ahead and lose the second generation of production and manufacturing to China, India, and soon to Africa and the Middle East.

This works. It has for decades. U.S. manufacturers were the first to make firecrackers and raincoats, and then decades ago, that production moved to China. That is still happening . . . but with flat screens, laptops, and so on. America has to invent and especially enterprise the future within that incoming $140 trillion of new economic energy. America has to create the next new way humans survive and thrive. It is very exciting because when American free enterprise is thriving, within that energy lies real human development . . . quality evolution of humankind. That's the core character of American exceptionalism.

WHO IS TO BLAME FOR THE U.S. LOSING JOBS? WHY?

Blame leadership. Always blame leadership. Everything turns on lousy or great leadership in government, business, and all organizations of all shapes and sizes. Leadership really does matter. Leadership fails especially when it works with failed assumptions. Failed assumptions and the wrong core thinking for the problems at hand. The worst failure is probably failure of vision. We have turned our national assets too much to those who "need" help versus toward those who can "offer" help—the small and medium businesses that are the primary job creators and employers.

I am not just talking the usual free enterprise line of too many taxes, regulations, over empowerment of unions, and all the other usual suspects that serve the people who need help with general well-being and survival. Americans get behind the people we identify as heroes and we subsequently swing virtually all strategies, policies and thinking that way. So will our heroes come in the image of a great equalizer like Barack Obama or a great pioneer like Steve Jobs? This isn't about voting, it's about the ideology and assumptions behind winning the best jobs in the world. Do we focus money and policies and speeches primarily on the people who need America's help or those who can offer help, the small and medium businesses. Because we can't have competing assumptions and win the coming jobs war. If we don't swing our hero worship quickly to great entrepreneurs, not only will we not get the old jobs back, we won't get new ones either.

For Class Discussion

1. One economic-political perspective that is popular now in the United States believes that the wealthy, big corporations, and private enterprise are job creators (and therefore should be minimally regulated). How do Clifton's assumptions, claim, and reasoning about job creation echo or differ from this view?

2. What oppositional views does Clifton address and how does he argue against them?

3. What does Clifton mean by "the jobs war" and "American exceptionalism"? How does Clifton provide evidence and support for his loaded terms "war" and "exceptionalism"?

4. How does Clifton's knowledge and position as head of the Gallup Organization influence this argument's persuasiveness?

5. What ideas in Clifton's argument do you find useful in considering the national and global economic problems explored in this chapter?

So If We Stop Buying
Jeff Danziger

Jeff Danziger is a political cartoonist and a Vietnam veteran, who has taught journalism and writing. His cartoons are syndicated by the *New York Times* and published worldwide and regularly in *The Huffington Post*. He creates the comic strip *The Teeds* and has published several books of cartoons, including *Wreckage Begins with W* (2004) and *Blood, Debt, and Fears: Cartoons of the First Half of the Last Half of the Bush Administration* (2006). In a YouTube video, Danziger speaks about his love of drawing, his use of visual metaphors and humor, and his desire to provoke a strong response from readers. Danziger identifies with old-fashioned conservative values but harshly critiques the faults he currently sees in politics. He received the Herblock Prize in 2006 and the Thomas Nast Prize in 2008 for political cartooning. This cartoon was published on September 5, 2011.

What is your initial impression of this cartoon?

For Class Discussion

1. On the surface, what causal argument does this cartoon convey?

2. The cartoon's rhetorical effectiveness derives from readers' interpretation of the characters. Who are they and what do they represent?

3. Some readers might interpret this cartoon as a satire on proposed solutions to the trade imbalance and the national unemployment problem. Whom do you think Danziger is satirizing? Does the cartoon clarify or complicate the issue?

4. How does the message of this cartoon differ from that of Wuerker's cartoon on page 97? What are both cartoons saying about ethical shopping?

Tariffs and the Perils of Freer Trade: It's Complicated

Allan Tanny

The motivating occasion for this opinion piece, which appeared in *The Gazette* of Montreal, Canada, on October 7, 2011, is the ongoing debate about countries looking out for their own industries, which is often dubbed "protectionism." Tanny is responding directly to the op-ed piece of another Canadian who advocated for protectionism. Allan Tanny manufactures industrial equipment—snowblowers and airport-runway sweepers. He also works as a business consultant.

How has the context of a citizen responding to a citizen in a regional newspaper influenced the main claim in this op-ed piece?

Derek Cooperberg ("When people are losing their jobs, let's hear it for protectionism," Opinion, Sept. 30) makes some interesting points in asking for a renewal of import tariffs as a way to counteract the effects that globalization has had on our unemployment rates. If it were only so simple.

To reimpose tariffs on imported goods, a way must be found to act unilaterally. The problem is that it cannot be to the long-term benefit of any country to contravene trade treaties that it has previously negotiated. On the other hand, it is just as bad to do nothing in the face of nations that violate trade agreements to your detriment.

In the case of Canada, it becomes even more complicated. If we were to reimpose tariffs, we should expect retaliation in kind. Many of our industries that have succeeded under the new freetrade rules have expanded to service these larger markets. If retaliatory rules are instituted against us, these companies will suffer horribly. Also, because new or existing smaller companies may be restricted to the Canadian market because of retaliatory tariffs, the small size of that market would lead to great inefficiencies, making us uncompetitive once open-trade rules again ruled the roost. So the question of adjusting import tariffs is a double-edged sword; it may help in the short term, but certainly not in the long term.

One example of the downside that freer trade can have is the great loss of business that Canadian manufacturers of airfield snow-removal equipment have suffered since the North American Free Trade Agreement came into effect. U.S. companies have virtually taken over the business in Canada now that their equipment can enter the country duty-free. On the other hand, the Federal Aviation Administration in the U.S., which funds most equipment purchases, insists that any purchase using its money comply with the Buy America Steel Act. This has effectively shut Canadian companies out of this industry altogether. Denied sales to the large U.S. market, Canadian companies are fighting to just hold on. The lack of sales has forced them to reduce spending on research and development, resulting in their inability to keep up with developing technologies, which in turn causes them to lose even more ground worldwide. Our government has stood by and done nothing to help.

Globalization has certainly not had many of the positive effects that were promised. Helping developing countries to export their goods was supposed to create new consumer societies for countries in the developed world to sell their goods to. It hasn't worked out as planned. The lesser-developed countries have not grown enough to help first-world countries make up for the job losses that free access to their home markets has caused.

Even worse, it has created several monster economies—such as China, the world's second-largest—that still receive the benefits the rest of the world gives to emerging economies. While they are taking millions of jobs away from the developed world, we allow them to manipulate their currency to further our disadvantage. And to their increased benefit, they do not have to play by the same environmental rules that add costs to our products. We have allowed China, India and Brazil and others to grow at our expense, often by not playing by the same rules as we do.

But not all the problems that now plague us can be blamed on others. Governments, especially in the United States, have allowed companies to take advantage of lax tax laws and loopholes to allow multinationals to transfer and declare large profits in low-tax jurisdictions rather than in North America. This has also helped to speed the flight of jobs from our shores.

Every day we see the damage globalization has done to our economies, but what to do about it is a complicated question.

Certainly simply raising tariffs is not the answer. History shows that erecting trade barriers was one of the leading causes of the Great Depression.

And unfortunately, instituting specific barriers against the most egregious offenders is not really possible, as these same countries hold such a great proportion of U.S. debt that erecting trade barriers against them could cause them to dump that debt, with the result that interest rates would soar.

A worldwide, long-term answer depends on the United States, given the size of the U.S. economy. Unfortunately, given the political climate there at the moment, a real solution looks a long way off.

For Class Discussion

1. How does Allan Tanny's conciliatory first sentence set the tone for his op-ed piece?

2. What does your knowledge of Tanny's line of work contribute to your impression of his reliability and authority?

3. What evidence and reasoning regarding treaties, tariffs, and the trade policies of different countries work well in this argument?

4. Why would you agree (or disagree) with the assertion that this argument leans toward the inquiry/exploratory end of the argument continuum?

5. How does this piece contribute to your understanding of the issues entangled in the free trade–global production–jobs web?

CHAPTER QUESTIONS FOR REFLECTION AND DISCUSSION

1. Some of the arguments in this chapter explore the big issue of free trade as a global economic system—its benefits, costs, successes, and problems. List five to ten specific ways that global trade affects your life, such as how you shop, what jobs relatives have, what car your family drives, and so forth.

2. Student writers Tiffany Anderson and Nicole Cesmat were inspired to write about issues regarding free trade, consumerism, and sweatshops based on their own work experiences, shopping habits, and academic interests. Using the list you generated from question 1, decide which connection you might be inspired to investigate.

3. Many of the arguments in this chapter make different assumptions about free trade, global production, global workers, corporate responsibility, outsourcing, national economic security, protecting domestic industries, and consumerism. Choose a pair of contrasting readings from one of the groups below. Identify the audience, genre, and writer's background for each. What underlying issue question is each writer addressing? Describe the major differences in the way the writers frame the issues: differences in their claims, reasons, and assumptions. Where do they look for evidence to support their claims? What counterarguments does each writer acknowledge?

   Ha-Joon Chang or Global Exchange and Daniella Markheim
   Bob Jeffcott or Ed Finn (Chapter 2, pages 29–31) and Jeffrey Sachs
   Nicole Cesmat and Matt Wuerker's cartoon "Made in China"
   Steven Rattner or Jeffrey Sachs and "Buy American, Buy Union" or Ralph Gomory
   Daniella Markheim and Jeff Danziger "So If We Stop Buying" cartoon or Ralph Gomory
   Dan Schawbel/Jim Clifton and Paul Craig Roberts

4. Identify and summarize common assumptions, reasons, or evidence in one of the following groups of readings and explain how these arguments are compatible or complementary.

Daniella Markheim, Steven Rattner, Allan Tanny, Dan Schawbel/Jim Clifton
Ha-Joon Chang, Ralph Gomory, Paul Craig Roberts
Nicole Cesmat, "Buy American, Buy Union," Bob Jeffcott, Jeffrey Sachs,
    Jeff Danziger cartoon, and Ed Finn (from Chapter 2, page 31)

5. The readings in this chapter explore a number of themes and issues pertaining to trading goods and jobs from different perspectives: (1) American consumerism, values, and global production and workers; (2) American consumerism, values, and the nation's economic prosperity; (3) corporate responsibility to workers and the nation; (4) the global competition over jobs; and (5) the role of national government in directing national trade policy. Choose *one* of these issues; list three or four readings that address it; and based on your developing understanding of the issue, state what you consider to be two or three main points or principles for an informed, responsible policy on that issue. (For example, what do you think are the responsibilities of corporations to the nation? What should ethical shoppers consider when they make purchases?) After you have listed your points, state which reading in this chapter contributed most to your understanding and why.

6. Because free trade, sweatshops, the United States' trade imbalance, the power of corporations, and consumerism are hot controversial topics today, political cartoons often focus on them. Find a political cartoon that takes a position on one of these issues and analyze it by sketching its characters and storyline, its claim and condensed argument, its angle of vision, and its appeal to values and emotions. What values and assumptions do readers have to hold to agree with this cartoon? How does this cartoon's message differ from the Wuerker and Danziger cartoons in this chapter?

7. Working individually or in a group, research one of the following economic problems related to this chapter's readings and prepare a short presentation in which you teach your class about your findings. Prepare a graph, chart, other numeric display of data, or some visual mapping of information.

- What household appliances can you "Buy American"? Check the following Web sites and any others you find: Still Made in USA.com (www.stillmadeinusa.com) and Made in USA Forever.com (www.madeinUSAforever.com). What are your impressions of these sites? What points stand out for you on the issue of American-made goods?

- What is the difference in salaries for the following occupations in top offshore outsourcing countries as compared to salaries in the United States, Canada, or the EU countries?

  Software engineer
  Mechanical engineer
  Accountant
  Payroll manager
  Medical transcriptionist

Information technology manager
Call center agent
Other outsourced jobs you think of

- Corporations are always looking for new cost-cutting offshore outsourcing sites for their businesses, factories, and assembly plants. What are three new popular locations for outsourcing? What types of companies are using these sites? What specific advantages do these sites offer? (You might investigate the growth in outsourcing to the Philippines, for example.)

- Various indexes list the top global corporations, their revenues, their locations, and their profiles. Consult one of these indexes, such as the *Fortune* Global 500, select information that you find interesting about the top ten companies, and find a way to display it memorably for the class.

WRITING ASSIGNMENTS

Brief Writing Assignments

1. **Reflective Writing.** Write a brief narrative in which you describe a moment that made you think in a new way about your consumer habits. You could describe a personal experience (1) when you became aware of the consumer benefits of free trade; (2) when you realized some of the production problems of free trade; or (3) when you confronted the question of ethical shopping in a new way.

2. Choose one of the following claims and write informally for twenty minutes, supporting or contesting this claim. Use examples from your reading, personal experience, and knowledge to provide evidence and specific examples to support your views. As a variation on this assignment, your instructor might ask you to write a short response in favor of the claim and then a short response against it.

   A. We should build and buy American products to strengthen our nation's economy.

   B. Consumers in developed countries have a responsibility to know about the supply chain and production conditions of the goods they buy.

   C. Corporations should not be criticized for pursuing offshore outsourcing as a means to reduce costs and maintain their competitive edge.

   D. The federal government should use the corporate tax code and tax incentives to compel corporations to invest in R&D in the United States.

   E. Economic policies in developed countries should not favor concentrating wealth and power in the hands of the corporate elite.

3. Using the readings in this chapter and some searching on your own, track one of the rhetorically loaded phrases that pops up frequently in public

debates about corporate responsibility, the global free trade of goods and jobs, and its impact on the U.S. economy: "job creators," "class warfare," "protectionism," "corporate welfare," "socialism," "level the playing field," "1 percent and the 99 percent," and "corporate rule." Choose two or three text or visual arguments, and briefly explain how each writer's use of one of these terms in the argument reveals the writer's angle of vision (values, assumptions, background, and position on the argument's subject).

4. **Analyzing Arguments Rhetorically.** The following groups of writers share similar perspectives on one of the issues covered in this chapter, yet their arguments differ in prominent ways. Choose a pair of writers in each group, and contrast their arguments in terms of genre, audience, and use of rhetorical appeals. (For example, how do Gomory's and Roberts's claims, use of evidence, and tone differ?) Briefly list and explain your points in preparation for discussion or formal writing.

Jeff Danziger's cartoon and Allan Tanny
Bob Jeffcott and Nicole Cesmat
Ralph Gomory, Paul Craig Roberts, and Ha-Joon Chang
Global Exchange and David Sirota
Steven Rattner and Dan Schawbel/Jim Clifton
Ralph Gomory and Dan Schawbel/Jim Clifton

Writing Projects

1. **Reflective Writing.** In response to one of the following questions, write a reflective essay that includes both narrative and analysis. Build your essay on your narration of one or two specific incidents or extended examples. In your analysis, infuse an awareness of your thoughts and feelings on the subject and a probing of why you think and feel this way.

A. Jim Clifton discovered through his Global Gallup Poll that "having a good job is the great global dream; it is the number one social value for everyone" (page 121). Reflect on this statement by generating your own criteria for what you consider a "good job." When have you experienced what a "good job" for you might be? Can you describe someone you know who has high job/career satisfaction? What do you see as the main personal, social, and economic obstacles to attaining a good job?

B. Are you the man or woman in Wuerker's cartoon or one of the characters in Danziger's cartoon? In the spirit of the cartoon "Made in China," author John Atcheson criticizes American citizens/consumers for selling our souls for material possessions and giving away our power as a consumer group to corporations.* Reflect on this claim by narrating a

---

*"The Walmartization of America Redux: How the Relentless Drive for Cheap Stuff Undermines Our Economy, Bankrupts Our Soul, and Pillages the Planet," Common Dreams.Org (December 16, 2011).

consumer experience you have had and analyzing your own thoughts and feelings on Americans' addiction to cheap, new goods and gadgets. Explore your own values.

2. **Analyzing Arguments Rhetorically.** Thinking about the contribution one of the writers in this chapter has made to your understanding of one of this chapter's issues, write an essay in which you analyze the rhetorical strategies of one of the following: Ha-Joon Chang, Jeffrey Sachs, Paul Craig Roberts, David Sirota, Nicole Cesmat, Allan Tanny, or Bob Jeffcott. In your analysis, you might focus on the writer's use of analogy, questions, evidence, description and narrative, or personal experience as support for his or her claim and reasons; the writer's credibility and authority; or the match between the genre of the argument, the audience for the argument, and the writer's word choice and level of formality. You may want to include a short summary of the argument in your introduction. Write to attract readers like yourself to this writer's argument or discourage them from reading it.

3. A number of the readings in this chapter (as well as Ed Finn's "Harnessing Our Consumer Power" in Chapter 2, pages 29–31) put pressure on the link between consumers in rich nations and the condition of workers in sweatshops around the world. Consider the case of the manufacturing of Apple products—or any personal electronic equipment. Although the activism of Nike and Gap consumers led to "a demand for better conditions in overseas factories," currently "there is little impetus for radical change" because right now, customers care more about a new iPhone than working conditions in China.* On this subject of ethical shopping, write either (A) a policy proposal for a consumer group or (B) a reflective op-ed piece with a personal angle and an exploratory tone using an approach like that of Nicole Cesmat, Ed Finn (pages 29–31), Susan Wilkinson (pages 81–82), or Allan Tanny. Express your informed/personal view of shopping with your values. You might argue your case for boycotting irresponsible companies, for pressuring companies to make their manufacturing practices transparent, for rewarding socially responsible companies with your business, or for political action to encourage economic development in poor countries; or you might ponder the market complexities facing consumers in developed countries.

4. Pretend you are a junior researcher assigned to write a policy analysis that could be posted on a think tank Web site. Your analysis should include summaries and explanations of different positions on the issue and conclude with a reasoned recommendation for a course of action—adoption of a policy or recommendations for further research. Choose one of the following issues to research and investigate by consulting a range of sources and views. You might find the following think tanks useful in your

---

*Charles Duhigg and David Barboza, "In China, the Human Costs That Are Built into an iPad," *New York Times*, January 26, 2012, A1+.

research: Center for Economic and Policy Research; Economic Policy Institute; Pew Research Institute; Brookings Institute; Center for American Progress; Horizon Project; The Heritage Foundation; the Peterson Institute for International Economics.

- Many business leaders and policymakers, along with analysts such as Jim Clifton in his book *The Coming Job War*, believe that leaders with a vision for job creation, local businesses, and cities hold the greatest promise for reviving the U.S. economy and preparing it for future global competition. Research some of the following: the National Small Business Association, the National Community Reinvestment Coalition, the growing popularity of credit unions, state banks, and co-ops, and organizations such as Local First. Write a policy analysis and proposal concerning the potential for local businesses to foster economic recovery.

- With high unemployment, home foreclosures, and credit card debt, many Americans have found themselves financially strapped. Some analysts have said that Americans must value savings over spending, following the example of other countries. Research the practice of saving. You might begin with *247 Wall Street's* "The Ten Countries Where People Save the Most Money." What can the United States learn from other countries regarding saving? Consider the question that financial analyst Adam Davidson of NPR's "Planet Money" raises, "What does a reasonable balance between consumption now and consumption deferred actually look like?"*

- Since the beginning of what economists are calling the Great Recession of 2007, U.S. unemployment rates have been high for the country as a whole but especially for certain age, ethnic, and education groups and some regions of the country. The phrase "the Lost Generation" has been applied to young adults who have been unable to find suitable employment, are carrying the burden of big college loans, or have had to move back to live with parents. Choose a group of people and research the unemployment rate for that group in your state over the last three years. What contributing factors stand out? What possible solutions (for example, canceling college debts, federal support of specialized training programs, funding for local businesses to hire) offer promise?

5. Identify an economic or social problem related to the readings in this chapter, research it, and write a policy proposal in the form of a letter to your U.S. senator or representative or an editorial for an online news commentary site such as CommonDreams.org or a conservative blog. Write as a concerned, informed citizen with the purpose of compelling your audience to support your proposal. Look for a global issue with a local dimension or a local issue with a global dimension and for one that touches your life in

*"Indicate This," *New York Times Magazine* (December 18, 2011), 14.

some way. Some examples might be a company or industry in your area that has recently outsourced jobs; an influx of foreign ownership of businesses or property; federal investment in a local green energy company; or problems facing activist groups that are protesting corporate greed. How would you like your political representative to speak out on this issue? Or what view do you think your community should consider?

6. Role-play that a family friend is interested in starting a clothing or food company that will be located in the United States and market heavily to Americans. Knowing that you are studying global and local issues, this person has asked you for advice about successful American companies. Research several of the following companies—Florsheim shoes, Biogreen Clean, Munro shoes, Not Your Daughter's Jeans, American Apparel, and USA Coffee Company. Analyze the Web sites of several of these companies and draw up some ideas for consumer appeal. What insights can you gain from the companies' histories, targeted consumer groups, and marketing angles? Write a short proposal argument for your family friend in which you identify and argue for three to five ingredients for success for a new company with American appeal.

7. Write a Rogerian letter (after Carl Rogers, the psychologist who believed that establishing nonthreatening, nonjudgmental listening is necessary for real communication to take place). Choose one of the chapter's issues that matters to you and one of the arguments in this chapter with which you disagree. Compose a letter to the writer that seeks to open up a dialogue with him or her about the issue. Maintain a respectful, engaged tone throughout your letter. Include a fair, accurate summary of the writer's argument—one that the writer would accept. Then include a discussion of several assumptions about the issue and values that you share with the writer and at least one point you could agree on. Include examples to show that you and the writer can meet on some common ground. Toward the end of the letter, offer several reasons of your own that you would like the writer to consider. Try to keep the conversation open even as you end the letter.

4

Crossing Borders
Immigration

CONTEXT FOR A NETWORK OF ISSUES

In Fremont, Nebraska, the meatpacking industry for years has drawn Latino workers, many illegal, who have established their own businesses, restaurants, and Spanish-language radio stations. This influx of immigrants has evoked uneasiness and resistance from some Nebraskans, with many now favoring laws denying employment and housing to undocumented immigrants. Similarly, in Alabama, an anti-immigration bill even harsher than Arizona's House Bill 1070 has scared immigrants by prohibiting work opportunities, house ownership and rental, and travel without proof of documentation. These fear-infused, anti-immigrant conflicts have counterparts in the European Union countries. For example, in spring of 2011, thousands of Tunisians fled the revolution in their country and landed by boat in Ventimiglia in southern Italy. Italians resented the refugees sleeping in train stations and the streets, and Italy and France argued about which country should absorb these people. In another part of the EU, the small Danish town of Odense, car burnings and violence between Danes and Palestinian and Somali youth revealed brimming anger over conflicting views of integration. Clearly, at this historical moment, economic and social/cultural problems with migration have outstripped the government policies and citizens' abilities to handle them.

Population growth and the changes in the racial and ethnic composition of countries are reflected in the population statistics for the United States and the European Union. According to the 2010 census, in the United States with its population of 313,074,000, approximately 38 million (or 12 percent of the population) are foreign-born; another 11 percent are native-born with at least one foreign-born parent as of 2009. Out of every five people, one is either a first- or second-generation U.S. resident.* According to *The Statistical Yearbook of the Immigration and Naturalization Service*, 1,042,625 people became legal permanent residents (green card

---

*"Nation's Foreign-Born Population Nears 37 Million," October 19, 2010, accessed February 22, 2012, www.census.gov/newsroom/releases/archives/foreignborn_pop.

holders) in 2010; in 2010, 34 percent of this group of legal immigrants came from China, India, the Philippines, Ethiopia, Mexico, and El Salvador. Meanwhile in the EU with a population of 502.52 million, "the total number of non-nationals (people who are not citizens) living on the territory of an EU Member State on 1 January 2010 was 32.5 million persons, representing 6.5 percent of the EU-27 population" and two-thirds of these persons came from non-EU countries, with the largest groups from Turkey, Albania, Ukraine, northern Africa, India, and China. The EU countries receiving the most immigrants were Great Britain, Spain, and Italy.[*] In addition, "the number of Muslims in Europe has grown from 29.6 million in 1990 to 44.1 million in 2010, or about 6% of Europe's total population."[†] These statistics show a sizable flow of immigrants and notable presence of cultural diversity in both the United States and the EU.

In the United States, the effort to control this volume of immigration through legislation and physical restraint has a problematic history. The McCarran-Walter Act of 1952 repealed the 1924 Immigration Act and ended the ban on Asian immigration, but it established a quota system by which immigrants were limited by national origin, race, and ancestry. Then in 1965, the Immigration and Nationality Act Amendments ended the discriminatory national origins quota system, which was replaced with a first-come, first-served system, giving preference to uniting families and establishing numerical restrictions according to the Eastern and Western Hemispheres. Another significant piece of legislation was the Immigration Reform and Control Act of 1986, which attempted to fix the problem of the large number of illegal immigrants by granting permanent resident status to those who had lived and worked in the United States since 1982; but it failed to establish a workable system for managing further illegal immigration. The number of illegal immigrants now residing in the United States is somewhere around 11.2 million, down from 12 million in 2007, 80 percent of whom are from Latin America, according to estimates by the Pew Hispanic Centers.[‡] Governmental strategies to restrain immigration physically along the 1,951-mile U.S.–Mexican border—a national security issue, complicated by violent drug trafficking—have entailed millions of dollars spent on fences, helicopters, drones, and border patrols, and have been moderately successful. However, tighter surveillance in border cities such as El Paso and Laredo, Texas, and San Diego, California, has compelled

---

[*]"Migration and Migrant Population Statistics-Statistics Explained," accessed February 24, 2012, http://epp.eurostat.ec.europa.eu/statistics_explained/index.php/Migra.

[†]"The Future of the Global Muslim Population," *Pew Forum on Religion, January 27, 2011, accessed February 24. 2012,* www.pewforum.org/future-of-the-global-muslim-population-regional-europe.aspx.

[‡]Jeffrey Passel and D'Vera Cohn, "Unauthorized Immigrant Population: National and State Trends, 2010," accessed February 22, 2012, www.pewhispanic.org/2011/02/01/unauthorized-immigrant-population-brnational-and-state-trends-2010/.

people to take more dangerous routes through the Sonora Desert, where many have died of thirst, hunger, and heat.

U.S. and EU immigration issues are part of the larger global picture of political, economic, and social forces. The movement of masses of people across national borders continues to increase in our globally connected world: "The UN estimated the stock of international migrants at 214 million in 2010, meaning that 3.1 percent of the world's 6.9 billion people were living outside their country of birth."* Some are refugees fleeing political or ethnic persecution, political upheaval, and unstable states, leaving countries such as Haiti, Bosnia, Kosovo, Sudan, Myanmar, Iraq, Bhutan, Libya, and Tunisia. However, most immigrants move for economic reasons. Some college-educated persons and professionals choose to head to developed countries, where they can use their training and education under better conditions for substantially higher pay, a phenomenon called the **brain drain**. Underlying all this migration is the dominant pattern: flows of people from poorer, developing **sender countries** to the more prosperous, stable, developed **receiving** or **destination countries** such as the United States, Canada, and the countries of the European Union.

STAKES AND STAKEHOLDERS

Citizens of developed countries as well as citizens of developing countries hold stakes in the potential gains and costs of global immigration. Policymakers, analysts, and citizens around the world are speculating about the reasons that so many people are leaving their countries of origin, and they are arguing about the most effective, socially just ways to manage immigration. Here are some key issue questions and some of the positions arguers are taking.

How Is Globalization Fueling Immigration?   Some analysts emphasize "pull" factors such as the enticing lifestyle of the world's wealthiest nations that is broadcast globally by television and other media, and that insidiously suggests the superiority of these values, customs, and opportunities to live the "good life." Other analysts, such as former U.S. Ambassador to Mexico Jeffrey Davidow, posit the dominance of "push" factors—the conditions compelling people to move from developing countries to developed countries. Davidow asserts that emigration from Mexico "will continue at high rates until the Mexican economy can provide sufficient work opportunities and decent standards of living for a far greater percentage of its population."† Some politicians, analysts, and policymakers believe that the way

---

*"Global: UN Migrants, Population," *Migration News* 17, no. 1 (January 2010), accessed February 24, 2012, http://migration.ucdavis.edu/mn/more.php?id=3585_0_5_0.

†"Immigration, the United States, and Mexico," Mexidata.Info, www.mexidata.info/id350.html.

to solve U.S. immigration problems with Mexico and other Latin American countries, and to stop the further erosion of U.S. workers' economic base is to address the income disparity between the United States and these developing countries.

The best way to bring prosperity to Mexico and Latin America is the subject of much debate. Free trade proponents argue that more emphasis on free trade will bring economic improvement and greater economic equality to these countries. However, other activists and analysts contend that free trade dominated by corporations, and influenced by global institutions, such as the International Monetary Fund (IMF) and the North American Free Trade Agreement (NAFTA), has been a major source of economic disruption and devastation in these Latin American countries. They argue that when giant agribusinesses buy up small subsistence farms in Mexico, they displace the poor and force these farmers to seek food, work, and dignity in the United States. These activists are working instead for more independence, social justice, and restoration of local/regional control in these countries. Besides these economic push factors, political upheaval, wars, and natural disasters cause people to seek asylum and new opportunities through migration.

A key piece of the migratory picture is the role of **remittances**—money earned by immigrants abroad and sent back to their own countries in the form of money orders, personal checks, or electronic transfers—which often constitutes a substantial percentage of developing countries' GDP and amounts to a large foreign aid package supported by these countries' own citizens. For example, remittances to Latin America and the Caribbean in 2012 are estimated to total $69 billion. Some analysts question this dependence model and emphasize the need for countries like Mexico and the Philippines to build their own economies by bolstering education and job creation at home.

How Much Should Receiving Countries Focus on Their National Interest and How Should They Integrate Immigrants for the Economic and Social Benefit of All?   Leaders and groups within both the European Union and the United States argue about the advantages and drains of taking in immigrant workers—either poor and uneducated or educated—particularly in hard economic times when unemployment is high. Citizens and politicians of the rich EU nations are debating whether to impose restrictions on immigration from the ten new EU members from eastern Europe who, like Slovakia and the Czech Republic, have high unemployment rates. Many British citizens, journalists, U.S. citizens, policymakers, and activists debate how and to what degree they should restrict immigrants' access to social benefits, such as the dole (welfare) and housing in Britain, and driver's licenses, welfare, food stamps, Medicaid, and financial support for higher education in the United States. Many European analysts and politicians argue that immigrants are beneficial, even necessary to supply labor to offset western

Europe's aging population and low birthrate. Similarly, in the United States, analysts point out that illegal workers pay Social Security taxes that benefit the country, but not them, while this huge subclass of undocumented workers work for low wages at some of the most necessary but least appreciated jobs in manufacturing, agriculture, and the service sector. Indeed, businesses, hospitals, restaurants, and other parts of American society, including American households that hire gardeners, nannies, and housecleaners, lean heavily on this inexpensive labor. The agricultural sector, which depends on inexpensive, hard-working immigrants, 50 to 85 percent of whom are illegal, has protested the new E-Verify system for checking the status of all immigrant workers upon employment, arguing that implementing this system will leave huge crops unharvested, hurting the economy and consumers. With these economic facts in mind, stakeholders are debating how to regulate the need for both low-skilled and highly educated immigrants and how to ensure that immigrants' contributions outweigh their costs.

The phenomenon of **transnationalism**—the process of immigrants' maintaining connections, loyalties, and cultural, social, and political involvement with their countries of origin through remittances, voting, or travel—is also controversial. Does transnationalism nurture or hinder immigrants' integration and participation in receiving countries?

To What Extent Are the Most Urgent Problems of Immigration Cultural Problems? Some analysts, politicians, and groups of citizens frame immigration problems in terms of religious and cultural differences affecting national identity and cultural integrity. One question under debate in the EU, Canada, and the United States is to what extent the presence of large groups of immigrants should be allowed to change the "character" of communities in these countries and the countries themselves. What practices of intercultural relations are good for the countries as a whole and socially just to the newcomers? The EU is struggling with its philosophy and practice of **multiculturalism**, which has encouraged new groups of people, largely Muslim, to remain in separate communities within their host countries or has demanded a complete adoption of European ways. Confronted with increasing numbers of Muslim immigrants from Turkey, Southeast Asia, North Africa, and the Middle East, some Europeans are speaking out in favor of preserving traditional European values. Some voices in this controversy, such as France's former President Nicolas Sarkozy and the late political theorist Samuel P. Huntington in the United States, believe that large immigrant groups must assimilate into the dominant culture of their receiving countries. In opposition, some immigrants and groups on the left label these attitudes as fear-driven and racist and instead advocate for tolerance and more inclusive social and political action; however, other voices warn that tolerance of immigrant groups that themselves are intolerant or defiant may be an unwise course for host countries' societies and governments. Examples of these cultural conflicts are the debates over Muslim women wearing the burka in Europe and Canada and over Sharia law and bilingual education in the United States. These conflicts generate intense emotions, and sometimes violent backlashes, as seen in right-wing extremist Norwegian Anders Behring Breivik's mass killing of the children of liberals tolerant of Muslims in Norway in July 2011, the protests of the Islamic culture center near Ground Zero, the burning of the Koran in Florida, and the attacks on Latino men in Staten Island, New York.

How Should the United States Reform Its Immigration Policy? Political leaders, citizens, lawyers, analysts, and advocacy groups have been arguing about the urgent need for comprehensive immigration reform in the United States, which political wrangling, widely divergent national views, and the complexity of the issues themselves have stalled. Most stakeholders agree on the need for (1) an immigration policy that is fair to legal immigrants and presents a consistent message on illegal immigration and employment for undocumented workers; (2) a plan to address the large population of illegal immigrants; and (3) a plan to manage future immigrant flow. How to achieve these goals is the subject of intense debates.

- **State policy versus federal policy.** The failure to craft a comprehensive immigration reform, particularly to determine whether undocumented immigrants should have access to driver's licenses, tax benefits, or higher education for their children, has prompted states such as Arizona, Alabama, Georgia, and South Carolina to pass their own immigration laws to control illegal immigration. While lawyers, citizens, and immigrant groups contest states' rights and the effect of these laws on immigrants, other states have rallied to pass their own punitive or welcoming laws, and many people are questioning whether the proliferation of state legislation will spur federal reform.

- **Prioritizing enforcement.** The federal focus on enforcement has generated both praise and strong criticism. President Obama's approach to immigration reform has stressed the strengthening of border security; encouraging legal immigration to meet employment needs but cracking down on those who employ illegal immigrants; promoting Mexican economic development as a way to reduce illegal immigration; and establishing a system for "undocumented immigrants in good standing to pay a fine, learn English, and go to the back of the line for the opportunity to become citizens."* Supporters commend the Immigration and Customs Enforcement (ICE) under the Department of Homeland Security for detaining and removing over 360,000 foreign nationals in 2010, creating a program (called Secure Communities) that coordinates local and federal enforcement and uses the federal immigrant databases for fingerprinting

---

*April 20, 2009, www.whitehouse.gov/agenda/immigration/.

to identify and deport criminal aliens, drug and gun smugglers, and gang members. However, social justice and human rights activists and immigrant advocates claim this system is being used to catch illegal immigrants regardless of their criminal records and the danger they pose, increasing racial profiling, criminalizing of minor offenders and even citizens, splitting up families, terrifying hardworking immigrants, and making communities less safe. Another component of enforcement is military intervention at the border and in the war on drugs. Many policymakers, analysts, and citizens are arguing about how to reduce the extent and violence of drug trafficking and how to secure the border. Would legalizing drugs in the United States and regulating employment be more effective than physical barriers? How should the E-Verify system, which has resulted in the audits of the employment records of hundreds of companies, be used to crack down on employers of illegal immigrants? Should the system target employers that don't exploit their workers as well as those with questionable practices? Should long-term, hardworking, well-trained illegal immigrant employees be penalized?

- **Managing the need for workers.** Political leaders, businesses, and citizens continue to argue about temporary worker permits. President George W. Bush's 2004 "guest worker plan," which died in Congress in 2007, would have enabled immigrants to apply for renewable three-year worker visas. Businesses and employers would have been required to give evidence that they couldn't fill their jobs with American workers. The plan also proposed offering worker protection, retirement benefits, and tax savings accounts to immigrant workers, as well as temporary visas allowing workers to come and go across the U.S. border. Worker advocates argue for the need to improve conditions that exploit undocumented workers, who often work under the most dangerous conditions in construction jobs and agriculture and often suffer from the lack of safety equipment and job training. In April 2009, the two leading labor federations in the United States (the AFL-CIO and Change to Win) joined in a campaign to give illegal workers already in the country legal status, but they also strongly opposed any new program that would allow employers to bring in new workers on a temporary basis, a practice many labor advocates have claimed benefits employers much more than workers. The U.S. Chamber of Commerce, representing businesses, promptly came out in favor of a temporary worker program to meet business needs and thus ensured that the legislative struggle over this aspect of immigration reform would continue. Pragmatists worry about the bureaucratic structure and cost of a temporary worker permit program.

- **Citizenship as problem or solution.** Policymakers, citizens, and advocacy groups are arguing about who and how many people should be granted U.S. citizenship. Should the United States preserve birthright citizenship—"the automatic granting of citizenship to children born within a nation's borders or territories"—a practice only the United States and Canada among developed countries preserve?* What role do the need for sustainable population growth, demands on the environment and resources, and social justice play in determining policies for citizenship? Some citizens and anti-immigration groups—among them the Federation for American Immigration Reform (FAIR)—oppose any programs that reward illegal immigrants with visas or a path to citizenship, what they call a "backdoor amnesty." In opposition, Latin American politicians and immigrant advocacy groups argue that years of work in the United States should be a qualification for applying for citizenship. Social justice advocates acknowledge that the whole system of granting visas needs reform—"5 million citizens or residents are still waiting, sometimes after decades, after applying legally for their closest family members to join them"†—but they also actively seek a means to bring illegal immigrants out of living in fear. One key discussion related to citizenship has centered on the Development, Relief, and Education for Alien Minors (DREAM) Act, which has failed to pass Congress twice, in 2007 and 2010. This law would provide a path to higher education and citizenship for the children of illegal immigrants who were brought by their parents to the United States before they were sixteen, have been in the country at least five years, have earned a high school diploma or GED, and have demonstrated good moral character. They would have six years to earn permanent legal residency through completing two years of higher education or military service. Could creating more roads to citizenship for the country's illegal immigrant population promote integration for the country's economic and social benefit? Forums from scholarly journals to populist radio talk shows are hotly debating this question.

Thinking Visually

Illegal Immigration

The U.S. Immigration and Customs Enforcement (ICE) took this photo on February 12, 2012, revealing a person hidden inside a truck's engine compartment to get across the Mexico–United States border. In his book *The Devil's Highway*, Luis Alberto Urrea identifies this extreme transportation as a means that human smuggling rings offer immigrants who have little money. Locking people in trunks and tying them to engine blocks is called by smugglers "coffin loads."‡

---

*NumbersUSA, accessed February 24, 2012, www.numbersusa.com/content/learn/issues/birthright-citizenshp.

†Larry Gosset, Josefina Beecher, and Pramily Jayapal, "Taking a Moral Stand Against a Broken Immigration System," *Seattle Times*, May 26, 2010, A 13.

‡Luis Alberto Urrea, *The Devil's Highway* (New York: Back Bay Books, 2004), 70.

AP Photo/ICE

Human Smuggling Discovered by I.C.E. at the Mexico-United States Border

Questions to Ponder

1. How could someone use this photo rhetorically to support an argument calling for tighter border security and stricter punishment for illegal immigrants and smugglers? How could an advocate for immigration reform use this photo to promote understanding of the larger forces behind illegal immigration and compassion for illegal immigrants?

2. Unfortunately, crackdowns on border security in cities (for example, San Diego, Nogales, El Paso) have had unforeseen consequences. What questions about illegal immigration and U.S. immigration policies does this photo prompt you to ask?

 STUDENT VOICE: La Migra
by Esperanza Borboa

In the narrative that follows, student writer Esperanza Borboa shares her experience of the exploitation of illegal immigrants in the United States.

> I'm from Los Angeles, California, and in 1976, I worked in the garment industry in the heart of downtown where small and large cutting rooms employed anywhere from 5 to 100 people. Gender roles were clearly marked in this industry. Men were cutters, spreaders and pattern makers. Women were seamstresses. Salaries were oftentimes below minimum wage with no benefits, and women sat at

the bottom of that pay scale. I worked in the office as an assistant bookkeeper for minimum wage and no benefits. Most of the workers at our shop were Mexicans with a few Cubans. Everyone, including the boss, knew there were some who were undocumented, but we never talked about it. I was slowly becoming aware of how these people were exploited with no protection or recourse. Working and getting to know these men and women, I was learning what they were willing to risk and suffer just for the opportunity to work and provide for themselves and their children, something they couldn't do in their home countries. One day an experience made me feel the pain of their situation.

On that day I walked out to the cutting room to double-check some tickets with numbers I couldn't read. A young man came running by me, and all at once people were running in all directions. I asked Carmen, one of the lead workers, what was going on and she said the Migra (Immigration) was outside. There was a black passenger van in the alley half filled with workers from our shop and the one across the alley. One of the women being led to the van was crying and shouting to her co-worker "Vaya a mi casa y escoge a mis hijos y te llamo por teléfono!" ("Go to my house and get my children and I'll phone you!")

Although I knew they couldn't take me, a U.S. citizen, in that van, I was scared and stunned. I had known that raids were common, but this was my first experience of one. I asked Carmen what would happen to these people. She said, "They'll be deported to Mexico, and some of them will be back here by next week if they can come up with the money to pay a Coyote to cross them over the border. Their kids will stay here with friends till their mother or another family member can get here." As we watched the van pull away, my furious boss was ranting that he needed our help finding replacement workers and that we should let our friends know he was hiring. The Immigration official said they had received an anonymous call about illegal aliens working in this area. We all knew that someone always benefited from these raids, perhaps a competitor or the boss himself. Sometimes the raids would conveniently come the day before payday, enabling the boss not to have to pay "illegal" workers, even if they managed to come back.

That day my heart ached for all those picked up, and I felt powerless, voiceless, and guilty for working there, but as a young single mother I needed to work. I quit that job shortly after the raid and found another job with a company in the same industry only to see it happen again, but this time, most of us were pretty sure the boss had something to do with it because it was too close to a pay period. I quit that job too.

Many years later, I moved to Washington state, and while working with farm workers, I found out that the same practices were taking place in fields all across the country. The Migra would show up when the fields were almost completely cleared. The growers would deny they had anything to do with it just as the company owners did in Los Angeles, but we all knew better.

INTERNATIONAL VOICES

Analysts in Latin America, Mexico, and the United States are trying to determine how and why the push and pull factors affecting immigration from Mexico and Latin America have changed in the last few years. This article by Damien Cave, "Mexicans Finding That Home Is Now an Option: Illegal Migration to U.S. Sputters as Prospects and Education Improve," published in *The International Herald Tribune* on July 7, 2011, discusses how changes within the Mexican economy are contributing to immigration patterns in complex ways.

Factors Contributing to New Immigration Patterns in Mexico

A growing body of evidence suggests that a mix of developments— expanding economic and educational opportunities, rising border crime and shrinking families—is suppressing illegal traffic as much as economic slowdowns and immigrant crackdowns in the United States.

Here in the red-earth highlands of Jalisco, one of Mexico's top three states for emigration over the past century, a new dynamic has emerged. For rural families like the Orozcos, heading to El Norte without papers is no longer an inevitable rite of passage. Instead, their homes are filling up with returning relatives, older brothers who once crossed illegally are awaiting visas; and the youngest Orozcos are staying put.

"I'm not going to go to the States because I'm more concerned with my studies," said Angel Orozco, 18. Indeed, at the new technological institute where he is earning a degree in industrial engineering, all the students in a recent class said they were better educated than their parents and that they planned to stay in Mexico rather than go to the United States. . . .

The United States, of course, has not lost its magnetic appeal. Illegal traffic from Central America has not dropped as fast as it has from Mexico, and even in Jalisco town plazas are now hangouts for men in their 30s with tattoos, oversize baseball caps and a desire to work again in California or another state.

But more Mexicans are now traveling legally. A few towns away from Agua Negra, at the hillside shrine of St. Toribio, the patron saint of migrants, prayers no longer focus on asking God to help sons, husbands or brothers crossing the desert. "Now people are praying for papers," said Maria Guadalupe, 47, a longtime volunteer.

GLOBAL HOT SPOT: European Union

Day-to-day social friction among cultures, terrorist bombings (Madrid, 2004; London, 2005; Stockholm, 2010), the rise of right-wing extremist anti-immigrant parties in many EU countries, and the massacre of seventy-seven Norwegians, mostly youths, by fanatical anti-immigrant Anders Behring Breivik as a protest against Norwegian tolerance of Muslims have underscored Europe's problems with immigration. In this article, "Tide of Muslims Changes EU's Old Order: Nations Facing 'Identity Crisis,'" by Jabeen Bhatti, published May 12, 2011, in the *Washington Times*, several European leaders confront the negative consequences of their multiculturalist policies.

> In Germany, Chancellor Angela Merkel made headlines worldwide in October when she said, "Multiculturalism has failed."
>
> British Prime Minister David Cameron echoed her remark.
>
> What Mrs. Merkel said was that the notion of separate communities coexisting had failed. She called for a more integrative approach from both communities.
>
> "Islam is part of Germany," she said in March.
>
> Scholars say that many in the EU reject the notion that second- and third-generation Muslims in Europe are, indeed, Europeans.
>
> Some Muslim leaders, meanwhile, say their communities need to do more to integrate into European society.
>
> "We need to adapt and adjust to the host society better, not push for minarets or ninjas [burka-clad women]," said Taj Hargeym, chairman of the Muslim Educational Center of Oxford and a British imam of the Oxford Islamic Congregation. "We also need to acknowledge that self-segregation is not a way forward."
>
> European societies have a responsibility to fight "Islamaphobia" and to show European Muslims they are a valued part of society, some European leaders have said.
>
> "We have failed to provide a vision of society to young Muslims to which they feel they want to belong," Mr. Cameron told the Munich Security Conference in February.
>
> "Instead of encouraging people to live apart, we need a clear sense of shared national identity, open to everyone."

The readings in this chapter will help you approach globalization and immigration from different perspectives as you formulate your own views on how receiving and sender nations should respond to these migration issues.

READINGS

Lecture on International Flows of Humanity

Kofi Annan

Born in Ghana, and educated both internationally and in the United States, Kofi Annan became secretary-general of the United Nations (UN) in 1997 after having held various leadership positions there. He served two terms as secretary-general, and was awarded the Nobel Peace Prize in 2001. Annan remains a constant advocate for both human rights and the rule of law in his role on the board of directors for the United Nations Foundation. He is also chancellor for the University of Ghana. Annan delivered this speech at Columbia University on November 21, 2003, as the Emma Lazarus Lecture. (Emma Lazarus [1849–1883] was a well-known Jewish-American poet and political activist. Her famous sonnet "The New Colossus" was engraved on a plaque on the Statue of Liberty's pedestal in 1903. This poem helped enhance the statue's role as a symbol of the United States as a welcoming place of freedom and opportunity for immigrants. Copies of this poem are readily available on the Web.)

> How does Kofi Annan make use of the specific rhetorical context of this speech, and how does he try to connect with his audience in his introductory remarks?

There could be no place more fitting for a lecture on international flows of humanity than this great university, located as it is in a city which has been the archetypal success story of international migration.

And you could not have chosen a better person to name it after than Emma Lazarus, whose unforgettable lines are inscribed on the base of the Statue of Liberty, the Mother of Exiles. Just in case you have forgotten them, they are printed in your programme!

While Emma Lazarus's immortal words promised welcome to the tired, the poor, the wretched, and the huddled masses yearning to be free, another American poet, Walt Whitman, spoke of the vibrancy and vitality that migrants brought to the new world. He called New York the "city of the world" because, he said, "all races are here, all lands of the earth make contributions here".

How right he was—and still is. Today, more than one in three inhabitants of New York City was born outside the United States. The city boasts communities of 188 different national origins—only three fewer than there are Member States in the United Nations—and 47 per cent of them speak a second language at home.

New York, in other words, is a brilliant success story of migration, as are many other cities all around the world today. In fact, in the year 2000, some 175 million people, about 3 per cent of the world's population, lived outside their country of birth—more than at any other time in history.

Of these, around 16 million were recognized refugees—people who did not choose to leave home but were forced to. Another 1 million were asylum seekers—people who claimed to be refugees, but whose claims were in the process of being verified. The remainder, some 158 million, were deemed international migrants—that is, people who have chosen to move.

So much mobility and diversity should be cause for celebration. But migration also gives rise to many problems, leading people to ask: Can we absorb large numbers of new people? Will they take our jobs or absorb our social services? Are they a threat to our security, our way of life or our national identity?

These are understandable concerns, and they must be answered. The answers are not easy. But I have come here today to say that they do not lie in halting migration—a policy that is bound to fail. I say the answer must lie in managing migration—rationally, creatively, compassionately and cooperatively. This is the only approach that can ensure that the interests of both migrant and host communities will be looked after and their rights upheld.

It is the only approach that can effectively address the complex issues surrounding migration—issues of human rights and economic opportunity, of labour shortages and unemployment, of brain drain and brain gain, of xenophobia and integration, of refugee crises and asylum seekers, of law enforcement and human trafficking, of human security and national security. And it is the only approach that can, if we get it right, bring advantages to all parties—sender countries, countries of transit, host countries, and migrants themselves.

Many migrants, while not literally forced to move, choose to do so under duress. They see no opportunity at home to improve themselves, or perhaps even to earn a living at all. Their departure may be a source of sadness for themselves and their families, and also a loss for their home countries—often poor ones, which could have benefited from their talents. They are usually not free riders looking for an easy life, but courageous men and women who make great sacrifices in search of a better future for themselves or their families.

Nor are their lives always to be envied once they have left home. They often face as many risks and unknowns as they do hopes and opportunities. Many fall prey to smugglers and traffickers on their journey, and many more face a surly welcome of exploitation, discrimination and prejudice once they arrive. Many have little choice but to do dirty, dangerous and difficult jobs.

Undoubtedly more needs to be done to create opportunities in poor countries for individual self-improvement. This is yet another reason why we must strive harder to achieve the Millennium Development

Goals, including by forging a global partnership for development which, among other things, gives poor countries a fair chance to compete in the global market.

But migration itself can also be part of that global partnership—part of the solution to economic problems, not only in sender countries, but also in receiving ones. Sender countries benefit enormously from migrant remittances. They bring not only vital sustenance to the migrants' families. They also bring much-needed stimulus to the national economy. Last year alone, migrant workers in developed countries sent at least $88 billion back to their countries of origin—more than those same developing countries received in official development aid. These amounts are growing fast.

Emigration also relieves the pressures of overpopulation and unemployment, and in time endows sender countries with an educated diaspora who often bring or send home new skills, products, ideas and knowledge.

In short, migration is one of the tools we have to help put more of the world's people on the right side of—and ultimately, to eliminate—the vast divides that exist today between poor and rich, and between fettered and free.

Host country economies, too, can reap benefits. After all, the main reason any country attracts immigrants is its need for their labour. They perform many services that the host population is eager to consume, but is either unwilling or unable to provide for itself—from highly skilled work in research or information technology to less skilled jobs tending fields, nursing the sick and elderly, working on construction sites, running corner shops that stay open all night, or looking after children and doing housework while parents are out pursuing careers.

Increasingly, as birth rates in many developed countries fall, and populations age, immigrant labour, taxes and spending are becoming a demographic and economic necessity. Without them, pension schemes and health-care systems will be in danger of collapse. While immigration may not by itself be the answer to all these challenges, there is no answer to them that does not include immigration.

So migration has a demand as well as a supply side. Migrants are rational human beings who make economic choices. Up to now, rich countries have been far too comfortable with a policy framework that allows them to benefit from immigrant labour, while denying immigrants the dignity and rights of a legal status.

That is not good enough. Let us remember from the start that migrants are not merely units of labour. They are human beings. They have human emotions, human families, and above all, human rights—human rights which must be at the very heart of debates and policies on migration. Among those rights is the right to family unity—and in fact families reuniting form by far the largest stream of immigration into North America and Europe.

The more we try to deal with migration simply by clamping down on it with tighter border controls, the more we find that human rights are sacrificed—on the journey, at the border, and inside host countries.

Few, if any, States have actually succeeded in cutting migrant numbers by imposing such controls. The laws of supply and demand are too strong for that. Instead, immigrants are driven to enter the country clandestinely, to overstay their visas, or to resort to the one legal route still open to them, namely the asylum system. This experience shows that stronger borders are not necessarily smarter ones. And it shows that they can create new problems of law enforcement and lead almost inevitably to human rights violations.

The gravest violations come at the hands of smugglers and traffickers. Smuggling occurs with the complicity of migrants, usually because they can see no legal route to migrate. Trafficking is a modern form of slavery in which migrants are coerced and exploited. All too often, people who initially collaborate with smugglers later find themselves in the hands of traffickers.

Asylum processes, meanwhile, become clogged with doubtful cases, with the result that bona fide refugees are often detained for long periods. They are often denied the rights accorded to accused or convicted criminals—and, when free, they are objects of suspicion and hostility. This, in turn, undermines support for migration in host countries—despite the fact that many of them need migrants.

Those who manage to get in, or stay, illegally become acutely vulnerable to exploitation. If they attempt to assert their rights, they can be met with a threat of exposure and deportation. Migrant women and unaccompanied children are especially vulnerable to physical, psychological, and sexual abuse, sometimes involving the risk of infection with HIV/AIDS.

I am not suggesting that all these problems could be solved at a stroke simply by lifting all restrictions on migration. It is vital for States to harmonize their policies and maintain networks of cooperation and information sharing on smuggling and trafficking routes and trends, and on effective practices in prevention and assistance.

Nor do I suggest that a society can be expected to forego any process for deciding which immigrants it will accept, and how many at a time. But I do say that those decisions need to be positive as well as negative. And I say here, in the United States, that while I understand this nation's need to ensure that those who come here are not a threat to homeland security, it would be a tragedy if this diverse country were to deprive itself of the enrichment of many students and workers and family members from particular parts of the world, or if the human rights of those who would migrate here were compromised.

I also believe that States need carefully thought-out policies for integrating immigrants who are allowed in. Since both migrants and host societies stand to benefit from successful integration, both must play their part in making it happen. It is reasonable for societies to expect those who would become citizens to share certain basic values, to respect the law of the land, and to develop fluency in the local language, with assistance if they need it.

For their part, host societies must have effective anti-discrimination legislation and procedures, reflecting international standards and obligations, and should also take measures to promote appreciation of cultural diversity among all their citizens and residents.

But laws and policies are not enough. Leadership is vital too. All national leaders should be conscious that any form of discrimination against immigrants is a regression from the standards for a just society enshrined in the Universal Declaration of Human Rights and the binding treaties that derive from it.

Many people, in government and academia, in the private sector and in civil society as a whole, are showing the leadership that is needed to combat xenophobia and stigma. I salute them for it. But I am also disturbed by the vilification, in some quarters, of migrants—particularly of asylum seekers—often in an effort to achieve political gain.

Many of those vilified have fled their homelands in fear of their lives. States have a legal obligation not to return them to danger. They must establish fair procedures to determine the legitimacy of asylum claims. If, in extreme circumstances, asylum seekers must be detained, certain minimal standards must be provided, and enforced, to ensure respect for their human dignity and human rights.

The international regime for protecting migrant workers, set out in a host of human rights conventions that are either regional in scope or confined to particular categories of workers, should be made applicable to all categories of migrants, both regular and irregular, and to members of their families. Many States have recognized this need.

Recently, a step forward was taken with the entry into force of the International Convention on the Protection of the Rights of All Migrant Workers and Members of their Families—the bill of rights for migrant workers and their families in their new home countries. This step was important. But it was not enough. So far, only sender States have ratified the Convention, which means that it will have little practical effect. I call on all States, and in particular receiving States, to ratify the Convention, so that the human rights of migrant workers are protected by law.

The Migrant Workers Convention is but one instance of the efforts that are being made to address the issue of migration at the global level. But despite these efforts, consensus is lacking on many of the principles and policies which should be applied to the governance of international migration.

Internationally, we are not well organized to forge that consensus.

The United Nations does play an important role in dealing with many aspects of migration, and a leading role in helping refugees through the office of the High Commissioner. The International Labour Organization gives a voice to organized labour, and sets standards for fair labour practices, in conjunction with governments and the private sector. Outside the United Nations system, the International Organization for Migration (IOM) facilitates the movement of people, at the request of member States. United Nations agencies and the IOM have come together in the Geneva Migration Group to work more closely on this issue.

But we still lack a comprehensive institutional focus at the international level that could protect the rights of migrants and promote the shared interest of emigration, immigration and transit. No single agency works systematically across the whole spectrum of migration issues, and there is no complete legal framework in place to deal with this quintessentially global phenomenon.

I do not pretend that we can achieve such a framework overnight. And we should not await it before increasing bilateral and regional efforts. I am heartened by the efforts of some States—particularly those of the European Union—to find ways of coordinating their actions and harmonizing their policies.

Yet more and more people are coming to the conclusion that we also have to address this issue globally. Doing it regionally or bilaterally is not enough. I particularly welcome the decision taken by a core group of Member States from both North and South to form a Global Commission on International Migration to deepen our understanding of this issue and to make recommendations for improving international cooperation.

The Commission will have two distinguished co-Chairs in Jan Karlsson of Sweden and Mamphela Ramphele of South Africa. It has my full backing, and I hope it will receive support from States in all parts of the world and from institutions like yours. Most of all, I hope it will help us approach this issue creatively and cooperatively.

As the Commission's work proceeds, there are many questions I believe it should be asking, and that the rest of us should be asking too. For instance:

- Can greater cooperation be built between sender and receiver countries?
- Have the benefits of short-term and long-term temporary immigration been fully explored?
- Could more be done to work with the laws of supply and demand rather than against them?

- Might financial methods of discouraging illegal migration be more effective and more humane than some current practices?
- What are the best ways to speed up the integration of immigrants into host societies?
- Could more be done to harness the potential of migration as a force for development?
- Can developing countries do more to maintain contact with their emigrants?

No doubt there are numerous other equally important issues to be addressed as well.

Above all, I believe we must approach this issue with a strong ethical compass. The basic fairness and decency of any society can best be measured by its treatment of the weak and vulnerable. The principle of nondiscrimination has become an integral part of the universal moral code, one on which the defence of all other universal values depends. We should keep a firm hold upon it.

The willingness of rich countries to welcome migrants, and the way that they treat them, will be a measure of their commitment to human equality and human dignity. Their preparedness to adjust to the changes that migration brings will be an indicator of their readiness to accept the obligations as well as the opportunities of globalization, and of their conception of global citizenship. And their attitude to the issue will also be a test of their awareness of the lessons, and obligations, of history. After all, many migrants today are seeking to enter countries which not so long ago conquered and exploited their own. And many countries that are now attracting immigrants were until recently major exporters of emigrants.

Along with other countries, the United States falls into a third category—a nation built by immigration, a land where constant renewal and regeneration are essential elements of the national character. That character must never be lost.

And the hope and reality of a new future for those who would migrate must glow brighter today than ever before.

As Emma Lazarus wrote: "Send these, the homeless, tempest-tost to me, I lift my lamp beside the golden door."

For Class Discussion

1. Annan identifies the global stakeholders in immigration issues as "sender countries, countries of transit, host countries, and migrants themselves." According to Annan, what does each group lose and gain through migration? What are the responsibilities he identifies for each group?

2. What does Annan claim are the main immigration problems facing receiving countries? What role in regulating immigration does Annan advocate for global institutions?

3. One argumentative strategy that Annan adopts in this speech is to change his audience's idea of immigrants and to reframe immigration in terms of the problem of poverty. How does he work on his audience members' emotions and imaginations to recast the identity of immigrants and the nature of the immigration problem?

4. How does remembering that this argument was delivered as a speech affect your response to it?

5. What features of this piece contribute to making it a persuasive argument in favor of global migration?

Illegal Immigration Is Immoral
Victor Davis Hanson

Victor Davis Hanson is a neoconservative scholar, professor, public intellectual, journalist, and public affairs analyst and author. He writes on subjects as wide ranging as his own academic field of classical Greece and military history and fighting the war on terror, domestic politics, and culture. He has published numerous books, among them *Who Killed Homer? The Demise of Classical Education and the Recovery of Greek Wisdom* (1998); *Carnage and Culture* (2001); *Mexifornia: A State of Becoming* (2003), *Between War and Peace: Lessons from Afghanistan to Iraq* (2004); and (with Heather MacDonald and Steven Malanga) *The Immigration Solution: A Better Plan Than Today's* (2007). In addition to writing a weekly column for *National Review Online* and a syndicated column for Tribune Media Services, Hanson's writing is published regularly in the *New York Times*, the *Wall Street Journal*, the *Washington Times*, *Policy Review*, the *Weekly Standard*, and the neoconservative magazine *Commentary*. Hanson holds a PhD in classics from Stanford, is the recipient of various awards, including the National Humanities Medal (2007) and the Eric Breindel Award for opinion journalism (2002). He serves as a senior fellow at the Hoover Institution at Stanford University. This editorial was published in the conservative news commentary source *National Review Online* on December 7, 2011.

> Why does Victor Davis Hanson say he has reframed the illegal immigration issue as a moral issue?

Illegal immigration has been in the news daily during the Republican primary campaign, even though a depressed economy here, stronger border enforcement, and vast new finds of petroleum in Latin America may soon radically curtail the number of illegal entrants into the United States. But for now, conservatives are warned that coming down hard on illegal immigration (i.e., enforcing federal statutes) would lose them the all-critical Hispanic vote. Meanwhile, in California, some legislators want to grant de facto state amnesty to illegal residents. But lost in the continuing furor, pro and con, is the moral dimension. The strange notion has developed that supporting something as immoral as illegal immigration is somehow ethical. It is not, and there are several reasons why.

1. **Entry-level labor.** Real wages for the working poor in the United States have been stagnant for decades, especially in the Southwest—largely because of the influx of millions of illegal aliens, who, at least for a time, will work for considerably lower wages than Americans. In the last three decades, we have written off an entire class of Americans on the premise that "They won't do the work." Here in a California of 10 percent–plus unemployment, everyone from farmers to landscapers complains from experience that the citizen poor cannot or will not work manually. But in theory, why should they, when employers have a constant option of undercutting their wages, and when expanding entitlements make entry-level work an unattractive alternative, both financially and socially? We have expanded social services and decreased workers' incentives, and then we wonder that a subsidized welfare class lacks the spunk of people crossing the border illegally from an impoverished Mexico. Yet there is something abhorrent about the present American notion of giving up on incentives to promote American labor—among which would be the prevention of cheaper foreign workers entering the country illegally and undercutting wages. Advocacy for illegal immigration is now a de facto lack of concern for the American underclass.

2. **Ethnic chauvinism.** Illegal immigration is primarily a Hispanic phenomenon, in general from Latin America and in particular from Mexico. Advocates for open borders, other than cynical employers, are today largely Hispanic activists or those who seek political advantage by catering to them. They argue for changes in or relaxation of immigration law, both out of an understandable sense of ethnic solidarity and real concern for the downtrodden, and, yet in some cases, out of a more dubious notion that the more Latin Americans who enter the country by any means necessary, the more power will eventually accrue to Spanish-speaking American elites who represent the collective interest. Or as Los Angeles County supervisor Gloria Molina put it in an infamous 1996 rant, "We are going to talk to all of those young people that need to become registered voters and go out to vote, and we're politicizing every single one of those new citizens that are becoming citizens of this country. And what we are saying is by November we will have one million additional Latino voters in this country, and we're gonna march, and our vote is going to be important. But I gotta tell you, there's a lot of people that are saying, 'I'm gonna go out there and vote because I want to pay them back!'"

Immigration lobbyists, remember, are not really worried about the plight of Chinese or Indian students who overstay their visas. Somehow ethnic chauvinism has been cloaked with a thin humanitarian veneer, when in fact the concern is not for illegal aliens per se, but for a particular category of illegal aliens. Try a thought experiment. Ask the National Council of La Raza whether it would support offering fast-track citizenship to a commensurate 15 million economic refugees from an imploding Europe or an impoverished Africa, even on conditions not imposed on those from Latin America, such as legality, mastery of English, a college degree, and proof of sustenance. Unfortunately, present advocacy for illegal immigration assumes that race and race-based identity politics shall determine the winners and losers in the immigration lottery. And that seems to me immoral to the core.

3. **Legal immigration.** Hundreds of thousands from Asia, Africa, and Europe wait patiently and in legal fashion to apply for citizenship. "Crowding to the front of the line" is not a cheap talking point, but an accurate description of those who ignore the rules while others suffer. In essence, the United States has established that several million foreign nationals have precedence for citizenship by virtue of the facts that (a) they have already broken the law in entering the U.S., (b) they are currently residing illegally in the U.S., and (c) they are of a particular ethnic group. To question why a Ph.D. in electrical engineering from India must wait for years to gain permanent residence in the U.S. while someone from Oaxaca without a high-school diploma is exempt from such scrutiny is deemed illiberal; in fact, the reality, not the description of it, is the real illiberality.

4. **The law.** Much of the discussion focuses on the fact that illegal immigration flouts federal law. But the problem is less the initial entry into the U.S. without documentation, and more the succession of law-breaking that needs must follow. If one crosses the border illegally, then one is not likely to state the truth on dozens of subsequent official documents, from matters of identification to certification of employment and entitlement. At each juncture, the law itself is insidiously eroded and the calls for it to be ignored increase. The real immorality is not a law that is found oppressive, but the notion that anyone, most ironically a foreign national, has the right to pick and choose which laws he will obey. No civilization can survive when the law hinges on individual interpretation. If foreign nationals are not required to abide by U.S. law, why would American citizens think that they must?

5. **Mexico.** The largest ethical myth of illegal immigration is the notion of a Mexico morally concerned about the treatment of its

expatriates. Of all the players in the illegal-immigration tragedy, the government of Mexico has proven the most heartless. It facilitates its own citizens' leaving, going so far as to publish comic books on how to do it (apparently assuming both that its potential emigrants are illiterate and that they should act illegally). It counts on remittances as its second-largest source of foreign exchange, apparently cruelly calibrating that while it won't fully support its own people, they should help support it once they leave the country. It has opened dozens of new consulates to facilitate help for illegal aliens in the United States, when Mexican citizens in Mexico are in far more need of such government concern. And while Mexico is far more interested in luring wealthy Americans southward with prospects of selling vacation homes in Baja California than it is in helping its own people find housing in Oaxaca, it somehow poses as the protector of the rights of Mexicans in America, whom it never troubled to help when they were in Mexico. Without illegal immigration, Mexico would lose American cash, have to reform its own social and economic policies, and forfeit leverage on U.S. social and foreign policy.

6. **Poverty.** We do not know how many billions of dollars leave the U.S. economy each year bound for Latin America. Before the recession, the number was estimated at anywhere between $25 billion and $50 billion, more than half of it believed sent to Mexico. If it is true that millions of illegal aliens, who are the primary remitters, are poor and at some point in need of public assistance for their housing, sustenance, and health care, then their sending dollars home is a direct subsidy by American taxpayers to foreign governments. In California the cost of providing support for illegal aliens ranges from $8 billion to some $12 billion a year, a figure that might roughly match the amount of money sent to Mexico from California each year. In a moral universe, illegal aliens would not remit money home and then expect their hosts to make up the difference; a moral Mexico in turn would not expect its most impoverished to work abroad and live cheaply, in order to send billions home to alleviate Mexico City's responsibility for its own poor. And in a moral universe, to suggest all that would not be deemed a thought crime.

7. **Moral racketeering.** One of the most disturbing aspects surrounding illegal immigration is the attempt to silence debate with charges of racism, nativism, and bias. In fact, there are legitimate concerns that have nothing to do with race or ethnicity, but simply are not being voiced about the consequences of millions arriving illegally, without capital or education, and without English. At present, there may be anywhere from 20,000 to 30,000 illegal aliens incarcerated in the California penal system

(exact figures are rarely released). The high-school dropout rate among first- and second-generation Hispanic males in California now nears 60 percent. To say out loud that millions of illegal aliens have some connection to California's declining test scores, its insolvent finances, and the exodus of California citizens from the state is absolutely taboo, but it is generally and quietly assumed. More disturbingly, an entire edifice of victimization has been built on American culpability for purported oppression on the basis of class and race. It has now reached the point of an eerie Orwellianism, in which many in the Hispanic political establishment make moral claims against an America unwilling to grant blanket amnesty, and yet must simultaneously assume that such a morally suspect entity is a far more desirable place than is Mexico—though the reasons for that tacit assumption must never be voiced. A disturbing example of how this plays out was the recent booing of the American national soccer team in the Los Angeles Coliseum by the "hometown" crowd. A psychiatrist is needed to explain why thousands were booing symbols of a country that they risked their lives to reach, while cheering on a country that they were dying to leave. That schizophrenia was inculcated largely in America.

8. **Politics.** The Republican candidates have been advised to tread carefully in talking about illegal immigration, in fear of the wrath of Hispanic voters, which has so effectively been massaged by President Obama ("punish our enemies," "alligators and moats"). Indeed, even to talk of illegal immigration in any but the vaguest terms is considered near suicidal to one's career and reputation. But such a calculus ignores long-term reality. Closing the borders will hasten assimilation, integration, and intermarriage, as the success of third- and fourth-generation Mexican-Americans attests. Compliance with the law is the only mechanism to allow the full expression of a naturally conservative Hispanic culture. The Mexican-American community deals first-hand with the chaos of massive illegal immigration and is not always happy about the consequences. In contrast, open borders and amnesty will ensure a constant influx of illegal immigrants who become constituents of those who facilitate illegal entry and residence.

There are ways that are both moral and practical to deport recent arrivals, felons, and those entirely on public assistance, while offering mechanisms for long-residing aliens, employed and not convicted of felonies, to apply for citizenship—without automatic approval, however, and only after meeting logical criteria and paying fines. The only real issue is whether the qualified should obtain temporary residence cards while waiting for adjudication of their requests, or must return to Mexico to apply; but that is a decision that follows, not precedes, an end to open borders. A fence, changed economic conditions in both the United States and Latin America, and new public doubts about illegal immigration are already beginning to slow down the influx, suggesting that it is time to address the issue in ways that will lay the groundwork for better policies in the future.

But for now, it is also time to change the entire tenor of the discussion, and accept that the proponents of illegal immigration have lost all moral credibility.

For Class Discussion

1. Hanson's argument is well structured, yet complex. Restate his numerous reasons in your own words.

2. What assumptions does Hanson make about his readers' values and positions on illegal immigration? Who is his target audience for this argument?

3. Hanson's angle of vision exerts a strong domination of this piece. What points about illegal immigration does he leave out of his argument?

4. English professor Mark Bracher distinguishes between ethics, which he associates with philosophy, and morals, which he connects to "asserting values, passing judgment, and controlling behavior" as well as social action.* How does Bracher's distinction help you in understanding the moral dimension that Hanson claims should be involved in the United States' policy on illegal immigration?

5. Where is Hanson's use of evidence provocative and compelling? Where might you challenge his evidence, especially in light of current economic and migratory trends in Mexico?

Help Wanted—Stop Illegal Immigration
Steve Breen

Steve Breen is an editorial cartoonist who has worked for the *San Diego Union-Tribune* since 2001. He has won a Pulitzer Prize twice for his political cartooning, in 1998 and 2009, among numerous other awards. As a syndicated cartoonist, he publishes his cartoons regularly in the *New York Times*, *USA Today*, *Newsweek*, and *U.S. News and World Report*. This cartoon appeared in the *San Diego Union-Tribune* in 2010.

---

*Mark Bracher, "Teaching for Social Justice: Reeducating the Emotions Through Literary Study." *Journal of Advanced Composition* 26, no. 3–4 (2006): 464.

What is your initial impression of this cartoon?

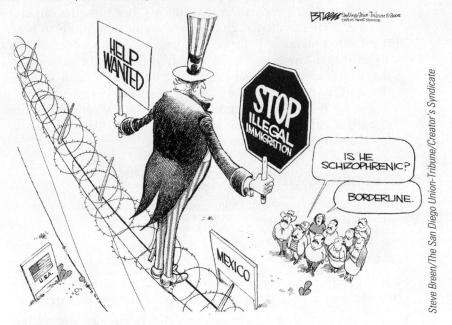

Steve Breen/The San Diego Union-Tribune/Creator's Syndicate

For Class Discussion

1. Who are the characters in this cartoon's narrative? What visual symbols are prominent in this cartoon?

2. What critique of the United States' policy on illegal immigration from Mexico does this cartoon voice? How does this cartoon condense, embody, and deliver its message?

3. How does Breen's play on words add a layer of meaning to his message?

4. Whom is Breen satirizing in this cartoon? What values and views do readers have to hold in order to agree with Breen's perspective?

5. In what new ways has Breen caused you to think about the United States' policy on illegal immigration?

Why Mexico's Drug War Is Unwinnable

Laura Carlsen

Laura Carlsen, who holds an MA in Latin American Studies from Stanford University, has worked as an international relations consultant, researcher, freelance writer, and speaker at national and international conferences. She is currently director of the Mexico City–based Americas Program of the Center for International Policy and author of the Americas MexicoBlog (www.americasmexico.blogspot.com). She coedited *Confronting Globalization: Economic Integration and Popular Resistance in Mexico* (2003) and contributes regularly to media in Mexico and the United States. Her writing has appeared in the *Washington Post*, *Boston Globe*, *Los Angeles Times*, and *Tom Paine*, among other publications, and she is a columnist for *Foreign Policy in Focus*. She has appeared on BBC, CBS, *Democracy Now*, and other television and radio programs and is considered an authority on NAFTA, Mexican agriculture, immigration, and U.S.–Central American politics. This policy proposal was published in *CounterPunch* on March 30, 2011. *CounterPunch* is a muckraking bi-weekly newsletter that critically examines and digs into political issues that are often not explored by either the political left or conservatives.

According to Laura Carlsen, by what criteria has the war on drugs been evaluated and found unsuccessful?

In Matamoros, Tamaulipas, schools close down after officials receive bomb threats. Newspapers timidly report that the threats "could be related to" Gulf Cartel retaliation for the killing of one of their leaders, Tony Tormenta, in a military operation days earlier. President Obama calls President Calderon to congratulate him on taking down the drug lord. Mexican authorities predict a new wave of violence in the state, as the Zetas move in to wrest control from the weakened Gulf Cartel.

Whether measured by increased public safety, reduced supply of illegal drugs on the U.S. market, or the dismantling of drug trafficking organizations, the war on drugs is failing. It has been four years since President Felipe Calderon announced the offensive and sent tens of thousands of soldiers into the streets. The results are a record 37,000 drug-war related homicides so far and thousands of complaints of human rights abuses by police and armed forces. Arrests of drug kingpins and lesser figures have set off violent turf wars, with no discernible effect on illicit flows. The murder of politicians, threats to civilians and disruption of daily life have furthered the downward spiral.

None of this should come as a surprise. Although Secretary of State Hillary Clinton has held up Plan Colombia as a model for Mexico, the drug war didn't work there either. A full decade and $7 billion after Plan Colombia began, regional drug production remains stable and smaller paramilitary groups have replaced the large cartels as traffickers. Some violent crimes, such as kidnappings, have gone down but corruption has deepened with scores of Congressional representatives under investigation, prosecution or sentencing for ties to paramilitaries.

Militarization with the combined rationale of the war on drugs and counterinsurgency has left Colombia with one of the worst human rights record in the hemisphere. Diplomatic relations have been affected as many neighboring nations view U.S. military presence and involvement in Colombia's drug war as a threat to regional self-determination.

Despite these results, the Obama administration has announced plans to extend indefinitely the Merida Initiative, designed by the Bush administration to last three years and cost $1.3 billion. The administration has requested $282 million for Mexico under the initiative in the 2012 budget.

The problem is, the drug war is not underfunded; it's unwinnable. As long as a lucrative market exists, the cartels will find a way to serve it. Eliminating operatives, even high-level leaders, merely diversifies and redistributes the business. Cartels have years of experience building flexible structures, with new leaders or rival gangs replacing displaced or weakened ones. At the lower levels, they draw from an inexhaustible pool of young men with few prospects in life, who have adopted the slogan, "Better to die young and rich than old and poor."

If the war on drugs is unwinnable, does that mean we have to resign ourselves to the unbridled power of the drug cartels?

No. The other tragedy of the war on drugs is that it precludes potentially more effective strategies by posing as the only option. As the U.S. government spends millions of taxpayer dollars to pay U.S. private security and defense firms to "fix" Mexico, it has done little to nothing to address the parts of transnational organized crime that exist within its borders—demand, transport and distribution, corrupt officials, gun-running and money laundering.

Rethinking the drug war is not tantamount to surrender. Here are a few key elements of an alternative strategy:

Follow the money. Instead of shoot-outs in the streets, far more could be done in both countries to attack the financial structures of criminal organizations. Billions of dollars are laundered in mainstream financial institutions and businesses. If we're serious about weakening organized crime, it's time to be serious about cracking down on illicit financial flows—even when it affects powerful interests.

Increase funding for drug abuse prevention and treatment. Approaching illegal drug use as a health issue is a win-win strategy. Education teaches young people the costs of addiction and abuse, and treatment and harm reduction programs can improve lives and reduce costs to society, as well as cut demand for illicit substances.

End prohibition, beginning with marijuana. Without the billions of dollars in revenue that pot provides, drug cartels have fewer resources to recruit youth, buy arms and corrupt politicians.

Give communities a role besides "victim." As Mexican funds and U.S. aid have been diverted to the drug war, social programs in Mexico have been severely cut back. This is exactly backward. Strong communities—ones with jobs, ample educational opportunities and coverage of basic needs and services—are better able to resist the infiltration of organized crime.

The war on drugs strategy lacks benchmarks or any real analysis of the root causes of the violence. Each day it digs itself deeper into a hole. That hole has become a mass grave for thousands of Mexicans, mostly youth.

The Obama administration has announced plans to intensify the drug war in Mexico and extend the model to Central American and Caribbean nations. Congress appears willing to follow suit. This would usher in a new era of military-led relations with our Latin American neighbors and unleash violent conflict in those countries as it has in Mexico.

If that happens, horror stories like the ones from Ciudad Juarez and Matamoros will sadly become the norm rather than the exception.

For Class Discussion

1. Carlsen's argument follows a problem–solution format. What evidence does she supply to elaborate on the problem her argument is addressing? Why does she oppose the Merida Initiative's allocation of funds for the war on drugs?

2. How does Carlsen use the failed precedent of Plan Colombia to build her case for a different approach to the drug war in Mexico?

3. What are the features of her proposal for addressing the drug war problem?

4. How does Carlsen convey her knowledge of Mexican social-political conditions and U.S. foreign policy in this piece? According to Carlsen, what are the high stakes in this drug war issue?

5. Carlsen's approach is direct and brief in this piece, and her style is clipped, brusque, and cautionary. What questions about her proposal or about the war on drugs would you like to ask her to develop further?

Free Trade: As U.S. Corn Flows South, Mexicans Stop Farming
Tim Johnson

This news story appeared on the Web site for the McClatchy Newspapers on February 1, 2011. The McClatchy Company, known for its award-winning journalism, is the third largest newspaper publisher in the United States with thirty daily newspapers as well as nondaily newspapers and digital assets. Tim Johnson is the McClatchy bureau chief in Mexico City.

According to Tim Johnson in this article, what are the repercussions of NAFTA on farming communities in Mexico and on emigration to the United States?

SAN JERONIMO SOLOLA, Mexico—Look around the rain-fed corn farms in Oaxaca state, and in vast areas of Mexico, and one sees few young men, just elderly people and single mothers.

"The men have gone to the United States," explained Abel Santiago Duran, a 56-year-old municipal agent, as he surveyed this empty village in Oaxaca state.

The countryside wasn't supposed to hollow out in this way when the North American Free Trade Agreement linked Mexico, Canada and the U.S. in 1994. Mexico, hoping its factories would absorb displaced farmers, said it would "export goods, not people."

But in hindsight, the agricultural elements of the pact were brutal on Mexico's corn farmers. A flood of U.S. corn imports, combined with subsidies that favor agribusiness, are blamed for the loss of 2 million farm jobs in Mexico. The trade pact worsened illegal migration, some experts say, particularly in areas where small farmers barely eke out a living.

That is the case in the rolling hills of western Oaxaca state, ancestral lands of indigenous Mixtecs who till small plots of corn, beans and squash between stands of jacarandas, junipers and eucalyptus. Eagles soar in the brilliant blue skies. Clumps of prickly pear and organ cactus attest to the sporadic nature of rainfall.

When a visitor arrives, the gray-haired men on the veranda of the village hall talk about the exodus of young men.

"When they hit 18 and finish secondary school, they leave for the United States or other states of Mexico," Duran said.

His cousin, Jesus Duran, said young men see little future as corn farmers and observe with dismay how the government aims subsidies at medium and big farms, leaving only a trickle for small family farms.

"If you go to the offices over there and ask for help," Duran said, nodding to the local agriculture agency, "they say there isn't any to give."

Mexican negotiators who signed the NAFTA agreement hoped that small corn farmers thrown out of work by rising imports of cheap U.S. corn would be absorbed into jobs in the fruit and vegetable export industry or in manufacturing.

"That turned out to be incorrect. The numbers of people displaced from family farming were much, much higher than the number of new wage jobs," said Jonathan Fox, an expert on rural Mexico at the University of California at Santa Cruz.

Then U.S. corn imports crested like a rain-swollen river, increasing from 7 percent of Mexican consumption to around 34 percent, mostly for animal feed and for industrial uses as cornstarch.

"It's been roughly a tripling, quadrupling, quintupling of U.S. corn exports to Mexico, depending on the year," said Timothy A. Wise, the director of research and policy at the Global Development and Environment Institute at Tufts University in Medford, Mass. "Is that a river? Yeah, that's a lot of corn."

Fox and Wise are among the collaborators on a study, "Subsidizing Inequality: Mexican corn policy since NAFTA," released last autumn.

Representatives of small farmers say Mexico's policymakers tossed the dice that trade-spurred growth would take care of rural disruptions—and lost.

"The great failure of this supposition is that there wasn't economic growth that would absorb these people," said Victor Suarez, the executive director of the National Association of Rural Producers, which represents 60,000 small farmers. "The result has left rural areas increasingly populated by the elderly and women."

Faced with deepening poverty, rural migrants have tried to escape regions of Mexico that never used to be sources of emigration.

"In Chiapas, there was hardly any migration before NAFTA," Suarez said, referring to Mexico's southernmost state. "Farm laborers were even brought in from Guatemala. Now, more than 50,000 rural people from Chiapas go each year to the United States."

Corn imports from the U.S. are only one component of what scholars say is a complex picture. In fact, Mexican corn production has risen since the trade pact, driven by domestic agribusiness and supported by subsidies biased to favor large producers that by one estimate surpassed $20 billion in the past two decades.

The Mexican government also has cash-transfer subsidies, known as ProCampo, for small farmers who are considered the free-trade pact's losers. But they reach only a portion of small corn growers, a quarter of whom are indigenous.

Some rural farmers no longer have enough corn to sell, sinking into subsistence living for themselves and their families.

"Of my generation," said 33-year-old Baldemar Mendoza, a Zapotec small corn farmer in the Sierra Juarez area of Oaxaca, "many people want nothing to do with farming because it doesn't pay. With all the changes in the weather, there is no certainty that your harvest will be good."

Unless the central government tweaks subsidies to make more small family farms economically viable, the result may be sustained migrant flows, experts said.

"The government didn't so much pull the plug on corn. The government pulled the plug on family farmers who grow corn because the big guys who grew corn got massive subsidies and protection from imports," Fox said.

Under the free-trade umbrella, several Mexican agro-industrial companies have become muscular global conglomerates.

"Before NAFTA, Grupo Bimbo was a big company. Now it is the largest industrial user of wheat in the world," Suarez said, referring to the world's No. 1 bread maker. "Maseca was a big company. Now it is a global company with a strong position in cornmeal worldwide."

Their powerful position in the market has kept prices high for consumers, while in the countryside, the social fabric frays as families disperse to find jobs.

The impact, Fox said, "unravels rural communities, separates families and makes it difficult for young people to see a future in their communities of origin."

Josefa Soriano, 74, doesn't need an explanation of what's happening. She sees it with her own eyes. As a rural exodus unfolds, families keep fewer of the animals such as goats, cattle and burros that provided manure for fields. Such livestock must have caretakers.

"You have no choice but to buy fertilizer now," she said. "If you don't fertilize, nothing grows, not even fodder."

As she ambled through the settlement, Soriano offered a running commentary on those who have migrated.

"The village is almost without people," Soriano said. "Many houses are empty. The fathers and the sons have gone."

She turned to a visitor and said, "If the young people always leave, what do you think will happen to us?"

"Free Trade: As U.S. Corn Flows South, Mexicans Stop Farming" by Tim Johnson. Copyright 2011 MCCLATCHY NEWSPAPERS.

For Class Discussion

1. This article makes a case that could be framed as either a causal argument (NAFTA has led to these unfortunate consequences . . .) or an evaluation argument (NAFTA is a detrimental trade policy for Mexico and the United States). Write out a claim like one of these and then reconstruct the reasons embedded in this article that support this claim.

2. What kinds of evidence does Johnson employ to make his case?

3. How effective is the open-form, journalistic style of this article compared to the impact the article would have as a tightly structured, explicit argument?

4. What do U.S. citizens gain by understanding the push factors behind immigration from Mexico? What ideas were new to you? You might investigate the Without Corn, There Is No Country National Campaign on the Web to understand the agricultural, food, and jobs problems faced by Mexican citizens as well as their love for their country.

From *Guide for the Mexican Migrant*

Mexico's Ministry of Foreign Relations

In January 2005, Mexico's Ministry of Foreign Relations issued a pamphlet titled *Guide for the Mexican Migrant*. This publication was produced as a supplement to *El Libro Vaquero*, an adult comic book romanticizing cowboy life and frequently read by uneducated male workers. In this pamphlet, the Mexican government addresses the reality of steady illegal migration and tries to protect its citizens who are seeking a new life in the United States. Soon after its publication, translations of the *Guide* began appearing in U.S. newspapers. *American Renaissance*, a monthly magazine that bills itself as "a literate, undeceived journal of race, immigration and the decline of civility," printed a version of the *Guide* in English, from which this excerpt is taken (www.amren. com/). To see the entire text of the *Guide*, go to this site or others on the Web.

As its title indicates, this pamphlet falls in the genre of guidebooks. How are the function and purpose of this guidebook like and unlike those of guidebooks you have used?

INTRODUCTION

Esteemed Countryman:

The purpose of this guide is to provide you with practical advice that may prove useful to you in case you have made the difficult decision to search for employment opportunities outside of your country.

The sure way to enter another country is by getting your passport from the Ministry of Foreign Affairs, and the visa, which you may apply for at the embassy or consulate of the country you wish to travel to.

However, in practice we see many Mexicans who try to cross the Northern Border without the necessary documents, through high risk zones that involve grave dangers, particularly in desert areas or rivers with strong, and not always obvious, currents.

Reading this guide will make you aware of some basic questions about the legal consequences of your stay in the United States of America without the appropriate migratory documents, as well as about the rights you have in that country, once you are there, independent of your migratory status.

Keep in mind always that there exist legal mechanisms to enter the United States of America legally.

In any case, if you encounter problems or run into difficulties, remember that Mexico has 45 consulates in that country whose locations you can find listed in this publication.

Familiarize yourself with the closest consulate and make use of it.

American Renaissance, 2005. Used with permission.

DANGERS IN CROSSING HIGH RISK ZONES

To cross the river can be very risky, above all if you cross alone and at night.

Heavy clothing increases in weight when wet and this makes swimming and floating difficult.

If you cross by desert, try to walk at times when the heat will not be too intense.

Highways and population centers are far apart, which means you will spend several days looking for roads, and you will not be able to carry foodstuffs or water for long periods of time. Also, you can get lost.

Salt water helps keep liquids in your body. Although you may feel more thirst if you drink salt water, the risk of dehydration is much less.

The symptoms of dehydration are:

- Little or no sweat.
- Dryness in the eyes and in the mouth.
- Headache.
- Tiredness and excessive exhaustion.
- Difficulty in walking and thinking.
- Hallucinations and visions.

If you get lost, guide yourself by [telephone poles], train tracks, or dirt roads.

BEWARE OF HUMAN TRAFFICKERS (COYOTES, POLLEROS)

They can deceive you with assurances of crossing in a few hours through the mountains and deserts. This is simply not so!

They can risk your life taking you across rivers, drainage canals, desert areas, train tracks, or highways. This has caused the death of hundreds of persons.

If you decide to hire people traffickers to cross the border, consider the following precautions:

Do not let them out of your sight. Remember that they are the only ones who know the lay of the land, and therefore the only ones who can get you out of that place.

Do not trust those who offer to take you to "the other side" and ask you to drive a car or to take or carry a package for them. Normally, those packages contain drugs or other prohibited substances. For this reason, many people have ended up in jail.

For Class Discussion

1. How is this guide designed to appeal to its target audience?

2. What does the use of comic book illustrations contribute to the rhetorical effect of this pamphlet? (If you find this *Guide* on the Web, you will see the numerous illustrations in color.) What do the illustrations suggest about the target audience?

3. How do you think the genre and appearance of the *Guide* have contributed to the strong emotional responses it has evoked, especially from some advocacy groups and politicians in the United States?

4. The *Guide* includes this disclaimer by the Mexican government: "This Consular Protection Guide does not promote crossing by Mexicans without legal documentation required by the government of the United States. Its purpose is to make known the risks, and to inform the migrants about their rights, whether they are legal residents or not." What features of the content, tone, and style of this pamphlet support this declaration? What features, if any, suggest an ambivalent attitude toward illegal migration?

5. Do a brief investigation of the *Guide* on the Web. What have people in Mexico and in the United States said about this pamphlet? What is at stake for those who take the strongest stances?

The Special Case of Mexican Immigration

Samuel P. Huntington

Samuel P. Huntington (1927–2008) was a major scholarly voice on issues of national security and strategy, democratization and development of less-developed countries, cultural factors in world politics, and American national identity. He was chair of the Harvard Department of Government and its Academy for International and Area Studies, the cofounder of *Foreign Policy* magazine, a vocal neoconservative, and a prolific writer. His famous book *The Clash of Civilizations and the Remaking of the World Order* (1996) posits the thesis that the main conflicts of our global age will not be economic, political, or environmental; instead they will center on the values of groups of people (civilizations) and will involve their history, culture, and religion. Huntington sparked even more controversy with his argument about the threat and challenge of Mexican immigration to U.S. national identity in an article titled "The Hispanic Challenge" and in the book *Who Are We? The Challenges to America's National Identity* (2004). "The Special Case of Mexican Immigration" is an adaptation of these longer writings. It appeared in 2000 in *American Enterprise*, the online publication of the American Enterprise Institute, a conservative think tank. This publication says it seeks to appeal to a wide range of readers and to promote informed, independent thinking by offering well reasoned and highly readable arguments.

Many of the articles in this chapter focus on economic issues related to immigration. In contrast, where does Samuel P. Huntington think the main U.S. problems with immigration lie?

America is often described as a country defined by commitment to a creed formulated in the writings of our Founders. But American identity is only partly a matter of creed. For much of our history we also defined ourselves in racial, religious, ethnic, and cultural terms.

Before the Revolution we thought of ourselves in religious terms: 98 percent of Americans were Protestants, and Catholic Spain and France were our enemies. We also thought of ourselves in racial and ethnic terms: 80 percent of Americans at the time of the Revolution were from the British Isles. The other 20 percent were largely German and Dutch.

America is also often described as a nation of immigrants. We should distinguish immigrants, however, from settlers. Immigrants are people who leave one society and move to a recipient society. Early Americans did not immigrate to an existing society; they established new societies, in some cases for commercial reasons, more often for religious reasons. It was the new societies they created, basically defined by Anglo-Protestant culture, that attracted subsequent generations of immigrants to this country.

Demographer Campbell Gibson has done a very interesting analysis of the evolution of the United States' population. He argues that if no immigrants had come to this country after 1790, the population of the United States in 1990 would have been just about half of what it actually was. Thus, the American people are literally only half an immigrant people.

There have been great efforts in our history to limit immigration. In only one decade in the nineteenth century did the annual intake of immigrants amount to more than 1 percent of the population each year. In three other decades it was slightly over eight-tenths of 1 percent, while in six decades it was less than four-tenths of 1 percent. Obviously immigration has been tremendously important to this country, but the foreign-born population has exceeded 10 percent of our total population only in the seven census years from 1860 to 1930. (When the 2000 census results come out we will be back above the 10 percent level again.)

As I began to investigate the question of immigration, I came to the conclusion that our real problem is not so much immigration as assimilation. Seventy-five or 100 years ago there were great pressures to ensure that immigrants assimilated to the Anglo-Protestant culture, work ethic, and principles of the American creed. Now we are uncertain what immigrants should assimilate to. And that is a serious problem.

As I went further in my research, I concluded there was a still more significant problem, a problem that encompasses immigration, assimilation, and other things, too—what I will refer to as the Mexican problem. Much of what we now consider to be problems concerning immigration and assimilation really concern Mexican immigration and assimilation. Mexican immigration poses challenges to our policies and to our identity in a way nothing else has in the past.

There are five distinctive characteristics of the Mexican question which make it special. First, Mexican immigration is different because of contiguity. We have thought of immigration as being symbolized by Ellis Island, and perhaps now by Kennedy Airport. But Mexicans do not come across 2,000 miles of ocean. They come, often easily, across 2,000 miles of land border.

Our relationship with Mexico in this regard is in many respects unique in the world. No other First World country has a land frontier with a Third World country—much less one of 2,000 miles. The significance of this border is enhanced by the economic differences between the two countries. The income gap between Mexico and us is the largest between any two contiguous countries in the world.

The second distinctive aspect of today's Mexican immigration concerns numbers. Mexican immigration during the past several decades has been very substantial. In 1998 Mexican immigrants constituted 27 percent of the total foreign-born population in this country; the next largest two contingents, Filipinos and Chinese, each amounted to only 4 percent. Mexicans constituted two-thirds of Spanish-speaking immigrants, who in turn were over half of all new arrivals between 1970 and 1996. Our post-1965 wave of immigration differs from previous waves in having a majority from a single non-English language group.

A third distinguishing characteristic of this Mexican immigration is illegality. Illegal immigration is overwhelmingly a post-1965 and Mexican phenomenon. In 1995, according to one report, Mexicans made up 62 percent of the immigrants who entered the United States illegally. In 1997, the Immigration and Naturalization Service estimated Mexican illegals were nine times as numerous as the next largest contingent, from El Salvador.

The next important characteristic of Mexican immigration has been its concentration in a particular region. Mexican immigrants are heavily concentrated in the Southwest and particularly in southern California. This has very real consequences. Our Founders emphasized that immigrants would have to be dispersed among what they described as the English population in this country. To the extent that we have a large regional concentration of immigrants, it is a departure from our usual pattern.

Now obviously we have previously had high concentrations of immigrants in particular areas, such as the Irish in Boston, but by and large the immigrants have dispersed to different cities, and those cities have simultaneously hosted many different immigrant groups. This is the case still in New York, where there are many immigrants today, but no group that dominates. In Southern California, though, two-thirds or more of all the children in school are Spanish speaking. As Abe Lowenthal and Katrina Burgess write in *The California-Mexico Connection,* "No school system in a major U.S. city has ever experienced such a large influx of students from a single foreign country. The schools of Los Angeles are becoming Mexican."

Finally, there is the matter of the persistence of Mexico's large immigration. Previous waves of immigration fairly soon came to an end. The huge 1840s and '50s influxes from Ireland and Germany were drastically reduced by the Civil War and the easing of the Irish potato famine. The big wave at the turn of the century came to an end with World War I and the restrictive legislation in 1924.

These breaks greatly helped to facilitate the assimilation of the newcomers. In contrast, there does not seem to be any prospect of the current wave, begun over three decades ago, coming to an end soon. Mexican immigration may eventually subside as the Mexican birth rate slows, and possibly as a result of long-term economic development in Mexico. But those effects will only occur over a very long term. For the time being we are faced with substantial continued immigration from Mexico.

Sustained high levels of immigration build on themselves. After the first immigrants come from a country, it is easier for others from that country to come. Immigration is not a self-limiting process, it is a self-enhancing one.

And the longer immigration continues, the more difficult politically it is to stop. Leaders of immigrant organizations and interest groups develop a vested interest in expanding their own constituency. Immigration develops political support, and becomes more difficult to limit or reshape.

For all these reasons Mexican immigration is unique. What are the implications of this for assimilation?

The answer appears uncertain. In education and economic activity, Mexicans rate much lower than other immigrant groups. The rate of intermarriage between Hispanics and other Americans appears to be decreasing rather than increasing. (In 1977, 31 percent of all Hispanic marriages were interethnic; in 1994, 25.5 percent were.) With respect to language, I suspect Mexicans will in large part follow the pattern of earlier immigrants, with the third generation being fluent in English, but quite possibly, unlike previous third generations, also fluent in their ancestral language.

All of the characteristics I have mentioned lead to the possibility of a cultural community evolving in the Southwest in which people could pursue their lives within an overwhelmingly Mexican community, without ever having to speak English. This has already happened with the Cubans in Miami, and it could be reproduced on a larger and more significant scale in the Southwest. We know in the coming decades people of Hispanic origin will be a majority of the people in California and eventually in other southwestern states. America is moving in the direction of becoming a bilingual and bicultural society.

Without Mexican immigration, the overall level of immigration to this country would be perhaps two-thirds of what it has been—near the levels recommended by Barbara Jordan's immigration commission a few years ago. Illegal entries would be relatively minor. The average skill and education level of immigrants would be the highest in American history, and the much-debated balance of economic benefits versus costs of immigration would tilt heavily toward the positive side. The bilingual education issue would fade from our agenda. A major potential challenge to the cultural, and conceivably political, integrity of the United States would disappear.

Mexico and Mexican immigration, however, will not disappear, and learning to live with both may become more and more difficult. President-elect Vicente Fox wants to remove all restrictions on the movement of Mexicans into the United States.

In almost every recent year the Border Patrol has stopped about 1 million people attempting to enter the U.S. illegally from Mexico. It is generally estimated that about 300,000 make it across illegally. If over 1 million Mexican soldiers crossed the border, Americans would treat it as a major threat to their national security and react accordingly. The invasion of over 1 million Mexican civilians is a comparable threat to American societal security, and Americans should react against it with comparable vigor.

Mexican immigration looms as a unique and disturbing challenge to our cultural integrity, our national identity, and potentially to our future as a country.

For Class Discussion

1. What key points would you include in a summary of Huntington's ideas in this article?

2. The American Enterprise Institute is a conservative think tank. What features of this article's structure, depth of material, main points, and kinds of evidence indicate that its publication, *American Enterprise*, seeks to reach a broad audience?

3. Many people responding to Huntington's book *Who Are We?* and his article "The Hispanic Challenge," which develop the views presented in this piece, have criticized Huntington for fostering racism and nativism (privileging native-born residents over immigrants). What ideas in this article could fuel those attitudes toward immigrants?

4. Huntington's values and views dominate this argument in its approach and points. What points about immigration, especially Mexican immigration, is Huntington *not* factoring into his argument? In your view, how would including those points affect the logic and credibility of his argument?

5. Carefully describe the assumptions about Mexican immigration and immigrants an audience would have to hold in order to agree with Huntington's main points. What points would a rebuttal challenging those assumptions need to include?

MALDEF and LULAC Rebuke Samuel Huntington's Theories on Latino Immigrants and Call on America to Reaffirm Its Commitment to Equal Opportunity and Democracy

Mexican American Legal Defense and Educational Fund (MALDEF) and League of United Latin American Citizens (LULAC)

This policy statement, dated April 23, 2004, is a formal response to Samuel P. Huntington's publications on Mexican immigration. The Mexican American Legal Defense and Educational Fund is a national, nonprofit, nonpartisan organization headquartered in Washington, D.C. Also centered there, the League of United Latin American Citizens is the oldest grassroots organization committed to the education, civil rights, and employment of Latinos. Both of these organizations are large, well established, and highly reputable. On the "About Us" page of its Web site, MALDEF states its mission: "to bring Latinos into the mainstream of American political and socioeconomic life, providing better educational opportunities, encouraging participation in all aspects of society, and offering a positive vision for the future" (www.maldef.org/about).

How does the mission of MALDEF itself refute Samuel Huntington's underlying thesis? What impression of the Latino community does this refutation of Huntington's views convey?

On May 27th, Samuel P. Huntington will publish his new book, alleging that Latino immigration threatens "Anglo-Protestant values" which are the "creed" of American culture. Since the release of his article announcing his new theory in *Foreign Policy* magazine in March,[1] Huntington's methodology and conclusions have been proven wrong by experts across the board.[2] As national Latino civil rights groups, we further believe that Huntington's writing is dangerously biased against Latinos and goes against fundamental American values.

Huntington's biases are un-American. The United States is a nation of immigrants from around the world. In the U.S., individual accomplishment is valued. The very foundation of American democracy is the Bill of Rights, respecting and even guaranteeing individual rights. By passing various civil rights laws in the 1960's, Congress reestablished that our Constitution also means that not one race, religion or ethnicity should dominate another. The American dream is built upon the hard work of immigrants and the fundamental value of equal opportunity. We must not go back to a system where one's race, class or religion determines one's fate, regardless of one's intellect or willingness to work hard.

Huntington has made astonishing and unsupported generalizations about Latinos. His generalizations about Latinos being "persistent" in immigrating to the U.S., being exceedingly fertile, having less interest in education and not wanting to learn English are not based on fact and appear to emanate from a prejudice against Latinos. He has no proof that every Latino/a, or even the majority of Latinos/as and their families, fall into these stereotypes, nor any proof that Latinos are very different from other ethnic groups. This kind of

---

[1]S. Huntington, "José, Can You See?" Samuel Huntington on how Hispanic immigrants threaten America's identity, values, and way of life (*Foreign Policy*, March/April 2004) (cover story).

[2]*See*, e.g., D. Glenn, "Critics Assail Scholar's Article Arguing that Hispanic Immigration Threatens U.S.," *Chronicle of Higher Education* (Feb. 24, 2004)(disproving methodology/ citations); D. Brooks, "The Americano Dream," *New York Times* (Editorial, Feb. 24, 2004); A. Oppenheimer, "Racists Will Love New 'Hispanic Threat' Book," *Miami Herald* (Feb. 26, 2004)(assimilation trend); R. Navarrette, "Professor Huntington Has Short Memory of Past Immigrants," *Dallas Morning News* (Mar. 3, 2004) (immigration facts wrong); Lexington, "A Question of Identity—Despite new arguments to the contrary, Latino immigration is still good for America," *The Economist* (Mar. 6th–12th, 2004 issue); F. de Ortego y Gasca, "Something About Harvard-Dreaming in English," *Hispanic Vista* (Mar. 14, 2004); M. Casillas, D. Rocha & M. Hernandez, "The Hispanic Contribution," *Harvard Crimson* (Mar. 18, 2004); C. Fuentes, "Looking for Enemies in the Wrong Places," *Miami Herald* (Mar. 28, 2004); A. Lanier, "Stigmatization of Hispanics is Unwarranted," *Chicago Tribune* (Editorial Board Member)(April 4, 2004); M. Elliott, "New Patriots In Our Midst—A forthcoming book says Mexican Americans won't assimilate. It's wrong," *TIME Magazine* (April 12, 2004)(citations wrong and do not prove conclusions).

analysis harkens back to the justifications for legal segregation and discriminatory policies that were commonplace prior to the civil rights laws of the 1960's.[3]

Mexican-Americans and Latino immigrants are not inferior to white Anglo-Protestants. A recent *New York Times* poll found that Latino immigrants are hard-working, have strong family values, do not take public benefits, and generally epitomize the American dream.[4] Latino immigrants are contributing billions of dollars to the economy and even creating jobs for U.S. citizens.[5] Studies consistently find that immigrants contribute far more in taxes to the government than they use in government services.[6]

Latina/o parents value education and encourage their children to do well in school at the same rates as Anglo parents, with more than 90 percent of Latina/o children reporting that their parents want them to go to college.[7] Moreover, studies demonstrate that Mexican Americans support American core values at least as much as Anglos.[8]

---

[3]V. Ruiz, "We Always Tell Our Children They Are Americans" *Méndez v. Westminster* and the California Road to Brown v. Board of Education, Review No. 200, Fiftieth Anniversary of the Supreme Court Ruling (College Board, Fall 2003), at p. 20–23 (Detailing history of Latino school segregation, along with other forms of segregation, "justified" by racial myths alleging Mexican Americans [are] not like "Americans"; social scientists were needed to disprove these myths in a 1944 *Méndez v. Westminster* school desegregation case.)

[4]S. Romero & J. Elder, "Hispanics in U.S. Report Optimism," *New York Times* (Aug. 6, 2003).

[5]D'Vera Cohn, "Immigrants Account for Half of New Workers—Report Calls Them Increasingly Needed for Economic Growth" *New York Times* (Dec. 2, 2003)(analyzing Center for Labor Market Studies report). See also R. Hinojosa-Ojeda, "Comprehensive Migration Policy Reform in North America: The Key to Sustainable and Equitable Economic Integration." North American Integration and Development Center, University of California, Los Angeles (2001).

[6]*See*, e.g., M. Fix & J. Passel, "Immigration and Immigrants. Setting the Record Straight." Urban Institute (1994) at [p.] 6 ("Overall, annual taxes paid by immigrants to all levels of government more than offset the costs of services received, generating a net annual surplus of $25 billion to $30 billion.").

[7]A. Ginorio & M. Huston, *!Sí Se Puede! Yes We Can! Latinas in School*, Values, Expectations and Norms (American Assn. of Univ. Women, 2001), at 22–24.

[8]R. de la Garza, A. Falcon & F. C. Garcia, "Will the Real Americans Please Stand Up: Anglo and Mexican-American Support of Core American Political Values," Vol. 40, No. 2 *American Journal of Political Science* (May 1996), pp. 335–51 (Results were that: "At all levels of acculturation, Mexican-Americans are no less likely and often more likely to endorse values of individualism and patriotism than are Anglos."). Also, 9 out of 10 Latinos new to the U.S. believe it is important to change so they can fit into American society. R. Pastor, *Toward a North American Community; Lessons from the Old World for the New World* (Wash, D.C., Institute for International Economics, 2001), pp. 164–166 (*citing* Washington Post, Kaiser Foundation and Harvard Univ. comprehensive poll).

Huntington alleges that Latinos do not want to become American, despite the fact that Latino immigrants consciously choose to leave their home countries and migrate to the U.S. in order to become American and live the American dream, especially for their children. Everything that is traditionally thought of as "American," Latinos live out fully. They are family-oriented, religious, hard-working and loyal to the U.S. In fact, Latinos have won more medals of honor for their service in the U.S. military than any other ethnic group.

Huntington fails to take into account that the significant accomplishments of Latinos have occurred in spite of the long and shameful history of discrimination specifically directed against Latinos in the U.S. When Huntington alleges that Latinos have not achieved as much as whites in education, he neglects to acknowledge the history of segregation against Latinos, and Mexican Americans in particular, especially in the Southwest. Even today, when legal segregation is outlawed, Huntington does not take into account that Latinos are attending the most segregated schools in the country, which are providing a lesser quality of education as compared to majority white schools.[9] Predominantly minority schools have less-qualified teachers, more overcrowding, worse educational facilities, and less access to advanced curricula. Despite all these barriers, children of Latino immigrants are succeeding at a very high rate.

It is ironic that Huntington blames Latinos for segregation.[10] Latinos and other people of color know from tough experience that such segregation is not voluntary, as it [is] still difficult for Latinos to gain equality in white communities, and there is still discrimination in jobs and housing. However, like African-Americans, Latinos have been segregated and mythologized as "different," and subject to unfair criticism, because of their ethnicity.

Huntington criticizes Latinos' use of Spanish and falsely alleges that Latinos do not want to learn English. The majority of Latinos speak English. Among Spanish-speaking Latinos, poll after poll shows

---

[9]Associated Press, "Latinos Segregated 50 Years After Brown v. Board of Ed" (April 6, 2004)(also reporting that no national policies specifically address Latino school education).

[10]"Majority of Americans Prefer to Live in Mixed Neighborhoods," *Diversity.com* (April 9, 2004)("According to the 'Civil Rights and Race Relations' survey conducted by Gallup, 68 percent of African Americans, 61 percent of Latinos and 57 percent of whites prefer to live in mixed neighborhoods.").

that Latinos want to learn English.[11] Their ability to learn English is sometimes limited if they entered the U.S. at an older age and when they do not have access to English classes because they are working more than one job and there are limited English classes offered. As far as the ability to speak Spanish, Huntington portrays it as a negative, whereas in the global economy, many see such language capabilities are a positive.

Huntington mischaracterizes the history between the U.S. and Mexico and the causes for migration patterns between the two countries. Huntington characterizes Mexican immigration as "persistent" and a "massive influx" post-1960's civil rights laws. This characterization fails to recognize the unique, historical relationship between the two countries. In 1848, the U.S. acquired a significant portion of Mexico, which became what is now known as the Southwest in the U.S. Those people living in that region were Mexican citizens prior to the acquisition. When the U.S. experienced severe labor shortages while its soldiers were fighting in the world wars, the U.S. entered into several agreements with Mexico to bring temporary migrant laborers from Mexico who worked under abusive conditions in the agricultural fields for decades. Most of these workers did not have the opportunity to become citizens, making it difficult to exercise full political participation. During the Great Depression, the U.S. government and a number of state and local governments forced repatriation of one-third of the Mexican American population to impoverished conditions in Mexico. Shockingly, most of those who were deported were U.S. citizens who happened to be of Mexican ethnicity.[12] Despite this checkered past, Mexican immigrants continued to come to the U.S. to fill U.S. economic needs and to pursue economic opportunities not available in Mexico.[13]

---

[11]Moreover, comprehensive studies demonstrate that the rate of linguistic assimilation of immigrants is just as rapid as it has been in previous generations. See S. Nicolan & R. Valdivieso, "The Veltman Report: What it Says, What it Means," Intro, C. Veltman, The Future of Spanish Language in the United States (New York, Wash. D.C.: Hispanic Policy Dev. Project, 1988) at i–x. Among first-generation native born Mexican Americans, 95% are proficient in English. K. McCarthy & R. Burciaga Valdez, *Current and Future Effects of Mexican Immigration in California* (The Rand Corp. 1985).

[12]F. Balderrama & R. Rodríguez, *Decade of Betrayal: Mexican Repatriation in the 1930's* (1995).

[13]*See*, e.g., "The Hispanic Challenge? What We Know About Latino Immigration," Woodrow Wilson International Center/Migration Policy Institute Panel of Experts (R. Suro, E. Grieco, D. Gutierrez, M. Jones-Correa, R. Stanton-Salazar)(Mar. 29, 2004).

Characterizing past non-Mexican immigration as "legal" and current Mexican immigration as "illegal" is false and misleading. Prior to 1939, it was not illegal to enter the U.S. without the U.S. government's permission. Millions of immigrants, mostly from Western Europe, entered the U.S. without proper visas.[14] Currently, many Mexicans enter the U.S. legally. The U.S. legal immigration system, however, is in need of serious overhaul. The current system is not meeting the economic or family reunification principles it was designed to meet. The backlogs in legal visa processing for the spouses and children of Mexican legal immigrants living in the U.S. are causing families to be separated for 13 years. In order to reunite with their families, some Mexican citizens do enter without proper documentation.

Present high levels of migration between the U.S. and Mexico are based on geographic proximity and economic interdependence of the two countries. Many Mexicans come here because Mexico is our close neighbor and trading partner. Mexico is closer than Europe so the voyage to America is more natural. The U.S. and Mexican fate and economies are inextricably intertwined. That is, the U.S. is just as dependent on Mexico and Mexican migration as the opposite is true.

For Class Discussion

1. Which segments of this policy statement seem to respond most directly to Huntington's points?

2. What is the rhetorical effect of the extensive documentation (by way of footnotes) in this argument?

3. In your mind, does this article incorporate key points about immigration that Huntington omits? How does MALDEF seek to reframe the controversy over cultural integration?

4. Where or how could this argument acknowledge alternative views? Do you think a more balanced approach would better serve the two organizations' rhetorical and political goals?

5. This is a bare-bones argument, a policy statement structured as a rebuttal to Huntington's articles and book on Mexican immigration. What reasoning and evidence are persuasive? What points would need more development in order to be persuasive to a general neutral or dissenting audience?

---

[14]D. Weissbrodt, *Immigration Law and Procedure*, Ch. 1. History of U.S. Immigration Law and Policy (West 1998).

The Arizona Syndrome: Propaganda and the Politics of Fear

David L. Altheide

David L. Altheide, a sociologist and Regents Emeritus Professor in the School of Justice and Social Inquiry at Arizona State University, is known for his scholarship and publications on mass communication and social control. He has received academic awards for his research, including the Cooley Award from the Society for the Study of Symbolic Interaction in 2007 for his book *Terrorism and the Politics of Fear* (2006). In his work on mass media and information technology he has authored other books, among them *Creating Fear: News and the Construction of Crisis* (2002) and *Terror Post 9/11 and the Media* (2009). This op-ed piece was published on May 23, 2010, in the *Seattle Times*.

What role does David Altheide say the media plays in shaping people's fear of the dangers of illegal immigration?

Fear is driving the legislation and emotions in Arizona these days. Fear is being manipulated through the mass media and inaccurate information to construct a moral panic about the threat of undocumented immigrants to our collective well-being.

Arizona state Rep. John Kavanagh, a supporter of the state's new immigration law, SB 1070, said: ". . . our intention is to make Arizona a very uncomfortable place for them to be so they leave or never come here in the first place."

Law trumps justice. My research on propaganda and the politics of fear convinces me that Pogo, the star of the old comic strip, had it right. Famously, Pogo proclaimed, "We have met the enemy and it is us."

The enemy is the unique political culture of Arizona that permits people who rally against "big government" to embrace a policy that requires police officers to zero in on any potentially undocumented person—30 percent of the state's population. Welcome to Arizona, Pogo.

Call it the Arizona Syndrome:
Promote fear at every turn.

Arizona has a long tradition of claiming to have more crime than it has, and politicians court voters by promoting numerous threats from outsiders, be they newcomers, politicians in Washington and new ideas. Maricopa County Sheriff Joe Arpaio raids Mesa City Hall in the middle of the night and arrests a janitor, while feasting on sound bites about toughness and his "tent-city jail."

The man credited with ramming SB 1070 through Arizona's Legislature boasts about being one of Sheriff Joe's former deputies. Arizona politics embraces the symbol of the gun, the individual's defense against bad things. Recent legal changes permit loaded guns to be carried into bars, and even concealed weapons can now be carried without a special permit.

The border is said to be "less secure" despite a drastic reduction in the number of people who cross it and a decrease in the violent crime rate. Any criminal activity, such as drug smuggling, along the border is framed as the "illegal immigration problem," and is used as a way of criticizing the federal government.

Arizona citizens are more likely to hear Arizona's Republican congressional members claiming that violence on the border "continues to increase at an alarming rate." A border-county sheriff disagreed in The Arizona Republic: "This is a media-created event. I hear politicians on TV saying the border has gotten worse. Well, the fact of the matter is that the border has never been more secure."

Believe the opposite of what is true as long as it fits the prevailing narrative about fear, threats and enemies, and the economy.

Arizona politicos deride "big government" even though Arizona benefitted directly from the federal government's role in constructing Roosevelt Dam. About a third of Arizona's territory consists of federally regulated Indian reservations, and military bases provide a sizable chunk of Arizona's economy. Arizonans pay fewer taxes than most of the country, and receive disproportionately more federal money per capita.

Many reports suggest that undocumented people commit more crime, do not pay an equitable share of taxes, use excessive social services and are an economic drain. None of this is true, according to research by the National Research Council and the President's Council of Economic Advisers, but it does not matter because long-held beliefs and prejudices are impervious to evidence.

Arizona's economy, including the construction and hospitality industries (hotels, restaurants, etc.), has depended on undocumented workers for decades. Yet, immigrants are blamed for economic problems and taxes. Indeed, architects of the Arizona immigration law claim that crime and taxes will go down as fear drives out many Arizona residents.

Have one common and very visible enemy.

Arizona thrives on identity politics. Politicians wrap themselves in the flag; those opposed to the new immigration law are said to be unpatriotic and unwilling to "protect our borders." Despite many claims by the architects of fear that they "love the Latino people," many problems associated with poverty (e.g., gangs) are attributed to race and ethnicity, and therefore undocumented residents.

The Arizona Syndrome becomes part of regional and national scripts and identities the more that it is repeated, and especially as sound bites reduce the conflict to two sides: one side proclaiming patriotism and self-defense, while the other is cast as defending unwanted invaders.

Arizona's politics of fear may be embraced in those states where Latinos lack political influence. More opportunistic politicians will try to connect with uninformed masses by jumping on the bandwagon of immigration reform. Now there is a national enemy, conveniently demonized along with the Taliban and al-Qaida. But as Pogo always knew, we didn't really need those outside enemies; we had the real one all along—us.

For Class Discussion

1. What is Altheide's main claim in this op-ed argument?
2. To what extent and in what ways does Altheide address alternative views? What evidence does he use to support his views? What rhetorical function do the three brief passages in italics serve in delivering Altheide's argument?
3. How would you describe the tone and approach of Altheide's argument? What values and perspective does he bring to the issue of Arizona's new hardline stance against immigrants?
4. Research the comic strip *Pogo*. What does Altheide gain and risk by alluding to this comic strip throughout his op-ed piece?
5. How might Altheide extend the appeal of this argument to reach apathetic or dissenting readers?

"Tennessee Daily Life"
Brandon Dill, Associated Press

According to The Statistical Yearbook of the Immigration and Naturalization Service, 613,913 persons were naturalized in 2010. Public naturalization ceremonies are held throughout the country with the most flamboyant taking place on the Fourth of July. This photo was taken on December 16, 2011 at the naturalization ceremony at Victory University in Memphis, Tennessee, an event involving over "200 immigrants and their families from dozens of countries," as the Associated Press caption to this photo indicates. Pictured in this photo are immigrants from the UK, Mexico, and Iran reciting the Pledge of Allegiance.

After studying the expressions on the new citizens' faces, their clothing and demeanor, how would you describe the mood of this photo?

New Citizens Pledging the Flag at a Naturalization Ceremony

Brandon Dill/The Commercial Appeal/AP Images

For Class Discussion

1. This photo has more of an informative than a persuasive purpose. However, what emotional responses might this photo evoke in readers?

2. How could a proponent of immigration reform policy use this photo for the rhetorical purpose of promoting humane policies, acceptance of immigrants, and more expansive access for immigrants to citizenship? How could this photo serve the rhetorical purpose of promoting a more restrictive policy for immigrant access to citizenship?

3. Considering this chapter's introduction to immigration problems and stakeholders in these issues and the readings in this chapter, what questions about immigration and citizenship does this photo prompt you to ask and investigate?

4. How might this photo contribute to discussions of cultural immigration and national identity?

 STUDENT VOICE: Arizona's HB 2281's Attack on Education and Equality: Let's End the Ban on Ethnic Studies by Carlos Sibaja Garcia

Carlos Sibaja Garcia is an international student from Mexico. He is majoring in English and plans to get a master's degree in teaching English as a second language (ESL). His interests are Latino/a literature and sociolinguistics. He also volunteers as an ESL tutor for adult learners. Carlos wrote this researched policy proposal for a class on argumentation.

According to Carlos Sibaja Garcia, what is the role of education in cultural conflicts over immigration and integration?

Although Arizona's and Alabama's anti-immigration laws designed to apprehend undocumented immigrants have dominated the news, Arizona's House Bill 2281 also merits concern. HB 2281, which went into effect on December 31, 2010, bans the teaching of ethnic studies in K–12 public schools. Ethnic studies includes history, literature, and culture and incorporates the viewpoints of groups marginalized due to their ethnicity and race. The stated purpose of HB 2281 is to prohibit classes that "promote the overthrow of the United States government, promote resentment towards a race or class of people, are designed primarily for pupils of a particular ethnic group, and advocate ethnic solidarity instead of treatment of pupils as individuals" (Stevens and Stovall 296). According to this new law, the ethnic studies program in Tucson was determined to have violated HB 2281 and must stop teaching ethnic studies or risk losing ten percent of its state funding—about 14.9 million dollars (Zehr, "Tucson District").

Why should we be concerned? Laws like HB 2281 undermine the democratic education of American students by censoring schools' curriculum and damaging successful educational programs. The larger implications and potential consequences of HB 2281 are so serious that all Americans, regardless of their ethnicity, should oppose it. HB 2281 should be repealed for three main reasons: (1) it ends a program that has worked against ignorance and racism by promoting knowledge of other cultural and racial groups; (2) it undermines the gains of the Civil Rights Movement by threatening the exchange of knowledge and targeting certain racial and ethnic groups; and (3) it stops an educational program that has had a positive effect on the academic success of minority students.

Some say ethnic studies "threaten the United States' government." In actuality, ethnic studies classes aim to dispel ignorance and racism and promote knowledge of other cultural and racial groups. Those who claim that ethnic studies classes "favor" a particular agenda and create segregation among students, ignore that these classes promote critical thinking by giving different perspectives (Finkel 58). These courses actually give students an opportunity to learn a broader, more balanced view of history: "Ethnic studies is a way of correcting inaccuracies in American history. It's a way of compensating for the way that blacks or Latinos and American Indians and other groups have been left out of American history" . . . (Wright 152). In fact, people of color in America have been arguing for more representation in history textbooks. Instead, figures like César Chávez and Harriet Tubman, who represent America because they strove to end unjust working conditions and slavery, have been removed (Wright 151). Students should be able to learn this history and the history of their local communities, which often involves minorities.

The law claims that ethnic studies excludes students through its main purpose of building ethnic solidarity; however, Tucson's ethnic studies classes benefit all students, not just students of color. Mr. Tom Horne, former Superintendent of Public Instruction in Arizona and chief supporter of this law, ignores that the classes are open to all students and that a state audit found that all students are treated as individuals and taught to be accepting of others (Biggers, "Arizona's Next Scandal?"). As a student from Mexico, I am often surprised by the lack of knowledge American college students have of other ethnicities and countries. Americans often seem to have heard partial stories about other countries. For example, they have heard and read reports about gun violence in Mexico's drug war but have not heard much about the source of most of these guns: the United States. One might ask, Why are special classes needed to teach the history of minorities when minorities are part of the American culture at large? One answer concerning the value of the history taught in Mexican American studies in Tucson was recently expressed by students and parents. Dr. Katerina Sinclair stated, "As a white parent of a white student . . . I want my daughter to learn about the values and history of culture outside of that in which she was raised" (Standing on the side of love.org). How are we going to teach young students about diversity in a state that makes it illegal to teach it?

Furthermore, although supporters of HB 2281 say they are defending the United States, this law itself attacks the country's values and progress. It represents a strike against the gains of the Civil Rights Movement in the United States. In Arizona, it was not until 1951 that a court case ended segregation in schools. In that Arizona ruling, the judge wrote, "a paramount requisite in the American system of public education is social equality" (McCormick and Ayala 28). Even after overturning the segregation laws in the 1950s and 1960s, the African American and Latino community had to file a lawsuit against the Tucson Unified School District in the 1970's claiming racial bias (Finkel 58). As a result, ethnic studies classes began to be offered to address social injustices. Now, some teachers and administrators have filed a federal lawsuit against HB 2281, identifying it as a product of racial bias (especially towards Hispanics) and a violation of the 1st and 14th Amendments of the U.S. Constitution (Zehr, "Tucson District"). The recent federal lawsuit filed against HB 2281 states that "[a]mong the many flaws contained in HB 2281 is the unmistakable message to our youth that the promise of the Constitution to protect them all equally is a myth; that the history, literature and culture of at least one group is not worthy of being taught in school" (Biggers, "Ethnic Studies Court Emergency in Arizona"). We need to abolish laws like HB 2281 that try to silence minority viewpoints and that violate the American values of diversity, freedom of speech, and opportunity.

Lastly, HB 2281 must be repealed because ethnic studies has a strong record of helping minority students succeed in obtaining high school and college degrees. According to Augustine Romero, director of Student Equity, and Martin Arce, director of Academic Equity for Mexican American Studies from the Tucson Unified School District, their ethnic studies program began in 1998 when the community advocated for the academic achievement of Hispanic students (180). Romero and Arce state, "when the cultural diversity of our students is embraced, appreciated, understood, and honored, students will respond in favorable ways that many never knew they could respond" (179). The state of Arizona's own audit of the Tucson ethnic studies found that students graduated "at a rate of eleven percent more in 2010" (Biggers 2011). In Tucson, students in ethnic studies programs have gone to college "at a rate that is 129% greater than the national average for Chicana/o students" (Romero and Arce 181). If high school students are not allowed to take ethnic studies classes, they miss valuable preparation for college. In addition, graduates of Arizona State University, which has a nationally prestigious department in history including the history of ethnic groups in America, will not be able to teach their areas of expertise in Arizona public schools. HB 2281 is destructive of a program that has been empowering minority students to succeed in academia and society.

Finally, just as Arizona and Alabama's anti-immigration bills have encouraged other states to consider similar laws, HB 2281 could influence other states. As a citizen of the world, I am concerned about how banning education damages our future. My previous years in college have taught me how, from the women's suffrage movement to the Civil Rights movement, marginalized groups have fought for equality and inclusion in the mainstream and academia. It is our responsibility to oppose anti-minority laws that repeat destructive patterns from the past and promote racism, discrimination, and prejudice. Students need to acquire cultural and historical knowledge to continue working against social inequality, and minorities need to be given access to educational routes to success to create and sustain a just society.

Works Cited

Biggers, Jeff. "Arizona's Next Scandal? Tea Party State Official Says Ethnic Studies Violates Ban." *The Huffington Post*. 16 June 2011: n. pag. Web. 30 Dec 2011.

————. "Ethnic Studies Court Emergency in Arizona: Only an Injunction Can Prevent Irreparable Harm." *The Huffington Post* 15 Nov 2011: n. pag. Web. 30 Dec 2011.

Finkel, Ed. "DIVIDING Arizona." *District Administration* 46.9 (2010): 54–61. Academic Search Complete. EBSCO. Web. 29 May 2011.

"In Tucson, People of Faith, Students & Parents Defend Embattled Ethnic Studies Program." *Standing on the Side of Love.* 5 May 2011: n. pag. Web. 1 June 2011. http://www.standingonthesideoflove.org/tag/hb-2281/

McCormick, Jennifer, and César J. Ayala. "Felícita 'La Prieta' Méndez (1916–1998) and the end of Latino school segregation in California." *Centro Journal* 19.2 (2007): 12–35. Academic Search Complete. EBSCO. Web. 29 May 2011.

Romero, Augustine F., and Martin Sean Arce. "Culture as a Resource: Critically Compassionate Intellectualism and its Struggle Against Racism, Fascism, and Intellectual Apartheid in Arizona." *Hamline Journal of Public Law & Policy* 31.1 (2009): 179–217. Academic Search Complete. EBSCO. Web. 29 May 2011.

Stevens, Lisa Patel, and David Omotoso Stovall. "Adolescent Literacy Policy." *Journal of Adolescent & Adult Literacy* 54.4 (2010): 295–298. Academic Search Complete. EBSCO. Web. 29 May 2011.

Wright, Stephanie. "From the Editorial Board Problematizing Recent Educational Decisions." *The High School Journal* 93.4 (2010): 151–155. Research Library, ProQuest. Web. 27 May. 2011.

Zehr, Mary Ann. "Tucson District Holds Firm Despite State Ultimatum on Ethnic-Studies Classes." *Education Week* 30.15 (2011): 20–21. Academic Search Complete. EBSCO. Web. 29 May 2011.

For Class Discussion

1. How does Carlos build momentum in this argument with the development of his reasons? For what readers might a different organization and order of points have been even more effective?

2. Both Carlos's personal conviction as an international student and future teacher and extensive research shaped this policy proposal. Where do his personal background and scholarly investigation of the issue contribute to the argument's rhetorical impact?

3. Carlos uses the words and ideas in HB 2281 as the alternative views he addresses. How might it have strengthened his argument to engage more fully with alternative views?

4. What values, assumptions, and beliefs does Carlos envision that his audience shares with him? In a longer argument, how might he have provided support for these values?

5. What points in his argument did you find the most thought-provoking and/or persuasive in terms of influencing your views on cultural immigration? What authors and readings in this chapter would endorse Carlos's perspective?

The Next Immigration Challenge
Dowell Myers

Dowell Myers holds a Master of Planning from the University of California at Berkeley and a PhD in urban planning from MIT. He is a professor of urban planning and demography at the School of Policy, Planning, and Development at the University of Southern California. Myers has served as an adviser to the U.S. Census Bureau. He supervises the Population Dynamics Research Group and has published books on population and growth, including *Housing Demography: Linking Demographic Structure and Housing Markets* (1990), *Analysis with Local Census Data: Portraits of Change* (1992), and his latest book, *Immigrants and Boomers: Forging a New Social Contract for the Future of America* (2007). This op-ed piece was published in the *New York Times* on January 12, 2012.

> What bold, optimistic claim drives this argument and how does Dowell Myers link immigrants and the baby boomer generation?

The immigration crisis that has roiled American politics for decades has faded into history. Illegal immigration is shrinking to a trickle, if that, and will likely never return to the peak levels of 2000. Just as important, immigrants who arrived in the 1990s and settled here are assimilating in remarkable and unexpected ways.

Taken together, these developments, and the demographic future they foreshadow, require bold changes in our approach to both legal and illegal immigration. Put simply, we must shift from an immigration policy, with its emphasis on keeping newcomers out, to an immigrant policy, with an emphasis on encouraging migrants and their children to integrate into our social fabric. "Show me your papers" should be replaced with "Welcome to English class."

Restrictionists, including those driving much of the debate on the Republican primary trail, still talk as if nothing has changed. But the numbers are stark: the total number of immigrants, legal and illegal, arriving in the 2000s grew at half the rate of the 1990s, according to the Census Bureau.

The most startling evidence of the falloff is the effective disappearance of illegal border crossers from Mexico, with some experts estimating the net number of new Mexicans settling in the United States at zero. The size of the illegal-immigrant population peaked in 2007, with about 58 percent of it of Mexican origin, according to the Pew Hispanic Center; since 2008, that population has shrunk by roughly 200,000 a year. Illegal immigrants from Asia and other parts of the globe have similarly dwindled in numbers.

This new equilibrium is here to stay, in large part because Mexico's birthrate is plunging. In 1970 a Mexican woman, on average, gave birth to 6.8 babies, and when they entered their 20s, millions journeyed north for work. Today the country's birthrate—at 2.1—is approaching that of the United States. That portends a shrinking pool of young adults to meet Mexico's future labor needs, and less competition for jobs at home.

If the number of immigrants is declining, what about that other nativist bugbear, assimilation? There's little doubt that immigrants' potential as economic contributors turns on their ability to assimilate. Fortunately, recent studies by John Pitkin, Julie Park and me show that immigrant parents and children, especially Latinos, are making extraordinary strides in assimilating.

Today, barely a third of adult immigrants have a high-school diploma. But the children of Latino immigrants have always outperformed their parents in educational achievement. By 2030 we expect 80 percent of their children who arrived in the 1990s before age 10 to have completed high school and 18 percent to have a bachelor's degree.

But it is immigrants' success in becoming homeowners—often overlooked in immigration debates—that is the truest mark of their desire to adopt America as home. Consider Latinos. Among those in the wave of 1990s immigrants, just 20 percent owned a home in 2000. We expect that percentage to rise to 69 percent—and 74 percent for all immigrants—by 2030, well above the historical average for all Americans.

Who will be selling these homes to these immigrants? The 78 million native-born baby boomers looking to downsize as their children grow up and leave home. Fortunately for them, both immigrants and their children will be there to buy their homes, putting money into baby-boomer pockets and helping to shore up future housing prices.

Indeed, with millions of people retiring every year, America's immigrants and their children are crucial to future economic growth: economists forecast labor-force growth to drop below 1 percent later this decade because of retiring baby boomers.

Immigrants' extraordinary progress in assimilating would be faster if federal and state policies encouraged it. Unfortunately, they don't. This year, the Department of Homeland Security plans to spend a measly $18 million—far less than a tenth of 1 percent of its budget—on helping immigrants assimilate. Meanwhile, states with large immigrant populations are cutting the budgets of community and state colleges, precisely where immigrant students predominantly enroll.

How do we change course and begin treating immigrants as a vast, untapped human resource? The answer goes to the heart of shifting from an immigration policy to an immigrant policy.

For starters, the billions of dollars spent on border enforcement should be gradually redirected to replenishing and boosting the education budget, particularly the Pell grant program for low-income students. Some money could be channeled to nonprofits like ImmigrationWorks and Welcoming America, which are at the forefront of helping migrants assimilate.

Second, the Departments of Labor, Commerce and Education need to play a greater role in immigration policy. Yes, as long as there remains a terrorist threat from abroad, the Department of Homeland Security should have an immigration component. But immigration policy is all about cultivating needed workers. That means helping immigrants and their children graduate from high school and college. It means that no migrant should have to stand in line for an English class. It means assistance in developing migrants' job skills to better compete in an increasingly information- and knowledge-based economy.

Thanks to our huge foreign-born population (12 percent of the total), America can remain the world's richest and most powerful nation for decades. Shaping an immigrant policy that focuses on developing the talents of our migrants and their children is the surest way to realize this goal.

For Class Discussion

1. According to Myers, what push factors have changed in Mexico?

2. By what criteria does Myers measure success in assimilation?

3. What are the features of Myers's proposal and what evidence does he use to support these points?

4. How does Myers distinguish between an "immigration policy" and an "immigrant policy"?

5. What questions would you like to ask Myers in order to understand his vision of the role of immigration in America's future society? How does knowing that he is an authority on demographics influence your response to his proposal?

Let's Fashion a Made-in-Canada Approach to the Burka

Sheema Khan

Sheema Khan holds a PhD in chemical physics from Harvard, works as a patents agent on drug delivery technology, and publishes columns frequently in Toronto's largest circulating national newspaper, *The Globe and Mail*, a centrist paper currently endorsing the conservatives in Canada. In 2009, Khan published her book *Of Hockey and Hijab: Reflections of a Canadian Muslim Woman*, which collects her columns on wide-ranging topics, from women and Islam to politics in the Middle East. Khan founded the Canadian Council on American-Islamic Relations and often speaks at nongovernmental organizations (NGOs) and government agencies on Muslim matters. She is known for her blend of spiritual conviction and modern, liberal views. This editorial appeared in *The Globe and Mail* on February 1, 2010.

> How does Sheema Khan both broaden and deepen the political-social conversation on Muslim women's right to wear the burka in Canada?

Following last month's call by the Muslim Canadian Congress to ban the face-covering *niqab*, or *burka*, about 30 Muslim groups across Canada denounced the proposal. Their basis: The state has no business dictating what a woman should wear, nor infringing on individual freedoms.

It is a compelling argument, echoing the message of U.S. President Barack Obama in his 2009 Cairo speech. And as France contemplates a *burka* ban, pragmatists there point out the difficulty of enforcing such a prohibition. Others warn of a backlash: *More* women will adopt the *burka* in defiance of the government. Also, fewer than 2,000 women wear the *niqab/burka* in France, or about 0.004 per cent of the population. These WMDs (women in Muslim dress) are perceived as the new WMDs—like a biological weapon, an infinitesimal concentration has the potential to destroy the very fabric of *la Republique laïque*. Who knew?

Yet, *laïcité* is a long-standing French tradition, dating back to the Third Republic of 1905, when the church was officially extracted from the education system, and from much of public life. According to John Bowen, author of *Why the French Don't Like Headscarves*, *laïcité* defines the character of public space as essentially "neutral." Any threat to neutrality can be interpreted as a threat to the state. Especially, it seems, in the face of high unemployment and March regional elections. The New York Times is more blunt, calling Nicolas Sarkozy's approach "hate-mongering" that fans "anti-Muslim prejudices" by using *burka*-clad women as a "cheap electoral target" to deflect the electorate's anger.

The French concept of *laïcité* is distinct from the Anglo-Saxon view of secularism, due in part to the different philosophies of Jean-Jacques Rousseau and John Locke. For Rousseau, the individual had to abstract oneself from particular traditions and accept the transfer of certain rights to Republican Law—a move from pluralism to unity. The individual gains freedom through the state, which has the right to regulate the public, organized face of religion. On the other hand, Locke believed freedom of conscience to be the foundation for individual rights, which guarantee freedom from the state. These views have permeated societies that have evolved from former French and British rule.

Not surprisingly, the Canadian Charter is more akin to Lockean principles. Individual rights, such as freedom of religion, carry heavy weight.

Some *burka*-banners argue that such a prohibition is not a violation of religious freedom, there is no religious basis for the garb. They quote the Grand Imam of Al-Azhar University, who recently said that the face-veil had nothing to do with Islam. A minority of clerics disagree. Yet, Canada's Supreme Court has ruled that the state is not an "arbiter of religious dogma"—what matters is the sincerity of the individual's beliefs. If a woman honestly believes it is part of her faith to cover her face in public, the state cannot counter that a different religious opinion carries greater religious legitimacy.

Legalities aside, many Canadians feel uncomfortable seeing the face-veil here. It represents a physical barrier, which has no precedent in our culture. It has also become a misogynous icon, due to the Taliban, and Saudi "religious" police. Security is an added concern. Finally, many assume veiled women are coerced into wearing "that thing."

Yet, the intentions of these women are diverse. For some, it is an act of faith to get closer to God. Some incur the disapproval of family, friends and community for taking this step; others are forced to do so by family members. Youthful defiance may play a role. As for security, veiled women readily comply with identification protocols when required.

Let's not forget our politicians have shamelessly used veiled women as cheap electoral targets. In the 2007 Quebec election, complaints forced the chief electoral officer to ban the face veil at the voting booth (even though veiled women never asked for an exemption). In a 2008 by-election, Prime Minister Stephen Harper seized on Quebec discontent with the face-veil by adding his disapproval. The political stigmatization and ensuing "mob mentality" created a climate of fear for a minority who wished to exercise their democratic right to vote.

Will an imported French-style ban settle these tensions? Are we ready to deny access to health care, education and public transportation based on a person's belief or dress? This is the French solution.

Or shall we fashion a made-in-Canada paradigm, guided by the principles enshrined in our Charter?

For Class Discussion

1. What is the motivating occasion for Khan's writing of this column?
2. How does Khan seek to capture the complexities of the discussion of the burka? What would you say is her claim?
3. What evidence and chain of reasoning does Khan draw on to support her view?
4. How effectively does she engage opposing views in this piece? What perspectives are not mentioned?
5. How compelling is the challenge or appeal to her readers with which she ends this piece? How has this piece enlarged your thinking about religious-cultural rights?

How to Integrate Europe's Muslims
Jonathan Laurence

Jonathan Laurence, who holds a PhD from Harvard University, is an associate professor of political science at Boston College. He has authored several books on religion and politics in Europe: *Integrating Islam: Political and Religious Challenges in Contemporary France* (2006) (with Justin Vaisse) and *The Emancipation of Europe's Muslims: The State's Role in Minority Integration* (2011). He has served as a senior fellow at the Brookings Institution in the Foreign Policy Studies division and the Transatlantic Academy. Along with numerous scholarly articles, book chapters, and policy reports for think tanks in the United States and Europe, he has written articles and reviews for the *Wall Street Journal*, *Foreign Affairs*, *Foreign Policy*, *Daily Kos*, and *New Statesman*. This op-ed piece was published in the *New York Times* on January 23, 2012. One of Laurence's key words in this piece is "anomie," which means both lawlessness and disconnection from normative standards, or social isolation.

> According to Jonathan Laurence, what are the stakes in the issue of Europe's integration of Muslims?

Two weeks ago, dozens of cars were set alight in the French city of Clermont-Ferrand after a 30-year-old truck driver, Wissam El-Yamni, was roughed up and then died while in police custody. The uproar underscored the hostility of young minority men toward authority across communities in Europe, an antipathy that has at times led to deadly violence.

The failure of Islamic integration in Europe is often attributed—especially by right-wing parties—to an excess of tolerance toward the large-scale Muslim immigration that began in the mid-1970s.

By recognizing Muslim religious requirements, the argument goes, countries like France, Britain and the Netherlands have unwittingly hindered assimilation and even, in some cases, fostered radicalism. But the unrest in gritty European suburbs stems not from religious difference, but from anomie.

Europeans should not be afraid to allow Muslim students to take classes on Islam in state-financed schools and universities. The recognition and accommodation of Islamic religious practices, from clothing to language to education, does not mean capitulation to fundamentalism. On the contrary, only by strengthening the democratic rights of Muslim citizens to form associations, join political parties and engage in other aspects of civic life can Europe integrate immigrants and give full meaning to the abstract promise of religious liberty.

The rise of right-wing, anti-immigrant parties has led several European countries to impose restrictions on Islamic dress, mosque-building and reunification of families through immigration law. These policies are counterproductive. Paradoxically, people for whom religion is otherwise not all that important become more attached to their faith's clothing, symbols and traditions when they feel they are being singled out and denied basic rights.

Take, for example, the French debate over whether to recognize the Jewish Day of Atonement, Yom Kippur, and the Muslim festival of Eid al-Adha as official holidays. Yes, the French state clings to the principle of "laicite," or secularism—but the state's recognition of Easter and Christmas as official holidays feels, to some Jews and Muslims, like hypocrisy. It is Islam's absence in the institutions young European Muslims encounter, starting with the school's calendar, classroom and canteen, that contributes to anger and alienation.

In the last few months, there have been some signs that the right-wing momentum has slowed. A French bill to ban headscarves from day care centers was killed in committee. The Dutch Parliament voted down a bill to outlaw Islamic animal slaughter. And Germany's most populous state helped offset a judicial ban on school prayer by announcing equal access to religion courses for Muslim students.

European countries could use a period of benign neglect of the Islam issue—but only after they finish incorporating religion into the national fabric. For too long, they have instead masked an absence of coherent integration policy under the cloak of "multiculturalism." The state outsourced the hard work of integration to foreign diplomats and Islamist institutions—for example, some students in Germany read Saudi-supplied textbooks in Saudi-run institutions.

This neglect of integration helped an unregulated "underground Islam" to take hold in storefronts, basements and courtyards. It reflected wishful thinking about how long guest workers would stay and perpetuated a myth of eventual departure and repatriation.

In Britain, for example, race-based equality laws protected Sikhs and Jews as minorities, but not Hindus and Muslims, since they were still considered "foreign."

Institutional exclusion fueled a demand for religious recognition, and did much to unite and segregate Muslims. Islamist organizations became the most visible defenders of the faith. It is crucial now to provide the right mix of institutional incentives for religious and political moderation, and the most promising strategy for doing that is for governments to consult with the full range of law-abiding religious institutions that Muslims have themselves established.

The French Council for the Muslim Faith, the German Islam Conference, the Committee for Italian Islam and the Mosques and Imams National Advisory Board in Britain—all state-sanctioned Islamic organizations set up in the past decade—represent a broad cross-section of mosque administrators in every country. They have quietly begun reconciling many practical issues, from issuing mosque permits to establishing Islamic theology departments at public universities to appointing chaplains in the military and in prisons.

Ultimately, however, elected democratic institutions are the place where the desires of individual Muslims should be expressed. Ever since 1789, when a French legislator argued that "the Jews should be denied everything as a nation, but granted everything as individuals," Europeans have struggled to resolve the tension between rights derived from universal citizenship versus group membership.

Over the next 20 years, Europe's Muslim population is projected to grow to nearly 30 million—7 to 8 percent of all Europeans—from around 17 million. Granting Muslims full religious freedom wouldn't remove obstacles to political participation or create jobs. But it would at least allow tensions over Muslims' religious practices to fade. This would avoid needless sectarian strife and clear the way for politicians to address the more vexing and urgent challenges of socioeconomic integration.

For Class Discussion

1. What description of the treatment of Muslims by European governments and societies does Laurence say is *not* accurate?

2. In this proposal argument, what change of attitudes and practices in Europe is Laurence advocating? What does he mean by "integration"?

3. What examples of how his proposal would work does he offer?

4. What reasons and arguments that you have encountered regarding the clash of European and Muslim cultures and tolerance of religious practices

(clothing, prayer, the preparation of food, and so forth) does Laurence not mention in his op-ed piece? How would mentioning these points have affected the impact of his argument?

5. What points in this argument concerning the problems of cultural immigration and integration did you find persuasive?

CHAPTER QUESTIONS FOR REFLECTION AND DISCUSSION

1. How has immigration affected your region, city, or local community? Describe some of the political, economic, or social-cultural influences of immigration on the place where you live. You might think in terms of the kinds of stores and restaurants (variety of food), religious buildings, radio stations, and the racial-ethnic composition of the student body of schools.

2. A number of the readings in this chapter explore the forces and conditions fueling immigration and posit very different interpretations of push and pull factors. Choose four of the following writers, identify their reasoning and assumptions about the causes of migration, and determine which writers are in agreement about these causes: Kofi Annan, Victor Davis Hanson, Laura Carlsen, Steve Breen, Tim Johnson, Mexico's Ministry of Foreign Relations, Samuel P. Huntington, MALDEF and LULAC, and Dowell Myers.

3. According to the following writers, what myths and misconceptions about immigrants permeate and distort debates about immigrants in the United States and Europe: MALDEF and LULAC, David L. Altheide, Laura Carlsen, Victor Davis Hanson, Carlos Sibaya Garcia, Jonathan Laurence, Sheema Khan, Dowell Myers, and Samuel P. Huntington? How do the angle of vision and political values of the writer influence what he or she identifies as myths and misconceptions?

4. Both (the late) Samuel P. Huntington and Victor Davis Hanson are scholars and public intellectuals writing for conservative forums, the American Enterprise Institute and *National Review Online,* respectively. How do the ways they frame their arguments against Mexican immigration coincide and differ?

5. **Analyzing Arguments Rhetorically.** Thinking of the trends and numbers in global migration, Kofi Annan asserts that we should celebrate "mobility and diversity" but admits that absorption of these people and maintaining national security in receiving countries are big issues. He charges that "the answer must lie in managing migration—rationally, creatively, compassionately and cooperatively" (page 148). Which of the arguments in this chapter do you think makes the most persuasive case for a way to address the needs of both "migrant and host communities"? Identify three or four points in this argument and several key features of the way it is written to explain its rhetorical effectiveness.

6. **Analyzing Arguments Rhetorically.** Many visual arguments—political cartoons, photos, posters, ads, and even bumper stickers—make strong emotional appeals on immigration issues. Find a visual argument in one of these genres that contrasts with a visual argument in this chapter in its stand on immigration reform or immigration enforcement. How does the use of symbols, relationship of image to text, abbreviated argument, and shock, irony, or humor work in this visual text? What insights does this text contribute to the public conversation?

7. What intersections do you see between Jonathan Laurence's and Sheema Khan's assessment of European and Canadian political and cultural integration of Muslims?

8. Working individually or collaboratively, research one of the following subjects related to immigration policy, enforcement, or reform. Prepare a presentation for the class that includes a graphic or some visual display of information.

   • Research the kinds of visas the United States offers, how many are given each year, and who gets them. Is it true that the U.S. immigration policy favors wealthy, educated foreigners? What arguments are people offering that more visas of different kinds should be granted?

   • A number of states—Arizona, Alabama, Georgia, and South Carolina—have passed harsh anti-immigration laws. Research how these laws have affected the immigrant populations—legal and illegal—and the economy of the states.

   • Research the federal E-Verify system mandating that businesses electronically verify employees. How does the system work, which companies have been audited, and how effective is the system in decreasing illegal immigration?

   • Europe has experienced a number of terrorist attacks and outbursts of violence related to immigration in the last ten years. Research these attacks and violent cultural conflicts. What perpetrators and motivations were involved? How did the different countries in which these problems occurred respond?

WRITING ASSIGNMENTS

Brief Writing Assignments

1. **Reflective Writing.** Write a short informal personal essay that uses one incident or experience as a departure point for an exploration of your thoughts and feelings about immigration. Your incident or experience could be your family's or a friend's immigration story, an experience of acceptance or alienation you had while living in another country, an experience you had working with immigrants, or even a thought-provoking

movie about immigration you have seen. Try to capture a few insights you have gained about immigration and make some connections between experience and ideas gleaned from readings in this chapter.

2. Imagine a dialogue or debate between one of the following pairs of writers from this chapter. List the main points that you think each writer would include in a summary of his or her views on immigration, what points he or she would concede, and how the writer would rebut opposing views. You may want to write the full script of this dialogue.

| A. Samuel P. Huntington | Jonathan Laurence, Dowell Myers, or Carlos Sibaya Garcia |
| B. Victor Davis Hanson | Tim Johnson, Laura Carlsen, Mexico's Ministry of Foreign Relations, or David L. Altheide |

3. **Reflective Writing.** Answer the following questions with a brief reflective discussion for each reading you select: (1) Which reading in this chapter is most successful in deepening understanding of and compassion for immigrants? (2) Which reading most effectively clarifies a problem related to immigration? (3) Which reading does the best job of showing how immigration problems are connected to forces of globalization? (4) Which reading provides the most compelling solution to an immigration problem?

4. Choose one of the following controversial claims and write for twenty minutes supporting or rebutting the claim. Use examples from the readings, your own background knowledge, and your experiences as evidence to develop your view. You might exchange papers with someone in your class and try to write the points that you think would further develop or refute your partner's case. Include specific examples from the readings or your own background knowledge to elaborate on your points.

A. Immigrants—even undocumented ones—are beneficial to Americans and to the United States.

B. U.S. policy toward immigration, especially illegal immigration, is contradictory and hypocritical.

C. Politicians and the media have allowed fear to distort the public discussion of immigration.

D. The United States should reconsider its own role and responsibility in the drug wars in Mexico.

E. Americans should be more aware of the immigration procedure, including the granting of visas and the steps in naturalization.

F. Receiving/host countries should acknowledge and accept the cultural-religious practices of immigrant subcultures.

Writing Projects

1. **Reflective Writing.** Write a reflective, exploratory essay that has a focus but not necessarily a thesis. Write for yourself and an audience of close friends or family—people who know you well and would be interested in your thinking. Often as citizens of a country, we may feel overwhelmed, confused, irritated, or even threatened by an influx of foreigners or by a problem with immigration that seems unsolvable. Reflect on a reading in this chapter that has shaken up, enlarged, or in some way changed your thoughts and feelings about immigration. Begin with a description of an incident, reading, or position that captures your earlier views on immigration. Explore your values and assumptions. Then analyze how the reading you have chosen has moved you. Use this essay to demonstrate how you have wrestled with ideas and worked your way to a more complicated understanding of immigrants and immigration.

2. **Analyzing Arguments Rhetorically.** Choose one of the following articles that you think is very effective for a general audience: Kofi Annan, Victor Davis Hanson, Samuel P. Huntington, Carlos Sibaya Garcia, David L. Altheide, Laura Carlsen, Tim Johnson, Sheema Khan, or Jonathan Laurence. With the readership of a general news commentary magazine such as *TIME*, *Newsweek*, or *U.S. News and World Report* in mind, analyze the argument you have chosen and explain its persuasiveness. In what ways does it make a valuable contribution to the public debates on global immigration? Include a short summary of the piece and an analysis of several of its rhetorical features (for example, the clarity of its claim, the strength of its evidence, its emotional impact, the author's credibility). How has this article changed your views of immigration?

3. For a variation on the rhetorical analysis in the preceding prompt, imagine that you are writing your analysis for an audience that is either openly politically conservative or definitely liberal. Write an interpretive argument that shapes your analysis for the readership of one of these publications: on the political right—*American Spectator*, *National Review*, *Reason On-line*, townhall.com, the *Washington Times*; on the left—*The Nation*, *The American Prospect*, *Mother Jones*, *Utne Reader*, or salon.com. Analyze the political values held by the readers of this publication. Why should these particular readers consider the piece you are discussing?

4. Choose one of the arguments in this chapter with which you disagree. Write an open letter to the writer in which you take a respectful collaborative, negotiating approach. In your letter, (1) introduce yourself and your encounter with the writer's argument; (2) summarize the writer's argument fairly and accurately; (3) discuss values and goals that you share with the writer; (4) identify some points of disagreement; and (5) present some key points of your own view of the issue that you think the writer should consider. Conclude your letter with remarks that would keep the conversation open.

5. After considering Carlos Sibaya Garcia's and Jonathan Laurence's perspectives on education's role in nurturing the integration of immigrant populations and creating a more harmonious, diverse society, and after researching the citizen and advocacy campaigns that were launched to support the DREAM Act in 2010 promoting higher education for immigrants, write an argument directed to voters of your age group. Construct your own informed vision of the role of education in incorporating immigrants. (For example, how and when should the history and culture of immigrant groups be taught? Why should education for immigrants be promoted?)

6. After doing field research about local (often nonprofit) organizations that seek to support immigrants in your community or region, create a brochure or series of ads informing the general public about how individuals can facilitate the work of one or several of these organizations. Your product could be a Web page designed to encourage volunteerism.

7. As one woman journalist has written, "Whenever Islam clashes with the West, women's bodies are the fiercest battleground"* The battle over the wearing of the hijab and burka in public spaces rages within the Muslim community as well as between Muslim's and non-Muslims and touches on multiple subjects: among them, women's rights versus repression and oppression, religious freedom, and citizenship and the rights of subcultures. Many prominent Muslim women have spoken out on these issues, including Sheema Khan, Farzana Hassan, and Raheel Raza from Canada and Nabila Ramdani from Great Britain. After researching these or other Muslim women writers on the controversy over the hijab and the burka, as well as the views of women outside Islam, write an argument directed to American citizens that presents your informed position.

8. After researching a particular immigration problem affecting your state or region (for example, a shortage of workers to harvest crops), write an editorial for your college or university newspaper that alerts students to the problem and proposes a course of action they should follow to bring legislative or community attention to this problem.

9. Imagine that you are an intern in the office of a state or nationally elected representative or senator. Besides tracking bills and corresponding with constituents, your responsibility is to conduct legislative research. Choose one of the following scenarios, research the issue from multiple perspectives, and write an informed policy proposal suggesting which position your congressional employer should take on this issue:

   A. Your employer has read David L. Altheide's op-ed piece "The Arizona Syndrome: Propaganda and the Politics of Fear" as well as an article

---

*Margaret Wente, "Ban the Burka? No, but . . . ," *The Globe and Mail* (June 25, 2009): A17.

by an immigration lawyer claiming that Immigration and Customs Enforcement's program Secure Communities is rounding up and deporting people without criminal backgrounds, leading to racial profiling and disrupting immigrant communities and families. Currently, counties and cities can choose to opt out of this program. Your task is to determine whether the program Secure Communities is working effectively to increase the safety of American citizens. Should local governments continue to be able to choose not to participate?

B. Your employer has read Dowell Myers's upbeat editorial calling for an "immigrant policy" that instead of focusing on trying to keep people out of the country "encourag[es] migrants and their children to integrate into our social fabric"; however, you have also encountered the voices of concerned citizen advocacy groups such as numbersusa.org, which emphasizes the negative effect of a large legal and illegal immigrant population and the growth rate of this population on the country. Research the question of immigrant demands on social services such as the school system. Should the country focus on restriction of immigrant flow or on integration? Will the growth of the immigrant population enrich the country or drain it?

C. Your employer has read Laura Carlsen's article "Why Mexico's Drug War Is Unwinnable," arguing that the United States is wasting millions of dollars and failing to curtail drug trafficking by following a course of militarization. Research alternative proposals for dealing with the drug war and choose one (for example, legalization of drugs) to pursue in depth. Write a policy proposal that advises your legislative employer to endorse this course of action.

5

Protecting the Environment

Water Issues and Competing Energy Technologies

CONTEXT FOR A NETWORK OF ISSUES

The global community is wrestling with conflicting views of the earth's natural resources. These are classified as **renewable resources**, which include renewable energy (solar, wind, and geothermal power), and **nonrenewable resources** such as minerals and **fossil fuels** (coal, oil, and natural gas). Whereas some corporations envision the earth as an expansive space with vast, lucrative resources to be tapped and marketed, other groups see the earth as our life-support system that has finite resources that need careful management. Recently, scientists have been wondering whether some renewable resources—trees, fertile soil, and water—are being depleted or contaminated at a rate that exceeds their replenishment and have been warning that the world's population growth over the next fifty years will only increase this threat to the environment. In addition, greenhouse gas emissions and changes in climate may very well be affecting the availability of resources.

Two concepts that regularly appear in controversies over natural resources, human dependence on the environment, and global interdependence are **sustainable development** and the **commons**. In 1987, the World Commission on Environment and Development (often called the "Brundtland Commission" after its chair Gro Harlem Brundtland) articulated this now widely accepted definition of "sustainable development" as "development that meets the needs of the present without compromising the ability of future generations to meet their own needs."* The concept of the

---

*1987, *Brundtland Report* (an easy-to-read version of the report is available at www.worldinbalance.net/intagreements/1987-brundtland.php).

commons asks people to think of the earth's resources as belonging equally to all nations and peoples of the world. The commons include "the air we breathe, the freshwater we drink, the oceans and the diverse wildlife and plant biodiversity of the world, . . . and among indigenous peoples, communal lands that have been worked cooperatively for thousands of years."[*] Clearly, the ideas of sharing environmental resources with future generations and with all peoples directly oppose the practices of environmental overuse and competition.

Freshwater is a prime example of a finite natural resource that is subject to global competition. The award-winning musical *Urinetown* depicts a fictional city where one company owns the water system and manipulates accessibility and cost according to its own whims. The poor must pay a fee to use the restrooms, and it is illegal *not* to use the facilities. The penalty for breaking the law is banishment to Urinetown, a death sentence. Although *Urinetown* is a melodramatic postmodern self-parody, its main conflict between "the people" and a powerful corporation that controls the water imitates real-world conflicts over water. For example, between 1999 and 2002 in Cochabamba, Bolivia, hundreds of thousands of poor people protested against a group of corporations (among them, the Bechtel Corporation) that controlled the city's water distribution system. Rallying behind the slogans "Water is God's gift and not merchandise" and "Water is life," the Citizen Alliance compelled the government to regain control of the water system. The Bolivian crisis and the musical raise serious environmental, political, and economic questions about the scarcity of usable water, the privatizing of water supplies, the money and technology required to manage water systems, and the consequences of corporate control of environmental resources.

What is the global status of water? The following facts give some idea of global problems with water:

WATER: A LIMITED RESOURCE

- 97.5 percent of the earth's water is saltwater and undrinkable.
- Polar snow and ice hold most of the freshwater.
- Less than 1 percent of freshwater is usable, amounting to only 0.01 percent of the earth's total water.
- 70 percent of water goes to agricultural use; 22 percent to industrial use; 8 percent to domestic use.[†]
- Although the United Nations Millennium Development has set a goal to halve the number of people with no access to clean drinking water, they

---

[*]The International Forum on Globalization, *Alternatives to Economic Globalization: A Better World Is Possible* (San Francisco: Berrett-Koehler, 2002), 81.
[†]"Water the Facts," *New Internationalist* (March 2003).

estimate that in 2015, one in ten will still not have sustainable access. More than 2.6 billion people still lack basic sanitation.[*]

- "Diarrhoeal diseases account for some 2 million deaths of children under age 5 each year, and the most recent estimates indicate that improved sanitation and drinking water could save 2.2 million children a year, or some 5,500 a day."[†]
- Water is wasted through misuse, inefficiency, leakage, evaporation, and allocation of pure water to tasks that don't need it, such as Americans using "18.5 gallons per day per person on flushing the toilet."[‡]
- It is projected that in twenty years, the demand for water will increase by 50 percent and two-thirds of the world population will be water-stressed.[§]

Clearly, water is a precious global resource that requires efficient, equitable management worldwide.

Present and future equitable treatment of the environment is also at issue in the global controversies over atmospheric pollution and climate change. **Climate change** is affecting rainfall patterns, the intensity and frequency of storms, and the longevity of droughts. Most of the international scientific community agrees that pollution from greenhouse gases (mostly carbon dioxide caused by the burning of fossil fuels), which trap the earth's heat like a greenhouse, is playing a role in raising average surface temperatures and that changes in temperatures are causing changes in the earth's climate. According to the Global Carbon Project, fossil fuel carbon emissions in 2010 were the highest in human history, with a total of 9.1 billion tons emitted to the atmosphere.[¥] Furthermore, countries have unequally contributed to this atmospheric pollution: Each American emits about 19.8 tons of carbon dioxide a year compared with 4.6 for each person in China (however, factor in China's population) and 0.29 ton emitted by each Bangladeshi.[€] Most climatologists believe that the growing population and industrialization of third world countries will magnify problems with greenhouse gases and their effect on the earth's atmosphere and climate.

---

[*]United Nations Development Programme, *The Millennium Goals Development Report 2011* (New York: Macmillan, 2011), 53–55.

[†]United Nations Development Programme, *Human Development Report 2011* (New York: Macmillan, 2011), 53.

[‡]Kathleen Parker, "Clean Water Down the Toilet: More Than a Drop in the Bucket," *Seattle Times*, May 30, 2011.

[§]Richard Steiner, "The Real Clear and Present Danger," *Seattle Post-Intelligencer*, May 30, 2004.

[¥]"Carbon Budget Highlights," *Global Carbon Project*, accessed January 10, 2012.

[€]Adam Vaughan, "Carbon Emissions per Person, By Country," *Guardian Online* (September 2, 2009), accessed January 10, 2012, www.guardian.co.uk/environment/datablog/2009/sep/02/carbon-emissions-per-person-capita. Though outranked by the United States in per capita emissions, because there are more people in China, China is now the world leader in total carbon emissions.

As a result of global concern over atmospheric pollution and climate change, scientists, corporations, and governments have begun to seek out environmentally friendly **alternative energy**, such as biofuels, solar power, and wind energy, in order to provide for the world's continuing energy needs. Other factors that contribute to this search include the increasing scarcity of fossil fuels (which are nonrenewable resources), the difficulty of accessing the remaining untapped deposits of fossil fuels, and the instability of the price of oil, coal, and natural gas in global markets.* Another discussion centers around questions of energy security and energy independence. Fossil fuel deposits are not evenly distributed around the globe, and political instability in some of the major oil-producing countries, including Nigeria, Iran, and Brazil, have prompted the United States, among other nations, to pass legislation urging the development of alternative fuels to lessen the country's dependence on foreign sources.

This chapter explores water scarcity and competing strategies for energy development as global environmental issues.

STAKES AND STAKEHOLDERS

Because all humans need fresh air, safe water, and energy to light our homes, produce our food and goods, and fuel our transportation, we are all prime stakeholders in global environmental issues, along with governments and corporations, who often control the access to natural resources. These and other stakeholders are debating issues related to the following key questions.

What Are Some of the World's Major Problems with Environmental Resources?   As stakeholders battle over defining the problems, many scientists are now saying that the amount of resources humans consume (as well as the damage we do to the earth—our "ecological footprint") is 20 percent over Earth's carrying capacity; we are overusing Earth's resources at too great a rate. Furthermore, ecologists point out that developed countries, roughly 20 percent of the world's population, consume between 70 and 80 percent of the planet's resources, a level of use that cannot continue.† Considering the excessive consumption of developed countries, environmentalists and social justice activists are now worried about the increasing drain on environmental resources as giants China and India as well as third world countries adopt the developmental pattern of Europe and the United States in their effort to industrialize and

---

*"Oil Prices Top 147 U.S. Dollars per Barrel," *The Sydney Morning Herald*, July 12, 2008.
†Thomas Pugh and Erik Assadourian, "What Is Sustainability, Anyway?" *World-Watch* (September–October, 2003): 17.

advance economically. Studies have projected that if people in the developing world were to take on the American lifestyle, the world would need the resources of five or six Earths to maintain that level of consumption. In contrast, many political leaders, policymakers, economists, and businesses acknowledge the increasing pressures on the environment caused by population growth and the economic development of third world countries, but they disagree about the severity and urgency of the problem.

The question of what kinds of energy sources we should be seeking is entangled with concerns over the immediacy, magnitude, and implications of climate change. The reputable Intergovernmental Panel on Climate Change* cites the critical temperature changes causing the warming of the oceans and the melting of the polar ice caps, erratic weather, more intense storms, the rapid thawing of the northern permafrost with its release of tons of methane, earlier blooming of plants, changes in animals' seasonal ranges, and cooling of the Northern Hemisphere as signs of climate change. They also speak in terms of the complex, cumulative interplay among many factors (such as ocean currents, ocean warming, snowfall, etc.) and regard climate change as not fully understood or calculable. For many, climate change is a human rights and social justice issue because rising sea levels and coastal flooding as well as changes in rainfall and violent storms hit hardest the most vulnerable, climate-dependent people—the poor. At issue is how serious and urgent climate change is. Stakeholders such as the fossil fuel industry and corporate leaders disagree about how much human contributions affect the changes that are taking place and whether the issue deserves priority in light of humans' immediate needs for energy.

Questions about environmental problems and climate change also involve conflicts among scientists, politics, and the way the media represent environmental issues to the public. Both environmentalists and global warming skeptics accuse the other side of violating principles of science, of oversimplifying causes and effects, and of pursuing a political agenda; both groups claim the media are biased. Arguments about what science can deliver in the way of certainty and predictions are entangled with scientists' government funding and affiliations with the fossil fuel industry and environmental organizations.

---

*The Intergovernmental Panel on Climate Change, established in 1988 by the World Meteorological Organization (WMO) and the United Nations Environment Programme (UNEP), focuses on evaluating "scientific, technical and socioeconomic information relevant for the understanding of climate change, its potential impacts, and options for adaptation and mitigation." The IPCC issues regular reports (1990, 1995, 2001, and 2007) to provide an assessment of the state of knowledge on climate change; a fifth report is expected to be issued in 2014 (www.ipcc. ch/about/index.htm).

As Third World Countries Develop and the Global Population Increases, How Can Environmental Resources Be Conserved and Fairly and Wisely Managed?   Many nongovernmental organizations (NGOs), governments, indigenous peoples, and activist groups call for respect for the environmental commons and an environmental ethic of sustainable development. They advocate immediate changes in consumption patterns and the adoption of alternative clean-energy sources, such as wind and solar power and hybrid and hydrogen-fueled cars. These stakeholders want voluntary limits on the production of greenhouse gases through international controls like the **Kyoto Protocol**. This global agreement, which went into effect in February 2005 and had been signed and ratified by 192 states as of 2011, compelled thirty-five developed nations, by 2008–2012, to reduce their greenhouse gas emissions by 5.2 percent compared to 1990. In late 2011, 200 delegates from the United Nations met in Durban, South Africa, to discuss a second commitment period spanning 2013 to 2017. The European Union has vowed to extend its commitment, but Russia and Japan have declared that they would not adopt the new targets. The United States has never ratified the protocol; Canada withdrew from the agreement; and China and India, particularly, resent restrictions on their economic development while they see little change in the practices of countries like the United States. Though the conference closed with a commitment to develop a new agreement by 2015 to take effect in 2020, and a Green Climate Fund was established to assist developing nations with adapting to climate change and converting to clean energies, many feel it simply postponed the attempt to achieve an equal binding agreement on reducing carbon emissions. Meanwhile, many worried environmentalists are calling for radical changes and reductions in emissions, beyond 50 percent and even 70 percent over the next few years to return to preindustrial levels of greenhouse gas emissions.

In contrast, some economists, corporate leaders, and politicians claim that major shifts in energy use would be too economically disruptive and damaging. They characterize concerns about climate change as abstractions or luxuries that we cannot afford to indulge when energy and jobs are needed right now and consumers, hit by the economic crisis, cannot pay more for energy.

What Is the Role of Economics and the Market in Managing Environmental Resources?   Renowned environmentalist, author, and entrepreneur Paul Hawken poses the question, "How did we create an economic system that tells us it is cheaper to destroy the earth and waste certain people?" and he argues that sustainably caring for the environment, all living things, and all people is the only way to ensure there will be a world for markets to operate in.* Environment and social justice advocates object

---

*Kristi Heim, "The Compelling Case for Action," *Pacific Northwest* (January 3, 2010): 11.

that free trade agreements and institutions like the World Trade Organization, the World Bank, and the International Monetary Fund grant corporations the freedom to act without accountability, promote the privatization of resources, and enable corporations to override national governments' efforts to protect resources. The biggest water corporations, Vivendi Environment and Suez-Lyonnaise des Eaux, hold water interests in 120 countries. Vandana Shiva, an Indian physicist and environmental and political activist, claims that big corporations in India can easily take advantage of the scarcity of environmental resources: ". . . water markets will take the water from the poor to the rich, from impoverished rural areas to affluent urban enclaves. It will also lead to overexploitation of water, because when access to water is determined by the market and not by limits of renewability, the water cycle will be systematically violated and the water crisis will deepen."* Arguing that these resources are the commons belonging to everyone, environmental advocates insist that governments should regulate and protect these resources for the public interest and that access to safe water should be declared a human right so that water cannot be sold for profit.

Economic questions also drive recent conflicts over energy, including short-term versus long-term gains; what benefits businesses; what benefits the economy overall, including jobs; and what preserves the environment for the future and for everyone. These conflicts are playing out in the public and political debates over the building of the Keystone XL Pipeline from Canada to the Gulf of Mexico across the Great Plains states; the new hydraulic process called **fracking** for extracting natural gas and shale oil by fracturing the underground shale fields; and the renewed agitation over closing down nuclear power plants or building new ones. These controversies turn on questions of priorities, regulation, and safety for the public and the environment. Some self-termed "realists" maintain that alternative energy is not ready for widespread adoption and argue for more technological means to tap existing energy sources such as the remaining deposits of oil. Some people argue that we should embrace existing "cleaner" (compared to coal) forms of nonrenewable fuels, such as the 100-year supply of natural gas that fracking makes available, or the small quantity of nuclear fuel required to produce a large amount of energy. However, environmentalists, political cautionaries, citizens, and analysts point to the BP Gulf Oil Spill of 2010; the nuclear reactor disaster in Fukushima, Japan, after the March 2011 earthquake and tsunami; the recent earthquakes and incidents of contaminated groundwater in fracking areas in Ohio, Oklahoma, Colorado, Texas, and Pennsylvania; and the potential for widespread pollution of the Ogallala Aquifer from leaks in the Keystone XL Pipeline. As these opponents point out, both the contamination of freshwater supplies and

---

*Vandana Shiva, "World Bank, WTO, and Corporate Control over Water," *International Socialist Review* (August–September 2001).

the increasing contribution of carbon emissions to air quality and climate change are involved, and therefore, these market strategies need at minimum more stringent regulations.

In contrast, many corporate leaders and economists think that *more* market involvement in natural resources will foster good stewardship. They claim that government subsidies encourage waste and that the task of managing environmental resources is so huge and expensive that only capital-rich companies can take on the job. Between 2003 and 2010 for instance, the Chicago Climate Exchange allowed more than 400 member organizations (including corporations, states and municipalities, and educational institutions) to purchase carbon credits. Farmers and landowners could then earn income by storing carbon in their soil, thereby offsetting members.[*] Encouraging the positive role of the market, Thomas L. Friedman, in his book *Hot, Flat, and Crowded* (2008), argues that the U.S. government and U.S. corporations should take the initiative to develop alternative energy to lead to greater economic security and a greener world.[†]

In the absence of a clear governmental policy for environmental protection, some businesses have decided that embracing limits on their own is shrewd. Anticipating the need to meet European Union emissions standards, companies such as Dupont, IBM, General Electric, United Technologies, Baxter International, and International Paper are embracing the Kyoto restrictions on their own. Some American companies, along with EU and Chinese companies, are using these restrictions to spur innovation with low-carbon technologies and clean energy.

What International Organizations Should Regulate Conflicts Between Nations over Natural Resources and Encourage Global Cooperation in Establishing Sustainable Practices? In the 1970s, when scientists began to understand that most environmental problems are global and interrelated (for example, weather patterns, rainfall, and growing seasons), the need for global institutions to tackle these problems became apparent. Conflicts over resources can be politically destabilizing, weakening poor countries and making them vulnerable to terrorists and dangerous political forces; indeed, environmental problems are security problems requiring global solutions. Still, people disagree about how to measure sustainability and what goals and timetables to establish.

Nations are also realizing that dependence on foreign countries for natural resources can lead to political instability. To prevent takeover by multinational companies and to ensure that domestic businesses stay

---

[*]"Chicago Climate Exchange," *IntercontinentalExchange* (2011), accessed January 10, 2012.
[†]Thomas L. Friedman, *Hot, Flat, and Crowded: Why We Need a Green Revolution—and How It Can Renew America* (New York: Farrar, Straus, and Giroux, 2008).

competitive with foreign businesses, many analysts, policymakers, and businesses are calling for strong, clear national water and energy policies.

In particular, many developing nations are turning to the United Nations and its various programs and agencies to help them protect the environmental rights of their people. By designating water a human right, the United Nations could further encourage global cooperation and help ward off water wars. Because approximately 260 rivers flow through two or more countries and numerous bodies of water are bounded by multiple countries, intergovernmental organizations are needed to regulate the rights to and use of this water. Advocates of global cooperation are arguing that countries should have legal recourse when they suffer from climate change damages and water exploitation. For example, developing countries should be able to seek reparations from multinationals in world courts; perhaps the International Court of Justice should mandate that rich polluting countries pay poorer developing countries for damages to their environment. Finally, many NGOs and policymakers are calling for global strategies for water conservation, reclamation, and efficiency and for equitable, sustainable environmental practices to prepare for the world's population growth.

What Can Technology Contribute to Encouraging Sustainability and to Solving Problems with Environmental Resources? Some more radical ecologists (deep ecologists) would argue that humans have created environmental problems by interfering with nature and that more technology represents more interference. Some ecofeminists like Vandana Shiva argue that we must consider power relationships: Who owns the technology? Who decides how it will be used? Will it harm nature? Many environmentalists would say that wise investment in technology—for example, to find renewable energy alternatives—should supplement a drastic reprogramming of our habits. Some environmentalists call for completely new designs for energy systems, cars, insulation, lighting, household appliances, and water systems. Many corporate leaders believe in technology and have embraced environmental problems as incentives and business opportunities. They cite the improvement in car fuel economy from 1977 through 1985, the advances in energy-efficient refrigerators and air conditioners, and the current work with desalination of water. And on the far protechnology extreme, some people assume that technology will be able to solve our environmental problems, remedy all our mistakes, and renew the environment; therefore, they see no need for new habits of consumption or energy use.

Thinking Visually

Water Use

Megaresorts—hotel-casinos of around 4,000 rooms with names like Mandalay Bay, Excalibur, Caesar's Palace, and the Mirage—feature blazing lights and lavish water displays in Las Vegas, Nevada, a desert city with an

© June Johnson

The Bellagio's Dancing Fountains in Las Vegas, Nevada

average of four inches of rain a year. Although Las Vegas has converted to xeriscaping (low-water landscaping with desert ground material) and water recycling and wastewater treatment, the eight-acre lake and choreographed fountains of the Bellagio, shown in the photo, raise questions about decorative water use when the Colorado River and Lake Mead, the water's source, are low from drought years and overuse. Yet Las Vegas resorts have money to pay top water rates to support the illusion of escaping reality.

Questions to Ponder

1. How would you use this photo rhetorically to promote tourism in Las Vegas? Alternatively, how might environmentalists use this image rhetorically to advocate for water conservation or rethinking water policy?

2. Given the facts about water you've learned in this chapter, what questions about water policy at the city, state, national, and international levels does this photo inspire you to raise and investigate?

The three sections that follow—Student Voice, International Voices, and Global Hot Spot—take you deeper into the network of environmental issues connected to water resources, competing energy technologies, and climate change.

STUDENT VOICE: Changing Lives with Water
by Malia Burns-Rozycki

For some Americans like Malia Burns-Rozycki, experiencing the great
need for water elsewhere in the world—in this case, in rural Benin, West
Africa—has led to a deeper awareness of how Americans take water for
granted.

> The dash board read 43 degrees Centigrade. Reaching for my
> second bottle of water I calculated the temperature to be around
> 110 Fahrenheit. It was almost unbearable, even inside the air-
> conditioned SUV. It was during times like these that I questioned
> what I was doing in Benin, West Africa. Why hadn't I found an
> internship in Washington DC like all my other friends? And yet
> here I was, camera in hand, bumping over winding dirt roads,
> miles from the nearest flushing toilet.
>
> Stepping out of the car, I was blasted in the face by the heat. The
> sun seared the barren landscape, preventing grass from growing. A
> few brave trees seemed to stand in defiance of the elements saying
> "look at me, I can survive the heat." I was amazed at how flat and
> monochromatic everything was. Even the huts in the village were
> made out of red dirt, making them disappear into the horizon.
>
> Fifty people were gazing intently at a large piece of machinery.
> I cannot imagine what this kind of technology would have looked
> like to a community where not one person owns a car, women
> walk miles to sell their goods at market, and few speak the national
> language. For a brief moment all villagers had put down their work
> to witness this momentous event, the drilling of a community well.
>
> The project coordinator explained to me that the nearest well
> was in the next village, more than two hours on foot, I estimated.
> Each morning women from the village set out with large metal
> bowls on their heads, returning in time to prepare the morning
> meal. Four hours a day are spent on this commute. Village life is
> not easy. Indicators can be seen everywhere, on the weathered
> faces, in the tired eyes, the muscular arms. A little girl who barely
> reached my hip carried an infant on her back and twigs on her
> head, proving that literally everyone who was capable worked.
>
> I wondered how Catholic Relief Services even found this village,
> when so many of these northern communities need water. In Benin
> only 23 percent of the population has access to improved sanitation
> and only 63 percent have sustainable access to an improved water
> source. Catholic Relief Services funded the drilling as part of its
> education program, conceptualizing water as a prerequisite for formal
> education. The village is in no way unique; it is one of many that need
> water, though I never found out why this one had been chosen.

The drilling had already been going for a few hours and the drillers were not yet pleased with their soil samples; they were still too dry. Yet with their superior technology and expertise, they had no doubt that water would soon be reached.

It wasn't until I got home and looked at the photos that I really understood. Looking through the lens I missed the magic of the moment, the marvel on their faces, and the true importance of what was taking place. I am constantly humbled by how much I take for granted. The showers, the laundry, the dishes—all the water—this valuable resource goes down the drain without a second thought. And yet this hole in the ground will fundamentally alter the way of life in the village. For most of the women there will be more hours in the day. The crops will have a much larger chance of survival during the two dry seasons. Hygiene could improve dramatically if people are able to wash their hands after they use the latrine. Sanitation in food preparation can prevent the spread of illness-causing bacteria. Life will change because the village now has water.

INTERNATIONAL VOICES

The disparity between developed and developing countries' access to safe water is pronounced: "The average American uses 90 gallons of water a day, says the EPA. A European uses only 53 gallons; a sub-Saharan African, 5 gallons."[*] Recognizing these disparities and the centrality of water in sustaining and improving life, the United Nations General Assembly in 2003 declared that 2005–2015 would be the International Decade for Action, "Water for Life," and it targeted Africa as a special focus. The **Millennium Development Goals** for water include halving the "proportion of people without access to safe drinking water," halting "unsustainable exploitation of water resources," and creating "integrated water resource management and efficiency plans."[†] Africa, which has some 288 million people without access to safe drinking water and 36 percent of the population without access to basic sanitation,[‡] is particularly in need of water. However, Africans' problems with water are entangled in complex economic,

---

[*]Micah Morrison, "Will We Run Dry?" *Parade*, August 24, 2005, 4.
[†]"International Decade for Action: Water for Life, 2005–2015," www.un.org/ waterforlifedecade/.
[‡]Inter Press Service, "PanAfrica; Water, Water Everywhere . . . ," *Africa News* (August 23, 2005). "The eight Millennium Development Goals include a 50 percent reduction in poverty and hunger; universal primary education; reduction of child mortality by two-thirds; cutbacks in maternal mortality by three-quarters; the promotion of gender equality; the reversal of the spread of HIV/AIDS, malaria, and other diseases; environmental sustainability, including access to safe drinking water; and a North-South global partnership for development."

political, and environmental conditions as shown in the news story "Swaziland: Coping with Diminishing Water Resources" from *Africa News*, March 22, 2005. (Swaziland is a tiny country surrounded by South Africa and Mozambique.)

Comments from Water Authorities in Swaziland

Rivers that were once perennial have now begun to run dry during the winter months, from June to September, when little or no rain falls. Dams throughout the country were below their usual level for this time of year. The largest of these, the Maguga dam in the mountainous northern Hhohho region, a joint venture between Swaziland and South Africa, had not reached even half its capacity since it opened two years ago.

Melvin Mayisela, senior water engineer in the rural water supply department, said, "We encourage communities to use boreholes and streams instead of rivers—if a river is used, it would mean qualified technicians would have to monitor the project to ensure a safe water supply."

He recently denied the residents of rural Hosea community permission to use water from the Ngwavuma river in southern Swaziland, due to its high level of toxic pollutants. River pollution is a lethal byproduct of Swaziland's push for industrialization, and has further compromised the nation's water supply.

GLOBAL HOT SPOT: Africa

African countries are engaged in numerous strategies to solve their water problems. These countries are seeking both big solutions involving large investments of foreign capital and technological equipment and small, community-based solutions that nurture independence and sustainable development. In the following excerpt from the news article "PanAfrica: Water, Water Everywhere . . . " from the August 23, 2005, issue of *Africa News*, South Africa's minister of water affairs and forestry gives a big-picture sketch of Africa's water problems and reaches toward solutions.

"In spite of a few large rivers like the Congo and the Nile, twenty-one of the world's most arid countries, in terms of water per person, are located in Africa," South Africa's minister of Water Affairs and Forestry told a symposium marking "World Water Week" in the Swedish capital.

The Nile and its tributaries flow through nine countries: Egypt, Uganda, Sudan, Ethiopia, Democratic Republic of Congo (DRC), Kenya, Tanzania, Rwanda, and Burundi. The Congo, the world's fifth longest river, flows primarily through DRC, People's Republic of Congo, Central African Republic, and partially through Zambia, Angola, Cameroon, and Tanzania.

Addressing over 1,400 water experts and representatives of nongovernmental organizations, Buyelwa Sonjica said that in arid and semi-arid countries, rivers only flow for short periods in the rainy season, "and you need dams to store water for dry periods."

"The need for water resource infrastructure in Africa is clear. The same arguments are also applicable to many countries in the developing world," she added.

But she warned that the construction of dams should be conditioned on two factors: first, people affected or displaced by a dam should be guaranteed benefits of some nature—"and they should also be better off after the construction of the dam than they were before." Secondly, she said, the impacts on aquatic and terrestrial ecosystems should be mitigated. . . .

As you read the articles in this chapter, think about the interconnection of environmental, political, and economic issues, and note how assumptions about the environment, science, and technology operate in these arguments' interpretations of problems and proposed solutions.

READINGS

Address to the UN General Assembly on Need to Conserve Water

Maude Barlow

Maude Barlow is the national chair of the Council of Canadians and has served as senior adviser on water to the president of the United Nations General Assembly. She also founded the Blue Planet Project, chairs the board of Washington-based Food and Water Watch, and is a Councillor with the Hamburg-based World Future Council. Her books include *Blue Covenant: The Global Water Crisis and the Coming Battle for the Right to Water* (2007), and (with Tony Clarke) *Blue Gold: The Battle Against Corporate Theft of the World's Water* (2002), which has been published in seventeen languages and over fifty countries. Barlow gave this speech to the General Assembly of the United Nations on April 22 (Earth Day), 2009.

How does Maude Barlow ask her audience to reframe the way humans regard and use water?

It is a great honour to share this wonderful day with such distinguished panellists and to be present at the founding of Mother Earth Day, now officially recognized by the UN General Assembly.

I want to take these few moments to speak about the urgency of the global water crisis and the need for more concerted action on the part of the global community. Recently, the findings of the 3rd United Nations World Water Development Report alarmed the world. This report and others tell us the frightening story that, in spite of the excellent work being done by many UN agencies and the progress made in some parts of the world in reaching the MDGs with respect to water, the fact is that the crisis is galloping ahead of the solution and our collective attempts to solve it.

Simply put, the global water crisis now threatens billions around the world and the ecology of the earth itself. It is my strong contention that there is only one body in the world capable of rising to this challenge and it is the General Assembly of the United Nations. It is time for the General Assembly to adopt an agreement to tackle this urgent issue and work toward a sustainable plan for action. I would argue that it is important to be guided by a set of principles as we set out on this journey and I would argue they be the following:

1) Water as a Commons

One of the fiercest disputes in the world is who gets to make allocation decisions over the world's dwindling water supply. Is water a commodity to be put on the open market for sale like running shoes or Coca Cola or is it part of the heritage of all humans and other species to be protected as a commons for the future? Who will determine who has access, a locally elected council or the CEO of a transnational corporation in another country? Will we allow the creation of "water banks" where water is traded on the open market to those who can pay? Who will protect the needs of those who cannot?

I strongly believe that water is a commons and a public trust that must be declared to belong to the citizens of every community and to the ecosystem and the future. While both the public and private sectors can access water, no one owns it; rather it belongs to all. This does not mean that water access should be a free-for-all. We need to have highly managed water systems that protect water at every stage of use based on a set of priorities. Nor does it mean that there is no commercial dimension to water. Clearly water is used in the production of everything from food to cars. However, the private sector should not be able to determine the allocation of water; that is the role of government and local communities. If water is seen as a market commodity, those who can pay will have preferential access and nature will be further plundered for its declining water supplies.

Water belongs to all living beings and is part of our global heritage. Surely this must form a core message on Mother Earth Day.

2) Equitable Access to Water

The second practical principle is that everyone has the right to clean safe water regardless of ability to pay. The answer to the current inequitable access to water is water justice, not charity. Millions of people live in countries that cannot provide clean water to their citizens as they are burdened by their debt to the global North. At least 62 countries need deep debt relief if the daily deaths of thousands of children are to end. As a result, poor countries are forced to exploit both their people and their resources, like water, to pay their debt. As well, foreign aid in many northern countries falls far below the recommended .7 percent of GDP.

To deal with the water crisis in the South, we must cancel or deeply cut the debt, substantively increase foreign aid, fund public services, and invest in water reclamation programs to protect source water. UNDP estimates that it would cost less that $14 billion to meet the Millennium Development Goals on water and sanitation, a pittance compared to the recent bank and industry bailouts that have been announced in many wealthy countries. We should also promote a tax on financial speculation; even a modest tax could pay for every public hospital, school and water utility in the global South. And we must challenge the devotion of so many leaders to unlimited growth, which has left countless millions in its wake. We need to create a whole new set of rules for global trade based on sustainability, cooperation, environmental stewardship and fair labour standards.

The equitable access to water should also be enshrined once and for all in a United Nations covenant and in nation-state constitutions. A United Nations right to water covenant would set the framework for water as a social and cultural asset and would establish the indispensable legal groundwork for a just system of distribution. It would serve as a common, coherent body of rules for all nations and clarify the right to clean, affordable water for all, regardless of income. A UN right to water covenant would establish once and for all that no one *anywhere* should be allowed to die or forced to watch a beloved child die from dirty water simply because they are poor.

3) Watershed Restoration

Finally, watersheds must be protected from plunder and we must revitalize wounded water systems with widespread watershed restoration programs. Simply put, we must leave enough water in aquifers, rivers and lakes for their ecological health. This must be the priority: the precautionary principle of ecosystem protection must take precedence over commercial demands on these waters. This means that we will have to abandon the "hard path" of large-scale technology—dams, diversion and desalination—in favour of the "soft path" of conservation, rainwater and storm water harvesting, recycling, alternative energy use, municipal infrastructure investment and local, sustainable food production. Living in and with nature instead of over nature is our path to a water sustainable future.

As a crucial next step, nature must be seen as having inherent rights beyond its use to us. Most Western law has viewed natural resources as the property of humans. We need new laws to regulate human behaviour in order to protect the integrity of the Earth and all species on it from our wanton exploitation. Rivers have rights to flow to the sea.

We, none of us, can live on a dry planet. Let us celebrate moving waters on this first United Nations International Mother Earth Day.

For Class Discussion

1. In this proposal argument, what is Barlow asking the United Nations to do? What is the main reasoning in her proposal?

2. How does she establish the urgency of the issue? What are the stakes? What types of evidence does Barlow provide to convince her audience and us of the global water crisis?

3. What oppositional viewpoints is Barlow responding to in her argument?

4. Explain in your own words what Barlow means by the "inherent rights" of nature. How would recognizing these rights change people's attitudes toward water and water management policies? What values do you have to hold to accept Barlow's views?

5. Thinking of your own region of the country, to what extent is "large-scale technology" involved in water management versus the "'soft path' of conservation"? How could you find out more about water issues in your area? You might begin with your state's Department of Ecology or Department of Natural Resources, your city's water department, or the Environmental Protection Agency (www.epa.gov).

Droughtbusters
Anita Hamilton

Anita Hamilton is a contributor for *TIME* magazine and its Web site, (www.time
.com), covering technology, business, and lifestyle topics. She has also written
for *PC World* and *Time Out New York* and was a founding editor of the technology news site *CNET*. This policy proposal was printed in the October 3, 2011,
edition of *TIME*, a general-interest weekly news magazine.

> As a journalist writing for a general audience, how does Anita Hamilton
> establish reader interest in her topic?

THE WORLD IS GETTING THIRSTIER. FIVE WAYS WE CAN KEEP FROM GOING DRY

Record droughts have parched the earth's crust from Somalia to Texas
this year. The effects on the world's drinking-water supply have been
enormous. The level of China's Yangtze River, the third largest in the
world, sank so low this spring that about 400,000 people along its
shores were stuck without a local drinking-water source until the government opened the gates of its massive Three Gorges dam to help
counteract the crisis. In East Africa, some 10 million people have been
punished by the region's worst drought in 60 years. And in Texas,
where wildfires scorched 4 million acres (1.6 million hectares) this
summer, the financial losses from starving cattle and blighted crops
have reached $5 billion.

Things will likely get worse. According to a new report from
McKinsey, by 2030, global water supplies will meet just 60% of the
total demand. Meanwhile, we'll spend an estimated $50 billion to $60
billion per year trying to bridge that gap. But while water scarcity is
real, it's not happening because we have any less than we did a century
ago. "We have the same amount of water," says James Famiglietti, a
professor of earth-system science and civil engineering at the University
of California at Irvine. But we have 250% more people drinking it.
What's more, climate change means that water is "moving around to
different places, even as populations are growing," notes Famiglietti.
The result is not only a shortage but also a mismatch between where
water is and where it's needed.

In the past, we beat water shortages by drilling for groundwater,
building dams and erecting massive pipelines. But the enormousness of
the problem today demands radical solutions that promote conservation
as well as boost supply. "One of the reasons we have been so wasteful in
the past is because it has been so easy to find another source of water,"
says Peter Gleick of the Pacific Institute. "But those days are over."

Novel ideas abound. In the Punjab region of India, for example, 6,500 rice and wheat farmers are testing out a $7 device called a tensiometer that analyzes ground moisture in order to prevent overwatering crops. In 2010, farmers using the tensiometer cut their water use by 22%. The trial, sponsored by PepsiCo and Columbia Water Center, will expand to some 50,000 farmers by 2012. Since agriculture accounts for 70% of global water consumption, a large-scale rollout of such devices could create massive savings.

While no single solution makes sense everywhere because of differences in climate, geography and local politics, a few are gaining traction. The best strategy often involves combining several tactics. Here are five smart ways that communities around the globe are fighting back against water scarcity:

1   Tackling the toilet-to-tap taboo / Windhoek, Namibia

The idea of drinking water that was once in your toilet bowl may seem like a bad joke, but it's not. Stripped of its impurities and rigorously tested to ensure its safety, reclaimed water is one of the most inexpensive and reliable supplies of water on earth. "This is where we have to use our rational brains to overcome our natural aversion," says Alex Prud'homme, author of The Ripple Effect. In Namibia, the driest country south of the Sahara, such recycled water accounts for 35% of the drinking supply in the country's capital city of Windhoek.

Located some 5,000 ft. (1,500 m) above sea level and surrounded by mountains, Windhoek receives a paltry amount of precipitation— just 14 in. (36 cm) a year on average—which quickly evaporates in the region's hot, windy clime. Although Namibia sits on the western Atlantic, Windhoek is too high for desalination to be feasible and too far from big rivers to the north and south to build expensive pipelines to them. So this fast-growing city first turned to wastewater processing in 1968 when local reservoirs began running dry. Upgraded in 2002, the New Goreangab Water Reclamation Plant, which cost about $16 million to build, now delivers 2 billion gal. (7.6 billion L) of water a year to the city's more than 300,000 residents, who use it for everything from drinking to bathing.

Forced through a series of sand and carbon filters as well as ultrafine membranes—some with pores less than one-hundredth the width of a human hair—before being chlorinated and tested for impurities, the treated water is then blended with freshwater piped in from a network of three different reservoirs in a 35%-to-65% ratio. The process is 37% cheaper than pumping in water from distant reservoirs, and the recycled wastewater costs the city less than two-tenths of a penny a gallon to treat.

The economics are persuading many to put aside their prejudices. In 2008, Orange County, California, began treating about 70 million gal. (265 million L) of sewage water that it then pours into its underground aquifers. Meanwhile, Zimbabwe's capital city of Harare will begin recycling some 21 million gal. (79 million L) of wastewater a day by 2014 for use as drinking water.

2 Success with seawater desalination / Perth, Australia

Most of our planet's surface is covered by oceans, so finding a way to turn our salty seas into something palatable is an obvious solution. Desalination, which typically involves using high pressure to force water through membranes that keep the brine behind, has become increasingly popular, with more than 15,000 desalination plants churning out about 17 billion gal. (64 billion L) of freshwater a day.

One place where desal makes sense is Perth (pop. 1.7 million), the largest city in Western Australia. With daytime watering bans firmly in place and most homeowners already collecting rainwater in backyard barrels to hydrate their gardens, Western Australia's capital city turned to desal in 2007 as a drought-proof insurance policy when water levels in dams dipped to less than a quarter of their maximum capacity.

Today, a third of Perth's 96 billion gal. (363 billion L) annual water supply comes from government-owned desalination plants in nearby Kwinana and Binningup. By the end of 2012, half the city's freshwater will come from the two plants, which will be powered by renewable-energy credits from wind and solar farms. Households will pay an extra $50 on top of their average annual bill of $700 to cover building and maintenance costs for the additional supply.

Desal is no cure-all. Even as the technology has taken off in much of Australia, Israel and the Persian Gulf, residents in some coastal communities in California, for example, are balking at the costs, which can be up to five times more than for wastewater recycling.

But new measures to reduce desalination's ecological impact, combined with smart thinking on how to lower the costs of powering the plants, are making desalination much easier to swallow. In July, Siemens announced that it had successfully tested a new desalination technique called electrodialysis that mimics the human kidney's electrochemical filtering process and uses less than half the power of traditional desalination methods.

3 Mandating rainwater harvesting / Bangalore, India

Water scarcity is a problem not just in desert climates. Even Bangalore, in southern India, which gets more than 38 in. (97 cm) of rain a year and is nicknamed the Garden City for its lush, hilly terrain, has been rationing tap water for its 9.5 million residents in recent years. The population has increased nearly 50% since 2001, thanks to an influx of workers to the city, the heart of India's Silicon Valley. Now half of Bangalore's 2,000 wells—which account for some 40% of the city's water supply—have gone dry, and running water is available only two to three hours a day. Shortages have become so bad that some people use bottled water for bathing or buy tanks of it from privately run trucks that drive around town when the city taps shut down.

In 2009, when Bangalore's water supply fell 25% below the estimated 112 billion gal. (424 billion L) needed each year, the city finally resorted to mandatory rainwater collection on both commercial and residential plots larger than 2,400 sq. ft. (223 sq m). In less than two years, half of the 60,000 households covered by the order began harvesting rainwater on their properties.

Those who have complied have done so without a government subsidy of any sort, even though a typical setup costs about $500. That rate of compliance can be attributed to government threats to cut off the water supply, a rather draconian stick. To ease the transition, the state has set up educational fairs, trained 1,300 plumbers and developed low-cost, compact filters to replace the larger, less effective sandpits used in other areas of the country. In addition, the city plans to offer a 2% property-tax rebate for those who comply by the end of the year. With the program expanding to smaller plots as well as all commercial and government buildings, A.R. Shivakumar, one of the program's architects, hopes that 40% of the city's water supply will come from rainwater harvesting within the next few years.

4   Incentivizing conservation / Albuquerque, New Mexico

Graced with an abundance of freshwater resources, Americans have long been the poster children for water gluttony, consuming an estimated 147 gal. (556 L) of water per person per day—several times more per person than their counterparts across the pond in England. But even water hogs can change their ways: Albuquerque (pop. 550,000), once one of the most wasteful cities in the U.S., has decreased its per capita water use 38%—from 251 gal. (950 L) to 175 gal. (662 L) per person per day—since 1995, in large part by handing out more than $14 million in rebates for everything from low-flow toilets to more climate-friendly landscaping.

With just 9 in. (23 cm) of rain per year on average, Albuquerque, the largest city in New Mexico, had long gulped down massive amounts of water for outdoor landscaping. As recently as the 1980s, lawns were actually required for residential plots, despite that fact that the city is located on the northern edge of the Chihuahuan Desert.

But since 1996, Albuquerque's water authority has been paying residents 75¢ per square foot (7¢/sq m) to rip out their thirsty lawns and replace them with native plants that need little water to thrive. To date, some 6 million sq. ft. (557,000 sq m) of turf has been replaced with agave plants, Joshua trees, hyacinths and other desert-appropriate vegetation in a style known as xeriscaping, which has taken off everywhere from Las Vegas to San Antonio.

To get consumers to cut back indoors, Albuquerque has instituted another set of rebates, including $200 off the price of low-flow toilets, $75 for waterless urinals, and $100 off high-efficiency washing machines. The city even pays residents $20 each to attend classes on conservation. "The most effective thing we do is educate our customers," says Albuquerque's water-conservation manager, Katherine Yuhas.

Fines and rate hikes play a key role in that education. Since 1995 the city has brought in $1 million in fines, which are levied on homeowners who let water run off their property or turn on sprinklers between 11 a.m. and 7 p.m. from April to October. A new rate hike set to kick in next year will increase residential customers' bills by about $3 a month, for a total price increase of 154% since 1995. That may sound extreme, but some think the price of water should be even higher. "If you compare the price of water with the price of gasoline, it is grossly underpriced," notes Upmanu Lall, director of Columbia Water Center.

The city's mostly gentle nudging has paid off. Since 1994, Albuquerque has saved more than 100 billion gal. (380 billion L) of water. That's a three-year supply.

5 Closing the water loop / Singapore

The world leader in water conservation is arguably the tiny island nation of Singapore. Smaller than New York City and packed with some 6 million residents, this economic powerhouse located just north of the equator gets plenty of rain but has little room to store it. Its densely populated terrain and sandy soil don't hold groundwater. As a result, Singapore has had to import up to 40% of the 380 million gal. (1.4 billion L) of water it uses each day from neighboring Malaysia, from which it gained political independence in 1965.

To achieve its goal of water independence before 2061, when its contract with Malaysia expires, Singapore has moved fast to exploit new technologies, promote conservation and ensure that every drop of water used is also recycled.

The Singapore solution has four main "faucets." First, 17 reservoirs, many of which were created by damming rivers, collect the nation's 100 in. (254 cm) of annual rainfall. Second, all rain that flows into the city sewers gets recycled as drinking water. Third, the county desalinates water from the surrounding seas to supply another 10% of its drinking water. Most impressive, however, is Singapore's $3 billion wastewater-recycling system, which channels all water from toilets and other household uses into a 30-mile (48 km) underground tunnel, then sends it out to four water-recycling plants that use reverse osmosis and ultraviolet light for purification. This water is not reused for drinking but instead gets piped to the island's silicon-wafer plants for use in their water-intensive manufacturing process. The recycled water is also used to cool commercial air-conditioning systems in the country's many high-rise buildings.

The government's tiered pricing structure penalizes those who use too much water. Use of dual-flush toilets (which vary the amount of water per flush for liquid or solid waste) and other efficient appliances is strongly encouraged.

"They've become the world's ultimate water conservationists," notes Cynthia Barnett, author of Blue Revolution, a new book on water scarcity. In 2010, Singaporeans used just 41 gal. (155 L) of water per person per day—a fraction of that consumed by Americans—all while enjoying one of the highest standards of living on earth. Even the city's many reservoirs double as water parks, where boating and other aquatic sports can be enjoyed by all. It's real-world proof that conservation doesn't have to mean deprivation.

For Class Discussion

1. How could you restate Hamilton's implicit core argument more explicitly for policymakers?

2. How do Hamilton's examples illustrate that water shortages are a global problem that will require global solutions? What does she suggest about the role of technology and business in the conservation and management of environmental resources?

3. What language does Hamilton use to appeal to the casual reader who might pick up a copy of *TIME* or encounter her work on the Web site?

4. How does Hamilton acknowledge the limitations of the various strategies proposed in this argument?

5. Hamilton's argument frequently employs numerical data to illustrate its points. If you were to create a visual argument using data from this article, what numbers would you choose to represent and what format would be most effective?

Water for Life
Sandra Postel

Sandra Postel directs the Global Water Policy Project, which "fosters ideas and inspiration for redirecting society's use and management of freshwater toward conservation and ecosystem health" (www.globalwaterpolicy.org). She is also the Freshwater Fellow of the National Geographic Society, serving as the lead water expert for its Freshwater Initiative. Postel's books include *Last Oasis: Facing Water Scarcity* (1993), *Rivers for Life: Managing Water for People and Nature* (coauthored with Brian Richter [2003]), and *Liquid Assets: The Critical Need to Safeguard Freshwater Ecosystems* (2005). This piece appeared as a guest editorial in *Frontiers in Ecology and the Environment* for March 2009. This is a scholarly journal with wide, interdisciplinary appeal.

> How does Sandra Postel indicate her desire to reach a wider audience than environmentalists?

Now for the million-dollar questions: Why has so much of modern water management gone awry? Why is it that ever greater amounts of money and ever more sophisticated engineering have not solved the world's water problems? Why, in so many places on this planet, are rivers drying up, lakes shrinking, and water tables falling?

The answer, in part, is simple: We have been trying to meet insatiable demands by continuously expanding a finite water supply. In the long run, of course, that is a losing proposition: It is impossible to expand a finite supply indefinitely, and in many parts of the world the "long run" has arrived.

For sure, measures to conserve, recycle, and more efficiently use water have enabled many places to contain their water demands and to avoid or at least delay an ecological reckoning. Such tried-and-true measures as thrifty irrigation techniques, water-saving plumbing fixtures, native landscaping, and wastewater recycling can cost-effectively reduce the amount of water required to grow food, produce material goods, and meet household needs. The conservation potential of these measures has barely been tapped.

Yet something is missing from this prescription, something less tangible than drip irrigation lines and low-flow showerheads, but, in the final analysis, more important. It has to do with modern society's disconnection from nature's web of life and from water's most fundamental role as the basis of that life. In our technologically sophisticated world, we no longer grasp the need for the wild river, the blackwater swamp, or even the diversity of species collectively performing nature's work. By and large, society views water in a utilitarian fashion—as a "resource" valued only when it is extracted from nature and put to use on a farm, in a factory, or in a home.

Overall, we have been quick to assume rights to use water but slow to recognize obligations to preserve and protect it. Better pricing and more open markets will assign water a higher value in its economic functions, and breed healthy competition that weeds out wasteful and unproductive uses. But this will not solve the deeper problem. What is needed is a set of guidelines and principles that stops us from chipping away at natural systems until nothing is left of their life-sustaining functions, which the marketplace fails to value adequately, if at all. In short, we need a water ethic—a guide to right conduct in the face of complex decisions about natural systems that we do not and cannot fully understand.

The essence of such an ethic is to make the protection of freshwater ecosystems a central goal in all that we do. This may sound idealistic, yet it is no more radical a notion than suggesting that a building be given a solid foundation before adding 30 stories to it. Water is the foundation of every human enterprise, and if that foundation is insecure, everything built upon it will be insecure, too. As such, our stewardship of water will determine not only the quality but the staying power of human societies.

The adoption of such a water ethic would represent a historic shift away from the strictly utilitarian approach to water management and toward an integrated, holistic approach that views people and water as interconnected parts of a greater whole. Instead of asking how we can further control and manipulate rivers, lakes, and streams to meet our ever-growing demands, we would ask instead how we can best satisfy human needs while accommodating the ecological requirements of freshwater ecosystems. It would lead us, as well, to deeper questions of human values, in particular how to narrow the wide gap between the haves and have-nots within a healthy ecosystem.

Embedded within this water ethic is a fundamental question: Do rivers and the life within them have a right to water? In his famous essay, "Should Trees Have Standing? Toward Legal Rights for Natural Objects," legal scholar Christopher D. Stone argued more than 35 years ago that yes, rivers and trees and other objects of nature do have rights, and these should be protected by granting legal standing to guardians of the voiceless entities of nature, much as the rights of children are protected by legal guardians. Stone's arguments struck a chord with U.S. Supreme Court Justice William O. Douglas, who wrote in a famous dissent in the 1972 case Sierra Club v. Morton that "contemporary public concern for protecting nature's ecological equilibrium should lead to the conferral of standing upon environmental objects to sue for their own preservation. . . . The river, for example, is the living symbol of all the life it sustains or nourishes—the fish, aquatic insects, water ouzels, otter, fisher, deer, elk, bear, and all other animals, including man, who are dependent on it or who enjoy it for its sight, its sound, or its life. The river as plaintiff speaks for the ecological unit of life that is part of it."

During the next three decades, U.S. courts heard cases brought by environmental groups and other legal entities on behalf of nature and its constituents. In water allocation, concepts such as "instream flow rights" began to take hold, although these rights often received too low a priority to offer meaningful protection of river health.

With freshwater life being extinguished at record rates, a more fundamental change is needed. An ethical society can no longer ignore the fact that water-management decisions have life-or-death consequences for other species. An ethically grounded water policy must begin with the premise that all people and all living things should be given access to enough water to secure their survival before some get more than enough.

On paper, at least one government has grounded its water policy in precisely such an ethic. South Africa's 1998 water law establishes a water reserve consisting of two parts. The first is a non-negotiable water allocation to meet the basic drinking, cooking, and sanitary needs of all South Africans. (When the African National Congress came to power, some 14 million poor South Africans lacked water for these basic needs.) The second part of the reserve is an allocation of water to support the long-term sustainability of the nation's aquatic and associated ecosystems. The water determined to constitute this two-part reserve has priority over licensed uses, such as irrigation, and only this water is guaranteed as a right.

At the core of South Africa's policy is an affirmation of the "public trust," a legal principle that traces back to the Roman Empire, that says governments hold certain rights and entitlements in trust for the people and are obliged to protect them for the common good. In addition to the public trust, another rule fast becoming essential for freshwater ecosystem protection is the "precautionary principle," which essentially says that given the rapid pace of ecosystem decline, the irreversible nature of many of the resulting losses, and the high value of freshwater ecosystems to human societies, it is wise to err on the side of protecting too much rather than too little of the remaining freshwater habitat.

The utilitarian code that continues to guide most water management may fit with prevailing market-based socioeconomic paradigms, but it is neither universal nor unchanging. The American conservationist Aldo Leopold viewed the extension of ethics to the natural environment as "an evolutionary possibility and an ecological necessity." More recently, Harvard biologist Edward O. Wilson noted in his book, *Consilience*, that ethical codes historically have arisen through the interplay of biology and culture. "Ethics, in the empiricist view," Wilson observes, "is conduct favored consistently enough throughout a society to be expressed as a code of principles."

In other words, ethics are not static; they evolve with social consciousness. But that evolution is not automatic. The extension of freedom to slaves and voting rights to women required leaders, movements, advocates, and activists that collectively pulled society onto higher moral ground. So it will be with the extension of rights to rivers, plants, fish, birds, and the ecosystems of which they are a part. As societies wrap their collective minds around the consequences of global environmental change—rising temperatures, prolonged droughts, chronic water shortages, disappearing species—it may well be that a new ethic will emerge, one that says it is not only right and good but necessary that all living things get enough water before some get more than enough. Because in the end, we're all in this together.

For Class Discussion

1. What does Postel's claim show that she is arguing against? Why does she object to the current dominant view of water management?

2. Postel relies heavily on numerical data to expose the weaknesses in the current economic models of water management and to support her reasoning in this argument. How might this data appeal to business-oriented readers? Which numerical facts did you find particularly persuasive?

3. How does she seek to recast the issue of water management?

4. Where does she acknowledge potential objections to her argument and respond to them?

5. How would you describe Postel's tone and approach in this argument, including the wording of the title? What does this editorial contribute to the global debates about water scarcity?

Health and Environment
United Nations Environment Programme

This poster is one of a series sponsored by the United Nations Environment Programme for an exhibition at the World Summit on Sustainable Development, held August 26–September 3, 2002, in Johannesburg, South Africa. The United Nations Environment Programme's mission is "to provide leadership and encourage partnership in caring for the environment by inspiring, informing, and enabling nations and peoples to improve their quality of life without compromising that of future generations" ("About UNEP," www.unep.org). The posters in this series have a dual educational and persuasive aim.

If you look only at the title of the poster, "Health and Environment," and the photo, what connections between environmental, economic, and social problems can you see? What background knowledge does it expect of its audience?

United Nations Environment Programme Poster (This poster has been reproduced by kind permission of the United Nations Environment Programme. This poster on "poverty and the environment" can be found at www.unep.org/wssd/Pictures/Posters/HEALTH.2.jpg.)

For Class Discussion

1. What are the impressions and ideas that this poster conveys?

2. In your own words, how would you state the main claim of this poster? What evidence does it offer in support of its claim?

3. What ideas about water, sanitation, and health does this poster convey?

4. What is the rhetorical effectiveness of using a photo of children? How does this poster appeal to the emotions and values of a global audience, especially people living in developed countries?

5. In what ways does this poster argue causes and consequences? In what way does it make a proposal and support it? How effective is it in communicating its argument?

The Most Important News Story of the Day/Millennium

Bill McKibben

Bill McKibben is a writer and environmental activist. Among his twelve books about the environment are *The End of Nature* (1989), the first book on climate change targeted at a general audience, *Deep Economy* (2007), and *Eaarth: Making a Life on a Tough New Planet* (2010). He is also a founder of the grassroots climate campaign site 350.org. In 2010, the *Boston Globe* called him "probably the country's most important environmentalist." First posted on the *Daily Kos,* a progressive community blog, this commentary was reposted December 5, 2011, on CommonDreams.org, a site that publishes "breaking news from a progressive perspective [and] the latest ideas, opinions, and in-depth analysis by some of the world's best progressive writers, thinkers, and activists."

> How would you describe Bill McKibben's tone in this blog posting and what does it contribute to the rhetorical effect?

The most important piece of news yesterday, this week, this month, and this year was a new set of statistics released yesterday by the Global Carbon Project. It showed that carbon emissions from our planet had increased 5.9 percent between 2009 and 2010. In fact, it was arguably among the most important pieces of data in the last, oh, three centuries, since according to the *New York Times* it represented "almost certainly the largest absolute jump in any year since the Industrial Revolution."

What it means, in climate terms, is that we've all but lost the battle to reduce the damage from global warming. The planet has already warmed about a degree Celsius; it's clearly going to go well past two degrees. It means, in political terms, that the fossil fuel industry has delayed effective action for the 12 years since the Kyoto treaty was signed. It means, in diplomatic terms, that the endless talks underway in Durban should be more important than ever—they should be the focus of a planetary population desperate to figure out how it's going to survive the century.

But instead, almost no one is paying attention to the proceedings, at least on this continent. One of our political parties has decided that global warming is a hoax—its two leading candidates are busily apologizing for anything they said in the past that might possibly have been construed as backing, you know, science. President Obama hasn't yet spoken on the Durban talks, and informed international observers like Joss Garman are beginning to despair that he ever will.

Who are the 99%? In this country, they're those of us who aren't making any of these deadly decisions. In this world, they're the vast majority of people who didn't contribute to those soaring emissions. In this biosphere they're every other species now living on a disorienting earth.

You think OWS is radical? You think 350.org was radical for helping organize mass civil disobedience in DC in August against the Keystone Pipeline? We're not radical. Radicals work for oil companies. The CEO of Exxon gets up every morning and goes to work changing the chemical composition of the atmosphere. No one has ever done anything as radical as that, not in all of human history. And he and his ilk spend heavily on campaigns to make sure no one stops them—the US Chamber of Commerce gave more money than the DNC and the RNC last cycle, and 94% of it went to climate deniers.

Corporate power has occupied the atmosphere. 2011 showed we could fight back. 2012 would be a good year to step up the pressure. Because this time next year the Global Carbon Project will release another number. And I'm betting it will be grim.

For Class Discussion

1. Given the references that McKibben makes, including to Occupy Wall Street (OWS), the Kyoto treaty, and the Keystone Pipeline, what assumptions can we make about his audience? What background information does he expect his readers to have, and what does this suggest about their shared values?

2. How does McKibben challenge our assumptions in his characterization of politicians, wealthy businesspeople, and members of the fossil fuel industry?

3. "The 99%," used by Occupy Wall Street to describe everyone but the wealthiest one percent of Americans (who tend to run corporations and governments), has become an emotionally and politically loaded term. How does McKibben's list of "the 99%" stakeholders play off of or extend the term's meaning?

4. What organizations or actions would you need to learn more about in order to assess McKibben's argument more fully? You might refer to the readings in this chapter by Dave Coles and Sarah Bean for information on the Keystone Pipeline, for instance.

5. How does McKibben's commentary provide context for the alternative energy readings in the rest of this chapter?

Stop the Keystone XL
Dave Coles

Dave Coles is president of the Communications, Energy, and Paperworkers Union of Canada (CEP), a union that represents 130,000 workers in Canada's forestry, energy, telecommunications, and media industries. As a labor and community activist, he helped found progressive national groups such as the Council of Canadians, the Canadian Centre for Policy Alternatives, and the Parkland Institute. This practical proposal appeared in the May/June 2011 issue of *Canadian Dimension*, which describes itself as "an independent forum for Left-wing political thought and discussion."

> How does Dave Coles characterize Canadian relations with the United States in this proposal?

The battle to stop the Keystone XL pipeline is being fought on three fronts: in defence of the environment, in defence of jobs, and in defence of Canada's energy security.

The 9,600-kilometre pipeline is designed to ferry black bitumen from the Canadian bitumen sands due south to planned refineries on the Gulf of Mexico.

So far, as more Canadians and Americans wake up to the environmental challenges of our oil economy, the bitumen sands carbon footprint is making most of the headlines. Clearly, Canada cannot make its 2020 greenhouse gas emission targets unless we have controlled bitumen sands growth and the XL pipeline at one million barrels per day is out of control.

But the project has other negative implications that are not getting the same exposure. For example, many Canadians remain blissfully unaware that despite having plenty of oil, our country could experience real shortages. Or that sending raw, unprocessed bitumen from Canada to spanking new oil refineries in the US is the equivalent of shipping millions of raw logs for others to cut the two-by-fours and create the wood furniture. Like forestry, the best jobs are in processing. We are left with the bitumen sands' massive mess.

The first Keystone, built by TransCanada Corp., cost Canada thousands of jobs. An analysis by the Informetrica think-tank demonstrated that besides exporting 400,000 barrels of heavy crude a day, it also shipped out 18,000 high-paying Canadian jobs. Twice the size of TransCanada's first Keystone is the new project, Keystone XL. It will shoot out 900,000 barrels of heavy crude in a one-way ride to the US. The number of jobs lost is expected to be more than double the 18,000 already gone.

Though the Conservative government has ignored our arguments that the export of raw bitumen also exported thousands of jobs to the US, last December Natural Resources Minister Christian Paradis, seeking their support for the project, told a conference of American businessmen that the pipeline would create 342,000 jobs in the US.

In our appeal of the National Energy Board decision to green light the project our union, the CEP, argued that it is in Canada's best interest to stop Keystone XL, keep the good jobs at home, and safeguard our energy needs. To do that we need to process the oil in Alberta, and points east, using various upgrader and refinery projects, out west and in Ontario. That means we need infrastructure to connect eastern Canada to western supply.

A pipeline located entirely in Canada would also restructure the way oil and gas are being delivered on this continent. Right now, oil travels thousands of kilometres south of the border, before it re-enters our country around Sarnia. So most of Canada remains vulnerable to off-shore oil supply disruptions. And we are virtually alone among oil producing nations in not having the means to supply our own needs. Canada is locked into a staggeringly lopsided deal with the US under NAFTA. Whatever volume of oil Canada ships south can never be cut back. No matter how desperate our needs might become, we are trumped by Brian Mulroney's gift that keeps on giving—to his American friends.

But despite our arguments, it came as no surprise when the board swept aside our case, and rubber-stamped the construction of Keystone XL. That's because there is a cozy connection between the oil lobby and the Conservative government. Many board members come straight from the energy sector and for the past several years, it has said yes to every major export pipeline project put before it.

The project is stalled right now only because the US State Department and the US Environmental Protection Agency seem to be listening to the environmental argument. US regulators have asked for a delay while they take a closer look at the project.

For Class Discussion

1. What is the central claim of Coles's argument? To whom is it addressed?

2. How does Coles develop his reasons in proposing an alternative to the Keystone XL Pipeline?

3. What values or attitudes does Coles appear to share with his audience? How does his outside perspective paint a different picture of American motives and values?

4. The author credits the U.S. State Department and the U.S. Environmental Protection Agency for considering the "environmental argument" against the Keystone XL Pipeline. Where could you find more information about the environmental effects of the proposed pipeline?

5. Though Coles argues that the battle is being fought on "three fronts," his solution does not address the environmental argument when he advocates for building the pipeline entirely in Canada rather than not building it at all. What is the rhetorical effect of not developing this argument?

Building the Keystone XL Pipeline: A Necessary Evil

Richard Korman

Richard Korman is the managing senior editor of the *Engineering News-Record* Web site, enr.com. *Engineering News-Record* is a weekly magazine targeted at construction industry professionals including contractors, project owners, engineers, architects, government regulators, and industry suppliers. This editorial was published in the print edition on October 17, 2011.

> Richard Korman begins his argument by acknowledging the dangers of building the Keystone XL Pipeline before advocating for its construction. What is his rhetorical strategy and what effect do you think he wants it to have on his readers?

Every pipeline is ugly, intrusive and potentially dangerous, no matter how barren the land that it crosses. In the best of all worlds, we would be charging our car batteries with hundreds of thousands of megawatts of electrical power from solar panels or wind turbines. That day isn't here yet, so the controversial TransCanada XL Keystone pipeline, which is set to run from Alberta to Texas, is a necessary economic evil, like all pipelines.

With more than 1,711 miles of 36-in.-dia steel pipeline, there is much that could go wrong, beginning with between one or two spills a year greater than 2,100 gallons, according to the State Dept.'s draft environmental impact statement. Crude oil and bitumen could be pumped out of any break under high pressure. Land and water—including the Northern High Plains Aquifer system, which supplies almost eight out of every 10 gallons of water to Nebraska—could be exposed to toxicity from a spill.

BOND THE RISK OF SPILL CLEANUP

The risk of damage is unfortunate, and we urge all federal authorities to require TransCanada to bond or in some form post security for the possible environmental and economic damage from spills.

However, it's important to keep in mind the realities of the current situation in light of the environmental risks. All forms of energy involve regrettable trade-offs, such as the need for new electrical transmission lines on public or private land or erecting huge turbines on land or sea.

Recovering oil from the Alberta oil-sands region has always involved much damage to the environment, but we don't see it as our place to lecture Canadians about pollution and the exploitation of natural resources. The idea of turning away the oil from Canada because of its higher greenhouse-gas profile—about 17% higher than other fossil fuels, according to some sources—strikes us as a luxury, not a life-and-death issue. Climate change is important, but not as urgent as the need for ample energy security and putting people to work. We note that members of the laborers' union who have participated in the "Occupy Wall Street" protests support construction of the pipeline.

The U.S. and the rest of the world will be dependent on fossil fuels for the foreseeable future. The risks posed by the Keystone XL pipeline are not substantially more catastrophic than the risks we run every day with the hundreds of thousands of miles of pipeline that crisscross our country. Acting as if the future of climate change hinges on this one big pipeline is just the kind of apocalyptic nonsense we don't need.

Industry sources suggest building the pipeline would take up much of the work capacity of pipeline contractors. That's good, unless you put amorphous goals about climate change ahead of a higher level of energy security and the need to put more people to work.

For Class Discussion

1. How does Korman structure his argument? Is this pattern effective in presenting the reasons for his claim?

2. At a time when public opinion seems to be calling for the development of alternative energy and a lessening of our dependence on fossil fuels, how does Korman characterize the relative risk of different energy sources?

3. What value does Korman's audience place on business and technology's ability to manage environmental resources? How might this be a reflection of their deeper personal values?

4. Given that Korman's intended audience stands to benefit from the construction of the pipeline, how might they respond to the tone and style he adopts? How might a different audience respond?

5. How would Bill McKibben or Sarah Bean respond to Korman's dismissal of the concerns of the climate change movement as "apocalyptic nonsense," and his assertion that objections to the pipeline's higher greenhouse-gas profile are "a luxury, not a life-and-death issue"?

Reflections on Tar Sands Action: The Collective Will to Address Climate Change
Sarah Bean

Sarah Bean recently completed a bachelor's degree in psychology with a minor in comparative religion. From her increasing concern for our environment and her desire to live in accordance with her deepest values, she is currently exploring Buddhist monasticism. To address her concern for the effects of climate change and tar sands oil extraction, Bean chose to participate in the Tar Sands Action in August 2011. To protest the building of the Keystone XL Pipeline, demonstrators staged a two-week sit-in at the White House. Over the two weeks, she and over 1,200 other citizens were arrested for their act of civil disobedience. After returning home, Bean wrote this letter to friends and family who had been following her journey.

What values are exhibited by Sarah Bean in this letter?

I am writing to share my heart-felt reflections on my participation in the civil disobedience campaign against the construction of the Keystone XL pipeline at the White House. I joined this campaign because I feel a deep concern about climate change and a sense of horror at the environmental degradation of the Alberta tar sands, a toxic wasteland so vast it can be seen from space.

I had planned to participate on Inter-Faith day of the two week sit-in. I chose this day for two main reasons. First, in light of humanity's long history of religious violence and extremism, I feel it is important to raise the voice of inter-faith collaboration. Second, I believe the wisdom teachings of compassion, love, and our ultimate inter-connection have a great deal to offer us. The ability to see through our differences to recognize our common humanity will be just what is necessary to help repair our planet.

I missed Inter-Faith day, however, because Hurricane Irene pummeled the East Coast, delaying my travels. So, I participated the next day, accompanied by 72 others, many of whom were from Vermont, a state which was hard-hit by the powerful storm. Hurricane Irene directly reminded us of our vulnerability to the forces of nature, and added a sense of urgency to our protest aimed at subduing the devastating effects of a hotter planet.

As I lined up in front of the White House with my fellow demonstrators, I felt a deep sense of privilege to be able to express my concern for the earth with others in this way. While watching the police preparing to arrest us and supporters cheering us on, I thought about the earth's natural beauty which I find so nourishing—the beauty of forests and rivers, meadows and glacial-peaked mountains, and the aliveness of birds and wild animals who inhabit this world with us. I thought, too, of my young niece and nephews and my friends' small children—their delightful freshness and uniqueness. Sitting there on the concrete, hot and thirsty, for a moment I felt the profundity of love—softness and tenderness in the chest—and I imagined this love spreading out into the world healing all wounds and injustices. When my moment came to be arrested, I hoped, and I continue to hope, that the small gesture may help this ailing planet, in the complex way small gestures affect the larger world.

In the moments and days since my arrest, I have wondered at our collective ability to address climate change and environmental degradation. This concern was shared by my fellow protesters. Riding in a paddy-wagon to the U.S. Park's Police Anacostia Substation with five other hot and thirsty women, we discussed the day's action. Despite the sense of empowerment we felt as we participated in the day's action, we also felt the discouraging weight of our predicament. The oil industry, with its staggering profits (to which we all contribute), is a powerful force to be up against. How can we loosen the knots of our broken system while we are so embedded in it? Will we intensify our efforts to lower CO_2 in the atmosphere and preserve the earth's ecosystems? And, if we don't, how will we respond in the direct presence of intense suffering and death as food and water resources diminish, and as our beautiful landscapes are lost?

Early in the morning following my arrest, I walked to the Martin Luther King Jr. Memorial. On the front of my tourist map was a photograph of King speaking to thousands of people, as far as the eye can see, on the National Mall. I believe the photograph captures a still moment of his famous "I Have a Dream" speech. As I made my way to his memorial, I wondered what awoke in people's hearts that day to bring them to the mall. What did they feel as they heard him speak? Walking through the memorial's Mountain of Despair to find the engravings of King's words etched into the monument's walls, I think I began to understand. Two quotations particularly inspired me:

> *Darkness cannot drive out darkness, only light can do that. Hate cannot drive out hate, only love can do that.*

> *Make a career of humanity. Commit yourself to the noble struggle for equal rights. You will make a greater person of yourself, a greater nation of your country, and a finer world to live in.*

In these words, in his memory, I felt the possibility of human goodness and courage to overcome adversity. And, so I wonder, will the climate movement grow? Will we all commit ourselves to non-violence as Martin Luther King did, even as challenges intensify?

I think our predicament is so profound—it involves each and every one of us directly. Because climate change is a problem the entire world faces together, it requires all of us to collaborate to solve it. It demands that we all decide what this earth, life itself, means to us, and to look deeply into our actions to see how they affect the web of life. May we remind ourselves, as we live the challenges of our personal lives, that although the details of our stories are different, we share a common humanity. May this recognition awaken in us a sense of deep connection to, and compassion for, all others.

My deep hope is that you will help me to raise the collective will to address climate change.

Injustice anywhere is a threat to justice everywhere. We are caught in an inescapable network of mutuality, tied in a single garment of destiny. Whatever affects one directly affects all indirectly. —MLK

For Class Discussion

1. What is the motivating occasion for this letter? How does Bean move beyond the specific occasion to a greater concern?

2. How do Bean's personal narrative, her moral convictions, and descriptions of her emotions invite her readers to identify with her cause and support her argument?

3. How might the presentation of evidence need to be expanded or altered for a different audience?

4. What values and challenges does Bean imply are shared by the civil rights movement and the climate movement? What are some of the shared tactics employed by each?

5. Rather than suggest a specific action that her readers can take (such as joining the Tar Sands Action or a similar campaign), Bean's call to action is more abstract. How might this be effective for her readers? Or would she be better off asking for a specific, concrete response?

Shale Gas Revolution
David Brooks

David Brooks is an op-ed columnist for the *New York Times*, in which this opinion essay was printed on November 4, 2011. He is the author of *Bobos in Paradise: The New Upper Class and How They Got There* (2000) and *On Paradise Drive: How We Live Now (And Always Have) in the Future Tense* (2004). He is also a commentator on *The Newshour with Jim Lehrer* and a frequent analyst on NPR's *All Things Considered*.

How does David Brooks frame the process of fracking to cultivate his readers' receptive—even positive—attitude toward it?

The United States is a country that has received many blessings, and once upon a time you could assume that Americans would come together to take advantage of them. But you can no longer make that assumption. The country is more divided and more clogged by special interests. Now we groan to absorb even the most wondrous gifts.

A few years ago, a business genius named George P. Mitchell helped offer such a gift. As Daniel Yergin writes in "The Quest," his gripping history of energy innovation, Mitchell fought through waves of skepticism and opposition to extract natural gas from shale. The method he and his team used to release the trapped gas, called fracking, has paid off in the most immense way. In 2000, shale gas represented just 1 percent of American natural gas supplies. Today, it is 30 percent and rising.

John Rowe, the chief executive of the utility Exelon, which derives almost all its power from nuclear plants, says that shale gas is one of the most important energy revolutions of his lifetime. It's a cliche word, Yergin told me, but the fracking innovation is game-changing. It transforms the energy marketplace.

The U.S. now seems to possess a 100-year supply of natural gas, which is the cleanest of the fossil fuels. This cleaner, cheaper energy source is already replacing dirtier coal-fired plants. It could serve as the ideal bridge, Amy Jaffe of Rice University says, until renewable sources like wind and solar mature.

Already shale gas has produced more than half a million new jobs, not only in traditional areas like Texas but also in economically wounded places like western Pennsylvania and, soon, Ohio. If current trends continue, there are hundreds of thousands of new jobs to come.

Chemical companies rely heavily on natural gas, and the abundance of this new source has induced companies like Dow Chemical to invest in the U.S. rather than abroad. The French company Vallourec is building a $650 million plant in Youngstown, Ohio, to make steel tubes for the wells. States like Pennsylvania, Ohio and New York will reap billions in additional revenue. Consumers also benefit. Today, natural gas prices are less than half of what they were three years ago, lowering electricity prices. Meanwhile, America is less reliant on foreign suppliers.

All of this is tremendously good news, but, of course, nothing is that simple. The U.S. is polarized between "drill, baby, drill" conservatives, who seem suspicious of most regulation, and some environmentalists, who seem to regard fossil fuels as morally corrupt and imagine we can switch to wind and solar overnight.

The shale gas revolution challenges the coal industry, renders new nuclear plants uneconomic and changes the economics for the renewable energy companies, which are now much further from viability. So forces have gathered against shale gas, with predictable results.

The clashes between the industry and the environmentalists are now becoming brutal and totalistic, dehumanizing each side. Not-in-my-backyard activists are organizing to prevent exploration. Environmentalists and their publicists wax apocalyptic.

Like every energy source, fracking has its dangers. The process involves injecting large amounts of water and chemicals deep underground. If done right, this should not contaminate freshwater supplies, but rogue companies have screwed up and there have been instances of contamination.

The wells, which are sometimes beneath residential areas, are serviced by big trucks that damage the roads and alter the atmosphere in neighborhoods. A few sloppy companies could discredit the whole sector.

These problems are real, but not insurmountable. An exhaustive study from the Massachusetts Institute of Technology concluded,

"With 20,000 shale wells drilled in the last 10 years, the environmental record of shale-gas development is for the most part a good one." In other words, the inherent risks can be managed if there is a reasonable regulatory regime, and if the general public has a balanced and realistic sense of the costs and benefits.

This kind of balance is exactly what our political system doesn't deliver. So far, the Obama administration has done a good job of trying to promote fracking while investigating the downsides. But the general public seems to be largely uninterested in the breakthrough (even though it could have a major impact on the 21st-century economy). The discussion is dominated by vested interests and the extremes. It's becoming another weapon in the political wars, with Republicans swinging behind fracking and Democrats being pressured to come out against. Especially in the Northeast, the gas companies are demonized as Satan in corporate form.

A few weeks ago, I sat around with John Rowe, one of the most trusted people in the energy business, and listened to him talk enthusiastically about this windfall. He has no vested interest in this; indeed, his company might be hurt. But he knows how much shale gas could mean to America. It would be a crime if we squandered this blessing.

For Class Discussion

1. What types of evidence does Brooks present in support of his claim?

2. What assumptions and values underlie the criticism of those who oppose fracking?

3. Like Richard Korman, Brooks argues that fossil fuels are necessary until renewable energy sources mature. For Brooks, how does shale gas measure up against its fossil fuel counterparts?

4. How does Brooks address the potential dangers of shale gas extraction? What is the rhetorical effect of his language in these paragraphs?

5. How has this op-ed piece influenced your thinking about fracking and the value of other new means to extract fossil fuels?

Safety First, Fracking Second
Scientific American

This editorial appeared in *Scientific American* on October 19, 2011. *Scientific American* is the oldest continuously published magazine in the United States, founded in 1845, and is produced in fourteen different languages. Its purpose

is to provide science and technology information and policy for a general audience. More than 140 Nobel laureates have written for the magazine, in addition
to world and U.S. government officials, economists, and industrialists.

What specific concerns do the editors of *Scientific American* voice about
fracking that have yet to be addressed by the government, oil exploration
companies, and the public?

Drilling for natural gas has gotten ahead of the science needed to prove it safe

A decade ago layers of shale lying deep underground supplied only
1 percent of America's natural gas. Today they provide 30 percent.
Drillers are rushing to hydraulically fracture, or "frack," shales in a
growing list of U.S. states. That is good news for national energy security, as well as for the global climate, because burning gas emits
less carbon dioxide than burning coal. The benefits come with risks,
however, that state and federal governments have yet to grapple with.

Public fears are growing about contamination of drinking-water
supplies from the chemicals used in fracking and from the methane gas
itself. Field tests show that those worries are not unfounded. A Duke
University study published in May found that methane levels in dozens
of drinking-water wells within a kilometer (3,280 feet) of new fracking
sites were 17 times higher than in wells farther away. Yet states have let
companies proceed without adequate regulations. They must begin to
provide more effective oversight, and the federal government should
step in, too.

Nowhere is the rush to frack, or the uproar, greater than in New
York. In July, Governor Andrew Cuomo lifted a ban on fracking.
The State Department of Environmental Conservation released an
environmental impact statement and was to propose regulations
in October. After a public comment period, which will end in early
December, the department plans to issue regulations, and drilling most
likely will begin. Fracking is already widespread in Wyoming, Colorado,
Texas and Pennsylvania.

All these states are flying blind. A long list of technical questions
remains unanswered about the ways the practice could contaminate
drinking water, the extent to which it already has, and what the industry
could do to reduce the risks. To fill this gap, the U.S. Environmental
Protection Agency is now conducting comprehensive field research.
Preliminary results are due in late 2012. Until then, states should put
the brakes on the drillers. In New Jersey, Governor Chris Christie set
an example in August when he vetoed a bill that would permanently
ban fracking, then approved a one-year moratorium so his state could
consider the results of federal studies. The EPA, for its part, could speed
up its work.

In addition to bringing some rigor to the debate over fracking, the federal government needs to establish common standards. Many in the gas industry say they are already sufficiently regulated by states, but this assurance is inadequate. For example, Pennsylvania regulators propose to extend a well operator's liability for water quality out to 2,500 feet from a well, even though horizontal bores from the central well can stretch as far as 5,000 feet.

Scientific advisory panels at the Department of Energy and the EPA have enumerated ways the industry could improve and have called for modest steps, such as establishing maximum contaminant levels allowed in water for all the chemicals used in fracking. Unfortunately, these recommendations do not address the biggest loophole of all. In 2005 Congress—at the behest of then Vice President Dick Cheney, a former CEO of gas driller Halliburton—exempted fracking from regulation under the Safe Drinking Water Act. Congress needs to close this so-called Halliburton loophole, as a bill co-sponsored by New York State Representative Maurice Hinchey would do. The FRAC Act would also mandate public disclosure of all chemicals used in fracking across the nation.

Even the incomplete data we now have suggest specific safety measures. First, the weakest link in preventing groundwater contamination is the concrete casing inside well bores [see "The Truth about Fracking," by Chris Mooney, on page 80]. Inspection of casings should be legally required. Second, the toxic fluid that is a major by-product of fracking is routinely stored in open pits, which can overflow or leach into the soil. It should be stored in tanks instead. Third, gas companies should inject tracers with the fracking fluid so inspectors can easily see whether any of the fluid ends up in the water streaming from residents' faucets. Finally, companies or municipalities should have to test aquifers and drinking-water wells for chemicals before drilling begins and then as long as gas extraction continues, so changes in groundwater are obvious.

It is in the industry's interest to accept improved oversight. Public opinion is turning against fracking. That is unfortunate, because more natural gas could benefit everyone. With basic precautions, we can enjoy both cleaner energy and clean water.

For Class Discussion

1. In this proposal argument, what specific actions or policies are called for by the editors before fracking continues?

2. What examples do the editors provide of science influencing political decisions, and vice versa?

3. How do the editors' choice of words and examples signal that this piece was written for a general audience rather than an audience composed of

science professionals? What points might be expanded or what details might be provided if it were written for scientists?

4. Like David Brooks, the editors of *Scientific American* generally support fracking. How do their approaches differ, though, in presenting the potential dangers of the technology? What values appear to underline their approach?

5. What are some other examples of new technologies that have been embraced before the science existed to prove its safety?

Nuclear Power After Fukushima
Rod Adams

Rod Adams blogs at *Atomic Insights* and produces the podcast *The Atomic Show*. On his blog, he calls himself a "pro-nuclear advocate with extensive small nuclear plant operating experience." He received his nuclear training as a submarine officer in the U.S. Navy, where he served for twenty-nine years. This opinion piece was published in the *National Review* on June 20, 2011. According to the magazine's Web site, the *National Review* is America's "most widely read and influential magazine [for] Republican/conservative news, commentary, and opinion." This piece appeared three months after a massive earthquake and tsunami crippled the Fukushima Daiichi nuclear power plant on the eastern coast of Japan. It is the largest nuclear disaster since the 1986 explosion at Chernobyl in the Ukraine, and has caused several countries including Japan, Taiwan, Germany, Spain, Mexico, and Venezuela to reevaluate their plans for or even shut down their nuclear energy programs.

> Rod Adams chooses to spend the first part of his argument describing the Fukushima Daiichi disaster. What is the rhetorical effect of his choice to delay the presentation of his claim until almost halfway through this piece?

Does nuclear energy have a future, in light of the events at Fukushima? Fukushima Daiichi is the six-unit nuclear-power station on the northeast coast of Japan that was hit by a powerful tsunami, preceded by one of the strongest earthquakes on record. The extent of the damage is considerable: The three reactors that were operating at the time of the earthquake were destroyed by the high-pressure steam produced by heat from radioactive decay and the explosive reaction of hydrogen inside the structures. The hydrogen was produced by chemical reactions between water and the protective, corrosion-resistant layer of zirconium alloy that normally seals radioactive material in a controlled location.

Those who design, build, and operate nuclear-energy facilities know that bad things can happen. They understand energy, shock absorption, chemistry, physics, and radiation, and they invest a great deal of time and effort to build facilities with layers of defense that can undergo a number of failures while still succeeding in protecting against public harm.

In a nuclear plant, the core contains the fuel materials that generate the heat that produces the steam that turns the turbines and creates massive quantities of electricity from tiny quantities of uranium. A single fuel pellet the size of the tip of my pinkie produces as much heat, when it fissions in a conventional nuclear-energy facility, as a ton of high-quality coal does when it is burned in a modern plant. When things are going right, nuclear-fuel pellets do not produce any atmospheric pollution at all, while burning a ton of coal releases between two and four tons of waste into the environment. In the U.S., we consume about a billion tons of coal each year to produce about 45 percent of our electricity.

Nuclear facilities have occasionally suffered core damage. Sometimes core damage is a result of design mistakes, sometimes it is due to actions taken or not taken by human operators, and sometimes it is caused by external forces that were not considered sufficiently probable to be factored into the design requirements. The Fukushima disaster resulted from that last risk. The facility experienced a natural disaster that was considered too improbable to require specific protective measures, but it has happened and may happen again.

The contractor teams that are bidding to clean up the facility estimate that it will require between 10 and 30 years to do the job right, depending on how "right" is defined. The recovery effort will cost tens of billions of dollars. Replacing the power capacity of Fukushima will require Japan to import an average of roughly 700 million additional cubic feet of natural gas per day. After evaluating the other nuclear plants in the country in light of the early lessons learned from the accident, the Japanese government decided to shut down the three-unit Hamaoka nuclear station located in an especially active seismic region. That decision brings the power deficit caused by the tsunami and earthquake to the equivalent of about 1.1 to 1.3 billion cubic feet of natural gas per day. Some of that deficit can be made up by the reduction in power demand that is a result of a damaged industrial infrastructure and concerted conservation efforts.

There are additional costly effects. A plume of radioactive isotopes that are either gaseous or water-soluble left the facility and spread in a northwesterly direction, contaminating areas as far as 30 miles from the plant. Everyone living within a twelve-mile radius of the plant was evacuated in the first few hours after the event, but there have been additional evacuations as radiation surveys have shown that the material moved out farther in some areas. Tens of thousands of people are still living in temporary shelters and are not sure whether they will ever be allowed to return home.

Based on the announced results of the surveys, at least part of the area that has been evacuated could safely be repopulated today, although officials are understandably cautious. Even in areas where measured radiation levels are still higher than allowable under currently accepted international standards, the levels are steadily dropping as a result of an inherent characteristic of radioactive material: It loses strength over time. A major component of the radiation level immediately after the accident was iodine-131, an isotope that loses half of its intensity every eight days and is virtually undetectable after 80 days. By the time you read this article, that period will already have passed. But for the people who have been living in gymnasiums and have had no access to personal possessions for many months, the accident has already imposed a high cost. If you add in the inevitable deterioration of unoccupied structures, there is no way to ignore the widespread nature of the effects. Some individuals or even towns may never recover from the impact of this disaster.

Given the extensiveness of the damage and the expectation of still-uncounted costs, it is legitimate to wonder whether nuclear energy is worth the risk. There are plenty of other ways to generate power, and people flourished for several thousand years before nuclear fission was even discovered. As some who are opposed to nuclear energy remind us, there are only about 435 reactors producing commercial energy today. In many places around the world, nuclear-energy-plant construction stopped several decades ago, as costs seemed to go out of control and people were repeatedly told that nuclear power involved a high level of risk.

On the other hand, it remains almost unbelievable that a few obscure minerals contain so much densely packed, emission-free energy. Every kilogram of uranium or thorium contains as much potential energy as 2 million kilograms of oil. And that relatively small number of facilities does produce the energy equivalent of about 12 million barrels of oil per day. (That is as much energy as the daily output of Saudi Arabia and Kuwait combined; the total world petroleum output is about 80 million barrels of oil per day.)

So far, our economy has focused on only a narrow selection of the available options for harnessing this energy. The majority of the nuclear reactors in operation today are large, central-station electrical-power plants that produce a steady output and use ordinary water to cool the cores, transfer the heat, and turn the turbines. Though this approach works well and has proven its safety and reliability, there are other options, which offer improvements in fuel-use rates, thermal efficiency, and power-output flexibility. Uranium dioxide pellets are not the only fuel form available; advantages might be obtained if some reactors used metal-alloy fuels, and different advantages might result from using thorium or uranium dissolved in fluoride salts.

Society will not likely turn its back on a fuel source with so much potential, although the path will not be smooth, and there will be strong opposition from competitors and from the people who seem to dislike all forms of reliable power. Whatever happens in the U.S., nuclear-energy development will not be suppressed everywhere: China announced a program to review its planned nuclear expansion in light of Fukushima, but has already concluded that there is no reason to stop or even slow down its building of nuclear plants. And developers in the U.S. are working to incorporate the lessons of Fukushima into their designs. One possibility that seems to be particularly advantageous is to build larger numbers of smaller units that have an easier time getting rid of excess heat, even when the power goes out.

Any decision to slow down nuclear-energy development needs to be taken in full understanding that nuclear fission competes almost directly with fossil fuels, not with some idealized power source that carries no risk and causes no harm to the environment. The electricity that Germany has refused to accept from seven large nuclear plants that the government ordered closed after Fukushima has not been replaced by the output of magically spinning offshore wind turbines or highly efficient solar panels. It has been replaced by burning more gas from Russia, by burning more dirty lignite in German coal plants, and by purchasing electricity generated by nuclear-energy plants in France.

People have learned to accept that burning coal, oil, and natural gas carries risks of fires, explosions, and massive spills, and causes continuous emissions of harmful fine particulates and possibly deadly gases that are altering the atmospheric chemical balance. We accept those risks because we are acutely aware of the benefits of heat and mobility.

With nuclear energy, the benefits are substantial and the risks, relative to all other reliable energy sources, are minor. Since Fukushima, there has been a remarkable void of pro-nuclear-energy advertising, which has been filled by efforts by the natural-gas industry to convince Americans that it has recently discovered a 100-year supply.

In my opinion, something close to the worst-case scenario for nuclear power happened at Fukushima. By some calculations, the earthquake and tsunami together hit Japan with a force that was equivalent to several thousand nuclear weapons. Looking at the photos of the area around the Fukushima nuclear station makes me, a career military officer, whistle with wonder at the incredibly successful attack that nature launched.

In the midst of all of the destruction, an important fact frequently gets lost: Not a single member of the plant staff or a single member of the general public has been exposed to a sufficient dose of radiation to cause any harm. The highest dose to any of the workers involved in the recovery effort has been less than 250 millisieverts (25 rem), which is beneath the internationally accepted limit for people responding to a life-threatening accident.

The doses received by the celebrated "Fukushima Fifty" recovery workers are roughly the same as the dose that the young Lt. Jimmy Carter and several hundred other people received when responding to a December 1952 accident at an experimental reactor in Chalk River, Canada. President Carter, like many others involved in that effort, is alive and apparently healthy today.

Even after the Fukushima disaster—affecting six 30-to-40-year-old plants that had primitive control systems, inadequate backup-power supplies, and insufficient protection against the potential effects of earthquakes and tsunamis—nuclear energy has compiled a remarkable safety record. It will be an important, reliable, affordable, and clean energy source for the foreseeable future.

For Class Discussion

1. What course of action does Adams advocate in this argument, which has an exploratory-inquiry structure and strategy?

2. How would you characterize Adams's depiction of the risks and consequences of nuclear power? What is the rhetorical effect of knowing that Adams is pro-nuclear? What do you make of his dismissal of the long-term effects of radiation exposure, including his reference to former president Jimmy Carter?

3. Adams acknowledges the financial and emotional costs incurred by those directly affected by the Fukushima disaster. How does this contribute to his ethical appeal?

4. How does Adams compare nuclear energy's output and impact to other energy sources, particularly fossil fuels?

5. Given that this article was written shortly after the disaster, which aspects of Adams's argument are tied to its historical moment, and which aspects transcend its motivating occasion?

After Fukushima

America

This brief editorial appeared in the July 4, 2011, edition of *America,* a national Jesuit Catholic weekly magazine. The magazine considers itself "a forum for discussion of religion, society, politics, and culture from a Catholic perspective. The Ignatian traditions of 'finding God in all things' and the promotion of justice shape our commentary." Like Rod Adams's opinion piece, this was printed three months after the disaster at the Fukushima Daiichi plant.

> How do the editors use numerical projections to emphasize the scale and reach of the Fukushima disaster?

Twenty-five years after the world's worst nuclear disaster took place at Chernobyl, in Ukraine, that reactor's molten core is still leaking. The radiation released there equaled 400 times that of the bomb dropped on Hiroshima, and radioactive emissions remain high locally. Since Chernobyl, all reactors are built with a containment shell to minimize possible damage. But the destructive power and half-life of radiation have not changed. The world's second-worst nuclear disaster took place in March, when three reactors at the Fukushima Daiichi nuclear plant in Japan melted down. There has been no explosion, and the initial release of radiation was a fraction of that at Chernobyl. But the multiple leaks continue to flow into land, air and ocean and will likely do so for decades.

Nuclear energy has been promoted not only as a cost-effective source of power but also as a safer and environmentally cleaner option than fossil fuels. But is it? Proponents tout the industry's international safety record: Out of 33 nuclear accidents of varying impact since 1952, according to The Guardian, a British newspaper, only the one at Chernobyl in 1986 resulted in mass deaths—31 people died immediately. Yet because cancer and leukemia cells take time to multiply, no one knows how many survivors did or will contract a fatal disease. Projections range from 4,000 to one million disease-related deaths.

Can nuclear power still be described as safe and clean if one factors in the harm to life and planet from reactor meltdowns and hazardous waste? Is nuclear energy "cost effective" if one calculates the full cost, including regular and thorough plant inspections, preventive maintenance, the retirement of outdated reactors and the disposal of radioactive waste? The accident-related costs are now borne mostly by taxpayers, not the nuclear industry. The full costs of nuclear energy are seldom spelled out. That must change. Sound energy policies must be based on accurate cost-benefit analysis and risk assessment.

Fukushima may be a game-changer. Italy, Germany, Switzerland and Japan just scrapped their plans to expand nuclear power. Switzerland and Germany also plan to retire their aged reactors without replacing them, phasing out nuclear power entirely. Instead, Germany will increase conservation and investments in solar and wind power.

After Fukushima, the U.S. Nuclear Regulatory Commission reviewed facilities and monitoring procedures at this country's 66 nuclear power plants. A commission report is expected in August. That information will help policymakers and the public to evaluate the nation's energy policy, much of which has been stalled in Congress. The public should learn how well many reactors are aging; which plants have a history of safety violations; which are located near major population centers (like the Indian Point power plant, 35 miles from New York City); which are vulnerable to an earthquake, hurricane or combination of natural disasters; and what can be done to enhance the safety of nuclear reactors, especially the 23 that use the same cooling vent design by General Electric that failed at Fukushima. What do the industry and government propose to do? And what would improvements actually cost?

Convening a conference in June to discuss nuclear safety and security, Yukiya Amano, head of the U.N. International Atomic Energy Agency, urged countries to conduct a thorough risk assessment of their nuclear operations. He also outlined a plan to separate regulators from the nuclear industry. "National nuclear regulatory bodies must be genuinely independent, adequately funded and staffed by well-trained people," he said. Two controversial issues were raised: whether U.N. experts should conduct random inspections of all 440 nuclear plants; and whether international safety standards, which now are nonbinding, should be made compulsory.

Even so, radiation poses extreme risks. The consequences of an accident, a natural disaster or sabotage are grave and far-reaching. And as more reactors are built, these risks increase. The old comparison between nuclear energy and fossil fuels is becoming obsolete as renewable energy sources become practical alternatives. Forward-looking nations should reduce their dependence on nuclear power while converting to less risky, renewable alternatives.

Given the urgency of reducing emissions and oil dependency, U.S. presidential candidates should be asked to state in some detail their energy plans. The case for increasing renewable sources is strong. Consider: What are the risks to health, planet and peace of renewable energy, like that powered by the sun and the wind? What are the gains, political and economic, from using safe, available sources? What are the costs of aggressively developing renewable energy now, so that it can replace nuclear power when the last reactor is retired? Any other course of action would be a waste of this year's disastrous warnings.

For Class Discussion

1. What argument—claim and reasons—do the writers of this editorial draw out of the lesson of the Fukushima disaster?

2. How do the editors employ rhetorical questioning to explore the ethical and social dimensions of nuclear power and its risks?

3. What arguments in support of nuclear power are acknowledged and refuted in this editorial?

4. How might the editors of *America* respond to Rod Adams's claims that the only realistic alternative to nuclear energy is fossil fuel? On what other points do Adams and this piece disagree?

5. How do pieces like this editorial and Sarah Bean's letter, for instance, invite us to consider the value of the commons in sustainable development? (See the chapter introduction for more information on these terms.)

Wind Versus Tidal Energy
Adrian Raeside

Adrian Raeside, born in New Zealand, has been an editorial cartoonist for the *Victoria Times Colonist* (Canada) for over thirty years. His editorial cartoons appear in over 250 magazines and newspapers worldwide. This cartoon is from his widely distributed comic strip *The Other Coast*.

What does the angle of vision in each of these cartoon panels suggest about the value and attention afforded to different environmental issues?

For Class Discussion

1. How does this cartoon employ humor and the element of surprise to convey its argument?

2. In your own words, how would you describe this cartoon to a friend? What additional context might you need to provide to help your friend understand the issues?

3. Who is the intended audience for this cartoon? How might different audiences interpret its argument?

4. In what ways does this cartoon present the trade-offs inherent in adopting one form of energy production over another?

___

STUDENT VOICE: A Letter to Ken Salazar
by Tine Sommer

Tine Sommer is originally from Denmark, where she earned a master's degree in engineering and then worked as a bridge planner and designer. When she wrote this researched proposal argument, she was pursuing a post-baccalaureate degree in English, having accompanied her partner, an engineer working on wind turbines, to Seattle. For this paper, she chose to address her argument to Ken Salazar, the U.S. secretary of the interior in the Obama administration. As secretary, he oversees federal agencies including the National Park Service, the Bureau of Land Management, the Fish and Wildlife Service, and the U.S. Geological Survey.

How does Tine Sommer establish her credibility in this argument?

Dear Mr. Secretary:

I am writing in response to your February 10, 2009, speech "Statement on Offshore Energy Strategy" (Salazar). In your speech, you called for more public opinions on offshore energy, and I am hereby offering you mine. As you will see, I am suggesting an approach to offshore energy that will benefit America's suffering economy as well as the environment, help the United States gain more independence from foreign oil markets, and achieve the same benefits from wind power that Denmark has gained. The financial crisis is affecting the development of wind power as an alternative source of energy; however, contrary to inclinations, the U.S. government needs actually to increase its investment in wind energy. A U.S. resident, originally from Denmark where wind turbines are widespread, I have a background in engineering and a knowledge of wind energy. My suggestions could be useful to you, as secretary of the U.S. Department of the Interior, and I hope you will consider them. The United States should contribute to the solution of a crisis that is affecting us all.

In this time of serious financial crisis, the United States needs to boost the economy by supporting projects that will benefit the country financially now and in the future. If you, in the Obama government, would support investments in new wind turbine projects, offshore and onshore, the United States could be helped out of this financial crisis. The main reason that the economy would benefit is that building wind farms would create new jobs for both highly skilled and unskilled workers. The Global Wind Energy Council, which represents wind energy companies and organizations, has in cooperation with Greenpeace published the report *Global Wind Energy Outlook 2008.* The Council finds that, based on experience from Europe, every additional megawatt of energy produced from wind turbines creates 15 new jobs a year. If growth in the wind energy industry continues at the current rate in North America, the United States will increase its yearly production of wind energy from 18,664 megawatts in 2007 to 92,000 megawatts in 2020, creating 84,000 new jobs in thirteen years. If we continue to increase our production of wind energy even more with the help of government incentives, in the most optimistic scenario, the United States would create 270,000 new jobs by 2020. The annual increase in new jobs would be highest in the beginning of the period, yielding an immediate effect on the number of employed Americans, increasing consumption and tax revenues. By supporting the wind energy industry you will therefore be supporting the American economy.

Another huge benefit of supporting the wind energy industry is that environmentally it is the right thing to do. Since global warming is increasing, we cannot wait any longer to reduce our carbon dioxide emissions from fossil fuels, recession or not. As Mark Hertsgaard, environment correspondent for the *Nation*, explains: "You wouldn't know it from our politicians or TV shows, but the climate crisis is even more serious than the financial crisis. The financial crisis, while painful and severe, can be resolved, given time and wise policies. The climate crisis, not so." Wind energy benefits the environment by allowing us to lower the amount of electricity we derive from coal and natural gas and thereby lower our carbon dioxide emissions. (Carbon dioxide builds up in the atmosphere, causing higher temperatures, rising sea-levels, melting of the inland ice, and extermination of certain animal and plant species.) Furthermore, coal mining and drilling for natural gas have bigger impacts on the environment than building wind turbines. For example, coal mining affects larger areas of land and causes air and water pollution. Compared to offshore production of natural gas, offshore wind farms are less harmful to the marine ecosystem. Wind farms only have an impact on the sea while they are being built, while natural gas production has a continuing impact on the marine environment. In their recent objections to drilling off the coast of Virginia, the Southern Environmental Law Center (SELC) ". . . compared the meager amount of recoverable oil and gas with the potentially drastic impacts of drilling to important marine species, including the endangered northern right whale and humpback whale, dolphins, sea turtles, and many migratory birds. . . . [SELC] also asks the agency to integrate offshore wind power into its 5-year plan." Offshore wind power is far more attractive than offshore drilling and offers a way to benefit the environment in the short and long term.

In addition to creating new jobs and benefiting the environment, supporting wind energy would also address the problem of dependence on foreign oil. In the very near future the world oil supply will decrease drastically and this, in combination with increasing costs of extracting less accessible oil, will increase oil prices. By investing in wind energy we can support the United States with electricity generated in our own country and thereby decrease our dependence on increasingly expensive foreign oil. Although wind energy will never be able to replace oil, in the long run it can help ensure that our society can keep on developing even when oil resources shrink. Being economically dependent on foreign oil is not wise; the geopolitical balance of power would drastically change if the U.S. found itself at the mercy of oil-producing countries who chose to use their power corruptly and dangerously.

Finally, other countries, especially Denmark, offer a model of successful governmental investment in wind energy. In Denmark the government provides an economic supplement for companies that sell electricity from wind turbines, so the cost difference between producing electricity from oil, gas, or coal and producing electricity from wind decreases. Wind energy has created many jobs in design, manufacturing, and operations. According to the Danish Wind Industry Association, by the end of 2007, 23,500 Danes were employed in the wind energy business. Denmark's knowledge and experience with wind turbines have increased the demand for Danish engineering services and wind turbine parts, boosting Denmark's exports and reducing the impact of the financial crisis. Supporting the wind energy industry in America would have the same beneficial effects on the U.S. economy.

Despite the compelling case for the government's support of wind energy, a number of people have opposing views on the subject. If we invest in wind energy, some people argue, we could not "buy American" as Louis Uchitelle explains in his article "'Buy American' in Stimulus (But Good Luck With That)" in the *New York Times*, because 70% of wind turbines in America are imported. Even though some money will leave the country, we would be creating American jobs for those who design and plan wind farms (highly skilled workers) and for the people who build and operate them (unskilled and skilled workers). In the long term, the United States would build its experience with wind turbines so there would be a basis for manufacturing them here. Eventually, we could "buy American."

Another objection to supporting wind energy is fluctuating oil prices. When oil prices are low, some ask why we should use money on developing wind energy. The underlying assumption is that if people can afford to buy oil there is no reason to invest in alternative forms of energy such as wind turbines. However, we should realize that oil prices will rise again as soon as the recession turns and the demand for oil rises. When oil prices start rising we will be prepared by having other energy sources.

Perhaps the most consistent argument against supporting investment in wind energy is that it is very expensive to build and use wind turbines, especially when money is scarce. Although it is a problem to obtain money in a financial crisis, I advise that we have to think long term. Consider that once a wind turbine is built it uses a source of energy that is free and unlimited, the wind. Even though wind energy is more expensive to harvest and transport than traditionally obtained electricity, the price gap is closing. The difference in the cost of energy from coal-produced electricity and from wind power is down to about $10 per megawatt hour. According to the Energy Information Administration, an average home in America uses around 11 megawatt hours per year (2007), so the difference in the price the consumer has to pay is minimal. With further development of wind technologies, this gap will continue to decrease. Since this is a time when banks are hesitant to lend, the government should guarantee repayment of loans for investments in wind energy instead of providing a tax credit. The problem these days is that many companies don't have a high positive income to take advantage of a tax credit. I therefore suggest that we alter the tax credit system: Instead of having to apply the tax credit on income the same year that a company invests in wind energy, it should be able to postpone using the credit to future profitable years.

However, some conservative opponents of wind energy say that we shouldn't use taxpayers' money to support an industry that can't make it on its own; the market should regulate itself. The Heritage Foundation, for example, suggests that we should instead allow offshore oil and gas drilling because it is privately financed (Lieberman). Even though drilling for offshore oil and gas was encouraged by the previous administration, it is an inefficient solution as it will not significantly increase the supply of oil. It would be a drop in the ocean so to speak. Because this oil would be sold on the free global markets, it would neither lower the price of oil for the United States nor would it significantly decrease our dependence on foreign oil. Drilling for offshore oil and gas would probably benefit the companies that invest in it, but it will have no impact on oil prices and therefore have no advantages for the average American. Besides, do we really want to increase our harmful impact on the environment by burning more oil when there are alternatives? Furthermore, the recent financial crisis has refuted the theory that the market can regulate itself. By regulating some minor areas, we would be using the taxpayers' money in a beneficial way that will eventually create jobs and lower the cost of energy in the long term.

For all these reasons, I am asking you, Mr. Secretary, to support a government guarantee on loans for investments in wind energy and the postponement of tax credits on income from these investments. By doing so, you would help the U.S.'s suffering economy, reduce the destruction of the environment, as well as take steps toward national independence from foreign oil. Let the U.S. take advantage of the experiences of other countries who have shown that these measures work and embrace this avenue of economic prosperity and growth.

Sincerely,
Tine Sommer

Works Cited

Danish Wind Industry Association. "Sector Statistics 2008." *Windpower.org*. Danish Wind Energy Association, 2008. Web. 23 Mar. 2009.

Energy Information Administration. Office of Coal, Nuclear, Electricity, and Alternative Fuels. "U.S. Average Monthly Bill by Sector, Census Division and State 2007." Dept. of Energy, Jan. 2009. Web. 13 Feb. 2009.

Global Wind Energy Council. *Global Wind Energy Outlook 2008*. Global Wind Energy Council and Greenpeace International, Oct. 2008. Web. 23 Mar. 2009.

Hertsgaard, Mark. "Wanted: A Climate Bailout." *Nation*. Nation, 17 Nov. 2008. Web. 21 Mar. 2009.

Lieberman, Ben. "The Obama Administration Should Not Delay Offshore Oil and Gas Leasing." *Heritage Foundation*. Heritage Foundation, 19 Feb. 2009. Web. 22 Feb. 2009.

Salazar, Ken. "Statement on Offshore Energy Strategy." Speech. Dept. of the Interior, 10 Feb. 2009. Web. 11 Feb. 2009.

Southern Environmental Law Center. "Environmental Groups Call for Withdrawal of Offshore Drilling Proposal for Virginia." Press release. Southern Environmental Law Center, 13 Jan. 2009. Web. 9 Feb. 2009.

Uchitelle, Louis. "'Buy American' in Stimulus (But Good Luck With That)." *New York Times*. New York Times, 21 Feb. 2009. Web. 23 Feb. 2009.

For Class Discussion

1. What aspects of the issue make Ken Salazar a good choice as the audience for Tine's letter?

2. What are Tine's main claim and reasons?

3. How does she establish the impetus for her argument? How does this motivation influence her claim and choice of evidence?

4. What assumptions does Tine make about her audience's knowledge of the problems with oil? What information might she need to add to draw in a broader audience?

5. How effectively does Tine anticipate and address potential objections to her recommendations?

6. Tine Sommer, Dave Coles, and Richard Korman all emphasize job creation as one of the reasons for their argument. What role does the economy play in supporting one form of energy over another?

Pedaling Our Way to Energy Independence

Jonathan Facelli

Jonathan Facelli is a corporate attorney in Cambridge, Massachusetts. This article is from the March/April 2009 edition of *The Humanist*, a magazine that describes itself as applying "humanism—a naturalistic and democratic outlook informed by science, inspired by art, and motivated by compassion" and specifies its goal of providing "alternative ideas" (www.thehumanist .org). This column originally appeared under the heading "Satirically Speaking." In satire, the author employs wit in order to attack a folly or vice with the aim of exposing or correcting it. The target may be people, institutions, ideas, or things, and the methods include exaggeration, distortion, humor, ridicule, and irony.

How does Jonathan Facelli apply the formal principles of argument to his humorous proposal?

During the 2008 U.S. presidential campaign the buzzword "energy independence" reemerged atop the nation's political agenda. U.S. policymakers and talking heads have increasingly declared the need for energy self-sufficiency. According to economist Daniel Yergin, writing for the *Wall Street Journal*, the United States is presently over 70 percent self-sufficient, a higher percentage than many Americans realize. But the pundits insist we must do better. How can we achieve that additional 30 percent without sending billions of U.S. dollars to OPEC nations and that big pink country to the north?

If you listen to the John McCains and the Sarah Palins, we should start by drilling in Alaska and building nuclear power plants. If Barack Obama and Al Gore are more to your tastes, the answers are in hybrid cars, clean coal technology, and investment in renewable energy sources such as wind and hydroelectric power. But maybe there's another option, one our pundits and political leaders have overlooked.

Wind, water, and steam turbines generate energy by using natural kinetic sources to rotate drive shafts connected to electric generators. At work are basic principles of physics, which instruct that an electric current is generated by cranking a loop of wire between stationary magnets. A massive steel windmill generates electricity the same way as a science experiment with two magnets and a coil of wire; the wire and magnets are merely larger in the windmill.

That got me thinking—how else might we crank generators to produce electrical energy? How do we gain that final 30 percent of energy we currently import? Maybe the question we should be asking is, how can we do more cranking? It's not an energy deficit we're dealing with—it's a cranking deficit.

Once the question is properly posed, the answer becomes obvious— foot pedals.

Tens of millions of students and white-collar employees in the United States spend their days seated at a desk. Instead of idling all day, these people could be pedaling. Accountants, attorneys, and academics could be winding their legs under the desk as they work. Students could be pedaling away while they listen and learn. If every cubicle desk, office chair, and board room were equipped with pedals, we could harness millions of kilowatt hours of electricity per day. Consider the possibilities in exercise facilities. Treadmills, stationary bikes, circuit trainers—all could be harnessing energy if equipped with a small generator.

An esteemed physics professor, who wishes to remain anonymous, conservatively estimates that an office worker could generate one kilowatt hour of electricity per day pedaling a small sub-desk generator. When we consider the total number of workers and work days in a year, we're talking about the potential for billions of kWhs generated annually from human movement alone. That's a big number. Then take into account the international possibilities—India's call centers alone could power the world if equipped with pedals. Let's get those telemarketers winding.

To be sure, there will be skeptics. The infrastructure required to install all those pedals and generators would be staggering, opponents will surely suggest. Granted, it will take some time and a bit of R&D, but leave that to the engineers and smart people like Bill Gates and Al Gore—if they can figure out how to make the Clapper, the Segway, and an iPod the size of a credit card, I'm sure they can whip up the portable pedal generator (or PPG) in no time. Other skeptics will argue that, with all of that churning and spinning, people will require greater food intake, which would offset the harnessed energy. This argument fails to consider the substitution effect: by churning away all day, students and office workers will have less need to exercise independently. Instead of running or biking after work, people will simultaneously stay fit and solve the energy crisis. On account of the obesity epidemic, we're already carrying around colossal amounts of excess energy in our guts and upper thighs; the PPGs will enable us to convert that blubber into a more usable form.

It's almost too simple. In fact, I'm surprised efforts haven't already been taken to install PPGs in office spaces and public classrooms. There's a lot of work to do, and there's no time like the present to get started.

We can install pedals on everything: restaurant booths, airplane seats, subway trains, toddler car seats, and church pews. Let's make it fun— employer-sponsored prizes, private office pools for energy production, bragging rights for best pedaler and most improved. The sky's the limit.

Who needs more windmills and oil rigs when we can collectively crank our way to energy independence? Call your local representative; write a letter to the Department of Energy. No more dependence on foreign oil—let's get cranking!

For Class Discussion

1. Though this proposal is meant to be humorous, the technology for human-powered generators exists. What features of Facelli's writing help readers identify his tongue-in-cheek tone?

2. What is Facelli's main claim, and how does he use evidence to support it? Could his audience find the argument reasonably convincing?

3. What other problems faced by Americans does Facelli argue would be solved through his proposal?

4. Facelli ties certain alternative energy options to different political points of view. Based on the readings in this chapter, do you agree with how he categorizes technologies such as nuclear, wind, and fossil fuel power? ■

CHAPTER QUESTIONS FOR REFLECTION AND DISCUSSION

1. Would you say you are a heavy, moderate, or light user of water? How have the articles in this chapter influenced your views on your own water use and on access to clean water, water conservation, or bottled water?

2. According to the authors in this chapter, what attitudes about water need to be examined or changed in order to meet our needs in the future? Which articles make the case that water is a human right? What is the argument for water as a good or service?

3. Choose a pair of writers from the following list and analyze where they agree and disagree about effective and ethical approaches to natural resources. Specifically examine their assumptions, reasoning, and interpretation of facts. Identify where their use of language reveals their values and challenges alternative views.

   A. Anita Hamilton and Maude Barlow or Sandra Postel

   B. Maude Barlow and Richard Korman or David Brooks

   C. Dave Coles and Sarah Bean

   D. David Brooks and the editors of *Scientific American*

   E. Rod Adams and the editors of *America*

4. Choose one of the readings in this chapter that argues for important connections between economics (such as the creation of new jobs or the economic feasibility of different technologies) and environmental problems. What connections does the reading make and how persuasive is its approach or solution?

5. Increased awareness of climate change informs many of the readings in this chapter. How do authors acknowledge the role of climate change in their arguments? Where do they place its importance in the decision-making process?

6. Having read the articles on competing energy technologies, what would you say is the most reasonable and compelling approach to solving our energy problems and why? What are the biggest obstacles?

7. Working in groups or individually, calculate your Water Footprint using the calculator provided at the National Geographic Web site (http://environment.nationalgeographic.com/environment/freshwater/water-footprint-calculator/). What has this quiz shown you about your use of environmental resources?

8. Working individually or in groups, research and report to your class on one of the following topics, and include a graphic to display your findings:

   A. China, in its rapid industrialization, is experiencing serious problems with water pollution, smog, growing energy needs, and conflicts over damming its major rivers. In 2007, it overtook the United States in total carbon emissions. Research the recent crises related to these problems. How is China dealing with these problems? What is the response of the global community?

   B. A number of the world's rivers cross national borders. For example, in Africa, the Nile and Congo Rivers are potential sites of international conflict and cooperation, as are the Mekong River in South Asia and the Colorado and Owens Rivers in North America. What countries and governments are competing for the water from these rivers? What intergovernmental agreements for equitable use of this water exist?

C. Indigenous peoples, citizens of developing countries, and the poor everywhere are the most vulnerable to environmental disasters. Research the concept of "environmental refugees." How have events like the 2004 Indian Ocean tsunami, Hurricane Katrina in 2005, drought in the Darfur region of the Sudan, the 2010 Haiti earthquake, or the 2011 Japanese earthquake and tsunami exposed this vulnerability?

D. Different energy options are more feasible for some regions of the United States than for others. Some of the options are discussed in this chapter, including wind, nuclear, and natural gas; other options include solar, geothermal, tidal, and clean coal energies. What energy sources are being discussed in your region? Are there any controversies attached to potential development of these resources?

9. Working individually or in groups, create a visual map of the range of views expressed in a group of readings from this chapter. Consider the political, social, or ethical perspectives, the value placed on different resources, the attitudes toward climate change, and the role of technology and business in the these approaches.

WRITING ASSIGNMENTS

Brief Writing Assignments

1. **Reflective Writing.** As Sarah Bean mentions in her letter, we all contribute in some way to those industries that consume our shared environmental resources. Briefly reflect on how the readings in this chapter have influenced your thinking about your own use of water and energy. What reading in particular did you find the most eye-opening, disturbing, or inspirational? What ideas or habits of yours did this reading cause you to question, rethink, or see from some new perspective?

2. **Analyzing Arguments Rhetorically.** Watch an animated short on YouTube or another online source that addresses a concept from this chapter. (Two of many options available on YouTube are "Fracking: Things Find a Way" and "Polar Bears Discussing Global Warming.") How do the characterizations use humor or irony in making their claim? Consider the use of images, sound effects and music, and text in the presentation of the video's point of view. How do visual arguments such as these reach a different audience or have a different effect than articles on the issue might?

3. **Analyzing Arguments Rhetorically.** A number of the writers in this chapter (Maude Barlow, Sandra Postel, Bill McKibben, Sarah Bean, and Rod Adams) act as spokespersons for particular stances in global environmental debates. Select one of these writers' arguments and examine it rhetorically. How directly and explicitly does the writer present his or her claim? How specific, relevant, and effective is his or her evidence? How does this writer use emotional and imaginative appeals to the audience and treat alternative views?

4. As with most controversial issues, discussions of environmental problems are often serious in tone. Briefly explain how arguments such as Jonathan Facelli's and political cartoons serve to lighten the mood while still addressing real concerns. In fact, what specific insights does their lighter approach offer?

5. Freewrite for twenty or more minutes on one of these propositions using ideas and examples from the readings in this chapter. To force yourself to think from different perspectives, you might try writing in agreement with the statement and then writing against it:

   A. Water should be a human right, not a commodity for sale.

   B. Technology is more important than conservation in finding solutions to water shortages and energy needs.

   C. We should invest in alternative energy technologies rather than try to access the remaining deposits of fossil fuels across the globe.

   D. The concept of climate change is too immense and abstract to tackle. We should focus our attention on energy sources that will put people to work and provide for our current needs.

   E. The benefits of nuclear power outweigh the risks associated with the technology.

6. Briefly explore your own environmental ethic by first writing a short summary of an article with which you disagree and a short explanation of the values that you believe the writer holds. Then in a paragraph explore ways that you could connect with this writer. For example, if you disagree on the urgency of the water shortage problem, step back and find some points on which you do agree with the writer. If you disagree on the necessity of using fracking or installing the Keystone XL Pipeline, take a bigger view and find some common concerns you could share with this writer.

Writing Projects

1. Write a synthesis paper for your peers in which you explain how the readings in this chapter have shaped your view of problems related to water or energy. You might sketch out your view (for example, on the need for access to freshwater to be treated as a health issue or on the need for people to encourage investment in alternative energy technologies) or simply present and explain your view as a series of key questions you think individuals and countries need to address. Use ideas from the arguments in this chapter to support your view or questions, and document these sources.

2. Make an advocacy poster for your residence, community, or university similar to the United Nations Environment Programme poster on page 229 supporting use of the environment that aids the poor. Your poster might urge people to use water or energy more efficiently. Think in terms of a powerful main image or photo and a small amount of text that reinforces or interprets the image and that calls people to action.

3. Using fieldwork and research, investigate the water, electricity, or waste-water system in your area: What is the source of this resource? Who owns it? Are the records regarding the quality of water or the safety of the electrical production system available to the public? Who sets the standards? How efficient and sustainable is this system? Then write an argument addressed to your community in which you either (a) support or criticize this system or (b) propose strategies for individual and communal conservation of water or energy.

4. **Reflective Writing.** Environmental issues can often seem overwhelming, and we sometimes feel powerless about our ability to make an impact. Still, it is often the actions of one committed individual that raise awareness of an issue or start a movement. Sarah Bean and thousands of others traveled to Washington, DC, to participate in the Tar Sands Action. Bill McKibben founded the grassroots climate action site 350.org. Colin Beavan spent a year living as No Impact Man. Abigail Borah, a 21-year-old Middlebury College student, spoke out at the Durban climate talks in late 2011 out of her concern that the U.S. delegates were not taking action. Research the story of one of these or another environmental activist. Summarize his or her story and then respond with your own reflections. What event, ethic, or emotion motivated that person to act? What example do you think this person has set? How have their individual actions contributed to or initiated a larger response to an environmental issue? What will you take away from this person's story, and is there an issue for which you have a similar passion?

5. Argue that water management or energy efficiency is a political issue that calls for political solutions in the form of national policies that promote government–business collaboration. You might research one of the following examples: France has had good results through taxing gasoline, encouraging industries to shift from oil to other fuels, and promoting diesel-powered cars. In the 1970s, Brazil financially motivated farmers, investors in distilleries, and automakers to develop a domestic ethanol fuel industry. Responding to the 1970s oil embargo, the United States lowered the speed limit to 55 miles per hour and promoted the manufacture of small cars with high gas mileage. South Africa has instituted a two-tier pricing system for water that provides 25 liters per day free but charges users beyond that amount. Australia has instigated a new system of government ownership of water and of pricing and trading. Make the case, directed toward a political representative, that political power can help solve environmental problems.

6. Suppose a friend says to you, "OK, I recycle all my plastics, newspapers, and cans. I carpool once a week to campus and take a bus once a week; I keep the heater in the apartment at sixty-two degrees; and I turn off all lights and electrical appliances when I am not using them. But some analysts, both liberals and conservatives, tell me that these individual efforts

are pretty useless in saving energy and affecting environmental issues like climate change." What argument would you make to your friend, affirming or rebutting this claim that individual efforts to change energy consumption are insignificant? What values would you build your argument on?

7. **Analyzing Arguments Rhetorically.** Environmental advocacy organizations are often thought of as appealing to a very specific audience, often white, middle- to upper-class Americans or Europeans with liberal political views. Using three or four of the following criteria, write a rhetorical analysis of an organization's Web site or one of its Web campaigns directed to the organization that created it. Identify the target audience for the organization, explain the strengths of the site's rhetorical features, and propose a set of recommendations for the organization to help it reach its target audience more effectively or broaden its outreach. You might consider these criteria: (a) visual appeal and functionality of the site; (b) clear explanation of the problem and sufficient evidence to support the organization's position; (c) strong appeal to readers' emotions, sympathies, and values, including how specific language choices might affect the site's appeal; (d) good credibility or currency of the information presented; (e) clear requests and directives indicating what the organization wants its audience to do.

Natural Resources Defense Council (www.nrdc.org)

Global Water Policy Project (www.globalwaterpolicy.org)

UN Global Alliance for Water Security (http://iwlearn.net)

International Rivers Network (www.internationalrivers.org)

Water Aid (www.wateraid.org)

Water for People (www.waterforpeople.org)

Global Strategy Institute (http://csis.org/program/global-strategy-institute)

Water Partners International (www.waterpartners.org)

Center for Global Safe Water (www.sph.emory.edu/CGSW/)

New Economics Foundation (www.neweconomics.org)

World Wind Energy Association (www.wwindea.org)

The Energy and Resources Institute (www.teriin.org)

African Rural Energy Enterprise Development (www.areed.org)

World Energy Council (www.worldenergy.org)

International Network for Sustainable Energy (www.inforse.dk/)

World Renewable Energy Network (www.wrenuk.co.uk)

American Energy Initiative (http://naturalresources.house.gov/issues/issue/?IssueID=34108)

6

Merging and Clashing Cultures
Graffiti, Comics, and Music

CONTEXT FOR A NETWORK OF ISSUES

Cultural globalization is as widely analyzed and disputed as economic globalization. The influence of globalization on several sites of cultural exchange—graffiti and street art, comics and cartoons, and hip-hop or rap music—are the focus of this chapter. Of course, cultural exchange has been going on for millennia, and yet globalization has stepped up cultural contact through business, media, and travel. These contemporary cultural interactions have brought new problems and possibilities. Think of the effect of rap and reality TV on the Arab world, of fast food on Asian countries, of Japanese anime (animation) on American cartoons, and of zumba and Bollywood style on the U.S. fitness and dance scenes. Because culture encompasses the material, intellectual, artistic, and spiritual practices of a society—including food and diet, art, music, literature, traditions and lifestyles, beliefs and values—it is bound up with national identity, preservation of heritage, cultural self-respect, and people's sense of home and belonging.

The sociologist Jan Nederveen Pieterse provides a useful theoretical framework in which to discuss cultural globalization. He posits three main paradigms of intercultural relations or cultural difference: that is, cultures can interact in these ways: "**cultural differentialism** or lasting difference, **cultural convergence** or growing sameness, and **cultural hybridization** or ongoing mixing."* According to Pieterse, each paradigm suggests a politics of multiculturalism. The following chart highlights some of Pieterse's key ideas of cultural interaction.

---

*Jan Nederveen Pieterse, "Globalization and Culture: Three Paradigms," *Readings in Globalization: Key Concepts and Major Debates*, ed. George Ritzer and Zeynep Atalay (West Sussex, UK: Wiley-Blackwell, 2010), 309.

PARADIGMS OF INTERCULTURAL RELATIONS*			
Model or Paradigm	**Cultural Differentialism**	**Cultural Convergence**	**Cultural Hybridization**
Images and language used to talk about the paradigm	• Cultures as static, distinct mosaic tiles • Clashing billiard balls (best-known advocate of this view is Samuel P. Huntington in his book *The Clash of Civilizations*)	• Homogenization • McDonaldization • Americanization • Westernization	• Crossover culture • Postmodern mixing • Synthesis, yielding new variety • The local in the global and the global in the local • Glocalization
Politics of multiculturalism associated with the paradigm	• Apartheid • Closed separation • Regionalism	• Assimilation to a dominant culture • Globalization as Westernization • One-way flows of culture • Cultural imperialism	• Integration • Continuous mixing and remixing without losing cultural identity • Multidirectional flows (for example, East to West as well as West to East and South to North as well as North to South)

These paradigms and theories become more concrete when we look at several dynamic sites of cultural exchange.

Conflicts over Graffiti.   Worldwide, graffiti and street art are challenging the uses, perceptions, and experiences of urban space.[†] Tourists visiting Venice, Italy, for the first time are often disappointed to find the famous Rialto Bridge over the Grand Canal marred with ugly scribbling; on the other hand, Melbourne, Australia, draws visitors and street artists from other countries with its lively graffiti scene. Shaping the images of the cities

---

*Ibid., 309–318.
[†]Alison Young, "Negotiated Consent or Zero Tolerance? Responding to Graffiti and Street Art in Melbourne," CITY: *Analysis of Urban Trends, Culture, Theory, Policy, Action* 14, nos. 1–2 (February–April): 100.

in which it appears, graffiti and street art grow from and are tailored to the specific urban landscape. The lettering art form of graffiti also includes stencils, posters hung with wheatpaste, stickers, etchings, and reverse graffiti (creating an image by wiping away dirt from a surface). Whether graffiti is in New York, Cape Town, Sao Paulo, Barcelona, or Beijing, it shares similar features yet represents its distinctive cultures. It is also constantly changing, as graffiti writers compete with each other in their creative self-expression and now even disseminate their pieces on the Web. This loosely connected global graffiti movement faces common problems and raises common questions.

In parallel and intersecting conflicts, global cities—Beijing, London, Berlin, New York, Sao Paulo, and Melbourne, among others—are arguing about whether to control graffiti and street art and about its intrusion in public space and its illegality. For example, the "Noffitti" international conference in Germany in 2006 drew people from Germany, seven European countries, and the United States. Many representatives at the conference argued that graffiti is vandalism and a gateway crime, which should be harshly punished for its costly damage to public and private property. Cities around the world are following the lead of the Scandinavian countries, which have instituted zero-tolerance policies toward graffiti, and New York City, which has made it illegal for people under twenty-one to possess spray paint. Many cities are intensifying the "war on graffiti" with surveillance equipment and more arrests. In defiance, many graffiti writers around the world insist on their right to act out their anger, underscore the allure of dangerous illegality, and boast of their knowledge of their urban landscapes and their strategies for outwitting law enforcement in their "bombing" of sites. Graffiti writers from different cultures also protest the domination of public space by commercial forces who, backed by the power of money, inflict billboards and advertising on city residents. Furthermore, graffiti writers from different cultures value the potential for graffiti as free speech and democratic expression to critique politics and give voice to the marginalized and powerless.

Other major conflicts over graffiti taking place globally question the incorporation of graffiti into the marketplace, the public realm, and art establishments. Global debates are occurring about the cooptation of graffiti's rebellious spirit and expression. If advertising campaigns exploit graffiti style, are they legitimizing graffiti or destroying its spirit? Another conversation worldwide centers on the need to draw distinctions between graffiti as vandalistic tagging and street art as creative expression with potential to humanize and enliven sterile public space; from Canada to New Zealand the debate rages over whether legal walls foster this distinction or promote a wider spread of all graffiti. Yet another challenge to global graffiti comes from the art establishment itself. If world-renowned British street artist Banksy sells his work for hundreds of thousands of dollars, is he giving in to commercial forces? If museums in Paris, Los Angeles, and New York feature exhibits of graffiti and street art, are they controlling and killing its potential as rebellion and critique? Can street art placed in a museum be *street art*?

Conflicts over Cartoons and Comics.   Cartoon images have proved to be politically and culturally inflammatory, particularly in the complex tensions between Islam and Western countries. In September 2005, a Danish newspaper printed twelve cartoons that caricatured the Prophet Mohammed as part of an effort to open up the debate about the relationship between Islam and terrorism. One of these cartoons showed Mohammed with a bomb for a turban. The cartoons aroused the anger of the Muslim community in Denmark and throughout the EU, and four months later they and other cartoons considered blasphemous and strongly anti-Muslim incited the bombing of the Danish Embassy in Pakistan and other countries, the burning of the Danish flag in Muslim countries, and the boycotting of Danish goods. At least fifty people died in these protests. For Danes and many Europeans, the crisis over images illuminated the conflict between freedom of expression in a secularized society and the sensitivities and values of a religion that prohibits all images of the Prophet Mohammed. In October 2011, a similar but less catastrophic conflict in Tunisia arose over the showing of the film *Persepolis*, based on the autobiographical graphic novel by Iranian Marjane Satrapi. The image that provoked the Islamist storming of the private television channel that broadcast the film shows God as a bearded man speaking to the girl Marjane, whom he cradles in his palm. Again, the stakes were freedom of speech versus the preservation of conservative religious values. These incidents and the furor in the United States over the Kuwaiti children's superhero comic series *The 99* and its supposed indoctrination of Muslim values show how cultural products such as political cartoons, graphic novels, and comic books and films—intended as satire, cultural critique, and entertainment—are embroiled in the clash of cultures involving religion and politics.

As these, hip-hop music, and other sites of cultural contact reveal, respecting cultures and their rights is challenging and the stakes in cultural globalization are high.

STAKES AND STAKEHOLDERS

Many stakeholders, including international institutions, nongovernmental organizations, multinational corporations, cultural critics, religious groups, and citizen groups, are striving to influence the way that globalization affects their own cultures and the cultures of other nations. Here are some of the big issue questions with which these groups are wrestling.

How Is Increasing Global Cultural Contact Affecting Cultural Diversity?
Some activists and cultural critics assert that cultural contact is creating
uniformity, standardization, **homogenization**—a global monoculture
that is sterile, dull, and artificial. For example, some American travelers
express frustration when they find many foreign cities looking like home
with Starbucks, Kentucky Fried Chicken, Walmart, Pizza Hut, Taco Bell,
and Hard Rock Café, and the most current American films playing. More
than monotony and homogenization, the issue for some linguists, anthropologists, activists, and spokespeople for indigenous cultures is the loss
of cultural heritage and cultural identity. Anthropologists, environmentalists, and activists are striving to preserve languages that are dying out
as some formerly remote cultures are drawn into more contact with the
outside world. Scholars and activists like Helena Norberg-Hodge, founder
of the International Society for Ecology and Culture, argue that language
is bound to culture and that culture is connected to the deep values and
structures that hold societies together. Some advocates for indigenous cultures argue that many of the smaller threatened cultural groups—such as
the people of Ladakh, an ancient culture nestled next to India, China, and
Tibet—possess knowledge of peaceful lifestyles and social cooperation that
the world needs. As Norberg-Hodge writes in her book *Ancient Futures*
(1991), "There is more than one path into the future."*

In contrast, proponents of free trade, corporate leaders, some cultural
analysts, and many citizens around the world applaud the opportunity
and cross-fertilization engendered by globalization's stepped-up cultural
contact and sharing. For example, some people examining the international music scene contend that cultural globalization has brought new
possibilities of pleasing everyone. Some music critics say the American
music industry is stimulating healthy competition, spurring musicians and
performers to create more innovative hybridized expressions of their own
national cultures. In a 2001 special edition of *TIME* magazine on global
music, executive editor Christopher Porterfield claims that the Internet
and television have created "a vast electronic bazaar through which South
African kwaito music can make pulses pound in Sweden, or Brazilian
post-mambo can set feet dancing in Tokyo."†

What Are the Power Dynamics of Cultural Globalization?   Many
critics contend that the United States and other rich countries are dom-
inating developing countries through **cultural imperialism**. Just as rich
nations imposed political power and economic control on third world
countries in earlier centuries (and became rich nations partly through this

---

Ancient Futures: Learning from Ladakh (San Francisco: Sierra Club Books, 1991), 1.
†"Planet Pop. Music Goes Global," *TIME*. http://www.time.com/time/magazine/article
/0,9171,1000785,00.html.

imperialism), many critics, policymakers, activists, and citizens assert that rich nations are imposing their own culture and undermining the cultural diversity and integrity of poor, developing nations. For example, how can poor countries lacking information, communication technologies, and the financial resources to support their own domestic music, arts, and film possibly compete with the production and distribution systems of affluent Hollywood? Some cultural critics point out that major labels and big money are not promoting world music. As Pino di Benedetto, the marketing director for EMI Africa, a main African recording company, has said, "There is a lot of music that comes out of Africa that would be marketable in the States and Europe. . . . Nobody gives us a chance. We just are not seen as hit makers."*

Still other cultural critics and citizen groups in some countries say that it is arrogant and simpleminded to assume that American culture is "conquering" the cultures of countries around the world. Many critics reject sociologist George Ritzer's McDonaldization model and claim instead that **glocalization**, whereby local cultures take an active part in adopting and adapting foreign culture, is more accurate.† After all, many McDonald's restaurants are owned and managed by people from those countries, and these McDonald's in different countries serve culturally distinctive menus. Similarly, MTV throughout the world has incorporated much local programming.

Other critics argue that American and Western cultures are already mixed, diverse cultures themselves, having been changed by other cultures around the world for centuries. America and Europe have experienced an influx of people from developing countries and have become new composite cultures. Using words like *integration*, *cultural fusion*, and *hybridization*, these analysts claim that the mixing of cultures is inevitable, healthy, and enriching. Other arguers claim that many countries and groups of people are welcoming American and Western cultures, which they see as modernization and progress. The people watching American movies and buying Kentucky Fried Chicken want to be included in the new global society and are embracing the modern Western "good life."

---

*Sharon LaFraniere, "Africa, and Its Artists Belatedly Get Their MTV, *New York Times* (February 24, 2005).

†Sociologist George Ritzer posits the global spread of McDonald's as a business model and a cultural force in *The McDonaldization of Society* (2000). However, sociologist Ronald Robertson speaks of glocalization (a term combining *globalization* and *localization*). He adopted this term from Japanese business, which used it to describe customizing products made for the global market to fit local cultures. See Habibul Haque Khondker, "Glocalization as Globalization: Evolution of a Sociological Concept," *Bangladesh e-Journal of Sociology* 1, no. 2 (July 2004). Thomas Friedman's definition of glocalization is given in Chapter 1: "Exploring and Defining Globalization" on p. 5.

Can Cultural Exchange Be an Instrument for Promoting Global Understanding, Cooperation, and Peace?   One global organization that is addressing tensions and attempting to shape global cultural exchange for the benefit of all countries is the **United Nations Educational, Scientific, and Cultural Organization (UNESCO)**. In 2001, this group, consisting of about two hundred member nations, formed the Convention on Cultural Diversity and wrote the **Universal Declaration on Cultural Diversity**, grounded in the principles that "cultural diversity is as necessary for humankind as biodiversity" and that "cultural rights are an integral part of human rights."* UNESCO supports the idea that protecting cultural rights and diversity has the potential to promote peaceful international relations. Its Universal Declaration on Cultural Diversity states that "affirming that respect for the diversity of cultures, tolerance, dialogue and cooperation, in a climate of mutual trust and understanding [is] among the best guarantees of international peace and security."† However, critics disagree about whether cultural forms such as a comic book series for children or the global street art movement can create solidarity or reshape the global perceptions of a religious group.

Thomas L. Friedman, a well-known American journalist, posits connections between global cultural and economic exchanges and peaceful relations in his Golden Arches Theory of Conflict Prevention. Friedman asserts that the spreading of McDonald's is closely bound up with the economic development of a strong middle class and that "people in McDonald's countries [don't] like to fight wars anymore," preferring instead "to wait in line for burgers" and not risk their economic and cultural prosperity.‡ Friedman's critics, however, cite the number of McDonald's in other countries as an example of the United States' cultural imperialistic encroachment. Other analysts argue that because cultural imperialism—or at least, very imbalanced cultural exchanges—is usually the reality, increased cultural contact frequently does not foster peace; instead, it engenders resentment and antipathy, as seen in the Arab world's growing hostility toward American culture and European antagonism to Muslim culture.

How Can Cultural Contact and the Marketing of Culture Be Regulated to Promote and Preserve Cultural Diversity?   Friedman proposes that countries engage in active glocalizing by filtering powerful cultures. He urges cultures to become active agents learning how "to assimilate aspects of globalization into [their] country and culture in a way that adds to [their]

---

*UNESCO, Thirty-First Session, "Universal Declaration on Cultural Diversity" (Paris, November 2, 2001).

†Ibid.

‡*The Lexus and the Olive Tree* (New York: Anchor Books, 2000), 249.

growth and diversity, without overwhelming it."* However, Friedman admits that glocalization must be supplemented by other "filters" such as governmental intervention to ensure the preservation of cultural heritage, educational programs, and wise promotion of tourism. UNESCO's Universal Declaration on Cultural Diversity seeks to advance **cultural pluralism** and to prevent culture from being turned into a commodity controlled by multinational corporations. A legal agreement still in progress, the declaration calls on national governments, international governmental and nongovernmental organizations, civil society, and private businesses to work together to prevent consumerism from overrunning culture and to stop the free trade advocates, multinationals, and the WTO from controlling the marketing of culture. The UNESCO supporters of cultural diversity assert that national and local bodies must maintain the power to decide how cultural exchanges will be managed and must preserve the right to create and protect their own cultural industries.

What Do Global Cultural Conflicts Reveal about the Need for Social and Political Change?   Many culture analysts and even political leaders note that intracultural conflict and intercultural conflict over cultural forms point to cultural, social, and political problems that need to be addressed. For example, what does the explosive effect of cartoon images related to Islam indicate about multiculturalism in Europe? What does American rejection of children's comics based on Muslim values say about integration in the United States? Or what social and political conclusions can be drawn from the controversies over graffiti that are pitting multiple stakeholders—artists and graffiti writers, residents, business owners, galleries and museums, crime prevention agencies, transportation and construction companies, police, young people, people who like street art, and tourists and visitors—against each other? Does the global omnipresence of conflicts over graffiti shed light on economic globalization's effect on cultures and societies? Cultural critic Michael Krimper points out that beneath the tensions lie deeper cultural and sociological questions with global cultural relevance about the "symptoms in our cities that have generated graffiti." He asks, "What is happening to our public space? Who has a right to this public space? Do our laws regarding property rights, in the public and private spheres, require revision?"†

Thinking Visually

Street Art as Activism and Advertising

This photo of a street art image, taken by Michael Caster in December 2008, shows an alleyway in the ethnically diverse part of Toronto, Canada. It depicts

---

*Ibid., 295.

†Michael Krimper, "Art in the Streets, in a Museum," *Hydra Magazine* (May 8, 2011).

a Native American in headdress with the word "hero" written on the left. The image functions as somewhat of an advertisement for the activist organization 4Real. According to its Web site (www.4real.com/), "4REAL connects individuals with people, projects and tools to make change real."

Michael Caster

Street Art in Toronto, Canada

Questions to Ponder

1. What is the rhetorical effect of locating this bold image of the Native American labeled "hero" in an alleyway next to trash cans? How well does this image work as an advertisement for 4Real?

2. How does the use of graffiti for advertising purposes affect your appreciation or position on graffiti? Would you think differently about using graffiti to advertise a nonprofit, socially conscious organization versus using it to advertise a corporate profit-maximizing company?

This chapter—first in the Student Voice, International Voices, and Global Hot Spot sections and then in its readings—explores how the big issues of cultural identity, values, and political voice are embedded in a variety of global cultural controversies.

STUDENT VOICE: A Fascination with Anime
by Owen Johnson

Many Americans have appreciation of and fondness for food, music, and art forms from other cultures. Student writer Owen Johnson talks about the importance of Japanese anime to him and explains some reasons for its growing popularity in the United States.

My adventure started nine years ago with a haircut. Sitting in a barber's chair, I became bored and began looking at the various pictures and drawings posted around my barber's station when an unfamiliar form of cartoon caught my eye. The drawing showed a complaining customer sitting in a barber's chair. The barber, grinning maliciously behind the customer, was holding a giant pair of open scissors, each blade on one side of the customer's neck. I found the drawing humorous, but at the same time it caused me to glance in the mirror at my barber, an Asian fellow in his late twenties. Catching the slightly concerned look on my face, and realizing that I had been observing his drawings, he laughed and said that his friend who drew many of those pictures was an animator, and when I asked why the characters in the drawings had bigger eyes and sharper features than most cartoon characters, he replied that these were done in Japanese animation style, which had not yet become hugely popular in the United States. He explained that anime characters have bigger eyes because in the Japanese culture, the eyes are seen as "windows to the soul." He told me about a Japanese animated show that aired on Sunday (not the usual Saturday morning cartoon time) called *DragonBall Z*. When I turned on the TV the next day, I was exposed for the first time to the wonderful world of anime, forever changing my perspective on cartoons.

Japanese animation has brought a whole new dimension to American cartoon watching and American cartoons, which tend to be children's entertainment—like *Sponge Bob Square Pants*—with pretty colors, slapstick comedy, and hardly any real substance. In contrast, Japanese animated shows such as *One Piece*, *Naruto*, and *Cowboy Bebop* cross genres—action, adventure, science fiction, and even comedy—and have more meaty plots for even the deepest thinkers. Animes also have good character development. Viewers can easily connect with the characters' misery, joy, sorrow, or fear and with the themes that deal with subjects like boldness and loyalty without being obvious or cheesy. I have always been a fairly imaginative kid, but watching hours of anime has pushed my imagination to new levels of possibility.

As America has become more diverse and open to other cultural influences, Japanese animation has become a regular part of Cartoon Network's (a network dedicated entirely to animation) programming. Anime started out being shown in a two-hour afternoon block and occasionally at midnight, but in the past few years anime has evolved into the most viewed shows on the network, my guess making up forty percent of CN's shows. Japanese animation has also influenced American cartoons. Recently I noticed that the flare of anime style has given one of my favorite childhood shows, *Teenage Mutant Ninja Turtles* (TMNT), new and much needed pizazz. Similarly, in *Batman Beyond*, the new Batman's martial arts seem more . . . well, to put it bluntly, more kick ass like animes' fighting. Clearly, countries learn from those who do an art best, and in the case of animation, that's Japan.

I can't imagine, even with my anime-stimulated imagination, how different my life would have been if I hadn't met that barber and seen *DragonBall Z* years ago. That show was a gateway to even better Japanese animation and to my interest in Japanese culture, which in turn inspired me to take Japanese for four years and to travel all throughout Kyushu (Southern Japan) during one high school summer. My cultural fascination continues, and I am planning to study in Japan during my college career.

INTERNATIONAL VOICES

During the last eight years, Iraq has experienced an immersion in some aspects of popular American culture. According to Bushra Juhi's article, "U.S. Military's Legacy Rubs Off on Iraqi Youth," subtitled "Rap, Hip-Hop, Tattoos, and English Lessons," published in the *Seattle Times* on November 24, 2011, the war has Westernized and Americanized the Iraqi youth culture, leaving intense—if warped—impressions of American culture.

Iraqis Comment on Their Adoption of American Cultural Forms

Sporting baggy soldiers' camouflage pants, high-top sneakers and a back-turned "N.Y." baseball cap, the chubby 22-year-old was showing off his break-dancing moves on a sunny afternoon in a Baghdad park. A $ sign was shaved into his closely cropped hair.

"While others might stop being rappers after the Americans leave, I will go on (rapping) till I reach N.Y.," said Mohammed, who teaches part time at primary school.

His forearm bears a tattoo of dice above the words "GANG STAR." That was the tattooist's mistake, he said; it was supposed to say "gangsta."

Eight million Iraqis—a quarter of the population—have been born since the U.S.-led invasion of 2003, and nearly half the country is under 19, according to Brett McGurk, a fellow at the Council on Foreign Relations in New York and until recently, senior adviser to the U.S. Embassy in Baghdad.

So after years of watching U.S. soldiers on patrol, it's almost inevitable that hip-hop styles, tough-guy mannerism and slangy English patter would catch on with young Iraqis.

Calling themselves "punky" or "hustlers," many are donning hoodie sweatshirts, listening to 50 Cent or Eminem, and watching "Twilight" vampire movies. They eat hamburgers and pizza and make death-defying Rollerblade runs through speeding traffic. Teens spike their hair or shave it Marine-style. The "Iraq Rap" page on Facebook has 1,480 fans.

To many of their fellow Iraqis, the habits appear weird if not downright offensive. But to the youths, it is a vital part of their pursuit of the American dream as they imagine it.

GLOBAL HOT SPOT: Nigeria

Musical styles, youth culture, and national identity are also at stake in African countries, particularly Nigeria, where members of the older generation are lamenting the loss of a rich national heritage of multiple genres of music as Western processes of commercialization are taking over. The following editorial by Juwe Oluwafemi, "Music Yesterday, Today—A Nation's Identity Crisis," was published on the AllAfrica.com site on January 22, 2012.

> In today's Nigeria, the most impactful musicians are the ones who rule the air waves, parties, and the tubes with their dance hall music. Talk about: Tu Face, D'Banj, MI, Ice Prince, Ikechukwu, Naeto C. Wiz Kid, Faze Ruggedman, Mode Nine, Sauce kid, Sasha, 9ice, Bouqui, Mo'cheddah, Teeto, P-Square, Don-jazzy, Wande Coal, Black Face, Dr. Sid, D'Prince, K-Switch, Timaya, to mention a few. . . .
>
> "At public functions, they mime . . . they do not have a real band in the sense of what it should be. They rely on computer generated tunes and sessions to sing. They are not artists, they may pretend to perform, but they are not necessarily composers, and even good dancers . . .their dance steps are not original and they are strange to our culture!" [Babagbenleke, a retired civil servant] declared.

[Another music critic, Reuben Abati gave his interpretation of the Nigerian music scene.]

"Nigeria's hip hop is bringing the country so much international recognition. All those strange names are household names across the African continent, so real is this that the phrase "collabo" is now part of the vocabulary of the new art. It speaks to an extension of frontiers. In Nigeria, it is now possible to hold a party without playing a single foreign musical track. The great grand-children of Nigerian music are belching out purely danceable sounds which excite the young at heart. But the output belongs majorly to the age of meaningless[ness] and prurience. The lyrics say it all," he expressed.

. . . So much sound is being produced in Nigeria, but there is very little sense, shape and skills. They call it hip-hop. They try to imitate Western hip pop stars. They even dress like them. . . .

According to him, unlike the music of yesteryears, most of the music being produced now will not be listenable in another five years and this perhaps is the certain fate of commercial art that is driven by branding, show and cash. . . . A country's character is indexed into its arts and culture, eternal purveyors of tones and modes. Nigerian youths now sing of broken heads, raw sex, uselessness and raw aspiration, emotionalism. A sign of the times? Yes, I guess, " he added . . . .

The readings in this chapter examine various cultural pressure points around the world by looking at cultural exchanges involving graffiti, comics, and hip-hop or rap music.

READINGS

Is Graffiti Art or Vandalism?
Mugambi Kiai

Mugambi Kiai holds an MA in law from Harvard Law School. He has worked in human rights advocacy in various organizations: as head of the program with the Kenya Human Rights Commission; as head of the Central Depository Unit monitoring electoral violence in Kenya; as senior program officer for the Canadian International Development Agency; and, currently, as program officer with the Open Society Initiative for Eastern Africa (OSIEA) and the OSI Africa Governance and Monitoring Project, related to monitoring, research, grant making, and advocacy in East African involvement with the African Union. This analytical commentary appeared on the AllAfrica.com site on March 24, 2012.

AllAfrica describes itself as "a voice of, by and about Africa—aggregating, producing and distributing 2000 news and information items daily from over 130 African news organizations and our own reporters to an African and global public."

How do the title and the opening examples in this piece establish the exploratory purpose and tone of this commentary?

It's been impossible not to take notice of the low-octane debate that has raged around graffiti, especially this past month.

On the one hand, there is the reported case where assistant minister Ferdinand Waititu is facing arrest following the expiry of a notice for him to remove the "display of illegal graffiti namely; 'Waititu for Governor'" on flyovers, underpasses, buildings and walls within the Nairobi area. Since this revolves around sloganeering, it is quite easy to resolve.

On the other hand, there is the more complex example where graffiti is an art form and part of social commentary, conversation and debate: a constitutionally-protected form of expression. Take the case of the political graffiti that suddenly sprouted earlier in March around the City Market, Muindi Mbingu Street and Kenyatta Avenue. Here's one description of it: "One of the images on the city market wall depicts a villain-like politician taking his seat in Parliament; he has conned voters into electing him to the lavish position but uses his power to impoverish them. The text caption reads 'I'm a tribal leader; they loot, rape, burn and kill in my defence while I steal their taxes and grab land, but the idiots will still vote for me.'"

The issues addressed include corruption, tribal clashes, land grabbing, political assassinations and other high profile crimes committed by the Kenyan elite. One of those reportedly behind this project was quoted: "We're using images of a vulture MP stomping on a face, of protests and Parliament, to tell Kenyans that when you sell your vote, you're mortgaging our future."

Should this be banned too? One view, emphatically articulated by Nairobi Town Clerk Philip Kisia earlier this week, is that it should. In fact, the City Council has reportedly begun to paint over this political graffiti. This view is shared by Peter Vallone who was a key sponsor of new anti-graffiti legislation in New York City that took effect in 2006. Vallone's view was that, "At its best graffiti is just a way for immature vandals to seek notoriety and at its worst it is messages between rival gangs and drug dealers." And he was strongly dismissive of the freedom of expression rationale: "I have a message for the graffiti vandals out there—your freedom of expression ends where my property begins!"

Vallone also noted there were numerous requests from the public to clean up with reports indicating that by April 2006, there had been

13,000 requests to clean graffiti. It was then approximated that it cost approximately $15 to $18bn annually to remove graffiti in the United States.

But there is a strong alternative view. This view supports graffiti as a legitimate and powerful form of social, economic and political protest. As one pro-graffiti advocate put it: "Nowadays, urban public spaces are reserved for those who have enough money. Advertising dominates the urban landscape, and we are constantly bombarded with slogans from multinationals everywhere we go. . . . Architecture and the streets are shaped by commercial interests, not by the residents of the city. It is impossible to avoid, the public have no access to these spaces, that is, unless we claim them for our own. . . . Graffiti and street art are the only ways that people can interact with public spaces actively. These art forms can, for example, express emotions, give critique on current politics or society, or offer venues for public art."

Graffiti is also seen as an alternative source of news, especially where credible information is not available. Here's how one Kashmiri graffiti artist put it: "Mainstream media will never say a word of truth. In 2008 and 2010 when our brothers were falling to the bullets of security forces, people remained uninformed about the real stories. We used graffiti as an alternative channel to the mainstream media, to disseminate the true information, which often was kept back by the latter. Somehow we succeeded."

So this is the argument: public spaces (including the media) have an exclusivist character based on, among others, expense, accessibility, knowhow, political, social and economic realities and networks and legal restrictions. Graffiti provides those who are excluded in this manner with an avenue to challenge the exclusion and articulate their aspirations in a simple and accessible way. This way it can inform, reinforce and amplify public demand for change at minimum cost and at a level that provides for greater inclusivity.

Of course, there are those who find graffiti to be untidy and invasive. Here is a comment by Cindy reacting to an internet story on the political graffiti in Nairobi titled "Graffiti That Inspires: Vultures Swoop In" "I wasn't inspired . . . I was saddened. I have become so proud of my city. The streets are being cleaned, park benches, beautification etc. Nairobi CBD is truly becoming the once famed city in the sun. There are many ways to make a point, desecrating our beautiful city is just not one that makes me rally behind your cause. Sorry."

Interestingly, this same attack is rarely ever levelled against other forms of public art that are commercialised, for example billboards and posters. Yet, it all boils down to taste. So why is it that we are prepared to tolerate the forms of commercialised art that we find distasteful but not graffiti? Whose opinion of "cleanliness," "desecration," and "beautification" are we pandering to?

The cost argument is another issue but here is one response: "While complaining about malicious damage, they clean the spray-painted, pasted walls, just to see them sprayed over again almost immediately. It would be a much more effective use of public resources to invest the money used for cleaning in workshops and painting lessons, in order to raise the quality of the graffiti."

So is graffiti art or vandalism? Perhaps we could look to Berlin where "graffiti was, above all, a symbol of freedom in the West. . . . Freedom of speech and movement made it possible for graffiti all over the Western side of the Berlin Wall to starkly emphasise the tighter restrictions of society in the East. The city recognised the symbolism of the graffiti and in this sense, welcomed it."

For Class Discussion

1. What are the different major views of graffiti that Kiai presents in this piece?

2. How does Kiai draw on evidence from both Kenya's conflict over graffiti, which he is targeting, and international conflicts over graffiti to give context and depth to his commentary?

3. How does this commentary engage with the arguments taking place globally about the use of public space and the creation of city image?

4. By choosing to end this commentary with the West Berlin example, what impression of his views does Kiai leave with readers? Which of Kiai's points in this piece struck you as the most persuasive?

Photo of Street Art
Shepard Fairey

Shepard Fairey, the graphic artist who made the Obama "Hope" poster and whose work is now exhibited in major museums such as the Victoria and Albert Museum in London, the Smithsonian, and the Museum of Modern Art in New York, painted a mural in Copenhagen in August 2011 on a seventy-foot-high wall at the former site of a radical left-wing youth culture center, which had been torn down. The mural depicted a peace dove in a target symbolizing Fairey's hope for global peace and a protest against the wars in Iraq and Afghanistan. This mural upset young people from the former youth center who saw it as a propaganda provocation paid for by the city officials who had been responsible for tearing down the original youth culture center. In anger, someone painted over the mural with graffiti. After Fairey explained that the street art was not commissioned by the city but rather was initiated by the Copenhagen gallery that was showing his work, he collaborated with artists from the former youth center who painted a riot scene in the lower part of the mural, depicting the history of the site. However, this collaborative work was later bombed with a fire extinguisher and destroyed. You can see photos of the collaborative work online.

What do the details of this photo suggest to you about the differences between street art and graffiti?

Street Art with Graffiti in Copenhagen

Tommi Ronnqvist

For Class Discussion

1. Some protesters of the mural objected to its image, its message, and its location. What potential problems with context, use of public space, choice of images and messages, and creator of these images do graffiti and street art illuminate?

2. Fairey wrote in his blog after the incident: "I think street art is one of the most democratic, accessible, empowering, and inspiring art forms there is. . . . Street art also is an outlet for the most competitive, frustrated, anarchic, and sometimes downright barbarically hostile people" (from his Facebook post August 13, 2011). Given the anti-American feelings expressed in the graffiti and the fate of the mural, what view of graffiti emerges from this incident?

3. What paradigm or paradigms of intercultural relations have operated in this incident surrounding Fairey's mural?

4. Would you be inclined to identify with Fairey, the protesters who collaborated with him, or the people who ultimately destroyed the mural? Explain why.

Graffiti Taggers Are Just a Pain in the Arts

Michael Pernar

Michael Pernar is the chief executive officer at Laverton Community Center, a nonprofit organization in Melbourne, Australia, which offers a range of education, care, and crisis aid services. This op-ed piece was published in the major Melbourne newspaper, the *Herald Sun*, on March 20, 2012.

In the opening of this op-ed piece, how does Michael Pernar distinguish between graffiti and art?

To many, graffiti is art.

In the outer suburbs of Melbourne, it is blatant vandalism where zero tolerance should be enforced.

A great deal of graffiti that people see in the outer suburbs is plain trash. If the words and images used are not vile they are meaningless and there is next to no artistic skill involved. There are no design principles behind the scrawl—no regard for colour, composition or style. It simply looks bad and it makes people feel unsafe. Graffiti is a social menace.

Let's face it, the perpetrators are defacing private and public property. This is a criminal act in itself, not an expression of art. Why should we condone it? Their work is unsightly and damaging and costs the community millions of dollars a year. The finished product also devalues the neighbourhood and damages the aesthetics. Businesses give up on the high and constant cost of removal as the tags multiply.

That is not to say there is no place for public art. I do concede that there is a need for young people to express themselves. When it comes to expressing themselves through public art, street art, this must be in controlled environments. It might be in the form of commissioned art as a mural on a business or alleyway, or on designated walls that local governments provide.

In these circumstances, this would be art and furthermore it would not be vandalised by "taggers". We know that there is a code among street artists that prevents them from defacing the "works" of others. Indeed, thoughtful, stylish street art is a good deterrent—a form of graffiti reduction, in areas where there are many "hits" by taggers. Install a mural and the tags disappear.

I have previously worked on the governance group of the Goodbye Graffiti program run by the Brotherhood of St Lawrence.

This was an employment program that set up long-term unemployed people into traineeships in management. During the traineeship they also obtained many other qualifications that allowed them to work along the Werribee/Williamstown rail corridor. Over a 12 month period, they removed 26,000 square metres of unsightly graffiti, predominately "tags". If the taggers came back and ruined the rail corridors that had just been cleaned up, the clean-up team would be out there very quickly. Their message was clear: post your tag and we will remove it.

Such vandalism of public and private assets and infrastructure continues and it is rampant. But who should foot the bill for the expensive removal?

Many assume that it is the local council's responsibility.

This is true if the graffiti is offensive or on a council-owned asset. If it is on a private dwelling or business, it is the responsibility of the dwelling or business owner.

This is where graffiti on rail corridors gets tricky.

The rail corridor has many owners or operators—Vic Track, Metro M and local councils. So where does the buck stop? Commuters deserve better and they deserve to feel safe. We know there are links between vandalism and petty crime.

Goodbye Graffiti was successful because the Department of Transport ensured that everyone interested was involved.

As well as funding the majority of the project, DoT ensured that all health and safety issues were addressed prior to workers accessing the track and sections.

The majority of graffiti removal is done by painting over the scrawl, especially the back fences of residences along the rail corridor. These residents are typically grateful that the clean-up has occurred and so, too, are the owners of surrounding businesses.

We all treat graffiti removal as an expense, like rubbish removal. I implore all supporters of graffiti to take notice of the spray-painted chaos abutting rail corridors and freeway fences next time they visit the suburbs. Would you want this scrawl on your property?

For Class Discussion

1. What is Pernar's main claim in this op-ed piece? What is the meaning of the title of the article?

2. Who do you think is the target audience for this argument? What values does Pernar assume his audience holds?

3. Where and how effectively does he respond to alternative views?

4. What are the ingredients of a successful campaign against graffiti? How might this op-ed piece be useful to cities in other countries facing a problem with graffiti?

Public Art, Political Space: The Rearticulation of Power in Post-Revolutionary Tunisia

Michael Caster

Michael Caster holds a master's degree in conflict studies and human rights from the University of Utrecht, in the Netherlands. His research interests focus on analyzing the symbolic interactions between power and resistance. He has also spent several years working in the nonprofit sector on issues of human rights in Asia. A self-styled cosmopolitan, Caster has lived in the United States, the Netherlands, China, Turkey, and Tunisia, and has traveled through over thirty-five countries. He blogs about social commentary, travel, and photography at http://michaelcaster.com. This commentary is a synthesis of a series of articles on Tunisia that appeared on his blog between October and December 2011.

> How does Michael Caster help readers understand the political context for graffiti in Tunisia?

Street art, such as graffiti, wheat pasting, or stenciling, continues to crop up in more cities around the world. Not just in the Paris, Berlin, New York, or London streets of the past but in Buenos Aires, Melbourne, Chongqing, and others is the epithet 'global graffiti capital' being contested. Some people are intrigued and aesthetically drawn to 'reading' the visual texts on previously monochrome brick and plaster. Some are horrified and angry at the perceived vandalism of public space, aghast at the signs of urban decay. Others are confused by the meaning of the images and unable to disentangle the arguments about graffiti. Is it art or crime, an egotistical plea for attention or the rearticulation of power by those who were previously marginalized?

Well known for his 2005 activist murals on the Palestinian side of the Israeli Security Barrier, UK artist Banksy stated in his 2001 book, *Banging Your Head Against A Brick Wall,* that, "Graffiti has been used to start revolutions, stop wars and generally is the voice of people who aren't listened to. Graffiti is one of the few tools you have if you have almost nothing" (1). Democratic countries have generally been the primary public space in which this hypothesis has been tested, primarily as a challenge, at times purposefully absurd, to mainstream consumer culture. However, we can turn to authoritarian countries, or formerly authoritarian countries such as Tunisia, as a more drastic case study to understand the social power of street art. In Tunisia, symbolically repressive public space magnified the repression of Ben Ali's twenty-three year dictatorship. With his removal, was public space affected by an artistic revolution parallel with the political and social revolution? A critical examination of street art in Tunisia reveals this contentious art form's ability potentially to foster democratic discourse and stimulate public participation, and I claim that this understanding is globally transferrable.

Tunisian artist and theorist, Mohamed Ben Soltane told me at our first meeting that before the revolution, "the art scene was closed so artists couldn't make art in public spaces. There was real fear from almost everybody. We can say that it was hell and it is now paradise." Ben Ali's reign was marked by rampant corruption and totalitarian control of social and political space. Disappearances and torture were reported by international organizations, and Tunisian public space was a canvas for the regime to remind its subjects of this domination. Posters of Ben Ali were ubiquitous fixtures on public surfaces. Several Tunisians told me that these posters conveyed a kind of Orwellian omnipresent surveillance. The walls belonged to Ben Ali and his party, the *Rassemblement Constitutionel Démocratique* (RCD) and aside from the occasionally scrawled reference to one of Tunisia's football clubs, the people of Tunisia saw very little on their walls that did not reaffirm their subjugation. The domination of public space foreclosed any public discussion or inscription of counter-discourses and in this way served as a metaphor of a greater lack of freedom. But that changed with the revolution. The country opened for the first time to democratic elections, and public space was laid bare for the free expression of artistic activism.

In Tunisia, as elsewhere, writing on the wall can be the beginning text for widespread public discussion, portent of a changing mood, or the final remark to an episode of contention. One example of tagging representing a discussion that also happened to play out in street manifestations is the comparison of the interim government with the *ancien regime*. After Ben Ali fled Tunisia on 14 January 2011, Mohamed Ghannouchi, Prime Minister under Ben Ali, proclaimed himself acting President, sparking a proliferation of contentious graffiti. Amid accusations of connection to the corrupt Ben Ali years, Ghannouchi was forced from office on 27 February 2011. He was replaced by Beji Caid el Sebsi, who ran the government until December 2011. While Sebsi was generally far more popular than Ghannouchi, both figures were attacked in paint with such graffiti as "Sebsi = Trabelsi:" a reference to Ben Ali's despised wife Leila Trabelsi, a symbol of corruption for many Tunisians, often compared to Imelda Marcos, the wife of former Filipino dictator Ferdinand Marcos. Such emotive writing sparked heated discussions between passersby, particularly between those who supported Sebsi and those who agreed with the tags. Such public discussion was practically unheard of under Ben Ali.

I am not arguing that every spray painted surface carries a critical political message. Graffiti for football club Espérance Sportive de Tunis saw the highest growth of public inscription. However, to become preoccupied with the form of a sign or performance and to neglect the symbolic meaning runs the risk of missing a great deal. What is written in public is not always as important as the fact that it *is written in public.*

Moving beyond a focus on the form—the specific text or image painted on the wall—we begin to gain a deeper appreciation for the meaning of graffiti as an inherently political act. Chantal Mouffe, the Belgian political theorist, encourages us to examine the political character of certain varieties of art—artistic activism being distinct from commercially motivated studio art for example. For Mouffe, and Radical Democratic Theory, the political is conceived of separately from politics. Where politics is strictly the realm of creating order by legislators and parliaments, the political is the public space of contestation and discourse. When individuals feel that political lines are blurred or that their participation is meaningless, alienation, disenchantment, and violence can occur. Encouraging a forum for public participation in the political is at the root of 'Radical Democratic Theory,' and for many, the potential social function of graffiti as public art. Art as public participation positions a challenge to the dominant discourse on power through a kind of democratic uprising. However, those in a position of power often see graffiti as merely another commodity to be owned, or a criminal element in society in need of eradication.

One criminal element presages another, claim social theorists James Q. Wilson and George L. Kelling in their "Broken Window Theory," which has been quoted by many antagonists of street art from law enforcement officials to academics. The theory holds that the condition of urban environments is causally related to crime rates, claiming that indicators such as broken windows or graffiti convey a social signaling of lawlessness and a lack of monitoring of crimes. The idea is that when someone else has already noticeably committed a crime, others will feel emboldened to follow suit, instituting a positive feedback loop. The argument rests on the premise that street art is perceived as a criminal element in society. But should a tag that reads "Ben Ali and his Forty Trabelsi Thieves" or "Sebsi=Trabelsi" be conceived of as "a broken window" or as public participation in the political where previously such forums had been closed off? I argue that we should see it as the latter.

After the revolution, the surge in street art, a social signal not of vandalism but of inscribed free expression, served as a forum for greater awareness and civic participation in a country still mostly distrustful of politics. The positive feedback of greater public participation was not confined to locals spray painting a few sentences of dissenting opinion but grew to invite a global participation in solidarity with Tunisia, a demonstration of graffiti as a conduit for a cosmopolitanism that its critics fail to acknowledge. I personally observed this cosmopolitanism on the streets of Tunisia.

One autumn afternoon, as I strolled through Tunis' more than a thousand-year-old Medina (old city), passing gypsum white walls, cyan and azure ornately decorated doorways, minarets rising in both hexagonal Arab and circular Ottoman styles, through crowded *souks* and cafes, past men watching football or smoking water pipes, I watched the dynamic cityscape unfold in much the same way as it has for centuries, with walls that have outlived empires. I rounded a corner and was suddenly confronted with a life-size caricature, painted simply in black and white, with a splash of blood red on his cheeks. In a note of unplanned poetics, the trash strewn at his feet produced a kind of symbolic insistence that he was emerging from a discarded past. Written on the right side of this image was a name: Mohamed Hanchi, and a date: 25/02/2011. This was a leftover piece of graffiti from Zoo Project, an Algerian graffiti artist who lives in Paris.

Between March and April 2011, Zoo Project visited Tunis and created a series of street art pieces, forty life-sized figures signifying some of the more than 200 people who were killed during the revolution, mostly during clashes with security forces during Ghannouchi's interim government. Mohamed Hanchi was a nineteen year old who was murdered by security forces. This piece and others such as a man sweeping 'RCD' off a wall or a group of children on each other's shoulders playing hopscotch toward *Democratie* are examples of localized remembrance that many Tunisians hope will serve to keep the message of the revolution alive in public conversation. This is an example of the role of street art in not only returning a voice to the voiceless, by prolonging the discussion of those who died, but of renegotiating the

Mohamed Hanchi was killed on February 25, 2011 by Tunisian government security forces.

This street art depicts children playing hopscotch toward democracy.

subjective meaning of public space. While the metaphor of domination existed under Ben Ali, the metaphor of freedom after the revolution is represented by the increase in street art throughout Tunisia.

At the end of Tunis' grand French colonial leftover, Avenue Habib Bourguiba, painted on the pylons of an overpass are countless murals by different artists, each one a distinct style and specific interaction between artist and public. Tunisia Live, a local media outlet, explained that for one of the artists, Mourad Khalsi, artists are always revolutionary. Others who participated in this action reiterated feelings of intense political engagement. There is nothing inherently revolutionary about abstract, multicolored smiling faces, but the fact that they were freely painted in public serves as a signifier of increased freedom of expression and, for the artist, stimulates a conversation on healing after years of suffering. The location for the project, which was approved by the municipality, was selected particularly for its high traffic, thus maximizing the artists' desire to spread their message. However, for Mohamed Ben Soltane, "If you go to the municipality and take authorization to make street art, it's not street art." A contention exists whether street art can convey a repositioning of public democratic discourse if it is permitted by the power structure. In response, Tunisia's radical art collective Ahl Al Kahf's work is a synthesis of the kind of street art that is both an impetus for deeper public participation in democratic discourse and a forum for challenging conceptions of dominant power through anarchistic creative action.

Ahl Al Kahf describe themselves as an anonymous collective of youth forged in the crucible of revolution and prepared to stand against Globalization and Orientalism.* Their graffiti can be found in many cities across Tunisia. They describe their work as an homage to all international resistance against dictators. One of their largest and most famous actions was the symbolic reclamation of the house of the nephew of Leila Trabelsi, Imed Trabelsi, in La Marsa, an affluent coastal suburb of Tunis.

As much as Leila Trabelsi was a symbol of corruption, so too was her family, those who profited from nepotism and the regime's abuse. As Ben Ali fled the country so did many members of the Trabelsi family. Many of their houses were ransacked, targeted with the unfettered destructive force of generations of subjugated individuals. Windows were broken, furniture was stolen or destroyed, and walls were torched. In this state of ruin, certain houses were left as brutalized effigies of their previous corrupt inhabitants. It was in this state of broken windows and detritus that Ahl Al Kahf, with no permission sought or publicity issued beforehand, set upon Imed

---

*Orientalism has grown to have a negative meaning since the publication of Edward Said's book by the same name. The term refers to the lingering colonialist oppression inherent in mainstream Western literary, artistic, or political examinations and analysis of the global South, often through a process of 'exoticization' or 'eroticization.'

A stencil of a footballer, where instead of a ball the artist has painted Ben Ali's head. This image appears on the side of Imed Trabelsi's mansion. On this wall graffiti is written in three languages, French, English, and Arabic.

In this Ahl Al Kahf stencil, the Arabic voices a plea for freedom of expression. But one is left to ponder why naked women are synonymous with freedom of expression.

Trabelsi's mansion with spray cans and stencils to reclaim that which belonged to the oppressor, as a symbolic interaction with the past and an encouragement for the future. As pioneering French street artist Blek le Rat has insisted, graffiti is a way to reclaim the street; or, as one Tunisian artist expressed to me, these actions should be seen as part of the realization that "for the first time the street and the walls are ours."

Ahl Al Kahf's work, along with other graffiti artists in Tunisia, has been featured on blogs and art magazines. Groups like the Wooster Collective are spreading street art to global audiences. In this way, not only has the broadening of a democratic voice been emboldened by street art in Tunisia, but, as I have observed, similar encounters of reclaiming public space are occurring around the world. The work of street artists in Detroit, Buenos Aires, Xi'an, and Tunis is being uploaded and discussed around the world; the exchange of symbols and ideas is contributing to a dialogue outside of mainstream structures of power. Thus, the potential for increased democratic voice engendered in the free expression of street art should not be considered simply location-specific nor should street art be dismissed and denigrated as vandalism. It should not be encouraged as commodity art relegated to philosophizing in art galleries or the walls of private collectors. Street art should be conceived and encouraged as part of a repertoire for an increase in, potentially, global awareness and political participation in the public sphere.

For Class Discussion

1. What interpretation of graffiti in postrevolutionary Tunisia does Caster want readers to accept?

2. Caster incorporates several important theories related to graffiti, political engagement, and public space. What are these theories? Which does he accept? Which does he refute?

3. How and how effectively does Caster weave his knowledge of graffiti, his personal experience, and visual evidence into this argument?

4. What opposing views does Caster acknowledge and how does he answer them?

5. How could you support the statement that cultural hybridization is the paradigm that underlies Caster's argument?

Photo of Street Art in Beijing, China
Michael Caster

This photo, taken by Michael Caster in winter 2010, depicts a street art mural in Beijing, China. The playful image from Beijing transforms traditional Chinese architecture into an anthropomorphic cartoonish creature. This image appears on the wall of an abandoned warehouse in the 798 Art District, formerly a machine works factory and now the site of numerous galleries and art spaces. The process of gentrification has forced many smaller artists to move.

What is your first impression of the graffiti depicted in this photo? What is most visually striking?

Street Art in Beijing, China

Michael Caster

For Class Discussion

1. How does this image convey the claims often made for graffiti that it is playful freedom of expression and an outlet for creativity?

2. In color, this cartoon figure is bright blue against a brick wall daubed with bright pink. Even without cultural background, why would you—or would you not—find this image more interesting than a blank wall?

3. How does knowing that this graffiti is on the wall outside a sanctioned art gallery influence your thinking on the nature of graffiti as art? Does art need to be in a museum to be considered art?

4. In what ways could this image be used in arguments about the possible social role of graffiti as commentary or art?

Photo of Street Art in Managua, Nicaragua
Michael Caster

This is an image of artwork from a series of concrete walls along Pista Juan Pablo II (Pope John Paul II Road) surrounding the University of Managua in the capital of Nicaragua, a city rich in graffiti, which has been profiled in many leading graffiti blogs and Web sites. (This photo was taken by Michael Caster in spring 2008.) Despite the large presence of graffiti, Nicaragua is generally considered the safest country in Central America and the second safest in all of Latin America. The text in Spanish in this image reads: "Ignorance is the greatest offense of a people, and the best weapon for a leader."

   What is your first impression of the graffiti depicted in this photo? What is most visually striking?

Michael Caster

Street Art in Managua, Nicaragua

For Class Discussion

1. What do you think was the artist's intent in depicting the human form in such a contorted, alien form?

2. If you first noticed the visual aspect of this piece of graffiti while walking down an unfamiliar street, without knowing what the Spanish means or before reading it, how do you think you would respond? Would you find it appealing, or would it make you feel at risk, or uncomfortable, for example?

3. Do you think that this graffiti is capable of conveying a social message to a global audience, even for those who do not know what the text means?

4. This graffiti promotes education as a bulwark against abusive rulers, in this sense playing a social advocacy and political role in the community. Look online for ways artists in other countries have used graffiti to engage in social/political commentary. Do you notice trends or similarities? How does this piece fit into your observations?

Marvel Comics and Manifest Destiny

David Adesnik

David Adesnik, a research analyst in Washington, DC, received his doctorate in international relations from Oxford University. Doublethink Online sponsors his blog as a "bright young mind of the Right." This cultural analysis was posted January 28, 2005, on the Web site of the *Daily Standard* (www.weeklystandard .com), a British daily online publication affiliated with the *Weekly Standard*, a news commentary magazine.

> This piece is more exploratory than argumentative. What claims does it make about comic superheroes? What questions does it raise about popular culture and cross-cultural exchanges?

Devarajan's aspirations are noble, yet it's interesting to wonder if American audiences will recognize this Spider-Man after his translation into the local idiom. Or, conversely, if Devarajan, born in New York to parents from India, will preserve too much of Spider-Man's American heritage and wind up with a character that won't resonate with Indian audiences.

In short, Devarajan's attempt to transform Peter Parker into Pavitr Prabhakar forces him to confront the age-old challenge of separating the universal aspects of human nature from the particular characteristics of a specific culture. The success (or failure) of Devarajan's effort matters, because it may tell us something important about the validity of Americans' faith in the universality of our most cherished ideals.

The first issue of *Spider-Man: India* demonstrates that Devarajan was dead serious when he spoke of preserving the Spider-mantra that "with great power comes great responsibility." In 1962, Spider-Man learned this enduring lesson when a security guard asked him to stop an armed robber in the midst of making his getaway. At that time, Peter Parker was an embittered teenager with no sense of obligation to the greater good. He refused to apprehend the robber.

Later that same night, Peter returns home to find out that his beloved Uncle Ben has been murdered. Enraged, Peter hunts down the murderer, only to discover that it is the tough he let go. This tragic coincidence provokes his epiphany.

In *Spider-Man: India*, young Pavitr Prabhakar learns his lesson in an almost identical manner. While swinging across Mumbai, Pavitr hears the cries of a young woman surrounded by a gang of thugs. He does nothing and swings away. Moments later, Pavitr's beloved Uncle Bhim hears the cries of the same young woman and decides to confront her assailants. They warn Uncle Bhim that they will hurt him if he does not walk away. Bhim stays. He is murdered. Later that night, Pavitr learns of his uncle's death, hunts down the murderers, and experiences an epiphany of his own.

Although its innovations seem trivial, *India's* reworking of the Spider-myth brilliantly enhances the painful irony of the American original. Whereas Ben's murder is a matter of pure coincidence, Bhim dies because he had the courage to confront precisely the same evil that his nephew wouldn't. In both instances, the punishment for selfishness is the death of a loved one. Yet in *India*, that loved one is also a martyr whose death becomes the embodiment of the ethos to which Spider-Man must aspire.

The counterpoint to *India's* subtle reworking of the death of Uncle Ben is its ambitious recasting of Spider-Man's powers as the worldly incarnation of a purposeful, mystical force rather than the accidental outgrowth of a scientific experiment. In a recent interview, Devarajan observed that the diametrically opposed forces of science and magic represent the fundamental contrast between Eastern and Western culture.

At a time when IBM is outsourcing thousands of high-tech jobs to Bangalore, it may seem strange to hear an Indian-American insist that magic is the essence of Eastern culture. Nonetheless, Devarajan's decision to build his story on a mythological foundation provides a much better testing ground for the hypothesis that the superhero ethic is part of a "universal psyche" rather than an American one.

As a literary device, the replacement of science with magic functions smoothly. In both accounts of Spider-Man's origins, there is a seamless integration of plot and metaphor. Although Peter Parker is now a married man in his thirties, he was a bespectacled teenage bookworm when Spider-Man debuted in the 1960s. A friendless outcast, Parker devoted all of his time to academic pursuits, such as the public science exhibit at which he was bitten by a radioactive spider. Although nominally an accident, the spider bite is a metaphorical expression of the American faith that knowledge is power and that science is the engine of progress. Initially taunted because of his devotion to science, Parker ultimately becomes all the more powerful because of it.

In *Spider-Man: India*, Pavitr Prabhakar is an outcast not because of his academic talent, but because of the traditional clothing that he wears to an expensive private school in cosmopolitan Mumbai. As a scholarship student from a small village in the countryside, it is all Pavitr can afford. One day, while being chased by the bullies who taunt him for wearing harem pants reminiscent of the glory days of MC Hammer, Pavitr stumbles upon an ancient mystic who warns him of an impending battle between ancient forces of good and evil. The old man endows Pavitr with the power of the spider and tells him "This is your destiny, young Pavitr Prabhakar. Rise to the challenge . . . fulfill your karma." In the same manner that Parker embodies the ideals of modern America, Prabhakar embodies those of traditional India.

At first, the suggestion that Pavitr has a destiny that he must fulfill may strike some readers as un-American. In the land of opportunity, we reject out of hand the notion that individuals must resign themselves to their fate. Instead, we believe that there are no limits to what can be achieved by a combination of hard work and ingenuity.

Yet is the concept of destiny really so foreign? Was it not under the banner of Manifest Destiny that the young United States claimed for itself the Great Plains and the northern reaches of Mexico? Was it not Ronald Reagan who constantly reminded the citizens of the United States that they had a "rendezvous with destiny"? To what else did George W. Bush refer to in his second inaugural address when he stated that "History has an ebb and flow of justice, but history also has a visible direction, set by liberty and the author of liberty"?

The most important difference Spider-fans will notice between the Indian and American notions of destiny is the Indian belief that tyranny and evil are primal forces no less powerful than freedom and good. Yet there is also a considerable measure of doubt embedded in the American vision of progress. Although one scientific accident gave Spider-Man his powers, other scientific accidents were responsible for the creation of his arch-nemeses, Dr. Octopus and the Green Goblin. In the final analysis, that which makes Pavitr Prabhakar authentically Indian does not make him in any way un-American.

Today the Republic of India is the most populous democracy on the face of the Earth. Someday, it may rival the United States in terms of wealth and power. Conventional thinking suggests that the emergence of a second superpower would threaten the security of the United States of America. Yet if India's first superhero recognizes that with great power there also comes great responsibility, perhaps we should look forward to the emergence of an Indian superpower.

For Class Discussion

1. What are the main changes that Devarajan has made in translating Spider-Man into an Indian comic book superhero?

2. What does this cultural analysis suggest are the important connections between the popular heroes and the values and identities of nations?

3. What is the rhetorical effect of the title of this article? How does Adesnik use the concept of "Manifest Destiny"?

4. Do you think the *Spider-Man: India* comic exemplifies a positive or a negative cultural exchange? Why? What paradigm of intercultural relations does it exemplify?

Image from *Spider-Man: India*
Jeevan J. Kang

This image is part of the Gotham Comics press release of the *Spider-Man: India* series, drawn by famous Indian artist Jeevan J. Kang. The comic ran for four issues in India in 2004, and in 2005 was released to a U.S. audience. The series was later collected into a trade paperback. In this comic, Pavitr Prabhakar, a poor Indian boy from the country and the counterpart of Peter Parker, discovers his karma and embraces the fight against evil. See the cover images at (www.marvel.com/digitalcomics/titles/SPIDER-MAN~colon~_INDIA.2004).

As an American reader, what is your spontaneous response to the drawing of this character?

SPIDER-MAN © 2004 Marvel Characters Inc.

Spider-Man:™ and © 2005 Marvel Characters, Inc. Used with permission. Illustration by Gotham Studios Asia.

For Class Discussion

1. In its press release, Gotham Comics calls *Spider-Man: India* a "transcreation," by which it means an Indian retelling of the American superhero's story. What signs of adaptation and cultural contextualizing do you see in this image?

2. What other characters from popular U.S. culture have crossed cultures in this way?

3. Based on what you have read in Adesnik's article, do you think these kinds of cultural transpositions are effective, creative, and interesting? Why? Why do you think American audiences would or would not enjoy this new comic?

4. How could you make a case that "transcreation" is an example of "glocalization" rather than an example of cultural imperialism? ∎

The 99 Aspires to Teach Muslim Principles
Brian Truitt

Brian Truitt writes articles about comics and pop cultural topics for *USA Today*, the American daily newspaper with the widest circulation. *USA Today* leans center-conservative in its political views. This short informative and promotional piece appeared in *USA Today* on September 20, 2011.

> According to Brian Truitt's coverage of this superheroes comic, what is the main theme of *The 99*?

Superman has been espousing the virtues of truth, justice and the American way for decades. It's 99 virtues and a global way, however, that power the Muslim-inspired superheroes of The 99.

Launched as a comic-book series in the Middle East by Kuwaiti-born psychologist Naif Al-Mutawa in 2006, The 99 has found a following that's just as international as its group of heroes.

Powered by magic gemstones, each member of The 99 hails from a different country and is a literal version of one of the 99 attributes of Allah. For example, Jabbar the Powerful from Saudi Arabia is super-strong, Hadya the Guide is a London woman who's also a walking GPS, and Darr the Afflicter (a guy from St. Louis named John Weller) inflicts his "painwave" on evildoers.

But they're not just limited to comics anymore. A theme park based on The 99 opened in Kuwait in 2009, and a second park in the region is now in the discussion phase. Al-Mutawa and his heroes were the subject of the documentary Wham! Bam! Islam! (which premieres Oct. 13 on PBS), and the animated feature The 99: Unbound will be unveiled to American audiences on Oct. 2 at the New York Film Festival.

"If I had these kinds of expectations, I'd be the one locked up at Bellevue and not the one seeing the patients there," quips Al-Mutawa, who hatched the idea for The 99 with his sister Samar in the back of a London cab in 2003.

"I knew that by creating it the way I create it—they're from 99 different countries, stuff like that —that it could one day maybe be able to be a global thing. It wasn't so much that I thought I could do something global. It was more trying to protect myself against what happens in my part of the world."

Al-Mutawa, 40, is himself a pretty worldly guy—these days, he divides time between Kuwait and New York City. His education has been mostly in the USA, including a doctorate in psychology from Long Island University, two master's degrees from Columbia and a love for comics that dates back to attending a Jewish summer camp in New Hampshire when he was 9. (His first comic: an adaptation of the Bible.)

Risky on many levels.

When he was rounding up comic-book writers such as Fabian Nicieza and Stuart Moore and $7 million in initial capital from investors, Al-Mutawa knew The 99 was a risky venture, both financially and culturally, especially in Muslim countries because of the subject matter. It was important to him that this new franchise give Arab children new heroes and teach about Muslim principles in a post-9/11 world.

He expected a lot of flak—he likens the situation to white blood cells attacking something new introduced to the human body.

"We also have people in our communities who are the white blood cells who will attack anything that's foreign and new," Al-Mutawa says. "This is repackaging something they felt shouldn't be repackaged, and no one had actually taken that initiative.

"I'm one of those people who believes that the only way to beat extremism is through arts and culture. That's what happened in Europe during the Reformation and the Renaissance, and that's what has to happen in the Muslim world."

Yet The 99 was never really banned in the Arab world, he says.

It wasn't approved to get into Saudi Arabia for a while, but now a network will air the first season of The 99 animated series—the first four episodes make up the Unbound movie—in that country and in others in the Middle East this fall. In addition, Cartoon Network bought the rights to air the show in Asia, and the cartoon also will air in Australia and Ireland.

The one place where Al-Mutawa has met the most resistance? The superhero-loving USA.

The 99 has even teamed with Batman and Superman in a crossover series with DC Comics' Justice League to appeal to fans in the USA, but Al-Mutawa says some have attacked him for promoting sharia law to American kids, even though he has made sure religion doesn't play a major role in the comics or the cartoon. (The Hub, an American cable venture from Discovery and Hasbro, bought the rights to The 99 animated series last year, but as of yet has no plans to air it.)

"I'm not on my turf here," Al-Mutawa says. "I've met these same kind of people in my part of the world, and I've been able to give like I get. I don't want to say I won the battle, but there's a truce there. They understand I'm not the bad guy.

"The stuff that we're being accused of, like we're out there trying to radicalize young children? Some of the responses on the blogs was stuff like, 'We can't let the Muslims brainwash our children like the Mexicans did with Dora the Explorer.'"

However, The 99 won't "radicalize" anybody, "unless your definition of radicalism means to tolerate other people," says Stan Berkowitz, story editor on The 99 animated series.

A superhero subtext.

A writer on American shows such as Justice League and Batman Beyond, Berkowitz says every superhero story has subtext, and he particularly likes the underlying themes of The 99.

"The Superman story, the subtext is the Moses story, finding the child in the basket. The Batman subtext is about vengeance," he says. "This one, it's not about the fight of the weak or who has what power. It's about everyone finding a gift, a skill or talent that they have and then developing it."

Al-Mutawa's five sons, ages 2 to 14, are all fans of The 99. "I told my wife, 'Five down, 94 to go,' but she's not interested," he jokes.

But he also has an admirer in President Obama, a comics lover who gave a shout-out to The 99 last year during a presidential summit on entrepreneurship.

"When you're in school and you write something great, your teacher says, 'Good job' and gives you a happy face," Al-Mutawa says. "That was like getting three happy faces."

For Class Discussion

1. What impressions of the author of *The 99,* Naif Al-Mutawa, does Truitt seek to give his readers?

2. What ideas and issues about cultural globalization mentioned in the "Stakes and Stakeholders" questions in the introduction to this chapter does this article speak to? How has this series been received globally?

3. From what this article says about the comic series, its characters, its purpose, and its theme, would you say *The 99* represents cultural convergence or cultural hybridization?

4. How does the title of the article run the risk of increasing readers' resistance to the comic series? What might a better title be both to match the content of the article and to be more rhetorically effective?

Poster of *The 99*
Naif Al-Mutawa

The 99 is a new superheroes comic book series, film, and now a theme park created by Naif Al-Mutawa, a Kuwaiti psychologist with graduate degrees from Long Island University and Columbia University. The title refers to 99 characters, each representing 1 of the 99 virtues of Allah. The TED talk Naif Al-Mutawa presented (available on the Web) explains his motivation, the underlying concepts, and the process of developing this new series. Dr. Al-Mutawa speaks at global conferences as a successful entrepreneur in the Middle East and as a culture maker. He has said that he was looking for Islamic role models for his five sons: "the only people using our culture were the wrong people . . . people who have basically weaponized our religion. The only way to de-link religion from their negative message is to link the same source and go back to the Koran (teachings) and create positive messages that highlight tolerance, multiculturalism and acceptance of other people's differences."* He has explained, "The message I send here is that the values of those Muslims are the same values of everybody else. So, it does not matter what religion you have because at the basic human level we are all the same."†

After studying the figures in this poster, what is your emotional response to them?

Copyright © 2012 Teshkeel Media Group, Inc.

Poster of the Characters from *The 99*

---

*Oralandar Brand-Williams, "Small Talk with Naif Al-Mutawa," *Detroit News,* October 3, 2011.
†"Muslim Comic Book Is 'The Antidote to bin Laden,'" *The National,* October 14, 2011.

For Class Discussion

1. What details of this poster suggest that this comic series is based on Islamic culture?

2. What details suggest it belongs in the broader genre of superhero comics?

3. Based on your understanding of this genre, what questions would you want to ask about the characters, plots, conflicts, and themes of *The 99*?

4. Without any introduction from their parents, how do you think American children would respond to this comic series?

5. As the incidents involving the Prophet Mohammed cartoons and the film of the autobiographical graphic novel *Persepolis* show, cartoon images have been very problematic in the Middle East and in Muslim cultures recently. Spend some time looking at the covers and characters from *The 99* on the Web (www.the99.org). How does this comic series try to cross cultures and reach out to a global audience with its images?

Trading Cape for the Burqa
Andrea Peyser

Andrea Peyser is a conservative columnist for the daily newspaper the *New York Post,* which has one of the largest circulations in the country. She is known for her lively, biting tone and her focus on public figures and scandal. Peyser worked for the Associated Press and CNN in several cities before becoming a reporter and then a columnist for the *New York Post*. Peyser's writing has appeared in *Cosmopolitan* and *Glamour*, and she has won several awards for women journalists as well as authored two books: *Mother Love, Deadly Love: The Susan Smith Murders* (1995) and *Celebutards: The Hollywood Hacks, Limousine Liberals, and Pandering Politicians Who Are Destroying America* (2009). This opinion column appeared in the *New York Post* on October 11, 2011.

> According to Andrea Peyser, on what basis do some Western and American viewers object to the comic series *The 99*? What cultural paradigm does this thinking represent?

Hide your face and grab the kids. Coming soon to a TV in your child's bedroom is a posse of righteous, *Sharia*-compliant Muslim superheroes—including one who fights crime hidden head-to-toe by a burqa.

These Islamic butt-kickers are ready to bring truth, justice and indoctrination to impressionable Western minds.

Scheduled for release on the new network The Hub—formerly Discovery Kids—which launches today (Time Warner and DirecTV carry it in the city), is a cartoon beloved in the Arab world and received timidly in Britain last year, "The 99."

The program chronicles the adventures of 99 superheroes, each of whom embodies an attribute of Allah.

Jabbar is a Muslim Incredible Hulk. Mumita is wicked fast. But Wonder Woman-style cleavage has been banned from the ladies. And, in this faith-based cartoon, hair-hiding head scarves are mandatory for five characters, not including burqa babe Batina the Hidden.

In another break from standard world-saving fare, male and female characters are never alone together. (Imagine the stoning super-strong characters would dish out.) "The 99" even has the seal of approval of a *Sharia* board—which polices Muslim law—affiliated with an Islamic bank from which the show received financing.

What a great time to come to the United States!

No higher an authority than President Obama praised the work of the comic's creator, Kuwaiti psychologist Naif Al-Mutawa. At an April meeting with Arab entrepreneurs, Obama said, "His superheroes embody the teachings of the tolerance of Islam."

There was no stopping it.

The Hub, a joint venture with Hasbro toys, announced in May that it would produce and air episodes of "The 99." But then, murmurs of dissatisfaction turned into a cry.

How can a secular nation endorse a children's show aimed at pushing one religion?

A Times of London columnist wrote last year that the show's mission was "to instill old-fashioned Islamic values in Christian, Jewish and atheist children."

Then last month, the conservative Family Security Matters think tank published a piece titled "Meet the Muslim Superheroes Who Are Ready to Indoctrinate American Kids."

Acknowledging Mustawa's efforts to bridge cultures, editor Adrian Morgan asked, "Are we going to see ass-kicking Christian superhero nuns called Faith, Hope and Charity whooping sinners' butts and sending Satan into hell? It's doubtful."

The effect was quick.

The debut of "The 99" has been pushed back at least until January, said a Hub source who asked not to be named. He blamed unspecified "production issues" for the delay.

Some New York parents don't want to see it at all.

"They're taking advantage of the fact that in every middle-class household, Mom and Dad are working their asses off," said Andy Sullivan, a Queens construction worker and dad who's been fighting the Ground Zero mosque.

"They know the kids are watching TV or on the Internet. So maybe *Sharia* becomes OK. It's a game. It gradually becomes more and more in their lives."

Mom-of-two Trish Mobley said, "I have no problem with Muslim superheroes, but lose the burqa. A female superhero should not wear a symbol of subservience to men. It's also completely impractical when fighting bad guys."

"Muslim superheroes?" asked Rich Pecorella, who lost his fiancée on 9/11. "They're dragging religion into an area that we don't drag religion into in this country."

Now we're getting a comic book based on a wheelchair-bound Muslim superhero. What's next?

I have no doubt Muslims are as fast and strong as any Supermen. But we don't need religious icons masquerading as good guys.

Cancel "The 99" before it starts.

For Class Discussion

1. What is the core of Peyser's argument against showing the television version of *The 99* in the United States?

2. On what assumptions about her audience and her subject—*The 99*—does Peyser build her argument?

3. What kinds and quality of evidence and reasoning undergird this argument?

4. Peyser employs a sarcastic, dramatic, and alarmist tone in this op-ed piece. What examples of this tone do you see in her choice of language and what are the potential rhetorical risks and gains of using this language?

5. What questions about *The 99* does this op-ed piece inspire you to investigate?

Super Muslims
Suzy Hansen

Suzy Hansen formerly worked as an editor for the *New York Observer* and *Salon* and now works as a freelance writer living in Istanbul. She has published in *The Atlantic*, the *New York Times*, *The New Republic*, *GQ*, and *Bloomberg Businessweek*, among other publications. She received a fellowship from the Institute of Current World Affairs in 2007. This analysis/review appeared as a "Religion" column in *The Atlantic* for May 2010. *The Atlantic* magazine features news and analysis of politics, business, foreign affairs, technology, and culture for readers who are generally well educated.

According to this article, what stance does creator Naif Al-Mutawa take toward politics and religion in *The 99*, his comic series for children?

On especially thick and gritty days in Kuwait, everything must be done indoors—in cars, malls, hotels, or office buildings. Often, it's not until you're in one of those violently airconditioned high-rise office buildings that you can take in the whole of Kuwait City: urban cylinders of silver and black improbably growing out of nothingness. It's a strangely drab backdrop for the hyperkinetic Naif al-Mutawa, who sat in a nice tan suit on a couch, and spoke with great enthusiasm and speed. On the walls of his office hung drawings of multicolored characters from his brainchild: *The 99,* a comic book rooted in Islam that has recently been recast into an animated television series, which may debut in the United States this fall.

"When I gave the direction to the writers in Hollywood for the animation series," he was saying, "I told them, 'Only when Jewish kids think these heroes are Jewish, and Christian kids think they're Christian, will we have achieved something—which is universality.' Too many people find differences and fight about them. Not enough people are talking about the things that are the same."

But they seem to want to. *The 99's* fledgling success is a publicity story for our times: in 2006, amid growing controversy over a Danish newspaper's publication of cartoons depicting Muhammad, a few articles about al-Mutawa's project appeared. So when people Googled variations of *Islam, cartoon, Muslim,* and *comic,* up popped the piece about *The 99.* Never mind that back in 2006, *The 99* didn't even exist yet in book form. Amid a miserable East-West cultural conflagration, searchers discovered a happier tale (Islam! Heroes! Children!), and al-Mutawa's phone at his tiny company, Teshkeel, began to ring.

Since then, *The 99* has been distributed in Indonesia, Saudi Arabia, China, India, the United States, and elsewhere. But the comic books (which veteran illustrators and writers produce under al-Mutawa's direction) were never the endgame, al-Mutawa told me; television was crucial to making his idea financially viable. In 2008, the European TV conglomerate Endemoi snatched up *The 99* for an animated series and is currently negotiating to broadcast in Western markets.

The first episode, "Origins," is set in Baghdad in 1258, when the Islamic world's most cherished library was destroyed by descendants of Genghis Kahn. In "Origins," scholars manage to preserve the wisdom of the world's great books in 99 stones. That there are 99 of them is, of course, no accident; in Islamic tradition, Allah is said to have 99 names, or virtues.

After that issue, the books mostly forgo history for the exploits of the crime-fighting multinational superheroes, who are imbued with special powers from those stones. They come from different countries, and have names like Noora the Light (from the UAE), whose holograms expose the evil in people's souls; Widad the Loving (the Philippines), who can make people feel love or "the emptiness of hatred"; Sami the Listener (Sudan/France), who is mute but can hear everything; and a curious character from the United States who can "manipulate nerve endings, allowing him to cause or prevent pain."

"People think it's political that I put the American hero in a wheelchair," said al-Mutawa, who is a clinical psychologist educated at Long Island University and Columbia University.

"I thought it was political because you called him the Afflicter," I replied.

"Nooooo! Honestly, I didn't make that decision, it was the [other writers]," he laughed. "My kids are all U.S. citizens, by the way. All five of them."

Al-Mutawa reiterated that he'd scrubbed the books clean of overt political references. Except for, say, a character wearing a hijab, and a scarcity of violence and skimpy clothing, it's just a typical comic book—all action, and good triumphing over evil. Al-Mutawa didn't want to give the censors in Kuwait or Saudi Arabia any opportunity to stop delivery. He also didn't want to scare off Westerners easily freaked out by all things Islam. In one example of such line-walking, al-Mutawa decided that *The 99*'s characters should work in teams of three, since pairing an unrelated male and female to work together might be problematic from an Islamic point of view. Even still, one Saudi scholar has suggested that al-Mutawa was sent by the pope to preach the trinity.

"So you can't win," he said. "It's fascinating to watch."

Al-Mutawa's creation has its admirers. But he may not necessarily win over one crucial and notoriously hard-to-please international group: adult comic-book geeks.

"The problem with the Islamic context of *The 99*, for me as a reader," the American comics critic Douglas Wölk told me, "is that it's *not* subtext: it's simply the setting, and the religious content of the series is so neutered that even having that context doesn't provide any opportunities for actually saying something about what it means to live in the world of Islam as a young person."

I wondered whether a Kuwaiti expert would feel the same. Faisal al-Duwaisan, a 36-year-old filmmaker, photographer, and comic-book enthusiast, met me at a Caribou Coffee in the Arraya Center, an extravagant but empty shopping mall. Al-Duwaisan, wearing jeans and New Balance sneakers, follows Kevin Smith on Twitter and identifies strongly with Batman. "This culture doesn't understand the importance of comics," he explained. "Here, there are no superheroes for kids, no role models. Most writers write about social or political issues. We don't even have science fiction."

He looked wistful when I brought up *The 99*. "I like the image Dr. Naif is bringing with *The 99*, but unfortunately it's not very successful here," he said. Al-Duwaisan still preferred his *Batmans* to *The 99*—and not because of too little Islamic subtext, but too much. Al-Duwaisan felt that groups of heroes working collectively missed the very point of the Western comics he adores: the triumph of the individual.

"In the West, there's one hero," he said with visible longing. "If there are too many of them, you can't idolize anyone. I don't feel the heroism. I am reading *Batman* because I see part of myself in it."

"Super Muslims" by Suzy Hansen from The Atlantic, May 2010. Copyright 2010, The Atlantic Media Co. as published in The Atlantic Monthly. Distributed by Tribune Media Services.

For Class Discussion

1. What is the philosophy undergirding *The 99* series? What does its creator, Naif Al-Mutawa, mean by "universality"?

2. In creating this series, where has Al-Mutawa made choices to accommodate Islamic values?

3. Why do comic book enthusiasts in the Middle East think *The 99* might not succeed in their culture?

4. How would you describe the position Hansen takes on *The 99* in this article and how does it differ from the view of this series presented by Brian Truitt and Andrea Peyser? In your mind, how successfully does this review promote this comic superhero series?

5. What questions about intercultural mixing and this comic series does Hansen raise?

The Secret Virus of Hip-Hop
Kris Saknussemm

Kris Saknussemm is a novelist, poet, essayist, and cultural critic. His novels include *Zanesville* (2005), *Private Midnight* (2009), *Enigmatic Pilot* (2011), and *Reverend America* (2012); the latter has a CD of jazz, gospel, and popular music that is in conversation with it and that exhibits Saknussemm's knowledge of music. Saknussemm has also authored an award-winning collection of poems, a play, and the short story collection *Sinister Miniatures*. A longtime expatriate in Australia and the Pacific Islands, he writes often about the exportation of American culture and its effects on local cultures around the world. This cultural commentary appeared on the blog Clockworkfather on March 24, 2010.

Why is it important that Kris Saknussemm recaps the history of hip-hop music early in his argument?

Think of it. A lone Indian boy tending cattle on a rainy hillside in the highlands of Melanesian Fiji . . . a group of Zulu kids in a smoking camp in Soweto . . . Maori street youths in Auckland . . . white boys in a desolate skate park in a dusty small town in rural Australia . . . they all look like what they believe Afro-American rappers should look like. From New York City to the jungles of New Ireland . . . LA to Lagos . . . the virus has spread.

Hip-Hop is widely agreed to have begun in the South Bronx in the late 1970s as a folk art form pioneered by young DJs, who demonstrated their skill and flamboyance on the turntables, mixing and intercutting songs and rhythms at dance parties. Over and in between the dance music, they had the opportunity to interject raps, which further served to distinguish the individuality of their particular style (and were of course advertisements for themselves).

It was a fresh and inventive new kind of expression that truly emerged at street level—and it had the energy and urgency that grassroots forms often exhibit.

Rap meanwhile drew on some rich older traditions. Poetry at large for one—and there's a long history of African-American excellence in deploying and reconfiguring the possibilities of Western poetics, as well as turning to some unique forms of African derived oratory, such as the ritual insult humor of traditional verbal games like "The Dozens" and the exaggerated personal celebrations of "Toasting."

It was a compelling blend of technical innovation and verbal/poetic tradition—and it seemed to offer tremendous flexibility. The grooves could be fun and funky while the words could go in many directions—from demonstrations of pyrotechnic street corner boasting for its own sake . . . to sharp political messages that built on the work of established artists like The Last Poets, Oscar Brown Jr and Gil Scott-Heron.

Very early, you can see and hear the contrast across the spectrum in the song "Rapper's Delight" by the Sugarhill Gang and the seminal track "The Message" by Grandmaster Flash and the Furious Five. I clearly remember pulling over in traffic in heavy Seattle rain the first time I heard the latter. I wasn't alone. Major American songwriters like Leiber & Stoller recall the same experience. It was powerful. There was suddenly something new, that like rock 'n' roll and punk, also had some primitive pull—and it had the capacity to enliven the art of poetry in seemingly endless ways. It also brought with it the influential collateral of the related dance styles and physical posturing (throwing hand signs) and the style of dress associated with the performers. To say the result became immensely popular is an understatement.

Hip-Hop culture synthesized dance styles, fashion, words, imagery and sound as no pop trend ever had before. It helped partially unite competitive Afro-American and Hispanic cultures. It appealed to people of color around the world, and had an infectious impact on young white American audiences searching for the hip, new rebellious thing. (As Eminem famously said, "If I'd have been black, we would've sold half.")

No one can take away from Hip-Hop its global appeal. It has proven itself as a gigantically popular form without question. But something bad happened—and it happened extremely quickly.

Commercialization is seen as the usual villain. Many would say that a street level art form that had some real rebel cred simply got absorbed and exploited too fast and lost its vitality as a consequence.

The fun, boppy aspect of Hip-Hop became completely sanitized and turned into the soundtracks for TV commercials, while the harder, political edge degenerated into "gangsta" messages of violence, sexual explicitness straining into the realm of audio pornography, and homophobia. The visual side as presented in the corresponding videos literally followed suit—and what had been quirky individual fashion quickly became a standard uniform that was, like all uniforms, readily imitated and caricatured.

This has happened before with pop trends of course. But in the case of Hip-Hop, it happened on a scale and at a speed that was breathtaking.

We live in a far more commercialized world than existed at the beginning of the rock 'n' roll era. It was much easier for marketers to turn something fresh and authentic into a KFC ad. And who would blame the various artists for wanting to cash in when the big money started to flow? Those wanting to preserve some street cred quickly had little conceptual choice but to exaggerate the hardcore elements—the gangsta swagger, the tough talk.

Bear in mind too, that the factors which gave rise to Hip-Hop had everything to do with the strained race relations in the USA . . . the fallout and residual damage to urban culture that the Reagan Era left as its sad legacy . . . and the Crack Epidemic. The gangsta raps about "Fuck the damn police" were indeed more than just commercialized swagger. They had a legitimate political intent to them, and they resonated with those sensing oppression around the world.

However, once the forms of rebellion have been commercialized and mainstreamed, they've been subverted, and Hip-Hop unquestionably peaked in vitality very quickly . . . descending into a parody of itself almost as fast as it had won over hearts and minds. (And still the body count from the crack gang wars rose.)

But I would argue that there's a bigger problem with Hip-Hop than simply its too rapid commercial success—and it takes two longer term and broader scale forms: musical and the Americanization of world culture.

While the superficial fashion and image of Hip-Hop became ever more exploited, one fundamental fact got conveniently overlooked—*the absence of real music*. Virtually no new music was being written, as in being composed. It was assembled music. The producer became the artist, the studio the instrument. Try to find sheet music for any major Hip-Hop act.

When you went to a Public Enemy concert, you saw rappers on stage. You didn't see a band—you heard a sound system.

For all the talk about how the money corrupted Hip-Hop, you rarely hear it pointedly said that Hip-Hop MEANT THE EMPLOYMENT OF FEWER REAL MUSICIANS.

One key reason why it was so fully embraced by the major record labels was that it was so cost effective to produce—the same argument that has made Reality TV popular. This also made smaller independent recordings possible as never before. You didn't need to hire musicians—and you didn't need to have any musical ability yourself to possibly hit the big time. All you needed was attitude and image.

Composition skills were eroded, music theory was undermined, and actual physical competence on any instrument became irrelevant. The effect of this on American popular music has been profound, and its downstream influence can be attested to by teachers of music, nightclub and entertainment venue owners—anyone connected with pop music.

The effect on world music has been devastating, and the irony has been particularly biting in the case of world black music. Just at the point when African and Caribbean music culture had reached the level of the world stage, along came Hip-Hop.

It froze in time the "Jamaican Sound" where it showed signs of going off in its own interesting directions (BECAUSE IT HAD A REAL BASE OF MUSICAL TALENT TO BUILD ON).

In the cities and villages of countries like Ghana, the Ivory Coast and Nigeria it undermined interest in traditional musical expression. Why go to all the trouble to learn how to play the drum, when you can just manipulate some samples? In South Africa, where vocal skill is highly valued and harmony is a major art form—just as that expertise was becoming finally appreciated by a global audience—it was suddenly not "commercially viable."

The great innovations of African music, which contributed so crucially to the rise of African-American music, were very directly denigrated. Professional musicians, proud of their ability, were cut out of jobs, while recorded American music (which was really re-recorded, manufactured pseudo music) played. And too often won.

Hip-Hop's inherent dependence on synthesized rhythms was a direct attack on the drum kit, the djembe, the Talking Drum, the congas, the timbales . . . and the list of instruments goes on. The attack on the vocal art of actually singing can't be overstated.

Hip-Hop began as the Art of the DJ/MC. What was initially a kind of ghetto-clever, culture hacking postmodernist piracy turned into the open discouragement of real music played by real musicians.

More importantly, the export flood of American product into foreign markets drowned indigenous music and emerging commercial culture. It drove recording studios and fledgling record companies out of business. It blitzed its own roots.

For the sake of a few American millionaires, thousands upon thousands of lives were changed, musical directions and traditional art paths not taken.

Few Americas can fully appreciate the effect American culture has had around the world. You have to have traveled widely—and ideally lived outside America a long time to see it. It's taken me twenty years and thousands of miles. You may get the general idea quick enough—you hear about it, you read about it as you are now. *But it takes a lot to have the message really sink in.*

When you're in a stilt village on the Sepik River in Papua New Guinea and you hear through the native language and the blur of pidgin the mention of "the hood" you begin to get an understanding of the problem.

When the carved wooden crocodile (duk-duk) drum that would've been played sits unattended and American music is listened to, that's not good.

That this so-called music was manufactured with no musicians—at a mixing desk, with a vocal performer who doesn't know how to sing . . . cannibalizing earlier true music—that's worse still.

For all its wonderful, vigorous in-your-face energy at the start, Hip-Hop now stands as the ultimate parody of modern culture, not the voice and rhythm of progressive change. (Look at the career of someone like Ice Cube, who took his street cred and gangsta edge and became a film star in dismal middle of the road children's comedies.)

Punk made an ironic and subversive comment on the nature of pop music. Hip-Hop became the first global musical form that has the least to do with music of any popular music trend. It has become one of the most manifest signs of the American Pandemic.

For Class Discussion

1. In the claim that Saknussemm argues in this piece, what evaluation does he make of hip-hop as an art form?

2. This evaluation argument uses causal reasoning. According to Saknussemm, what ruined the grassroots vitality of hip-hop?

3. What concessions does Saknussemm make to other viewpoints? How does he refute some of the alternative views? What arguments would you bring against his perspective?

4. How does Saknussemm draw on his experience as a world traveler to give authority to his argument?

5. Think of the meaning of the title of this piece. What is the rhetorical effect of calling hip-hop a "virus" and a sign of the "American Pandemic"?

6. In his critique of global hip-hop music as a site of cultural interaction, which paradigm does Saknussemm examine?

Leveraging Hip-Hop in US Foreign Policy

Hishaam Aidi

Hishaam Aidi holds a PhD in political economy from Columbia University. He teaches at Columbia University's School of International and Public Affairs and is a fellow at the Open Society in New York. He researches the United States' and Europe's cultural policies toward their Muslim communities and movements within the Muslim communities. Aidi's writing has been published in *Africana, Middle East Report, ColorLines,* and the *New African.* He is coeditor of *Black Routes to Islam* (2009) and contributing editor of *Souls: A Critical Journal of Black Culture, Politics and Society.* This commentary was published on the Al Jazeera Internet site on November 7, 2011. Al Jazeera is a broadcasting news network, centered in Doha, Qatar, known for its bold coverage of controversies and its presentation of dissenting views; it is considered a strong example of the free press.

> Why do U.S. Secretary of State Hillary Clinton and the State Department think that hip-hop is a good diplomacy tool? What political and cultural goals do they have in mind?

In April 2010, the US State Department sent a rap group named Chen Lo and The Liberation Family to perform in Damascus, Syria.

Following Chen Lo's performance, US secretary of state Hillary Clinton was asked by *CBS News* about US diplomacy's recent embrace of hip hop. "Hip hop is America," she said, noting that rap and other musical forms could help "rebuild the image" of the United States. "You know it may be a little bit hopeful, because I can't point to a change in Syrian policy because Chen Lo and the Liberation Family showed up. But I think we have to use every tool at our disposal."

The State Department began using hip hop as a tool in the mid-2000s, when, in the wake of Abu Ghraib and the resurgence of the Taliban, Karen Hughes, then undersecretary of state for public diplomacy, launched an initiative called Rhythm Road. The programme was modelled on the jazz diplomacy initiative of the Cold War era, except that in the "War on Terror", hip hop would play the central role of countering "poor perceptions" of the US.

In 2005, the State Department began sending "hip hop envoys"—rappers, dancers, DJs—to perform and speak in different parts of Africa, Asia and the Middle East. The tours have since covered the broad arc of the Muslim world, with performances taking place in Senegal and Ivory Coast, across North Africa, the Levant and Middle East, and extending to Mongolia, Pakistan and Indonesia.

The artists stage performances and hold workshops; those hip hop ambassadors who are Muslims talk to local media about being Muslim in the US. The tours aim not only to exhibit the integration of American Muslims, but also, according to planners, to promote democracy and foster dissent.

"You have to bet at the end of the day, people will choose freedom over tyranny if they're given a choice," Clinton observed of the State Department's hip hop programme in Syria—stating that cultural diplomacy is a complex game of "multidimensional chess".

"Hip hop can be a chess piece?" asked the interviewer. "Absolutely!" responded the secretary of state.

Much has been said about the role of hip hop in the Arab revolts. French media described the Arab Spring as *le printemps des rappeurs* ["The spring of the rappers"]. *Time Magazine* named Tunisian rapper Hamada Ben Amor (aka El General)—a rapper who was arrested by Tunisian dictator Zine El Abidine Ben Ali—as one of the "100 Most Influential People of 2011", ranking him higher than President Barack Obama.

HIP HOP REVOLUTION

It is true that since protests began in Tunisia in December 2010, rap has provided a soundtrack to the North African revolts. As security forces rampaged in the streets, artists in Tunis, Cairo and Benghazi were writing lyrics and cobbling together protest footage, beats and rhymes, which they then uploaded to proxy servers. These impromptu songs—such as El General's *Rais Lebled*—were then picked up and broadcast by Al Jazeera, and played at gatherings and solidarity marches in London, New York and Washington.

But the role of music should not be exaggerated: Hip hop did not cause the Arab revolts any more than Twitter or Facebook did. The cross-border spread of popular movements is not a new phenomenon in the Arab world—the uprisings of 1919, which engulfed Egypt, Libya and Tunisia, occurred long before the advent of the internet, social media or rap music.

And the countries in the region with the most vibrant hip hop scenes, Morocco and Algeria, have not seen revolts. Western journalists' focus on hip hop—like their fixation on Facebook and Twitter—seems partly because, in their eyes, a taste for hip hop among young Muslims is a sign of moderation, modernity, even "an embrace of the US".

What is absent from these discussions about rap and the breakdown of Arab authoritarianism is the role that states—in the region and beyond—have played in shaping and directing local hip hop cultures. From deposed Tunisian dictator Ben Ali's mobilisation of hip hop culture against Islamism to the embattled Syrian regime's current support of "pro-stability rappers", to the US government's growing use of hip hop in public diplomacy, counter-terrorism and democracy promotion, regimes are intervening to promote some sub-styles of hip hop, in an attempt to harness the genre towards various political objectives.

The jazz tours of the Cold War saw the US government send integrated bands led by Dizzy Gillespie, Louis Armstrong, Duke Ellington and Benny Goodman to various parts of Africa, Asia and the Middle East to counter Soviet propaganda about American racial practices, and to get people in other countries to identify with "the American way of life".

The choice of jazz was not simply due to its international appeal. As historian Penny Von Eschen writes in her pioneering book *Satchmo Blows Up the World*, in the 1950s, the State Department believed that African-American culture could convey "a sense of shared suffering, as well as the conviction that equality could be gained under the American political system" to people who had suffered European colonialism.

Similar thinking underpins the current "hip hop diplomacy" initiatives. The State Department planners who are calling for "the leveraging of hip hop" in US foreign policy emphasise "the importance of Islam to the roots of hip hop in America", and the "pain" and "struggle" that the music expresses.

A Brookings report authored by the programme's architects— titled "Mightier than the Sword: Arts and Culture in the US-Muslim World Relationship" (2008)—notes that hip hop began as "outsiders' protest" against the US system, and now resonates among marginalised Muslim youth worldwide. From the Parisian banlieues to Palestine to Kyrgyzstan, "hip hop reflects struggle against authority" and expresses a "pain" that transcends language barriers.

AN IRONIC CHOICE

Moreover, note the authors, hip hop's pioneers were inner-city Muslims who "carry on an African-American Muslim tradition of protest against authority, most powerfully represented by Malcolm X". The report concludes by calling for a "greater exploitation of this natural connector to the Muslim world".

The choice of hip hop is ironic: The very music blamed for a range of social ills at home—violence, misogyny, consumerism, academic underperformance—is being deployed abroad in the hopes of making the US safer and better-liked. European states have also been disptaching their Muslim hip hop artists to perform in Muslim-majority countries. Long before the fall of the Gaddafi regime, the British Council was organising hip hop workshops in Tripoli, and sponsoring Electric Steps, "Libya's only hip hop band", as a way to promote political reform in that country.

Rap is also being used in de-radicalisation and counter-terrorism initiatives. American and European terrorism experts have expressed concerns over "anti-American hip hop", accenting the radicalising influence of this genre. Others have advocated mobilising certain sub-genres of hip hop against what they call "jihadi cool".

Warning that Osama bin Laden's associate Abu Yahya al-Libi has made al-Qaeda look "cool", one terrorism expert recommends that the US respond "with one of America's coolest exports: hip hop", specifically with a "subgroup" thereof.

"Muslim hip hop is Muslim poetry set to drum beats," explains Jeffrey Halverson in an article titled Rap Is Da Bomb for Defeating Abu Yahya. "Add in the emotional parallels between the plight of African-Americans and, for example, impoverished Algerians living in ghettos outside of Paris or Palestinian refugees in the West Bank and the analogy becomes even clearer."

But it's unclear how "Muslim hip hop" will exert a moderating or democratising influence: Will a performance by an African-American Muslim group trigger a particular calming "effect", pushing young Muslim men away from extremist ideas? Nor is it clear what constitutes "Muslim hip hop": Does the fact that Busta Rhymes is a Sunni Muslim make his music "Islamic"?

Moreover, while references to Islam in hip hop are—as these public diplomacy experts note—legion, they are not necessarily political or flattering. In December 2002, Lil Kim appeared on the cover of *OneWorld* magazine wearing a burqa and a bikini, saying "F*** Afghanistan".

50 Cent's track "Ghetto Quran" is about dealing drugs and "snitchin'". Foxy Brown charmed some and infuriated others with her song "Hot Spot", saying, "MCs wanna eat me but it's Ramadan."

More disturbing was the video "Hard" released in late 2009 by the diva, Rihanna, in which she appears decked out in military garb, heavily armed and straddling a tank's gun turret in a Middle Eastern war setting. An Arabic tattoo beneath her bronze bra reads, "Freedom Through Christ"; on a wall is the Quranic verse: "We belong to God, and to Him we shall return"—recited to honour the dead, and not an uncommon wall inscription in war-torn Muslim societies.

The point is that not all Islam-alluding hip hop resonates with Muslim youth. Those hip hop stars—Lupe Fiasco, Mos Def, Rakim— who are beloved among Muslim youth are appreciated because they work their Muslim identity into their art and because they forthrightly criticise US foreign policy.

At the recent BET Hip Hop Awards, Lupe Fiasco performed his hit "Words I Never Said", with a Palestinian flag draped over his mic. ("Gaza Strip was getting burned; Obama didn't say sh**," he rapped.) But neither Lupe nor Mos are likely to be invited on a State Department tour.

For State Department officials, the hip hop initiatives in Muslim-majority states showcase the diversity and integration of post-civil rights America. The multi-hued hip hop acts sent overseas represent a post-racial or post-racist American dream, and exhibit the achievements of the civil rights movement, a uniquely American moment that others can learn from.

But it's unclear how persuasive this racialised imagery is. Muslims do not resent the US for its lack of diversity. Where perceptions are poor, it is because of foreign policy, as well as, increasingly, domestic policies that target Muslims.

Perhaps the greatest irony of the State Department's efforts to showcase the model integration of US Muslims, and to deploy the moral and symbolic capital of the civil rights movement, is that these tours—as with the jazz tours—are occurring against a backdrop of unfavourable (and racialised) media images of Quran burnings, anti-mosque rallies and anti-sharia campaigns, as one of the most alarming waves of nativism in recent US history surges northward.

US diplomacy's embrace of hip hop as a foreign policy tool has sparked a heated debate, among artists and aficionados worldwide, over the purpose of hip hop: whether hip hop is "protest music" or "party music"; whether it is the "soundtrack to the struggle" or to American unipolarity; and what it means now that states—not just corporations—have entered the hip hop game.

Hip hop activists have long been concerned about how to protect their music from corporate power, but now that the music is being used in diplomacy and counterterrorism, the conversation is shifting.

The immensely popular "underground" British rapper Lowkey (Kareem Denis) recently articulated the question on many minds: "Hip hop at its best has exposed power, challenged power, it hasn't served power. When the US government loves the same rappers you love, whose interests are those rappers serving?"

For Class Discussion

1. In this exploratory piece, what questions does Aidi raise about hip-hop as a tool of cultural diplomacy?

2. A precedent for using hip-hop as cultural diplomacy is the jazz tours of the Cold War. What message was the U.S. government trying to send with the jazz tours?

3. In his efforts to show the complexity of the issue, Aidi suggests that hip-hop should not be used in U.S. foreign policy. What reasons does he state and imply?

4. Imagine if Aidi had written this piece as a straightforward editorial. What claim and reasons might he have used? Why do you think this piece would have been more or less effective rhetorically if it had presented a direct argument?

5. In what ways does this commentary contradict or agree with Saknussemm's argument against hip-hop?

The Mixtape of the Revolution
Sujatha Fernandes

Sujatha Fernandes earned a PhD in political science from the University of Chicago. She is an associate professor of sociology at Queens College and the Graduate Center of the City University of New York. Fernandes has authored several books, including *Cuba Represent! Cuban Arts, State Power, and the Making of New Revolutionary Cultures* (2006); *Who Can Stop the Drums? Urban Social Movements in Chavez's Venezuela* (2010); and *Close to the Edge: In Search of the Global Hip Hop Generation* (2011). She has published articles in *Economic and Political Weekly, The Nation, The Huffington Post*, and *ColorLines*. She has received various prestigious academic awards and fellowships for her outstanding research on the role of culture in social movements and cultural politics, among other subjects. This op-ed piece appeared in the *New York Times* on January 30, 2012.

> According to Sujatha Fernandes, what is the appeal of rap music in Senegal, Guinea, Libya, and the Republic of Djibouti?

Def Jam will probably never sign them, but Cheikh Oumar Cyrille Touré, from a small town about 100 miles southeast of Dakar, Senegal, and Hamada Ben Amor, a 22-year-old man from a port city 170 miles southeast of Tunis, may be two of the most influential rappers in the history of hip-hop.

Mr. Touré, a.k.a. Thiat ("Junior"), and Mr. Ben Amor, a.k.a. El Général, both wrote protest songs that led to their arrests and generated powerful political movements. "We are drowning in hunger and unemployment," spits Thiat on "Coup 2 Gueule" (from a phrase meaning "rant") with the Keurgui Crew. El Général's song "Head of State" addresses the now-deposed President Zine el-Abidine Ben Ali over a plaintive background beat. "A lot of money was pledged for projects and infrastructure/Schools, hospitals, buildings, houses/but the sons of dogs swallowed it in their big bellies." Later, he rhymes, "I know people have a lot to say in their hearts, but no way to convey it." The song acted as sluice gates for the release of anger that until then was being expressed clandestinely, if at all.

During the recent wave of revolutions across the Arab world and the protests against illegitimate presidents in African countries like Guinea and Djibouti, rap music has played a critical role in articulating citizen discontent over poverty, rising food prices, blackouts, unemployment, police repression and political corruption. Rap songs in Arabic in particular—the new lingua franca of the hip-hop world—have spread through YouTube, Facebook, mixtapes, ringtones and MP3s from Tunisia to Egypt, Libya and Algeria, helping to disseminate ideas and anthems as the insurrections progressed. El Général, for example, was featured on a mixtape put out by the dissident group Khalas (Enough) in Libya, which also included songs like "Tripoli Is Calling" and "Dirty Colonel."

Why has rap—an American music that in its early global spread was associated with thuggery and violence—come to be so highly influential in these regions? After all, rappers are not the only musicians involved in politics. Late last week, protests erupted when Youssou N'Dour, a Senegalese singer of mbalax, a fusion of traditional music with Latin, pop and jazz, was barred by a constitutional court from pursuing a run for president. But mbalax singers are typically seen as older entertainers who often support the government in power. In contrast, rappers, according to the Senegalese rapper Keyti, "are closer to the streets and can bring into their music the general feeling of frustration among people."

Another reason is the oratorical style rap employs: rappers report in a direct manner that cuts through political subterfuge. Rapping can simulate a political speech or address, rhetorical conventions that are generally inaccessible to the marginal youth who form the base of this movement. And in places like Senegal, rap follows in the oral traditions of West African griots, who often used rhyming verse to evaluate their political leaders. "M.C.'s are the modern griot," Papa Moussa Lo, a.k.a. Waterflow, told me in an interview a few weeks ago. "They are taking over the role of representing the people."

Although many of these rappers style themselves as revolutionary upstarts, they are most concerned with protecting a constitutional order that they see as being trampled by unscrupulous politicians. On "Coup 2 Gueule," Thiat accuses President Abdoulaye Wade of election fraud and of siphoning money from Senegal's Chemical Industries company (I.C.S.) and the African air traffic management organization (Asecna). He raps in Wolof, the dominant language in Senegal, "Old man, your seven-year presidential reign has been expensive/As if it wasn't enough that you cheated during the last elections/You ruined the I.C.S. and hijacked Asecna's money." (It flows better in Wolof.)

Most of these rappers made music prior to the political events that swept their countries. But by speaking boldly and openly about a political reality that was not being otherwise acknowledged, rappers hit a nerve, and their music served as a call to arms for the budding protest movements. In Egypt, the rapper Mohamed el Deeb told me in a recent interview, "shallow pop music and love songs got heavy airplay on the radio, but when the revolution broke out, people woke up and refused to accept shallow music with no substance."

As the Arab revolutions and African protests are ousting and discrediting establishment politicians, the young populations of these regions are looking to rappers as voices of clarity and leadership. Waterflow raises money at his shows to support his community because, like many of his fans, he believes that "waiting for our political leaders to give us opportunities is a waste of time." Other Senegalese rappers helped found the movement Y'en a Marre ("We're Fed Up"), which has crystallized opposition to President Wade and led a campaign to register young voters for the elections next month. Some are even supporting candidates for president. The rapper Keyti does not back the candidacy of Mr. N'Dour, because he thinks he's trying to run out of self-interest, but acknowledges that it "was much needed to make people realize how politicians have failed."

Rappers are hoping to inaugurate a different kind of politics. They would sooner make a pilgrimage to the South Bronx than to the Senegalese, Sufi holy city of Touba; they reject the predefined roles available within the political arena. And we shouldn't forget that despite being thrust into the spotlight at a historic moment, rappers are also artists who want to make their music. As Deeb raps in his song "Masrah Deeb" (Deeb's Stage)—written in the early days of the Egyptian revolution to remind people why they were taking to the streets—"I'm not a dictator/Deeb's a doctor in the beat department."

For Class Discussion

1. What is Fernandes' purpose in writing this op-ed piece about rap for a *New York Times* audience? What assumptions does she make about her audience's knowledge of rap?

2. What does Fernandes claim about the political and social power of rap music?

3. How does Fernandes' use of evidence and examples in this piece both testify to her knowledge of and expertise on this subject and support her argument? How persuasive is this evidence?

4. What alternative views of rap might Fernandes have acknowledged and thus have made her argument even stronger?

5. What intercultural paradigm does Fernandes' argument exemplify?

CHAPTER QUESTIONS FOR REFLECTION AND DISCUSSION

1. Explain your choice of which reading in this chapter best represents each of the following intercultural paradigms:
   - Cultural differentialism (lasting difference)
   - Cultural convergence (homogenization)
   - Cultural hybridization (mixing of cultures)

2. Each of the following groups of writers makes similar observations about cultural exchanges; in effect,—they subscribe to the same intercultural paradigm. Choose one of the following groups of readings and map out their points of agreement and disagreement. Consider their target audiences, their assumptions and values, their main claims and reasons, their use and quality of evidence, their angle of vision, the points that each overlooks or ignores, and their engagement with controversy and alternative views.
   - Michael Caster, Mugambi Kiai, Sujatha Fernandes, David Adesnik, Suzy Hansen, *Spider-Man: India* image
   - Shepard Fairey, Kris Saknussemm, Andrea Peyser, AllAfrica excerpt about Nigerian hip-hop (from the chapter introduction)
   - Mugambi Kiai, Hishaam Aidi, excerpt about Iraqi hip-hop (from the chapter introduction), Brian Truitt, Suzy Hansen

3. Mugambi Kiai, the Shepard Fairy incident, Michael Caster, and Michael Pernar all address the problems with graffiti's intrusion into public space and public–private distinctions. What points raised in these readings or images clarify or complicate the view of graffiti as vandalism?

4. What do the comic superhero images of *Spider-Man: India* and the superheroes of *The 99* have in common? You might want to investigate the Marvel Web site (http://marvel.com) and *The 99* site (www.the99.org). To what extent do you think these comics represent cultural hybridization and glocalization? How could these comics promote cultural understanding?

5. Much of the discussion about cultural forms and issues focuses on empowering people or depriving people of cultural identity. Which writer in this chapter do you think most directly and credibly confronts the problems of power dynamics in cultural exchanges? Think about the arguments over cultural forms as free speech and creative expression, as commercialization, and as cultural homogenization and Western domination. What does this writer see as cultural losses and gains?

6. Which reading or readings in this chapter make the most effective and persuasive use of appeals to readers' values, imaginations, and emotions? Which reading had the most impact on you, either by reinforcing or challenging your own values?

7. The film industry, the comic book industry, and the music industry are thriving in the United States, yet other countries are developing or have

the potential to develop strong industries. In groups or individually, research one of the following cultural forms and prepare an informative presentation for the class that sketches important facts and issues. Plan to show examples with images and short film or sound clips.

- Research Bollywood or the film industry in Europe or Africa. If you look at Bollywood, you might also consider the crossover film by British writer/director Gurinder Chadha *Bride and Prejudice* (2004) and this director's other popular film *Bend It Like Beckham* (2002), Mira Nair's *Monsoon Wedding* (2001), or other recent Indian films.

- Research anime or the comic book industry in Japan, the Philippines, Egypt, India, or Kuwait. You might explore the local comic book industries in the Philippines (Mango Comics, Summit Publishing, and Culture Crash), anime in Japan, AK Comics from Cairo, or *Spider-Man: India*, or you might investigate the reception of *The 99* around the world and the spin-offs from this series.

- Research the music industry in a specific country. You might explore the Middle Eastern hip-hop scene, the different genres of Afro Pop in Africa, or *corrido* or *rock nacional* in Mexico.

WRITING ASSIGNMENTS

Brief Writing Assignments

1. **Reflective Writing.** Thinking about Owen Johnson's narrative about his first encounter with anime and thinking about your own identity, personal style, and cultural choices, write a short reflection in which you explore what part of foreign or international culture is most important to you. You could focus on food, music, clothing, sports, film, animation, language, television programming, religion, art, philosophy, or literature. You might focus on one incident as a departure point (for example, when you became an international soccer fan, when you fell in love with Thai food, when you learned yoga or Bollywood dancing, and so on).

2. Using the readings in this chapter as a source of inspiration and the global quiz in Chapter 1 on pages pages 2–4 as a model, create a quiz about cultural phenomena (food, clothing, sports, film, music, art, trendy brands, advertising, architecture, international travel spots, street art, and comics) for an audience of your peers. Create ten to fifteen multiple-choice items. You will need to choose different regions in the world and research specific cultural areas for those regions (for example, the main professional competitive sports in Australia; the main protest singers in South America). Include answers separately and keep track of your sources so that your classmates can take your quiz or pursue these topics further.

3. Choose one of the following claims and write for twenty minutes in support of it or against it. Use evidence from the readings and from your own experience to develop your claim persuasively. To force yourself to think

from a different point of view, you may want to write in agreement with the statement and then write against it:

A. Americans can't get away from home because cultures around the world have become Americanized and homogenized.

B. Cultures should work to preserve their distinctive cultural identities.

C. The marketing, buying, and selling of culture is inevitable and mostly benefits everyone.

D. Street art should be distinguished from graffiti and allowed access to public space without legal penalties.

E. Cultural exchanges can fuel peaceful relations among countries.

4. A number of the writers in this chapter represent divergent views on cultural conflicts. Imagine a dialogue or debate between one of the following pairs of writers. Consider these writers' angles of vision, values, main claims, reasoning, and evidence.

What would the writers you have chosen say to each other on these cultural issues?

- Michael Caster and Michael Pernar on the meaning and value of graffiti
- Suzy Hansen and Andrea Peyser on the impact and value of *The 99*
- Kris Saknussemm and Hishaam Aidi or Sujatha Fernandes on the cultural impact and importance of rap

5. **Analyzing Arguments Rhetorically.** A number of the readings in this chapter actually take more of an exploratory or analytical approach than an argumentative one. Choose one of the analytical/exploratory readings and sketch out how you would turn it into an argument. What ideas and parts of the reading would you emphasize? Why do you think that writing about culture often fits an exploratory or analytical purpose more than an argumentative one?

Writing Projects

1. **Reflective Writing.** You may live in a community or city in which immigrants preserve their transnational identities by maintaining lively cultural ties to their home countries through ethnic restaurants, music on radio stations, films, ethnic fairs or parades, and stores that sell ethnic clothing and products. These cultural practices may or may not attract or invite people from outside the culture. On the other hand, your community or region may not have felt the effects of cultural globalization. How real are the intercultural paradigms in this chapter in your experience? Reflect on your own insulation from or involvement in intercultural contact. Have you experienced cultural interaction as billiard balls or a mosaic, as homogenization, or as hybridization? Have contacts with other cultures threatened you or added rich variety to your life? Describe particular experiences and reflect on their significance. Write for yourself and a group of your friends.

2. Writing for an uninformed audience, build a strong case that one of the following cultural forms—or one you know from your own experience—has had a profound, transformative influence on American life: anime (from Japan); music from Africa, Latin America, or the Caribbean; food from Asia; film from India or Europe; television programs from Britain; dance from Africa; soccer from Europe or South America. You might write an argument as a feature story for your university or local newspaper.

3. Investigate the contemporary music scene of some country such as Brazil, Mexico, Nigeria, South Africa, or Japan—perhaps focusing on a particular style of music (such as hip-hop, punk rock, or folk). You might think of Jamaican reggae artist Bob Marley and his son Ziggy; Nigeria's Femi Kuti; Brazil's samba and hip-hopper Max de Castro and Marisa Monte of samba and art-pop fame; diva Brenda Fassie from South Africa; Shakira from Colombia; Thalia from Mexico; and Charlotte Church from Wales. Argue that the selected country's music has had an important effect on world music. Or you could argue that this music/music style/recording artist should receive world attention. You will need to provide criteria to evaluate the importance of this music or artist. Tailor your argument to your chosen audience.

4. Choose an internationally marketed product, such as a soft drink, brand of car, food, or television franchise, and research how that product is marketed differently in different countries. You might consult the producer's Web pages for different countries to view their branding or print advertising, or check YouTube (www.youtube.com) to locate international commercials. What aspects of the advertising remain consistent across cultures? How has the product changed its image to appeal to different cultures? Can you argue that this is a successful example of glocalizing or does this marketing exemplify cultural imperialism? Write a short editorial for your university's newspaper to interest readers in your discoveries and views.

5. Prepare to write a policy proposal or a commentary on graffiti and street art—cultural forms which touch all of us in one way or another. Choose either (1) the audience of a cultural commentary magazine or (2) the voters in your city. You might think about the following questions: Would you rather look at a product advertisement or street art on the sides of city buses and buildings? Should your city have legal graffiti walls, a street art program, or a zero tolerance policy? Has graffiti harmed neighborhoods of your city? Has it added visual interest and color? Do you believe that graffiti and street art should be exhibited in galleries and museums? Take a stand on one of these questions. In your research, you might want to consult your city's current laws; scholarly articles on the urban war on graffiti; films such as *Bomb It!, Exit Through the Gift Shop, Style Wars, Spray Paint Beijing,* and others; and the following Web sites:

Urban Art Core (www.urbanartcore.eu)

The Wooster Collective (www.woostercollective.com/#grid-view)

Brooklyn Street Art (www.brooklynstreetart.com/theblog/)

UK Street Art (www.ukstreetart.co.uk/)

Graffiti Hurts (www.graffitihurts.org)

The Anti-Graffiti Association (http://theaga.org.uk/)

6. **Reflective Writing.** Some of the writers in this chapter think that culture can be used to promote global understanding, cooperation, and peace, while others see culture as profoundly alienating, threatening, or divisive. Choose a reading that moved you to think seriously about culture in this role—of promoting understanding or enhancing division—and write a reflective analysis in which you explain how this writer caused you to think in this way. Try to create a synthesis that integrates ideas from this reading, your emotional and intellectual response to this reading, and your own experience. For example, if you are a fan of street art, comics, or rap, you could interact with one of the readings that argues about that cultural form.

7. **Analyzing Arguments Rhetorically.** Choose one of the readings in this chapter that speaks with a strong authorial voice or a command of the subject achieved through experience or research: Michael Pernar, Michael Caster, Andrea Peyser, Kris Saknussemm, David Adesnik, or Sujatha Fernandes. Write a rhetorical analysis considering the writer's angle of vision, target audience, genre of argument, assumptions and values, main claims and reasons, use of language, and the points that each emphasizes and overlooks. Write for your university community. Why should your own audience read, or not read, the argument of this writer? What cultural understanding or values are at stake that make this argument a valuable or negative contribution to public discussion?

8. This is a two-part writing project. First, write an exploratory essay in which you pose a significant, perplexing, open-ended question about a cultural conflict. As you research this question, write a summary of and thoughtful "talk-back to" response to each source. Weave these responses together into an essay that presents the chronological development of your own answer to your research question. As you are researching your question, has the issue become more complicated or have you synthesized ideas and formulated your own views? For the second part of the project, write an analysis or an argument that persuades an audience of your choice of the importance of cultural globalization as it relates to the cultural conflict you researched. For these projects, for a research question, you might focus on the effect of the marketing of rap, reality TV, or MTV in the Middle East or Africa; the dangers of cross-cultural images such as political cartoons and satire; the reductive or distorting representation of a culture in film; the need to promote cultural understanding in children through art forms directed to them; the historical and cultural importance of preserving World Heritage sites; and so forth.

7

Global Netizens
Social Media's Role in Social and Political Change

CONTEXT FOR A NETWORK OF ISSUES

On December 17, 2010, Mohamed Bouazizi set himself on fire in the small, interior Tunisian town of Sidi Bouzid, sparking countrywide protests, many organized via Facebook and blogs, which eventually toppled the twenty-three-year dictatorship of President Zine El Abidine Ben Ali on January 14, 2011. On January 25, popular protests against Hosni Mubarak flared up in Cairo and other parts of Egypt, leading to the end of Mubarak's thirty-year presidency less than one month later. Again, many activists used Facebook, Twitter, and YouTube to organize and communicate. These two events were the catalysts for what has been called the Arab Spring or, in some circles, the Facebook or Twitter Revolution. Similarly, in June 2009, in Iran, contested presidential elections brought thousands of Iranians to the streets of Tehran. Mobilized by Twitter and other social media, the Iranian episode was called both the Green Revolution and the Twitter Revolution. However, in Iran there was a brutal crackdown by the state; rampant censoring and infiltration of social media sites followed, and the contested regime remained in power. Are the different outcomes of these similar events a matter of time and place, or connectivity (having or being able to maintain an Internet connection) and international attention? What is the role of social media in a global context? What should it be?

In the last few years there has been a dramatic increase in attention to **social media**, Web applications that facilitate participatory information sharing between **prosumers**, users who produce and consume content, and networking. This increase in attention from journalists, academics, and activists follows a dramatic increase in global connectivity of **netizens**, active social media users. In July 2011, Facebook co-creator and CEO Mark Zuckerberg announced that Facebook had reached a total of 800 million active users, reporting that 350 million users a month connect via mobile devices, such as cell phones.* Similarly, in May 2011 Twitter announced that its global users surpassed 300 million.† In China, where both Facebook and Twitter have been banned, their Chinese equivalents, QQ and Renren, report totals of 990 million registered users, 448 million active users,‡ and 117 million registered users,§ respectively. Taken together with the myriad of other social media such as Google+, Wordpress, Tumblr, and Vimeo, there is a constantly evolving array of social media for different desires and purposes. Whereas proponents of social media as a catalyst for social change look expectantly to increasing numbers of activity, Evgeny Morozov, a Belarusian researcher and writer, and social media's outspoken skeptic, warns against **iPod liberalism**, the assumption that anyone with mobile devices and a social media connection will favor a Western liberal political system. As examples from around the world show, netizen behavior is still very much influenced by cultural and historical factors; there is no universal pattern.

As a result of global concerns over the role and use of social media, a number of organizations (such as Global Voices, Threatened Voices, Electronic Frontier Foundation, and the Open Society Foundation) have continued to search for innovative approaches to both fulfilling social media's empowering potential and acting on behalf of social media users in danger. In addition, social media's enthusiasts, advocates, skeptics, and critics are complicating and enriching the lively public debate about this new phenomenon. For example, critic Mark Bauerlein, author of *The Dumbest Generation: How the Digital Age Stupefies Young Americans and Jeopardizes Our Future (Or, Don't Trust Anyone Under 30)* (2008), argues that because of the rapid increase in digital connectivity and social media, "new identities have emerged or been fabulously empowered—the angry citizen with a video camera handy, the hyper-social networking teenager, the blog 'troll,' avatars."¥ This chapter shows the importance of understanding these diverse responses and social media's role in a global context.

---

*Nathan Olivarez-Giles. "Facebook F8: Redesigning and Hitting 800 Million Users" Los Angeles Times (September 22, 2011). http://latimesblogs.latimes.com/technology/2011/09/facebook-f8-media-features.html

†Chris Taylor. "Social Networking 'Utopia' Isn't Coming." CNN (June 27, 2011) http://articles.cnn.com/2011-06-27/tech/limits.social.networking.taylor_1_twitter-users-facebook-friends-connections?_s=PM:TECH

‡http://www.alexa.com/siteinfo/qq.com

§Michael Kan. "China's Facebook, Renren, Faces Stiff Competition." PC World (May 4, 2011) http://www.pcworld.com/businesscenter/article/227052/chinas_facebook_renren_faces_stiff_competition.html

¥Mark Bauerlein. Ed. *The Digital Divide: Arguments for and Against Facebook, Google, Texting, and the Age of Social Networking* (New York: Jeremy P. Tarcher/Penguin, 2011), xiv.

STAKES AND STAKEHOLDERS

Citizens of developed and underdeveloped countries hold stakes in the potential use and manipulation of social media, and as more people become connected globally we are all becoming stakeholders in these issues. Also, governments, transnational corporations, journalists, nongovernmental organizations, and free speech and human rights activists regularly analyze social media conditions. Here are some major issue questions and some of the positions arguers are taking.

What Are the Major Causes of the Global Digital Divide and How Are People Trying to Bridge Them?   The last decade has seen a drastic increase in digital connectivity. China alone has 485 million Internet users, an increase from 22 million in 2000. India has reported an increase from 5 million to 100 million, while still only accounting for 8.4 percent of the population. Sweden has one of the highest numbers of Internet users at 92.4 percent. Meanwhile, for the entire continent of Africa the percentage with Internet access is a mere 11.5 percent. Clearly, the digital divide is not rapidly receding despite the claims of voices such as *New York Times* columnist Thomas Friedman. Even after a decade of digital development in mobile technologies, the world Internet connectivity remains at around 30 percent.*

Policy analysts, academics, and corporations have proposed multiple approaches to the **global digital divide (GDD)**, the disparity in Internet access and the potential for information sharing, social networking, and educational or entrepreneurial opportunities. Many voices in the GDD argument prefer to focus on issues expedient to their own interests, such as when computer or cell phone manufacturers promote campaigns to send their hardware into rural African or South Asian villages.

The most common view is that if we could only send more computers or cell phones to poor areas, the GDD would be filled. Donating computers is a common practice among international organizations and companies, such as Microsoft's Computers 4 Africa program. Furthermore, with the growth in Internet-ready mobile technologies, cell phones have become highly popularized.

In response, some argue that cell phones are still too expensive a solution for much of the world. In poor communities, daily needs such as food and health concerns trump home computer or smartphone purchases, even with the availability of cheap technology in black markets, from Bangkok and Nairobi, to Istanbul and Marrakech. The globally popular Nokia 1100, not a smartphone, has text messaging as its most advanced feature. While text message banking may be revolutionizing rural business in some places, it is hardly a panacea for the GDD. As another option, some point to **Internet cafés**, single-computer kiosks to multifloor complexes, in parts of

---

*http://www.internetworldstats.com/stats.htm

the world where home computer ownership is still very low, as an attractive counter to inadequate cell phone solutions. Internet cafés offer an array of possibilities for a variety of needs.

A number of nongovernmental organizations (NGOs) argue in favor of social solutions. This perspective, common to the Open Society Foundation, holds that the GDD is linked to broader social injustices, such as gender inequality and educational differences. For example, in South Asia, Africa, and the Middle East, men are far more likely to have access to cell phones than women, and in many countries, the percentage of educated citizens with connectivity is much higher than that of uneducated citizens.

Is Social Media Capable of Empowering Individuals and Introducing Narratives Beyond Mainstream Control?   Many activists and citizen journalists believe social media is facilitating the exchange of information outside of mainstream media control and allowing individuals, often those that were previously marginalized, greater freedom of expression. For Chinese artist and dissident Ai Wei Wei, social media gives people "the chance to really discuss, no matter what level they are on, and freely give out their opinions."*

Journalist Dan Hind theorizes that social media and mainstream media forge a different relationship between the media and the audience. In a **mass society** paradigm, "communication is a broadcast that delivers one unanswerable voice," which prevents dialogue or political action; in contrast, the Internet has nurtured a **public society**, where communication allows for "virtually as many people to express opinions as to receive them,"† and thus encourages political participation and action. The ability of social media to foster public society interaction is also important to Clay Shirky, professor of New Media and Internet technologies at New York University. He notes, "whereas the phone gave us the one to one pattern, and television, radio, magazine, books gave us the one to many pattern, the internet gives us the many to many pattern."‡ When public society is given a voice and can produce and spread information, social media creates opportunities for alternatives to mainstream media's construction of news.

As examples of Hind's and Shirky's theories, global citizens have employed social media to shape domestic and international awareness of issues previously unheard or underrepresented in mainstream media. Farmers in central India can upload videos to YouTube on suicides of desperation in response to feelings of exploitation by multinational corporations, such as Monsanto, or reach global audiences by blogging against genetically modified organisms as with the GM Genocide blog. Gay men

---

*http://www.paleycenter.org/special-event-ai-weiwei-jack-dorsey-richard-macmanus
†Dan Hind. "Mass Media, or Public Media? AlJazeera.net (October 20, 2011) http:// english.aljazeera.net/indepth/opinion/2011/10/201110207714864929.html
‡Clay Shirky. TED: How Social Media Can Make History (June 2009) www.ted.com/ talks/clay_shirky_how_cellphones_twitter_facebook_can_make_history.html

and lesbians can publish blogs and editorials, bringing the issue of social reform more saliently into public attention anonymously in Uganda, where same-sex relationships are illegal and often violently punished. In opposition, naysayers and skeptics question how inclusive this public society is or point to instances of cooptation by repressive forces.

Is Social Media an Effective Tool for Mobilization and Social Change?
Disagreement rages about the use of social media as a tool for social change and about its effects on users' identities and consciousness. While it's true that some people use social media politically and it can theoretically increase global perspective, empower, and educate, other people use it simply as a source of entertainment, whether at home, on their mobile devices, or in an Internet café playing online games or uploading personal photos. Evgeny Morozov has labeled these types of users "cyberhedonists." Many analysts focus on users' psychological involvement with social media and on its effects on identity and socialization. Some argue that many users simply seek to enhance their material-social lives or noncommittally follow campaigns on Twitter; some of these analysts argue for a distinction between digital and "real-world" identities. Other cyberanalysts, such as media theorist Nathan Jurgenson, find the connection between on- and offline activity and identities more complexly interconnected and blurred.

Some academics and journalists such as linguist, philosopher, and activist Noam Chomsky maintain that communication through social media "erodes normal human relations. It makes them more superficial, shallow, evanescent."* Such critics cite **Dunbar's number**, after the British anthropologist Robin Dunbar who postulated that the number of people with whom one can maintain stable social relationships, not including general acquaintances, is usually only around 150. With Facebook topping out at 5,000 friends and no limit to followers on Twitter, skeptics argue that the superficiality of social media technologies render them ineffective for large campaigns or mobilizations. They contend that few major activist projects succeed through Facebook or Twitter, and that **clicktivism**, clicking "like" on a Facebook campaign, is not a substitute for more traditional forms of engagement. In opposition, some people praise social media's alternative model for social activism. For example, *Adbusters*, the counterculture magazine credited with initially organizing the **Occupy Wall Street (OWS)** movement launched in fall of 2011 in New York City to protest the role of Wall Street and banking in causing the economic recession and concentrating more wealth in the hands of the upper 1% of Americans, lauds the power of social media. *Adbusters* and other advocates emphasize how social media's informality and potential for anonymity make it more attractive than traditional forms of organization.

---

*See Noam Chomsky "Interview with Noam Chomsky" Brightest Young Things.com March 9, 2011 http://www.brightestyoungthings.com/articles/the-secret-of-noam-a-chomsky-interview.htm

Some international organizations and citizens argue that a broad-based, international campaign proliferated via social media can provide timely assistance by spreading news of arrests and detentions, eliciting responses from hundreds or thousands, and providing public notice and support to endangered individuals. Granted, it requires minimal commitment to send an e-mail, fill out an online petition, or click "like," but Amnesty International has had tremendous success with this sort of advocacy model for over fifty years. A campaign by thousands of citizens around the world, although started on social media, can grow to put substantive economic or political pressure on abusive regimes.

Does Social Media's Vulnerability to Control Through Censorship Undermine Its Potential to Serve Social Change? Social media's potential to frame, voice, and disseminate alternative narratives (alternative views of news events) allows for prosumers to freely generate and share information. For example, the flood of videos from the U.S. OWS movement—which were posted to YouTube, tweets, blogs, and elsewhere—prevented mainstream manipulation and control of the news coverage surrounding the protest. A number of activists have argued that the prevalence of social media during OWS allowed for a challenge to police narratives, as opposed to the 1999 World Trade Organization (WTO) protests in Seattle, where the authorities engineered stories to legitimize police use of force.

Although some academics and social media experts agree with Navi Pillay, United Nations High Commissioner for Human Rights, who asserts that social media has made it so that "governments no longer hold the ability to monopolize the dissemination of information and censor what it says,"* others take a more pessimistic view. The very open-ended, democratic, nonhierarchical, quasi-anonymous form of social activism engendered by social media may weaken its potential to maintain activist causes and make it vulnerable to appropriation by dominant powers for social control. Many think movements formed by social media tend to become incoherent or unsustainable. Furthermore, many analysts and users point out that maintaining this independence of views and freedom of expression is precarious because the majority of technologies are owned by corporations. Noam Chomsky and Edward S. Herman argue in their book *Manufacturing Consent: The Political Economy of the Mass Media* (1988), on political control and mass media, that wealthy persons, governments, and corporations will use social media (as they did television) to manipulate and dominate the public narrative. Digital activism may be appropriated by the dominant powers to maintain social control, a phenomenon Evgeny Morozov has termed **spinternet**, when regimes distort the perception and

---

*"Inspired by Global Events, UN Launches Social Media Campaign to Celebrate Rights." UN News Centre (December 1, 2011) http://www.un.org/apps/news/story .asp?NewsID=40584

coverage of a given social phenomenon through social media tools on the Internet, sometimes by hiring bloggers to flood the Internet with counter-views.* Responding to those who stress the limitations of social media's potential, other academics and activists point out that there are hidden costs to all forms of activism.

Furthermore, purportedly democratic governments and authoritarian regimes may simply block Internet access in order to silence dissent. For example, after the July 5, 2009, ethnic riots in Urumqi, the capital of the Xinjiang Uyghur Autonomous Region in northwest China, the government blocked Internet access to the entire province for close to a year in hopes of choking international media attention and future mobilization. In less extreme cases authoritarian regimes will simply block access to certain Web sites, from Human Rights Watch to YouTube or Facebook. The U.S. government blocked access to WikiLeaks after WikiLeaks exposed reports of illegal or unethical foreign policies and actions.

In response, proponents of digital activism encourage the development and spread of **virtual private networks (VPNs)** and **proxy servers**, downloadable programs that allow for the circumvention of blocked Web sites, as a viable means of outwitting regime control. However, there is a serious contention about how these services can be made most effective for social change. Should they be **open source**—that is, peer designed, reviewed, and freely accessible—or paid services?

Should a "Universal Declaration of Digital Rights" or Social Media Laws Be Adopted to Protect Internet Users?   On December 10, 2011, Human Rights Day, the anniversary of the December 10, 1948, ratification of the Universal Declaration of Human Rights, the UN announced that the year's focus would be social media and human rights. For some members of the international community, 2011, and the UN's conflation of social media and human rights, was a wakeup call for an examination of social media and international laws on freedom of expression and the right to privacy.

Human Rights Watch and other NGOs have teamed up with Google, Yahoo, and Microsoft to develop the Global Network Initiative, a voluntary code of conduct that encourages Internet companies to deny the demands of repressive regimes and shield their users. However, Facebook and Twitter are not members. Meanwhile, in the United States academics and activists including constitutional lawyer and writer Glenn Greenwald; Julian Assange, the controversial founder of WikiLeaks; and progressive journalist Amy Goodman, among others, point out the decrease in digital rights to privacy for U.S. citizens, and the increase of censorship and surveillance technologies employed in the United States. Digital activists such as Tunisian blogger Sami Ben Gharbia and Canadian journalist Naomi Klein protest the hypocrisy of Western governments and companies and claim that before a durable

---

*See Evgeny Morozov's *The Net Delusion*.

system of digital rights can take hold globally, Western governments and companies must acknowledge their complicity in undermining Internet freedom by manufacturing and promoting censor ware and filtering software.*

Thinking Visually

The Global Digital Divide

This photo from Africa appeared on the cover of *The Economist,* a weekly London-based political and economic news commentary magazine with a pro–free trade perspective. This March 12, 2005, issue featured articles about the digital divide.

Christian Als/Panos Pictures

Cover Image from *The Economist*

---

*See Ben Gharbia's blog: https://ifikra.wordpress.com

Questions to Ponder

1. What is the rhetorical effect of the smiling little boy and the mud cell phone in this photo? How might this photo appeal to the magazine's audience of business executives and political leaders? What audience assumptions might this image challenge?

2. What different arguments about the global digital divide and social media could this image be used to support?

The three sections that follow—Student Voice, International Voices, and Global Hot Spot—take you deeper into the network of issues connected to the role of the Internet and social media in civil society and politics around the world.

 STUDENT VOICE: The Ripples of a Tunisian Twitter Experience by John Wood

In the narrative that follows, student writer John Wood shares his experience of the power of social media in the service of social justice causes.

Having a chance to visit a friend, a graduate student doing field research, during my own study abroad year, I traveled to Tunisia in the fall 2011. This visit seemed like a perfect chance to investigate the hype surrounding the so-called Facebook Revolution. Along with the rest of my generation, I have been using Facebook to upload pictures or chat with friends for years, but the people of Tunisia had enlisted online tools in overthrowing their authoritarian president, and I was curious.

I gained much of what I learned about social media in Tunisia at the Third Arab Bloggers Meeting, which set out to highlight and strengthen the impact of bloggers on society and provide a platform for the exchange of ideas through presentations and workshops. I had recently signed up for Twitter, so I started following a number of the speakers' blogs and Twitter feeds. Global Voices co-founder Rebecca MacKinnon began the conference with the challenge that it is time to move beyond arguing whether the Internet can bring about social change and begin addressing how it should be structured to empower users. MacKinnon was followed by presentations by bloggers from a number of countries including Egypt, Morocco, Yemen, and Syria. By the end of the first day I was amazed at the complexity of the issue.

After the conference concluded, the attendees began venturing back to their respective countries, but Twitter flashed with parting comments as bloggers, journalists, and activists boarded flights or waited in airports. One comment from Syrian blogger and human rights activist Razan Ghazzawi, known as Red Razan, caught my attention. I responded to something she tweeted, and a couple of hours later she was following me on Twitter. A spark of ego flashed up with the thought that a well-known blogger was now following me on Twitter, but I soon gave no more thought to the matter until about two months later.

On December 4th several tweets announcing that Razan had been taken into custody by the Syrian police while she was trying to cross the border into Jordan flashed on the screen of my Macbook. For some reason, perhaps our Twitter connection, I felt personally called into action to show my support. I tweeted and retweeted a number of messages left by activists from Iraq to Morocco and the United States, and received notice that one of my tweets had likewise been retweeted. I joined the Facebook campaign and posted the link to my wall. Before I went to sleep that night, there were about 400 supporters of the Free Razan Facebook campaign. The next morning there were close to four thousand, within a day, more than five thousand. Within the first few days, tens of thousands of tweets referencing Razan's detention were sent through cyberspace and countless blog and Facebook profile pictures were changed to the Free Razan Campaign image. Then, after fourteen days in captivity, she was released by the Syrian authorities on bail, and she later tweeted that the campaign's threat of publicity had influenced her treatment; she had not been tortured.

Even if the tweets, blogs, and Facebook campaigns didn't secure her release, they at least affected her peace of mind during a traumatizing experience, but I couldn't help feeling as though I, along with thousands of others online, had participated in some way in protecting her.

INTERNATIONAL VOICES

One of the difficulties with social media's proclaimed goal of promoting global awareness and positive change is the language barrier. Global Voices, a meta-media Web site of more than 500 bloggers and translators founded by Rebecca MacKinnon and Ethan Zuckerman in 2004, seeks to bridge language barriers and provide a platform for otherwise unheard global voices by translating citizen media into nearly twenty languages. The following excerpt is from Dr. Hussein Ibish's interview of Mona Kareem, a Global Voices journalist and human rights activist. Dr. Ibish, a senior fellow at the American Task Force on Palestine, originally posted this interview to his blog, Ibishblog, on December 19, 2011. It demonstrates the value and influence of Global Voices' translations of international blogs and Twitter.

Translators at Global Voices Make Social Media Messages Widely Available

One of the most interesting people I've come to know through Twitter is Mona Kareem, a poet, journalist, blogger and tweep who also happens to be bidoun jinsiya—"without citizenship"—from Kuwait. First, it's almost impossible to follow events in Kuwait quickly and efficiently in English—and in many cases at all—without consulting her Twitter feed (@monakareem), which does the work of 20 typical Middle East journalists. I'd go so far as to call it indispensable. More significantly, through her tweets and blogs she's introduced me, and I'm sure a lot of other people, to not only up-to-date information but background details on an issue we either didn't know about or, in my case, knew about only very vaguely: the plight of the stateless of Kuwait.

GLOBAL HOTSPOT: Russia

On December 4, 2011, Russian citizens went to the polls to cast their votes in a legislative election that has been criticized by participants and international observers for irregularities and the potential of corruption, including ballot stuffing and voter fraud. Before the elections, individuals and organizations had reservations about the fairness of the proceedings. Following the elections, Russia experienced large-scale demonstrations that on December 10 reached sizes not reported since the 1990s. While much of the criticism came from Russian youth and was directed at the ruling United Russia party, claims focused on the annulment of election results and the opening of an investigation. Demonstrations and claims were widely organized and broadcast throughout Russia and around the world via social media sites. Pro-government tweeting and social media activity critical of the protests was also reported.

According to Alexander Kolyander, these rallies and social media exchanges "showed the power of the Internet to raise money for anti-Kremlin causes." The following excerpt from Kolyander's article "Internet Activism Increases in Russia," which was published in the January 9, 2012, *Wall Street Journal*–Europe News, illuminates the power of social networking sites in Russia's new activist landscape.

> For years, the Kremlin's tight control over business and civic life has made fund-raising one of the biggest challenges for the government's opponents. The task requires painstaking and delicate talks with donors fearful of official reprisals.
>
> "People are afraid of donating money openly. They are scared for their businesses, their families," said Sergei Parkhomenko, a publisher and a main organizer of both December rallies. . . .
>
> The Internet offered a solution. Systems such as the one operated by Yandex NV, Russia's leading search company, offer relative anonymity to donors. . . .

[To raise money for a bigger stage and stronger sound system for the large rallies] organizers turned to the Internet. More than 5,000 contributions flooded in, from as little as 30 rubles, or about one dollar, to 15,000 rubles, the maximum set by Yandex. The system accepts payments only from inside Russia, rendering allegations of foreign funding moot.

"It was fast, easy and transparent. We well understood that there would be a lot of people wanting to catch us on some questionable transactions, which we have none with this system," Mr. Parkhomenko said.

The following readings in this chapter explore social media and the diversity of positions and arguments concerning its place and potential in a global context.

READINGS

When Here Sees There
George Packer

George Packer is an award-winning journalist who is a staff writer for the *New Yorker*. He has written many articles for *Harper's*, *New York Times Magazine*, *Mother Jones*, and *Dissent*, works of nonfiction, and novels, including *Blood of the Liberals* (2001), the anthology *The Fight for Democracy* (2003), *The Assassin's Gate: America in Iraq* (2005), and most recently, *Interesting Times: Writings from a Turbulent Decade* (2009). He maintains a blog on the *New Yorker* Web site, "Interesting Times: Semi-Regular Thoughts on Foreign Affairs, Politics, and Books." His writings support liberal views regarding world issues. This op-ed piece appeared in the *New York Times* on April 21, 2002.

> What does George Packer claim is wrong with "the global communication system" and its effect on the world?

An Arab intellectual named Abdel Monem Said recently surveyed the massive anti-Israel and anti-American protests by Egyptian students and said: "They are galvanized by the images that they see on television. They want to be like the rock-throwers." By now everyone knows that satellite TV has helped deepen divisions in the Middle East. But it's worth remembering that it wasn't supposed to be this way.

⋇ The globalization of the media was supposed to knit the world together. The more information we receive about one another, the thinking went, the more international understanding will prevail. An injustice in Thailand will be instantly known and ultimately remedied by people in London or San Francisco. The father of worldwide television, Ted Turner, once said, "My main concern is to be a benefit to the world, to build up a global communications system that helps humanity come together." These days we are living with the results—a young man in Somalia watches the attack on the south tower live, while Americans can hear more, and sooner, about Kandahar or Ramallah than the county next to theirs.

⁎ But this technological togetherness has not created the human bonds that were promised. In some ways, global satellite TV and Internet access have actually made the world a less understanding, less tolerant place. What the media provide is superficial familiarity— images without context, indignation without remedy. The problem isn't just the content of the media, but the fact that while images become international, people's lives remain parochial—in the Arab world and everywhere else, including here.

"I think what's best about my country is not exportable," says Frank Holliwell, the American anthropologist in *A Flag for Sunrise,* Robert Stone's 1981 novel about Central America. The line kept playing in my mind recently as I traveled through Africa and watched, on television screens from Butare, Rwanda, to Burao, Somalia, CNN's coverage of the war on terrorism, which was shown like a mini-series, complete with the ominous score.

Three months after the World Trade Center attacks, I found myself sitting in a hotel lobby by Lake Victoria watching Larry King preside over a special commemoration with a montage of grief-stricken American faces and flags while Melissa Etheridge sang "Heal Me." Back home, I would have had the requisite tears in my eyes. But I was in Africa, and I wanted us to stop talking about ourselves in front of strangers. Worse, the Ugandans watching with me seemed to expect to hear nothing else. Like a dinner guest who realizes he has been the subject of all the talk, I wanted to turn to one of them: "But enough about me—anything momentous happening to you?" In CNN's global village, everyone has to overhear one family's conversation.

 What America exports to poor countries through the ubiquitous media—pictures of glittering abundance and national self-absorption— enrages those whom it doesn't depress. In Sierra Leone, a teenage rebel in a disarmament camp tried to explain to me why he had joined one of the modern world's most brutal insurgencies: "I see on television you have motorbikes, cars. I see some of your children on TV this high"—he held his hand up to his waist—"they have bikes for themselves, but we in Sierra Leone have nothing." Unable to possess what he saw in images beamed from halfway around the world, the teenager picked up an automatic rifle and turned his anger on his countrymen. On generator-powered VCR's in rebel jungle camps, the fantasies of such boy fighters were stoked with Rambo movies. To most of the world, America looks like a cross between a heavily armed action hero and a Lexus ad.

Meanwhile, in this country the aperture for news from elsewhere has widened considerably since Sept. 11. And how does the world look to Americans? Like a nonstop series of human outrages. Just as what's best about America can't be exported, our imports in the global-image trade hardly represent the best from other countries either. Of course, the world is a nonstop series of human outrages, and you can argue that it's a good thing for Americans, with all our power, to know. But what interests me is the psychological effect of knowing. One day, you read that 600 Nigerians have been killed in a munitions explosion at an army barracks. The next day, you read that the number has risen to a thousand. The next day, you read nothing. The story has disappeared—except something remains, a thousand dead Nigerians are lodged in some dim region of the mind, where they exact a toll. You've been exposed to one corner of human misery, but you've done nothing about it. Nor will you. You feel—perhaps without being conscious of it—an impotent guilt, and your helplessness makes you irritated and resentful, almost as if it's the fault of those thousand Nigerians for becoming your burden. We carry around the mental residue of millions of suffering human beings for whom we've done nothing.

It is possible, of course, for media attention to galvanize action. Because of a newspaper photo, ordinary citizens send checks or pick up rocks. On the whole, knowing is better than not knowing; in any case, there's no going back. But at this halfway point between mutual ignorance and true understanding, the "global village" actually resembles a real one—in my experience, not the utopian community promised by the boosters of globalization but a parochial place of manifold suspicions, rumors, resentments and half-truths. If the world seems to be growing more, rather than less, nasty these days, it might have something to do with the images all of us now carry around in our heads.

For Class Discussion

1. What assumptions about the potential of global media might Packer's audience have? How does he work these assumptions into his writing?

2. How does Packer challenge the position that social media and Internet technologies broaden our worldviews and produce globally connected and active citizens? Can you think of examples to counter the evidence he presents?

3. Part of the rhetorical power of this piece derives from Packer's skillful use of language. List as many memorable phrases like "technological to-getherness" and "global-image trade" as you can and explain what these phrases capture and why they are rhetorically effective.

4. Where and how does Packer acknowledge alternative views?

5. After encountering Packer's views in this argument, what thoughts and feelings do you have about the ability of media to bridge gaps among people and cultivate understanding? How do your views differ from Packer's?

Are Mobile Phones Bridging the Digital Divide or Deepening It?

Brett Davidson

Brett Davidson is a senior program officer at the Open Society Foundation's Public Health Program. The Open Society Foundation is an NGO started in 1993 by George Soros, which lists among its aims to "shape public policies that assure greater fairness in political, legal, and economic systems and safeguard fundamental rights (www.soros.org/)." Davidson writes for the Open Society blog, a platform designed for reflections on issues of human rights and justice. Prior to joining the Open Society Foundation, Davidson worked in journalism in South Africa doing advocacy work for NGOs. This blog editorial was originally published on the Open Society Foundation's blog on July 7, 2011. You can follow Davidson on Twitter at @brettdav.

> What assumptions does Brett Davidson make about his audience's background knowledge and view of mobile phones and the digital divide?

Mobile phones are often touted as the solution to the digital divide and the answer to a range of development problems. There is undoubtedly a huge growth in mobile phone access in the developing world, and the possibilities this presents are indeed exciting (as my colleague Mary Joyce blogged previously,* innovations in mobile health are helping to transform people's lives).

But these positive developments should not blind us to a range of problems and concerns (such as research in poor communities showing that expenditure on mobile phone use often comes at the expense of other needs, such as food). Two recent articles highlight the fact that the digital divide is very much still with us, and in fact new kinds of divides may be opening up.

In a paper published by Audience Scapes,† Gayatri Murthy acknowledges the unprecedented proliferation of mobile phones in the developing world: the developing world's share of mobile phone subscriptions increased from 53% in 2005 to 73% in 2010; mobile phone subscriptions increased by 16% in the developing world last year, as opposed to 1.6% in the developed world. But she goes on to

---

*http://www.soros.org/voices/using-digital-media-improve-health-marginalized-populations
†http://www.globaldashboard.org/2011/06/22/is-the-mobile-phone-revolution-in-africa-really-for-everybody/

show that gender and income disparities mean that not everyone is able to reap the benefits of the growth in mobile penetration.

In South Asia, Africa, and the Middle East, men are much more likely to have access to cell phones than women. In Sub-Saharan Africa, where the "mobile divide" is slightly smaller than in the other two regions, a woman is 23% less likely to own a mobile phone than a man. Unequal educational opportunities present another divide. For example, 93% of Kenyans with formal education had access to a mobile phone, as opposed to 50% of those without. Since a higher proportion of men than women have access to formal education, this reinforces the gender imbalance.

Furthermore, according to Murthi, women are less likely to receive information via mobile phone, relying more on interpersonal communication. This challenges assumptions that new technologies are, in and of themselves, going to democratize the information environment.

In addition to gender, Claire Melamed, a self-proclaimed "technological optimist," highlights some other divides, in a recent blog post on Global Dashboard.*

Firstly, there's a geographical divide: while heavily populated areas have excellent signal coverage, there are vast expanses of almost every African country where there is no signal at all. Secondly [there's] a literacy divide: even when people have mobile phones they may not be able to take advantage of access to a range of information services if they cannot read (despite the existence of projects that use mobile phones to promote literacy). And finally, there's a financial divide: for example she says, despite the advance of cheap mobile banking, in parts of Kenya making a money transaction using the MPESA mobile banking service costs the same as a bag of maize.

These two articles reinforce the fact that as exciting as the advances in mobile technology are, they're not a "one size fits all" solution for promoting development and democracy—and as much as they may help us solve some problems they are also creating new divides and inequities.

For Class Discussion

1. What features of this piece show that it is part of a blog conversation?

2. What is Davidson's main claim and how does his argument complicate and refute those who, like journalist Thomas Friedman, believe the digital divide is rapidly diminishing?

3. How well does Davidson's use of evidence convey the currency of his knowledge of the issue?

4. By the conclusion of this blog editorial, what position on mobile technologies, development, and democracy has Davidson reached?

*http://www.globaldashboard.org/2011/06/22/is-the-mobile-phone-revolution-in-africa-really-for-everybody/

The Revolutionary Force of Facebook and Twitter

Jillian C. York

Jillian C. York is a writer and digital rights activist and outspoken proponent for social media. She works with the Electronic Frontier Foundation (EFF), formed in 1990 as an international nonprofit digital rights advocacy and legal organization. In addition, she is on the board of directors of Global Voices Online and regularly writes on free expression, politics, the future of journalism, and digital activism for various publications, including Al Jazeera, *The Guardian*, and *Bloomberg*. Her personal Web site is http://jilliancyork.com/, and you can follow her on Twitter at @jilliancyork. The following argument appeared in the fall 2011 online version of *The Nieman Reports* published by the Nieman Foundation for Journalism at Harvard. *The Nieman Reports* explores the rights and responsibilities of news organizations to promote and elevate the standards of journalism.

> What major questions about mainstream journalism and the new social media underlie this piece?

In the wake of the Arab Spring, a vigorous debate is taking shape. While Facebook and Twitter are recognized broadly for playing a pivotal role in broadcasting information from inside the demonstrations in Cairo's Tahrir Square and elsewhere, views differ on the fit they will—or should—have in territory that has been the traditional reserve of journalists.

Throughout the Arab region, Web forums—general and themed—have long served as hosts for civic discussion. These online spaces held the place of social media before global sites like Facebook and Twitter came along. From 2004 to 2007, when I lived in Morocco, Facebook was nascent, still closed off to users outside certain networks, and Twitter, launched in 2006, had not yet emerged there. Blogs were still new, so much so that the Moroccan blogosphere, now a force to be reckoned with, consisted of just a handful of largely disconnected writers posting in diary style, dipping briefly into politics or sports. It was Yabiladi, Bladi and others—Morocco's forums—that were sources of unreported news, discussion and social commentary.

Morocco is not a dictatorship like Tunisia was before its revolution or as Syria remains today. It is a parliamentary monarchy with democratic norms followed to varying degrees, depending on the issue at hand. Its press is considerably freer than that of its neighbors in the region, with only a few off-limits subjects such as Islam, the king, and the Western Sahara, to name a few. Yet a few journalists there do broach even the most taboo subjects, sometimes to the detriment or demise of their careers.

On the Moroccan Internet, otherwise verboten topics are discussed routinely. Trilingual and multicultural, the country's blogosphere thrives and expands as Moroccans communicate via Facebook and Twitter. As they do, the topic of conversation changes, leaning more toward the political. Individuals' blogs fill in perceived gaps in local mainstream reporting while group blogs like Mamfakinch publish information about the ongoing protests sparked by the February 20th movement. Using Twitter and Facebook, people share videos of demonstrations, debate the movement's relevance, and analyze the mainstream media's depiction of what's happening in the streets and in the halls of power.

Social media now hold a vital place in this media ecosystem, filling informational voids left by the still bridled state and traditional media. Words written on them also round off the unknowing edges of reporting done by foreign media who fail at times to understand certain cultural, political or societal dimensions of their stories.

A similar dynamic exists throughout the Arab world—and beyond. In January, a global community followed Egyptians as they live-tweeted their uprising. We remain riveted by the horrific videos coming out of Syria as authorities brutally crack down on protesters and the hopeful ones coming from Saudi Arabia where women record their attempts to drive. In all of these examples, social media were not only effective, but also vital in spreading information.

MEDIA OR JOURNALISM?

While there is little question that online commentary adds value to the media landscape, is it journalism or is it activism? Or is it, perhaps, both? The answer, though complex, lies in the existing roles of state, mainstream and alternative media in the region.

Arab state media, in large part, assume the role of propagandist. To those who might challenge this description, I offer an illustrative example: Back in September 2010, just a few months before Egyptians rose up and ousted him, President Hosni Mubarak was the subject of a social media scandal. Al-Ahram, a state-run newspaper, had published a doctored image of the five leaders of the Israeli-Palestinian peace process. In it Mubarak was leading the pack, instead of U.S. President Barack Obama, as was actually the case. But alas, readers caught on quickly and used digital media to debunk Al-Ahram's image and spoof the scandal.

The region's independent news organizations must also be careful of firm lines drawn in shifting sands. Reporters and editors know to avoid certain topics or stick to safe talking points—stopping short of regurgitating propaganda—lest they find themselves without a job, or worse. And Western news entities with Arabic editions, such as CNN or the U.S. government-funded Alhurra, are seen as harboring a pro-American political agenda.

All of this leaves a large gap to be filled, often by small independent outfits relying to some extent on user-generated content. Working against the backdrop of the flagrantly biased state media and international media that, at best, have their own agendas, this emerging band of online writers strives to provide a corrective, alternative view that is inherently impartial, in the vein of public interest media.

Today's Arab media landscape is polarized, lacking either the tradition of or interest in the American concept of objective reporting. As media scholar Adel Iskandar observed in 2008, "Government media and alternative agendas alike pose an inherent problem for advocates of objectivity." Citizen-generated content adds a new dimension with its range of perspectives. But just as they can serve to challenge the mainstream forces, they can be tools of government propaganda, as seen most recently in Bahrain and Syria, where masses of Twitter and Facebook users have attempted to uphold state views by flooding services with pro-regime sentiment.

Though these pro-state users present a worrying development, the overall trend is toward a diversity of views. As George Washington University professor and Middle East blogger Marc Lynch observed in 2007, the Arab blogosphere is "chipping away at the encrusted structures of the Arab punditocracy." Social networking sites serve a similar purpose while encouraging quick updates and communication. While blogging allows for reactive punditry, Twitter and Facebook allow for rapid-fire commentary. Their use during major events is often immediately corrective, providing context or amending errors in mainstream journalism.

In reporting on the Egyptian uprising, for example, various U.S. media outlets repeatedly credited Facebook, Twitter, WikiLeaks and even nonviolence strategist Gene Sharp for the revolution. Through social media, Egyptians challenged these reports, such as when Twitter users mocked The New York Times with the hashtag #GeneSharpTaughtMe.

Blogs and social networking sites—and the Arabic Internet itself—are what Iskandar called in 2007 the "only regional venue for consistently non-hierarchical, socially-concerned, counter-hegemonic information, thereby making it the region's most appropriate 'alternative medium.'"

This active participation in journalism, made possible by social networking sites, is therefore changing the region's journalistic landscape and allowing for commentary not possible in even the most alternative of venues. As Internet access rates continue to grow and social media continues to be adopted as a venue for free expression, we will continue to see this landscape shift and expand, becoming more participatory and in turn more democratized.

Will there be journalists and news organizations? Certainly, and the roles they play will likely be significant ones in strengthening democratic impulses. But right alongside will be the social media entrepreneurs and enlivened citizenry, pushing and prodding, as has been their role so far in these seasons of Arab revolution.

For Class Discussion

1. According to York, what is the role of social networking sites in the journalistic landscape in the Middle East and what tensions does she cite within this landscape?

2. What does the complexity of York's mapping of the issue suggest about her knowledge and authority and about her audience's background and interest?

3. What evidence does York draw on to flesh out her claim about social media's significant alternative status?

4. What short quotation from this piece do you think best sums up York's argument?

5. How has this piece complicated, clarified, informed, or in some way changed your perspective on social media's influence on recent events in the Middle East?

Small Change
Malcolm Gladwell

Malcolm Gladwell is an internationally best-selling Canadian author and award-winning journalist who currently writes for the *New Yorker*; formerly, he wrote for the *Washington Post*. His personal Web site is (www.gladwell.com/index .html), and he tweets at @Malcgladwell. In 2005, he was named one of *TIME* magazine's 100 Most Influential People. He is perhaps best known for his books *Tipping Point: How Little Things Can Make a Big Difference* (2000), *Blink: The Power of Thinking Without Thinking* (2005), and *Outliers: The Story of Success* (2008). Gladwell, a cultural analyst, incorporates academic studies from fields such as sociology and psychology to support his insights, although his writing heavily employs stories and anecdotes. This editorial appeared in the *New Yorker* on October 4, 2010.

> What is the rhetorical effect of Malcolm Gladwell's beginning his piece with the well-known Greensboro sit-in event from the early days of the American civil rights movement?

At four-thirty in the afternoon on Monday, February 1, 1960, four college students sat down at the lunch counter at the Woolworth's in downtown Greensboro, North Carolina. They were freshmen at North Carolina A. & T., a black college a mile or so away.

"I'd like a cup of coffee, please," one of the four, Ezell Blair, said to the waitress.

"We don't serve Negroes here," she replied.

The Woolworth's lunch counter was a long L-shaped bar that could seat sixty-six people, with a standup snack bar at one end. The seats were for whites. The snack bar was for blacks. Another employee, a black woman who worked at the steam table, approached the students and tried to warn them away. "You're acting stupid, ignorant!" she said. They didn't move. Around five-thirty, the front doors to the store were locked. The four still didn't move. Finally, they left by a side door. Outside, a small crowd had gathered, including a photographer from the Greensboro *Record*. "I'll be back tomorrow with A. & T. College," one of the students said.

By next morning, the protest had grown to twenty-seven men and four women, most from the same dormitory as the original four. The men were dressed in suits and ties. The students had brought their schoolwork, and studied as they sat at the counter. On Wednesday, students from Greensboro's "Negro" secondary school, Dudley High, joined in, and the number of protesters swelled to eighty. By Thursday, the protesters numbered three hundred, including three white women, from the Greensboro campus of the University of North Carolina. By Saturday, the sit-in had reached six hundred. People spilled out onto the street. White teen-agers waved Confederate flags. Someone threw a firecracker. At noon, the A. & T. football team arrived. "Here comes the wrecking crew," one of the white students shouted.

By the following Monday, sit-ins had spread to Winston-Salem, twenty-five miles away, and Durham, fifty miles away. The day after that, students at Fayetteville State Teachers College and at Johnson C. Smith College, in Charlotte, joined in, followed on Wednesday by students at St. Augustine's College and Shaw University, in Raleigh. On Thursday and Friday, the protest crossed state lines, surfacing in Hampton and Portsmouth, Virginia, in Rock Hill, South Carolina, and in Chattanooga, Tennessee. By the end of the month, there were sit-ins throughout the South, as far west as Texas. "I asked every student I met what the first day of the sitdowns had been like on his campus," the political theorist Michael Walzer wrote in *Dissent*. "The answer was always the same: 'It was like a fever. Everyone wanted to go.'" Some seventy thousand students eventually took part. Thousands were arrested and untold thousands more radicalized. These events in the early sixties became a civil-rights war that engulfed the South for the rest of the decade—and it happened without e-mail, texting, Facebook, or Twitter.

The world, we are told, is in the midst of a revolution. The new tools of social media have reinvented social activism. With Facebook and Twitter and the like, the traditional relationship between political authority and popular will has been upended, making it easier for the powerless to collaborate, coördinate, and give voice to their concerns. When ten thousand protesters took to the streets in Moldova in the spring of 2009 to protest against their country's Communist government, the action was dubbed the Twitter Revolution, because of the means by which the demonstrators had been brought together. A few months after that, when student protests rocked Tehran, the State Department took the unusual step of asking Twitter to suspend scheduled maintenance of its Web site, because the Administration didn't want such a critical organizing tool out of service at the height of the demonstrations. "Without Twitter the people of Iran would not have felt empowered and confident to stand up for freedom and democracy," Mark Pfeifle, a former national-security adviser, later wrote, calling for Twitter to be nominated for the Nobel Peace Prize. Where activists were once defined by their causes, they are now defined by their tools. Facebook warriors go online to push for change. "You are the best hope for us all," James K. Glassman, a former senior State Department official, told a crowd of cyber activists at a recent conference sponsored by Facebook, A. T. & T., Howcast, MTV, and Google. Sites like Facebook, Glassman said, "give the U.S. a significant competitive advantage over terrorists. Some time ago, I said that Al Qaeda was 'eating our lunch on the Internet.' That is no longer the case. Al Qaeda is stuck in Web 1.0. The Internet is now about interactivity and conversation."

These are strong, and puzzling, claims. Why does it matter who is eating whose lunch on the Internet? Are people who log on to their Facebook page really the best hope for us all? As for Moldova's so-called Twitter Revolution, Evgeny Morozov, a scholar at Stanford who has been the most persistent of digital evangelism's critics, points out that Twitter had scant internal significance in Moldova, a country where very few Twitter accounts exist. Nor does it seem to have been a revolution, not least because the protests—as Anne Applebaum suggested in the Washington *Post*—may well have been a bit of stagecraft cooked up by the government. (In a country paranoid about Romanian revanchism, the protesters flew a Romanian flag over the Parliament building.) In the Iranian case, meanwhile, the people tweeting about the demonstrations were almost all in the West. "It is time to get Twitter's role in the events in Iran right," Golnaz Esfandiari wrote, this past summer, in *Foreign Policy*. "Simply put: There was no Twitter Revolution inside Iran." The cadre of prominent bloggers, like Andrew Sullivan, who championed the role of social media in Iran, Esfandiari continued, misunderstood the situation. "Western journalists who couldn't reach—or didn't bother reaching?—people on the ground in Iran simply scrolled through the English-language tweets post with tag #iranelection," she wrote. "Through it all, no one seemed to wonder why people trying to coordinate protests in Iran would be writing in any language other than Farsi."

Some of this grandiosity is to be expected. Innovators tend to be solipsists. They often want to cram every stray fact and experience into their new model. As the historian Robert Darnton has written, "The marvels of communication technology in the present have produced a false consciousness about the past—even a sense that communication has no history, or had nothing of importance to consider before the days of television and the Internet." But there is something else at work here, in the outsized enthusiasm for social media. Fifty years after one of the most extraordinary episodes of social upheaval in American history, we seem to have forgotten what activism is.

Greensboro in the early nineteen-sixties was the kind of place where racial insubordination was routinely met with violence. The four students who first sat down at the lunch counter were terrified. "I suppose if anyone had come up behind me and yelled 'Boo,' I think I would have fallen off my seat," one of them said later. On the first day, the store manager notified the police chief, who immediately sent two officers to the store. On the third day, a gang of white toughs showed up at the lunch counter and stood ostentatiously behind the protesters, ominously muttering epithets such as "burr-head nigger." A local Ku Klux Klan leader made an appearance. On Saturday, as tensions grew, someone called in a bomb threat, and the entire store had to be evacuated.

The dangers were even clearer in the Mississippi Freedom Summer Project of 1964, another of the sentinel campaigns of the civil-rights movement. The Student Nonviolent Coordinating Committee recruited hundreds of Northern, largely white unpaid volunteers to run Freedom Schools, register black voters, and raise civil-rights awareness in the Deep South. "No one should go *anywhere* alone, but certainly not in an automobile and certainly not at night," they were instructed. Within days of arriving in Mississippi, three volunteers—Michael Schwerner, James Chaney, and Andrew Goodman—were kidnapped and killed, and, during the rest of the summer, thirty-seven black churches were set on fire and dozens of safe houses were bombed; volunteers were beaten, shot at, arrested, and trailed by pickup trucks full of armed men. A quarter of those in the program dropped out. Activism that challenges the status quo—that attacks deeply rooted problems—is not for the faint of heart.

What makes people capable of this kind of activism? The Stanford sociologist Doug McAdam compared the Freedom Summer dropouts with the participants who stayed, and discovered that the key difference wasn't, as might be expected, ideological fervor. "*All* of the applicants—participants and withdrawals alike—emerge as highly committed, articulate supporters of the goals and values of the summer program," he concluded. What mattered more was an applicant's degree of personal connection to the civil-rights movement. All the volunteers were required to provide a list of personal contacts—the people they wanted kept apprised of their activities—and participants were far more likely than dropouts to have close friends who were also going to Mississippi. High-risk activism, McAdam concluded, is a "strong-tie" phenomenon.

This pattern shows up again and again. One study of the Red Brigades, the Italian terrorist group of the nineteen-seventies, found that seventy per cent of recruits had at least one good friend already in the organization. The same is true of the men who joined the mujahideen in Afghanistan. Even revolutionary actions that look spontaneous, like the demonstrations in East Germany that led to the fall of the Berlin Wall, are, at core, strong-tie phenomena. The opposition movement in East Germany consisted of several hundred groups, each with roughly a dozen members. Each group was in limited contact with the others: at the time, only thirteen per cent of East Germans even had a phone. All they knew was that on Monday nights, outside St. Nicholas Church in downtown Leipzig, people gathered to voice their anger at the state. And the primary determinant of who showed up was "critical friends"—the more friends you had who were critical of the regime the more likely you were to join the protest.

So one crucial fact about the four freshmen at the Greensboro lunch counter—David Richmond, Franklin McCain, Ezell Blair, and Joseph McNeil—was their relationship with one another. McNeil was a roommate of Blair's in A. & T.'s Scott Hall dormitory. Richmond roomed with McCain one floor up, and Blair, Richmond, and McCain had all gone to Dudley High School. The four would smuggle beer into the dorm and talk late into the night in Blair and McNeil's room. They would all have remembered the murder of Emmett Till in 1955, the Montgomery bus boycott that same year, and the showdown in Little Rock in 1957. It was McNeil who brought up the idea of a sit-in at Woolworth's. They'd discussed it for nearly a month. Then McNeil came into the dorm room and asked the others if they were ready. There was a pause, and McCain said, in a way that works only with people who talk late into the night with one another, "Are you guys chicken or not?" Ezell Blair worked up the courage the next day to ask for a cup of coffee because he was flanked by his roommate and two good friends from high school.

The kind of activism associated with social media isn't like this at all. The platforms of social media are built around weak ties. Twitter is a way of following (or being followed by) people you may never have met. Facebook is a tool for efficiently managing your acquaintances, for keeping up with the people you would not otherwise be able to stay in touch with. That's why you can have a thousand "friends" on Facebook, as you never could in real life.

This is in many ways a wonderful thing. There is strength in weak ties, as the sociologist Mark Granovetter has observed. Our acquaintances—not our friends—are our greatest source of new ideas and information. The Internet lets us exploit the power of these kinds of distant connections with marvellous efficiency. It's terrific at the diffusion of innovation, interdisciplinary collaboration, seamlessly matching up buyers and sellers, and the logistical functions of the dating world. But weak ties seldom lead to high-risk activism.

In a new book called *"The Dragonfly Effect: Quick, Effective, and Powerful Ways to Use Social Media to Drive Social Change,"* the business consultant Andy Smith and the Stanford Business School professor Jennifer Aaker tell the story of Sameer Bhatia, a young Silicon Valley entrepreneur who came down with acute myelogenous leukemia. It's a perfect illustration of social media's strengths. Bhatia needed a bone-marrow transplant, but he could not find a match among his relatives and friends. The odds were best with a donor of his ethnicity, and there were few South Asians in the national bone-marrow database. So Bhatia's business partner sent out an e-mail explaining Bhatia's plight to more than four hundred of their acquaintances, who forwarded the e-mail to their personal contacts; Facebook pages and YouTube videos were devoted to the Help Sameer campaign. Eventually, nearly twenty-five thousand new people were registered in the bone-marrow database, and Bhatia found a match.

But how did the campaign get so many people to sign up? By not asking too much of them. That's the only way you can get someone you don't really know to do something on your behalf. You can get thousands of people to sign up for a donor registry, because doing so is pretty easy. You have to send in a cheek swab and—in the highly unlikely event that your bone marrow is a good match for someone in need—spend a few hours at the hospital. Donating bone marrow isn't a trivial matter. But it doesn't involve financial or personal risk; it doesn't mean spending a summer being chased by armed men in pickup trucks. It doesn't require that you confront socially entrenched norms and practices. In fact, it's the kind of commitment that will bring only social acknowledgment and praise.

The evangelists of social media don't understand this distinction; they seem to believe that a Facebook friend is the same as a real friend and that signing up for a donor registry in Silicon Valley today is activism in the same sense as sitting at a segregated lunch counter in Greensboro in 1960. "Social networks are particularly effective at increasing motivation," Aaker and Smith write. But that's not true. Social networks are effective at increasing *participation*—by lessening the level of motivation that participation requires. The Facebook page of the Save Darfur Coalition has 1,282,339 members, who have donated an average of nine cents apiece. The next biggest Darfur charity on Facebook has 22,073 members, who have donated an average of thirty-five cents. Help Save Darfur has 2,797 members, who have given, on average, fifteen cents. A spokesperson for the Save Darfur Coalition told *Newsweek,* "We wouldn't necessarily gauge someone's value to the advocacy movement based on what they've given. This is a powerful mechanism to engage this critical population. They inform their community, attend events, volunteer. It's not something you can measure by looking at a ledger." In other words, Facebook activism succeeds not by motivating people to make a real sacrifice but by motivating them to do the things that people do when they are not motivated enough to make a real sacrifice. We are a long way from the lunch counters of Greensboro.

The students who joined the sit-ins across the South during the winter of 1960 described the movement as a "fever." But the civil-rights movement was more like a military campaign than like a contagion. In the late nineteen-fifties, there had been sixteen sit-ins in various cities throughout the South, fifteen of which were formally organized by civil-rights organizations like the N.A.A.C.P. and CORE. Possible locations for activism were scouted. Plans were drawn up. Movement activists held training sessions and retreats for would-be protesters. The Greensboro Four were a product of this groundwork: all were members of the N.A.A.C.P. Youth Council. They had close ties with the head of the local N.A.A.C.P. chapter. They had been briefed on the earlier wave of sit-ins in Durham, and had been part of a series of movement meetings in activist churches. When the sit-in movement spread from Greensboro throughout the South, it did not spread indiscriminately. It spread to those cities which had preëxisting "movement centers"—a core of dedicated and trained activists ready to turn the "fever" into action.

The civil-rights movement was high-risk activism. It was also, crucially, strategic activism: a challenge to the establishment mounted with precision and discipline. The N.A.A.C.P. was a centralized organization, run from New York according to highly formalized operating procedures. At the Southern Christian Leadership Conference, Martin Luther King, Jr., was the unquestioned authority. At the center of the movement was the black church, which had, as Aldon D. Morris points out in his superb 1984 study, "The Origins of the Civil Rights Movement," a carefully demarcated division of labor, with various standing committees and disciplined groups. "Each group was task-oriented and coordinated its activities through authority structures," Morris writes. "Individuals were held accountable for their assigned duties, and important conflicts were resolved by the minister, who usually exercised ultimate authority over the congregation."

This is the second crucial distinction between traditional activism and its online variant: social media are not about this kind of hierarchical organization. Facebook and the like are tools for building *networks*, which are the opposite, in structure and character, of hierarchies. Unlike hierarchies, with their rules and procedures, networks aren't controlled by a single central authority. Decisions are made through consensus, and the ties that bind people to the group are loose.

This structure makes networks enormously resilient and adaptable in low-risk situations. Wikipedia is a perfect example. It doesn't have an editor, sitting in New York, who directs and corrects each entry. The effort of putting together each entry is self-organized. If every entry in Wikipedia were to be erased tomorrow, the content would swiftly be restored, because that's what happens when a network of thousands spontaneously devote their time to a task.

There are many things, though, that networks don't do well. Car companies sensibly use a network to organize their hundreds of suppliers, but not to design their cars. No one believes that the articulation of a coherent design philosophy is best handled by a sprawling, leaderless organizational system. Because networks don't have a centralized leadership structure and clear lines of authority, they have real difficulty reaching consensus and setting goals. They can't think strategically; they are chronically prone to conflict and error. How do you make difficult choices about tactics or strategy or philosophical direction when everyone has an equal say?

The Palestine Liberation Organization originated as a network, and the international-relations scholars Mette Eilstrup-Sangiovanni and Calvert Jones argue in a recent essay in *International Security* that this is why it ran into such trouble as it grew: "Structural features typical of networks—the absence of central authority, the unchecked autonomy of rival groups, and the inability to arbitrate quarrels through formal mechanisms—made the P.L.O. excessively vulnerable to outside manipulation and internal strife."

In Germany in the nineteen-seventies, they go on, "the far more unified and successful left-wing terrorists tended to organize hierarchically, with professional management and clear divisions of labor. They were concentrated geographically in universities, where they could establish central leadership, trust, and camaraderie through regular, face-to-face meetings." They seldom betrayed their comrades in arms during police interrogations. Their counterparts on the right were organized as decentralized networks, and had no such discipline. These groups were regularly infiltrated, and members, once arrested, easily gave up their comrades. Similarly, Al Qaeda was most dangerous when it was a unified hierarchy. Now that it has dissipated into a network, it has proved far less effective.

The drawbacks of networks scarcely matter if the network isn't interested in systemic change—if it just wants to frighten or humiliate or make a splash—or if it doesn't need to think strategically. But if you're taking on a powerful and organized establishment you have to be a hierarchy. The Montgomery bus boycott required the participation of tens of thousands of people who depended on public transit to get to and from work each day. It lasted a *year*. In order to persuade those people to stay true to the cause, the boycott's organizers tasked each local black church with maintaining morale, and put together a free alternative private carpool service, with forty-eight dispatchers and forty-two pickup stations. Even the White Citizens Council, King later said, conceded that the carpool system moved with "military precision." By the time King came to Birmingham, for the climactic showdown with Police Commissioner Eugene (Bull) Connor, he had a budget of a million dollars, and a hundred full-time staff members on the ground, divided into operational units. The operation itself was divided into steadily escalating phases, mapped out in advance. Support was maintained through consecutive mass meetings rotating from church to church around the city.

Boycotts and sit-ins and nonviolent confrontations—which were the weapons of choice for the civil-rights movement—are high-risk strategies. They leave little room for conflict and error. The moment even one protester deviates from the script and responds to provocation, the moral legitimacy of the entire protest is compromised. Enthusiasts for social media would no doubt have us believe that King's task in Birmingham would have been made infinitely easier had he been able to communicate with his followers through Facebook, and contented himself with tweets from a Birmingham jail. But networks are messy: think of the ceaseless pattern of correction and revision, amendment and debate, that characterizes Wikipedia. If Martin Luther King, Jr., had tried to do a wiki-boycott in Montgomery, he would have been steamrollered by the white power structure. And of what use would a digital communication tool be in a town where ninety-eight per cent of the black community could be reached every Sunday morning at church? The things that King needed in Birmingham—discipline and strategy—were things that online social media cannot provide.

The bible of the social-media movement is Clay Shirky's "Here Comes Everybody." Shirky, who teaches at New York University, sets out to demonstrate the organizing power of the Internet, and he begins with the story of Evan, who worked on Wall Street, and his friend Ivanna, after she left her smart phone, an expensive Sidekick, on the back seat of a New York City taxicab. The telephone company transferred the data on Ivanna's lost phone to a new phone, whereupon she and Evan discovered that the Sidekick was now in the hands of a teen-ager from Queens, who was using it to take photographs of herself and her friends.

When Evan e-mailed the teen-ager, Sasha, asking for the phone back, she replied that his "white ass" didn't deserve to have it back. Miffed, he set up a Web page with her picture and a description of what had happened. He forwarded the link to his friends, and they forwarded it to their friends. Someone found the MySpace page of Sasha's boyfriend, and a link to it found its way onto the site. Someone found her address online and took a video of her home while driving by; Evan posted the video on the site. The story was picked up by the news filter Digg. Evan was now up to ten e-mails a minute. He created a bulletin board for his readers to share their stories, but it crashed under the weight of responses. Evan and Ivanna went to the police, but the police filed the report under "lost," rather than "stolen," which essentially closed the case. "By this point millions of readers were watching," Shirky writes, "and dozens of mainstream news outlets had covered the story." Bowing to the pressure, the N.Y.P.D. reclassified the item as "stolen." Sasha was arrested, and Evan got his friend's Sidekick back.

Shirky's argument is that this is the kind of thing that could never have happened in the pre-Internet age—and he's right. Evan could never have tracked down Sasha. The story of the Sidekick would never have been publicized. An army of people could never have been assembled to wage this fight. The police wouldn't have bowed to the pressure of a lone person who had misplaced something as trivial as a cell phone. The story, to Shirky, illustrates "the ease and speed with which a group can be mobilized for the right kind of cause" in the Internet age.

Shirky considers this model of activism an upgrade. But it is simply a form of organizing which favors the weak-tie connections that give us access to information over the strong-tie connections that help us persevere in the face of danger. It shifts our energies from organizations that promote strategic and disciplined activity and toward those which promote resilience and adaptability. It makes it easier for activists to express themselves, and harder for that expression to have any impact. The instruments of social media are well suited to making the existing social order more efficient. They are not a natural enemy of the status quo. If you are of the opinion that all the world needs is a little buffing around the edges, this should not trouble you. But if you think that there are still lunch counters out there that need integrating it ought to give you pause.

Shirky ends the story of the lost Sidekick by asking, portentously, "What happens next?"—no doubt imagining future waves of digital protesters. But he has already answered the question. What happens next is more of the same. A networked, weak-tie world is good at things like helping Wall Streeters get phones back from teen-age girls. *Viva la revolución.*

For Class Discussion

1. What main reasons does Gladwell use to build his case that technical innovation and social media do not pose a significant advancement in activism? Summarize his argument in several sentences.

2. Gladwell draws distinctions between "strong ties" and "weak ties," levels of motivation and participation, and hierarchies and networks. How does he explain these concepts and employ them in his argument? What assumptions underlie his framing of these ideas?

3. What kinds of evidence and emotional and imaginative appeals does Gladwell enlist to build his case and how effective are they?

4. Gladwell's title for this piece is a play on words. What are the multiple meanings of the phrase "small change," and why does it make a good title for this editorial?

5. Gladwell published this piece before the outbreak of revolution in Tunisia, Egypt, and Libya and before the violence in Syria and the election protests in Russia. How would these recent historical events affect the persuasiveness of Gladwell's argument?

Digital Dualism Versus Augmented Reality
Nathan Jurgenson

Nathan Jurgenson is a social media theorist, a photographer, and a PhD student in sociology at the University of Maryland. His research is informed by the understanding that people's online and offline presences are increasingly enmeshed. Jurgenson has written for *The Atlantic, Salon.com,* and academic journals, including the *Journal of Consumer Culture* and *Surveillance and Society.* He is a regular contributor to the multidisciplinary social science blog *The Society Pages,* based out of the University of Minnesota. He and University of Maryland colleague PJ Rey founded *Cyborgology,* a blog focused on new technologies and social interactions, which invites contributions from academics and journalists alike. This blog argument appeared in *Cyborgology* on February 24, 2011. You can follow Jurgenson on Twitter at @nathanjurgenson.

What is Nathan Jurgenson's main claim in this blog argument?

The power of social media to burrow dramatically into our everyday lives as well as the near ubiquity of new technologies such as mobile phones has forced us all to conceptualize the digital and the physical; the on- and off-line.

And some have a bias to see the digital and the physical as separate; what I am calling **digital dualism**. Digital dualists believe that the digital world is "virtual" and the physical world "real." This bias motivates many of the critiques of sites like Facebook and the rest of the social web and **I fundamentally think this digital dualism is a fallacy**. Instead, I want to argue that the digital and physical are increasingly meshed, and want to call this opposite perspective that implodes atoms and bits rather than holding them conceptually separate **augmented reality**.

In a 2009 post titled "Towards Theorizing An Augmented Reality," I discussed geo-tagging (think Foursquare or Facebook Places), street view, face recognition, the Wii controller and the fact that sites like Facebook both impact and are impacted by the physical world to argue that "digital and material realities dialectically co-construct each other." This is opposed to the notion that the Internet is like the Matrix, where there is a "real" (Zion) that you leave when you enter the virtual space (the Matrix)–an outdated perspective as Facebook is increasingly real and our physical world increasingly digital.

I have used this perspective of augmentation to critque dualism when I see it. For instance, last year I posted a rebuttal to the digital-dualist critique of so-called "slacktivism" that claimed "real" activism is being traded for a cyber-based slacker activism. No, cyber-activism should be seen in context with physical world activism and how they interact. Taken alone, yes, much of the cyber-activism would not amount to much. But used in conjunction with offline efforts, it can be powerful. And, of course, my point is much, much easier to make with the subsequent uprisings in the Arab world that utilize both digital and physical organizing. This *augmented dissent* will be a topic for another post.

Recently, I have critiqued "cyborg anthropologist" Amber Case for her use of Turkle's outdated term "second self" to describe our online presence. My critique was that conceptually splitting so-called "first" and "second" selves creates a "false binary" because "people are enmeshing their physical and digital selves to the point where the distinction is becoming increasingly irrelevant." [I'll offer my own take for what that digital presence should be called in a soon-to-come post.]

But the dualism keeps rolling in. There are the popular books that typically critique social media from the digital dualist perspective. Besides Turkle's *Alone Together*, there is Carr's *The Shallows*, Morozov's *The Net Delusion*, Bauerlein's *The Dumbest Generation*, Keen's *The Cult of the Amateur,* Siegel's *Against the Machine,* Lanier's *You Are Not a Gadget*, and the list goes on (we can even include the implicit argument in the 2010 blockbuster movie *The Social Network*). All of these argue that the problem with social media is that people are trading the rich, physical and real nature of face-to face contact for the digital, virtual and trivial quality of Facebook. The critique stems from the systematic bias to see the digital and physical as separate; often as a zero-sum tradeoff where time and energy spent on one subtracts from the other. **This is digital dualism par excellence. And it is a fallacy.**

I am proposing an alternative view that states that our reality is both technological and organic, both digital and physical, all at once. We are not crossing in and out of separate digital and physical realities, ala *The Matrix*, but instead live in one reality, one that is augmented by atoms and bits. And our selves are not separated across these two spheres as some dualistic "first" and "second" self, but is instead an augmented self. A Haraway-like cyborg self comprised of a physical body as well as our digital Profile, acting in constant dialogue. Our Facebook profiles reflect who we know and what we do offline, and our offline lives are impacted by what happens on Facebook (e.g., how we might change our behaviors in order to create a more ideal documentation).

Most importantly, research demonstrates what social media users already know: we are not trading one reality for another at all, but, instead, **using sites like Facebook and others actually increase offline interaction**. This is not zero-sum dualism. As the famous *Network Society* theorist Manuel Castells stated earlier this month,

"Nobody who is on social networks everyday (and this is true for some 700 million of the 1,200 million social network users) is still the same person. It's an online/offline interaction, not an esoteric virtual world."

None of this is to say that social media and the web should not be critiqued. Indeed, it should be, and I hope to do that work myself. However, critiques of social media should begin with the idea of augmented reality. **Is a reality augmented by digitality a good thing?** My job with this post is not to answer that question, but to help make it possible.

For Class Discussion

1. What is the alternative view and who are the stakeholders that Jurgenson is arguing against in this piece?

2. What reasoning and evidence does Jurgenson use to refute the digital dualists and their assumptions about "slacktivism"?

3. Jurgenson is writing for a blog aimed at undergraduate and graduate students in the social sciences. What challenges or benefits does this forum offer the development of his argument?

4. How does Jurgenson's notion of augmented reality shed light on this chapter's controversies over cyberactivism?

5. Why do you agree (or disagree) with Jurgenson that using sites like Facebook increases offline interaction? How has this article challenged the way you conceptualize your online and offline persona and interactions?

Social Media Venn Diagram
Justin Sewell, Despair Inc.

Justin Sewell founded Despair Inc. with his business partners in 1998 after they lost their jobs at a startup Internet company. Despair sells "demotivational" posters, coffee mugs, t-shirts, calendars and other items with dark quotations that parody inspirational platitudes. This visual argument comes from a T-shirt design.

> In your own words, how would you articulate the argument that is being made in this design?

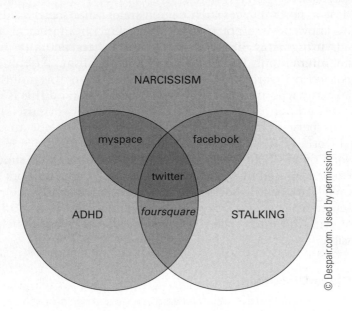

© Despair.com. Used by permission.

For Class Discussion

1. What cultural and social background does Sewell expect readers to bring to this design?

2. What stakeholder perspective of social media does this graphic draw on and what assumptions would readers have to accept to find this design humorous?

3. Can you think of reasons in support of and in rebuttal to the argument made by the design?

4. What role can satire play in advancing or detracting from the critical development of a complex issue, and how does this graphic affect your thinking on social media's value and use?

The Rise of the Occupy Insurgency, The World's First Internet Revolution #OWS

Nozomi Hayase

Originally from Japan, Nozomi Hayase now lives in the United States and writes for *Culture Unplugged*, the Web site for a new media studio aimed at promoting the sharing of stories and experiences for the enrichment of the global community. She also writes for *Journaling Between Worlds,* a blog where she advocates for imagination and the cultivation of a global civil consciousness. In addition, she contributes content to *A World Beyond Borders,* a blog "for all the people who believe that we are moving into an era where our human connection across the globe is more important than our national racial heritage" (http://aworldbeyondborders.com/). This argument appeared on the *World Beyond Borders* blog on October 23, 2011. Hayase tweets at @nozomimagine.

> What global connections does Hayase draw in her argument among protests around the world?

The 1980's popularization of the computer and the birth of the Internet was a quantum shift in communication and an evolutionary step for human society. The Digital Revolution marked the latest stage of the information age. People in distant parts of the world now connect instantly and information flow has shrunk the world. One of the biggest changes recently is the interconnected immediacy of social networking. This is a communication revolution in itself.

The word revolution has roughly three different meanings. The first is political, signifying fundamental change in political institutions, such as the overthrow of a government and replacement with another form. The second describes a fundamental change in technology or society in general, such as the Industrial Revolution. The Digital Revolution brought a shift in how we communicate as well as a sea change in a vast array of technology. And lastly in astronomy, revolution is the orbiting of one heavenly body around another.

Until recently, the Digital Revolution has not been fundamentally linked to serious political change. Yet, it created the foundation for the ubiquitous social media that is now being linked with political revolution on a global scale.

The first signs were the rise of online journalism, where bloggers and crowd-sourcers worked to fill the slack of mainstream media, much of which has been controlled through moneyed interests. In addition, the popularity of social websites like twitter and You Tube has contributed to the eventual decline of many traditional newspapers and TV news. The new digital press is more and more running roughshod over the old printing press; it is gradually replacing much of the existing system of journalism, which often filtered and slanted perception toward particular commercial interests.

The people's uprisings in the Middle East marked the maturation of this digital revolution where it merged with a new current of human passion. In Egypt, we saw social media playing a vital role in people assembling and taking action at Tahrir Square to throw off the Mubarak regime.

Social media facilitated uprisings are spreading, as in China, where active mobilization toward freedom is on the rise. The effect of social media in the arena of social and political empowerment is becoming undeniable.

How has this move toward social revolution come about? One answer is in the inherently democratic and immediately egalitarian nature of digital communication.

"The internet is direct democracy." Anthropologist Paul Jorion's statement might have captured a glimpse of a possible future society. Jorion noted that with the Internet, "there's no hierarchy and everyone can express themselves."

Although inequality of access to this technology is a problem, the Internet has opened the door to an incredibly fast changing and relatively unmediated world. The Internet is borderless. It can take one to virtually any corner of any street. The world has become literally a click away. People who go online can have direct communication with those in other countries through social networking on platforms such as Facebook and Internet Relay Chat. This relates a person immediately to events happening around the world and to masses of like-minded people.

WIKILEAKS WINTER

> *I think the politicization of the youth connected to internet is the most significant thing that happened in the world since the 1960s. This is something new, a real revolution.*
>
> —Julian Assange

The first ones to pioneer this unknown new land on the web were hackers and programmers. They have blazed through a wild cyberspace, not bound in the same way by the laws and traditions of society.

Through the wild currents of net-neutrality, the fresh thoughts and ideas of people that are exiled from the mainstream find refuge in offshore digital asylums. In this domain, one can explore and carve out a different identity. In relative anonymity, one with technical savvy can connect, travel and embody wishes and ideals via digitized avatars and move freely beyond prescribed societal roles. Despite increasing

Internet surveillance and censorship, many still feel safer finding like-minded people online to share their grievances toward government than through traditional structures.

WikiLeaks put its roots down on this new neutral infrastructure as the first stateless whistle-blower publisher that exists only on the internet. By revealing government and corporate abuse, this organization has inspired people the world over to unite in a struggle for justice.

Long before the uprisings in the Arab world, the seeds of revolution have been growing underground. WikiLeaks arose in the winter before the Arab Spring. After a long political chill, it welcomed whistle-blowers and kept that torch of justice burning. For many, alleged whistle-blower Bradley Manning and WikiLeaks founder Julian Assange became global symbols of a new era, modeling courage, idealism and a commitment to justice, especially for the younger generations. These two were recently nominated for the Nobel Peace Prize and won it hands-down in popular polls. Despite the US government's war on whistle-blowers, all around the world the trend of dissent and willingness to speak out against corruption is growing.

Another crucial component of the WikiLeaks Winter was the leaderless group Anonymous. Following WikiLeaks's lead, the online collective came on the scene to stake a strong claim in this growing stateless web culture. Ethical hackers and information activists showed how it is possible to move freely online by breaking down firewalls, collectively sitting in with DDoS (Distributed Denial of Service) attacks and defacing websites of corporations and corrupt government institutions. All this empowered ordinary people by showing that it is possible to effectively challenge old power structures.

FROM THE ARAB SPRING TO THE AMERICAN FALL

> *All civilization has from time to time become a thin crust over a volcano of revolution.*
>
> —Henry Ellis

2011 has become the year of revolution. The seeds of a global uprising that sprouted in the Arab spring blossomed into the European summer, and now with OccupyWallStreet it has entered a new season in the American fall. In the light of the law of empires, some see the dual meaning of the word "fall" as prescient.

In this online era, resistance within a particular country and community immediately gains global support. In late August, something was in the air. Just prior to the explosion of OccupyWallStreet, the online global collective Anonymous launched OpBART against the Bay Area Rapid Transit police for their repeated pattern of brutality.

With quick mobilization through the web, what started out as a distinctly local effort quickly got international attention, partly because of the mysterious international allure of Anonymous and the highly charged and sensitive digital atmosphere. Interactive Twitter feeds across oceans brought waves of the hashtag #MuBARTek, uniting Egyptians and San Franciscans in global solidarity against censorship and abuse of power. It was small, but was a shot across the bow just as the 99% movement was finding its spark.

The OccupyWallStreet movement that is now exploding across the world follows the revolving seasons of year-round Internet revolution. "OccupyWallStreet is a hashtag revolt," wrote Jeff Jarvis, a professor at City University; "A hashtag has no owner, no hierarchy, no canon or credo. It is a blank slate onto which anyone may impose his or her frustrations, complaints, demands, wishes, or principles."

The Twitter connected and bred action OccupyWallStreet was at first a group of committed individuals who gathered to camp out in the Financial District. People in a half dozen European cities: London, Valencia, Milan and Amsterdam soon joined in the operation.

Egyptian activist Mohammed Ezzeldin came to NY to join in solidarity with OccupyWallStreet. Acknowledging the connection between this and the protests against Mubarak and other despots he said:

> I am coming from there—from the Arab Spring. From the Arab Spring to the fall of Wall Street. . . . From Liberation Square to Washington Square, to the fall of Wall Street and market domination and capitalist domination.

Live tweets circulating from the ground as the rally moved downtown were mirrored in cyberspace. From lower Manhattan to Union Square, eyes behind the screen crossed borders and followed the crowd through the streets of New York. Verve and passion were spreading across the globe. Occupy movements started to pop up in various cities in the US and overseas. On Oct 15 global day of rage, people around the world raised their voices in solidarity.

This 24 hour Internet Revolution never sleeps. Through IRC and Twitter, people around the world communicate with one another, taking turns to pass the baton in a relay of revolution. What's behind this impulse?

2.0 OPEN SOCIETY

> *We ARE the Internet. You are actually dealing with a collective mind. Controlled by individuals and yet you don't understand what it means.*
>
> —@AnonymousIRC

What is striking is how this Internet-enabled revolution is different than traditional protests. It is a reality online as much as in physical space. What happens across the computer and I-phone screens is the tip of the iceberg of a massive movement. Like waves of unknown faces behind Guy Fawkes masks, the underground culture moves as a mysterious tide.

One thing that is unique about online culture is the relative anonymity that comes with the territory of the Internet. By crossing computer screens, people can leave their traditional social identities behind. They become relatively free from the underlying oppressive force of hierarchy based on gender, class and race. This 2.0 open society on the web levels the playing field, distributing the power to people, regardless of political or social standing. With an evolving digital dialogue, a common universal language of justice and fairness can flourish in this online culture. It naturally enables the users to exercise a kind of egalitarian democracy. Many IRC chats have created a Quaker-style dialogue, where the conversation is moderated to check the balance of power and make sure each person has an equal share in the dialogue. In this, values held by many indigenous cultures such as collaboration and sharing are finding a new place, counteracting the pitfalls of a domination and exploitation mentality common to Western civilization.

Learning through the inherently democratic nature of the Internet, the younger generation has been experiencing first hand this new approach to democracy. Yet, outside the screen, democracy has become a myth. Everyday life is now shaped by corporate values of hierarchy, efficiency and profits at any cost. Most political systems have also been taken over by this. A cognitive dissonance is growing between apparent powerlessness over the course of their lives in the outer world and relative freedom on line. People have been living double lives, as in the movie *The Matrix*, where Neo asks the question, "What is real?" Now ideals that have been submerged for too long are coming to the surface. It is this global culture that is growing online, that comes into opposition with the Wall Street world. The revolutions spreading around the world are simply a testimony of those who say no to this unjust reality and see the borders dissolving all around them.

> *#OWS participants realized that the online and offline worlds aren't separate after all. Now the underground current is bursting into mainstream consciousness.*
>
> —@virtadpt The Doctor

The egalitarian use of the Internet is now being translated onto the streets. This movement is bringing back unmediated oral traditions. With open mic and general assembly call and response, people practice face-to-face active listening and a new way of speaking together. Levi Asher shared her first hand experience of the people's mic.

It's called "the People's mic," and it's designed to allow a large group to hold an assembly in the middle of a noisy city without speakers or amplification. One of the facilitators explained it to the crowd: first, a speaker says a few words in a normal voice, no more than half a sentence at a time. The speaker will then pause while many people sitting nearby will repeat the same words together loudly, thus amplifying the speaker.

People are saying we don't need amplifiers. The echoing diffuses power from would be leaders and responsibility is shared by all.

Action in the streets reveal what has been incubating beneath the surface. Ideals, compassion, and creativity are the insurgent forces battling against the one-sided development of corporate culture. Naomi Klein remarked how she was moved by a sign at OccupyWallStreet saying "we care about you." Values traditionally held as the province of religious faiths are now finding their way into revolutionary action.

With the insurgency of these diverse ideals rising from the underground onto the streets, the online network Anonymous has become an Icon of Internet activist culture. In *The Real Role of Anonymous in Occupy Wall Street*, Sean Captain noted that there weren't many people wearing masks or those who claimed to be associated with Anonymous at the actual site. He described how the role of an online collective lies in its power to affect mass media and raise awareness about the movement.

"Beneath this mask there is more than flesh. Beneath this mask there is an idea, . . . and ideas are bulletproof" (*V for Vendetta*). The absence of GuyFawks masks at the protests does not mean their absence in the movement. Ideals behind the mask find their way into the 99% tumblr, and from there go viral. These are ideals that cannot be killed or arrested. They survive through the harsh winter of political persecution without being captured by religion, nationality or ideology. They continue to grow like seeds of hope.

In a recent article on *V for Vendetta* masks, Rich Johnston, an animation commentator was quoted saying, "The film *V for Vendetta* ends with an image of a crowd of Londoners all wearing Guy Fawkes masks, unarmed and marching on Parliament. It is that image of collective identification and simultaneous anonymity that is appealing to Anonymous and other groups."

By blending into the collective of the 99%, people are perhaps becoming anonymous in a new way. In principle, everyone is Anonymous and everyone is the 99% if they but choose to recognize it. The story that each person brings is unique and individual, yet in the majority the stories are tied together with a common thread, forming a new sense of individuality, not in isolation but in relationship to others.

The Digital Revolution was initially a technological one. It is now being humanized by people re-birthing the old ideals of justice into a new era. "The revolution will not be televised" said Gill Scott-Heron in 1970. Decades later with the spread of the Internet, "The revolution will be tweeted." Now people can see what's going on. So, what is next?

A CALL FOR DIRECT DEMOCRACY

> *To petition an establishment is to deny that from us can come*
> *fresh political movements through which power is exercised.*
> —@x7o

The New York Times article, *As Scorn for Vote Grows, Protests Surge around Globe* looked for the roots of people's uprisings around the world. It concluded that the global wave of revolution is a sign of a deep-seated distrust toward the system and that people are "taking to the streets, in part, because they have little faith in the ballot box."

"People realize that it's a show; it's a charade," author Lawrence Lessig echoes, adding "When you just look a little bit deeper, it's clear that what's driving both parties is whatever is the thing that's going to maximize the money." Through social media, people's voices are getting bolder in sharing their distrust of authority.

> *Imagine: Your citizens can think on their own now. Scary?*
> *Didn't expect it? Just pathetic. WE DO NOT BELIEVE YOUR*
> *LIES ANYMORE.*
> —@AnonymousIRC

Independent journalist, Kevin Gosztola described how the Occupy WallStreet movement is challenging the rigged 'two party' political system. While the importance of Occupy Wall Street was dismissed and belittled in the media, labor unions quickly recognized its potential. On the second week, Wed Oct 5, they joined the activists for a march.

Recently, unions have lost power and become mostly window dressing for corporate structures and a prop for this semblance of democracy. After having so much of their power stripped away, unions are joining the protesters and bypassing the traditional political system.

Is OccupyWallStreet calling for a direct democracy? People are now starting to challenge the notion of representative democracy when this has mostly become a system of moneyed interests corrupting elected politicians. At first the Mainstream Media criticized the lack of concrete demands of the occupiers and the lack of apparent leaders. Yet, many acknowledge that this is actually the strength of the movement. Out of what appears on the surface unformed and chaotic, consensus is gradually being built and because of the lack of hierarchy, decision-making processes become more democratic rather than top-down.

In essence, OccupyWallStreet is an experiment in direct democracy. In the conventional method of protest, people march for one day and put forward their demands. They then have no choice but to wait for politicians to deliver (which rarely happens). Before the invasion of Iraq in 2002, the global antiwar protest brought millions to the streets. Yet, they were ignored by the media and shut out by the government. The wars based on lies still continue. In contrast, OccupyWallStreet is not a one day event. When asked by the interviewer what he wants to see at the end of this occupation, a protester responded, "As far as seeing it end, I wouldn't like to see it end. I would like to see the conversation continue."

It is a new form of sit-in. Through encampment, people are starting to learn to live together, creating an alternative society. Leaderless movements encourage each person to become their own leader and really work with others. Decentralization means power is rendered by the people back into the hands of the individual.

Despite the media ridiculing occupiers, calling them hippies and trying to discredit them, it has been noted that the occupiers have been very articulate. The general public had been led to believe that they were not qualified to participate in democracy. Now it seems they are showing up ready to take matters into their own hands.

"One of the most abundant resources on earth is smart, creative, imaginative people," said one of the organizers; and yet 99.9% of the power of the human race is not being marshaled right now except to find something to eat. So all we need to do is open up that spigot a little bit and we could come up with endless ways to create and produce and distribute. That's what these assembly movements are about: people sitting down and saying, here's how we can do this.

Ordinary people's efforts are dissolving walls, whether it is the facade of opposition of a two party system or hanging onto nationalism. The divide between rich and poor was put up to exclude and divide people. Now action on the streets is decolonizing the space that has long been occupied by what is symbolized by Wall Street. From the Berlin Wall to Tahrir Square, from Tienanmen to the Gaza Strip, the message is resounding across time: We will no longer tolerate walls that separates us. What is happening with this movement is opening the space for a truly democratic dialogue. In the middle of seeming chaos and anarchy, an open space for imagination of the masses begins to move freely.

Ideals shared and acted on by the 99% are alive and constantly evolving, showing how democracy is a process, rather than an end-product of top-down decisions. Changes are already happening with an underlying shift in how we think about ourselves, our neighbors, and communities.

For Class Discussion

1. What different meanings of the word *revolution* does Hayase provide, and why do you think she begins her argument this way? What other key words does she use throughout this piece?

2. What are the main claims that Hayase makes about the functioning and benefits of the Internet in this piece? Briefly state them in your own words.

3. How does Hayase support her claim that we are in the midst of an Internet revolution? What evidence does she employ?

4. How would you describe the structure, tone, and style of this piece and how do they suit the forum in which Hayase is writing?

5. What stakeholders and readers would identify with this blog piece? What readers might not be reached by Hayase's reasoning? What insights or reservations about social media's potential has Hayase inspired for you?

Twitter Does Not Cause Revolutions, People Do

Harini Calamur

Harini Calamur lives in Mumbai, India, where she has worked in the broadcast media for more than ten years. She is a filmmaker, columnist, writer, and blogger. She teaches Media and Culture at Sophia College, Mumbai. Calamur also maintains a personal blog, *Point of View*, at http://calamur.org/gargi/, where she posts editorials and links to her articles that appear in various English language Indian publications. This editorial was first published in the Mumbai daily newspaper *Daily News and Analysis (DNA)* on February 20, 2011. Since 2005, *DNA* has become a very popular English language paper in India's economic capital Mumbai and has a print and digital distribution across the country and the globe. Follow Calamur on Twitter at @calamur.

> Which of this chapter's big introductory questions about stakes and stakeholders does Harini Calamur's argument address?

You need to have been stuck under a rock in Antarctica or living in the furthest reaches or China to have missed the popular protest in Egypt that led to the fall of the thirty-year-old dictatorship of President Hosni Mubarak.

The revolution didn't happen because one morning the people of Egypt woke up and said "Ah! Nice morning, we have nothing better to do, so let's get rid of our government".

Rather, the protests were the culmination of 30 years of repression, economic shackles, rampant corruption and above all—the inability of the bulk of the Egyptian population to have or meet aspirations of a better tomorrow. It was a popular revolution and the government fell because it could no longer get people to obey it—and that included the Army that refused to fire on its people.

However, if you were on-line and read or 'heard' comments from those in the know—you would think that it was a Facebook or Twitter revolution (17% of Egyptians have internet access and that was severely blocked during the revolution) or a social media-inspired revolution.

Ever since president Barack Obama won his election in the US, the power of the social media to garner support for a cause or elections has been talked about. What has been ignored is the sheer grassroots mechanism—individuals—who manned the campaign.

Dedicated workers—in various parts of the USA—who used social media as one of the tools to encourage voters to turn up and vote for their candidate on election day. These people didn't spam—rather they sent targeted e-mails to a mailing list of around 13 million voters (around 10% of the total voters), got around 3 million to donate and so on.

While these 10% might have been great and strong supporters for Obama, he would not have won if a substantial chunk of the remaining 90% who were not part of the social network didn't vote for him.

However, the hype was such that many believed that but for social networking Obama—who incidentally is a brilliant and tireless campaigner—would not have won. So much so, in the last general election the most visible part of the BJP's election campaign in India was its online 'LK Advani for Prime Minister campaign'.

There were internet groups, social media, web advertising and the rest of web marketing brought into play on this campaign. To no avail. If anything, the BJP fared worse than it did when it didn't use social media to campaign. On the other hand, the Congress, which, has an embarrassingly sad web presence, managed to win and do better despite the fact that it did not use the social media.

There is a genuine problem when you start mistaking the tool for the outcome. Just because you have a screw driver at home, doesn't make you an electrician.

While the analogy might sound nonsensical—that is exactly how those active on social media are seeing its use in polity and society. Internet penetration in India was around 5% in the last general elections, and while it should have grown since then, it is nowhere near the reach of television (around 50%). This means that 95% of voters have no internet, and 50% have no television. Campaigns in India have to be fought the old-fashioned way—household by household, constituency by constituency.

Revolutions happen because the bulk of the population rises up against a government. Parties win because a large chunk of the population votes for a party. While social media is great fun, and an effective networking tool—over reliance can lead to a certain kind of complacency.

You meet people from similar backgrounds, similar values, and you extrapolate this behaviour to the remaining population. There is a great danger in mistaking the wood for the trees if you take this approach.

So the next time someone tells you that the power of social media is going to bring down governments, or bring in government, don't argue with the converted—just smile—because it isn't true.

Expecting social media to deliver revolution or governments is a bit like expecting Coke or Pepsi to sell via social media without getting their ground distribution in place.

For Class Discussion

1. What specific political and social events are motivating Calamur to write this piece?

2. What stance does Calamur take on social media and political power in India and in a global context? What does Calamur mean when she warns against "mistaking the tool for the outcome"?

3. What do Calamur's analogies contribute to the logical and emotional appeal of her argument? Would you argue that they underscore her tendency to reduce social media to an all or nothing role or memorably enrich her argument?

4. If you were speaking back to Calamur from your own values, what assumptions and points would you identify as common ground or a place of agreement?

Agitprop 2.0 on Occupy Wall Street's Social Media Revolution
Kyle Chayka

Kyle Chayka researches and writes about art and culture. He has written for *The Atlantic* and *Leap: The International Art Magazine of Contemporary China*. Most recently Chayka has contributed to *Hyperallergic: Sensitive to Art & Its Discontents*, "a forum for serious, playful and radical thinking about art in the world today" (http://hyperallergic.com/), and Art Info, the online publication of Louise Blouin Media, a world-renowned cultural media group whose mission is to provide "unparalleled access to the world of art and culture" (www.artinfo .com/). The following article was published on the Art Info International Edition Web site on September 28, 2011. Chayka is on Twitter at @chaykak.

According to Kyle Chayka, what has been the relationship between social media and artistic activism in the Occupy Wall Street movement?

More than the ability to share photos with friends or keep everyone posted on your eating habits, the massive protests and resulting political change of the Arab Spring has driven home the point that online social media is the defining reality of our era. Now, the power of this new medium of communication has come to roost in New York City with Occupy Wall Street, a protest against the economic crisis and the excesses of the financial industry that has gone viral in much the same way that the Tahrir Square protests in Egypt did (albeit on a much more modest level).

Hundreds of protesters began meeting around Wall Street on September 17, and have since focused on the occupation of Liberty Park Plaza, across the street from finance hub One Liberty Plaza. Protesters have created a media hub in the park's center—not to meet with press, but to provide the infrastructure for protesters to broadcast their own motivations, critiques, and causes. The protest is occurring in digital and physical space simultaneously, as it has in Egypt, Libya, and Britain, as well as in youth-driven protests currently in progress all around the world, in Spain, in India, in Greece, and in Israel—this is revolution 2.0.

In an article on these global protests in the New York Times, Nicholas Kulish writes, "Increasingly, citizens of all ages, but particularly the young, are rejecting conventional structures like parties and trade unions in favor of a less hierarchical, more participatory system modeled in many ways on the culture of the Web." A Reuters article noticed the same phenomenon. It is the capabilities of the social web—instant communication, money transfer, media sharing—that are disrupting the traditional routes of communication and politics in New York City as much as in the Middle East. Here is how Occupy Wall Street has occupied the Internet even as it has occupied Liberty Park Plaza.

GOING VIRAL

Occupy Wall Street began on the Internet with calls from the activist coalition General Assembly and alternative publication Adbusters. The Wall Street protesters have made themselves known online by creating presences on traditional social networks. An @occupywallst Twitter feed currently has 18,133 followers, while the #occupywallstreet hashtag has provided an active venue for people both inside and outside New York to participate in the protests (Twitter has even been accused of censoring the #occupywallstreet hashtag from its "Trending Topics" list). An Occupy Wall Street Facebook page has 29,563 members and has seen 15 wall posts in the past 10 minutes alone. Page members post encouraging images, link to the latest press coverage, and share inspirational quotes. We Are the 99 Percent, a Tumblr blog, posts images of individuals holding up signs with their own complaints.

The online infrastructure of Twitter and Facebook has made it easy to pass along newsworthy documentation of the protests, which includes a now-notorious video of policeman Anthony Bologna spraying a female protestor in the face with pepper spray. Anonymous (the hacktivist group who pledged early support of the protests, though it did not come up with the idea) dug up Bologna's identity shortly after the video was released. It turns out the policeman was accused of civil rights violations in 2004. The incident has touched off even more controversy, and heightened mainstream media attention on the protest. This wouldn't have been possible without the protesters' own efforts—as the Observer noted, "Because the protest was continuously documenting itself, it was hard to tell who was participant, who was reporter, and who was tourist, snapping photos for their Instagram feed as they would of their cat or their breakfast." (NYPD commissioner Ray Kelly has since said that he will "look into" Bologna's actions.)

PORTRAITS & POSTERS

In the initial round of mainstream media coverage kicked off in a cynical piece by the New York Times, the protests were represented as a hippie-leaning crew still not united by a single cause or desired outcome (see the photo that accompanies the piece: an absurd marching band with a sardonic suited man strolling by). How the protesters represent themselves is much more urgent, and much more earnest.

Images of Occupy Wall Street posters and portraits of protesters have become popular ways of covering the events. Portrait series—like this extensive feature at the Observer and a Facebook album by Adam Nelson—show young people, professionals, students, and others, who identify with the idea that the financial industry's actions and the government's inaction have disrupted their lives. As Observer portrait subject Lou Panico says, "This is what everyone is always thinking about, but no one does anything. Glad it's finally happening."

Homemade signs have also provided a direct platform for protesters, as photos of the signs and posters have been distributed as internationally-consumed images. Art blog Hyperallergic has documented protest signs, with photos showing a quilt of signs laid on the ground. Others can be found in Nelson's album. They read, "Thank god for YouTube, cause my mom can't afford to send me to a good school," "This street is our street," and "do I look like a corporation?" Hyperallergic has also started an international call for artists to send in posters for the protesters. The results including a group of masked figures from the movie "V For Vendetta" (also Anonymous imagery) underneath the words #OCCUPYTHERICH. YouTube videos uploaded by miixxy document daily selections of posters and images, while one by Korgasmx documents violent protestor arrests.

These clips and images are the medium through which Occupy Wall Street's message spreads, far more than the mainstream media.

IN THE MAINSTREAM

In the past week, the mainstream media has paid ever-closer attention to the protesters and several significant public figures have visited the protest site in support. Noam Chomsky and the Atlantic's James Fallows have written backing the protests, while rapper Lupe Fiasco wrote a poem for the protesters and has tweeted his support. Documentarian Michael Moore visited the protest on Monday, as did Brooklyn city councilman Charles Barron on Tuesday.

A constant refrain in today's coverage of the protests is that Occupy Wall Street "could spark a movement." I would say that the protest has already created a movement—and it doesn't matter who notices. Now that the message has taken hold through the avenues of social media, and as long as participants are passionate enough to keep the tweets and signs and photos coming, it's going to be difficult to stop.

For Class Discussion

1. In this piece, Chayka discusses the stakes involved in the power of representation: Who has the right to represent whom? With which big issue questions about the role of social media in cyberactivism does this representation issue intersect?

2. What is the core claim of Chayka's argument about a social media revolution?

3. How does Chayka explain the role of social media in the diffusion and innovation process of global protest repertoires—symbols, slogans, and performances, particularly concerning the role of art and artists? In other words, how does the Internet relate to visual argument?

4. This argument was published in an arts and culture magazine. How do you think this forum shapes this piece's depth and development?

5. What feature of Chayka's argument did you find intriguing, compelling, or effective?

The Internet is a Tyrant's Friend
Evgeny Morozov

Originally from Belarus, Evgeny Morozov is a researcher and writer well known for his books, articles, and TED talks displaying his criticism of "cyberutopianism," the belief that the Internet and mobile technologies are inherently suited for promoting democracy and social progressiveness. Morozov, who identifies himself as a cyberskeptic, queries instead whether the Internet might be better suited to helping repressive regimes as well as to simply delivering entertainment. His book *The Net Delusion: The Dark Side of Internet Freedom* (2011) is stirring up much debate. Morozov has been a fellow at Stanford University, Georgetown University, and the Open Society Institute. He contributes to *Foreign Policy* magazine, the *New York Times*, *Financial Times*, the *Wall Street Journal*, *The Guardian*, *The Economist*, *The New Republic*, and *Newsweek International*, among other publications. This policy proposal first appeared in the March 5, 2011, issue of *New Scientist*, a general-interest science and technology related weekly magazine published in London. You can follow Morozov on Twitter at @evgenymorozov.

> What reasons does Evgeny Morozov offer to temper celebrations over the democratizing power of the Internet?

As recent events in Egypt and Tunisia so aptly demonstrate, technology is a double-edged sword: while pro-democracy protesters used sites like Facebook to organise, their governments used the same sites to suppress dissent.

Judging by the failed Iranian uprising of 2009, social media in particular provides dictators with all the information they need for an effective crackdown. Monitoring a revolutionary movement has never been easier—the secret police just need to collect enough tweets and pokes. Thus, while it's important to recognise the positive contribution that social media can and does make to popular uprisings, it's equally important to recognise its shortcomings and vulnerabilities.

Many authoritarian regimes have already established a very active presence online. They are constantly designing new tools and learning new tactics that range from producing suave online propaganda to cultivating their own easily controllable alternatives to services like Facebook or Twitter.

Why should we bother studying how dictators exploit the web? There are two main reasons. First, it may help us get a better grasp on how to promote "internet freedom," a cause that western governments are championing.

Promoters of internet freedom clearly need to understand what is going on. For example, it used to be that authoritarian regimes could tame the web simply by filtering or blocking "harmful" websites. Anyone who wanted to gain access to them would then need to use proxies and tools to get around censorship.

How things have changed. Now authoritarian governments rely on a rapidly expanding panoply of tools and tactics that range from distributed denial-of-service attacks to make websites temporarily unavailable, to spreading malware that helps them to spy on dissidents remotely. Merely funding censorship circumvention tools as a means of weakening authoritarian control no longer seems sufficient and may actually encourage dictators to replace technological controls with social ones, such as pressuring internet companies to remove political comments from their sites.

Another reason why those of us living in democracies should pay more attention to how dictators control the web is because it is the only way to identify and put pressure on western corporations that make such control possible by selling them the equipment.

The Egyptian government had the ability to monitor and intercept traffic passing through their networks thanks to "deep packet inspection" technology sold to state-owned Telecom Egypt by the American firm Narus (owned by Boeing). The Iranian government appears to have used similar equipment sold to them by western companies to spy on its opponents: last year the European parliament condemned Nokia Siemens for providing Iran's authorities with "censorship and surveillance technology." Some fear that the oppressive regime in Belarus used technology supplied by Ericsson to suppress political dissent.

Thanks to radical improvements in technologies such as face recognition, it may become even easier for the secret police to track their opponents. Here, too, there is a cut-throat competition among western firms, who rightly smell lucrative commercial opportunities— wouldn't it be wonderful if all those online photos of your friends could be tagged automatically? And yet you can almost guarantee that such technologies would be abused by authoritarian states. The way in which we choose to regulate such technologies in the west can really define—and perhaps, even limit—their contribution to political oppression.

Sadly, the likes of Facebook and Twitter do not have a spotless record on digital activism. For all the celebration of their role in facilitating democratic change, neither company has so far joined the Global Network Initiative, a group of companies, civil organisations and academics committed to upholding human rights and freedom of expression in telecommunications (Microsoft, Google and Yahoo have all joined). Many dissidents around the globe are unhappy that Facebook systematically deletes their accounts because their profiles bear pseudonyms, not their real names.

Realising the democratising potential of the internet won't be easy and, on the whole, it's perhaps a good sign that the US government is so keen on internet freedom. However, as activists in authoritarian states have told me, the biggest contribution that Washington can make to this fight is to first solve numerous problems in its own backyard. Getting US companies to stop selling technology to authoritarian states that are likely to abuse it would be a good first step; having Facebook, Twitter and others commit to some shared set of democratic norms would be a good second.

Companies aside, the biggest challenge to internet freedom lies in western democracies themselves, where law enforcement and intelligence agencies want to assert greater control over our networks. The rapid securitisation of cyberspace is particularly severe in the US, where the government, spooked by the WikiLeaks saga, is opting for a more aggressive watch over the internet.

The fact that the US government is trying to export internet freedom abroad while limiting it at home is not lost on its adversaries, who skillfully exploit such hypocrisy for propaganda. The push to promote internet freedom should aim as much inward as it does outward.

For Class Discussion

1. What background information does Morozov provide on the Internet's tools for repression and how does his presentation of this information suit the publication?

2. What reasons and evidence does Morozov offer to support his claim that we need to understand how dictators use the Web for their advantage?

3. How does Morozov reveal the complications and moral-political complexities of the internet in the second part of his proposal argument concerning the "securitization of cyberspace"?

4. How would you describe Morozov's tone, purpose, and attitude toward his audience in this piece? Why do you think he did not give more attention to alternative views?

5. With what other perspectives and writers in this chapter are Morozov's views aligned?

Stop, or I'll Tweet
Walt Handelsman

Walt Handelsman is a two-time Pulitzer Prize–winning political cartoonist for the New York–based tabloid style daily *Newsday*. His cartoons are published in more than 200 newspapers around the world, and he has published eight collections of editorial cartoons. This cartoon first appeared in June 2009 and was widely reprinted. It alludes to the contested 2009 presidential elections in Iran and the ensuing countrywide protests, sometimes dubbed the Green Revolution or the Twitter Revolution, whose organizers and participants used Facebook, YouTube, and Twitter.

Based on this illustration, do you think Walt Handelsman supports the label of the Twitter Revolution to describe the uprisings in Iran or not?

For Class Discussion

1. What story does this editorial cartoon tell, and who are the characters?

2. What condensed argument does this cartoon convey?

3. What arguments in this chapter does this cartoon support?

4. From your perspective, what role do political cartoons play in developing critical discussion on complex issues? How much attention do you pay to political cartoons, and have they ever sparked a conversation among you and your friends?

New Laws Needed to Protect Social Media
Kenneth Roth

Kenneth Roth is a human rights lawyer and, since 1993, the executive director of Human Rights Watch, a prominent global nongovernmental organization. Roth has also contributed over 100 articles to diverse international publications, including *Foreign Policy*, the *Los Angeles Times*, *The Guardian*, *East African*, and *Jerusalem Post*, as well as academic journals. This policy recommendation first appeared on the Human Rights Watch Web site on April 15, 2011. Roth tweets at @KenRoth.

In this piece, how does Kenneth Roth contrast a typical revolution with a social media revolution, and what is the importance of that contrast in this policy recommendation?

The use of social media such as Facebook and Twitter is transforming political activism. In the uprisings spreading across the Middle East and North Africa, the use of social media is spawning more diffuse and dynamic political movements. The possibilities are enormously exciting, but authoritarian governments are already catching on.

In this moment of celebration, it is worth thinking about the dangers ahead.

In the traditional model, revolution is guided by a handful of charismatic leaders—the classic vanguard—aided by a small group of disciples. That model is highly vulnerable. A repressive government can often stop political change by arresting the leaders and harassing supporters, as some governments did to limit the "color revolutions" of the last decade.

Social media makes possible a seemingly leaderless revolution, which cannot be so easily decapitated. In Egypt and Tunisia, for example, the revolutions did have people in leadership roles, studying other revolutionary movements and preparing strategies. But they could lead quietly, behind the scenes. Their lack of visibility allowed them time and room to maneuver without attracting government attention. Meanwhile, the movement built virally, with friends passing messages to friends, eclipsing any particular leader.

Facebook allowed political supporters to stand up and be counted virtually, without initially having to stand up physically and risk violent reprisal. Facebook could be monitored—Libya and Syria arrested some users—but as the number of virtual supporters grew, people became emboldened to use Facebook more freely, apparently figuring that the government couldn't monitor everyone. That drew in new constituents, many of whom showed up when demonstrations took place.

Social media allowed protesters to respond quickly when security forces attacked, warning others on Twitter with hand-held devices. They posted videos and photos of abuse on YouTube and Flickr. Al-Jazeera, in turn, beamed those images across the region—with enormous effect—even when its reporters were barred from a country. These communications generated outrage—and support for the demonstrators.

Some people rushed to the scene. Others applied pressure from abroad. Tunisians advised Egyptians through Facebook on how to protect themselves from tear gas. Text messages and email also allow such communication, but social media make mass interaction easy, quickly engaging many who have no acquaintance with each other.

But social media, like other technology, is double-edged, usable for repression or freedom. Unlike private conversations, social media leaves a virtual paper trail for governments to monitor and exploit. Facebook is especially dangerous because it doesn't allow pseudonyms even in repressive countries.

That paper trail might be what prompted Syrian President Bashar al-Assad to authorize the use of Facebook and YouTube just as the revolutions in Egypt and Tunisia were succeeding. But the growing protests in Syria suggest that Assad might have miscalculated. His secret police had long managed to arrest the leaders of Syria's small and embattled civil society. But social media followers can proliferate more quickly than secret police can multiply. Social media also helps activists circumvent government efforts to cover up repression.

Egypt and Libya were so exasperated by social media that they shut down internet and mobile phone communication. But that strategy is fraught, since it impedes commerce, inconveniences ordinary people and even undermines communication among security forces.

The Chinese government, with its massive resources, has so far managed to keep social media in check. Invoking Tunisia's Jasmine Revolution, activists cautiously announced "Jasmine rallies" in China, summoning supporters to stroll by crowded shopping areas on Sunday afternoons so the police would have a hard time distinguishing them. But the authorities flooded the areas with police, so few demonstrators risked taking part. Whether that is a successful long-term strategy remains to be seen.

Some governments order social media companies to reveal the identities of anonymous users or to block discussion of certain topics. Working with Human Rights Watch and other nongovernmental organizations, Google, Yahoo and Microsoft have developed the Global Network Initiative, an industry-monitored voluntary code of conduct that makes it easier for companies to resist these demands and for users to have confidence that companies are protecting their rights. Facebook and Twitter are not yet members. They should be.

Sympathetic governments also have a role. Businesses reflexively oppose regulation, but social media companies could better resist repressive demands if acquiescence were prohibited by law.

These governments should also fund a broad range of technologies and initiatives for circumventing censorship. Governments might also look for creative ways to fight censorship, such as including internet freedom in trade agreements, much as labor rights are now.

The use of social media has opened the door to dramatic new political possibilities. For the moment, the forces of freedom have the upper hand. But vigilance is essential before the inevitable reaction. As we savor recent advances, we should also prepare our defense.

For Class Discussion

1. What problem is Roth addressing and what action is he recommending that governments and businesses take?

2. What reasons and examples of users' danger and means of protecting them does Roth offer to give focus, depth, and urgency to his recommendation?

3. Based on his main claim, the development of his argument, and the site of publication, who do you think is Roth's primary intended audience?

4. According to Roth, what is hopeful about the role that mainstream media (such as CNN and Al Jazeera) is playing in relation to social media with regard to digital rights?

5. How do Roth's authority and policy position affect his contribution to the public discussion of digital rights and the progressive potential of social media? On the other hand, where might readers find this piece lacking or what questions might linger after reading it?

An Absence of Evidence
Malcolm Gladwell and Clay Shirky

The following exchange between Malcolm Gladwell, a journalist and author, and Clay Shirky, an author and professor of Internet technologies and new media at New York University, appeared in *Foreign Affairs* in the March/April 2011 edition in response to Shirky's earlier *Foreign Affairs* article, "The Political Power of Social Media." *Foreign Affairs*, published by the Council on Foreign Relations since 1922, describes itself as "the international forum of choice for the most important new ideas, analysis, and debate on the most significant issues in the world" (www.foreignaffairs.org).

Shirky has written several books, most recently *Here Comes Everybody: The Power of Organizing Without Organizations* (2008) and *Cognitive Surplus: Creativity and Generosity in a Connected Age* (2010). He publishes in academic journals as well as in *Business 2.0*, the *New York Times,* and the *Harvard Business Review*. He is on the advisory board at Wikipedia and is a proponent of peer-to-peer Internet services and their effect on the development of the Internet. He often speaks positively yet realistically of the Internet for its potential to advance society. Shirky's personal Web site is (www.shirky.com/) and he is on Twitter at @cshirky.

> What features of this exchange convey that you are reading a part of an argumentative conversation or debate?

While reading Clay Shirky's "The Political Power of Social Media" (January/February 2010), I was reminded of a trip I took just over ten years ago, during the dot-com bubble. I went to the catalog clothier Lands' End in Wisconsin, determined to write about how the rise of the Internet and e-commerce was transforming retail. What I learned was that it was not. Having a Web site, I was told, was definitely an improvement over being dependent entirely on a paper catalog and a phone bank. But it was not a life-changing event. After all, taking someone's order over the phone is not that much harder than taking it over the Internet. The innovations that companies such as Lands' End really cared about were bar codes and overnight delivery, which utterly revolutionized the back ends of their businesses and which had happened a good ten to 15 years previously.

The lesson here is that just because innovations in communications technology happen does not mean that they matter; or, to put it another way, in order for an innovation to make a real difference, it has to solve a problem that was actually a problem in the first place. This is the question that I kept wondering about throughout Shirky's essay—and that had motivated my New Yorker article on social media, to which Shirky refers: What evidence is there that social revolutions in the pre-Internet era suffered from a lack of cutting-edge communications and organizational tools? In other words, did social media solve a problem that actually needed solving? Shirky does a good job of showing how some recent protests have used the tools of social media. But for his argument to be anything close to persuasive, he has to convince readers that in the absence of social media, those uprisings would not have been possible.

SHIRKY REPLIES

Malcolm Gladwell's commercial comparison is illustrative. If you look at the way the Internet has affected businesses such as Lands' End, you will indeed conclude that not much has changed, but that is because you are looking at the wrong thing. The effect of the Internet on traditional businesses is less about altering internal practices than about altering the competitive landscape: clothing firms now have to compete with Zappos, bookstores with Amazon, newspapers with Craigslist, and so on.

The competitive landscape gets altered because the Internet allows insurgents to play by different rules than incumbents. (Curiously, the importance of this difference is best explained by Gladwell himself, in his 2009 New Yorker essay "How David Beats Goliath.") So I would break Gladwell's question of whether social media solved a problem that actually needed solving into two parts: Do social media allow insurgents to adopt new strategies? And have those strategies ever been crucial? Here, the historical record of the last decade is unambiguous: yes, and yes.

Digital networks have acted as a massive positive supply shock to the cost and spread of information, to the ease and range of public speech by citizens, and to the speed and scale of group coordination. As Gladwell has noted elsewhere, these changes do not allow otherwise uncommitted groups to take effective political action. They do, however, allow committed groups to play by new rules.

It would be impossible to tell the story of Philippine President Joseph Estrada's 2000 downfall without talking about how texting allowed Filipinos to coordinate at a speed and on a scale not available with other media. Similarly, the supporters of Spanish Prime Minister José Luis Rodríguez Zapatero used text messaging to coordinate the 2004 ouster of the People's Party in four days; anticommunist Moldovans used social media in 2009 to turn out 20,000 protesters in just 36 hours; the South Koreans who rallied against beef imports in 2008 took their grievances directly to the public, sharing text, photos, and video online, without needing permission from the state or help from professional media. Chinese anticorruption protesters use the instant-messaging service qq the same way today. All these actions relied on the power of social media to synchronize the behavior of groups quickly, cheaply, and publicly, in ways that were unavailable as recently as a decade ago.

As I noted in my original essay, this does not mean insurgents always prevail. Both the Green Movement and the Red Shirt protesters used novel strategies to organize, but the willingness of the Iranian and Thai governments to kill their own citizens proved an adequate defense of the status quo. Given the increased vigor of state reaction in the world today, it is not clear what new equilibriums between states and their citizens will look like. (I believe that, as with the printing press, the current changes will result in a net improvement for democracy; the scholars Evgeny Morozov and Rebecca MacKinnon, among others, dispute this view.)

Even the increased sophistication and force of state reaction, however, underline the basic point: these tools alter the dynamics of the public sphere. Where the state prevails, it is only by reacting to citizens' ability to be more publicly vocal and to coordinate more rapidly and on a larger scale than before these tools existed.

For Class Discussion

1. How do the ways that Gladwell and Shirky frame their arguments about social media and political activism differ?

2. Gladwell's style is journalistic, narrative, and personal. What specific ways does he try to appeal to readers and make his point?

3. What strategy does Shirky use to rebut Gladwell's argument? What reasoning and evidence does Shirky use?

4. Where do Shirky's evidence, concessions, and positioning of his views within the field confirm his authoritative knowledge and reliability?

5. Preferences for genres and styles of writing are always personal; however, what case could you make that either the argument about social media's applicability to political activism by Shirky, the scholar and academic, or Gladwell, the journalist, is more enlightening and persuasive? ▪

CHAPTER QUESTIONS FOR REFLECTION AND DISCUSSION

1. Thinking about how you use the Internet and social media on a daily and weekly basis, list as many uses as you can and give specific examples (for instance, post my response to good films and concerts on Facebook; follow my favorite pop culture heroes on Twitter). What are your primary purposes for using social media?

2. **Analyzing Arguments Rhetorically.** The readings in this chapter are built on different assumptions about the motivation of social media users; the relationship of social media to mainstream media; the potential for greater global communication and connection; social media's potential for galvanizing revolutionary change; and the degree to which social media has transformed social and political interaction. Choose one writer from each of the following rows and columns and (1) articulate the major differences in the way they frame the issues; (2) identify and briefly state their claims, reasons, and underlying assumptions; (3) comment on their kinds of evidence; and (4) explain how they address and respond to alternative views.

A. Jurgenson, Hayase, Chayka	Gladwell, Packer, Sewell
B. York, Roth, Handelsman	Morozov, Calamur
C. Hayase, Shirky, Chayka	Davidson, Calamur, Morozov
D. Roth, York, Shirky	Gladwell, Packer, Morozov

3. Morozov, Roth, and Handelsman share a concern for the ability of governments to censor and deny digital rights to individual citizens and protesting groups and for social media's empowerment of resistance. How do their critiques of regime control differ? What assumptions about the Internet as a tool for repression and resistance underlie each argument?

4. York, Jurgenson, Hayase, Chayka, Roth, and Shirky all in some way endorse the transformations social media has wrought in social interactions and the offline world. In one or two sentences, what is each writer's main argument? To what extent do you agree with Chayka that "online social media is the defining reality of our era" (366)? How do problems with the global digital divide challenge Chayka's claim?

5. Sewell, Morozov, Gladwell, and Calamur question the effectiveness and impact of the Internet. What do you see as the common threads in their arguments? How do their objections and reservations differ?

6. York, Roth, Shirky, Chayka, and Handelsman each in his or her own way celebrates the potential of social media to encourage political change. Based on your values, interests, and knowledge, which argument do you think makes the strongest case?

7. In arguments that take different approaches and have different tones, Roth and Morozov both advocate for greater awareness of the threats to the freedom of expression and freedom of access to information on the Internet and both discuss social media-driven revolution. Where do these writers' ideas coincide and clash and how do they propose to protect social media users?

8. In groups or individually, conduct research on the Web on one of the following questions related to this chapter's readings. Prepare to present your findings to the class using a video clip, handout, PowerPoint, or Web site for the class to examine.

   • What is The 550 Challenge and how can it overcome the global digital divide?

   • WikiLeaks.org, founded and edited by Julian Assange, "is devoted to exposing suppressed government and corporate corruption by publicizing many of their most closely guarded secrets"* Considering citizens' right to know and the need for national security, what are the main points in the case for and against WikiLeaks?

   • One form of online activism is the raising of awareness and money for natural disaster victims. Research Web-generated donations for the victims of the Haiti earthquake of January 2010; the Chile earthquake and tsunami of February 2010; and the Japan earthquake, tsunami, and nuclear power plant accidents of March 2011. What do these campaigns say about the social activist potential of the Internet and social media?

   • Use the Web to locate three or four cartoons from around the world on the role of social media and political activism. How do the arguments of these cartoons compare and contrast with the well-known "Stop, or I'll Tweet" in this chapter?

9. Contrast the more complementary or collaborative relationship between mainstream media and Internet/social media users that York and Roth describe with the antagonistic relationship discussed by Hayase and Chayka. To what do you attribute these writers' different views?

---

*Glenn Greenwald, "The War on WikiLeaks and Why It Matters," *Salon* (March 27, 2010).

WRITING ASSIGNMENTS

Brief Writing Assignments

1. **Reflective Writing.** A number of the writers in this chapter use the words *revolution* or *revolutionary* when they speak of social media in their arguments. Write a short response to these questions: How have the readings in this chapter affected the way you think about digitally driven social and political change? Which reading made the strongest impression on you personally—provoked deep thought or changed your views on the idea that dramatic transformations in human interactions driven by technology have taken place or are currently taking place?

2. Write informally for twenty minutes supporting or contesting one of the following controversial claims. Use evidence from your reading, personal experience, or knowledge to support your ideas and try to interweave specific examples with your general points. As a variation on this assignment, your instructor might ask you to write a short response in favor of the claim and then a short response arguing against it.

    A. Online and offline identities of social media users are distinctly different.

    B. More people are cyberhedonists than cyberactivists; that is, more people regard social media as entertainment and as part of their social lives than as a means to participate in socially and politically responsible action.

    C. Global citizens should actively oppose corporate and governmental censorship of the Internet.

    D. Overcoming the global digital divide should be a high priority for the global community.

    E. Social media as a means of giving voice to many should be celebrated in its potential to further democratic movements.

3. Imagine a dialogue between any two of this chapter's writers who take opposing positions on the way the Internet affects users or the value of social media to influence events in the physical world. Write a short conversational exchange in which these writers present some of their key views and respond to each other's views. For example, how would Hayase, who expresses the idea discussed by Jurgenson that online and offline worlds are part of the same reality, respond to Gladwell's emphasis on face-to-face interactions and his assertion that online activity represents diluted motivation and participation? How would Gladwell critique Hayase's points?

4. In groups, create a questionnaire of five to ten questions eliciting information on social media usage. Some questions should be fixed-choice questions (for example, asking how many hours a day a person spends on Facebook and giving the choices); some should be open-ended (What forms of social media would you say you and your friends use most regularly?);

and some should have a scaled answer (agree, strongly agree, disagree, and so forth). Include a brief note at the beginning of your questionnaire explaining its purpose. Do a test-drive of your questionnaire with other classmates and revise it per their suggestions. Then distribute your questionnaire in your university community and among neighborhood friends. Try for a sampling of at least twenty people. After compiling the data you gather, reflect on any trends that you noticed. What factors—age, gender, interests, place of origin—influenced the responses? Prepare a table and brief analysis of the availability, use, and value of social media. In what ways do your results confirm, contradict, or extend ideas about social media in this chapter?

Writing Projects

1. **Reflective Writing.** Write a reflective essay in which you respond from your own experience, values, and contemplation to one or both of the following statements by Nathan Jurgenson: ". . . people are enmeshing their physical and digital selves to the point where the distinction is becoming increasingly irrelevant" (356) or "cyber-activism should be seen in context with physical world activism and how they interact" (356). Think about specific times in your life when your experience refuted or confirmed Jurgenson's rejection of a dual reality and of digital participation in a cause as "clicktivism" or "slacktivism." (For example, has participation in a cause online ever led you to greater involvement in it offline? Why or why not?) Probe what you are thinking and feeling when you are online and how those thoughts and feelings affect your offline identity.

2. **Analyzing Arguments Rhetorically.** A number of writers in this chapter—particularly, George Packer, Malcolm Gladwell, Harini Calamur, Nozomi Hayase, Kyle Chayka, and Clay Shirky—have written passionate arguments about the role of media in global communication and social/political action. Thinking about the contribution one of these writers has made to your understanding of the issue, write an essay in which you analyze the argumentative strategies of one of these writers. In your analysis, you might focus on the writer's use of analogy, description, narrative, and evidence (the kinds, breadth, or sources of examples) as support for his or her claim and reasons; the writer's credibility and authority; or the genre, style, use of language, or formality/informality of the argument. You might speculate to what degree the forum of publication (newspaper, magazine, or blog) has shaped the argument. Include a short summary of the piece you are analyzing in your introduction. Through your interpretation of this argument, try to attract readers like yourself to this writer's piece or discourage them from reading it.

3. Choose one of the writers in this chapter with which you strongly disagree and write a letter to this person in which you seek to open a channel of communication on a common problem you both acknowledge concerning

the importance and potential of social media. Early in your letter, include a fair, accurate summary of the writer's argument that the writer would accept. Then explore the values that you and the writer share as well as your points of difference. Conclude your letter with a discussion of some of your own points that you would like the writer to consider. In your progression of ideas and tone, strive to make this letter a dialogue, a problem-solving negotiation or collaborative exchange, rather than an argument intended to sway your audience.

4. Imagine that you are interning for a state politician and have been assigned the task of researching the views of college students on online censorship, a major issue for people in China and other parts of the world and one that is heating up in the United States, as seen in Congress' recent debates about censorship and Internet blockage over the Stop Online Piracy Act (SOPA) in the House of Representatives and the Protect Intellectual Property Act (PIPA) in the Senate. According to a BBC summary of this controversy, these bills target various forms of online piracy, particularly "illegal copies of films and other forms of media hosted on foreign servers." Stakeholders in favor of these bills "include television networks, music publishers, movie industry bodies, book publishers and manufacturers" whereas "critics include Google, Facebook, Twitter, Wikipedia, Yahoo, eBay, LinkedIn, AOL and Zynga, Reddit, and Boing Boing," among others.* Would bills such as these cripple the spread of free knowledge, expression, and innovation on the Web? After researching the stakes and stakeholders and interviewing college students, write a policy recommendation for your political supervisor that summarizes the different perspectives and argues for a position with well-supported reasons and evidence.

5. As an alternative to a policy recommendation and the scenario in question 4, research these Internet censorship, privacy, and intellectual property issues, and either (a) design a brochure or flier for your residence hall, community, or city on how the issue of censorship affects the community; or (b) write an op-ed piece for your university or regional newspaper that takes a stand on this issue.

6. **Analyzing Arguments Rhetorically.** "Agitprop" refers to politicized art—that is, literature, pamphlets, drama, and visual art with an overt political message. In his article from this chapter, Chayka argues that the Occupy protestors occupied both physical spaces in cities and cyberspace. Many media analysts and commentators have cited the posts on Facebook, videos on YouTube, and posters featured on Occupy sites generated by participants as examples of direct democracy—political views voiced directly by the people. Write an interpretive argument in the form of an article for

---

*"Sopa and Pipa Anti-Piracy Bills Controversy Explained," *BBC News*, January 17, 2012, (www.bbc.co.uk/news/technology-16596577).

a news commentary magazine in which you rhetorically analyze one of the photo exchanges, YouTube videos, or Occupy posters that emerged from this political movement as agitprop for direct democracy. What is the message of the artifact, how does it make its appeals, and for what audiences would it be effective?

7. The United States is the source of a number of technologies that have been used for social control or surveillance around the world. At the same time, various voices—such as Evgeny Morozov, Amy Goodman of Democracy Now, constitutional lawyer Glenn Greenwald, and WikiLeaks founder Julian Assange—have pointed out that the United States itself struggles with balancing individual freedom, Internet privacy, and digital rights on the one hand, and national security, censorship, and monitoring on the other. What priorities and policies should the United States set in its role as global citizen? Write a policy proposal taking an informed position on this debate and direct it to either fellow American citizens or a governmental or corporate audience. Give your argument emotional impact by incorporating your own interests and concerns.

8. Should access to the Internet be a human right? A civil right? Should people have access to open source software and technologies or should corporate proprietary rights control these channels of digital communication? Does the protection of intellectual property rights or the free exchange of ideas lead to more innovation in digital technology? Choose one of these questions, brainstorm the meaning of terms (for instance, what is a human right?), and then research how these terms are defined in public discourse. After researching your issue question by examining a variety of sources that give you background, sketch the main arguments on the issue, provide evidence for the claim you will make, and write an ethical argument addressed to your peers that introduces them to the stakes and prominent stakeholders and that guides them to consider your position as an ethical view of this issue. You may find the following sites useful in developing your views:

International Freedom of Expression Exchange (www.ifex.org/)
Index on Censorship (www.indexoncensorship.org/)
The Tor Project (https://www.torproject.org/)
Open Source Initiative (www.opensource.org/)

8

Defending Human Rights

Human Trafficking, Forced Child Labor, and Rape as a Weapon of War

CONTEXT FOR A NETWORK OF ISSUES

Many people think all slavery ended several centuries ago. Britain's Abolition Act of 1833 launched the abolition of slavery throughout its empire; the United States banned the importation of slaves in 1808 and abolished slavery with the Thirteenth Amendment in 1865; and Brazil ended slavery in 1888. Yet a new form of slavery—human trafficking—is illicitly thriving globally despite progress with human rights. Estimates are that "more than 27 million people are enslaved" around the world*; that "some 2 to 4 million people are trafficked annually"; and that "as many as 17,500 people are believed to be trafficked into the United States each year and some have estimated that 100,000 U.S. citizen children are victims of trafficking within the United States."† These trafficked persons are moved within or across national borders against their will, intimidated by the loss of their visas and passports and by threats to their families, and coerced through violence to work for minimal or no pay.

Since World War II, the United Nations and advocacy groups have brought human rights to the attention of the world. The **Universal Declaration of Human Rights (UDHR)**, adopted by the General Assembly of the United Nations on December 10, 1948, declares that "recognition of the inherent dignity and of the equal and inalienable rights of all members of the human family is the foundation of freedom, justice, and peace

---

*Free the Slaves & Human Rights Center, University of California-Berkeley, "Hidden Slaves: Forced Labor in the United States," September 2004, www.freetheslaves.net/.

†Alison Siskin and Liana Sun Wyler, "Trafficking in Persons: U.S. Policy and Issues for Congress," CRS Report for Congress, December 23, 2010, p. 1

in the world" (www.un.org/en/documents/udhr). Along with the UDHR, two other main documents—the the International Covenant on Civil and Political Rights (ICCPR) and the International Covenant on Economic, Social and Cultural Rights (ICESCR), both adopted in 1966 and put into force in 1976—comprise the International Bill of Rights. Hundreds of further resolutions, covenants, and treaties have clarified and guided the global community's evolving conception and enforcement of human rights, which encompass basic rights: the political freedoms of speech, assembly, and suffrage, and the right to religion, work, welfare, and health. However, serious violations of these rights occur in many forms: the arbitrary detention and torture of individuals, the silencing of protest voices, genocide, the use of rape as a weapon of war, the abduction of children for child soldiers, and the trafficking of women and children for forced labor, among others.

The illegal business of **trafficking** of human beings, involving the buying and selling of people who are forced to work for the profit of others, is a problem affecting most countries, including European Union nations, Canada, and the United States. Girls and boys as well as men and women are "trafficked": that is, they are transported within countries or across national borders, traded for money, and kept subjugated by violence and brutality. The United Nations defines trafficking as

> the recruitment, transportation, transfer, harbouring or receipt of persons, by means of the threat or use of force or other forms of coercion, of abduction, of fraud, of deception, of the abuse of power or of a position of vulnerability or of the giving or receiving of payments or benefits to achieve the consent of a person having control over another person, for the purpose of exploitation. Exploitation shall include, at a minimum, the exploitation or the prostitution of others or other forms of sexual exploitation, forced labour or services, slavery or practices similar to slavery, servitude or the removal of organs.*

Although the exact number of persons trafficked is difficult to pin down because this trade is criminal, Human Rights Watch, a leading human rights organization, estimates that between 700,000 and four million persons are trafficked annually (www.hrw.org). The **International Labor Organization (ILO)** reports that about "8.4 million children are caught in 'unconditional' worst forms of child labour, including slavery, trafficking, debt bondage, and other forms of coerced labour, forced recruitment for armed conflict, prostitution, pornography, and other illicit activities."† These large numbers of adults and children are ensnared in

---

*Protocol to Prevent, Suppress, and Punish Trafficking in Persons, Especially Women and Children, Supplementing the United Nations Convention Against Transnational Organized Crime (2000).

†"Child Labor Remains 'Massive Problem,'" *World of Work*, no. 43 (June 2002): 4–5.

trafficking through abduction; through their vulnerability in orphanages, refugee camps, street life, poverty, and unemployment; or through the abuse of their earnest desires for a better life.

Shocking statistics only begin to convey the depth of human suffering that trafficking inflicts. For example, one of the main trafficking patterns involves the removal of women and girls from the former Soviet Union republics for sale and exploitation in Europe, the Middle East, and Japan. Lured and deceived by false job offers, women are sold for $2,500, raped and beaten into submission, and forced to service ten to thirty men a night, making between $75,000 and $250,000 a year for their "owners."* Terrorized into submission, these women are exposed to psychological abuse, rape, torture, and sexually transmitted diseases, including HIV/AIDS. When they are not working, they are often kept locked up, sometimes in filthy conditions. Similar exploitation is present in the burgeoning sex tourism industry in Southeast Asia, where girls as young as twelve are trafficked from Burma to Thailand, from Nepal to India, and from Vietnam to Cambodia.

Children, officially anyone under age eighteen, are also being sold and held in hopeless, dehumanizing labor. Activists distinguish between child labor, which is customary in some developing countries to supplement family income, and bondage. While the former can involve dangerous conditions, long hours, and low pay, the latter involves the abduction of children from their homes and entrapment in harmful, degrading work in other parts of their countries or outside their countries. Anti-Slavery International notes that only a small percentage of child labor is involved in manufacturing items for export. However, hundreds of thousands of children in Sri Lanka, Cambodia, India, Pakistan, Nepal, and African nations are trapped in bleak, arduous, isolated work as domestic laborers, and often exploited sexually as well. Children—boys and girls—are also abducted or coerced by military groups to serve as soldiers, forced wives, or sex slaves.

This human suffering calls for our compassion. In addition, these violations of human rights should concern us because human trafficking feeds crime domestically and contributes to the political and social destabilization of many regions of the world. The global trafficking of women and girls in the sex trade has fueled the AIDS pandemic, which in turn advances social disintegration, political instability, and potential terrorism. Currently, sex trafficking, the spread of AIDS, and subsequent social unraveling are threatening India, Nepal, and China. The huge potential profits encourage crime and corruption; wealthy traffickers can easily bribe local government officials and police. After trade in drugs and weapons, the trafficking of women and children is the most lucrative criminal business. Often the drug trade and the sex trade nurture each other by using the same routes

---

*Victor Malarek, *The Natashas: Inside the New Global Sex Trade* (New York: Arcade Publishing, 2003): 4–5.

and contacts. In addition, forced child labor and the recruitment of child soldiers jeopardizes the future of societies and perpetuates countries' cycles of poverty as worn-down children are denied education and opportunities to acquire skills that could help them improve their economic status.

The United Nations, the United States, and many other countries and numerous nongovernmental organizations (NGOs) are trying to address these human rights problems. The United Nations has formally proscribed trafficking and forced labor in Article 4 of its UDHR: "No one shall be held in slavery or servitude; slavery and the slave trade shall be prohibited in all their forms" (www.un.org/en/documents/udhr). Similarly, Article 32 of the UN Convention on the Rights of the Child adopted by the United Nations General Assembly on November 20, 1989, declares, "State Parties recognize the right of the child to be protected from economic exploitation and from performing any work that is likely to be hazardous or to interfere with the child's education or to be harmful to the child's health or physical, mental, spiritual, moral, or social development." In 2000, the U.S. Congress passed the Trafficking Victims Protection Act that established the tier system for measuring countries' efforts to combat human trafficking. Tier 1 includes the most cooperative countries, and Tier 3 includes the least diligent in fighting trafficking.*

This approach is intended to work by using shame and economic pressure to compel countries to confront their human trafficking problems. The United States has banned sex tourism involving children in the PROTECT Act of 2003 and has called on other nations to criminalize such behavior. Numerous organizations are working with governments on preventative strategies, detection and prosecution of traffickers, and rehabilitation of victims. For example, the Angel Coalition of the Moscow Trafficking Assistance Center has begun educational programs in orphanages and schools warning of trafficking, and it has established a free telephone helpline for Russian-speaking women and girls trafficked to Europe. As this chapter shows, the immensity and complexity of the human trafficking problems and human rights violations necessitate local and regional efforts as well as international cooperation.

STAKES AND STAKEHOLDERS

Many stakeholders—such as national governments, international advocacy groups, and civil society organizations around the world—are struggling to grasp the causes, extent, and possible solutions to these global human rights violations as they argue over these controversies.

---

*For more information on tier rankings of different countries, see U.S. Department of State, Office to Monitor and Combat Trafficking in Persons, *Trafficking in Persons Report 2009*, June 16, 2009.

How Has Globalization Affected the Trafficking of Women and Children?
Free trade proponents believe that many of the current violations of human rights, especially in developing countries, are part of the temporary conditions of economic development. They argue that global trade and growing prosperity will bring new freedoms and improve the societal and economic conditions that make people vulnerable to human trafficking. These advocates object to using economic sanctions to penalize countries for their human rights violations and trafficking problems. Some free trade supporters and governments and businesses in developing countries themselves argue that making money from their women and children, although harsh and unpleasant, is a practical way of dealing with economic needs, of paying their countries' debts, and of entering the global market.

In opposition, social activists and critics of economic globalization hold multinational corporations and free trade accountable for forcing rapid economic change, for undermining the social order and traditional societies in these countries, and for creating ready global markets for trafficked people. Kevin Bales, author of *Disposable People: New Slavery in the Global Economy* (1999) and activist in Anti-Slavery International, asserts that the emphasis on profits and speedy modernization has nurtured these countries' tolerance of human trafficking and that the lure of big money has fostered corruption in developing countries. Many critics also fault multinationals for indifference to human rights violations in developing countries.

Some analysts and critics stress the role of global communication and connections in facilitating the smuggling of slaves across national borders and the falsifying of passports, airline tickets, visas, and work contracts. Investigative journalist Victor Malarek, in his book *The Natashas: Inside the New Global Sex Trade* (2003), argues that the Internet is fueling the sex trade and calls the Internet "the biggest whorehouse on the planet"[*]

He claims that "in no time porn kings, pimps and traffickers were online promoting their products and services. Indeed, many observers believe that the Net is singularly responsible for the incredible explosion in the trafficking of women and girls worldwide."[†] The recent controversy in the United States over sex ads on the Web selling minors supports this theory.

Who Should Be Protecting Human Rights?   Despite various treaties and agreements, the global community is in conflict about who should enforce them. NGOs, activists, and some policymakers are calling for more UN and U.S. involvement in establishing laws to apprehend and punish traffickers and those who benefit from trafficked persons. Some advocacy groups and NGOs want the U.S. Department of State to emphasize human rights in

---

[*]Malarek, *The Natashas: Inside the New Global Sex Trade* (New York: Arcade Publishing, 2003), p. 80.
[†]Ibid, p. 81.

applying its tier system more rigorously. These activists and analysts criticize multinational corporations, trade agreements, institutions such as the World Trade Organization, and governments for valuing property over human lives. They challenge them to make human trafficking unprofitable and therefore unattractive, contending that protecting human rights creates political and economic stability beneficial for investment. Some advocates call for more consumer awareness of the conditions under which minerals are extracted and products are made. Other advocates urge citizen activism to put pressure on local, state, and national governments to pass and enforce laws related to human rights violations.

What Priorities Should Govern Intervention in Human Rights Violations?
Many conflicts arise over the need to decide which human rights violations will receive governmental and individual attention and financial aid. For example, will acknowledging sexual violence against men and boys take energy and money away from confronting rape as a weapon of war used against women and girls, as some feminist activists believe? On the other hand, workers within the human rights field emphasize that the international human rights system is a mutually reinforcing system: when human rights are lost in one area, they are often violated in others as well. In other words, human rights are interdependent. These advocates map human rights in two primary categories—civil and political rights; and economic, social, and cultural rights—creating a picture of the leading human rights issues today and how they are connected. According to this perspective, we can break down human rights into freedom from fear and freedom from want, as part of President Roosevelt's famous 1941 speech outlined, which later became foundational in the drafting of the UDHR. This big-picture approach to human rights calls for cooperation and collaboration, not competition among causes.

How Big Is the Human Trafficking Problem and What Are the Motives of Activists?   Some critics and public health officials argue that NGOs are exaggerating the problem in order to gain more governmental aid. The human trafficking issue has brought together conservative Protestants, Catholics, Jews, Buddhists, and feminists in the cause of international human rights; yet some politicians and critics suggest that these social activists are using the sex trade issue to fuel their campaign against prostitution. Some researchers, politicians, and analysts also contest the idea that certain groups of child laborers and sex workers are being trafficked, disagreeing over who are victims and who are willing workers using prostitution and servitude knowingly as solutions to their economic problems.

How Can We End Trafficking and Help Current and Potential Victims?
Controversies swirl around whether we need more legislation or better enforcement of the legislation we have. Many stakeholders are asking, How

can countries be held to their commitment to treaties such as the Convention on the Rights of the Child and to their own laws? Some NGOs, politicians, and activists point out that the people who have the highest stakes in human trafficking, the victims themselves, are first silenced by coercion and then by the legal processes that criminalize them or penalize them as illegal migrants. These activists are campaigning for new laws and procedures for victims to have access to greater protection and aid. Trafficking Programme Officer of Anti-Slavery International Elaine Pearson recommends "increased employment and migration opportunities; protection and support for those trafficked, including temporary or permanent residence in countries of destination; and opportunities for legal redress and compensation."*

NGOs, researchers, and policymakers disagree about what strategies and solutions to pursue. Some target root causes, prevention, and the connection between trafficking and poverty, noting that the dominant global patterns of trafficking are from east to west and south to north, from poorer countries to richer ones. Kevin Bales asserts that the trafficking victims and the poor need to own their own lives; he recommends that we "give them access to credit, let them choose their work, get rid of corruption, offer rehabilitation programs, and provide education."†

Some activists focus on the global market, for example, challenging sex work as an industry, promoting the curbing of sex tourism, or asking consumers to buy or not buy items produced by child workers. Other analysts, activists, and policymakers call for public support of local in-the-field groups that are in tune with specific regional conditions. Still others demand a rethinking of human trafficking in terms of migration patterns or global health problems.

Thinking Visually

The Trafficking of Girls

The International Organization for Migration seeks to "assist in meeting the growing operational challenges of migration management; advance understanding of migration issues; encourage social and economic development through migration; and uphold the human dignity and well-being of migrants" (from its mission statement, www.iom.org). The IOM works with governments and civil society on every continent. Its countertrafficking projects—of which this "For Sale" poster is a part—focus on information campaigns, counseling services, research, safe conduct and assistance for victims, and working with governments on their legal systems to stop trafficking.

---

*"Trapped in Traffic," *New Internationalist*, no. 337 (August 2001): 26.
†*Disposable People* (Berkeley: University of California Press, 1999): 257.

Questions to Ponder

1. How would you describe the girl in this poster and the emotional effect of the combination of the photo of the girl, the words "FOR SALE," and the placement of the words?

2. What primary and secondary audiences could this poster reach? How could this poster be used to clarify the connections and differences between migration and human trafficking?

The three sections that follow—Student Voice, International Voices, and Global Hot Spot—take you deeper into local and global dimensions of this chapter's human rights issues.

 ### STUDENT VOICE: A Human Connection by Victoria Herradura

Although Americans may feel removed from the problems of sex trafficking and forced labor, student writer Victoria Herradura shows how she became aware of these human rights abuses and decided to offer help.

As a first generation Filipino in the United States, I have been sheltered from the many hardships that my parents faced while growing up in the rural areas of the Philippines. My parents wanted to raise me as Americanized as possible, which meant not living the frugal lifestyle that they were raised in. Of course, this did not mean abandoning my relatives still trapped in the motherland unable to obtain visas. Every season, my mother would rummage through my belongings to find forgotten toys, clothes, and even unused school supplies to send overseas to my cousins in the Philippines. I would always put up a battle with her. There was no way I would let my mother simply give away my belongings to my cousins whom I had never met. I figured that if both of my parents were able to make it from the islands to America, there should be no reason why my aunts and uncles could not relocate here if that was what they truly desired.

As the years passed, I grew out of my bratty childhood attitude and personally sorted through my clothes and other belongings to send overseas. My mother thought that I was being more altruistic, but secretly I just wanted to make more room in my closet for better clothes, better shoes, and better accessories. During my junior year in high school, just before the seasonal closet clean-out, I purchased a pair of pastel pink Converse high-tops for a spirit day at school. Unfortunately, I was only able to wear those shoes once because a few days later, my mother packed them up and shipped them off. Several months after that, I found the need for those pastel pink shoes again. I searched through my closet, under my bed, in the backyard, and in the basement until my mother told me that my less-fortunate cousin in the Philippines was wearing them at that moment. The thought that she would dare give away something I bought with my own money to someone I did not even know temporarily made me livid.

It was not until the middle of senior year, when I watched the Lifetime movie, *Human Trafficking,* and saw the dire conditions and economic crisis of families in foreign countries, that I realized how horribly skewed my thoughts about my relatives had been. The movie traces three different stories, three different journeys out of human trafficking: that of a little girl, a teenager, and an older woman. The purpose of the film is to show that human trafficking is a global human rights issue, targeting women of all ages. In countries where there seems to be little hope of economic stability, any door that leads to opportunities and security is accessed without question, which allows the rich to take advantage of the poor and ignorant.

It seems odd that a four-hour movie highlighting the struggles of a form of prostitution could make me grasp the difficulties of life in the Philippines, but the story of the little girl did just that. The film portrays an American preteen girl on vacation in the Philippines with her parents, who befriends a poor Filipino boy lurking in the street market for girls to sell into prostitution. While her parents are searching for her, she meets a younger Filipina who was sold by her parents for a year to do physical labor for a rich European businessman. Sadly, parents from rural areas of the Philippines often sell their children to men who claim that their children will be well taken care of and returned in good condition without any idea of the actual work they have to endure. I now know that jobs in America with a minimum wage are not offered everywhere and that the opportunities of making a successful life are not the same for everyone. My cousins are not being sold to foreign human traffickers, but it is just as challenging for them to earn money and get by on their own. They appreciated every used item my mother sent more than I did when those very same items were new.

Since watching that movie, I have willingly donated my belongings, not only to my relatives, but also to local charities. I have even convinced my parents to sponsor children in the Philippines because what is considered pocket change to Americans is just enough to meet a child's daily basic needs and prevent one more child from entering the world of human trafficking. Although I am disgusted at my initial views of life outside of the comforts of the U.S. borders, I realize that we often need exposure to the outside world to feel the need to help globally.

INTERNATIONAL VOICES

In December of 2011, three women—Ellen Johnson Sirleaf and Leymah Gbowee from Liberia and Tawakkol Karman from Yemen—won the Nobel Peace Prize for their nonviolent work for democracy and gender equality. The following passage is an excerpt from Gbowee's 2011 acceptance speech, proclaiming the hope, generated by the courageous self-assertion and collaborative efforts of women, that is growing in the face of ongoing violence, mass rapes, and forced recruitment of child soldiers. This speech was published in *Africa News* on December 10, 2011.

Comments from Women Working for Peace and Equality

Early 2003, seven of us women gathered in a makeshift office/ conference room to discuss the Liberian civil war and the fast approaching war on the capital Monrovia. Armed with nothing but our conviction and $10 United States dollars, the Women of Liberia Mass Action for Peace Campaign was born.

Women had become the "toy of war" for over-drugged young militias. Sexual abuse and exploitation spared no woman; we were raped and abused regardless of our age, religious or social status. A common scene daily was a mother watching her young one being forcibly recruited or her daughter taken away as the wife of another drug emboldened fighter.

We used our pains, broken bodies and scarred emotions to confront the injustices and terror of our nation. We were aware that the end of the war will only come through nonviolence, as we had all seen that the use of violence was taking us and our beloved country deeper into the abyss of pains, death, and destruction. . . .

We worked daily confronting warlords, meeting with dictators and refusing to be silenced in the face of AK 47s and RPGs. We walked when we had no transportation, we fasted when water was unaffordable, we held hands in the face of danger, we spoke truth to power when everyone else was being diplomatic, we stood under the rain and the sun with our children to tell the world the stories of the other side of the conflict. . . .

This prize could not have come at a better time than this. . . . It has come at a time when unarmed citizens men and women, boys and girls are challenging dictatorships and ushering in democracy and the sovereignty of people.

Yes! It has come at a time when in many societies where women used to be the silent victims and objects of men's powers, women are throwing down the walls of repressive traditions with the invincible power of nonviolence. Women are using their broken bodies from hunger, poverty, desperation, and destitution to stare down the barrel of the gun. This prize has come at a time when ordinary mothers are no longer begging for peace, but demanding peace, justice, equality and inclusion in political decision-making.

I must be quick to add that this prize is not just in recognition of the triumph of women. It is a triumph for humanity. To recognize and honor women, the other half of humanity, is to achieve universal wholeness and balance. Like the women I met in Congo DRC over a year ago who said, "Rape and abuse is the result of [a] larger problem and that problem is the absence of women in the decision-making space." If women were part of decision-making in most societies, there would be less exclusive policies and laws that are blind to abuses women endure. . . .

GLOBAL HOT SPOT: Democratic Republic of Congo

One site with rampant, compounded human rights violations is Democratic Republic of Congo where political, economic, and social conflicts over mineral wealth are causing destruction in women's lives through rape and enslaved labor, as revealed in this excerpt from the article "Congo Rape Victims Face Slavery in Gold and Mineral Mines" by Diane Taylor from the British news source *The Guardian*, September 2, 2011.

Rape victims in eastern Democratic Republic of Congo are being forced to work in conditions of slavery in mines producing gold, coltan and the tin ore needed to manufacture jewellery, mobile phones and laptops, a *Guardian* investigation has found.

The girls and women fled their villages after being raped by one or more of the militias terrorising the region. Traditionally the women were engaged in farming but their fields are in forests occupied by rebels and growing food has become too dangerous. Instead they are forced into exploitative work in mines to survive.

"If you choose to get food from the field you have to accept that you're going to be raped," said Patience Kengwa, 30, who works at Kamituga gold mine. She fled her village, Luliba, after being raped five times in two and a half years. Now she pounds rocks and carries heavy sacks, earning between 50 cents and a dollar a day.

Dominique Bikaba, director of Strong Roots, an environmental charity that works with miners to improve their conditions, has condemned the situation.

"These girls and women are working in the mines in conditions of slavery. They earn less than a dollar a day and are often forced to work harder than they are physically capable of working," he said.

Various militias have been fighting each other in east Congo for more than a decade, raping and looting with impunity. . . .

Congo's mineral resources are estimated at $24 trillion, more than the combined GDP of Europe and America.

According to Bikaba, 98% of east Congo's mines have some involvement with one militia or another—either the militia control the mines or coerce people to work in them or demand "taxes" from workers.

East Congo was recently described as one of the worst places on earth to be a woman after a study in June by the *American Journal of Public Health* found that 1,152 women are raped every day in the African state, equating to a rate of 48 an hour. The perpetrators include the mainly Hutu Rwandan rebel group FDLR, a rival rebel group comprised mainly of Tutsis called CNDP, Congolese soldiers and the local Congolese Mai Mai militia.

From "Congo Rape Victims Face Slavery in Gold and Mineral Mines"
by Diane Taylor from The Guardian, September 2, 2011.
Copyright Guardian News & Media Ltd 2011.

The arguments in this chapter, which present policy statements, scholarly research, and calls to action, will help you explore the political, economic, social, health, and moral dimensions of the human rights issues discussed in this introduction.

READINGS

Human Trafficking
David A. Feingold

David A. Feingold is an anthropologist, author, filmmaker, and director of the Ophidian Research Institute, a nongovernmental organization focused on human trafficking. He has worked for UNESCO Bangkok as international coordinator for HIV/AIDS and Trafficking Projects. His documentary film *Trading Women* (2003) exposes the complexities of trafficking in Southeast Asia. In his film and writing, Feingold calls for more research and more accurate statistics. He says that trafficking involves two main elements, "migration and coercion," and that "trafficking is like a disease" that is constantly mutating and needs responses that are continuously being adjusted and refined in order to get at the underlying factors and to find an effective solution.* He favors work with local NGOs to improve the status and job opportunities of potential victims. This article appeared in the September–October 2005 edition of *Foreign Policy*, a politically nonbiased magazine about international politics and economics that is "dedicated to reaching a broad, nonspecialized audience who recognizes that what happens 'there' matters 'here,' and vice versa" (www.foreignpolicy.com).

> How does David Feingold show his double purpose of clarifying and complicating his audience's understanding of human trafficking?

Judging by news headlines, human trafficking is a recent phenomenon. In fact, the coerced movement of people across borders is as old as the laws of supply and demand. What is new is the volume of the traffic— and the realization that we have done little to stem the tide. We must look beyond our raw emotions if we are ever to stop those who trade in human lives.

"MOST VICTIMS ARE TRAFFICKED INTO THE SEX INDUSTRY"

No. Trafficking of women and children (and, more rarely, young men) for prostitution is a vile and heinous violation of human rights, but labor trafficking is probably more widespread. Evidence can be found in field studies of trafficking victims across the world and in the simple fact that the worldwide market for labor is far greater than that for sex. Statistics on the "end use" of trafficked people are often unreliable

---

*Vicki Silverman, "Trading Women Shatters Myths about Human Trafficking," America.gov, September 11, 2003, http://www.america.gov/st/washfile-english/2003/September/20030911115501namrevlisv0.2781031.html (accessed June 15, 2009).

because they tend to overrepresent the sex trade. For example, men are excluded from the trafficking statistics gathered in Thailand because, according to its national law, men cannot qualify as trafficking victims. However, a detailed 2005 study by the International Labour Organization (ILO) found that, of the estimated 9.5 million victims of forced labor in Asia, less than 10 percent are trafficked for commercial sexual exploitation. Worldwide, less than half of all trafficking victims are part of the sex trade, according to the same report.

Labor trafficking, however, is hardly benign. A study of Burmese domestic workers in Thailand by Mahidol University's Institute for Population and Social Research found beatings, sexual assault, forced labor without pay, sleep deprivation, and rape to be common. Another study, by the German Agency for Technical Cooperation (GTZ), looked at East African girls trafficked to the Middle East and found that most were bound for oppressive domestic work, and often raped and beaten along the way. Boys from Cambodia and Burma are also frequently trafficked onto deep-sea commercial fishing boats, some of which stay at sea for up to two years. Preliminary research suggests 10 percent of these young crews never return, and boys that become ill are frequently thrown overboard.

The focus on the sex industry may galvanize action through moral outrage, but it can also cloud reason. A recent example is the unsubstantiated press reports that tsunami orphans in Indonesia's Aceh province were being abducted by organized gangs of traffickers. How such gangs could operate in an area bereft of roads and airstrips remains unclear, but that did not stop some U.S. organizations from appealing for funds to send "trained investigators" to track down the criminals. Although the devastation wrought by the tsunami certainly rendered people vulnerable—mostly through economic disruption—investigations by the United Nations have yet to identify a single confirmed case of sex trafficking.

"TIGHTENING BORDERS WILL STOP TRAFFICKING"

Wrong. The trafficking issue is often used—some would say hijacked—to support policies limiting immigration. In fact, the recent global tightening of asylum admissions has increased trafficking by forcing many desperate people to turn to smugglers. In southeast Europe, a GTZ study found that more stringent border controls have led to an increase in trafficking, as people turned to third parties to smuggle them out of the country.

Similarly, other legal efforts to protect women from trafficking have had the perverse effect of making them more vulnerable. For example, Burmese law precludes women under the age of 26 from visiting border areas unless accompanied by a husband or parent.

Although Burmese officials say the law demonstrates the government's concern with the issue, many women believe it only increases the cost of travel (particularly from bribe-seeking police) and decreases their safety by making them dependent on "facilitators" to move them across the border. These women incur greater debt for their passage, thus making them even more vulnerable to exploitation along the way.

"TRAFFICKING IS A BIG BUSINESS CONTROLLED BY ORGANIZED CRIME"

False. Trafficking is big business, but in many regions of the world, such as Southeast Asia, trafficking involves mostly "disorganized crime": individuals or small groups linked on an ad hoc basis. There is no standard profile of traffickers. They range from truck drivers and village "aunties" to labor brokers and police officers. Traffickers are as varied as the circumstances of their victims. Although some trafficking victims are literally kidnapped, most leave their homes voluntarily and become trafficked on their journey.

Trafficking "kingpins," along the lines of the late cocaine boss Pablo Escobar, are rare. Japanese mafia, or yakuza, do control many of the venues in Japan where trafficked girls end up, but they are more likely to purchase people than transport them. Doing research in Thailand in 1997, I located the Luk Moo ("Piglet") network, which was responsible for about 50 percent of the women and girls smuggled into Thailand from Burma, China, and Laos to work in brothels. There were also other networks, such as the Kabuankam Loy Fah ("Floating in the Sky") network that specialized in girls for restaurants and karaoke bars. However, these networks have since faded in importance, owing to changes in the structure of the sex industry.

The worldwide trade in persons has been estimated by the United Nations Office on Drugs and Crime at $7 billion annually, and by the United Nations Children's Fund at $10 billion—but, of course, no one really knows. The ILO estimates the total illicit profits produced by trafficked forced laborers in one year to be just short of $32 billion. Although that is hardly an insignificant amount, it is a small business compared to the more than $320 billion international trade in illicit drugs.

"LEGALIZING PROSTITUTION WILL INCREASE TRAFFICKING"

It depends on how it's done. The intersection of the highly emotive issues of sex work and human trafficking generates a lot more heat than light. Some antitrafficking activists equate "prostitution" with trafficking and vice versa, despite evidence to the contrary. The U.S. government leaves no doubt as to where it stands: According to the State Department Web site, "Where prostitution is legalized or tolerated, there is a greater demand for human trafficking victims and nearly always an increase in the number of women and children trafficked into commercial sex slavery." By this logic, the state of Nevada should be awash in foreign sex slaves, leading one to wonder what steps the Justice Department is taking to free them. Oddly, the Netherlands, Australia, and Germany—all of whom have legalized prostitution—received top marks from the Bush administration in the most recent Trafficking in Persons Report.

Moreover, some efforts to prohibit prostitution have increased sex workers' risk to the dangers of trafficking, though largely because lawmakers neglected to consult the people the laws were designed to protect. Sweden, for example, is much praised by antiprostitution activists for a 1998 law that aimed to protect sex workers by criminalizing their customers. But several independent studies, including one conducted by the Swedish police, showed that it exposed prostitutes to more dangerous clients and less safe-sex practices.

Others argue that giving sex workers a measure of legitimacy short of legalization would actually discourage trafficking. In Thailand, many opposed to the commercial sex industry support extending labor and social security laws to sex workers. Such a move could hamper trafficking by opening establishments to inspection, allowing labor organization, and exposing underage prostitution.

"PROSECUTION WILL STOP TRAFFICKERS"

Not likely. In the United States, an odd but effective coalition of liberal Democrats, conservative Republicans, committed feminists, and evangelical Christians pushed a law through Congress in 2000 that aimed to prosecute traffickers and protect victims at home, while pressuring other countries to take action abroad. The Victims of Trafficking and Violence Protection Act recognized trafficking as a federal crime for the first time and provided a definition of victims in need of protection and services.

Despite the political energies expended on human trafficking, there is little evidence that prosecutions have any significant impact on aggregate levels of trafficking. For example, U.S. government figures indicate the presence of some 200,000 trafficked victims in the United States. But even with a well-trained law enforcement and prosecutorial system, less than 500 people have been awarded T visas, the special visas given to victims in return for cooperation with federal prosecutors. In fact, between 2001 and 2003, only

110 traffickers were prosecuted by the Justice Department. Of these, 77 were convicted or pled guilty.

Given the nature of the trafficking business, so few convictions will have little effect. Convicting a local recruiter or transporter has no significant impact on the overall scale of trafficking. If the incentives are right, he or she is instantly replaced, and the flow of people is hardly interrupted.

"SANCTIONS WILL STOP TRAFFICKING"

Wrong. The same U.S. law that made trafficking a federal crime also gave the United States the right to punish other states that do not crack down on human trafficking. The State Department is required to send a report to Congress each year ranking countries according to their success in combating trafficking and threatening sanctions for those with the worst records.

But international humanitarian agencies see the threat of U.S. sanctions against foreign governments as largely counterproductive. Practically speaking, sanctions will likely be applied only against countries already subject to sanctions, such as Burma or North Korea. Threatening moderately unresponsive countries—such as China, Nigeria, or Saudi Arabia—would likely backfire, causing these countries to become less open to dialogue and limiting the flow of information necessary for effective cooperation.

Although some countries certainly lack candor and create false fronts of activity, others actively seek Uncle Sam's seal of approval (and the resources that often follow) with genuine efforts to combat trafficking. Bangladesh, for example, received higher marks from the State Department this year by taking significant steps against trafficking, despite the country's poverty and limited resources. Incentives, instead of sanctions, might encourage others to do the same.

"TRAFFICKING VICTIMS SHOULD BE SENT HOME"

Not always. Sending victims home may simply place them back in the same conditions that endangered them in the first place, particularly in situations of armed conflict or political unrest. If criminal gangs were involved in the trafficking, they will likely threaten the safety of victims and their families.

To complicate matters, people may have no "home" to which they can return. Lack of legal status is a major risk factor in trafficking, impeding and often precluding victims' return and reintegration. That problem is particularly true for minorities, indigenous peoples, and informal migrants who often have no way to prove their nationality. In Thailand, for example, studies by the United Nations Educational, Scientific and Cultural Organization have demonstrated that a lack of proof of citizenship is the single greatest risk factor for a hill tribe girl or woman to be trafficked or otherwise exploited. Without citizenship, she cannot get a school diploma, register her marriage, own land, or work outside her home district without special permission. Lack of legal status prevents a woman from finding alternate means of income, rendering her vulnerable to trafficking for sex work or the most abusive forms of labor.

In developing countries, one's lack of legal status usually begins at birth. Without a birth certificate, a child typically has no legal identity: That is why international laws such as the Convention on the Rights of the Child stress that children have the right to be registered at birth. Many activists have never considered that a fix as simple as promoting birth registration in developing countries is one of the most cost-effective means to combat human trafficking.

"TRAFFICKING IS DRIVEN BY POVERTY"

Too simple. Trafficking is often migration gone terribly wrong. In addition to the push of poverty or political and social instability, trafficking is influenced by the expanded world views of the victims—the draw of bright lights and big cities. The lure of urban centers helps to account for why, in parts of Africa, girls from medium-sized towns are more vulnerable to trafficking than those in rural villages.

To fill the demand for ever cheaper labor, many victims are trafficked within the same economic class or even within a single country. In Brazil, for example, girls may be trafficked for sex work from rural to urban areas, whereas males may be sold to work in the gold mines of the Amazon jungle. In the Ivory Coast, children are frequently sold into slavery to work on cocoa plantations. In China, girls are trafficked as brides in impoverished rural areas, which are devoid of marriage-age females as a result of China's one-child policy and families' preference for baby boys.

Does this mean that "destination" countries or cities are the beneficiaries of trafficking? Not necessarily. What one area or industry may gain in cheap, docile labor, others—especially those situated near national borders—often pay for in terms of security, health costs, and, sometimes, political unrest. Trafficking may answer a demand, but the cost is too steep for this ever shrinking world to bear.

For Class Discussion

1. What assumptions and common views of human trafficking is Feingold challenging? What is his main claim about human trafficking?

2. What evidence strikes you as the most effective and persuasive?

3. How well does Feingold convince you of his knowledge and authority and of the reliability of his evidence?

4. This piece has been structured to fit *Foreign Policy's* "Forum," a regular feature that presents a loose, informal debate, highlighting opposing views and responding to them. If Feingold were to rewrite this piece as another kind of argument genre (for example, an op-ed piece, policy brief, or open letter to a public official), what claims, reasons, and evidence would you suggest he include? Think of the audience he would be trying to reach and the length and depth of the article.

5. How has Feingold disrupted or enlarged your view of human trafficking? What questions do you have after reading this article?

Supply and Demand: Human Trafficking in the Global Economy
Siddharth Kara

Siddharth Kara holds a law degree from England and an MBA from Columbia University. He worked as an investment banker at Merrill Lynch and as business executive of his own finance and consulting firm until he turned to research and advocacy on human trafficking. The experience of volunteer work in a Bosnian refugee camp made him aware of sex trafficking, and he has subsequently researched human trafficking all over the world. He is the author of two well-received books on trafficking: *Sex Trafficking: Inside the Business of Modern Slavery* (2008; co-winner of the Yale University 2010 Frederick Douglass Award for a nonfiction book on slavery) and *Bonded Labor: Tackling the System of Slavery in South Asia* (2012). Kara serves on the board of directors of Free the Slaves, a nonprofit organization dedicated to ending global slavery, and as an adviser to the United Nations, various governments, private organizations, and NGOs on policy related to antislavery. He is currently the first Fellow on Human Trafficking with the Kennedy School of Government at Harvard University. This policy analysis argument was published in the summer 2011 edition of the *Harvard International Review*, a student-run publication that seeks "to make the arguments of scholars, policymakers, and other international affairs actors available to a wider audience" ("About Us").

Siddharth Kara introduces his argument with a description of a historically significant site of the slave trade. Why is this opening an effective way to begin his argument?

On New Year's Day 2011, I flew to Lagos to research human trafficking in Nigeria. Towards the end of my trip, I visited a small town called Badagry, about a two-hour drive west of Lagos. In 1502, Portuguese colonists built one of the first slave-trading posts along the coast of West Africa in this city. The non-descript, two-story building still stands today as a museum, but for more than 300 years, it was one of the most active slave-trading outposts in West Africa. Estimates are that almost 600,000 West Africans were shipped from Badagry to the Americas to be agricultural slaves. That figure represents approximately one in twenty of all slaves transported from West Africa to the Americas during the entire time of the North Atlantic Slave Trade.

It was a haunting experience walking through the old slave-holding pens, gazing at the iron shackles, imagining the fear and terror that must have coursed through the veins of slaves as they awaited their fates. Like so many millions today, those 600,000 individuals transported from Badagry to the Americas were victims of human trafficking. In fact, all 12 to 13 million of the West African slaves transported across the Atlantic to the Americas were victims of human trafficking. While their lengthy journeys at sea are very different from the journeys of most human trafficking victims today, the purpose of those journeys remains the same: the callous exploitation of the labor of vulnerable people in order to maximize profit.

THE NATURE OF SLAVERY TODAY

However, unlike the agricultural and domestic slaves of the past, today's victims of modern-day slave trading are exploited in countless industries, and they are vastly more profitable. Whether for commercial sex, construction, domestic work, carpet weaving, agriculture, tea and coffee, shrimp, fish, minerals, dimensional stones, gems, or numerous other industries that I have investigated, human trafficking touches almost every sector of the globalized economy in a way it never has before. Understanding the reasons for this shift in the fundamental nature of human trafficking is vital if more effective efforts to combat it are to be deployed. The key thesis to understand is that the slave exploiter's ability to generate immense profits at almost no real risk directly catalyzed the pervasiveness of all forms of contemporary slave labor exploitation.

One point is crucial to establish from the start—slavery still exists. But what exactly is "modern slavery?" There is still considerable debate regarding the definition of terms such as "slavery," "forced labor," "bonded labor," "child labor," and "human trafficking." With "slavery," we can go as far back as the League of Nations Slavery Convention of 1926 and the International Labor Organization's Forced Labor Convention of 1930. These early definitions focused on the exercise of power attaching to a right of ownership over another human being.

Over the decades, international conventions and jurisprudence relating to slavery shifted away from targeting actual rights of ownership toward the nature of the exploitation, particularly as it involves coercion (physical or other), nominal or no compensation, and the absence of freedom of employment or movement. The term "forced labor" has generally come to replace the term "slavery," given the powerful historical and emotional connotations of the latter term. Similarly, "human trafficking" has come to replace the term "slave trade."

It is open to debate whether these terminological substitutions are helpful, but when it comes to "human trafficking," I believe the use of this term has done considerable disservice to the tactical prioritization required to combat these crimes more effectively. Definitions of the term "human trafficking," such as that found in the United Nations Protocol to Prevent, Suppress, and Punish Trafficking in Persons (the Palermo Protocol of 2000) or the US Trafficking Victims Protection Act (TVPA, of the same year), have historically suffered from a greater focus on the movement connotation of the term "trafficking" rather than the exploitation involved. The result has been a prioritization of efforts to stop cross-border migration instead of slave-like exploitation, the real purpose of trafficking; this approach has met with limited success.

Terminological debates aside, within the broad context of modern-day slavery, I estimate the number of slaves at the end of 2010 to have been between 30 and 36 million. Depending on how one specifies terms such as "coercion" and "held captive," the number of people considered slaves could be slightly lower or considerably higher. There are many modes by which slaves are exploited, and these can be aggregated into various categories. I have chosen three: bonded labor, forced labor, and trafficked slaves.

BONDED, FORCED LABOR, AND TRAFFICKED SLAVES

The economic model of bonded labor dates back centuries. In essence, individuals borrow money or assets and are bound in servitude until the debts are repaid, and often they never are. Forced laborers are similar to bonded laborers but without the intermingling of credit and labor relationships. However, the line between bonded labor and forced labor is easily blurred. The more farcical a debt becomes, the more the bonded laborer is actually a forced laborer.

Human trafficking is essentially modern-day slave trading, which ensnares millions of people in debt bondage or forced labor conditions in a plethora of industries. Regardless of the industry of exploitation, there are three common steps to the business model of most human trafficking networks: acquisition, movement, and exploitation, which often results in one or more counts of re-trafficking. Acquisition of trafficked slaves primarily occurs in one of five ways: deceit, sale by family, abduction, seduction or romance (with sex trafficking), or recruitment by former slaves. Poor or marginally subsistent individuals are the ones most vulnerable to exploitation because of their economic desperation.

Trafficked slaves are moved from countries of origin through transit countries into destination countries, except in the case of internal trafficking, during which the same country acts as origin, transit, and destination. However, trafficking victims often undergo multiple stops in several countries, where they are repeatedly resold and exploited. At each destination, victims are threatened, abused, and tortured. They may be told they must work off the "debt" of trafficking them between jobs. The accounting of these debts is invariably exploitive, involving deductions for living expenses and exorbitant interest rates. For others, no farce of debt repayment is provided—they are simply kept in a state of perpetual forced labor.

Slave exploiters often re-sell trafficked slaves to new exploiters. If the slaves do not escape, their cycle of exploitation may never end. Even if they do escape, they often return to the same conditions of poverty or vulnerability that led to their initial enslavement, resulting in one or more instances of re-trafficking.

Most importantly, slave exploiters and traffickers take advantage of the fact that movement in the globalized world is exceedingly difficult to disrupt. Borders are porous, documents can be forged, and it can be difficult to identify a potential victim of human trafficking before the forced labor has taken place. Movement is also inexpensive. Whereas ships from Badagry to the Americas had to spend weeks at sea at great expense to transport slaves to the point of exploitation, today's victims of human trafficking can be transported from one side of the planet to the other in a few days or less, at a nominal cost of doing business even when airfare is involved. For these and other reasons, any efforts to combat human trafficking by thwarting movement will prove highly challenging.

The final step in the human trafficking business model is exploitation. Exploitation of trafficked slaves primarily involves the coercion of some form of labor or services with little or no compensation. The location and nature of the coercion is industry-specific. In cases of commercial sex, exploitation involves multiple counts of coerced sex acts every day in physical confinement and under threats of harm to the slave or their loved ones back home. The brutality of this form of human trafficking cannot be overstated. It involves rape, torture, forced drug use, and the wholesale destruction of a human body, mind, and spirit.

Another common sector is construction, which may involve exploitation of human trafficking victims under strict confinement at construction sites, with little or no payment for months at a time. In agriculture, trafficked slaves are confined to the area of harvest and are coerced to work under threats of violence or eviction from tenant homes, and with minimal or no wages. When it comes to carpets, trafficked child slaves are locked inside shacks where they are drugged and beaten to work for eighteen hours a day, suffering spinal deformation and respiratory ailments.

For these and other products that are tainted by exploitative labor, I have traced the complete supply chains from the point of production to the retailers that sell the tainted products in the United States. This is an important step toward catalyzing the kind of corporate and consumer awareness campaigns required to strike back against the use of trafficked, slave, or child labor in products consumed in Western markets. However, in order to truly combat human trafficking, we must understand exactly why it has become so prevalent throughout the global economy. What compels those involved in this type of exploitation to engage in it?

INCENTIVES UNDERLYING TRAFFICKING

Just like most law-abiding citizens, criminals are rational economic agents, and when a near risk-free opportunity to generate immense profits emerges, they will flock to it. Modern-day slavery is immensely more profitable than past forms of slavery. This is the key factor driving the tremendous demand for new slaves through human trafficking networks. Whereas slaves in 1850 could be purchased for a global weighted average of between US$9,500 and US$11,000 (adjusted for inflation) and generate roughly 15 to 20 percent in annual return on investment, today's slaves sell for a global weighted average of US$420 and can generate 300 to 500 percent or more in annual return on investment, depending on the industry. In terms of risk, the laws against human trafficking and forced labor in most countries involve relatively anemic prison sentences and little or no economic penalties. Even where there are stiff financial penalties stipulated in the law, such as in the United States, the levels of prosecution and conviction of slave exploiters remain paltry.

As a result, the real risk of exploiting trafficked slaves is almost nonexistent. That is to say, the costs of exploiting a slave are miniscule as weighed against the immense profits that criminals can reap. This basic economic reality gives us a clear sense of some of the powerful forces of demand that promote the trafficking and slave-like exploitation of men, women, and children around the world. I believe these forces are also the ones we can most effectively disrupt in the near term.

However, there is also a supply-side to human trafficking, meaning those forces that promote the supply of potential human trafficking victims. We must also mitigate these forces, though it will prove difficult to effect a near-term impact on the human trafficking industry through supply-side efforts alone. The supply of contemporary trafficked slaves is promoted by longstanding factors such as poverty, lawlessness, social instability, military conflict, environmental disaster, corruption, and acute bias against female gender and minority ethnicities.

The policies and governance of economic globalization sharply exacerbated these and other forces during the 1990s. The deepening of rural poverty, the net extraction of wealth and resources from poor economies into richer ones, the evaporation of social safety nets under structural adjustment programs, the overall destabilization of transition economies, and the broad-based erosion of real human freedoms across the developing world all increased the vulnerability of rural, poor, and otherwise disenfranchised populations. These forces unleashed mass-migration trends that shrewd criminals and slave traders could easily exploit. While these global economic and sociocultural supply-side drivers of the contemporary human trafficking industry will require considerable, long-term efforts to redress, we do not have to rely on supply-side measures alone to severely mitigate, if not virtually abolish, human trafficking.

In fact, the demand-side of most human trafficking industries is highly vulnerable to disruption. The specific forces of demand that drive any industry will vary. For example, in commercial sex, male demand to purchase commercial sex is a key factor of demand that would not be present with construction or tea. However, there are always two forces of demand that are common to any human trafficking industry and they are both economic: slave exploiter demand for maximum profit and consumer demand for lower retail prices (the price elasticity of demand).

For almost any business in the world, labor is typically the highest cost component to overall operating expenses. Thus, throughout history, producers have tried to find ways to minimize labor costs. Slavery is the extreme of this. Slaves afford a virtually nil cost of labor. With a drastically reduced cost of labor, total operating costs are substantially reduced, allowing the slave owner to maximize profit. However, drastically lower labor costs also allow producers to become more competitive by lowering retail prices. The retail price of any product or service is largely based on the costs of producing, distributing, and marketing that product or service, along with the available supply of the product or alternatives, and whatever brand premium the market will bear. If a major component of cost is stripped out of the production model, then producers can finely balance their desire to maximize profit and lower retail price.

Depending on the product, the lower it costs, the more people will tend to purchase it. Conversely, the more expensive a product is, the less people will tend to purchase it. This concept is called the price elasticity of demand, and depending on the specific product or service, the "elasticity" can be high or low, implying changes in price can have large or small impacts on consumer demand. Because consumers in general almost always prefer the lower priced version of the same product or service (if all other variables such as quality are the same), producers often try to compete by minimizing price, and one of the most effective ways to do this while retaining profitability is to exploit labor.

In a globalized economy, where products are available in our nearby shops from all over the world, the need to be price competitive is greater than ever. A seller of t-shirts or rice no longer just competes with producers nearby, but with producers on the other side of the world. As an example, I was conducting research into bonded labor in South Asia during the summer of 2010, and an exporter of precious stones in Chennai told me quite candidly that he was forced to exploit low-wage labor (actually bonded and child labor) in order to compete with the Chinese, who he believed to be doing the same. Because transportation costs are 90 percent less than they were in 1920, and since all types of exploited labor can be used to minimize production expenses, the entire world is in competition, and human trafficking has evolved from the old world into the globalized world as a key way in which unscrupulous producers can minimize labor costs to advance profits and remain price competitive.

COMBATING TRAFFICKING

Understanding the twin economic forces of demand that have helped catalyze the accretion in levels of human trafficking throughout the global economy suggests two tactical priorities in efforts to combat these crimes. First, attack the profitability human traffickers enjoy. An attack on profitability will reduce aggregate demand for slave labor because slave owners will be forced to accept a lower-profit (hence less desirable) business, or they will pass the increased costs to the consumer by elevating retail price, which will in turn reduce consumer demand.

The most effective way to attack profitability is to elevate real risk. Depending on the type of industry, the tactics will vary, but such efforts will assuredly involve the following: elevated efforts by law enforcement to proactively investigate and intervene in human trafficking crimes; the expansion of community-based antislavery efforts; elevated funding for anti-trafficking police, prosecutors, and judges, especially in developing nations; fast-track courts to prosecute trafficking crimes quickly so as to minimize risks to the survivor-witness; and a massive increase in the financial penalties associated with human trafficking crimes, including enterprise corruption, asset forfeiture, and victim compensation, to help former slaves get their lives back on track.

An increase in penalties, along with increased prosecution and conviction levels achieved through the kinds of tactics described above, should elevate the real risk and cost of human trafficking to an economically detrimental level. Put in criminal law terms, we are trying to elevate the deterrent and retributive value of the real penalty associated with the commission of slave-related crimes to a far more effective level. In turn, criminals will likely diversify their operations to other, less toxic opportunities, just as quickly as they originally flocked to trafficking and labor exploitation.

The other main force of demand relates to consumers. While we typically prefer to buy our products at the best price, we are also far removed from the complex supply chains that may be tainted by trafficked or slave labor at the bottom end of the production process. However, we are also in control of our consumer force of demand, so it is up to us to demand that lawmakers enact provisions whereby corporations must investigate and certify that their supply chains are free of trafficked, slave, or child labor of any kind. Consumers must also demand that companies whose products they purchase take a leadership role in conducting the kind of investigation and certification required, and that such activities should be a regular aspect of their internal controls and operating model. By attacking the fundamental motivation behind the exploitation of trafficking slaves—profits—and by leveraging consumer power to shift the market away from the "cheap at all costs" product to the product that is morally and socially responsible, a powerful near-term impact can be achieved on the business of human trafficking.

The ugliness of human trafficking dates back centuries, and even though we agreed 150 years ago as a human civilization that slavery is unacceptable, it is more pervasive and expansive today than it was centuries ago when the slave port at Badagry was in its prime. The forces of globalization have made human trafficking a highly profitable and virtually risk-free enterprise. As a matter of ensuring basic human dignity and freedom, the global community must utilize every resource available to combat traffickers and slave exploiters by elevating the real risk and cost of the crime, while eliminating the immense profitability that human traffickers and slave exploiters currently enjoy.

The persistence of human trafficking is an affront to human dignity and a denial of any claims of moral legitimacy by contemporary capitalist civilization. The time is long overdue for the world to come together to deploy the kinds of sustained interventions required to eliminate this evil forever.

For Class Discussion

1. According to Kara, how has globalization affected human trafficking? Why is the causal thinking involved in understanding the global economics of human trafficking so important in tackling the problem?

2. In the first part of his argument, Kara focuses on definitional debates over the meaning and importance of terms: "forced labor" versus "slavery"; "slave trade" versus "human trafficking." What does he assert are the stakes or consequences of defining the problem using these terms?

3. How does Kara's analysis of "the business model of most human trafficking networks" draw on his expertise and authority? How could understanding the supply side and the demand side of human trafficking lead to more effective ways to combat human trafficking?

4. Instead of focusing on vivid incidents of human suffering, Kara has said that his writing on trafficking is "an attempt to unify outrage with economics" in a "new brand of global abolitionist movement."* How has understanding the economics and business of trafficking expanded your own view of the problem and potential solutions?

5. How rhetorically effective is Kara's concluding appeal to consumer power and to citizens' moral sense?

Look Beneath the Surface
National Human Trafficking Resource Center

This poster is one of a series that appears on the U.S. Department of Health and Human Services' National Human Trafficking Resource Center Web site

Administration for Children & Families

US Department of Health & Human Services

*"Interview with Siddharth Kara, Author of *Sex Trafficking*," Columbia University Press http:cup.columbia.edu/statid/siddarth-kara-interview.

under Campaign Toolkits. The NHTRC's goal is to "connect community members with additional tools to raise awareness and combat human trafficking in their local areas, as well as guide service providers and law enforcement personnel in their work with potential trafficking victims" (www.acf.hhs.gov/trafficking/index.html, "What We Do"). The Department of Health and Human Services has created this poster for social service organizations as part of its campaign against trafficking.

> Even if you had little knowledge of the human trafficking issue and the main problems it poses, what ideas could you glean from this poster?

For Class Discussion

1. One problem in fighting human trafficking is identifying the victims. A number of campaigns are directed at equipping workers such as law enforcement officers, social service workers, and medical personnel to identify victims. What features of this poster indicate its main target audience?

2. What assumptions is this poster addressing and arguing against?

3. After studying the image, the text, the use of type, and the layout of this poster, reconstruct the thinking of its creators. What creative choices did they make and why?

4. One of the projects of the NHTRC is a community-based campaign called "Rescue and Restore," currently established in twenty-four cities, regions, and states. If you were part of a design team assigned to create a comparable poster for your city or state for law enforcement or health care professionals, what image, text, and layout would you choose for your poster and why?

Trafficking and Health
Joanna Busza, Sarah Castle, and Aisse Diarra

Joanna Busza and Sarah Castle are lecturers at the Center for Population Studies at the London School of Hygiene and Tropical Medicine. Busza has researched reproductive and sexual health issues in Southeast Asia, and from 1997 to 2001, she focused on HIV prevention with migrant sex workers. Sarah Castle spent fifteen years in Mali, Africa, working with outmigration. Aisse Diarra, an independent consultant, has extensive experience with women's health and women's rights issues in Mali. This policy proposal appeared in the scholarly publication *BMJ* on June 5, 2004.

> This article follows a surprising-reversal format in that it sets up a common view of the trafficking of women and children and then argues that this view is erroneous and misinformed. What is the common view that Joanna Busza, Sarah Castle, and Aisse Diarra challenge? What is the new, surprising view that they seek to establish?

Trafficking in women and children is now recognised as a global public health issue as well as a violation of human rights. The *UN Protocol to Prevent, Suppress, and Punish Trafficking in Persons, Especially Women and Children* states that trafficking involves force, threat, or fraud and intent to exploit individuals.[1] Intermediaries often smuggle victims across international borders into illegal or unsafe occupations, including agriculture, construction, domestic labour, and sex work. A recent study identified trafficking to be associated with health risks such as psychological trauma, injuries from violence, sexually transmitted infections, HIV and AIDS, other adverse reproductive health outcomes, and substance misuse.[2] These risks are shaped by lack of access to services in a foreign country, language barriers, isolation, and exploitative working conditions. However, as this article shows, efforts to reduce trafficking may be making conditions worse for voluntary migrants.

RESPONSE TO TRAFFICKING

Multinational, governmental, and non-governmental groups working to counter trafficking sometimes misinterpret the cultural context in which migration occurs.[3] They often seek to eradicate labour migration rather than target specific instances of exploitation and abuse.[4,5] Regulatory measures, such as introducing new requirements for documentation and strengthening of border controls, criminalise and marginalise all migrants, whether trafficked or not. This exacerbates their health risks and vulnerability by reducing access to appropriate services and social care. Such approaches do not adequately distinguish between forced and voluntary migrants, as it is extremely difficult to identify the motivations of migrants and their intermediaries before travel.[6]

We illustrate these concerns with evidence from research conducted among child migrants in Mali who had been returned from the Ivory Coast and Vietnamese sex workers in Cambodia. The evidence draws from studies conducted between 2000 and 2002.[7,8] In both settings, the international media has reported emotively on the existence of "child slaves," "sex slaves," and "trafficking" and oriented donors and nongovernmental organisations to this agenda.[9–11]

CHILD MIGRANTS IN MALI

Although no substantiated figures exist, an estimated 15,000 Malian children have been "trafficked" to the cocoa plantations in the Ivory Coast.[12] This study responded to a demand from several international non-governmental organisations that wanted to improve their understanding of the situation.[7] We compiled a sampling frame with the assistance of nongovernmental organisations working with children and their governmental partners. It included young people from communities deemed to be at high risk of trafficking, as well as intercepted or repatriated children thought to have been trafficked. However, a survey of nearly 1000 young people from this list found that only four could be classified as having been deceived, exploited, or not paid at all for their labour. Rather, young people voluntarily sought employment abroad, which represented an opportunity to experience urban lifestyles, learn new languages, and accumulate possessions. For both boys and girls, the experience provided a rite of passage with cultural as well as financial importance.

For many of these migrants, movement across international borders depended on assistance from intermediaries, often family members. In Mali there is a longstanding tradition of using intermediaries to facilitate a range of social and economic activities, such as looking for employment, negotiating purchases, handling disputes, and even seeking a spouse. Our research found that intermediaries could protect the migrants during their journey and help them search for work. In destination areas, they advocated for young people in cases of non-payment of salary or abrupt termination of employment. Migrants also relied on intermediaries to negotiate with corrupt authorities that demanded bribes at international borders. Classifying such assistance as "trafficking" simplifies a much deeper cultural reality.

Local anti-trafficking policies and interventions, however, have not acknowledged these complex dynamics and have instead posed obstacles to safe, assisted migration. For example, interviews with Malian legal experts showed that new legislative measures do not enable them to distinguish between a trafficker with intent to exploit and an intermediary who, for a fee, facilitates a young migrant's journey and search for housing and employment. Local anti-trafficking surveillance committees have been established; these have come to view all migration as negative and local leaders seem to seek to arrest children if they attempt to leave. At the national level, a new child's passport is required for all children under the age of 18 who wish to travel. In reality, young people find the document difficult to obtain, and failure to possess it provides an easy excuse for law enforcement officers to extort additional bribes at borders.

These measures discourage community members from assisting in traditional labour migration and have the potential to force migrants to rely increasingly on corrupt officials to waive travel documents or provide forgeries. Clandestine migrants are generally more difficult to reach at destination points, as they may be reluctant to seek health care or other help if they fear being forcibly repatriated or detained. Child migrants who left home of their own free will report being returned home against their wishes by non-governmental organisations, only to leave for the border again a few days later.

The study found that rehabilitation centres for trafficked children run by two non-governmental organisations in the Malian town of Sikasso were usually empty. Such interventions are neither appropriate nor cost effective and do not tackle the exploitative conditions encountered by children in the Ivory Coast. Children would be better served through services offered in the Ivory Coast or support through protective networks of intermediaries and community members.

VIETNAMESE SEX WORKERS IN CAMBODIA

As with Malians in the Ivory Coast, it is difficult to obtain accurate data on the number of Vietnamese migrants in Cambodia. Some estimates suggest that up to 10,000 Vietnamese women are sex workers in Cambodia.[13] The research presented here was conducted in collaboration with a local non-governmental organisation as part of a wider investigation of sex workers' perceptions, motivations, and experiences.[8] The study formed one component of a service delivery programme to about 300 brothel based Vietnamese sex workers in Svay Pak district, Phnom Penh. Before the research, medical services, outreach, and counselling had been provided to sex workers for over five years, and a trusting relationship had been established between non-governmental organisation staff and both sex workers and brothel managers. Young, female, Vietnamese speaking project staff familiar to the sex workers conducted indepth interviews with 28 women and focus group discussions with 72 participants to explore patterns of entry into sex work.

Most women knew before they left Vietnam that they would be engaged in sex work under a system of "debt bondage" to a brothel. The work would repay loans made to them or their families. Some women showed clear ambition in their choices to travel to Cambodia for sex work, citing economic incentives, desire for an independent lifestyle, and dissatisfaction with rural life and agricultural labour. As in Mali, intermediaries from home communities were instrumental in facilitating safe migration. Many women were accompanied by a parent, aunt, or neighbour who provided transport, paid bribes to border patrols, and negotiated the contract with brothel managers.

Of the 100 participants in this qualitative study, six women reported having been "tricked" into sex work or betrayed by an intermediary. Many sex workers, however, expressed dissatisfaction with their work conditions or stated that they had not fully appreciated the risks they would face, such as clients who refused to use condoms, coercion from brothel owners, and violence from both clients and local police.

A policy focus on combating "trafficking" again seemed to threaten rather than safeguard migrants' health and rights. Local and international non-governmental organisations conducted raids on brothels during which sex workers were taken to "rehabilitation centres," often against their will. Police sometimes assisted in these raids, although they also conducted arrests independently.

Our research found that "rescued" women usually returned to their brothel as quickly as possible, having secured their release through bribes or by summoning relatives from Vietnam to collect them. Furthermore, police presence in the raids scared off custom[ers], thus reducing earnings, increasing competition for clients, and further limiting sex workers' power in negotiating improved work conditions. Bribes and other costs were added to sex workers' debts, increasing their tenure in the brothel and adding pressure to take on additional customers or agree to condom-free sex to maximise income. Raids and rescues could also damage the relationship between service providers and brothel managers, who restricted sex workers' mobility, including access to health care, to avoid arrest. These findings mirror recent reports from other sex worker communities throughout the region.[14–16]

THE WAY FORWARD

Our research in Mali and Cambodia shows disturbing parallels in ways that anti-trafficking measures can contribute to adverse health outcomes. Without wanting to minimise the issue of trafficking, these studies show that a more flexible and realistic approach to labour migration among young people is required. The needs of vulnerable young migrants, whether trafficked or not, can be met only through comprehensive understanding of their motivations and of the cultural and economic contexts in which their movements occur. Criminalising migrants or the industries they work in simply forces them "underground," making them more difficult to reach with appropriate services and increasing the likelihood of exploitation.

We do not dispute that in both settings migrants have suffered hardship and abuse, but current "anti-trafficking" approaches do not help their problems. The agendas need to be redrawn so that they reflect the needs of the populations they aim to serve, rather than emotive reactions to sensationalised media coverage. This requires deeper investigation at both local and regional levels, including participatory research to inform interventions from the experiences of the migrants and their communities. From the research that we have conducted in Mali and Cambodia, we recommend the following:

- Policy makers need to recognise that migration has sociocultural as well as economic motivations and seeking to stop it will simply cause migrants to leave in a clandestine and potentially more dangerous manner. Facilitating safe, assisted migration may be more effective than relying on corrupt officials to enforce restrictive border controls.

- Instead of seeking to repatriate migrants, often against their will, interventions should consider ways to provide appropriate services at destination points, taking into consideration specific occupational hazards, language barriers, and ability to access health and social care facilities.
- Programmes aimed at improving migrants' health and welfare should not assume that all intermediaries are "traffickers" intending to exploit migrants. Efforts to reach migrants in destination areas could use intermediaries.
- Organisations that have established good rapport with migrant communities should document cases of abuse and advocate for improved labour conditions. In the case of sex work, however, this can be politically difficult. For example, the United States Agency for International Development recently announced its intention to stop funding organisations that do not explicitly support the eradication of all sex work.

Ultimately, trafficking and other forms of exploitation will cease only with sustainable development in sending areas combined with a reduction in demand for cheap, undocumented labour in receiving countries. Non-governmental organisations and government partners therefore need to focus on the root causes of rural poverty and exploitation of labour as well as mitigating the health risks of current migrants. At the moment, trafficking is big business not just for traffickers but also for the international development community, which can access funds relatively easily to tackle the issue without investing in a more comprehensive understanding of the wider dynamics shaping labour migration.

References

1. United Nations. *Protocol to prevent, suppress and punish trafficking in persons, especially women and children, supplementing the United National Convention Against Transnational Organized Crime.* New York: United Nations, 2000.
2. Zimmerman C, Yun K, Shvab I, Watts C, Trappolin L, Treppete M, et al. *The health risks and consequences of trafficking in women and adolescents. Findings from a European study.* London: London School of Hygiene and Tropical Medicine, 2003.
3. Butcher K. Confusion between prostitution and sex trafficking. *Lancet* 2003;361: 1983. [CrossRef][ISI][Medline]
4. Marshall P. *Globalization, migration and trafficking: some thoughts from the South-East Asian region.* Bangkok: UN Inter-Agency Project on Trafficking in Women and Children in the Mekong Sub-region, 2001. (Occasional paper No 1.)
5. Taran PA, Moreno-Fontes G. *Getting at the roots.* UN Inter-Agency Project Newsletter 2002;7: 1–5.

6. Coomaraswamy R. *Integration of the human rights of women and the gender perspective: violence against women: report of the special rapporteur on violence against women, its causes and consequences.* New York: UN Economic and Social Council, 2000.
7. Castle S, Diarra A. *The international migration of young Malians: tradition, necessity or rite of passage?* London: London School of Hygiene and Tropical Medicine, 2003.
8. Busza J, Schunter BT. From competition to community: participatory learning and action among young, debt-bonded Vietnamese sex workers in Cambodia. *Reprod Health Matters* 2001;9: 72–81. [CrossRef[ISI][Medline]
9. Bobak L. For sale: the innocence of Cambodia. *Ottawa Sun* 1996 Oct 24.
10. Chocolate slaves carry many scars. *Daily Telegraph* 2001 Apr 24.
11. Child slavery: Africa's growing problem. *CNN* 2001 Apr 17.
12. United States Agency for International Development. *Trafficking in persons: USAID's response.* Washington, DC: USAID Office of Women in Development, 2001: 10–6.
13. Unicef. Unicef supports national seminar on human trafficking. www.unicef.org/vietnam/new080.htm (accessed 11 Nov 2003).
14. Jones M. Thailand's brothel busters. *Mother Jones* 2003 Nov/Dec.
15. Phal S. *Survey on police human rights violations in Toul Kork.* Phnom Penh: Cambodia Women's Development Association, 2002.
16. Sutees R. Brothel raids in Indonesia—ideal solution or further violation? *Research for Sex Work* 2003;6: 5–7.

For Class Discussion

1. This proposal argument addresses the complexities of child labor in Mali and Africa, and of Vietnamese sex workers (many of them young girls) in Cambodia. What assumptions about human trafficking does this argument challenge?

2. What clashes among stakeholders on the trafficking controversy and what complexities do Busza, Castle, and Diarra want readers to understand?

3. What claims do these writers make about stakeholders' conflicting agendas for dealing with global child labor and the sex trade?

4. In this researched policy proposal, how do the writers establish their credibility and authority? What makes their use of evidence effective and persuasive?

5. What proposal do these writers make for a more realistic and effective handling of the trafficking problem?

6. How has this article influenced your view of the trafficking of children and women? In what ways do you think free trade advocates would agree with the writers of this article?   ■

Sex Trafficking and HIV/AIDS: A Deadly Junction for Women and Girls
Amanda Kloer

In her writing and campaigns, Amanda Kloer focuses on such issues as human rights, HIV/AIDS, domestic violence, genocide, and LGBT (lesbian, gay, bisexual, and transgender) projects. She serves as program associate of the American Bar Association's AIDS Coordination Project. She is also editor of Change .org's human trafficking section, in which capacity she has authored reports and training materials on human trafficking nationally and globally. She has created documentaries and speaks publicly on these issues. This policy proposal was published in spring of 2010 in *Human Rights*, a publication of the Section of Individual Rights and Responsibilities of the ABA, which is dedicated to addressing issues related to civil rights, civil liberties, and human rights.

According to Amanda Kloer, why is it important that HIV prevention be seen as a human rights problem and sex trafficking be approached as a health crisis?

> *A way out of no way, it's flesh out of flesh, it's courage that cries out at night; A way out of no way, it's flesh out of flesh, it's bravery kept out of sight; A way out of no way, it's too much to ask, it's too much of a task for any one woman.*
>
> —"Oughta Be A Woman," by Sweet Honey in the Rock

The nexus of the global epidemics of sex trafficking and HIV/AIDS primarily manifests in the lives of women and girls. This intersection exists in sex trafficking victims' increased vulnerability to HIV infection, the proliferation of HIV infection through sex trafficking, and the perceived and actual clashes between HIV and sex trafficking prevention efforts. Holistically addressing these intersecting issues entails framing the elimination of sex trafficking as a tool to reduce HIV transmission. This article explores this deadly junction for women and girls and proposes tools to address it.

The direct and individual impact of sex trafficking and HIV on girls and women is illustrated by the experience of "Gita" (not her real name). Gita grew up in India, and was sold into sexual slavery by a family member when she was twelve years old. When she arrived at the brothel in Mumbai, she was locked in a room, raped, tortured, and abused until she was deemed sufficiently obedient. When the brothel owners began selling Gita, she was threatened with death if she refused to have sex with a customer. Most days she was forced to have sex with ten to twenty men. The brothel did not provide condoms, and she was not able to control which of her customers chose to practice safer sex. During her early teens, Gita contracted HIV from a customer. However, she was not allowed to seek testing or treatment and was forced to continue having unprotected sex with several men per day for several more years. Finally, Gita managed to escape to a local anti-trafficking organization and is now living in a shelter and receiving HIV treatment and counseling.

Gita contracted HIV as a direct result of her status as a victim of sex trafficking. She also, unknowingly and unintentionally, may have spread HIV to customers who bought her after she became infected. If Gita were never trafficked, she may not have ever become infected with HIV and, in turn, transmitted it to the men who bought her and their future sex partners. Preventing this multiplier effect of HIV transmission catalyzed by sex trafficking involves fighting two global phenomena—a deadly disease and a highly complex and lucrative criminal industry, both of which disproportionately affect girls and women around the world.

SEX TRAFFICKING VICTIMS' INCREASED VULNERABILITY

According to U.S. law, sex trafficking is a form of modern-day slavery in which a commercial sex act is induced by force, fraud, or coercion, or in which the person induced to perform such an act is under eighteen years of age. Precise statistics for the number of women and girls trafficked in the commercial sex industry are difficult to obtain. However, the U.S. Department of State estimates that up to 900,000 people are trafficked across international borders each year, the majority of whom are women and girls forced into commercial sex industries. See *U.S. Department of State Trafficking in Persons Report* (June 2003). International Labor Organization data indicates that 1.39 million girls and women are victims of sex trafficking at any given time. See *U.S. Department of State Trafficking in Persons Report* (June 2009).

Sex trafficking is a global epidemic, and cases of forced prostitution and sex trafficking have been identified in almost every country in the world. The United Nations Children's Fund estimates that in the past thirty years, more than 30 million women and children in Asia have been victimized in the commercial sex industry. See United Nations Children's Fund press release (2006). In Latin America, the International Organization for Migration estimates that the sex trafficking of women and girls is a $16 million-a-year business. See Association for Women's Rights in Development, "Sex Trafficking Now a $16 Billion Business in

Latin America" (2008). The scourge of sex trafficking also plagues Europe, Africa, and Australia. Even in the United States, the National Center for Missing and Exploited Children estimates that up to 100,000 American children are at risk for sex trafficking each year, and 83 percent of the 1,200 human trafficking allegations made to the U.S. Department of Justice in 2007 were sex trafficking cases. See *The Human Trafficking Data Collection and Reporting Project* (2010).

It is important to note, however, that women and girls also are trafficked into industries other than the commercial sex industry, including agricultural work, factory work, domestic servitude, and the service industry. They may be at increased risk of HIV transmission as well, because trafficked women in all industries become more vulnerable to sexual assault and rape and may not be able to access testing and treatment for HIV during their enslavement.

Sex trafficking victims, however, are at significantly increased risk for contracting HIV for a number of reasons directly related to the nature of their forced servitude. Sex trafficking victims are modern-day slaves, and thus are unable to make choices about or control some aspects of their lives, including their sexual activity. They are forced to sell sex acts on the street, in hotels, through escort agencies, at brothels, and many other places where they don't have access to safer sex tools. Even when trafficking victims are held in brothels or other places where condoms are made available, they may not be able to enforce condom usage and other safer sex practices. Women and girls enslaved in commercial sex also are forced to endure sex with multiple partners, many of whom may also have had unprotected sex with multiple partners, which increases victims' risk of contracting HIV. They further must endure the riskiest types of unprotected sex, such as anal sex, injurious sadomasochism, and violently abusive sex, which increases their risk of transmission. Often injuries inflicted during violent sex are not allowed to heal properly, as traffickers force victims to continue to serve men without seeking medical attention. As a result, trafficked women may have high-risk, unprotected sex with multiple partners despite having open genital cuts and abrasions.

It is difficult to determine how many sexual partners an "average" trafficking victim might have over the course of her captivity. Reports from nongovernmental organizations vary greatly, with some reporting only a handful of customers per day, others up to forty or fifty per day. However, between five and ten customers per day is often considered a conservative figure. If a victim is forced to have sex with only five customers per day, six days per week for one year, she will have had sexual contact with 1,560 men that year. Without the ability to enforce safer sex practices or screen potential partners for STDs, this much sexual contact clearly puts the victim at a heightened risk for contracting HIV.

Another risk factor for trafficked females is their age. According to the U.S. Department of Justice, the average age of entry into prostitution is twelve to fourteen years old, and every child under eighteen in prostitution in the United States and many other countries is considered by law a sex trafficking victim. Children and young teens sold into prostitution are at a greater risk for contracting HIV because their smaller, still-developing bodies are more susceptible to the genital tearing that often leads to HIV transmission during sexual intercourse. Because trafficked children in prostitution are even less likely to be in control of choices than adults, they may have less opportunity to insist on safer sex practices. Worse still, some men seek ever younger children for sex, based on the warped belief that there is less risk of HIV transmission with a younger partner. In turn, younger children are being recruited into prostitution, which provides a longer period during which they can become HIV-infected.

SEX TRAFFICKING AS A FACILITATOR OF GLOBAL HIV TRANSMISSION

While trafficked women and girls are individually at an increased risk for contracting HIV, sex trafficking as an international phenomenon is also a catalyst and facilitator of large-scale HIV transmission. According to AIDS prevention organization AVERT, in some parts of the world, such as West Africa, the AIDS epidemic appears to be driven in part by the commercial sex industry, including the abuse of those trafficked into it. AVERT found that 27.1 percent of people in the commercial sex industry in Dakar, Senegal, were infected with HIV in 2005. See AVERT, "Aids and Prostitution" (2010). Other studies have found commercial sex to be a significant factor in the AIDS epidemics in Ghana, Togo, and Burkina Faso. Similarly, a 2008 study out of the Harvard School of Public Health found that 38 percent of women trafficked from Nepal to India for sex were returned to Nepal HIV-positive. See *Harvard Public Health Review, Trafficked* (2007). In the United States, there are both high rates of sexual exploitation of African American teen girls within the commercial sex industry and by family members and high rates of HIV infection among African American females. In addition to the sexual risk factors, high rates of injection drug use within the commercial sex industry also increase the risk of infection and transmission on a global scale.

Human trafficking within the commercial sex industry, however, greatly exacerbates the spread of HIV infections. Traffickers frequently transport victims between cities or countries to both disorient the victims and provide "fresh faces" for the men who buy sexual services from them. For example, "Corina" was trafficked in her home country of Moldova, where she likely contracted HIV. Her trafficker then sold her in London, Prague, New York, and Miami for a month each to have sex with ten to twenty men per night. As a trafficking victim, Corina was unable to seek testing or treatment for her HIV, and may have unknowingly and unwillingly spread the disease. Corina also began using drugs to mask the pain of sexual slavery. Women and girls trafficked for sex may turn to drugs and alcohol, including injection drugs, thus increasing their risk of infection and widespread transmission.

Another example of how sex trafficking can spread HIV is the cultural belief in some parts of the world that sex with a virgin can cure HIV or AIDS. HIV-positive men who believe this myth will seek out traffickers to procure a virgin for them, often a child. They then have unprotected sex with that virgin, and in the process will sometimes transmit the disease. However, the transmission factor of this encounter is multiplied exponentially, because after this sexual contact, the man, thinking himself cured, may have unprotected sex with other partners. The child he used, now possibly infected, will often continue to be trafficked for sex. In these cases, HIV transmission is not merely a byproduct of sex with a trafficking victim, but is the impetus for the trafficking and the sexual contact. It is also an action that can spread the disease exponentially.

Human trafficking has also been implicated as a possible catalyst for the mutation of HIV into multiple subtypes. Dr. Chris Beyer of Johns Hopkins University has linked sex trafficking to both the spread and mutation of HIV, stating that the commercial sex industry in general, and sex trafficking in particular, are facilitating the global dispersion of various (and possibly drug-resistant) HIV subtypes. Another factor in the creation of mutations is inconsistent treatment for people infected with HIV. Even those few trafficking victims who are able to seek testing and treatment for their HIV may suffer repeated interruptions in care because of lack of access, lack of education, or re-trafficking. The role of sex trafficking in the mutation of HIV is extremely dangerous and must be recognized in the global fight against AIDS.

THE CLASH OF HIV AND TRAFFICKING PREVENTION EFFORTS

One reason the intersection of sex trafficking and HIV may be under-examined is the tension between those groups conducting HIV prevention and treatment initiatives, and those groups conducting human trafficking prevention or rescue operations. Historically, HIV prevention programs have focused on harm-reduction models, which involve supplying brothels and women in prostitution with condoms, access to HIV tests, and other tools to prevent infection and transmission of the virus. This model of prevention sometimes entails allowing illegal commercial sex enterprises to operate without involving the local authorities, based on the philosophy that cooperation with the commercial sex industry is the best technique for preserving the safety of those in it. Human trafficking raids and prevention activities, however, have historically focused on identifying human trafficking within the commercial sex industry as a criminal activity and arresting the perpetrators and facilitators of that crime. HIV prevention organizations have sometimes seen anti-trafficking raids in brothels or red-light districts as disrupting HIV outreach and prevention or harming local relationships. Anti-trafficking organizations have sometimes seen HIV prevention as ineffective in assisting trafficking victims, and seen relationship-building within the commercial sex industry as neglecting to address the criminal components of sex trafficking within it.

Another issue that has caused tension between HIV prevention and anti-trafficking initiatives was the Bush administration's policy of denying federal funding to any organization found to be "promoting prostitution." For the better part of the last decade, "promoting prostitution" was interpreted broadly to include everything from making condoms readily accessible to offering English classes for women trying to leave the sex industry. One way this debate played out was over the effectiveness of a 2008 anti-trafficking law in Cambodia. Some anti-trafficking organizations have claimed the law has led to better identification of victims, but some HIV prevention groups have argued that it has instead increased fear and stigmatization of condom use in the commercial sex industry. However, in July 2009, the U.S. Department of Justice dropped its appeal of a 2006 court injunction prohibiting enforcement of the "anti-prostitution pledge" under U.S. global AIDS policy. This move suggests strongly that the Obama administration will not continue the Bush policy in this regard.

As the Obama era moves forward, HIV and trafficking prevention groups will need to develop new strategies—collaboratively, one hopes—for addressing their concerns in and with the commercial sex industry. Overall, HIV/AIDS heretofore has received minimal attention in the context of addressing sex trafficking, and few HIV/AIDS-focused services exist for trafficking victims. Similarly, while some HIV/AIDS plans address the role of the commercial sex industry in HIV transmission, what often are not addressed are the trafficking, forced prostitution, and sexual violence against women and girls. Despite the historical tension between anti-trafficking and HIV organizations, more common ground than not exists between them and should be pursued by both.

ENDING SEX TRAFFICKING AS A TOOL FOR CURBING THE SPREAD OF HIV

One promising practice to reduce the global epidemics of HIV and sex trafficking, as proposed by Holly Burkhalter, former U.S. Policy Director of Physicians for Human Rights, during testimony before the

U.S. House of Representatives International Relations Committee, is to frame the ending of sex trafficking as a tool for preventing HIV/AIDS. This approach would be effective for a number of reasons. First, it would provide an immediate road map for anti-trafficking and HIV prevention organizations to work together. Once the positive correlation between the reduction of sex trafficking and new HIV infections is identified, groups with formerly disparate goals will have a common goal around which to unite. HIV/AIDS prevention and trafficking prevention organizations working together to find common ground is crucial to effectively addressing both of these epidemics.

Second, the Trafficking Victims Protection Act (TVPA) can be used as a tool to convince foreign countries to address the dual epidemics of HIV and sex trafficking. When the TVPA was initially passed in 2000, it authorized the U.S. Department of State to issue an annual Trafficking in Persons Report, which places countries on "tiers" appropriate to their efforts to combat human trafficking. Countries placed on Tier 3 do not fully comply with the minimum standards of the TVPA and are not making significant efforts to do so. Pursuant to the TVPA, governments of countries on Tier 3 may be subject to certain sanctions, whereby the U.S. government may withhold non-humanitarian, non-trade-related foreign assistance. These sanctions provide additional leverage with which to convince foreign nations that eliminating sex trafficking and reducing HIV is in their national best interest—in economic, diplomatic, humanitarian, and public health terms.

Finally, the TVPA provides a framework for the collection of data on the intersection of HIV and human trafficking, including a list of countries with limited resources and significant need for human trafficking prevention; the opportunity to collect epidemiological data on the relationship between HIV transmission and sex trafficking; tools to facilitate collaboration between HIV and trafficking prevention programs; and resources to assist victims of sex trafficking and HIV. However, the ability to fully utilize the framework provided by the TVPA to address the intersection of HIV and sex trafficking rests in the identification of common goals by advocates for both issues.

In conclusion, women and girls are the primary victims of the nexus of the global epidemics of sex trafficking and HIV/AIDS. As sex trafficking victims, women and girls are more vulnerable to HIV infection because of their lack of choice with regard to high-risk sexual activities. Similarly, HIV infection is spread through international and local sex trafficking. This intersection has not been the subject of significant scholarship, possibly in part because of the perceived and actual clashes between HIV and sex trafficking prevention efforts. However, the TVPA provides some tools for both HIV and sex trafficking advocacy groups to move forward collaboratively and identify promising practices for addressing this deadly junction, which has destroyed the lives of so many women and girls.

For Class Discussion

1. In the first part of her argument, Kloer seeks to establish the interrelationship of the spread of HIV/AIDS and the prevalence of sex trafficking. What main reasons does she offer to substantiate this intersection?

2. What target audience do you think Kloer is particularly trying to reach with this policy proposal?

3. Where does Kloer use evidence effectively in this argument? What examples stand out for you?

4. How does Kloer drive home the global and local dimension of both issues and the increased vulnerability of young girls?

5. Summarize the historical tensions between groups that have focused on HIV prevention and groups that have focused on anti-trafficking.

6. What reasons does Kloer provide that collaboration among these groups— that is, "fram[ing] the ending of sex trafficking as a tool for preventing HIV/ AIDS"—is necessary in order for progress to be made with these two problems?

This Man Wants to Rent Your Daughter
Shared Hope International

Shared Hope International is a faith-based nonprofit organization dedicated to the rescue, restoration, and education of women and children who are victims of sexual trafficking. Founded by former congresswoman Linda Smith, this organization describes itself as "leaders in a worldwide effort to prevent and eradicate sex trafficking and slavery through education and public awareness" (www.sharedhope.org). Shared Hope International and the American Center for Law Justice conducted research in order to establish "a national standard of protection against domestic minor sex trafficking." Based on this research and assigning grades (A, C, F, etc.) to states for their policies and laws to fight sex trafficking of children, these organizations created recommendations for policies for each state. Part of this research involved tackling the sex traffic market, which drives this trafficking, by creating public awareness to bring social and legislative pressure for better laws. This billboard is part of a national campaign launched in November 2011 to achieve these goals.

What features strike you immediately about this billboard?

Shared Hope International, Do You Know Lacy national billboard campaign

For Class Discussion

1. Why do you think the designers of this campaign billboard chose this particular image? What is significant about the clothing and hands of the man? What information can you reconstruct from this partial torso image?

2. What is the rhetorical impact of the designers' choice of words for the billboard's slogan?

3. Who do you think is the target audience for this billboard?

4. What is the emotional and mental impact of the combined text and image? How does this billboard localize and personalize the problem of sex trafficking?

Sex Trafficking Needs to Be Stopped
Representative Frank R. Wolf

Frank R. Wolf is a Republican congressional representative from Virginia. He chairs the House Commerce-Justice-Science Appropriations subcommittee and has been active in promoting the establishment of the Human Trafficking Task Forces. Representative Wolf wrote this open letter regarding the status of federal legislation prohibiting sex ads with minors to Attorney General Eric H. Holder, Jr., on April 4, 2012.

The *kairos* ("why now") of this letter involves a controversy over the online forum Backpage.com, owned by Village Voice Media, which is considered the major U.S. online forum for trafficking of underage girls. Many Americans, including *New York Times* columnist Nicholas Kristof, have spoken out about shutting down this online source. How does Wolf convey a sense of immediacy and urgency about this controversy?

The Honorable Eric H. Holder, Jr.
Attorney General
U.S. Department of Justice
950 Pennsylvania Ave NW Rm 5111
Washington DC 20530

Dear Attorney General Holder:

I am writing, again, about an issue of utmost importance—namely the blatant sexual exploitation of American girls and boys. This heinous crime is happening in plain view with little to no consequence for those involved, including those reaping massive profits from this system of modern day slavery.

With the explosive growth of the Internet, pimps, "johns," gangs, traffickers, "madams" and the like have expanded their criminal activity to dizzying new heights. They have penetrated our nation's neighborhoods, victimized our children while cloaking themselves in misguided claims of "free speech" whenever they or the Web sites they use come under scrutiny.

Backpage.com is among the online Web sites that have been found to serve as a conduit for the buying and selling of human beings—not just prostitution (which is itself illegal in 49 out of 50 states), but more specifically the trafficking of minors. New York Times columnist Nicholas Kristof, long an impassioned abolitionist, has written extensively about Backpage.com. In a March 18 column he wrote, "Backpage accounts for about 70 percent of prostitution advertising among five Web sites that carry such ads in the United States, earning more than $22 million annually from prostitution ads, according to AIM Group, a media research and consulting company. It is now the premier Web site for human trafficking in the United States, according to the National Association of Attorneys General [NAAG]."

Quite simply, where prostitution flourishes it is a magnet for sex trafficking. National Security Presidential Directive-22 explicitly makes the connection stating: "Prostitution and related activities, which are inherently harmful and dehumanizing, contribute to the phenomenon of trafficking in persons." This reality has been borne out on Backpage. com. Of particular note is what Kristof revealed in his most recent column on March 31—that household names like Goldman Sachs (until Kristof began digging) owned a 16 percent stake in Village Voice Media (Backpage.com's parent company) and that a Goldman managing director sat on the Village Voice Media board for several years.

The NAAG first raised concerns with Backpage.com in August 2011 saying that the site served as a "hub" for human trafficking, especially trafficking of minors. Shortly after NAAG sent its letter, a group of prominent clergy wrote an open letter to Village Voice Media, which ran in the New York Times expressing solidarity with the position of the 51 Attorneys Generals who had signed the original letter. These faith leaders urged the company executives to shut down the "adult section" of the web site so as to ensure that "no minor is exploited through advertisements on your Web site."

Since that time others have joined the cause in pressing Backpage .com to act. Thousands of Americans have signed an online petition "demanding that Village Voice Media . . . stop selling ads that others use to sell minors on Backpage.com by shutting down the Adult section of the website." On March 23 a bipartisan group of U.S. senators wrote a letter to the chairman and CEO of Village Voice Media in which they echoed "the sentiments of 51 Attorneys General, dozens of human rights and sexual assault organizations, The Seattle Times, faith leaders, and more than 90,000 Americans who signed a petition on this issue, and urge you in the strongest terms possible to follow Craigslist and remove the adult services section from Backpage.com."

And yet, in the face of public pressure and even shame, Backpage .com remains unmoved. I believe it is imperative that these efforts be complimented by the very real prospect of criminal prosecution. Law enforcement, notably the Department of Justice (DOJ), must engage.

In the consolidated appropriations bill signed into law last year, Congress directed each U.S. Attorney to "establish or participate in a U.S. Attorney-led human trafficking task force." The bill also included language indicating that "Task force meetings should focus specifically on combating human trafficking, with an emphasis on undertaking proactive investigations. Such investigations shall include, for example, the investigation of persons or entities facilitating trafficking in persons through the use of classified advertising on the Internet." This report language was largely aimed at targeting Web sites like Backpage.com.

When you testified before the Commerce-Justice-Science Appropriations subcommittee on February 28, I inquired as to the status of these taskforces and specifically asked if you had sent a directive to the field on this issue. You replied, "I don't believe that in fact I have and I'll have to check on the status."

To date, I have received no such update. By April 25, I want to know the status of that directive as it relates to individual taskforces, and, of equal importance, whether the taskforces have been charged with specifically focusing on classified advertising—the latest front in this ever evolving battle to combat human trafficking.

Further, if DOJ is of the mind that there are insufficient laws on the books to prosecute this activity, I respectfully request a broader legal analysis and recommendations to Congress of legislative initiatives that may be undertaken to fully equip law enforcement to tackle this problem.

Most Americans would be horrified to know that human trafficking isn't simply relegated to distant lands, rather it is happening right here at home. It is happening to our sisters, our daughters and our friends with devastating implications. Just last week, in my area, five northern Virginian men with alleged ties to the Underground Gangster Crips gang were arrested and charged with sex trafficking. The local teenage girls they victimized were allegedly recruited on Web sites like Facebook and then, according to a Washington Post story that reported on the arrests, "The teens were advertised on Web sites such as Craigslist and Backpage.com, according to court records." Here again, we see Backpage.com in the spotlight. When will this end?

Kristof rightly notes that were Backpage.com to shut down its "adult services" section, child sex trafficking would not be eliminated, but it would surely be curbed. He writes, "Let's be honest: Backpage's exit from prostitution advertising wouldn't solve the problem, for smaller Web sites would take on some of the ads. But it would be a setback for pimps to lose a major online marketplace. When Craigslist stopped taking such ads in 2010, many did not migrate to new sites: online prostitution advertising plummeted by more than 50 percent, according to AIM Group."

The media, civil society, faith leaders and more can and must continue to shine a bright light on the activities of Backpage.com and their ilk. Similarly, such groups can pressure their financers, as Kristof has done by exposing Goldman Sachs. But there is a unique role for law enforcement. And as our nation's chief law enforcement officer, that responsibility falls squarely on your shoulders. This administration needs to make this a priority.

Best wishes.
Sincerely,
Frank R. Wolf
Member of Congress

For Class Discussion

1. What course of action is Wolf imploring Attorney General Holder to take? What reasoning does Wolf use to support his claim?

2. According to Wolf, what is the critical role of the Internet in promoting the business of sex trafficking? How does Wolf's letter address the issue of the demand side of human trafficking that Siddharth Kara describes in his argument?

3. What precedent does Wolf cite in this letter to support his argument?

4. How does Wolf's handling of alternative views contribute to his argument?

5. How does Wolf contribute to your understanding of the national and local dimensions of this global problem?

Child Soldiers: A Worldwide Scourge

Jo Becker

Jo Becker holds an MA in political science from the Maxwell School of Citizenship and Public Affairs at Syracuse University. She was executive director of the Fellowship of Reconciliation, joined Human Rights Watch in 1997, founded the International Coalition to Stop the Use of Child Soldiers, and was instrumental in the United Nations' adoption of the treaty Optional Protocol to the Convention on the Rights of the Child in 2000, prohibiting the use of child soldiers. In her current role as advocacy director for the children's rights division of Human Rights Watch, she has researched child soldiers in Sri Lanka, Nepal, Burma, and northern Uganda, and she frequently speaks out in government and media forums on child soldiers and the abuse of child laborers. This advocacy piece appeared in the *Los Angeles Times* on March 22, 2012, and it was published on the Human Rights Watch Web site on March 23, 2012.

> What is the immediate motivating occasion for Jo Becker's writing of this advocacy piece? In other words, what assumptions and ideas does she believe her readers hold that need to be addressed at this time?

Last week in The Hague, the International Criminal Court, or ICC, found the Congolese warlord Thomas Lubanga guilty of recruiting and using child soldiers in the armed conflict in that country, sealing his fate as the court's first convicted war criminal.

At the same time, the viral video "Kony 2012" has seemingly achieved its goal of making Joseph Kony, another rebel commander facing an ICC arrest warrant, notorious for his alleged crimes, including the abduction of an estimated 30,000 children for his Lord's Resistance Army. Millions of people have viewed the video, with millions more learning about Kony, who is still at large, through mainstream media coverage of the campaign.

Kony, Lubanga and Charles Taylor could be regarded as the three most infamous child soldier recruiters in the world today. Taylor, the former president of Liberia, is awaiting a verdict from the Special Court for Sierra Leone on charges of recruiting child soldiers and other crimes.

Together, the three may bear responsibility for forcing tens of thousands of children into brutal and deadly wars.

But the use of child soldiers extends far beyond Central and West Africa. Today, child soldiers are fighting in at least 14 countries, including Colombia, Myanmar (also known as Burma) and Afghanistan. In most of these cases, there have been no arrest warrants, no trials and no convictions for those responsible.

The United Nations has identified more than a dozen "persistent perpetrators," governments and armed groups that are known to have used child soldiers in active conflict for more than 10 years. The Revolutionary Armed Forces of Colombia, or FARC, rebels in Colombia, for example, have recruited children as young as 7 and forced them into combat. They execute fighters who try to desert.

In some cases, military recruiters not only escape punishment but are rewarded for bringing children into their forces.

On the Thailand-Burma border, I interviewed boys who had escaped from Burma's army. Some were only 11 years old when recruiters threatened or coerced them into joining the army. They said that when they arrived at the recruitment center, the commanders not only turned a blind eye to the boys' young age but gave the recruiters cash and bags of rice.

The situation in a few countries is becoming notably worse. In Afghanistan, the Taliban has stepped up its use of children for suicide attacks. In Somalia, the Islamist armed group Shabab has increasingly targeted children for forced recruitment, often abducting children as young as 10 from their homes or schools.

Lubanga's conviction is a landmark. But more action is needed to address the problem globally.

At the national level, governments need to crack down on commanders who recruit children. Burma has prosecuted some low-level soldiers but no high-ranking officers. In the Democratic Republic of Congo, not only is Bosco Ntaganda, one of six wanted by the ICC for recruiting child soldiers, still at large, but he has been promoted to the rank of general in the national army.

Other governments may be complicit in the use of child soldiers by other countries. The United States, for example, continues to provide military assistance to governments using child soldiers in their national forces, including the Democratic Republic of Congo and Yemen, despite U.S. laws prohibiting such aid.

Lubanga and Taylor are facing real consequences for their use of child soldiers. Kony, if apprehended, could also face decades in prison.

But the scourge of child soldiers reaches around the globe. To end the use of child soldiers, we can't stop with these three.

For Class Discussion

1. What is Becker's main message in this argument? In this policy proposal, what does Becker ask readers to do?

2. According to Becker, what role do the United States and other governments play in the human rights violations of the forced recruitment of child soldiers?

3. How successful is Becker in making her argument persuasive? If she were to expand and deepen her argument, what questions would you want her to address? What points should she develop?

4. What knowledge of the child soldier human rights issue did you bring to your reading of this argument and what were the sources of this previous information? For example, what have you heard about Joseph Kony? How has this article contributed to your knowledge of the recruiters and military leaders responsible for using children in combat?

Chadian Eight-Year-Old Soldier Smoking
Luc Novovitch

Advocacy organizations believe that around 300,000 children from more than thirty countries are fighting in wars around the world. Many of these children— both boys and girls—have been abducted or coerced into military service,

Luc Novovitch/Reuters/Corbis

tortured, sexually abused, forced to participate in violence, and compelled to witness terrible atrocities. These children are fighting in armies in Nepal, Sri Lanka, Indonesia, Colombia, Guatemala, Burma, Peru, Sudan, Uganda, Sierra Leone, and Liberia, among other countries. Many countries have signed the UN protocol of 2002 to stop the military recruitment of children; however, Asian and African signatories who have violated the protocol have not been brought before the International Criminal Court. This photo, one of many taken by news agencies reporting the problem of child soldiers, shows an eight-year-old soldier in Chad.

> The more readers know about the horrors experienced by child soldiers, the more disturbing photos of these children are. What details of this photo stand out for you?

For Class Discussion

1. What features of this photo suggest that this boy has suffered?

2. With this photo in mind, list some of the psychological problems that child soldiers may have while they are serving in these armies and when they are liberated.

3. Investigate the problem of child soldiers by consulting the Web sites for such advocacy organizations as Human Rights Watch (www.hrw.org/), the Anti-Slavery Society (www.anti-slaverysociety.addr.com), and Save the Children (www.savethechildren.org/). What key facts from these sources would you use in a report for your peers on this human rights issue? What makes a photo rhetorically effective to protest child soldiers?

4. How has this photo influenced your thinking about forced child labor? ∎

Rape as a Weapon of War: Men Suffer, Too
Emily Rauhala

Emily Rauhala is a reporter, writer, editor, and Web producer. She is a graduate of Columbia University's Graduate School of Journalism. Currently, she is associate editor of *TIME* magazine and a contributor to *This Magazine* and the *International Herald Tribune*. Originally from Canada, she has lived recently in Hong Kong. This editorial appeared on August 3, 2011, on the Web publication affiliated with *TIME*, *Global Spin*, which calls itself "a blog about the world, its people, and its politics."

> According to Emily Rauhala, why is sexual violence against men and boys a little known and understood human rights problem?

It's talked about in whispers, if at all. But men and boys are all-too-frequently subjected to sexual violence, particularly in times of conflict, forced confinement or war. The problem is persistent and global. For the most part, though, nobody wants to talk about it. Over the last few months, however, a handful of reports from West Africa show that rape and sexual violence are being used as a weapon against men and boys, as well as women and girls. In a dispatch for the *Observer*, British journalist Will Storr chronicles the stories of men raped during the conflict in Congo. In Kampala, Uganda, he meets a refugee who was kidnapped and then raped three times a day, every day, for three years. "There are certain things you just don't believe can happen to a man," he said.

Indeed, sexual violence against men and boys, though common, is little understood or studied. One notable exception is the work of UCLA's Lara Stemple, who looks at the phenomenon of male rape through the prism of international human rights. Though females are certainly more likely to be raped in conflict, she finds, males comprise a "sizable minority" of victims. There are documented cases in conflicts in Chile, Greece, Iran, the Democratic Republic of Congo and other places, too. At a torture treatment center in London, 21% of Sri Lankan Tamil males said they'd experienced sexual abuse during the war, she notes. One study of the conflict in the former Yugoslavia found that 80% of the 6000 inmates at a prison camp in Sarajevo reported rape.

The Abu Ghraib fiasco was a high-profile example of sexual violence in a military detention center. However, rape is also prevalent in civilian facilities. One in five male inmates in America said they'd had a pressured or forced sexual encounter while incarcerated, one study found. In South Africa's overcrowded, under-funded prisons, rape and sexual violence are used to define and maintain a strict social hierarchy in which "victims are humiliated, dominated and feminized," Stemple writes. Here, as elsewhere, men who identify as gay, or are perceived to be 'feminine' are particularly susceptible to abuse. (See also Ross Kemp's investigation of sexual violence in one South African prison.)

Shame and social stigma silence many survivors. They are often plagued by injury, ashamed and wary of speaking out. Here's Storr's account of one survivor's life after surviving gang rape and sexual torture in Congo:

> Today, despite his hospital treatment, Jean Paul still bleeds when he walks. Like many victims, the wounds are such that he's supposed to restrict his diet to soft foods such as bananas, which are expensive, and Jean Paul can only afford maize and millet. His brother keeps asking what's wrong with him. "I don't want to tell him," says Jean Paul. "I fear he will say: 'Now, my brother is not a man.'"
>
> It is for this reason that both perpetrator and victim enter a conspiracy of silence and why male survivors often find, once their story is discovered, that they lose the support and comfort of those around them. In the patriarchal societies found in many developing countries, gender roles are strictly defined.

Though patriarchy and homophobia are certainly not limited to poor countries, Storr rightly highlights the ways in which stigma prevents men from getting help. Survivors are often assumed to be gay, which is a crime in 38 of 53 African nations and carries considerable social stigma elsewhere. Also, relatively few groups are able, or willing, to help male survivors. In her paper for *Hastings Law Review*, Stemple notes that of the 4000+ organizations that address rape as a weapon of war, only 3% mention the men in their informational materials. And few doctors, anywhere, are trained to recognize signs of male rape, or counsel survivors, she says.

There is concern, too, that highlighting male rape will somehow take away from efforts to stop sexual violence against women. I understand the fear, but think it short-sighted. Talking about sexual violence against men and boys helps shatter stigma, which, hopefully, will result in more support for survivors. It also challenges rigidly-defined gender roles that cast men as hyper-masculine sexual aggressors and women as passive victims. Tackling this narrative is one step toward ending violence against women, as well violence against men.

For Class Discussion

1. How does Rauhala use the opening of her article to attract readers' attention to the problem of sexual violence against men and boys?

2. In a categorical argument where the arguer asserts "X is a major problem," the main support strategy is to provide abundant, relevant, and persuasive examples. How effective is Rauhala at using evidence to build a case for her claim?

3. How does Rauhala appeal to readers' emotions and values?

4. What objections does Rauhala acknowledge against focusing on male rape and how does she respond to them?

5. How does this argument illustrate the principle held by human rights analysts and advocates that all human rights issues are interconnected?

Ten Radical Acts for Congo in the New Year

Eve Ensler

Eve Ensler is a feminist playwright, a performer, and a social activist for women's rights globally. Her best known play is *The Vagina Monologues*, which continues in performance around the world and has been translated into over forty languages. She made a film of this play in 2002. Some of her other plays are *The Good Body, Necessary Targets, Conviction, Extraordinary Measures,* and most recently, *Here,* and she has published articles in *The Guardian, Marie Claire,* the *Huffington Post,* the *Washington Post,* and *Glamour* magazine, among other publications. In addition to her writing that focuses on raising consciousness and stopping violence against women, she created V-Day (VDay .org), a nonprofit movement that works globally to educate, support women, change attitudes, and campaign to raise money for the cause of stopping violence against women. One of Ensler's most recent projects, supported jointly by V-Day, UNICEF, and the Panzi Foundation and developed by women of Democratic Republic of Congo, is the creation of the City of Joy in Bukavu, DRC. This retreat center for survivors of sexual violence educates women about their rights; helps them cope with the social shame of rape; and teaches self-defense, leadership, reproductive health, and economic opportunity. This op-ed piece was published in the *Huffington Post* on January 11, 2010.

> What background or contextual information about the conflicts in Democratic Republic of Congo does Eve Ensler incorporate in this piece?

Having just been in the Congo for the last month, it is evident that the more than 12-year economic war in the Democratic Republic of Congo rages on. Almost 6 million dead. Almost 500 thousand raped. Here is what I propose:

1. Please stop endlessly repeating these phrases:

- "The Congo has been like this forever."
- "There is nothing we can do."
- "It's too complicated. I just don't understand."
- "It's a cultural thing."

A. Violence against women and girls is rampant across the entire planet.

B. Sexual terrorism was imported into the DRC like a plague about 12 years ago years ago, after a 1996 military operation know as Operation Turquoise—a plan supported and implemented by the international community which allowed murdering Hutu militias of Rwanda (FDLR) into Eastern Congo. Since then, this sexual terrorism has been sustained by these and other parties interested in the minerals (coltan, gold, tin), that are serving you. Like a plague, this rape and sexual violence has spread, infecting the Congolese Army and even the UN peacekeepers who are there to "protect" the women. Put pressure on the international community to remove all outside militias. They brought them there, they are responsible for getting them out.

2. Stop asking women survivors in the Congo to tell their stories over and over

A woman activist told me yesterday they were going to shut up now. "There is no reason to keep telling the story or paying expats lots of money to research the story of women and girls in the Congo. We all know the story."

Visit these sites:

Read the latest U.N. human rights reports from the NYT AFEM

Friends of Congo

Read the recent Human Rights Watch reports

Read the history

We know what is happening in the DRC. Now is the time for action.

3. Deconstruct and abolish subterranean and learned racism

Deconstruct and abolish subterranean and learned racism that lies at the bedrock of human consciousness and arranges and expects and accepts the doom of black and brown people. Undo the brutal and evil indifference to the suffering of the people of Congo, the women in particular.

4. Shoes, shoes, shoes, for everyone who needs them

5. Insist on support for thousands of trained Congolese women police officers

Insist on support for thousands of trained Congolese women police officers who can protect their sisters in the bush. Don't let Security Council resolutions 1820 and 1325 continue to be random insider numbers UN policy bureaucrats refer to when they are trying to prove they are doing something about sexual violence. Insist they be resolutions with grit that get applied regularly with sincerity and substance. Begin application by insisting that the UN not collaborate with rapists and former warlords in military operations.

Write to Secretary of State Hillary Clinton and ask her to allocate funding for a women's police force in the Congo:

Secretary of State Hillary Clinton
US Department of State
2201 C Street NW
Washington, DC 20520

6. Serve the Congolese and take their lead

Support their initiatives. Get out of the way. Support the local groups and campaigns that already exist, that have existed. They need your support to continue to exist. Fight to make sure the money headed for Eastern Congo actually gets to the women on the ground—the grassroots groups who need it most. Believe in grassroots women and men. Send them your confidence, your solidarity, and your money.

Give to V-Day's **Stop Raping Our Greatest Resource** campaign as it continues to support local groups on the ground like AFEM, the

South Kivu Women's Media Association, Panzi Hospital in Bukavu and Heal Africa Hospital in Goma, women's collectives like I Will Not Kill Myself Today and AFECOD, and the Women's Ministry and Laissez l'Afrique Vivre.

7. Tell President Obama to step up to femicide

Insist that as a Nobel Peace Prize winner, President Obama ask questions about the history of the conflict in the Congo. Ask him to find out how and when this war began. Ask him to put his attention to what's happening to the women in the Congo, to femicide—the destruction of the female species that is spreading to other countries and will continue to spread if he, himself does not make this a front and center issue. The Congo needs to be more than a phrase reference in one of his speeches. He needs to come to the Congo. He needs to meet the women and bring them to the table with himself and leaders of Rwanda and Uganda and Burundi. He needs to help facilitate a diplomatic plan for peace that does not involve more violence.

Write to President Obama and ask him to make finding a non-military solution to the war in Congo a priority in his foreign policy agenda.

8. Acknowledge what's fueling this war and your part in it

Educate yourself about how conflict minerals are illegally and inhumanely pillaged from the Congo and make their way into your cell phones and the computer you are using to read this post right now. Demand that electronics companies alter their mining and trade policies so that conflict-free minerals are used in our electronics. Until this happens, we all literally have blood on our hands.

Investigate where and how your electronics companies are purchasing their materials. As a consumer, demand that they use conflict-free minerals in their parts.

9. Talk about the Congo everywhere you go

Be a pain in the ass. Ruin cocktail parties. Stop traffic. Give sermons. Insert facts about Congo in every possible occasion, i.e., in response to "How are you today?," you might say: "Well, I would be okay if women weren't being raped in the DRC."

Host teach-ins and screen V-Day's film *Turning Pain to Power*. Visit vday.org to access both.

10. Get angry and stop being polite

Feel what your sister, mother, grandmother, daughter, wife, girlfriend would be feeling if she were being gang raped or held as a sex slave for years or if her insides were destroyed by sticks and guns and she could never have another baby.

Feel feel feel.

Open yourself to feeling.

For Class Discussion

1. Often articles about human rights conflicts around the world leave readers overwhelmed and confused about what they can do to help. How does Ensler's forceful directive approach and no-nonsense format in this piece confront that problem? How would you describe her tone?

2. What are Ensler's main claim and reasons in this argument? What is she proposing?

3. What opposing beliefs, assumptions, and views about Africa, women, and rape does Ensler address in this piece? How rhetorically effective is her treatment of these?

4. What role does Ensler urge for consumers in the United States?

5. Ensler makes appeals to emotions in this piece. What rhetorical risks does she take in her appeals and her authoritative approach to her subject and her readers? What ideas about human rights conflicts and campaigns have you gained from this piece?

CHAPTER QUESTIONS FOR REFLECTION AND DISCUSSION

1. How do the readings in this chapter suggest that globalization has nurtured human rights violations? List at least five ways and cite specific examples from the readings.

2. **Analyzing Arguments Rhetorically.** The following writers agree on the urgency and magnitude of the sex trafficking problem, but their views also differ. Think about the professional backgrounds of each writer and the audience he or she is addressing. Then map out the way these writers disagree in their perspectives and values, assumptions, claims, reasons, and evidence/interpretation of facts. If you do find common ground and agreement in any points, list those as well.

   - David A. Feingold and Siddharth Kara
   - Siddharth Kara and Joanna Busza and her coauthors
   - Amanda Kloer and Joanna Busza and her coauthors

3. How do the following writers complement, reinforce, or extend each other's argument about human rights?

   - Frank R. Wolf and Siddharth Kara or the National Human Trafficking Resource Center
   - Emily Rauhala and Eve Ensler
   - Jo Becker and Luc Novovitch

- Siddharth Kara and the National Human Trafficking Resource Center
- Shared Hope International and Frank R. Wolf

4. A number of writers in this chapter insist that emotional appeals, using sensational stories of suffering, have muddied human rights issues or even done damage to the efforts to combat the problems. What do David A. Feingold, Joanna Busza and coauthors, and Siddharth Kara say about the danger of emotional appeals and the need to infuse more complex thinking, accurate data, and involvement of the people most affected into problem-solving projects?

5. Using the visuals in this chapter, sketch out a case that visual arguments can be particularly useful in human rights advocacy?

6. Explain which reading in this chapter you think presents the clearest, most thorough, and most compassionate and respectful argument about human rights violations.

7. The human rights violations discussed in this chapter suggest many questions for further investigation. Choose one of the following topics, and individually or in groups, do some research to help you formulate an informed answer to questions about it. Prepare a report with a visual display of data for your class.

A. Many policymakers discourage the boycotting of companies and products as a way to combat human rights violations; however, consumer power was successful in the Rugmark Campaign in improving the treatment of child workers in the rug and carpet industry in India. Currently, the problem of forced child labor in the cotton fields of Uzbekistan is receiving global attention. Investigate the AFL-CIO's "List of Shame: Goods Made with Forced, Child Labor" to determine what products and their supply chains consumers should know about. What can American consumers do to protest these exploitative practices?

B. A number of NGOs have decided to involve children in their search for ways to stop the exploitation of children. Choose one of the following organizations and examine its Web site. What are some of the ways that this organization is including children and working to help them?

Global Movement for Children, (www.unicef.org/gmfc/)

The Childwatch International Research Network, (www.childwatch.uio
    .no/)

Save the Children, (www.savethechildren.net/)

South Asian Coalition on Child Servitude (Bachpan Bachao Andolan),
    (www.bba.org.in/)

C. In some countries, efforts to stop trafficking and tighten borders has led to human rights violations of immigrants, refugees, asylum seekers, and the victims of smuggling rather than to stopping the traffickers. Investigate the detention problems raised by Canada's Protecting Canada's Immigration System Act (Bill C-31). What problems have arisen? How could these problems be corrected?

D. Research Nicholas Kristof's numerous columns about the sex trade and abuse of girls and women written for the *New York Times.* Summarize Kristof's main views. Prepare to share with your class both his main points and some of his most moving emotional appeals.

E. Two strategies that seem to be gaining traction in the struggle to stop the widespread use of rape and exploitation of women are to educate and train the people of a country, particularly the women, to confront the deep-seated political, economic, social, and cultural problems that are creating the conditions in which these violations flourish. Investigate the efforts of the Women of Liberia Mass Action for Peace Campaign or the City of Joy in DRC. Report on how women are learning new roles and taking action.

WRITING ASSIGNMENTS ████████████████

Brief Writing Assignments

1. **Reflective Writing.** Write for twenty minutes informally about what surprised, shocked, or disturbed you the most about the trafficking of women and children and rape as a weapon of war. Briefly discuss which reading had the most impact on you. What values that you hold did it cause you to reexamine?

2. After considering the readings in this chapter, use one of the following prompts to begin sorting out your own thinking on the views of human rights you encountered in this chapter:

   A. The arguments in this chapter have particularly clarified my understanding of _____ (some aspect of the human trafficking issue).

   B. The arguments in this chapter have changed my views on the (urgency, magnitude, or nearness) of the trafficking and forced labor problem in these ways: _____.

   C. After reading these articles (fill in titles), I have major questions about _____.

3. Summarize one of the longer arguments in this chapter: David A. Feingold, Siddharth Kara, Busza and coauthors, or Amanda Kloer. Try to capture the writer's main claim and reasoning in your own words in a way that the writer would accept as fair to his or her ideas.

4. **Analyzing Arguments Rhetorically.** Publicity of human rights causes can be problematic: for example, the viral video sponsored by the advocacy group Invisible Children about Joseph Kony's the Lord's Resistance Army in Uganda. After watching this video (and perhaps its sequel), and researching the controversy it has generated, including WikiLeaks' response, prepare a brief rhetorical analysis of this video for your class. Why is (or is not) this video effective as an advocacy tool? How does it affect the public's understanding of the human rights problem of child soldiers? You might consider Jo Becker's argument in your analysis as well.

5. Working in groups or individually, consult the Poster for Tomorrow project (www.posterfortomorrow.org) and view the gallery of posters on human rights topics (one theme per year) that individuals have contributed. Then design a poster on one of the subjects in this chapter: human trafficking, forced child labor, enslaved labor, child soldiers, or rape as a weapon of war against females or males. Prepare either your idea or the poster itself for presentation to your class. As a source for ideas for your poster, you might consult the U.S. Department of Health and Human Services' set of outreach and training materials to aid local social service organizations, law enforcement, and health care professionals in identifying and offering support to trafficking victims.

Writing Projects

1. **Reflective Writing.** Sometimes we distance ourselves from human rights violations, particularly if they are very disturbing, as in the case of rape used as a weapon of war and human trafficking. We may take shelter in a sense of immunity, superiority, or sheer geographical distance. It may take a jolt from a film, reading, volunteering experience, or research to evoke our concern and compassion and move us to action. Write a reflective essay in which you honestly confront your new awareness of a human rights violation or explore why the subject has not moved you yet. You might write a narrative like Victoria Herradura's in the introduction to this chapter on pages 391–393, which shares your personal experience and reasons for caring about a particular human rights issue, or you can analyze the obstacles to your personal involvement.

2. **Analyzing Arguments Rhetorically.** A number of the readings in this chapter make powerful rational, emotional, or moral appeals to readers. Choose one of the following readings and analyze how it presents its interpretation of the problem; creates and supports an argument tailored to its audience; and uses emotional and imaginative appeals. Write an interpretive argument that analyzes how the piece you have chosen works rhetorically. Write for average citizens who are trying to grasp this human rights problem. How successful is this piece at helping these readers become informed? Justify your analysis of this reading by citing specific examples and

explaining your points. Choose from these writers: Siddharth Kara, Joanna Busza and her coauthors, Amanda Kloer, Frank R. Wolf, and Eve Ensler.

3. One of the main obstacles to combating sex trafficking centers on the controversy over distinguishing between victims of sex trafficking and sex workers in prostitution. Several writers in this chapter address this issue: David A. Feingold, Siddharth Kara, Joanna Busza and coauthors, and Amanda Kloer, In April of 2012, the *New York Times* reported on the increase in prostitution *and* sex trafficking in Spain and throughout the EU. Does prostitution nurture sex trafficking or does allowing and monitoring prostitution provide a legal channel for controlling sex trafficking? Investigate this issue and write a policy proposal directed at other puzzled citizens who are trying to take an informed stand on this question.

4. Use Shared Hope International's "Protected Innocence Initiative" link to determine how your state has been graded with regard to its human trafficking policies and laws. You might also research the social services resources available to help trafficking victims. Consider your state's geographical location, borders, ports, and waterways; main sources of revenue such as agriculture; and major cities. Based on your fieldwork and research, write either (1) a letter to your state legislator proposing how he or she might improve your state's grade and invigorate your state's anti-trafficking policies or (2) a newsletter or brochure for your city or community informing citizens of the status of your state's laws (your state's current grade) and proposing a course of action citizens can pursue to improve your state's policies and laws.

5. Using the "Look Beneath the Surface" poster and the "This Man Wants to Rent Your Daughter" billboard as your departure point, create the design for an anti-trafficking campaign billboard for your city using some combination of image and text. Then write a commentary that explains your target audience, the appeals you are making to that audience, your intended rhetorical effect on viewers, and a justification for why your city should support this campaign. You might investigate how much it would cost to rent a billboard. (If you consult with Shared Hope International, this organization will allow you to use its logo should you decide to pursue the actualization of your campaign.)

6. The controversy in the United States over Village Voice Media's sex ads at Backpage.com, which advertise trafficked minors, involves a debate over free speech and the free market versus human rights and criminal actions against youth under sixteen. Investigate this controversy over Backpage.com through research on the Web. Determine your own views, and choose someone who holds an opposing view: a person, business, or organization. Write an open letter to this person or group in which you try to win a hearing for your position. Summarize the controversy neutrally, try to establish some common values and interests with your audience,

and finally propose a compromise position and negotiate with your audience to consider it. This approach (called a Rogerian letter) acknowledges that a straightforward attack or forceful effort to persuade often does not work rhetorically in situations involving strong disagreement and differing values. Try to achieve a problem-solving tone even when you are addressing views with which you don't agree. Accept that in some situations some negotiation is better than a standoff.

7. Sometimes the complexity of human rights issues can be overwhelming and discouraging. However, some activists offer hope: activists such as Don Cesare Lo Deserto and his home for rescued victims of the sex trade in Italy; Mara Radovanovic of the Lara organization in Bosnia; Eve Ensler's founding of the City of Joy in DRC; politician Linda Smith and Shared Hope International; former Ambassador John Miller and the anti-trafficking legislation he has sponsored; and Ellen Johnson Sirleaf, Leymah Gbowee, and Tawakkol Karman, the three women who won the Nobel Peace Prize in 2011 for their nonviolent action for democracy and gender equality. Investigate and research one of these activists or one you discover on your own. Then write an editorial or journalistic profile for your university or community newspaper explaining what you found impressive and inspirational about this person's contribution to the fight against trafficking violations of human rights.

8. Imagine that a wealthy relative has left you $25,000 in her will with the stipulation that you will donate $5,000 to a human rights advocacy organization that helps women and children. Knowing that you are a good Web researcher and also a student of globalization issues, your relative has asked you to choose the organization, advocacy group, or NGO that you think is most effective at educating the public about the horrors of the trafficking of women and children and at providing practical, life-changing help to victims of trafficking. Your task is (1) to investigate several of the following organizations; (2) to use the following criteria to evaluate the effectiveness of the one you are going to choose to support; and (3) to write an argument in the form of a letter to your relatives justifying your choice.

Human Rights Watch (www.hrw.org)
Anti-Slavery International (www.antislavery.org)
Free the Slaves (www.freetheslaves.org)
Save the Children (www.savethechildren.org)
Media Voices for Children (http://mediavoicesforchildren.org)
The Human Trafficking Project (www.traffickingproject.org)
The Protection Project (www.protectionproject.org)
The Polaris Project (www.polarisproject.org)
Global Movement for Children (www.unicef.org/gmfc/)
United Nations Children's Fund (UNICEF) (www.unicef.org)

Evaluate your organization's Web site using these criteria:

A. Clear explanation of the problem and credible information to support the organization's position

B. Strong appeal to readers' emotions, sympathies, and values

C. Good currency of the information presenting the organization's successes in addressing the problem

D. Clear requests and directives indicating what the organization wants readers to do

Fighting Global Disease

Pandemics, Antibiotic Resistance, AIDS, and Maternal Health

CONTEXT FOR A NETWORK OF ISSUES

Along with global trade, the world has been sharing diseases for centuries; in fact, "pandemics" (infectious diseases spreading rapidly to a high percentage of the populations of several continents simultaneously) were often transmitted from country to country by ships and merchants' overland caravans. One of the most deadly of these pandemics was the Black Death of 1347–1352. It began in China and then, following trade and shipping routes, spread to central Asia and Asia Minor and to ports in Italy and Egypt, to Europe, North Africa, and the Middle East. The Black Death killed around 25 million people, or between one-third to one-half the population of Europe.

Throughout the twentieth century and recently, pandemics have periodically had widespread deadly effects. The Spanish flu[*] of 1918–1919, a type of bird flu, swept around the world attacking the young and vigorous, including soldiers in the trenches in Europe in World War I, and left between 20 and 50 million people dead. Between 1957 and 1958, the Asian flu began in East Asia and reached the United States, killing 70 thousand Americans and 1 million people around the world. In November 2002, SARS (severe acute respiratory syndrome, a disease that fills the lungs with fluid) cropped up in China and spread to over 8,000 people in twenty-seven countries.

Yearly, the influenzas for which many people receive flu shots kill between 500,000 and 1 million people around the world. Three to four

---

[*]"Flu," or influenza, is a viral infection that involves the lungs and usually brings a fever, a cough, and severe muscle aches. It can involve a secondary bacterial infection.

times a century these viruses mutate to become influenza pandemics that are beyond the treatment ability of known vaccines and cures. For example, in 2005, avian flu (bird flu), a disease similar to SARS, appeared to pose global danger. Because avian flu spreads from ducks and wild birds to domestic poultry, such as chickens and turkeys, and can also jump from chickens to humans, whole farms of poultry were killed in an effort to prevent the spread of the disease. Between spring 2009 and summer 2010, the swine flu (H1N1) traveled from Mexico to the United States and around the world, causing alarm because it particularly affected older children and younger adults. Although deaths from SARS, avian flu, and swine flu have not reached the large tolls expected, the potential for a mutated virus to cause a lethal pandemic remains very real.

Globalization has collapsed time and space and heightened the complexity of controlling these influenza outbreaks. As scientists scramble to identify and create medicines and vaccines for mutating and migrating viruses, the global community puzzles over the most efficient ways to collaborate for the benefit of all. Kofi Annan, former secretary-general of the United Nations, framed disease control as a global security issue:

> The security of developed countries is only as strong as the ability of poor states to respond to and contain a new deadly infectious disease. . . . The incubation period for most infectious diseases is longer than most international air flights. As a result, any one of the 700 million people who travel on airlines in a year could unwittingly carry a lethal virus to an unsuspecting country. The 1918 influenza epidemic killed twice as many people in one year as HIV/AIDS has killed in the past 28 years. Today, a similar virus could kill tens of millions in a fraction of the time.[*]

Annan exhorts all countries to think as an interdependent global community, to commit to common goals, and to harmonize their efforts against these diseases.

One of the greatest weapons in the fight against pandemic disease has been the development and use of antibiotics and similar drugs, which together are referred to as antimicrobial agents. Since the 1940s, drugs in this category have greatly reduced the incidence of illness and death from infectious diseases caused by bacteria, viruses, fungi, or parasites. Yet due to various factors, including natural evolution or mutation of microbes, overprescription of antimicrobials, misdiagnosis by health care professionals, incorrect use of the drugs by patients, intensive hospital use of antimicrobials, and agricultural use of antibiotics in animal feed as a preventative measure, scientists are now finding that drug-resistant strains of many pathogens are emerging. Thus, infectious diseases such as HIV infection,

---

[*]Kofi Annan, "Courage to Fulfill Our Responsibilities," *Economist* (December 4, 2004).

staphylococcal infections, tuberculosis, influenza, gonorrhea, yeast infections, and malaria are becoming increasingly difficult to treat.[*] Beyond the fears that we may not be able to treat existing or emergent pandemics effectively, there are financial concerns associated with antimicrobial resistance. According to the Centers for Disease Control and Prevention (CDC), the estimated costs of antibiotic resistance in the United States alone add up to $20 billion a year in excess health care costs, $35 million in other societal costs, and more than 8 million additional days a year that people spend in the hospital.[†] To raise awareness of this problem, the World Health Organization's World Health Day 2011 spotlighted antimicrobial resistance as a key public health issue.

Another pandemic is HIV (human immunodeficiency virus)/AIDS (acquired immunodeficiency syndrome), which was first officially identified in the United States in 1981. HIV/AIDS continues to be especially serious in Africa, where it has reached a critical mass that is battering the social structures of countries. At the end of 2010, 34 percent of the 34 million people living with AIDS lived in sub-Saharan Africa. Although the number of newly infected people and the number of deaths in sub-Saharan Africa has declined, women and girls continue to be the most vulnerable part of the population, accounting for a majority of the population living with HIV/AIDS. The prevalence of HIV has increased in eastern Europe and Central Asia, North America and western Europe, Bangladesh, and the Philippines, among regions and countries, while the rate of new infections in India, Nepal, and Thailand fell in the last ten years.[‡] There are many repercussions of HIV/AIDS because people whose immune systems are compromised by AIDS are vulnerable to other diseases such as tuberculosis and malaria which, like AIDS, are fueled by and contribute to poverty.

In the global picture of AIDS, one main problem is that the resources to fight this disease are concentrated in developed countries. Although scientists have developed antiretroviral drugs[§] that halt the debilitating advance of AIDS, and even though the cost of these drugs has come down dramatically in the last ten years, they still remain expensive for the poor in most developing countries. In addition, these countries lack medical staff to treat AIDS patients, funds for education and prevention programs,

---

[*]National Institute of Allergies and Infectious Diseases, "Antimicrobial (Drug) Resistance," www.niaid.nih.gov/topics/antimicrobialResistance/Understanding/Pages/default.aspx.

[†]Centers for Disease Control and Prevention, "Antimicrobial Resistance Posing Growing Health Threat," April 7, 2011, www.cdc.gov/media/releases/2011/p0407_antimicrobialresistance.html.

[‡]UNAIDS Fact Sheets. UNAIDS frequently updates its fact sheets and displays data by region. For the most recent material, see www.unaids.org/en/mediaCenterPressMaterias/FactSheets.asp.

[§]HIV is a retrovirus that weakens the immune system. Antiretroviral drugs prevent HIV from replicating and spreading the virus within the body.

and people to implement the programs. As the death toll of the disease cuts deeper into the adult population—taking away parents, teachers, professionals, and workers, and striking hardest at women—economies and communities begin to stagger. With inadequate treatment and no vaccine to prevent AIDS even after thirty years, this damage threatens to stretch indefinitely into the future.

STAKES AND STAKEHOLDERS

Public health leaders, policymakers, pharmaceutical companies, NGOs, political leaders, health care workers, journalists, and ordinary citizens are seeking to persuade the global community that everyone is a stakeholder in pandemics, resistance to antibiotics, and the ongoing HIV/AIDS crisis. Indeed, confronting global health crises poses economic, social justice, security, political, medical-scientific, and cultural challenges, as the following broad questions suggest.

How Should the Global Community and Nations Manage Influenza Pandemics?   Much debate centers on what global collaborative strategies and emergency health procedures to establish and how money should be allocated to prepare for pandemics. Public health and political leaders seek to mobilize health/science/technology resources proactively. They are calling for national and international plans for vaccinations (for instance, deciding which part of a population should be vaccinated first), for quarantine, and for sharing information and decision-making power among international, national, and local authorities. Policy analysts and medical professionals argue for the need to identify social justice factors such as race, ethnicity, gender, and socioeconomic status that may affect a group's information about and access to prevention and treatment in the event of a pandemic.

People disagree about whether influenza viruses pose a global security threat. Some argue that these pandemics deserve as much funding as military spending and even merit military support. These advocates point out how easily viruses or deadly bacteria could be deployed in bioterrorist attacks and how swiftly such an infectious disease could disrupt transportation systems, manufacturing, businesses, schools, hospitals, and whole countries. In contrast, opponents see much less danger and urgency in biological attacks, bird flu, or other influenza pandemics.

Much of this debate over pandemics focuses on balancing national and global interests to ensure that countries work fairly and respectfully together on prevention and containment. Citing China's dangerous silence over SARS when it tried for months to cover up this virulent disease while it spread and was carried beyond China's borders, some voices stress that all countries must agree to be open and responsible about reporting virus outbreaks and to share scientific/medical information in timely ways.

How Should Nations and the Global Community Respond to the Problem of Antimicrobial Resistance and Overuse of Antibiotics?   According to the World Health Organization, "[a]ntimicrobial resistance is not a new problem but one that is becoming more dangerous."[*] Stakeholders, policymakers, and health professionals disagree about the most important steps to combat this problem. Some believe that global organizations such as the WTO and UN should regulate the over-the-counter availability of antibiotics. Others believe that countries and individuals should curb the prescription and consumption of antibiotics as a conservation measure to avoid further diminishing of the effectiveness of broad-spectrum antibiotics. Others think we should place emphasis on regulating the prophylactic use of antibiotics in animal husbandry, particularly relevant in the evolution of resistant *Escherichia coli (E. coli)*. Some who see the business/economic angle of the problem think the global community should provide an economic incentive for pharmaceutical companies, which are reluctant to invest in the development of new antibiotics with a limited life span or low profit margin.

What Is the Relationship Between the AIDS Pandemic, Poverty, and Global Security?   For the last decade, rich Western countries have tended to regard AIDS as largely a problem of the developing world.[†] While it is true that increasingly convenient and affordable advances in medicine, such as the recent development of one daily pill in affluent countries, have given AIDS patients options for longer life, the rate of new cases of HIV/AIDS has not slowed in the United States and western Europe.

- **Addressing Poverty First, Health Care First, or AIDS.** Some humanitarians argue that free trade agreements favoring rich countries have caused poverty, and poverty has nurtured AIDS as well as malaria, tuberculosis, and waterborne diseases. Condemning U.S. negligence, Jeffrey Sachs, the lead economist of the UN Millennium Development Project, recently wrote that poverty in Africa is killing 20,000 people a day.[‡] Advocates like Sachs say that poverty must be addressed directly along with AIDS, in part by ensuring that global trade works for developing countries. Recently, the U.S. Global Health Initiative argued that improving the health of women, newborns, and children is key to a sustainable response to HIV/AIDS. However, some stakeholders believe that developed nations should tackle the health crises of the

---

[*]World Health Organization, "World Health Day 2011", www.who.int/world-health-day/2011/en/index.html.

[†]Within the United States, the fight against AIDS has been—and still is—embroiled in moral and religious controversy over homosexuality and gay rights as well as in social justice, class, and race issues.

[‡]"Thousands Died in Africa Yesterday," *New York Times*, February 27, 2005.

AIDS pandemic immediately, before effective solutions to the deeper causes of poverty can be found and implemented. These analysts, activists, public health advocates, and philanthropists want the world to concentrate on achieving scientific breakthroughs and delivering these discoveries and treatments to the poor countries in need. Still others question whether the United States can pour money into the economies and health of developing countries when the country itself lacks a universal health care system, many Americans have no medical insurance, and the child and family poverty rate is increasing.

- **AIDS as a Security Issue.** In addition to treating the suffering from AIDS in developing countries as a social justice issue, many policymakers and activists believe the devastation of AIDS poses a major global security threat. They underscore the economic and social destruction caused by AIDS in Africa: food production interrupted by the death of farmers; social and governmental institutions weakened by the loss of professionals; children orphaned and left without adult guidance, income, or opportunity for education. These activists warn that desperate people and weakened countries create grounds for terrorism to germinate and destabilize the whole world.

What Prevention and Treatment Offer the Best Ways to Combat AIDS?   Prevention and treatment are tied up in politics, economics, and cultural values.

- **Control of Drugs.** Some economic and political conflicts over *how* to prevent and treat AIDS involve who should have control over donated funds for prevention and treatment programs. For example, the United States has tended to promote AIDS treatment in the form of brand-name antiretroviral drugs from big-name pharmaceutical companies that have been tested and approved. However, poor African countries have preferred less-expensive and simpler generic drugs from India that are easier for AIDS patients to learn how to take. One group of stakeholders includes scientists, research institutions, drug companies, and policymakers who emphasize the role of science and technology in combating and conquering AIDS. These stakeholders are pushing for improved drugs and a vaccine.

- **International Partnerships.** Another economic and political issue involves which governments and institutions should direct the administering of drugs: global institutions like the United Nations, its agencies, and the Global AIDS Fund; or the United States acting unilaterally or multilaterally? Some African leaders and countries like Mozambique have welcomed Western aid while insisting that they have a major role in managing these global contributions; otherwise, they say, this aid will become simply a new chapter in a history of Western domination. Establishing successful private–public and rich country–poor country partnerships is challenging. Brazil and Thailand offer examples of how strong government involvement and commitment coupled with effective public–private partnerships can help countries deal with AIDS.

A further dispute over prevention and treatment pits some of those African countries and activists who seek systemic, long-term change against Western benefactors who want to focus on the AIDS crisis only. While advocates for systemic change believe rich countries should help African countries build their own national health systems—a long-term solution that respects national sovereignty and fosters self-determination—in recent years, the U.S. government and some nonprofit aid organizations have objected to helping countries such as Liberia, Zimbabwe, and Swaziland that have corrupt governments. Other organizations protest that people suffering under these corrupt governments especially need help, and that such policies will prevent NGOs from critical work with groups of people who are especially endangered by HIV/AIDS.

- **The Role of Cultural Values, Ethics, and Religion.** Many leaders and human rights activists in developing countries endorse holistic approaches that work with cultural values and traditions from within the cultural frames of the people who need help. For instance, Marina Mahathir, president of the Malaysian AIDS Council and daughter of Malaysia's prime minister, rejects generic programs and stresses attuning AIDS prevention and treatment to specific countries, regions, and subgroups of people: "All the responses have to be tailor-made—sometimes even more locally, even to specific communities. . . . There's no way you can talk to women the same way you talk to men about this issue. Talking to young people has to be different than talking to old people."[*] Many people working with prevention and treatment in Africa stress the need to factor in male social, economic, and sexual dominance, which is seen in polygamy and male reluctance to use condoms. Prevention manuals given to women will not help when women lack sexual autonomy and have few economic rights. Instead, holistic and cultural approaches to the fight against AIDS focus on empowering women, especially through education. One example of Africans working within their culture for social change is popular Zimbabwean singer Oliver Mtukudzi, who has written songs about the pain of watching loved ones die of AIDS in the hope of combating the social shame of this disease.

Other stakeholders point out how AIDS prevention is entangled in ethics and religion. The 2004 vision for the U.S. President's Emergency Plan for AIDS Relief (PEPFAR), for example, limited funding for programs that did not emphasize abstinence-only as an AIDS prevention

---

[*]Rachel S. Taylor, "Interview: Marina Mahathir," *World Press Review*, November 25, 2002, www.worldpress.org/print_article.cfm?article_id=933&don't=yes.

strategy and programs that did not denounce prostitution. Though those restrictions were lifted when the plan was reauthorized in 2008, some faith-based Western organizations, both Protestant and Catholic, and African Catholicism stress abstinence and faithfulness, downplaying or rejecting entirely sex-positive measures such as the use of condoms.[*] For some Africans, condoms represent Western individualism and consumerism, which are at odds with African communal values. However, many public health workers and activists continue to argue for the value, even necessity, of condoms in the fight against the AIDS pandemic.

Thinking Visually

The Threat of Pandemics

This image depicts a scene from the 2011 film *Contagion*, about a flulike virus that jumps from wildlife to domesticated animals to humans and rapidly kills millions of people throughout the world. The disease path and evolution of the virus; the response of public health, medical, and government officials; and the development of a vaccine were imagined by W. Ian Lipkin, a professor at Columbia University's Center for Infection and Immunity, who served as a consultant for this film. He wanted to design a realistic virus for this film in order to alert the public and the government to the real need for better systems to handle health crises like pandemics.

Claudette Barius/Warner Bros/courtesy Everett Collection

---

[*]See the President's Emergency Plan for AIDS Relief, www.pepfar.gov, and the 2008 reallocation bill, which removed some of the funding restrictions, fpc.state.gov/documents/organization/110385.pdf.

Questions to Ponder

1. How could you emphasize the details of this scene and the overall impression it gives to support an argument that our federal, state, and local governments need to invest more money in preparation for pandemics? On the other hand, how might someone cite this scene as an example of the media's use of fear tactics to shape people's views on public health issues like pandemics?

2. What questions about a pandemic's ability to disrupt public services and create social and political disorder does this still from the film suggest?

The three sections that follow—Student Voice, International Voices, and Global Hot Spot—make these global controversies over the spread of disease more personal and concrete.

 STUDENT VOICE: Experiencing the SARS Pandemic by Mark Merin

In 2003, SARS unnerved the global community. Seeming to appear from nowhere in China, it was later discovered to have jumped from wild civets (weasel-like creatures eaten as a delicacy) to humans. Especially virulent, it sickened many of the medical staff caring for patients. Epidemiologists discovered that the SARS virus could survive outside the human body for hours, even days, and therefore could be transmitted even without direct contact; and there was no vaccine or cure. Showing how these facts generated social anxiety and triggered governmental restraints, student Mark Merin writes about experiencing this epidemic firsthand. In the following narrative, Mark recounts his effort to complete his senior year of high school in Taiwan while SARS was disrupting and transforming ordinary daily life.

We were all confident that Taiwan had taken the necessary precautions to prevent the SARS epidemic from reaching us. However, not even the doctors and high tech machinery on standby at the airport were enough to prevent SARS from coming. The numerous businessmen who traveled back and forth weekly from China and Hong Kong to Taiwan must have brought it. Soon enough, we were reading about it in the papers, seeing it on the news, hearing about it on the radio.

I went out every day armed with two essentials, a disposable mask and a small bottle of isopropyl alcohol. Whenever I entered a public area such as a bus or a movie theatre, I put on the mask, and afterwards I sprayed my hands with alcohol. Others around me did the same. Certain pharmaceutical companies soon began to raise the prices on masks. Some companies even developed better and more efficient ones. These disposable masks typically cost from four to twelve dollars apiece, so people were spending anywhere from twenty-eight to eighty-four dollars every week. It was ludicrous, but everyone was afraid. You would see people wearing masks everywhere you went, from restaurants to stores and most especially on airplanes.

Every day I would read in the paper of how several people were quarantined under suspicion of being infected by SARS. People didn't want to get SARS, and people also didn't want to be suspected of having it. They all feared that the government would quarantine them. As the virus infected more people, the government decided to pass a new law: any person with a fever had to report it to the nearest medical facility or be fined several thousand dollars. Thermometers became widely sold in Taiwan after several weeks. The government continually urged people to check their temperature at least three times a day. Fear began to grow and even the slightest feeling of discomfort or sickness would send people into a panic thinking they had SARS. When people sneezed or even coughed on buses or in any public area, those near them would immediately draw away in fear.

While all this was happening in the city, at home I was thinking, "Oh it won't ever affect me that much." I was wrong. My school soon initiated SARS prevention measures. We all had to have our temperatures taken before entering school grounds. Every morning at 7:45, hundreds of students from kindergarten to high school lined up at the doors waiting to get their temperatures taken. Many students were late to class. The school's fears were not unfounded. In fact, one student and the rest of his family were confined in a hospital because they had all been infected by SARS. Unfortunately, a week later I read in the school newspaper that the father had passed away. The school administrators panicked.

Our senior class started worrying about what would happen if SARS got any worse. It would mean an end to senior trips. Maybe colleges would re-evaluate us because we came from countries infected with SARS. Then it hit us. Classes were cancelled a month earlier than planned. A teacher suspected of developing SARS symptoms came into contact with the entire faculty of my school during a conference, and all classes were cancelled because all the teachers were put under quarantine. Advanced placement tests were in question, senior prom was cancelled, and graduation became a maybe.

Several of my friends left the country right away. They didn't care if they weren't there for their exams or for graduation as long as they were safe from the deadly epidemic. Most of us didn't even get to say goodbye. Up to this day, I haven't seen a majority of those friends. The good news, however, was that the school contacted various substitute teachers to sit in while we took our exams. Graduation was thankfully also not cancelled. However, before entering the graduation grounds, temperatures had to be taken.

By the time I had to leave for college, the SARS epidemic had been controlled. Occasionally, I still hear news of SARS resurfacing, but so far those reports have quickly faded away. I think the Taiwan government, having learned through this experience, would now be more efficient in dealing with the threat of SARS or other similar diseases.

INTERNATIONAL VOICES

While many developed nations worry about and plan for the potential outbreak of a pandemic flu or the threat of a bioterrorist attack, other nations, particularly in the developing world, deal with widespread disease as a fact of daily life and argue that we must address the root conditions that allow epidemic diseases to survive and flourish. According to the CDC, water- and sanitation-related diseases caused by unsafe water, inadequate sanitation, or insufficient hygiene are linked to 88 percent of diarrhea cases worldwide and result in 1.5 million deaths each year, mostly in young children. The president of Liberia, Ellen Johnson-Sirleaf, believes that we will not be able to achieve the United Nations' Millennium Development Goals without increasing access to basic sanitation. The following is an excerpt from her commentary titled "The Orphan Development Goal," which appeared in the *International Herald Tribune* on September 17, 2010. In it, she exhorts the UN General Assembly to go beyond the Millennium Development Goal of halving the number of people without access to sanitation and water and to commit to ending what she terms "water sanitation and poverty."

Liberian President Promotes Sanitation to Reduce Widespread Disease

We will hear much in the coming days about maternal health and child mortality, about gender equality and combating disease. These are critically important issues and it is absolutely right that we focus on safe motherhood, redouble our efforts to fight H.I.V./AIDS and malaria, and improve the lives of women and children in all developing countries. What we will almost certainly not hear much about, however, is the most off-track and possibly least fashionable Millennium Development Goal intervention—sanitation. . . .

There are 2.6 billion people who will go through today, just as they do every day, without a proper toilet. According to a recent report in the *Lancet*, the biggest killer of African children under five is diarrhea, which kills more children globally than AIDS, measles and malaria combined. The vast majority of these deaths could be prevented by investing in safe toilet facilities, clean drinking water supplies, and raising awareness of the need to improve hygiene practices—for example, washing hands with soap. These simple and cost-effective interventions can also significantly reduce other leading causes of child deaths, such as pneumonia and under-nutrition.

GLOBAL HOT SPOT: Sub-Saharan Africa

News reports, interviews, and personal accounts from sub-Saharan African countries show how AIDS has hurt children and women especially. Some of the most disturbing news tells of children who have experienced the death of one or both parents (called "double orphans") and who are now forced to live with grandparents or any other remaining relatives or are thrown into the streets to fend for themselves. Women's unequal access to education and economic opportunities, as well as their limited access to reproductive health services and susceptibility to gender violence, reveal how women's oppression contributes to the spread of AIDS. The following excerpt is from the article "Africa: Five Ways to Reduce Women's Vulnerability to HIV," published on the news site plusnews.org (IRIN) on March 8, 2011.

In many developing countries, women have very limited access to vital reproductive health services. A combination of biological and social factors means women are more vulnerable to sexually transmitted infections (STIs), which, if left untreated, increase their vulnerability to HIV. . . .

One in three women has been beaten, experienced sexual violence or otherwise been abused in their lifetime, according to the UN; one in five will be a victim of rape or attempted rape. More often than not, the perpetrators are known to the women.

Practices such as early marriage, FGM/C and human trafficking all increase women's vulnerability to HIV, but more accepted forms of violence, such as marital rape, also play a large part in increasing women's HIV risk.

Experiencing violence increases the risk of HIV infection by a factor of three. . . .

The readings in this chapter explore these global health controversies from different perspectives.

READINGS

The Age of Pandemics
Larry Brilliant

Larry Brilliant, MD, MPH, is president and CEO of the Skoll Global Threats Fund. He has also been vice president of Google and the executive director of Google.org, and he has worked as an epidemiologist for WHO and UNICEF on smallpox eradication, polio eradication, and blindness. His awards include the Peacemaker Award in 2005, the TED Prize in 2006, and a UN Global Leadership Award in 2008. This op-ed piece appeared in the *Wall Street Journal* on May 2, 2009, while Dr. Brilliant was serving as chair of the National Biosurveillance Advisory Subcommittee. The *Wall Street Journal* is a daily newspaper focusing on business news and financial information.

> How does Larry Brilliant tailor his public health argument to the *Wall Street Journal's* business audience?

In 1967, the country's surgeon general, William Stewart, famously said, "The time has come to close the book on infectious diseases. We have basically wiped out infection in the United States." This premature victory declaration, perhaps based on early public health victories over 19th-century infectious diseases, has entered the lore of epidemiologists who know that, if anything, the time has come to open the book to a new and dangerous chapter on 21st-century communicable diseases.

Indeed, to the epidemiological community, the Influenza Pandemic of 2009 is one of the most widely anticipated diseases in history. Epidemiologists have been shouting from rooftops that a pandemic (or, a world-wide epidemic) of influenza is overdue, and that it is not a matter of "if" but "when." The current pathogen creating the threat is actually a mixture of viral genetic elements from all over the globe that have sorted, shifted, sorted, shifted, drifted and recombined to form this worrisome virus.

No one knows if the 2009 swine flu will behave like the 1918 Spanish flu that killed 50 million to 100 million world-wide, or like the 1957 Asian flu and 1968 Hong Kong flu that killed far fewer. This 2009 flu may weaken and lose its virulence, or strengthen and gain virulence—we just do not know.

Here's the good news: Compared with a few years ago, the world is somewhat better prepared to deal with pandemic influenza. There have been training meetings, table-top exercises, dry runs and preparedness drills at virtually every level of government and civil society. World Health Organization member states have agreed on a set of regulations that require all members to report the status of diseases of global significance within their borders. We have two effective antiviral drugs, at least for the time being. There have been some breakthroughs to reduce the time required to get effective vaccines into the field, and there is even a small chance that last year's seasonal vaccine will help protect lives from H1N1. In the U.S. at least, influenza surveillance has improved.

Here's the bad news: Today, we remain underprepared for any pandemic or major outbreak, whether it comes from newly emerging infectious diseases, bioterror attack or laboratory accident. We do not have the best general disease surveillance systems or "surge" capacity in our hospitals and health-care facilities. We do not have enough beds, respirators or seasoned public-health staff (many of whom, because of the financial meltdown, ironically got pink slips from their state and county health departments days or even hours before WHO declared we are at a Phase 5 alert, one step short of its highest global level). We not only need to retain the public-health people we have, we quickly need to train a new generation of 21st-century workers who know both the old diseases and have mastered the computer and other digital technologies and genomic advances to keep them ahead of the newest emerging threats.

And there is worse news: The 2009 swine flu will not be the last and may not be the worst pandemic that we will face in the coming years. Indeed, we might be entering an Age of Pandemics.

In our lifetimes, or our children's lifetimes, we will face a broad array of dangerous emerging 21st-century diseases, man-made or natural, brand-new or old, newly resistant to our current vaccines and antiviral drugs. You can bet on it.

One of the top scientists in the world did bet on it. A few years ago, Lord Martin Rees, who holds three of the most distinguished titles in the scientific world (Astronomer Royal; Master of Trinity College, Cambridge; and head of the 350-year-old Royal Society, London) offered a $1,000 wager that bioterror or bioerror would unleash a catastrophic event claiming one million lives in the next two decades. Lord Rees said: "There's real concern about whether our civilization can be safeguarded without us sacrificing too much in terms of privacy, diversity and individualism."

Risks from bioterror are unpredictable, of course, but I think it's fair to say that world-wide access to infectious agents and basic biological know-how has grown more rapidly than even the exponential growth of computing power. According to Moore's law, the number of transistors on a chip doubles in 18 to 24 months—or, said another way, the "the bang for the buck" in computers doubles in less than two years.

The technologies supporting bioterror have exploded even faster than computing power. The cost of genomic sequencing, as one example of a supporting technology, has gone down from the nearly $1 billion it cost for the first full human DNA sequences to the low thousands for consumers in the coming years. Genetic engineering of viruses is much less complex and far less expensive than sequencing human DNA. Bioterror weapons are cheap and do not need huge labs or government support. They are the poor man's WMD.

Naturally occurring diseases with pandemic potential are much more ubiquitous and more certain to occur. Over the last decades, we have seen more than three dozen new infectious diseases appear, some of which could kill millions of people with one or two unlucky gene mutations or one or two unfavorable environmental changes. The risks of pandemics only increase as the human population grows, the world loses greenbelts, uninhabited land disappears and more humans hunt and eat wild animals.

Most pathogenic viruses that affect humans have originated in animals and jumped to humans; for that reason, we call them "zoonoses." They account for 60% of all infectious diseases, and 75% of all emerging infections.

Some of these diseases are well-known: bird flu, SARS, HIV/AIDS, West Nile, Monkey-pox and Ebola. Some are brand-new, like the arenavirus that was first found only a few months ago when it caused a handful of deaths in Africa and was genetically sequenced and identified by Ian Lipkin at Columbia University. He believes there may be as many as one million viruses that remain to be discovered.

Why are more new viruses with pandemic potential jumping from their traditional animal hosts to humans now? If I had to choose a single word answer it would be: "modernity." If I had two more words, I would add "human irresponsibility." And of course so much of this peril is made much worse by the Great Exacerbator—climate change and global warming.

Increasingly, humans push every conceivable barrier, and we now occupy more land that was historically the province of animals than ever before. More humans come in contact with animals and their viruses because there is less rain forest, jungle and wild lands separating them. Partly driven by poverty and lack of access to other food sources, Africans last year consumed nearly 700 million wild animals, about two billion kilograms of "bush meat." Scientists like Nathan Wolfe of the Global Viral Forecasting Initiative are taking matching blood specimens from the bush-meat hunters and the animals they kill, in an attempt to predict which virus will jump next.

If sub-Saharan Africa is the hotspot for blood-borne diseases, the Mekong area bounded by China, Myanmar, Laos, Thailand and Cambodia is the hotspot for respiratory diseases like SARS or pandemic bird flu. In these countries, the issue is not poverty but relative prosperity that has led to increased raising of cattle and chickens, and increased meat consumption. In China, the numbers of chickens raised for food has increased 1,000-fold over the past few decades. In parts of Southeast Asia, humans and chickens—and pigs—live so close together, exchanging viruses, it looks almost like a science experiment.

As climate change causes sea levels to rise and aquifers to dip dangerously into salty water, agricultural lands yield fewer calories of food per acre. That leads farmers to cut down jungle, creating deforested areas which once served as barriers to the zoonotic viruses that each day have more opportunities to jump from bats and rodents and monkeys and civet cats to humans. As temperatures rise and seashores change, animals head inland and to higher ground, moving into heavily populated human areas. Soon there will be human climate refugees on the move into land once thought uninhabitable. All of these changes increase the potential for humans and animals to exchange new viruses.

I chair the National Biosurveillance Advisory Subcommittee, created by a presidential directive in 2008, comprising some of the smartest and most dedicated public health professionals I have ever met. We've been working to understand our national capability to respond to these emerging threats. Our first report will be released shortly. I can't prerelease it, but its contents will come as no surprise. We are concerned that the nation and the world do not have adequate "early warning" or biosurveillance capabilities. We are recommending that governments need far better early warning systems for potential pandemics and other epidemic threats. We are also emphasizing that public health be restored to a position of respect and be given resources commensurate with its duty to protect us all from these and other threats to our health.

In the 1970s I had the great good fortune that my first job out of medical school was to be the junior-most member of the WHO's smallpox-eradication program in India. I was, in Silicon Valley terms, the third or fourth "hire" for the team that would create history and eradicate smallpox from India and South Asia. I stayed in India for nearly a decade and went back at the end of the program to turn off the lights and document this amazing success story, the only disease in history to be eradicated.

Smallpox killed 500 million people in the 20th century alone. The global smallpox program cost $150 million total in 1965 dollars; each year, in addition to lives saved from ending this terrible disease, the U.S. reaps economic benefits exceeding $2 billion from eliminating routine vaccination and the handful of very serious adverse consequences, including three or four vaccine-caused deaths, airport checkpoints (remember those little yellow cards?) and the loss of time away from work and school.

In analyzing the effect of loss of travel and trade in addition to the health-care costs of a possible bird-flu pandemic, Bank of Montreal chief economist Sherry Cooper estimated the global costs of a "mild" pandemic to be 2% of global GDP, which in 2005 dollars was $1.1 trillion. There is a stark contrast between savings in lives and treasure from investing in public health and prevention, increasing training programs, funding the research that leads to better vaccines, more lab capacity, improved antivirals and early warning systems—and the human and economic costs of not acting in time. The business community should be at the front of the line, advocating for prevention and public health, one of the history's best investments by any criteria.

There is hope for some good news on that front: Another disease may soon be checked off the list of human scourges. Because of the dedicated staff of WHO and Unicef, and the generosity of Rotary International, the Bill and Melinda Gates Foundation and others, polio, with only 1,500 cases in the world last year, may soon follow smallpox into the dustbin of history. The Carter Center has also brought Guinea worm close to its demise as well.

That is either one, two or three diseases that could be ticked off the list of humanity's worst afflictions, with great savings in lives, health and wealth. Reducing the number of terrible forms of suffering is what we all want, but I fear that if we don't take seriously the factors that could make the next decade the Age of Pandemics, we will start moving backward, adding lethal diseases to that list—instead of subtracting them.

For Class Discussion

1. How does Brilliant support his claim that we have entered "an Age of Pandemics" and that a pandemic virus is imminent?

2. What causal reasoning does Brilliant use to argue the role that environmental concerns such as climate change, population, and deforestation play in the likelihood of a pandemic virus?

3. How does Brilliant establish his credibility in this argument?

4. What role does technology play in bioterrorism and global health issues?

5. By what cost-benefit analysis does Brilliant make a case for the business angle on public health issues? What do you find persuasive about his argument in this piece?

The Impact of Disparities in Health on Pandemic Preparedness
David Satcher

Dr. David Satcher served as the surgeon general of the United States from 1998 to 2002 and simultaneously held the position of assistant secretary for health from 1998 to 2001. During his term, he focused on eliminating racial and ethnic disparities in health, and he released surgeon general's reports on topics including tobacco and health, mental health, sexual health and responsible sexual behavior, and obesity. He is currently director of the Satcher Health Leadership Institute at the Morehouse School of Medicine and serves on the board of directors for Johnson & Johnson and the Kaiser Family Foundation. Prior to serving as surgeon general, Dr. Satcher worked as director of the Centers for Disease Control and Prevention (CDC) and as president of Meharry Medical College. While at Meharry, Dr. Satcher founded the *Journal of Health Care for the Poor and Underserved*, a peer-reviewed journal focusing on the health care of medically underserved communities from a North American, Central American, Caribbean, and sub-Saharan African perspective. This commentary was published in the *Journal of Health Care for the Poor and Underserved* in 2011.

> According to David Satcher, what are the stakes in this argument about public health?

Pandemic illness would threaten family, community, and national security. Globally, pandemics such as smallpox, polio, and more recently HIV/AIDS have left a trail of destruction of individuals, homes, communities, and institutions. Pandemics have destroyed educational, economic, and political stability and progress. Well over 15 million orphans have been left in Africa by AIDS alone. Thus pandemic preparedness is one of the most important goals for us as individuals, families, and communities.

Health disparities and global health inequities represent some of the greatest barriers to pandemic preparedness. Elimination of disparities in health and the drive toward global health equity must be major components of our commitment to pandemic preparedness.

Some of the most striking areas of disparities in health in the United States are represented by differences in health outcomes between African Americans and the majority population. For example, African Americans are two and a half times more likely to die in the first year of life (infant mortality) and eight times as likely to be infected with HIV/AIDS as the majority.[*,†] African Americans are also 35% more likely to die of

---

[*]Mathews TJ, MacDorman MF. Infant mortality statistics from the 2006 period linked birth/infant death data set. Natl Vital Stat Rep. 2010 Apr 30;58(17):1–31.
[†]Centers for Disease Control and Prevention. Disparities in diagnoses of HIV infection between Blacks/African Americans and other racial/ethnic populations—37 states, 2005–2008. MMWR Morb Mortal Wkly Rep. 2011 Feb 4;60(4):93–8.

cancer and have the highest mortality rates in the four leading causes of cancer death in America (lung, colorectal, breast and prostate).* Similarly, African Americans are 30% to 35% more likely to die of cardiovascular disease.*

Why are disparities in health and health inequities major barriers to pandemic preparedness? Disparities in health include disparities in health outcomes, health care quality, and health access.† Major components of pandemic preparedness include health awareness, early detection of health problems (especially the onset of infectious diseases), access to vaccines to prevent infectious diseases, and early intervention to treat infectious diseases.

People who lack access to health care are more likely to be uninformed about the risk of a pandemic, less likely to trust messages they do hear, less likely to be immunized early against new infections, and more likely to ignore messages that they hear from the government about ways to protect themselves.‡

In the eradication of smallpox, a major component of the strategy for control and elimination of the disease was early detection and intervention, including virtual surrounding of persons with the disease with persons who were vaccinated such that the disease could not spread.§

This strategy was successful in Africa and India and other places throughout the world. But in order for the strategy to be implemented, village and religious leaders had to be first convinced that it was in the best interest of the community and then had to convince their people to cooperate.¥

Any successful strategy for pandemic preparedness in the United States must overcome the barriers of disparities in access to care, including lack of information, distrust of information, lack of access to early detection and to early intervention.

---

*Centers for Disease Control and Prevention. The burden of chronic diseases and their risk factors. Atlanta, GA: Department of Health and Human Services, 2004.

†Smedley BD, Stith AY, Nelson AR, eds. Unequal treatment: confronting racial and ethnic disparities in health care. Washington, DC: National Academies Press, 2003.

‡Vaughn E, Tinker T. Effective health risk communication about pandemic influenza for vulnerable populations. Am J Public Health. 2009 Oct;99 Suppl 2:S324–S332.

§Henderson DA, Inglesby TV, Bartlett JG, et al. Smallpox as a biological weapon: medical and public health management. Working Group on Civilian Biodefense. JAMA. 1999 Jun 9;281(22):2127–37.

¥Fenner F, Henderon DA, Arita I, et al. Smallpox and its eradication. Geneva, Switzerland: World Health Organization, 1988.

While it will be too late to change a system of care that has worked to create disparities for years, it would be critical to engage and convince community leaders that preparedness planning and the critical components of it are in the best interest of their community.

According to our study of the mortality ratios between African Americans and Whites in the United States, there are over 83,000 deaths among African Americans each year that would not occur if African Americans had the same health outcomes as the majority population. This is even in the absence of pandemics, while any pandemic will increase excess deaths. It will also be exacerbated by disparities in health and health inequities.*

Thus it is very clear that in order for us to succeed in pandemic preparedness we must attack disparities in health and the conditions that lead to disparities in health and health outcomes. Globally we must begin to work for global health equity as a way of protecting health of all of the people.

For Class Discussion

1. What is Satcher's central claim in this brief commentary?

2. What are some of the factors contributing to "disparities in health outcomes, health care quality, and health access" discussed by Dr. Satcher? What additional factors could you cite?

3. Although this piece is written for an audience educated in the field of public health, how does Dr. Satcher make his argument accessible to a broader audience?

4. According to Satcher, what are the causal connections between pandemic preparedness and questions of social justice?

5. While Larry Brilliant focuses on the conditions leading up to a pandemic illness, what would be the results of a pandemic according to Dr. Satcher?

6. Using Satcher's precedent of convincing village and religious leaders in Africa and India that preparedness is in the best interest of their community, who are the community leaders and influential voices in your or other American communities?

---

*Satcher D, Fryer GE Jr, McCann J, et al. What if we were equal? A comparison of the Black-White mortality gap in 1960 and 2000. Health Affairs. 2005;24(2):459–64.

Ten Years Later, What's Changed?
Ali S. Khan

Rear Admiral Ali S. Khan, MD, MPH, is an assistant surgeon general for the United States and the leader of the Centers for Disease Control and Prevention's (CDC) Office of Public Health Preparedness and Response. He received his MD from Downstate Medical Center in Brooklyn, New York, and his MPH from Emory University. He has worked for the CDC since 1991, and in the last decade, he has responded to and led emergency responses to health emergencies including hantavirus, Ebola virus, monkeypox, avian influenza (bird flu), and SARS, the Asian tsunami, and Hurricane Katrina. Dr. Khan served as one of the main architects of the CDC's public health bioterrorism preparedness program. This commentary was posted to the CDC's Public Health Matters blog on September 2, 2011. The blog is authored by members of the CDC who are on "the front lines of emerging infectious diseases and public health emergencies." According to Khan, it was created to "share our public health passions about the evolution of public health and the continual strides that are being made to protect and save lives through education, awareness, research, and promoting healthy lifestyles."

> What is the rhetorical effect of using the tenth anniversary of 9/11 to frame Ali Khan's argument about public health preparedness?

The events of 9/11 will forever be engrained in our memories. The attacks on the twin towers, Pentagon, and the anthrax attacks which followed were unimaginable at the time. Ten years after these tragic events, what's changed?

We now know that terrorist threats are ever present and that our nation must be in a constant state of vigilance in order to protect our communities. We've come a long way since 2001 in bolstering our nation's ability to prepare for and respond to catastrophic events whether natural, accidental, or intentional. We are also learning more and more every day that the resources we need for the big disasters are much the same as the ones we use for everyday public health activities.

Check out my list of **top 5 accomplishments** in the years after the 2001 attacks:

5. A much-needed **global perspective** that acknowledges that pandemics or terrorist threats don't stop at geographic borders. A number of programs have been established to rapidly detect and contain emerging health threats, including bioterrorism threats. Programs like CDC's Global Disease Detection are increasingly focused on building local capacity to support global

efforts directed at preparedness and response for disease out-breaks. This means identifying potential outbreaks or threats where they emerge and before they have a chance to spread globally.

4. Improved **communication and information sharing.** Response efforts following the 9/11 and anthrax attacks lacked the kind of integrated communication and unified command needed for a large scale response. Information critical for decision making was not shared between agencies and there were difficulties keeping local, state, and federal officials informed. Today we have systems such as Epi-X and the Health Alert Network (HAN), which allow health officials to access and share information quickly with other professionals and the public. In addition, public health departments in every state have established relationships and conducted exercises with key emergency management players such as law enforcement, fire departments, and hospitals.

3. **Establishment and expansion of federal resources.** The 2001 anthrax attacks were a wake up call to the realities of bioterrorism. Scientists in laboratories and doctors in hospitals had to be ready at all times to identify illnesses related to bioterrorism and treat victims of these attacks. This is no small feat as illnesses linked to bioterrorism often mimic the symptoms of more common maladies. Not to mention, once a cause is identified, treatment is not always something readily available. Before 1999, CDC performed all tests to detect and confirm the presence of biological threat agents such as anthrax. This took up valuable time when every second counted. Today, more than 150 laboratories across the nation belong to CDC's Laboratory Response Network and can test for biological agents, saving both time and money. Additionally, CDC's Strategic National Stockpile now ensures the availability of key medical supplies and all states have plans to receive, distribute, and dispense these assets. To help prevent improper use of select agents and toxins (e.g., anthrax, Ebola virus, botulinum), CDC's Division of Select Agents and Toxins helps provide oversight by licensing, registering, and identifying entities working with these agents.

2. **Federal funding for states and localities** to build and strengthen their ability to prevent and respond to disasters. The events of 2001 revealed our vulnerability to the use of weapons of mass destruction and made public health a new participant in the national security discussion. Significant investments were made in state and local preparedness and response infrastructure,

planning, and capability development for "routine" outbreaks and in the face of large scale disasters and epidemics. Today CDC provides funding to all 50 states, 4 metropolitan areas, and 8 territories. Grantees use this money to support laboratories, outbreak investigations, and risk communication, among other things.

1. Following the 2001 attacks there was a **cultural shift** in how we think about national security. It had become apparent that public health played an important role in national security. The terrorist attacks changed the way state and city health departments worked and interacted with other agencies and sectors. Health departments are increasingly becoming accepted as equal partners by traditional first responders, including law enforcement, fire departments and emergency medical services. These interactions are supported by the incorporation of public health components into the National Response Framework and National Incident Management System (the "playbooks" federal, state, and local responders use to plan for and respond to emergencies). Our ability to respond to disasters is strengthened with each area of government working together.

LOOKING AHEAD

Progress made in preparedness over the last decade has benefitted routine and surge responses, saving lives and preventing illness and injuries. There is growing recognition that preparedness and core ("routine") public health investments are synergistic. Large scale and unpredictable disasters and disease outbreaks require many of the same routine surveillance, laboratory, risk communication, and other core public health capabilities and systems. Although we are better prepared today, we continue to face new challenges with fewer resources. Looking ahead, we must increase our focus on communities and better define and enhance community and local resilience. We also need to enhance our focus on vulnerable populations that require additional assistance during emergencies and finally, improve the evidence base for preparedness activities to show that work before a disaster really does pay off.

For Class Discussion

1. With what reasoning and evidence does Khan develop his claim that the terrorist attacks of 2001 led to a better state of public health preparedness? Which pieces of evidence strike you as particularly effective?

2. What audience or audiences does Khan seem to be targeting in this blog? What audiences do you imagine might follow this blog or come across it online?

3. What rhetorical strategies does Khan employ to convince his blog readers of the increased need for preparedness?

4. How do Khan's authority and professional credentials empower this argument?

5. What does Khan suggest about the role of government in public health issues?

6. Khan wrote a version of this argument for the September 3, 2011 edition of the medical journal the *Lancet*. How might Khan's choice of language, level of technical detail, and tone in that article differ from this version?

Antimicrobial Resistance: No Action Today, No Cure Tomorrow
Anuj Sharma

Dr. Anuj Sharma works with the World Health Organization (WHO) country office for India on strengthening laboratory surveillance for diseases of importance to public health. He is a medical doctor and has a master's degree in medical microbiology from Lady Hardinge Medical College, and he worked for more than thirteen years in clinical microbiology at the Sir Ganga Ram Hospital in Delhi, India. Since 2000, he has worked on assignments for WHO, including developing guidelines for hospital-associated infections, strengthening health laboratories in India's neighboring countries, addressing antimicrobial resistance, and improving malaria microscopy. This editorial was published in 2011 in the *Indian Journal of Medical Microbiology*. Each year, WHO marks World Health Day on April 7 and declares a theme to call attention to a global health issue. For 2011, World Health Day's theme was antimicrobial resistance.

> How does Anuj Sharma call on his audience of microbiologists to play a role in preventing and managing antimicrobial resistance?

The discovery and development of antimicrobials has been hailed as one of the most important advances in the history of modern medicine— reducing the suffering from disease and saving lives. However, these "miracle drugs" are losing their efficacy due to the emergence of antimicrobial resistance. Infections caused by multi-drug resistant organisms are associated not only with higher morbidity and mortality, but also with a prolonged and more expensive treatment as well. Multi-drug resistant organisms are also an epidemiological concern as they may spread locally, regionally or globally through individual contacts, poor sanitation, travel, or the food chain.

Antimicrobial resistance is a serious problem that strikes at the core of infectious disease control and has the potential to halt, and possibly to even roll back, progress. Antimicrobial resistance and its global spread not only threatens the continued effectiveness of antimicrobials, but also risks jeopardising global health security. Hence, World Health Organisation (WHO) has declared antimicrobial resistance as the theme for the World Health Day, 2011.

The multi-drug resistant superbugs pose a therapeutic challenge to the treating physicians. In addition, antimicrobial resistance is also becoming a problem in some pathogens, with grave effects on some national disease control programmes. Chloroquine resistance in the malarial parasite has forced changes in the treatment strategy, necessitating introduction of the more expensive artemisinin-based combinations. Multi-drug resistant tuberculosis threatens to undo major gains in TB control, with an estimated 100,000 cases emerging every year. In TB drug resistance—as with all anti-microbial drug resistance—the human and economic costs of drug-resistance control are much greater than the missed opportunities for prevention. Inappropriate prescribing and dispensing of anti-TB medicines (i.e., incorrect regimens, monotherapy, inadequate compliance with treatment regimens) is a major public health concern. Drug resistance to first-line anti-retroviral treatment (ART) regimens in HIV has led to higher direct and indirect health costs. Second-line ART drugs cost six times more than the first-line ART regimen in the national programme.

The main drivers of the development of resistance are antimicrobial selection pressure and spread of resistant organisms. Use of a broad-spectrum antimicrobial to treat an infection not only impacts the specific pathogen causing the disease, but also kills populations of susceptible organisms that form a part of our normal flora. Indiscriminate antimicrobial use by physicians and the community, over-the-counter availability, and use of antimicrobials as growth promoters in agriculture and animal husbandry are a cause of concern.

It is important to understand the dynamics of antimicrobial use and resistance. National and international policy decisions backed by political and social will are needed to provide a more accurate assessment of the problem and interrupt the unacceptable trends. The two main factors that drive the rise and spread of resistant organisms are overuse and misuse of antimicrobials, and the spread of resistant organisms between individuals, communities, and countries. Surveillance of antimicrobial resistance and use is an essential prerequisite to monitor the situation, for effective prevention and containment of antimicrobial resistance and rational antimicrobial use. The WHO has supported the Indian Network for Surveillance of Antimicrobial Resistance (INSAR) by providing a platform for representative Indian microbiology laboratories, in both public and private sectors, to share and monitor the trends of antimicrobial resistance in few organisms of public health importance. There is a need to strengthen the capacity of laboratories in the quality analysis of antimicrobial resistance by providing reliable data for use at the local level as well as for national guidelines. Microbiologists could play a key role in antimicrobial stewardship by standardising antimicrobial susceptibility testing and sharing their data and trends in antibiograms.

The emerging multi-drug resistance and its global spread is a grim reminder that antimicrobial resistance and infection control are cross-cutting issues that can only be tackled effectively through a health system's approach. Concerted action is needed at the local, national, and global level by all stakeholders, working in both human and animal health, to ensure the adequate treatment of patients today and the preservation of the life-saving power of antimicrobials for future generations.

The World Health Day, 2011 provides an opportunity to launch sustainable action to contain resistance, to raise awareness and education, and to track and contain the spread of resistance with improved informatics, and clinical decision support by development and use of better diagnostics. WHO will provide technical support to all stakeholders to implement the policies and practices needed to prevent and counter the emergence of antimicrobial resistance.

To avoid the spectre of a post-antibiotic era, this is the time for action. WHO is committed to support the government in tackling this challenging public health problem to safeguard the health of all.

For Class Discussion

1. What is the motivating occasion and the urgency for Sharma's argument? In other words, what has called him to write this piece? Consider the significance of World Health Day.

2. What policy proposal is Sharma defending in this editorial?

3. What are the factors named by Sharma that contribute to antimicrobial resistance?

4. Though Sharma does not go into detail about the possible implications of a "post-antibiotic era," what scenarios might we face if antibiotics and antimicrobials lose their effectiveness?

Healthy Growth for U.S. Farms
Scientific American

This editorial was written for the April 2009 edition of *Scientific American*, which is the oldest continuously published magazine in the United States. Since its founding in 1845, more than 140 Nobel laureates have written on topics of science and technology for the magazine, as have world leaders, U.S. government officials, economists, and industrialists. The magazine's editorial staff is currently led by editor-in-chief Mariette DiChristina, a science journalist, former president of the National Association of Science Writers, and an adjunct professor in the Science, Health, and Environmental Reporting Program at New York University.

> How do the editors of this magazine present food and agricultural production as an emerging public health problem?

Congress and the FDA must upend the nation's agricultural policies to keep its food supply safe.

Agriculture has fueled the eruption of human civilization. Efficiently raised, affordable crops and livestock feed our growing population, and hunger has largely been banished from the developed world as a result. Yet there are reasons to believe that we are beginning to lose control of our great agricultural machine. The security of our food supply is at risk—in ways more noxious than anyone had feared.

The trouble starts with crops. Orange groves in Florida and California are falling to fast-moving blights with no known cure. Cavendish-variety bananas—the global standard, each genetically identical to the next—will almost certainly be wiped out by emerging infectious disease, just as the Cavendish's predecessor was six decades ago. And as entomologists Diana Cox-Foster and Dennis vanEngelsdorp describe in "Saving the Honeybee" [in the same issue], a mysterious affliction has ravaged honeybee colonies around the U.S., jeopardizing an agricultural system that is utterly dependent on farmed, traveling hives to pollinate vast swaths of monoculture. The ailment may be in part the result of the stresses imposed on hives by this uniquely modern system.

Plants and animals are not the only ones getting sick, however. New evidence indicates that our agricultural practices are leading directly to the spread of human disease.

Much has been made in recent years of MRSA, the antibiotic-resistant strain of Staphylococcus bacteria, and for good reason. In 2005, the most recent year for which figures are available, about 95,000 MRSA infections caused the deaths of nearly 19,000 Americans. The disease first incubated in hospitals—the killer bacterium is an inevitable evolutionary response to the widespread use of antibiotics—but has since found a home in locker rooms, prisons and child care facilities. Now the bacteria have spread to the farm.

Perhaps we should not be surprised. Modern factory farms keep so many animals in such a small space that the animals must be given low doses of antibiotics to shield them from the fetid conditions. The drug-resistant bacteria that emerge have now entered our food supply. The first study to investigate farm-bred MRSA in the U.S.—amazingly, the Food and Drug Administration has shown little interest in testing the nation's livestock for this disease—recently found that 49 percent of pigs and 45 percent of pig workers in the survey harbored the bacteria. Unfortunately, these infections can spread. According to a report published in Emerging Infectious Diseases, MRSA from animals is now thought to be responsible for more than 20 percent of all human MRSA cases in the Netherlands.

In April 2008 a high-profile commission of scientists, farmers, doctors and veterinarians recommended that the FDA phase out the nontherapeutic use of antibiotics in farm animal production, to "preserve these drugs to treat sick animals, not healthy ones" in the words of former Kansas governor John Carlin, the commission's chair. The FDA agreed and soon announced that it would ban the use of one widespread antibiotic except for strictly delineated medical purposes. But five days before the ban was set to take effect, the agency quietly reversed its position. Although no official reason was given, the opposition of the powerful farm lobby is widely thought to have played a role.

This is just one example of a food production system that protects a narrow set of interests over the nation's public health. Simple measures such as the reinstatement of the FDA's initial ruling are necessary and important steps. But Congress needs to take a far more comprehensive approach to realign the country's agricultural priorities with its health priorities, to eliminate subsidies that encourage factory farming, and to encourage the growth of polyculture and good old-fashioned crop rotation in the U.S. As the world is quickly learning, a civilization can only be as healthy as its food supply.

For Class Discussion

1. What is the central proposal claim this editorial sketches?

2. How do our food-production practices and our collective national appetite contribute to the problem, according to the editors of *Scientific American*? What evidence of the problem is especially compelling?

3. According to this editorial, what is the role of politics in this health issue?

4. This editorial sketches its solution but does not develop it. What courses of action would you want to investigate in support of this proposal?

5. As a citizen of the United States, what action could you take to address this issue?

Resistance Is Futile
Megan McArdle

Megan McArdle is a senior editor covering business and economics for *The Atlantic*, a magazine focusing on "foreign affairs, politics, and the economy" and cultural trends. The magazine is considered a moderate to politically conservative alternative to the more liberal view presented by the *New Yorker*. McArdle holds a bachelor's degree in English literature and an MBA from the University of Chicago. She began blogging on economics and business topics and has blogged for both the *Economist* and *The Atlantic*. This proposal argument was featured in the October 2011 edition of *The Atlantic*.

> How does Megan McArdle tailor her style and rhetorical approach to a more general audience in this piece?

On Christmas Eve 1947, George Orwell was admitted to a Scottish hospital with a case of galloping consumption. Orwell had first been diagnosed with tuberculosis almost 10 years earlier, but nonetheless, in what a biographer called "one of the many ill-judged decisions in a life littered with misjudgements," he had recently moved to a remote and primitive Scottish cottage, where he began work on *Nineteen Eighty-Four*. There, he developed the night sweats, fever, and weight loss that are hallmarks of active TB. By the time he was admitted to the hospital, *Mycobacterium tuberculosis* had husked nearly 30 pounds off his already slender frame.

When I was younger and more romantic, I imagined that tuberculosis made you a good writer. After all, so many great ones, from Keats to Chekhov to all three Brontës, seemed to have died of it. Indeed, in 19th-century Europe, the "White Plague" may have caused as many as a quarter of all deaths. Though that proportion had fallen by Orwell's time, writers from Camus to Bukowski were still contracting tuberculosis, as were millions of their less famous countrymen. Only antibiotics finally conquered the disease.

Victory arrived just barely too late for Orwell. His friends actually managed to obtain a supply of streptomycin, the brand-new anti-TB drug, from America, but it caused such a violent reaction that every morning when he woke, blood from the ulcers in his mouth had glued his lips shut. It had to be soaked off before he could speak. After several weeks, his doctors had to give up. A less powerful new drug called PAS, which he tried in 1949, didn't make him so sick, but apparently didn't much bother the tuberculosis bacilli, either. In January of 1950, an artery burst in his lungs, and at the age of 46, George Orwell drowned in his own blood.

It seems a medieval end for a very modern man. But we are not as far from TB as we like to think. It remains endemic in the developing world and is coming back in richer countries, thanks to travel and immigration, but also to a phenomenon that Alexander Fleming, the discoverer of penicillin, warned of in the 1940s: antibiotic resistance.

"What people might not know about resistance," says Eric Utt, a former antibiotic researcher now working in Pfizer's science public-policy division, "is that the resistant organisms are already there. This is why we find bacteria that are resistant to new antibiotics, even before those drugs reach the market." They're often the loners in the corner with the mutation that just happens to confer immunity to some super-drug. When we bombard their competition with lethal weapons, they get the place to themselves; and eventually, they take over. After generations of this, the super-drug loses its effectiveness.

Worse, *other* drugs lose their effectiveness, because many bacteria that are resistant to one drug will also resist other drugs in the same class. We are now learning that bacteria trade genes with each other promiscuously, even between different species, so that resistance developed by one strain of bacteria can be acquired by another. The more we use these drugs, the faster they begin to fail.

By 2004, more than 50 percent of staph infections were caused by methicillin-resistant *Staphylococcus aureus* (MRSA), up from 2 percent in 1987; some are also resistant to vancomycin, a common backup antibiotic. Other disease organisms show similar patterns: pneumococcus, *E. coli,* and, yes, *M. tuberculosis* now come in multidrug-resistant or extremely drug-resistant varieties. In 2001, the Food and Drug Administration warned:

> Unless antibiotic resistance problems are detected as they emerge, and actions are taken to contain them, the world could be faced with previously treatable diseases that have again become untreatable, as in the days before antibiotics were developed.

We are not quite on the brink of some dystopian Victorian future. But every year, the prognosis for infectious-disease patients gets a bit grimmer. Ramanan Laxminarayan, an economist at the Center for Disease Dynamics, Economics & Policy, says that even extremely drug-resistant TB "can be treated with a couple of drugs. They're just extremely toxic, and they're not something you'd want to take"— think blood-sealed lips. And more-powerful drugs tend to cost more than the old drugs. "Right now the cost is in the hundreds of dollars, but the next step will be thousands of dollars," Laxminarayan says. "In developed countries, it's manifested in slightly higher average prices of antibiotics. In poorer countries, it manifests as more people sick and dying of resistant infections."

Even in the rich world, death from infection still looms; MRSA alone kills thousands every year. And firms are not developing anti-biotics as fast as they used to. According to the Infectious Diseases Society of America (IDSA), between 1983 and 1987, the FDA approved

16 new antibacterial drugs for use in humans; from 2003 to 2007, it approved six.

Whom to blame for all of this depends on whom you ask. Patients, physicians, hospitals, drug companies, and even regulators have all taken their turn in the dock. But to an economist, when it's everyone's fault, it's really no one's fault: what we're witnessing is not a personal failure, but a market failure.

Almost no one develops something like MRSA in his or her own body. Resistance arises over generations of treatment, usually in hospitals with lots of patients. Though resistance is ultimately inevitable, we can slow its emergence considerably. However, doing so requires strict compliance with tedious and often expensive protocols. Each slip contributes only slightly to the problem, so there's a high temptation to free-ride: *Just this once, I'll skip washing my hands between patients*, or *Just today, I'll skip taking the last of the pills that upset my tummy*. Anyone who lived in a group house in college knows how this story turns out.

Markets and property rights give people incentives to avert the tragedy of the commons, and have yielded a steady stream of life-saving drugs and medical innovations. But antibiotics are different from most of the other drugs we use. As Kevin Outterson, a professor of health law and bioethics at Boston University, points out, 100 million people could be taking Lipitor and it would remain just as effective as the day it was first invented. Unless we discover something even better, patients could still be taking Lipitor 1,000 years from now. But antibiotics like penicillin inevitably begin to lose effectiveness.

Antibiotics are an exhaustible resource. We should be treating them like an oil field, or an endangered species. Instead, we handle them like consumer electronics. The patent system is designed to promote human invention, not conserve what has already been discovered. Patents are limited to 20 years, so that other inventors can build on earlier innovations. Arthur Daemmrich, a professor at Harvard Business School who studies the pharmaceutical industry, points out that the pharmaceutical patent life is actually much shorter, because the patent clock begins running before the start of multi-year clinical trials necessary to get the drug approved. And when companies finally get to market, they face the risk that a competitor will be close behind with a related drug. As Laxminarayan says, "The pharma companies don't have an incentive to conserve the effectiveness of their antibiotics. They have [intellectual-property] rights on a drug, but someone else could be developing a similar molecule that will create resistance to my molecule, so I need to sell it as fast as I can."

Tighter controls on prescriptions, or a tax on antibiotics, might address the conservation problem. But because resistance is inevitable, we also need drug companies to develop new antibiotics. For them, the cost of making more batches of pills is typically trivial; all the cost is in the R&D and the corporate overhead. That means that a profitable drug—the sort of drug that pharmaceutical firms work hard to create— is one that sells as many units as possible.

The problem is, efforts at promoting conservation may discourage innovation—and vice versa. Some hospitals now require infectious-disease doctors to sign off on the use of newer and more powerful antibiotics. But this has a cost. "When a new antibiotic comes out," Pfizer's Utt says, "physicians don't necessarily use it—they tend to hold it in reserve. So by the time it's being used, it's already used up part of its marketable patent life." As a result, fewer large firms may want to spend the time and money to get these drugs approved—according to the IDSA, only two major drug companies (GlaxoSmithKline and AstraZeneca) still have strong active research programs, down from nearly 20 in 1990. Antibiotics are not big moneymakers: Every time a doctor writes a prescription for Lipitor, Pfizer may gain a customer for decades. But short-course drugs like antibiotics sell perhaps a dozen doses.

Of course, we could always jack up the price. This idea is remarkably popular (at least if paired with conservation); even some people who have a pronounced distaste for pharmaceutical firms seem to like it. But extremely drug-resistant bacteria are still relatively rare, which means that in almost all cases, a new antibiotic is competing with an older antibiotic that actually works pretty well at curing a particular disease. If a drug company sets the new product's price too high, it won't sell enough units to earn back its investment. Also, reflexive Big Pharma critics would fill every op-ed page in the country with laments about greedy drug makers.

Those same critics suggest that perhaps we should take this out of the invisible hands of the market. Historically, we've solved tragedy-of-the-commons problems either through privatization, as Britain did with its land, or through nationalization, as many nations have done with their military and police. If the market doesn't work, why not try the government?

Even many libertarian types agree that the commons problem seems to call for stronger state controls over antibiotics. But how far should that go? Government and academia perform vital basic research, but they haven't delivered a lot of working drugs. "What would be nice," says Daemmrich, "would be to have free-market mechanisms reward new-drug discovery even as the use of antibiotics was limited to infections that don't go away on their own."

One possibility is to have the government buy all the antibiotics on a sliding scale: so many billion dollars for a first-in-class antibiotic, half that amount for a second-in-class, and so forth. The government could then restrict the antibiotic's use. I've posed this possibility to people at pharmaceutical companies and gotten a surprisingly warm reception. Another idea, proposed by Outterson and a colleague, Harvard's Aaron Kesselheim, is to change the reimbursement system so that companies get paid more when *fewer* of their drugs are prescribed, as part of a conservation plan. "Let's say Bayer had a diagnostic test that could quickly tell whether you had a bacterial or viral infection. Right now, the only thing that this would do is knock down their unit sales [of antibiotics]. We should reward companies like Bayer if they bring out a diagnostic like this—their unit sales might decrease by half, but if so, we should quadruple their unit price." Or we could have special rules for antibiotics patents: instead of a 20-year term, make them renewable annually for drug companies that promote conservation.

These ideas sound elegant and simple in a magazine article. In the real world, they'd be messy and controversial. The government would be getting into the business of fixing prices. Likely, it would overshoot, handing windfall profits to firms, or undershoot, leaving us without enough drugs to treat emerging resistant infections. But the potential for such mistakes shouldn't stop us from trying to pursue creative public-private solutions. We just need to be prepared to face a lot of yelling.

Especially since the way to reward conservation is not entirely clear. Laxminarayan notes, "Whether resistance develops is not entirely a function of what the manufacturer does—it's a function of what other manufacturers do as well." Not to mention doctors, and patients, not all of whom are, ahem, entirely compliant.

Rich countries such as the United States can—and should—solve the problem of new antibiotics discovery on their own; as Laxminarayan says, "Show up at a table with enough money, and someone is going to show up with an antibiotic." But they cannot practice conservation without involving the developing world, an involvement that will require almost unimaginable coordination and cooperation. Laxminarayan likens antibiotics resistance to global warming: every country needs to solve its own problems and cooperate—but if it doesn't, we all suffer. Coordinating a global response will require years, even decades; any serious revision to the patent system might have to go through the World Trade Organization. Presumably, if the resistance gets bad enough the world will come together on this—but maybe not before there is a real crisis. "The time when it happens," Laxminarayan tells me, "is when a lot of antibiotics have failed."

In the meantime, we here in the United States can make a start. "There are a lot of good things hospitals could be doing for infection control," Outterson says, "but there's no Medicare billing code for this. They won't pay a nickel for a hospital that's extra careful with hand-washing, or uses more-expensive equipment that resists infections." While we wait for global action, we can develop better guidelines, change Medicare and Medicaid reimbursements, and start building stronger multilateral institutions. We can also start the policy debate over more-radical action, like changing the patent system and revisiting the role of government in the marketplace.

But the troubling possibility remains that this effort may not be fast enough. We won't see life expectancies plummet—we have much better public health and nutrition than the Victorians did. But we could end up in a world where the risk of infection curtails life-enhancing surgeries such as hip and knee replacements; where organ transplants, which require suppressing the recipient's immune system, become too risky to justify their cost; or even where pneumonia, which used to kill most of its victims over the age of 60, once again becomes "the old man's friend." The longer we ignore our problem, as Orwell did, the more likely we are to share his fate.

For Class Discussion

1. How does McArdle's opening anecdote about George Orwell work to set up her argument? Compare this appeal to an alternative beginning she could have used, such as presenting facts about pharmaceutical companies' investment in antibiotic research.

2. Where and how does McArdle explain the interplay between diseases, drugs, and the market? What pieces of evidence that she employs were new to you?

3. McArdle applies the term "tragedy of the commons," usually related to the overuse and abuse of environmental resources, to the overuse and misuse of antibiotics, which cause antimicrobial resistance. According to McArdle, how do decisions made by individuals contribute to the problem and make it difficult to solve?

4. In this proposal argument, what is McArdle's tiered solution to the problem? In other words, what can the United States do right now, and what will take more global coordination and effort? How does McArdle employ confronting the problem of global warming as a precedent?

5. What is the rhetorical effect of admitting that this solution would be "messy and controversial" in practice? Does this concession contribute to or detract from McArdle's overall rhetorical effectiveness?

6. After reading this argument, why do you think it is important to consider economic and market perspectives on public health? Which authors in this chapter also acknowledge the value of the business approach?

Africa's Condom Conundrum: Fighting HIV in Africa

Kingsley Chiedu Moghalu

Kingsley Chiedu Moghalu is an internationally renowned Nigerian diplomat. He earned his Barrister at Law degree from the Nigerian Law School, a master's degree from the Fletcher School of Law and Diplomacy at Tufts University, and his doctorate in international relations from the London School of Economics and Political Science. He is widely sought after by the global media as an international correspondent and a popular keynote speaker on global issues. As a diplomat with the United Nations from 1992 to 2009, he worked with UN organizations all over the world, and he served as counselor to the UN International Criminal Tribunal for Rwanda. Moghalu has written on law and international affairs for scholarly journals and major newspapers and has authored several books, including *Global Justice: The Politics of War Crimes Trials* (2006). Since 2002, he has been head of global partnerships at the Global Fund to Fight AIDS, Tuberculosis and Malaria in Geneva, Switzerland. Currently, he is deputy governor of the Central Bank of Nigeria. This guest column was posted on the allAfrica.com site on December 1, 2005. All Africa Global Media is the "largest electronic distributor of African news and information worldwide."

> How does Kingsley Chiedu Moghalu shape his argument for both Africans and the larger global audience?

A controversy about preventing HIV/AIDS—the most profound strategic threat to Africa's future—has been raging over the past year in Uganda, a country that registered one of the early successes in the fight against the pandemic. Simply put, the debate is about the right mix between sexual abstinence and condom use to prevent and control the spread of AIDS.

In all of Africa, and not just in Uganda, the tension between these competing approaches is all too real, with the choice often presented as a dichotomy. Should condoms be promoted, along with an implicit endorsement of sexual freedom, or should they be discouraged in favor of advancing private morality as good public policy?

Call it the condom conundrum. The problem arises when, as is often the case, the debate is made into an ideological one that denies the evidence of the scientific benefits of condoms, on the one hand, or the importance of individual moral choices about premarital or extramarital sex as a legitimate response to the pandemic, on the other. Whatever one may think of the plastic contraption, the reality is that condoms play an important role in the fight against a disease that is spread in Africa mainly through heterosexual sex.

The condom conundrum confronts African societies at four main levels—culture, gender, political leadership and religion.

The issue of culture embraces technology and its impact on human behavior. Condoms have historically not been a part of sexual relations in African societies. Indigenous African technology never produced a device whose aim was to prevent pregnancy and sexually transmitted diseases at the same time.

Natural methods were used for birth control. This situation led to a culture in which condoms, ever since they became part of sexual mores in Africa, have remained an essentially urban phenomenon. Many people in rural Africa have never seen a condom, let alone used one.

At the same time, the gender dimension of the fight against AIDS has not been accorded an importance equal to its impact as a cause of the pandemic's spread. The face of AIDS in Africa is mostly female. Sixty per cent of those living with the disease in Africa are women, and the disparity is often even greater among younger age groups.

Use of the "c-word" is circumscribed by the history and psychology of how men and women relate in the bedroom and is intrinsically bound in wider issues of gender relations. In many societies, including those of the industrialized global North, women have historically been disempowered—whether by denying them voting rights until well into the 20th century or control over their bodies. African and Islamic societies are not unique in the restrictions they have placed on women, although they have been slower to change. Thus many women, married or unmarried, cannot insist that a man use a condom against his will.

This female disempowerment is what has led to the invention of female condoms and microbicides that can help women protect themselves from the HIV virus. But again, few women in Africa know about these things or have access to them.

The lack of political leadership is a third factor limiting condom use. The fact that condoms are often seen as a social taboo means that political leaders in Africa do not want to be seen a mile near one—in public at least. As one African leader reportedly told UN Secretary-General Kofi Annan, "I can't utter the word condoms. I'm the father of the nation".

That aversion is not universal. When Alpha Konare, the current president of the African Union Commission, was President of Mali, he is reputed to have waved one in public—on television, no less— while talking about sex education and AIDS prevention. Such political leadership and mobilization at the grassroots level is essential if African countries are to have any chance against HIV/AIDS. It should not be a matter of embarrassment. It is one of life and death.

Finally, the tension between religious and social morality and public policy is perhaps the most contentious issue when it comes to condoms. Abstinence, for reasons of spirituality or public health—or both—is a valid approach to fighting AIDS.

Posters in Nigeria asking young men and women to "zip up" are not advocating a lifetime ban on close encounters of the intimate kind.

They are asking young people to make a choice they can make—to reduce the chance of living with or dying from AIDS by delaying sexual debut, preferably until marriage. Campaigns aimed at delaying sexual debut amongst youth have also emerged in countries like Zambia and South Africa. This campaign is gaining ground even in liberal societies like the United States, where stunningly pretty young women now pop up on television telling their future husbands out there that "you are worth waiting for".

What is wrong with this message? Nothing. When we consider that the majority of those living with AIDS are young people in their prime, it becomes clear that their attitudes towards sex affect their health.

Many critics of the abstinence message are social libertarians who believe that individual freedom should not be restricted on moral grounds, as was argued among the free sex, marijuana-smoking youth culture of 1960s America. The Nigerian musician Femi Kuti, debunking the United States government's support for abstinence campaigns, recently argued in an interview with the American newsmagazine *Newsweek* that "we were born to have sex". He is entitled to his opinion, but I suspect that is not the advice many parents will be giving their daughters.

The political/ideological position that masquerades as a human rights campaign fails to recognize that the public space is often an aggregate of private actions. But the abstinence message runs into difficulties when it is presented as the only acceptable prevention method, especially on religious grounds.

The dilemma crops up in the positions of certain influential faiths towards condoms and AIDS. The Catholic Church, for example, has launched a "Marshall Plan" to fight AIDS in Africa, not by joining the condom-distribution chain—it says it will not—but by treating AIDS patients as part of the church's avowed mission to treat the sick.

Even here, however, the nagging dilemmas creep in. What of a case where one partner in a Catholic Christian marriage is living with the virus? Should that partner not use a condom to avoid passing it on to the other?

Whatever our personal or religious views about sex outside of marriage, the reality is that not all who wish to abstain succeed in doing so. To preserve their lives—and a chance for a possible latter-day spiritual conversion—they need condoms.

Expecting all faith-based organizations to actively encourage the use of condoms may be asking too much. But public health is a legitimate concern and responsibility of governments. They cannot—and should not—discourage or prevent condom use to promote religious doctrine.

This is why the "ABC" approach—abstinence, be faithful, and condoms—is the best approach to preventing the spread of HIV/AIDS. Emphasizing one of these three components to the exclusion of the others is not good public health policy. Let the churches and mosques play their role in prevention and treatment. And let the public authorities do their duty to safeguard public health. Neither should stand in the way of the other.

But all these methods together have no hope of success in Africa without effective public education about HIV/AIDS. Education, which informs effective prevention, holds the key to breaking the back of AIDS in Africa. When the uninformed man or woman in rural Africa gets to know what this potent virus is, how it is acquired, how to prevent it, and how to live with it when the all-important prevention fails, then he or she will know that the "wasting disease" is often a consequence of preventable behavior. It is not "witchcraft".

For Class Discussion

1. How does Moghalu show that sometimes the way that an issue is framed can contribute to the problem? How does the word "conundrum" serve his purpose?

2. In presenting the African controversy over using condoms in AIDS prevention, what main points does Moghalu make? How does he show his knowledge of African cultures, and what does his background contribute to the persuasiveness of his argument?

3. What various alternative views is Moghalu addressing?

4. Why do you think that Moghalu saves the full statement of his position on AIDS prevention until the end of his article? How rhetorically effective is the structure of this argument?

5. Whom does Moghalu hope to persuade with his argument? How has he influenced your thinking about AIDS prevention in Africa?

AIDS Prevention Images from Africa

The following two visuals illustrate the efforts of African countries to tackle their AIDS crisis by preventing the spread of HIV.

Using materials such as this "NO 'til we know" billboard, South Africa's loveLife is a national HIV-prevention initiative that seeks "to promote healthy, HIV-free living among South African teens." The program recognizes the individual factors (self-esteem), social factors (disempowerment of and violence against girls and women), and structural factors (poverty, unemployment, and school dropout rates) that put young people at risk. They work with a national corps of 1,200 full-time peer educators, ages 18 to 25, called groundBREAKERs.

The second image is a photograph of a billboard on the border between Namibia and Botswana taken by Australian Neil Shedden when he visited South Africa, Namibia, Botswana, and Zimbabwe.

What details and features stand out for you in these two billboards?

Billboard for HIV Prevention Campaign, South Africa

www.avert.org

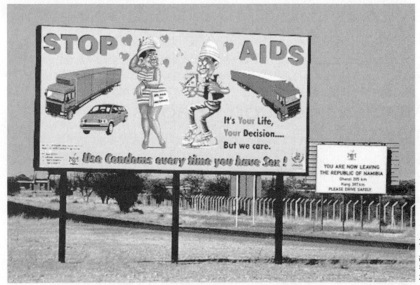

HIV Prevention Billboard, Namibia and Botswana

Neil Shedden

For Class Discussion

1. Briefly describe each image. What is the style (realistic, cartoonish, dramatic, glamorous) and tone (serious, cautionary, humorous, optimistic) of each? What do the figures in each billboard contribute to the message?

2. What does the text contribute to the rhetorical effect of the billboards?

3. How do the billboards appeal to viewers' emotions and understanding?

4. How do these images address the African cultural and social issues discussed in the readings in this chapter? What response would Kingsley Chiedu Moghalu have to these AIDS awareness campaigns? You might want to investigate Avert.org's media gallery for other AIDS awareness campaigns in Africa. What other strategies and appeals are these organizations using? Which poster campaigns appear to be speaking especially to each of these target groups: men, women, teens, and girls?

AIDS in America—Forgotten but Not Gone
Wafaa M. El-Sadr, Kenneth H. Mayer, and Sally L. Hodder

Dr. Wafaa M. El-Sadr researches the HIV and tuberculosis epidemics in the United States and globally. She received her MD from Cairo University, her master's degree in public health from Columbia University, and her master's degree in public administration from the Harvard University Kennedy School. She is director of the International Center for AIDS Care and Treatment Programs and director of the Center for Infectious Disease Epidemiologic Research at Columbia University's Mailman School of Public Health. She previously led the Division of Infectious Diseases at Harlem Hospital Center. El-Sadr has received grants for the National Institutes of Health, and in 2008 was named a John D. and Catherine T. MacArthur Foundation Fellow.

Kenneth H. Mayer received his MD from Northwestern University and is currently professor of medicine and community health at Brown University, director of the Brown University AIDS Program, and medical research director at Boston's Fenway Community Health Center. In the early 1980s, Dr. Brown was one of the first clinical researchers in New England to care for patients living with AIDS. He has coauthored more than 350 articles and other publications on AIDS and related infectious disease topics.

Sally L. Hodder, MD, is the director of HIV Programs at the New Jersey Medical School and a board member of the Forum for Collaborative HIV Research.

The authors' proposal argument was published in the March 18, 2010 edition of the *New England Journal of Medicine*, a journal that brings research and information to physicians "at the intersection of biomedical science and clinical practice."

How does the authors' use of statistics function rhetorically in this argument? Think of the comparisons between AIDS in Africa and the scope of AIDS in the United States.

Over the past decade, limited attention has been paid to the human immunodeficiency virus (HIV) epidemic in the United States. The global epidemic—particularly the epidemic in sub-Saharan Africa, where approximately two thirds of the world's population living with AIDS resides—has rightfully received most of the focus. Meanwhile, however, the prevalence of HIV infection within some U.S. populations now rivals that in some sub-Saharan African countries.

For example, more than 1 in 30 adults in Washington, D.C., are HIV-infected—a prevalence higher than that reported in Ethiopia, Nigeria, or Rwanda.* Certain U.S. subpopulations are particularly hard hit. In New York City, 1 in 40 blacks, 1 in 10 men who have sex with men, and 1 in 8 injection-drug users are HIV-infected, as are 1 in 16 black men in Washington, D.C.[†] In several U.S. urban areas, the HIV prevalence among men who have sex with men is as high as 30%[‡]—as compared with a general-population prevalence of 7.8% in Kenya and 16.9% in South Africa.

During the first two decades of the epidemic, remarkable advances in preventing mother-to-child transmission, screening of blood and blood products, and behavior change among men who have sex with men resulted in significant decreases in new HIV infections in the United States—from approximately 130,000 in 1984 to about 60,000 in 1991. For the past decade, however, progress has been stalled. It had been anticipated that effective antiretroviral therapy, with its suppressive effect on viral replication, would reduce the overall rate of new infections, but this expectation has not been realized. More than half a million Americans became infected with HIV in the past decade,

---

*District of Columbia HIV/AIDS epidemiology update 2008. Washington, DC: Government of the District of Columbia, Department of Health, HIV/AIDS Administration; 2008. (Accessed February 8, 2010, at http://dchealth.dc.gov/DOH/frames.asp?doc=/doh/lib/doh/pdf/dc_hiv-aids_2008_updatereport.pdf.)

[†]Nguyen TQ, Gwynn RC, Kellerman SE, et al. Population prevalence of reported and unreported HIV and related behaviors among household adult population in New York City, 2004. AIDS 2008;22:281-7.

[‡]HIV prevalence among selected populations: high-risk populations. Atlanta: Centers for Disease Control and Prevention, 2007. (Accessed February 8, 2010, at http://www.cdc.gov/hiv/topics/testing/resources/reports/hiv_prevalence/high-risk.htm.)

including about 56,000 in the past year.[*] It is estimated that there are now more than 1 million HIV-infected Americans, more than 20% of whom are unaware of their infection.

Unlike the generalized HIV epidemics in sub-Saharan Africa, the U.S. epidemic primarily affects certain discrete geographic areas— especially urban areas of the Northeast and West Coast and cities and small towns in the South.

Within these areas, specific neighborhoods are often disproportionately affected, in part because of residents' engagement in unprotected sex within relatively insular social-sexual networks. Many of the populations most affected tend to have limited social mobility; thus, partner selection tends to concentrate transmission patterns and amplify spread within defined geographic areas.

Traditionally, researchers and policymakers concerned with HIV acquisition have concentrated on specific high-risk transmission behaviors, including injection-drug use, sex with multiple partners, and failure to use protective measures such as condoms or safe injection practices. It is now evident that among men who have sex with men, the use of drugs such as crystal methamphetamine—especially at sex parties and in venues such as bathhouses—has contributed to risky behavior and HIV acquisition. Other disinhibiting substances, including alcohol and cocaine, are also associated with increased risk taking in these populations.

However, the extent of the risk of acquiring HIV in the United States today is largely defined by a person's sexual network rather than his or her individual behaviors. Understanding the context and settings in which risk is increased may lead to more robust and effective preventive interventions. For example, black men who have sex with men are at increased risk for HIV infection in part because of its high prevalence in their sexual networks and their likelihood of choosing racially similar partners; they have also been shown to be less likely than their white counterparts to be aware of their HIV status and thus are more likely to unknowingly transmit HIV.[†] Moreover, even those who are aware of their HIV infection may be less engaged in HIV care and less likely to avail themselves of antiretroviral therapy—behavior that limits the potential benefit of such therapy as a preventive strategy.

The situation is similar for black and Hispanic women, whose increased risk of HIV acquisition is attributable in greater part to their

---

[*]Hall HI, Song R, Rhodes P, et al. Estimation of HIV incidence in the United States. JAMA 2008;300:520-9.

[†]Millett GA, Flores SA, Peterson JL, Bakeman R. Explaining disparities in HIV infection among black and white men who have sex with men: a meta-analysis of HIV risk behaviors. AIDS 2007; 21:2083-91.

vulnerable social and economic situations and their sexual networks than to their own risky behaviors. Socioeconomic disadvantage and instability of partnerships due to high rates of incarceration among men in their communities may lead women to engage in concurrent relationships or serial monogamy. In addition, they may be unaware of their partners' HIV status or may be involved in abusive or economically dependent relationships and thus be unable to negotiate safer sex with their partners.

The specific characteristics of the U.S. HIV epidemic—low prevalence in the general population, high prevalence among the disenfranchised and socially marginalized, with a concentration in geographic hotspots—in combination with the various structural impediments to prevention create unique challenges for the design and implementation of effective interventions. Thus, a nuanced and targeted approach that avoids stigmatization of these populations is necessary. Structural interventions might include tackling the disproportionate incarceration of black and Hispanic men, urging health insurers to reimburse providers for preventive care, and using microcredit to help women out of poverty so that they avoid the perceived need to engage in commercial sex or other coercive sex.

Research tailored to specific populations is required if we are to gain the understanding needed to move forward. For example, how do we identify those people in the United States who are at greatest risk for HIV acquisition, especially among women? Although more than a quarter of new HIV infections in the United States occur in women (predominantly black or Hispanic women), identifying such at-risk women to engage them in prevention studies has proven particularly challenging. Research is also needed to identify interventions that will persuade men who have sex with men to undergo HIV testing, facilitate their disclosure of their HIV status to sexual partners, and promote negotiations for safer sexual practices; such interventions need to be implemented in the settings where such men may meet (e.g., in bars or on the Internet). Additional qualitative research is needed to understand how the targeted community uses various sources of information in making decisions about sexual risk taking.

Most glaringly, HIV disproportionately affects poor black Americans who have substandard education, unstable housing, and limited social mobility. This confluence of factors may result in high rates of incarceration, which threaten a community's social fabric. Such vulnerable populations must be engaged in research, program development, and interventions that are culturally relevant and address the socioeconomic milieu in which HIV transmission occurs.

Preventive interventions must be rooted in science, not driven by ideological concerns. Homophobia may have impeded the development of sexually appropriate prevention studies among men who have sex with men. Reluctance to fund studies of needle exchange or conditional cash transfer (providing financial incentives for healthy behavior) or to support work in high-risk venues, such as bathhouses, has hampered progress. Cash transfer has proved effective in achieving desirable health outcomes, including weight control, smoking cessation, and decreased use of crystal methamphetamine, but until recently it was not being studied for use in HIV prevention in the United States.

What will it take to control the U.S. HIV epidemic? First, there is an urgent need to acknowledge that HIV remains a major health threat in the United States. Second, concerted effort and substantial resource investment—especially in innovative and courageous approaches—are necessary. Focused studies of the sociocultural dynamics that facilitate transmission are needed, as well as large studies assessing the effectiveness of multidimensional interventions, including behavioral, biomedical, and structural components. Disenfranchised communities must be engaged as partners in such efforts, along with new researchers drawn from the affected populations, if the nuances of local epidemics are to be addressed. The time has come to confront this largely forgotten and hidden epidemic.

For Class Discussion

1. What factors do the authors cite that may have led to AIDS being "forgotten" in America? What do you think has contributed to this lack of attention?

2. How do El-Sadr, Mayer, and Hodder acknowledge and then reject common assumptions about who contracts HIV and why?

3. Where have stereotypes and/or prejudices stunted or hampered the research of HIV acquisition, even among medical professionals? Where could generalizations be helpful in targeting the most at-risk populations?

4. What claim do the authors make about "structural interventions" that could reduce the incidence of HIV in the named populations?

5. How do the professional credentials of Drs. El-Sadr, Mayer, and Hodder contribute to the effectiveness of their argument? How does this argument connect with the racial and ethnic disparities in public health that David Satcher explores in his argument?

Viral Vows
Regan Hofmann

Regan Hofmann is editor-in-chief of *POZ* magazine, a national magazine and Web site for people living with or affected by HIV and AIDS. Hofmann blogged as "Anonymous" in *POZ* for four years before disclosing her HIV-positive status in the April 2006 issue of the magazine when she became editor-in-chief. Hofmann believes that leadership from HIV-positive people is essential in fighting the spread of the pandemic, and she regularly speaks to students, health care professionals, government leaders, and the public about awareness and reducing the stigma of HIV/AIDS. She has appeared on *Good Morning America*, *The Oprah Winfrey Show*, CNN, and NPR, and has been featured in the *New York Times*, *Vogue*, the *London Daily Telegraph,* and the *China Post,* among many other publications. Her memoir, titled *I Have Something to Tell You,* was published in 2009. She is a board member of the Foundation for AIDS Research and an ambassador for the Elizabeth Glaser Pediatric AIDS Foundation, and she has served as U.S. delegate to the UN General Assembly Special Session on AIDS. The following editor's letter was printed in the January/February 2011 issue of *POZ.*

> How does your awareness of Regan Hofmann's personal experience with HIV influence your expectations of her argument?

One of the biggest and most dangerous myths around HIV is that the sanctity of marriage protects those in it from the virus. Certainly, if two people are tested, don't have HIV and don't go outside the marriage to sleep with others or inject drugs, marriage can provide a wonderful safeguard against diseases such as HIV. That's true for all committed partnerships, gay or straight.

But the truth is that global infidelity rates are high. And in many places across the world, marriages don't reflect consensual love but instead represent business arrangements between families. Such marriages can often place a woman's health in a particularly vulnerable situation. In many cases, women are powerless to advocate for the safety of their own bodies. And if they try to negotiate for safer sex, for example, when they know their husbands are cheating, they put themselves at further risk for violence. Some may even have their own fidelity questioned.

In the developing world, men often must live far from their families to earn a living. And, while away, some engage in risky behaviors such as using drugs or paying for sex—and in the process contract HIV. Then, they bring the disease home and give it to their spouse.

When infidelity or injection drug use enters the equation, people in marriage can actually be at a greater risk, as they are not as likely to be using condoms or be aware they might be at risk. And for those aware of their spouse's extramarital habits or drug use, the very ring around their finger prevents them from protecting themselves from their husbands or from seeking safe havens outside the home.

Marital infidelity is also dangerous because it's something people don't like to discuss. Many people may suspect it's going on but are too afraid to face whatever pain the truth may bring. And so, denial leads people to not protect themselves.

When I got married (I am now divorced), a syphilis test was required. Given the low incidence of syphilis and the high rates of HIV in the United States at that time, I was surprised.

Perhaps HIV testing should be a mandatory requirement for marriage. After all, being aware of and caring for your spouse-to-be's health should be a prerequisite for signing up for a life together. Infidelity can still bring HIV into the marriage (by either the man or the woman), but an initial test could help raise awareness and educate both partners about potential risks.

As is so often the case, tracing the infection route of HIV illuminates the ills of society. The tough news is we have to address some really difficult challenges, like the global inequality of women and the lack of their empowerment, in order to best stop the spread of HIV.

This year marks the 30th anniversary of the first reported case of HIV. Let's hope that 2011 brings us closer to effective vaccines—and the cure. And that as we try to solve those scientific conundrums, we also resolve intermediate steps like developing effective microbicides—a very good solution for people who need to protect themselves against HIV but who can't necessarily negotiate for condom use.

I wish you a wonderful and a very happy New Year!

For Class Discussion

1. What myth about HIV transmission does Hofmann seek to dispel? What reaction does she hope to get from her audience?

2. How does Hofmann link HIV to other issues like the global inequality of women?

3. Though Hofmann focuses on conditions of marriage in the developing world, which of these risks could just as easily apply to relationships in the United States?

4. What cultural concerns does Hofmann's editorial share with the argument by Kingsley Chiedu Moghalu?

Family Health Makes Moral and Economic Sense
Melinda Gates

Melinda Gates is best known as the co-chair of the Bill and Melinda Gates Foundation, which focuses on three main programs: global development, global health, and education in the United States. Working with partners, including nonprofits, businesses, and governments, they target public health issues such as epidemic diseases, maternal and child health, and family planning; development issues such as agricultural development, sanitation, and hygiene; and U.S. issues such as family homelessness, education, and libraries. Gates received her bachelor's degree in computer science and economics from Duke University and her MBA from Duke's Fuqua School of Business. She worked at Microsoft for ten years before directing her efforts toward the nonprofit world and cofounding the Gates Foundation. This guest editorial, written for CNN, appeared in the November 30, 2011 edition of the *St. Joseph News-Press*.

> How does Melinda Gates employ storytelling to engage her audience with her argument?

Last year I traveled to a small village in Uttar Pradesh, India, where I met a young mother named Rukmini, who had recently given birth to a daughter. It was the sixth day of baby Durga's life, and in keeping with Indian custom, Rukmini was preparing for a ceremony to celebrate the special bond between mother and child.

As Rukmini bathed and dressed her daughter in new clothes and then held Durga up to present her to the sun god to ask for blessings, I kept thinking about the incredible joy and hope I felt when each of my three children was born.

These are universal feelings mothers have, no matter where they live. Yet millions of women—especially in the world's poorest countries—never get to hold a healthy baby in their arms. Although advances in vaccines, nutrition and family health have dramatically reduced the number of child deaths in the past 50 years, nearly 8 million children younger than 5 still die every year.

For me, this number is unacceptable, because most of these deaths could be avoided.

Many of the children who die are newborns. Up to 70% of infants could be saved with inexpensive tools such as antibiotics for infections, sterile blades to cut umbilical cords and education about the importance of exclusive breastfeeding and keeping babies warm through skin-to-skin contact.

Mothers and children need food that is rich in vitamins and minerals, and when they don't get it, malnutrition increases the risk of pregnancy complications for mothers and infections and death for children.

And more than 200 million women in developing countries need access to effective contraceptives. Without it, there will continue to be unnecessary maternal and child deaths associated with unintended or unplanned pregnancies.

On a visit not long ago to Nairobi, I met a woman who used contraceptives and limited her family to three children, which meant she had the resources to open a sewing business. With earnings from that business—and a smaller family to care for—she was able to make sure all of her children were well-fed and attending school. No matter where

I go, this is what mothers want for their children—enough food and a chance to go to school so they can grow up healthy and prosperous.

By focusing on these fundamental issues and simple solutions, we can save millions of lives. And the great thing is we don't have to wait for a major scientific breakthrough to know exactly what to do next.

There are already simple, proven ways to save millions more children, reduce unwanted pregnancies and keep mothers strong and healthy. But for that to happen, people around the world need to speak up so that governments make family health a priority. Working together, we all can help create a future where women everywhere have the knowledge and the power to save their lives and the lives of their babies.

For Class Discussion

1. What common values does Gates tap and what emotional connections does she establish between herself, the women in developing countries, and the women in her reading audience?

2. What "simple solutions" does Gates propose that would have a profound impact on maternal and child health?

3. What objections or alternative views might readers raise in response to Gates' proposal?

4. How does she ask her audience to get involved with the issue?

5. What points about maternal or child health in developing countries does this piece bring up that you might want to research further?

CHAPTER QUESTIONS FOR REFLECTION AND DISCUSSION

1. From your reading in this chapter, what do you see as the main problems that the global community is facing in (a) its efforts to prepare for and treat pandemics; (b) its recognition and response to the problem of antimicrobial resistance; (c) its efforts to control the spread of AIDS; and (d) its efforts to improve the health of mothers and children? List these problems for each issue. Then identify the reading in the chapter that you think most clearly explains the problem.

2. After reading the arguments in this chapter, choose one of the following pairs of authors and sketch out their points of agreement and disagreement.

What assumptions and values do they share? Where do they differ or clash?

- Larry Brilliant and David Satcher or Ali S. Khan
- Megan McArdle and the editors of *Scientific American*
- Anuj Sharma and Megan McArdle
- David Satcher and Wafaa El-Sadr, Kenneth Mayer, and Sally Hodder
- Melinda Gates and Regan Hofmann or Kingsley Chiedu Moghalu

3. Choose the author in this chapter who you think draws most effectively on his or her professional experience and personal convictions to enhance the credibility and persuasiveness of his or her argument, and explain your choice.

4. The readings in this chapter approach global health issues from several different perspectives: economic/business, biomedical/technological, social justice/equal access to health care, national security, and culture. Choose one of these perspectives. From your examination of the readings in this chapter, make a list of reasons why you think this perspective deserves emphasis, even priority.

5. In groups or individually, research one of the following topics and bring your information and views back to share with your class. From your research, what have you learned that can deepen the public discussion about fighting diseases in a global community?

   A. The AIDS billboards in this chapter illustrate how two African countries are raising awareness about AIDS. Research AIDS awareness or prevention campaigns in another nation or region of the world. How are these programs tailored to the specific society and culture? How effective are they? You may want to start with AVERT (avert.org), an international AIDS organization whose media gallery is searchable by region.

   B. Oprah Winfrey, Bono, and other popular figures are using their star appeal and their financial resources to mobilize the global community in the worldwide fight against deadly diseases. Investigate Oprah, Bono, or some other celebrity who is working for global health. Which of the perspectives on diseases presented in the readings in this chapter does this person support? Where is this celebrity investing his or her efforts and resources?

   C. Investigate what kinds of psychological and medical care your state, county, or city is providing for local residents with HIV/AIDS. How many people are receiving health care and what is the cost of treatment?

   D. What are some of the key concerns regarding antibiotics and their overuse or misuse? What actions are different countries or organizations taking to avoid antibiotic and antimicrobial resistance? You might start with the World Health Organization's 2011 World Health Day materials (www.who.int/world-health-day/2011).

6. **Analyzing Arguments Rhetorically.** As the still from the film *Contagion* in this chapter's introduction shows, pandemics have the potential to bring wide-ranging destructive social consequences. Search the Web for a political cartoon, photo, or another still from this film or some other film that appeals to the emotions of viewers and to the value they put on security and being able to maintain a normal life. Analyze the details of the image to explain *how* it works rhetorically on readers. What do the creators of this image want readers/viewers to think and feel?

7. Think about how the spread of diseases in the global community is related to other topics in this text such as free trade (Chapter 3), immigration (Chapter 4), environmental problems with water and climate change (Chapter 5), and the trafficking of women and children (Chapter 8). Brainstorm a network of issue questions that highlight connected controversies. For example, how have free trade agreements between the United States and Africa affected African countries' resources to fight AIDS? How has our increasing population and environmental footprint worsened the threat of pandemics?

8. Which reading in this chapter does the best job of outlining a solution and calling citizens to take action to address a global health problem?

WRITING ASSIGNMENTS ▰▰▰▰▰▰▰

Brief Writing Assignments

1. **Reflective Writing.** Few people have had the experience Mark Merin describes in his narrative about living with a pandemic like SARS, and yet most have had the yearly flu or some contagious illness. Write a brief personal narrative about (a) a time when you had a serious case of the flu; (b) a time when your family, friends, residence hall, or community were threatened by some illness that made a lot of people around you sick; (c) a time when you or someone you knew got food poisoning or some foodborne illness. How was the disease caught? What was unpleasant or scary about it? How long did it take you or others to get well? How did this experience affect your thinking about diseases?

2. Summarize one of the more complex arguments in this chapter, such as the article by Larry Brilliant, David Satcher, Megan McArdle, or Kingsley Chiedu Moghalu. What are the main points that readers should take away from reading this article?

3. **Analyzing Arguments Rhetorically.** Skimming through the readings in this chapter, find either (a) an example of a powerful and rhetorically effective use of numerical data or (b) a powerful use of anecdote or examples. Briefly explain how your chosen passage works on readers to make some concept or problem comprehensible and meaningful.

4. Using ideas from the readings in this chapter, freewrite an informal defense or refutation of one of the following claims. If you will be writing a

formal argument on this issue later, you might briefly sketch out several reasons in support of this claim and then spend an equal amount of time questioning and refuting the claim with several points.

A. Countries experiencing epidemics need to consider the global community as much as their own citizens.

B. Disparities in access to health care and health information in the United States must be addressed if we hope to curb the AIDS epidemic and to prepare ourselves for a potential pandemic.

C. The developed countries of the world need to regard pandemic disease as a global security threat as serious and dangerous as a military threat.

D. Businesses need to be provided with incentives to tackle the challenges of antibiotic resistance and pandemic diseases.

E. Science and technology are the most powerful tools in the prevention and treatment of AIDS.

F. Unless we work to improve the rights of women around the world, we will not be effective in combating the spread of AIDS.

5. Consider the rise in popularity of zombies in television (AMC's *The Walking Dead* and BBC's *Dead Set*), film (*28 Days Later*, *Dawn of the Dead*, *Zombieland*, and *Shaun of the Dead*), books (the graphic novel series *The Walking Dead*, Max Brooks' *World War Z*, and Colson Whitehead's *Zone One*), and video games (the *Resident Evil* series). Many major cities organize annual "zombie walks," and the CDC's Public Health Matters blog even used zombies as a fun way to talk about disaster and emergency preparedness. Analyze one of these texts or another of your choosing. What does our obsession with zombies suggest about our collective fears or anxieties about pandemics? What real lessons about pandemic or disaster preparedness can be derived from the text?

Writing Projects

1. **Reflective Writing.** Although Sharma, McArdle, and the *Scientific American* article do not go into detail about the possible implications of a "post-antibiotic era," they do raise questions about the problems we might face if antibiotics and antimicrobials lose their effectiveness. Write a reflective essay in which you thoughtfully examine your own relationship to antibiotics in the medicine you take and the food you eat. How responsible are you in your use of antibiotics and choosing food? If your state or city conducted a campaign like these—"Antibiotics are not automatic" in France; "Get smart" promoting the wise use of antibiotics in the United States; and "Do bugs need drugs?" in Canada—would you participate? What factors have influenced your awareness and contact with antibiotics? How have the readings in this chapter opened up new avenues of thought for you on this subject?

2. **Analyzing Arguments Rhetorically.** Write an essay that analyzes and critiques the effectiveness of one of the readings in this chapter as a policy

argument that brings a health issue into focus for readers and proposes a course of action. What features of this piece make it particularly rhetorically effective or problematic? Consider its target audience and genre, its claim and use of evidence, its use of emotional appeals, the author's knowledge and reliability, and the contribution of this piece to the public understanding of global health issues. What argumentative strategies are worthy of imitation?

3. **Reflective Writing.** Write a reflective essay in which you explain which article in this chapter had the greatest intellectual and emotional impact on you as a global citizen. How did this article appeal to your values, emotions, and reason? How did this article compel you to grapple with assumptions or beliefs that you held before you read it?

4. If a flu pandemic were to reach your region or city, it could completely disrupt public life, taking many lives and costing businesses millions of dollars. Investigate the status of your city's emergency preparations by researching and interviewing public health officials and possibly representatives of the largest companies in your area. How would your city handle problems such as workers without sick leave who insist on going to work sick; companies with a large percentage of their employees ill; and interrupted public services such as sanitation, food supply, and public transportation? Write a brief argument in which you praise or criticize the status of preparations in your city. Try to motivate local citizens and businesses to become involved in this issue.

5. The controversy over successful means to combat AIDS in Africa (condoms, the availability of antiretroviral drugs, abstinence, empowering women through education) is complicated and touches on cultural, moral, spiritual, economic, and political issues. After researching a variety of perspectives—for example, the views of American Catholics and African Catholics; the results of research studies on the effectiveness of male or female condoms in sub-Saharan Africa; the findings of UNAIDS and other global organizations; views of African leaders; views of African health care workers and other relevant stakeholders—write a policy proposal addressed to your U.S. representatives or senators in which you argue for the most successful method to fight against AIDS in Africa.

6. Studies in the last few years have shown that young people in the United States (those born after the initial AIDS scare) are less concerned with or not afraid of contracting HIV/AIDS. Yet the CDC reports that, as of August 2011, over 1 million people in the United States were living with HIV infection and that transmission rates have remained steady over the past several years. Imagine that a friend has learned that you are reading about the AIDS pandemic and says, "I thought that AIDS was only a problem in Africa. Haven't we got it under control here in the United States?" What information (or lack of information) might have led your friend to believe this? Think about the role of HIV/AIDS in the media, of sex education in school, or the awareness of HIV/AIDS on your campus.

Write a commentary directed to your campus newspaper on "Why AIDS Is Still Our Problem," in which you appeal to your friend and others of your generation to regard AIDS in a more informed and realistic way.

7. The controversy over antibiotic and antimicrobial resistance brings up the intersection of public health and medical treatment with private industry. After researching the issue, write a policy proposal in which you argue (a) that government needs to provide financial incentives for antibiotic research; (b) that health care workers need to curb the prescription of antibiotics and pursue alternate courses of treatment to preserve antibiotic effectiveness; (c) that the agricultural industry needs to change its practices to avoid the overuse and misuse of antibiotics; or (d) that the global community should agree to prohibit the over-the-counter sale of antibiotics (where they are currently available, in large countries like China and India). Be sure to consult a range of think tanks such as the Hudson Institute, the Cato Institute, and the Center for American Progress. You could address this argument to a policymaker or to fellow American citizens.

8. The names of the following organizations pop up frequently in articles about world health crises. Choose one of these or another global or public health institute or organization and investigate it. Then prepare a short speech for your class in which you explain the role this organization is playing in the world health picture. Summarize and illustrate what you find important about this organization.

Family Health International (www.fhi.org)
Doctors without Borders (www.doctorswithoutborders.org)
World Health Organization (www.who.int)
U.S. Department of Health and Human Services (www.hhs.gov)
National Institutes of Health (www.nih.gov)
Centers for Disease Control and Prevention (www.cdc.gov)
UNAIDS Joint United Nations Programme on HIV/AIDS (www.unaids.org)
Institute of Medicine of the National Academies (www.iom.edu)
Center for Infectious Disease Research and Policy at the University of Minnesota (www.cidrap.umn.edu)

Glossary of Globalization and Argument Terms

agribusiness An industry engaged in the production, processing, manufacture, or distribution of farm goods.

alternative energy Energy derived from sources such as biofuels, solar power and hydropower, or wind, tidal, and geothermal energy that is proposed as an alternative to the continued consumption of nonrenewable resources such as oil, natural gas, and coal.

amnesty The granting of a pardon for offenses against a government, often related to issues of political dissent.

angle of vision The lens of values through which an argument's writer is interpreting the issue, determining what is omitted and what is emphasized in the argument.

appeal to *ethos* The ethical character of a writer that comes across in the argument in the writer's credibility, knowledge, and treatment of other viewpoints.

appeal to *logos* The logical structure, consistency, and development of an argument.

appeal to *pathos* How a writer engages the emotions and imaginations of the audience and taps into the audience's values in an argument.

argument A persuasive text that makes a claim and develops it with reasons and supporting evidence.

assumptions The principles behind the reasons given for an argumentative claim.

asylum seeker A type of refugee seeking relief from political or religious persecution.

attributive tags Language used by a writer to indicate that the ideas being expressed belong to another author.

audience The people whom a writer has in mind when making an argument, or the people whom the writer hopes to persuade of his or her position on an issue.

banana republic A term used to describe Latin American countries with economies focused on exporting one limited resource, often a crop. Banana republics typically had a vast economic divide between a small ruling elite of economic or political leaders and the masses.

blue collar Pertaining to working-class employees who perform manual labor such as factory work.

brain drain A phenomenon in which college-educated persons and professionals leave developing countries in order to take advantage of better conditions and substantially higher pay for their skills in developed countries.

capital Wealth and durable produced goods that are used in the production of other goods—farm equipment, property, or money, for example.

Central America–Dominican Republic–United States Free Trade Agreement (CAFTA–DR) A free trade agreement, similar to the North American Free Trade Agreement, between the United States and most Central American countries, ratified in 2005.

claim A statement that asserts an arguable answer to an issue question and functions as the core of an argument.

Clean Air Act A set of laws originally passed in 1963 that has since been expanded and revised. These laws aim to improve air quality and focus specifically on the ozone layer, acid rain, and emissions standards for factories and vehicles.

clicktivism A derogatory term that refers to activism consisting of reblogging or "liking" posts as part of awareness campaigns on sites like Facebook or Twitter.

climate change Changes in global temperatures and weather patterns that can result in changing patterns of rainfall and drought, greater intensity and frequency of storms, and melting of polar ice caps and glaciers. Formerly referred to as global warming, the phenomenon is currently discussed in relation to issues of atmospheric pollution caused by greenhouse gases.

colonialism Political, economic, social, and cultural domination and exploitation of a territory by a foreign power. This system was popular among the European powers in the nineteenth century, a notable example being Great Britain's presence in India.

commons A concept that considers the earth's resources as belonging equally to all nations and peoples of the world. Examples include air, fresh water, the oceans, and animal and plant biodiversity.

communication technology Technologies used to transmit data or exchange information.

communism A political system in which the government owns the means of production and equitably distributes the common goods among the people.

communitarianism A political philosophy, created in response to the rugged individualism of liberalism, which advocates the preservation and enhancement of the community.

comparative advantage David Ricardo's theory of economics, which states that all countries benefit when each nation specializes in producing and exporting goods it can produce at relatively lower cost and imports goods it produces at higher cost.

cost-benefit analysis A method of determining whether the benefits of a proposed policy outweigh the losses.

creative destruction In economics, an outcome of offshore outsourcing where the destruction of a company's existing infrastructure provides the opportunity for reorganization, redevelopment, and innovation, potentially creating new, different jobs.

cultural convergence One of Jan Nederveen Pieterse's three paradigms of intercultural relations, in this case indicating a growing sameness or increased homogenization over time.

cultural differentialism One of Jan Nederveen Pieterse's three paradigms of intercultural relations, in this case indicating a lasting difference despite the two cultures' relationship.

cultural diversity Differences in race, ethnicity, language, nationality, or religion among various groups within a community or nation.

cultural homogenization The act of making a formerly diverse cultural population uniform.

cultural hybridization One of Jan Nederveen Pieterse's three paradigms describing an intercultural relationship, in this case describing a continued mixing of two or more distinct cultures.

cultural imperialism Promoting the domination of the culture or language of one nation over another, disregarding cultural diversity.

cultural pluralism The existence of multiple culturally diverse groups within a larger shared culture.

dependency theory A theory of international relations which states that rich countries stay rich and keep poor countries poor by exploiting the resources and wealth of poor countries.

deregulation The reduction or elimination of government control of private economic activities, usually to the benefit of corporations.

developed countries/industrialized countries/ first world countries The wealthiest nations of the world, which enjoy high levels of education, health standards, and technological advancement.

developing countries/emerging economies/third world countries The poorer countries of the world, which are attempting to industrialize or reach the economic level of the developed countries.

diaspora People settled far from the homelands of their ancestry.

direct trade A form of trade in which private and respectful price-setting agreements are made directly between the grower or producer and the company selling that product so that both parties benefit.

Dunbar's number Named for its discoverer, Robin Dunbar, this refers to the maximum number of stable social relationships one person can maintain, not including casual acquaintances—generally around 150.

economic development Usually measured by an increase in a population's standard of living, economic development involves increases in technology, resources, and human capital.

economic globalization The movement from separate, national economies toward an international

or global economy in which goods, money, and workers are able to flow across national borders freely.

economic growth An increase in the total output of a nation over time, usually measured in terms of gross domestic product (GDP).

embargo A legal refusal to sell goods to a disfavored country.

emissions The release of greenhouse gases into the atmosphere.

Environmental Protection Agency An agency of the U.S. government created in 1970 to oversee coordinated governmental protection of the environment and natural resources.

epidemic A widespread disease that affects many individuals in a population in a relatively short period of time.

ethnicity Cultural characteristics that distinguish one group of people from another.

ethos See *appeal to* **ethos**.

European Union (EU) A federation of European states, originally created after World War II to prevent another war through economic integration by means of the establishment of a common currency and free movement of goods across borders. Currently, the European Union maintains common economic, foreign, and security policies. The agreement between fifteen countries (Austria, Belgium, Denmark, Finland, France, Germany, Greece, Ireland, Italy, Luxembourg, the Netherlands, Portugal, Spain, Sweden, and the United Kingdom) has expanded to twenty-seven countries, including Bulgaria, Cyprus, the Czech Republic, Estonia, Hungary, Latvia, Lithuania, Malta, Poland, Romania, Slovakia, and Slovenia.

evidence Examples, facts, numerical data, testimonies and quotations, or further reasoning that support an author's claim in an argument.

Export Processing Zone (EPZ) A region within a country aimed at attracting foreign investment from multinational corporations by relaxing tax and labor restrictions. Examples include apparel and textile factories in Saipan and the Philippines, and Motorola and Intel factories in Costa Rica. EPZs are often associated with sweatshops.

fair trade A trade movement characterized by concern for human rights and social responsibility that demands that workers and farmers be treated and paid fairly and that works to remove intermediate parties.

financial literacy An understanding of the multiple and cumulative ways that global financial institutions and personal financial choices affect individuals and others around the world, including an ability to understand financial regulations and agreements.

first world Originally used to indicate democratic nations during the Cold War, the term now describes the highly developed, rich nations of the Western world.

food security The ability of countries independently to provide adequate and reliable food at reasonable cost for their own people in socially acceptable ways to sustain healthy living.

food sovereignty   The right of people to define their own food and agriculture, free from pressures of the international market.

fossil fuels   Fuels formed over millions of years from dead plants and animals; examples include oil, natural gas, and coal.

fracking   The hydraulic process for extracting natural gas and shale oil by fracturing the underground shale fields.

free trade   An economic philosophy of reducing barriers to unrestricted trade, such as tariffs, taxes, subsidies, and quotas, in an effort to move raw materials, goods, and services freely across international borders. This ideology is largely embraced and promoted by the World Trade Organization, the International Monetary Fund, and the World Bank as the best way to benefit both developed countries and developing countries.

Free Trade Area of the Americas (FTAA)   A proposed trade agreement that would expand the benefits of the North American Free Trade Agreement to the entire Western Hemisphere.

fundamentalism   The belief in strict adherence to certain traditional doctrines and practices of a religion and the tendency to interpret scriptures literally.

General Agreement on Tariffs and Trade (GATT)   A negotiating framework for international trade aimed at eliminating tariffs and quotas in order to achieve free trade. GATT was created in 1947 and later absorbed by the World Trade Organization.

genocide   Deliberate and systematic annihilation of a racial, political, or cultural group.

genre   The type, kind, or category of argument, such as an editorial, scholarly argument, or advocacy advertisement.

global capitalism   The expansion of the system of capitalism (individual and corporate ownership of the means of production) as the primary economic system around the globe.

global digital divide (GDD)   The disparity in possession of technology and access to the Internet—and the related potential for information sharing, social networking, and educational or entrepreneurial opportunities—around the world, especially between developed and developing nations.

global financial system   The international interdependence of banks and other financial institutions, corporations, and governments.

globalization   A contested term, *globalization* is generally used in one of two ways: (1) to describe the way that transportation, communication, and technology have facilitated the movement of materials, goods, and ideas across continents and national borders; and (2) in reference to the dominant model and system of economic globalization.

global village   The drawing together of the world's diverse cultures through the advent of mass communication and technology, first articulated in 1964 by Marshall McLuhan.

glocalization   A term used by Japanese business to describe ways to tailor global products to local markets. Thomas L. Friedman popularized the term, describing it as the ability of a culture to assimilate aspects of other cultures in a way that enriches the home culture rather than overwhelms or replaces it.

grassroots   A political movement organized by a network of citizens at the local level.

Green Revolution   A dramatic increase of agricultural production, in both developed and developing countries, between the 1940s and 1970s as a result of the widespread use of pesticides, chemical fertilizers, hybrid seeds, and animal antibiotics.

gross domestic product (GDP)   The total monetary value of goods and services produced by and within a country during a specific period.

gross national product (GNP)   The total monetary value of goods and services produced by a nation at home and abroad during a specific period.

guest worker program   A plan proposed by former President George W. Bush that would enable both potential immigrants to the United States and those already working in the country illegally to apply for renewable three-year worker visas.

H-1B visa   A work visa allowing skilled international professionals and/or international students in specialty areas to work in the United States for up to six years. The visa is favored by high-tech, health care, and scientific companies, and it allows the holder to bring a spouse and family and to apply for a Green Card (legal permanent residency).

hegemony   The dominance of one power over another and a simultaneous acceptance of the commanding power's right to rule.

homogenization   A process by which distinct components or parts are converted or mixed into a uniform whole.

ideology   A unifying system of beliefs, values, philosophies, and attitudes that guides a society, particularly in the form of its government.

imperialism   The practice of one country extending its control over the territory, political system, or economic life of another country.

information technology (IT)   All forms of technology that deal with computers, telecommunications, or the storage, transmission, or retrieval of information.

infrastructure   The system of public works in a country that makes business activities possible—for example, roads, buildings, telephone service, electricity, and public transportation.

International Labor Organization (ILO)   A UN agency created in 1919 to maintain and promote fair and socially just international labor standards.

International Monetary Fund (IMF)   An international organization, one of the three main global economic institutions created in 1944, designed to lend finances to nations with debt problems and provide solutions that will enable international free trade, monetary cooperation, and economic growth. Some people protest IMF policies because membership is undemocratic; the countries that contribute the most money have the most voting power.

Internet cafe A shop or café in which patrons can purchase time on a computer equipped with Internet access. An Internet café may be a small kiosk with one computer or a massive shop with several floors. Internet cafés are especially popular in areas where home computer ownership is low.

iPod liberalism An ideology that asserts that Western values, especially democracy or liberal political systems, will necessarily develop in a society with greater access to mobile devices and social media; the philosophy generally assumes that every proponent of technology will have liberal values. The phrase was coined by Evgeny Morozov as part of a critique of the philosophy.

issue question A controversial question that can have many contestable answers and can lead to many different claims.

kairos The timeliness of an argument, as related to the motivating occasion.

Kyoto Protocol An international agreement, negotiated in 1997 in Kyoto, Japan, and effective in 2005, to reduce the rate of fossil fuel emissions to acceptable levels through legally binding commitments. The United States decided not to sign this agreement or adhere to its standards.

land reform Redistribution of land ownership to small farmers and peasants in order to destroy the concentration of landholdings among a few powerful landowners or corporations.

liberalism A political philosophy from the nineteenth century that embraces individual rights, civil liberties, and private property.

libertarianism An economic philosophy that promotes free trade and emphasizes the importance of personal freedom in economic and political affairs and the limitation of government intervention in the lives and choices of individuals.

local food Food produced in the same region in which it is sold or consumed, often linked to traditional regional or cultural diets.

logos See *appeal to* logos.

macroeconomics Factors that reveal the big picture of a state's economy, including GDP growth, inflation, interest rates, and productivity.

market A place where buyers and sellers interact and supply and demand control the fluctuation of prices of goods.

Marxism Marx's theory of socialism that includes class struggle and a dictatorship of the proletariat working toward the eventual realization of a classless society.

mass society Along with public society, one of two paradigms of communication in a society as theorized by Dan Hinds. In the mass society paradigm, information is broadcast from one source, such as mainstream media, and can't be answered or interacted with, which prevents dialogue or political action.

microbicide An antibiotic or chemical that kills microbes, currently being tested to see whether forms of the agent can destroy STIs and HIV.

Millennium Development Goals Eight goals set by the United Nations to tackle and conquer some of the world's worst problems, including the scarcity of safe water, extreme poverty and hunger, child mortality, and HIV/AIDS, and to achieve universal primary education, gender equality, environmental sustainability, and global partnership for development. The proposed time for reaching these goals is 2015.

monoculture The growing of plants or animals of a single species, absent of biodiversity.

most favored nation (MFN) A trade principle utilized by the WTO that states that all of a nation's trading partners must receive the lowest tariff rates the country offers.

motivating occasion The event, occasion, problem, or condition that prompts an arguer to speak out.

multiculturalism A philosophy and associated policies that allow new groups to form separate communities within their larger host country without forcing complete assimilation.

multinational/transnational corporations Corporations that have divisions in more than two countries.

nationalism Complete loyalty to and belief in the greatness of one's nation.

nation building Constructing or structuring a nation using the power of the state, often in the realms of political development, economic growth, and social harmony.

neoliberalism A political-economic philosophy that encourages deregulation, favors corporations, and suggests that the best way to achieve justice, progress, and growth is through free market economics.

netizen A portmanteau of "Internet" and "citizen" used to identify active social media users.

nongovernmental organization (NGO) A nonprofit agency unconnected to government or corporate or private actors and interests that is devoted to issues of social justice and resource management. Examples include Catholic Relief Services, the International Red Cross, the World Wildlife Fund, and Human Rights Watch.

nonrenewable resources Natural resources that are finite and exhaustible because of their scarcity or the length of time it takes for them to be replenished; examples include minerals and oil.

North American Free Trade Agreement (NAFTA) A trade agreement ratified in 1993 and put into effect in 1994 between the United States, Canada, and Mexico, created to encourage free trade and investment among the three countries.

Occupy Wall Street (OWS) A protest launched in the fall of 2011 that brought attention to the role of corporate donations in government and growing income inequality in the United States. Notable for its lack of central leadership and diffuse goals, OWS relied heavily on social media both for organization of protests and to prevent inaccurate depictions of its protests.

open source Software that is peer designed, reviewed, and made freely accessible.

outsourcing/offshore outsourcing Subcontracting some or all of a business's functions to a foreign company. This term is most often used to describe the movement of jobs to developing countries.

pandemic A widespread epidemic that crosses international boundaries and affects a large number of people on a number of continents simultaneously.

pathos See *appeal to* **pathos**.

potable water Water that is safe for human consumption.

privatization Turning over or selling state-owned industries to the private sector.

productivity The efficiency with which things are produced, usually with a focus on the amount of labor and time involved.

prosumers Users of social media who both produce and consume content.

protectionism Any policy used to protect domestic industries against competition from imports; tariffs are the most common form of protectionism.

public society Along with mass society, one of two paradigms of communication in a society, as theorized by Dan Hinds. In the public society paradigm, information is dispersed from a variety of sources; with nearly as many people dispensing and receiving information, this paradigm encourages political participation and action.

pull factors The conditions enticing people to move from developing countries to developed countries, such as the promise of higher-paying jobs and the suggestions made in the media about the superiority of the developed nation's lifestyle and customs.

purpose The writer's goal in making an argument.

push factors The conditions compelling people to move from developing countries to developed countries, such as the displacement of subsistence farmers from their traditional lands and livelihoods.

quota A form of protectionism that limits the total quantity of imports of a good during a set period of time.

rational choice theory The theory of human nature and interaction which states that people calculate the costs and benefits of any action and rationally decide which course of action would be the best to take.

real politik A German term describing foreign policy that is based on practical concerns as opposed to theoretical or ethical concerns.

reasons In argument, the statements that support the claim being made, explicitly and implicitly, and with the claim create the core of an argument.

receiving countries/destination countries A prosperous, stable, developed country experiencing an influx of immigrants.

recession A period of reduced economic activity characterized by rising levels of unemployment, a decline in GDP, and slowed production.

remittance Money earned by immigrants abroad and sent back to their home countries in the form of money orders, personal checks, or electronic transfers.

renewable resources Natural resources such as forests or fisheries that renew themselves through natural processes.

reshoring The return of jobs to a country that previously outsourced them; reshoring usually occurs after an increase in wages and other costs of doing business abroad.

rhetoric/rhetorical The persuasive use of language to accomplish certain ends in specific situations.

sectarianism Adherence to a particular form or sect of a religion to the exclusion of other sects.

secularism A governmental system that embodies the separation of church and state.

sender countries A country, generally poorer and less developed, that sees its citizens, often college-educated or professional, depart the country and head for receiving countries.

Smith, Adam The founding father of economics and capitalism, most famous for *The Wealth of Nations* (1776), in which he argued that people should be free from government interference to follow their own self-interests in the market, which would regulate economic activity like an "invisible hand." However, Smith believed that government intervention in the economy was at times necessary to provide public works such as roads and schools that would not be profitable for individuals alone to produce.

socialism A political and economic system in which a democratic community owns the means of production and distributes the benefits equitably among the community members.

social media Online applications that facilitate networking and participatory information sharing.

social safety nets Programs and benefits provided by a government that exist independently of a person's employment status. Examples include socialized health care in the European Union and Canada.

sovereignty A principle of government which holds that a state exercises absolute power over its territory and population.

spinternet A phenomenon, studied by Evgeny Morozov, that occurs when dominant powers in a country use digital activism to maintain social control. Regimes may use social media tools to distort the perception or coverage of social phenomena, such as hiring bloggers to produce content that supports their position but appears independent of them.

stakeholders People who have investments in the answers to issue questions.

STAR criteria The criteria for evaluating evidence in an argument. STAR stands for sufficiency, typicality, accuracy, and relevance.

Structural Adjustment Programs (SAPs) The package of free market reforms designed to create economic growth and generate income to pay off a nation's debt. These policies were promoted by the IMF and World Bank. Third world nations agree to SAPs in exchange for debt relief.

style The level of formality and complexity, tone, and use of language employed by a writer in an argument.

subcontracting To use a third party to complete all or part of the work required for a job.

subsidy Financial help from the government to the private sector of the economy.

sustainable development Development that meets the needs of the present while conserving resources so that future generations will be able to meet their own needs.

sweatshop A factory in which employees work for long hours under unhealthy or dangerous conditions for low pay.

tariff A tax on each unit of an imported good.

theocracy A political system in which political organization is based on religious organization.

third world Used during the Cold War to describe nations aligned with neither communism nor democracy, this term is now used to describe developing countries.

totalitarianism A political system characterized by dictatorial, one-party rule. Totalitarian regimes generally do not tolerate political opposition and attempt to control all aspects of citizen life.

trade barriers Policies utilized by governments to restrict importing and exporting with other countries; tariffs are the most common form of trade barriers.

trade deficit A term describing the balance of trade in a country whose exports are worth less than its imports. Also called a negative trade balance, or a trade gap.

trade imbalance The situation that arises when the value of a country's imports and exports are not approximately equal. If a country's exports are worth more than its imports, it is a positive balance, or a surplus. If a country's imports are worth more than its exports, it is a negative balance, or a trade deficit.

Trade-Related Intellectual Property Rights (TRIPs) Laws governing patents, copyrights, and other goods related to information that are hotly disputed in the international trading system; one example is patents in the pharmaceutical industry.

trafficking An illegal activity involving the international transport of drugs, weapons, or people, the latter by threat, force, or fraud.

transnationalism The process of immigrants maintaining connections, loyalties, and cultural, social, and political involvement with their countries of origin through remittances, voting, or travel.

United Nations An international organization created in 1945 by 51 countries to preserve peace and security through international cooperation and collective action. Current membership is 191 countries.

United Nations Educational, Scientific, and Cultural Organization (UNESCO) An international organization with about two hundred member nations that includes among its goals the assertion of cultural rights as human rights and the preservation of cultural diversity.

Universal Declaration on Cultural Diversity An international and intercultural agreement written by UNESCO in 2001 that seeks to make legal the principles that cultural diversity is a necessity for humankind and contributes to international peace and security, and that cultural rights are integral to human rights.

Universal Declaration of Human Rights (UDHR) A document adopted by the General Assembly of the United Nations on December 10, 1948, that recognizes the equal rights of all humans globally.

Uruguay Round The final set of trade negotiations under GATT that began in 1986 and closed in 1993. This round created the WTO as a permanent arena to address issues of international free trade.

virtual private networks (VPNs) and proxy servers Downloadable programs that allow the circumvention of blocked Web sites. VPNs and proxy servers are often pointed to as a means of outwitting or overcoming regime control online.

wastewater Used water that carries wastes like soap, chemicals, or fertilizers from homes, businesses, or industries.

white collar Pertaining to employees who do nonmanual desk work, often for higher compensation than blue-collar workers receive.

World Bank An international financial institution, one of the three main global economic institutions created in 1944, whose purpose is to lend funds and provide assistance for economic development in poorer countries, often prescribing policies that promote free trade.

World Health Organization (WHO) An agency of the United Nations that was founded in 1948 to promote the attainment of the highest level of human health through research, technical cooperation among countries, international conferences, and various other programs.

World Trade Organization (WTO) An international organization created in 1994 and active as of 1995 and responsible for the legislation and regulation of trade rules and the adjudication of trade disputes, aimed at maintaining free trade in the international trading system.

xenophobia Fear or hatred of foreigners.

Answers to Chapter 1 "Global Pursuit," pp. 2–4

1. Nestlé is the world's largest food company. Where is its corporate headquarters?

   d. Vevey, Switzerland

2. Match these world cities with their country of location.

   a. Pakistan, b. Ecuador, c. Vietnam, d. China, e. Romania

3. A raga is

   d. a particular kind of melody in Indian music.

4. Rank these international sports in terms of estimated global popularity.

   c, a, b, d

5. Which country is *not* one of the world's top oil-producing countries?

   d. India

6. How many American states border Canada.

   13

7. Nasi Goreng is considered the national dish of which country?

   Indonesia

8. Which of these nations is *not* a member of NATO?

   b. Australia

9. The United States owes billions of dollars around the world. China is by far its largest creditor. What country is number two?

   Japan

10. Pop star Lady Gaga was born in which country?

    b. United States (New York)

11. Which country has the largest Muslim population in the world?

    d. Indonesia

12. Which country on the continent of Africa is newly formed since 2008?

    d. Republic of South Sudan

13. The International Dateline generally runs which way?

    b. north-south along the 180 degrees of longitude while skirting around Russia

14. What do Guam, Puerto Rico and the Virgin Islands have in common?

    They are unincorporated territories of the United States.

15. In 2011, which nation experienced a significant popular political and cultural revolution?

    c. Egypt

16. African Mango refers to

    b. a controversial diet aid / weight loss program.

17. Anders Behring Breivik achieved international notoriety for what?

    b. Mass murder.

18. What does Pai Gow refer to?

    c. Chinese gambling game.

19. What is Hamas?

    c. The Palestinian Sunni Islamic party that governs the Gaza Strip.

20. Muammar Gaddafi, the assassinated dictator, was the head of state of which country?

    Libya

Credits

Index